Presidents' Secret Wars

Presidents' Secret Wars

CIA AND PENTAGON COVERT OPERATIONS FROM WORLD WAR II THROUGH IRANSCAM

JOHN PRADOS

Quill
William Morrow
New York

It is the policy of William Morrow and Company, Inc., and its imprints and affiliates, recognizing the importance of preserving what has been written, to print the books we publish on acid-free paper, and we exert our best efforts to that end.

Library of Congress Cataloging-in-Publication Data

Prados, John.
    Presidents' secret wars : CIA and Pentagon covert operations from
World War II through Iranscam / John Prados.
       p.   cm.
    Bibliography: p.
    Includes index.
    ISBN 0-688-07759-5
    1. Intelligence service—United States. 2. United States—
Cental Intelligence Agency. 3. Military intelligence—United
States. 4. United States—Foreign relations—1945– I. Title.
JK468.I6P7   1988   81-30440
327.1′2′0973—dc19   CIP

Printed in the United States of America

3 4 5 6 7 8 9 10

BOOK DESIGN BY VICTORIA HARTMAN

For Ritva

CONTENTS

INTRODUCTION

I t has been more than a decade now since 1975, "the Year of
Intelligence," during which the intelligence community
was investigated separately by a presidential commission, a
select committee of the United States Senate, and another select
committee from the House of Representatives. The wheel has
turned full circle since then: Now demands for intelligence reform
have given way to equally strident ones calling for an "unleashed"
CIA.

In any event, the reform movement proved abortive. Congress
made do with the half measure of "oversight," while the intelligence agencies have been as circumspect as possible in their reporting, and as creative as possible in formulating minimalist
interpretations of the existing laws. Meanwhile, the Reagan administration has effectively given free rein to the intelligence specialists, with one result being the uproar over the 1983–1984 mining of
the harbors of Nicaragua. But barely a year after the mining of Nicaraguan harbors, in which the oversight prerogatives of the Senate
Select Committee on Intelligence were flouted so flagrantly that its
vice-chairman was barely dissuaded from resigning, the problem of
the legal authority for and range of intelligence operations was
again swept under the rug.

At a conference in early 1985, a former general counsel of the
Central Intelligence Agency and senior staff members of the Senate
select committee agreed that it was a good thing that the pressure
for intelligence reform had passed.

The questions of which activities are appropriate for an intelligence organization in a democratic nation, and what is the legal

basis for those activities, are still with us today; they were not in any way resolved by the addition of formal oversight in the 1970s. Such questions are best considered calmly and not in the heat of another intelligence fiasco. Under present arrangements, it's only a matter of time before another Nicaragua mining, or, for that matter, another Bay of Pigs.

In order to show the problems in the starkest possible light, I have chosen to focus on covert, or secret, operations, and within that category specifically on paramilitary action: the use of armed forces supported by the United States to affect events in other nations. Influence peddling, espionage, and intelligence analysis are discussed only where germane to the major topics in this account. Paramilitary operations are not the sole type of covert action, but they are the most significant and have the greatest potential for damaging American national interests. Yet little effort has been made to assemble a balance sheet on the effectiveness of paramilitary techniques, or to compile a record of how such covert actions have been controlled. The CIA is forty years old, and the time has come for such assessments.

Just how much have paramilitary operations contributed to United States security? Can we identify general problems that have recurred in different operations. If some paramilitary capability is desirable, how should it be organized and maintained? What role has the President played and should he play in these matters? What about Congress? Because the literature has been overwhelmingly preoccupied with exposés of individual operations, it has not been possible to answer such broad questions.

With all due respect to the highly trained and skilled officers who staff the intelligence community, questions of intelligence policy are too important to be left to the practitioners of covert action, who have a vested interest in exercising their techniques. The only way to preserve our American democracy is to mandate limited authority to and demand proper accountability from the intelligence sector.

A good deal of the difficulty in thinking through these questions resides in our, the public's, not having been presented with the necessary information. This account makes a start toward filling that gap by broadly surveying paramilitary actions rather than fastening on to single cases, and by giving sustained attention both to the development of capabilities and to mechanisms for control.

The information contained in this book has been assembled entirely from the public record. Sources include memoirs, newspaper and periodical accounts, studies of individual paramilitary operations, and official histories. Numerous government documents have been consulted as well. The Freedom of Information Act and mandatory declassification review of documents have provided important sources, though they have been much less useful of late, given the present administration's attitude toward classification of information. That an account like this can be assembled, from the record, itself demonstrates the futility of attempting to forestall public discussion through the suppression of documentation.

One advantage of pursuing questions of intelligence policy through a study of paramilitary operations is that these activities inevitably become known, because of their nature, regardless of attempts at classification. This makes it impossible, or at least less believable, for intelligence officials to claim, by alluding to some higher body of (secret) knowledge, that the record is something other than it appears to be.

It is time to resume the debate on intelligence reform. "Unleashing" the CIA is not even good for the Agency itself: CIA deaths in the line of duty are commemorated by stars on the facade of the headquarters building at Langley, Virginia. The eight stars chiseled between the spring of 1983 and fall of 1984 represent a casualty rate *eight times the annual average* for all the preceding years of CIA's existence. Most of these deaths resulted from covert actions or acts of terrorism.

—John Prados
Washington, D.C., December 1985

·I·

THE COLD WAR CRUCIBLE

The men in the yard carried submachine guns. They did not threaten, but only asked for food. The German farmer gave them some and they left. No sooner were they gone than the farmer reported the incident to the local authorities. The police at Wildenranna also received other reports of armed men in the woods along the Austrian border. Investigation quickly confirmed that an armed band of some sort was abroad. Central police headquarters at Passau was asked to send reinforcements in order to apprehend the intruders.

Thus was the Passau police command thrown into a dilemma. It was September 1947 and Germany was occupied by the victorious Allies. Passau was in the American sector. Police there reported to the United States military officials. The news of an armed band north of the Inn River could signal some Soviet military move. In any case, German police were under standing orders: Anything to do with foreign nationals was the province of the Counter-Intelligence Corps (CIC) of the U.S. Army. A Passau police official telephoned American regional headquarters at Munich. The CIC decided to organize a manhunt in the hills along the Austrian border. Agents from Munich drove to Waldkirchen and then fanned out toward the border, joining with German police who had, by now, also equipped themselves with submachine guns.

At three o'clock in the morning, on September 10, one of the CIC search parties heard the voices of men in the forest, and found the band. They were indeed a large group—almost forty men—but they were sitting around a campfire and most of them were singing.

13

They wore Soviet uniforms. The search party carefully surrounded the camp, and moved in.

The intruders put up no resistance. In fact, they relaxed considerably when they learned that it was Americans who had apprehended them. It was quickly learned that the band was organized in a military fashion, and that they were armed with submachine guns, light machine guns, and hand grenades. Like their uniforms, the equipment they carried was Soviet, and they spoke what sounded at first like Russian. The intruders allowed themselves to be disarmed, after which they were taken to Passau, and then to a CIC base at Oberursel outside Frankfurt. There the CIC brought in its Soviet intelligence specialists to work with the men. Thirty-five soldiers had been captured at the campsite. Four more were apprehended in different places over the following days and turned out to be from the same band. The U.S. Army put the entire investigation under tight security.

The press reported some facts and more rumors. Even at this time, when Europe was inured to displaced persons and exchanges of prisoners between East and West, the appearance of armed bands in Bavaria was uncommon enough to be reported. A United Press International reporter who went to Passau a few days after the incident got a garbled version of the truth: The prisoners had told CIC they were anti-Soviet partisans from the Ukraine. But there were other speculations: The captured men were Soviet deserters; they were Polish anti-Soviet guerrillas; they were simply very-well-armed bandits.

The CIC debriefed the men for over three weeks. The interrogators soon discovered that the new arrivals were, in fact, Ukrainian partisans, who thought that a war against the Soviet forces was still going on in the Ukraine, Czechoslovakia, and southern Poland. They provided much information about their partisan units as well as political conditions in Eastern Europe. This intelligence was included in a report by CIC officers in Frankfurt on October 5, 1947.

Detailed information on anti-Soviet partisan activities in Eastern Europe was an intelligence windfall for the United States. Washington, however, saw the data as more than merely an opportunity to bring its political perceptions of the Soviet Union up to date. Instead, the intelligence on the Ukrainian partisans signaled, to some American officials, a chance to take secret military action against Russia. The Ukrainian movement offered the opening for an offensive move in the cold war, a classic covert operation. The United States was just then creating a capability to engage in intelligence and psychological warfare missions of all kinds, including covert operations.

American secret wars have been carried out on almost every continent since that day in 1947. These covert operations have involved thousands of native fighters, significant numbers of American clandestine agents, and even regular United States military forces. United States involvement has run the gamut from advice to arms, from supplying full support for invasions of independent nations to secret bombing in support of clandestine military operations. These techniques for international coercion are not new, nor were they first developed by the United States. But American participation in World War II opened many eyes to the potential uses of special operations and provided a nucleus of personnel well-versed in specialized clandestine capabilities.

World War II was crucial in many ways. The United States found its British allies to be avid practitioners of secret warfare. Europe was blanketed by networks of fighters resisting the German occupation. To cooperate with the resistance movements, the British established their own very successful Special Operations Executive (SOE). Agents of SOE provided arms and advice to small guerrilla units from such countries as Norway and Greece, as well as Burma. Others undertook special missions ranging from Czechoslovakia to Malaya. SOE propagandists helped the operations with a variety of information and misinformation campaigns.

Early American intelligence officers benefited from the British example. During the war, the United States created an Office of Strategic Services (OSS) to perform all kinds of intelligence tasks. Under the leadership of the irrepressible William J. "Wild Bill" Donovan, OSS functioned globally. There were major commands in the Mediterranean, northern Europe, Burma, and China. OSS teams parachuted into France and Norway, blew up bridges in the Balkans, worked with partisans in Italy, and led bands of tribesmen against the Japanese in Burma. OSS officers also spied on the enemy and supplied incisive intelligence analyses to American commanders.

The United States military also acquired experience with secret operations during the course of the war. Most often the military were asked to assist some operation, for example by covertly landing additional agents or supplies. The Navy did this using submarines and PT boats, the Air Force with planes. The Army actually ran a guerrilla force fighting the Japanese in the Philippines. The Army and the Marine Corps also established elite Ranger and Raider units for commando missions. The Army's 5,307th Composite Unit, probably better known as Merrill's Marauders, played an important part in the Burma campaign and worked closely with the OSS there.

It is the Burma campaign, in fact, that illustrates most clearly the embryonic forms of the standard operating procedures for the later secret wars. An OSS unit with the innocuous name of Service Unit Detachment 101 was sent to India to establish a base close to the area of interest. Agents from Detachment 101 infiltrated into the Burmese hill country, forged links with local Kachin tribesmen, and created a guerrilla movement to combat the Japanese. Weapons, supplies, and OSS officers were parachuted into the jungle or flown in by the planes of the "air commando groups" formed by the Air Force.

The OSS officers slowly built up the Kachin from local espionage networks to roving patrols of fighters to organized guerrilla units. By 1944 the Kachin were fighting in conjunction with Merrill's Marauders and the British Chindit brigades. There were over 10,000 Kachin fighting a year later, including a field force of seven 450-man battalions led by the OSS. The Kachin units planned their actions using information derived from more than 60 spies operating deep in the Japanese areas, plus about 400 agents surveying nearby enemy positions. The Kachin field force helped trap two very powerful Japanese divisions during the Allies' final offensives in Burma.

It was a remarkable achievement for the OSS. With a strength of about 300 men, Detachment 101 succeeded in mobilizing a military force over thirty times that size, and used that force to execute highly successful military operations. Service Unit Detachment 101 was awarded a special commendation by the United States Army.

Several features of the OSS tribesmen program are worth noting. Among them are the organization of formal units within the overall guerrilla force; the clearing of the enemy from zones within the operating area to serve as local bases; the use of espionage networks to shield the guerrillas during the period of their formation and training, and to find targets for them later on; the use of outside bases for specialized training and major support; and the use of clandestine air traffic for supply and communication between local and outside bases. These techniques became essential features of secret warfare tactics. The type of clandestine operation that creates forces resembling regular military units came to be called paramilitary.

OSS also participated in the European theater, of course. Teams there assisted the rescue and escape of Allied airmen downed over the Continent, carried out commando raids, and cooperated with resistance fighters. One of the biggest OSS operations of the war was launched in connection with the Normandy invasion of 1944. There, the intelligence part of the invasion plan, using the code name Sussex, called for special teams to be parachuted in to supplement the resistance. The OSS, British SOE, and French intelligence each contributed agents to form ninety three-man "Jedburgh" teams that were sent to specific resistance networks. The Jedburghs were parachuted in military uniform but carried civilian clothes with them. They were backed up by eleven Special Operations groups, which were thirty-two-man strike teams for commando missions.

The European operations were very successful. The OSS had 500 French and 375 American agents in France alone by the time of the invasion. More than half the Americans who served with Jedburgh teams received decorations for heroism or merit. Resistance operations are credited with slowing down the German response to the invasion and with furnishing the Allies with vital intelligence. Later in the campaign OSS succeeded in infiltrating as many as 200 agents directly into Germany. These, however, were engaged almost entirely in espionage missions.

In addition to the OSS, the Army's CIC was operating a parallel program through a much smaller network of agents on enemy territory. CIC activity had been going on since 1942, virtually from the moment Americans first arrived in the European theater. CIC agents proved especially useful in Italy, where they helped identify Nazi efforts to penetrate pro-Allied Italian partisan groups.

World War II not only provided experience, it formed and reinforced a certain way of thinking among participants from the intelligence community. The war as an issue was cast in black and white—it was a case of fighting Hitler and Tojo or not. Not to fight was a clear abdication of responsibility in the face of foreign aggression and pernicious ideologies. After the war it was easy to transfer wartime hostility and methods to the newly perceived adversary.

This hostile philosophy did not matter at first. The surrender of Japan in August 1945 brought a scramble to demobilize the armies, and this extended to the intelligence branch. The OSS had built itself up to a strength of about twelve thousand when President Harry Truman ordered its dissolution, in an executive order, on September 20. Under the new arrangements, the parts of OSS that had dealt with analytical intelligence moved over to State. The detachments of clandestine officers went to the War Department as a new Strategic Services Unit (SSU) under Brigadier General John Magruder, who had been the OSS special-warfare chief.

General Magruder's mandate was not to preserve or enlarge the SSU but mainly to liquidate it. The demobilization was accomplished by early 1946. Former OSS officers who had served with the Jedburghs, the Kachin, and elsewhere went back to their homes, law practices, to school, to the Army. Teams from OSS/SSU were pulled out of Vietnam, where, ironically, they had met Ho Chi Minh and advised against the type of American policy that eventually led us to war there. When Colonel William W. Quinn took over the SSU in 1946, it had been reduced to fewer than two hundred men operating out of seven field stations in foreign countries.

In addition to the SSU, the Army Counter-Intelligence Corps remained as a clandestine operations center. It was controlled by military intelligence, or G-2.

Given its role as the official intelligence branch of the Army, G-2 was ideally situated to operate in Eastern Europe and against the Soviet Union, because of the Army's presence in Germany, Austria, and Japan as part of the military occupation forces in those countries. The first American links with anti-Soviet Russian émigrés were forged by G-2, which also acted, as early as August 1945, to enlist the services of former German intelligence officers who had knowledge of the Russians.

One other aspect of the World War II experience had a fundamental influence upon American intelligence organization in the postwar period. The United States had entered the war as a result of the Japanese attack on Pearl Harbor in 1941, which had surprised the American commanders. Later investigations revealed a number of items that might have alerted leaders to the attack, but there had been no one responsible for gathering and interpreting intelligence at the national level. Thus the lesson was drawn that the United States needed some sort of organization for intelligence.

Even before President Truman abolished the OSS, there were many competing plans for structuring the peacetime intelligence agency. Important issues dividing the proponents of the various plans were the specific functions and degree of autonomy: to be accorded a peacetime intelligence agency. Truman's military advisers, the Joint Chiefs of Staff, favored a plan under which the President would establish an interagency group to supervise the intelligence unit. The State Department proposed a plan that was concerned only with supervisory authority, which they wanted to be in the hands of the secretary of state.

President Truman took part of the advice of his Joint Chiefs when, on January 22, 1946, he issued a directive that established a National Intelligence Authority (NIA) to oversee a Central Intelligence Group (CIG). The NIA was composed of the secretaries of state, war, and navy, plus Truman's personal representative. Under them was a director of central intelligence (DCI) who ran the Central Intelligence Group. Truman selected trusted individuals for both the DCI and his representative to the NIA, and he humorously referred to them as "personal snooper" and "director of centralized snooping." Truman's first DCI was Sidney W. Souers, a St. Louis businessman who was proud of his reserve commission as a Navy rear admiral and his wartime service with naval intelligence. Souers, anxious to return home from the war, served only five months as director of central intelligence. Army Chief of Staff General Dwight D. Eisenhower then recommended one of his top Pentagon planners, General Charles H. Bonesteel, for the job, but Truman selected Air Force Lieutenant General Hoyt S. Vandenberg instead. The President felt Vandenberg knew the job and was enough of a diplomat to get along with the State, War, and Navy departments.

Actually, Vandenberg had been a combat commander. His intelligence experience was limited. But he was a good organizer and began a sustained effort to build up the Central Intelligence Group. Under Souers CIG had operated out of a suite of three rooms next door to the White House, and was authorized to maintain less than 250 personnel. Vandenberg, however, soon established an office for research and evaluation plus administrative organs. Clandestine operators of the Strategic Services Unit moved back from the War

Department and were reconstituted as the Office of Special Operations (OSO). By the end of 1946 there were about 800 officers in OSO alone, out of 1,816 total personnel in CIG; Vandenberg had plans to expand to a strength of 3,000 over six months.

The peacetime intelligence agency thus grew quickly, but it was still a creation of the executive branch of government. CIG had no basis in the law of the land. Already several bills had been proposed in Congress, and the White House had held discussions with CIG lawyers in 1946. Clark M. Clifford of the President's staff helped draft legislation for a peacetime intelligence agency. In addition, President Truman was planning a reorganization of the entire military establishment, a proposal for which was sent to Congress in February 1947. Provision for the peacetime intelligence agency was included in the proposed legislation, which became the National Security Act of 1947.

Through the 1947 law, Truman created a National Security Council, to advise him on defense and foreign affairs. The separate War and Navy departments were merged into a single Department of Defense, under which the Air Force also gained autonomy as an independent armed service. As for the intelligence organization, the original legislative proposal did no more than say that a Central Intelligence Agency would be formed. In the letter Truman sent to congressional leaders along with the proposed legislation, he did not even mention this intelligence component of the bill.

Like the President, most congressmen concerned themselves mainly with those parts of the bill that were not about intelligence. Only late in the sequence of congressional hearings did the CIG come up, and then the attention of Congress centered on whether it should become some kind of secret police. Congressmen noted the lack of detail in the bill regarding the intelligence organization, and the legislation was then amended to prohibit it from possessing any police powers.

Some further amendments to the bill were inserted by Congress that specified responsibilities for the new Central Intelligence Agency (CIA). Essentially, Congress went back to Truman's January 1946 directive establishing the National Intelligence Authority and CIG, from which they extracted almost the exact language the President had used to assign responsibility. Under the National Security Act, the CIA was directly answerable to the President through the NSC. The National Intelligence Authority was abolished. The CIA was given five functions: advising the NSC on intelligence, making recommendations on related matters, producing intelligence estimates and reports, performing "additional services of common concern" for the government-wide intelligence community, and performing "such other functions and duties related to intelligence affecting the national security as the National Security Council may from time to time direct."

In later years it was this last provision that was said to furnish legal authority for the conduct of secret warfare by the CIA. It should be noted, therefore, that the terms *covert operation, clandestine operation, paramilitary operation, secret operation,* and *special operation,* all euphemisms for secret warfare, appear nowhere in the law authorizing the peacetime intelligence agency. The phrase "such other functions" was intended to cover unforeseen circumstances, but even there, as the legislative history of the law makes clear, Congress was not considering international coercion.

President Truman signed the legislation on July 26, 1947, and the National Security Act became law. Six weeks later, on September 8, the CIG became the CIA. The CIA soon became an expanding organization in search of roles and missions. It was at precisely this time that American agents in Germany apprehended the band of Ukrainian partisans. The Ukrainians were looking for help.

The formation of a peacetime intelligence agency in the United States occurred during the murky dawn of the "cold war," a conflict unlike any other before it, in which superpowers threatened each other but did not dare resort to war. The seeds of the cold war lay in the very outcome of World War II. The end of hostilities found the European economies a shambles, the Soviet Union in control of Eastern Europe, the Western Allies frustrated in their dealings with the Soviets, and both sides with powerful military forces in Germany. The Soviet Union and the United States emerged as the only clear victors, significantly more powerful than other nations—"superpowers" in a word coined as recently as 1944.

Conflict between the superpowers may not have been inevitable but avoiding it in 1945 required more wisdom and strength than either country commanded. Soviet Generalissimo Joseph Stalin persisted in an obsession with defending the borders of Russia through the device of a buffer zone of Soviet-dominated nations. In pursuit of this aim, Stalin repeatedly broke agreements reached by the wartime allies concerning Eastern European nations. The West bristled. Attitudes hardened on both sides.

One milestone of sorts occurred in early 1946. By this time troops garrisoning Iran under a joint occupation arrangement were to be withdrawn. The deadline came and passed, with Russian soldiers still in the country. Stalin did finally evacuate after blunt language from Truman, who explained to his secretary of state, James Byrnes, "I'm tired of babying the Soviets."

The Iran crisis proved a watershed for public opinion in the United States. British wartime prime minister Sir Winston Churchill received a standing ovation at Westminster College, in Fulton, Missouri, when he declared in a speech, only a few days after the expired Iran deadline:

> From Stettin in the Baltic to Trieste in the Adriatic, an Iron Curtain has descended across the Continent. Behind that line lie all the capitals of the ancient states of central and eastern Europe ... all subject, in one form or another, not only to Soviet influence but to a very high and in some cases increasing measure of control from Moscow.

Early efforts at negotiations between the West and Stalin expired in the increasingly tense atmosphere of Soviet-American relations. Within days of taking office, Truman was speaking to the Soviet foreign minister in very strong terms. Lend-Lease aid, which the Americans had provided to Russia since 1941, and which the Soviets were interested in extending, was halted. Truman met with Stalin and British leaders one time—at Potsdam, in Germany, during July 1945. There they talked of the arrangements for Eastern Europe and the operation of Allied Control Councils in the occupied countries, which were to be garrisoned until peace treaties were signed and ratified. After three top-level meetings, "summit" conferences if you will, over two years, the United States would not again meet the Soviets at the summit until 1955.

Another diplomatic device available was the Council of Foreign Ministers. This was a formal negotiating group composed of the secretaries of state of the Big Four powers—the United States, Soviet Union, Great Britain, and France—which met periodically. The foreign ministers discussed repeatedly Asian and European questions, making little progress except with peace treaties for Hungary,

Romania, and Bulgaria, minor participants in World War II. At the end of 1947 a conference ended with no accords at all. Even negotiations for a peace treaty with Austria were broken off in May 1948, not to be resumed for six years.

Stalin bears some responsibility for what happened. The Soviet dictator had a secret he dared not divulge—that Russia lay shattered, despite appearances. Soviet prisoners and forced laborers repatriated at the end of the war faced death or more long years of detention, and often merely exchanged German work sites for Russian ones. Unlike the United States, Russia's economy was so devastated that it could not absorb a mass of returning veterans reentering the labor force. So Stalin moved slowly on postwar demobilization, retaining large armed forces, including troops who manned occupation zones in Germany and Austria plus the Eastern European nations.

On Stalin's orders, Soviet diplomats and military authorities disrupted the functioning of many Big Four joint bodies. The Soviets also pressed unremittingly for a large share of war reparations from all the conquered nations, including those they occupied. This helped sour relations in the Council of Foreign Ministers and led to further acrimony. By January 1946 the Americans complained that the Allied Control Council in Bulgaria had been rendered ineffective. In Germany authorities in the American zone suspended all deliveries of reparations in May 1946.

The United States must also take some of the blame for the cold war. From the beginning of his administration, Harry Truman proved more eager to use muscle in relations with the Soviets than had his predecessor Franklin D. Roosevelt. Historians still debate whether Truman threatened the Russians with the atomic bomb (on which the United States then had a monopoly), especially in connection with forcing the Soviets to evacuate Iran in early 1946. Only a few months later the President dispatched major American naval forces to the Mediterranean Sea for the first time in response to reports of Soviet pressure on Turkey for a joint defense agreement. The suspension of reparations from Germany also had a coercive and punitive character.

France caused problems as well. It had been allotted occupation zones in Germany and Austria, and seats on the Allied Control Councils, as part of its role in the Big Four. The Americans had always intended to administer each of the occupied countries as a single economic unit, but the French were concerned that Soviet policies might come to dominate the unified economies. French representatives accordingly vetoed moves in the Allied Control Council designed to unify economic administration. As a result, in July 1946 the Americans offered to join their occupation zone in Germany with those of any other powers willing to participate. Suspecting a trap, the Russians resisted the plan while the French simply refused to go along. Only the British were willing. In December the United States and British sectors were reorganized into a hybrid entity called Bizonia, in which a new currency was introduced.

The Russians regarded Bizonia as the beginning of a British-American effort to create a separate German state. Stalin became even more intransigent. Soviet armies consolidated control over the Eastern European nations rather than preparing for withdrawal. After the peace treaties with Hungary, Romania, and Bulgaria, the Soviet troops stayed in place. Russian diplomats walked out of a meeting of the Council of Foreign Ministers.

Soviet-American relations crossed a watershed in 1947. In February, the British told American officials that they would be forced to terminate their foreign aid to Greece at the end of March. Europe faced a cruel winter, the worst in decades, and the British government felt it could not continue to support Greece, which had been receiving military and economic aid from it for over two years. Meanwhile, the Greek government faced a civil war against communist insurgents. President Truman approved a suggestion that the United States take over for the British, and added aid to Turkey for good measure. In mid-March the State Department offered aid, which soon grew into a substantial intervention in the Greek civil war.

This marked a shift in Truman's policy toward an active stance of countering perceived Soviet moves. The aid itself was not ultimately as important as the change in strategy. Under the new concept Soviet power was to be "contained" within the areas where it had already achieved dominance. George F. Kennan, then a foreign service officer, coined the term "containment" and this was elevated to the status of the Truman Doctrine.

From the initial aid to Greece and Turkey, it was but a short step to offering foreign aid more widely to European nations. Secretary of State George C. Marshall made this offer in a commencement address he delivered at Harvard University on June 5, 1947. The Marshall Plan was intended to further containment by helping rebuild the European economies, thereby eliminating social conditions hospitable to the growth of communism. As an extra benefit, rebuilt European economies would provide substantial markets for American goods and services. The Marshall Plan became the first sustained foreign assistance program ever adopted by the United States.

Soviet leaders were not mistaken in believing that the Truman Doctrine and Marshall Plan were designed to be used against them. Stalin forbade participation in the Marshall Plan by the occupied countries of Eastern Europe. The Czechs, whose political system was not yet controlled by the Russians, saw Marshall Plan aid as a counterweight to Soviet influence and initially responded favorably to the American offer. It is likely that their reaction served as a catalyst for Stalin's decision to consolidate Soviet control of Prague. Political pressures mounted until, in February 1948, a sort of constitutional coup was carried out. Noncommunist ministers in the Czech coalition government resigned, to be replaced by representatives of a minority party, the Czech communist party. Within a month a famous Czech patriot—Jan Masaryk, a prominent politician and government official—died under very suspicious circumstances.

These events in Czechoslovakia plus the rising tide of hostility in America created a "war scare." The American high commissioner in Germany, General Lucius D. Clay, cabled a warning on March 5 that war "may come with dramatic suddenness." Asked for its opinion, the CIA prepared a memorandum concluding that war was not in fact imminent, but it refused to predict for a period beyond the following sixty days.

It was in Germany that matters came to a head. The foreign ministers of the Big Three—now the United States, Britain, and France—had met recently in London for diplomatic discussions. At the meeting of the Allied Control Council on March 20, Soviet delegates demanded to be informed about the London talks and Allied representatives refused. The Russians then walked out of the session, declaring the council dissolved. Several days later Allied representatives in turn refused to attend meetings of Control Council subcommittees called by the Soviets.

On the last day of March the Russians suddenly informed the West that they would impose travel restrictions on the three land corridors connecting the western sector of Berlin with the Allied occupation area Bizonia. The restrictions went into effect at midnight on April 1. British and American trains en route to Berlin were halted at the Soviet zone boundary. The Allies shifted to aircraft for transport. On April 5 a British C-47 making its approach to the Berlin airfield at Gatow was destroyed when a Soviet fighter plane collided with it in midair. The Soviets apologized but the Allies then ordered fighter escorts for their transport planes.

By July 1948 travel restrictions had developed into a full-scale blockade of Berlin by the Soviets, and this lasted until May 12, 1949. During that time everything was carried to West Berlin by aircraft, in Operation Vittles: eighty tons the first day, and within a month over three thousand tons a day. During the course of the blockade, there were 733 incidents between Soviet and Allied aircraft; thirty-nine British, thirty-one American, and five German airmen were killed. The cold war began in earnest.

The years 1945 to 1948 thus had witnessed an accelerating cycle of misperception, provocation, and hostility on both sides. The wartime Big Four alliance became a thing of the past. Neither side saw much possibility for improving relations; Western leaders spoke instead of Soviet "aggression" and of the "captive nations" of Eastern Europe. President Truman wanted to strike back at the Russians and the CIA would be his instrument.

From its creation the CIA was caught up in the shifting currents of the cold war. In the fall of 1947 the first secretary of defense, James M. Forrestal asked the CIA if it would be capable of undertaking secret political action and paramilitary campaigns on behalf of the United States. The Agency replied that it could carry out any mission assigned it by the National Security Council and for which resources were made available.

At first the CIA concentrated on building up its capabilities. It occupied additional quarters in a complex of temporary office buildings on northwest E Street in Washington, which had also housed the Office of Strategic Services during World War II. Managed by a new DCI, Rear Admiral Roscoe H. Hillenkoetter of the Navy, in its first year, the CIA increased its budget by 60 percent and added hundreds of personnel. Stalwarts who had remained with the Office of Special Operations throughout its evolution from SSU to CIG to CIA began to see many old faces from OSS. A new wave of faces appeared as well, young men and women who believed that cold war competition with the Soviet Union was the most important challenge of the times.

But the CIA was not yet ready for covert operations and, in important ways, it actually lacked the authority to engage in them. In response to the initial Pentagon inquiries that fall, Admiral Hillenkoetter asked CIA's legal counsel for an opinion regarding whether the organization could conduct secret propaganda and paramilitary actions. General counsel Lawrence R. Houston replied with a memorandum on September 25, 1947, arguing that the National Security Act failed to provide CIA with the legal authority required. The famous language usually cited to justify covert operations was the provision that the CIA would fulfill such missions as the NSC might, "from time to time," direct. Houston noted that this provision was qualified by language that said the mission must be "related to intelligence." Covert operations were only tenuously related to intelligence. Furthermore, Houston noted, Congress had clearly directed that the agency mainly coordinate the government's intelligence reporting.

Houston did support one intelligence function already being performed that was related to covert operations. This was "acquisition of extensive indication on plans in Western Europe for [the] establishment of resistance elements in event of further extension of Communist control" including information on the training of agents, groups, radio operators, and their outside contacts. For secret propaganda and paramilitary missions, Houston felt, new offices would have to be established, entailing the procurement of "huge quantities" of all kinds of materials and involving large sums for expenses. The memo then declared that "we believe this would be an unauthorized use of the funds made available to CIA." If such operations were ordered by the NSC, Houston concluded, "it would, we feel, still be necessary to go to Congress for authority and funds."

In a published letter thirty-five years later, Houston recalled that Hillenkoetter expressed concern with his legal opinion. The DCI asked whether there were "other considerations" in the matter, whereupon the lawyer provided a second memorandum. Here Houston stated that "if the President, with his constitutional responsibilities for the conduct of foreign policy, gave the agency appropriate instructions and if Congress gave it the funds to carry them out, the agency had the legal capability of carrying out the covert actions involved."

Hillenkoetter then went to Truman with the problem. A proposal for secret propaganda was initiated for presidential consideration. In this connection, the State Department advised in December that Soviet covert operations threatened to defeat American foreign policy objectives unless the United States adopted similar measures. At its very first meeting, on December 13, the National Security Council discussed a program for secret propaganda. The following day President Truman signed a directive, NSC-4/A, approving a secret propaganda program and assigning responsibility for it to the CIA. A week later the CIA formed a Special Procedures Group within its Office of Special Operations to carry out the mission.

It is worth noting that these American decisions were made months before the Czech coup or the Berlin blockade. Events only served to heighten the American hostility and accelerate preparations for covert operations. George Kennan proposed the formation of a Special Studies Group under State Department control to serve as a small elite force for special missions. Since he was the department's senior policy planner, Kennan's views carried considerable weight. For their part, the Joint Chiefs of Staff favored expanding the special-mission capability of the CIA. Everyone agreed on the need for some action.

In June 1948 President Truman resolved this matter by expanding the functions not only of the CIA, but of the State *and* Defense departments and the National Security Council as well. Through a new directive, NSC-10/2, which he signed on June 18, Truman included both psychological warfare and paramilitary programs, the latter for the first time. Both kinds of missions would be carried out by a new organization that would take its operational orders from the CIA and its policy direction from a secret committee chaired by the director of central intelligence. The committee was made a unit of the National Security Council and thus worked directly for the President. The group was composed of representatives of the secretaries of state and defense. Under the "10/2 Panel," funds for the new organization would be included in the budget of the CIA, while the director would be nominated by the secretary of state and approved by the NSC. According to the 10/2 directive, "the overt foreign activities of the US Government must be supplemented by covert operations."

Three features of the NSC-10/2 directive were crucial to the postwar evolution of American covert operations. For the first time in a government decisional document, there appeared a mechanism designated by the President to approve and manage secret operations, and make them responsible to him. Second, and also for the first time, there appeared a comprehensive definition of covert operations. Finally, the CIA was again given primary responsibility for the mission, confirming the arrangement begun with NSC-4/A.

The new covert operations were to involve more than psychological warfare, more even than secret wars. The new definition specified that covert operations included all activities sponsored or conducted by the United States either in support of friendly governments or against hostile ones, with the stipulation that they be "so planned and executed that any US Government responsibility for them is not evident to unauthorized persons and that if uncovered the US Government can plausibly disclaim any responsibility for them." The core of the 10/2 definition explained that

> such operations shall include any covert activities related to: propaganda, economic warfare; preventive direct action, including sabotage, anti-sabotage, demolition and evacuation measures; subversion against hostile states, including assistance to underground resistance movements, guerrillas and refugee liberation groups, and support of indigenous anti-communist elements in threatened countries of the free world.

Virtually the only intelligence area left out of this definition is espionage, and as far as warfare is concerned, the scale ranged up to a level just short of "armed conflict by recognized military forces."

The definition of covert operations contained in NSC-10/2 endured for over three decades, and a new organization called the Office of Special Projects was created to carry them out. That office later merged into the CIA, but the mechanism for presidential approval prescribed by NSC-10/2 is with us to this day.

·II·
THE SECRET WAR
AGAINST RUSSIA

Stalin mobilized Russia for World War II by fanning the flames of nationalism in his country. The theme of the invaded motherland was so prominent that World War II is still called the Great Patriotic War in the Soviet Union. But nationalism in service of the state, plus Soviet ideology, did not bridge the deep ethnic and cultural differences among Russian peoples. The Soviet Union was, and is, a kaleidoscope of peoples and cultures governed from the center. The party papered over the differences of cultures ranging from Muslim to Eastern Orthodox and peoples ranging from Ukrainians to Uzbeks and Asians. Stalin himself was a Georgian from the mountainous Caucasus region. The motherland theme in propaganda cloaked a "nationality problem" that predates Soviet rule to the beginning of Russian expansion under the czars.

The "nationalities question," as it was often called in Soviet ideological debates, was sharpened by the regional distribution of the cultures under the Soviet banner. Unlike countries whose peoples intermix and migrate internally, Russian peoples continue to live in defined geographic areas. This is a matter of both racial and cultural heritage and history—with the czars, serfs were bound to the land; with the Communist Party (CPSU), resettlement requires special permission. To the Soviet leadership the "nationalities question" was a euphemism for control of over 130 Russian ethnic minorities; some of Stalin's prewar purges were sparked precisely by differences between him and other Soviet leaders over policy toward the minorities.

The problem grew along with Stalin's military success in World War II. With Russian troops in garrisons across Eastern Europe, Stalin had no difficulty in making certain changes in the European borders of Russia. Parts of Poland were annexed to the Ukraine and to White Russia, parts of Finland taken over, and some territory from the erstwhile Baltic republics annexed also to White Russia. The province of Moldavia was detached from Romania and it, together with three formerly independent nations—Latvia, Lithuania, and Estonia—became Soviet socialist republics.

In the case of the new socialist republics, Stalin claimed he was merely restoring prewar conditions. Soviet forces had occupied Moldavia and the Baltic Republics briefly in 1940 and 1941 as a result of a deal Adolf Hitler made with Stalin when Germany and Russia were still friends. The measures taken then by Soviet governors had included executions and mass deportations to Siberia. When Russian armies returned four years later, they confirmed these minorities' worst fears by resorting to the same behavior. Before the end of 1945 some 128,000 people were deported from the three Baltic states alone. Not surprisingly, this quickly provoked resistance.

There were other minorities that had been resisting right along, notably Cossacks and Ukrainians. Many from these minorities fought with the Whites against the communists during the Russian civil war. Ukrainian forces also arrayed themselves with the Poles during the Russo-Polish War of 1920. Ukrainians again fought the Russians, this time as German auxiliary troops, or *hiwis*, in the Great Patriotic War itself. While the war as a whole might have ended in 1945, the Ukrainian guerrilla armies continued to fight the Russians. The Ukrainians discovered by the American CIC near Passau in 1947 were part of these forces.

Among ethnic Russians there were also plenty of people resisting Stalin. Activists founded the National Labor Alliance (NTS for Natsionalno Trudovoi Soyuz) in Belgrade in 1930. Both NTS and the czarist groups carried out espionage missions in the Soviet Union before the war; some czarist former Whites also fought alongside the Germans. Another wave of emigration began with Soviet victory in 1945: Soviet deserters, defectors, former prisoners of war evading repatriation, and forced laborers becoming displaced persons, refilled the ranks of the Russian émigré groups.

Stalin's diplomats went to great lengths to get the West to send back certain Russians who had been Whites in the civil war or participants in the anti-Soviet Russian army formed by the Germans with General Andrei Vlasov, a Soviet military hero taken prisoner in the war. Vlasov himself was handed back by the Americans and executed by Stalin's secret police in Moscow in August 1946. Up to 90 percent of Soviet returnees disappeared into the Soviet *"Gulag"* system of penal camps. Repression heightened even the fears of ordinary citizens.

Beyond Soviet borders were the "satellite" states of Eastern Europe. These peoples, too, could not be expected to accept Soviet domination willingly. In a military sense the Eastern European states were indeed "captive nations." Organizing resistance there at first seemed simply a matter of making contact with the right people.

The captive nations, disaffected minorities, and groups of disillusioned social democrats and communists were fertile recruiting grounds, indeed irresistible ones, for Western intelligence officers as the cold war intensified, and the CIA was ordered to begin a secret war against Soviet communism.

The first unit at CIA intended for covert operations was the Special Procedures Group, formed at the end of 1947. This unit was upgraded following President Truman's NSC-10/2 directive to become the Office of Special Projects. As if that name did not sound innocuous enough, it was soon changed again to the Office of Policy Coordination (OPC). The unit was an action group that had little to do with policy or with coordination. The name was intended to conceal the true functions of the unit, which were political action, black propaganda, and paramilitary operations.

Although Harry Truman approved formation of OPC in the heat of the cold war conflict, government records show that it was originally intended that the Office of Policy Coordination maintain its capabilities only for extraordinary circumstances. At an early meeting of the 10/2 Panel, on August 12, 1948, a representative of the NSC made clear that the OPC should be controlled by the State Department during peacetime, and by the Pentagon during war. In turn, George Kennan, who represented the secretary of state, specified that his department be given detailed information about the objectives and methods to be employed in all proposed operations that involved political decisions.

But such decisions were inherent in the cold war situation. Blockade of Berlin began only days after formal approval of NSC-10/2. State Department officials were also impressed with the results of CIA's impromptu intervention in Italian general elections in the spring of 1948—State had been determined to use political action to forestall the possibility of electoral victory by the Italian communist party. So, because of the political atmosphere, little restraint came from the body designated by President Truman to oversee the covert action program.

Covert action also received a tremendous boost from the man selected by the secretary of state to head the Office of Policy Coordination. Frank Gardiner Wisner was a thirty-nine-year-old Mississippian then serving as deputy assistant secretary of state for occupied areas. A dynamo and a workaholic, third in his class at the University of Virginia Law School, he had practiced at the prestigious Wall Street law firm of Carter, Ledyard and Milburn. After being commissioned into naval intelligence during the war, he was quickly transferred to OSS and served in Africa, Turkey, Romania, France, and Germany. Wisner was determined to build an organization with the kind of positive can-do attitude that had characterized OSS. His method was to assign the same mission to several different officers, stay constantly in touch with the details, and hound his subordinates for results.

Wisner's energy provided critical impetus for the CIA's establishment of the Office of Policy Coordination. Much like the companion espionage staff in CIA's Office of Special Operations (OSO), OPC was divided into regional "divisions" and functional "staffs." The Eastern Europe Division handled operations in the "denied areas" of the Soviet bloc. There were functional staffs for political action and for psychological warfare. By the beginning of 1948 Wisner had obtained a budget of $4.7 million, a staff of 302 intelligence officers, and seven field stations.

Since Wisner had been warned not to poach on OSO territory—personnel from the espionage office were off limits to his recruitment drive—he turned instead to the cadre of OSS veterans and the fresh crop of Ivy League college graduates who had just returned from the war—men whom Wisner's journalist friend Stewart Alsop called "the bold Easterners." OPC, perched between CIA and the State Department, was ideally positioned for growth and it doubled and redoubled in size in the first six months of 1949. Wisner's shop appeared to be the hottest thing going at the CIA. But the boss reveled only in action and lacked patience for organizational issues. Rather than coherent, planned growth, there were bursts of wild activity as Wisner plunged off in one or another direction in search of a mission for OPC.

One of Wisner's favorite OPC programs was secret propaganda. The tools developed to carry out these activities Frank used to call his "Wurlitzer," after a popular brand name of jukebox. Wisner's "Wurlitzer" included, at that stage, a shortwave radio transmitter acquired from the Army, the first of a fleet of balloons that could be used to carry leaflets over the "denied areas," and a psychological warfare staff.

To conceal these operations it was deemed necessary to create visible public groups, to which the information activities could be attributed. This was contemplated from the program's inception, and Allen Dulles, who was in contact with Wisner during 1948 as a result of work on a report for President Truman, held several discussions that year with Wall Street colleagues and other prominent acquaintances on the possibility of forming such a group. George Kennan is credited with making a similar proposal within State. Secretary Dean Acheson also discussed the topic informally in late 1948 and early 1949 with several former American diplomats. Among them was Joseph C. Grew, who in turn contacted Dewitt C. Poole, an OSS veteran who had been the senior American diplomat in Moscow at the time of the Russian civil war. Grew and Poole proceeded to establish the National Committee for a Free Europe in June 1949. Allen Dulles was elected its first president. Such figures as the former high commissioner in Germany, General Lucius D. Clay, joined Free Europe's board of directors.

The committee in turn formed a broadcasting subsidiary called Radio Free Europe (RFE) with corporate offices in New York and studios in Munich, where it employed Eastern European émigrés as broadcasters. RFE was secretly given Wisner's radio transmitter while a search began for more powerful equipment. The OPC kept in close contact with RFE, assigning a couple of officers to the RFE staff, in addition to Wisner's direct contacts with many of its board members. Former OSS radio experts like Peter Mero and Robert E. Lang furnished technical assistance in the selection of a transmission site near Frankfurt. The first RFE broadcast was a half-hour program beamed into Czechoslovakia on July 4, 1950.

In 1951 Wisner followed up by initiating a similar organization for broadcasting propaganda directly into the Soviet Union. This was the American Committee for Freedom for the Peoples of the USSR and its broadcast station became known as Radio Liberty. The principal actor in the effort was corporate executive Franklin A. Lindsay, who also represented the CIA on important joint committees with the British. Dewitt Poole again played a vital role in the creation of the organization.

These "radios," as they were called at the CIA, became important resources in the secret war against Russia. They used increasingly powerful transmitters located in Germany, and from 1952, in Portugal as well. There was also the balloon program, which distributed printed materials. The first balloon was launched by an RFE crew from a German farm field in August 1951, which was the beginning of a stream that would deliver four hundred *tons*—up to three hundred million leaflets—over the "denied areas." The balloon launch was attended, as if it were a ceremonial occasion, by RFE president C. D. Jackson, politician Harold Stassen, journalist Drew Pearson, and representatives of the "radios" and émigré groups.

Another facet of Frank Wisner's activity was the creation of a capability for paramilitary operations. This interest cut in two directions. If there was a Russian invasion, and the Soviets did conquer Western Europe, the United States wanted to have stay-behind networks that would resist the Russians. If there was no invasion, the United States still wanted to conduct paramilitary operations on the Russians' own ground of the "denied areas." The OPC could not carry out missions of this sort by itself, and Frank Wisner went to the Pentagon for assistance.

A relationship with the Defense Department was formed despite some opposition. The secretary of the army initially prohibited the assignment of Army officers to OPC on the grounds that he wished his service to have nothing to do with covert operations. But in August 1948 the Joint Chiefs went on record to declare, not only that guerrilla warfare should be supported, under the direction of the NSC, but that the armed services should form no special-warfare units of their own, leaving the field by default to the OPC. Individual military men could be given special training, but OPC would be the only organization with a comprehensive capability to plan and conduct such missions.

In early August of 1949, Wisner asked the Army for extensive assistance, including the designation of an Army officer to serve as
chief of the OPC Guerrilla Warfare Group and the use of Army facilities for CIA training. While the request for an officer was later
withdrawn, in mid-November a conference between OPC and
Army representatives resulted in the selection of Fort Benning,
Georgia, for some CIA training. One of the OPC men at the conference was in fact on detached service from the Army. He was Colonel Richard G. Stilwell, who had served with Detachment 101 of
OSS in Burma. As an officer with firsthand experience in wartime
paramilitary operations, Stilwell played a major role in the CIA-
Army meetings.

There were also certain Army assets in the field, especially in
Germany, that would be of use to OPC. The main one was G-2's
Counter-Intelligence Corps (CIC), with its 66th CIC Detachment
headquartered at Stuttgart from September 1949. The 66th CIC
had the major responsibility of screening displaced persons and refugees, who would be the main source of OPC agent recruits. Some
forty-two thousand people were screened by the 66th during 1949
alone. As late as 1951 some 500 defectors a month were coming
from behind the Iron Curtain. The 66th CIC also carried out "positive intelligence" missions in the Soviet zone—2,211 of them in
1949—that provided information useful to OPC in the planning and
preparation of secret missions.

Probably the most important resource that Frank Wisner got
from the Army was an entire intelligence agency, a German one.
This came about in a circuitous way, with a story that stretches
back to 1945. The Germans had had a military intelligence unit
called Foreign Armies East that handled Soviet intelligence. As the
end neared, the unit evacuated southwest toward the American
armies. The director of Foreign Armies East, Reinhard Gehlen, ultimately ordered the Soviet intelligence files buried and contrived to
have himself captured by the Americans. He then offered to cooperate with the Americans against the Soviet Union.

Gehlen was given a preliminary interrogation by G-2 and OSS officers to evaluate his offer. One of the inquisitors was Frank Wisner.
Gehlen was moved to the United States in August 1945 and began
an alliance with G-2 that ultimately took him back to Germany to
create an organization that worked for G-2 and CIC. The Gehlen
organization was installed at Pullach, near Munich, in December

1947. Gehlen assembled a cadre of German specialists on the Soviets without regard for their pasts; some of his best experts were in fact former Nazis. This and similar Army connections with Nazis would prove embarrassing for the United States many years later.

By 1949 the Gehlen organization was in place and fully functional. Since the Army was winding down its activities in Germany and wished to give up its association with Gehlen, Wisner stepped into the breach. The OPC continued American support for the Gehlen unit and a formal agreement to this effect was signed in June 1949.

American capabilities for covert operations came too late for some, for instance the Baltic States, where nationalist partisans waged a tragic struggle against the reimposition of Soviet control over their countries. In this struggle Western cooperation did come before the end, but it was too little and too late to affect the outcome.

There was a moment of intense hope at the end of the war, when news of the atomic bomb reached Lithuania. In Siaulai, Kaunas, and Vilnius, one heard speculation that the Americans would present Stalin with an ultimatum to force Soviet withdrawal from the occupied territories. To enthralled partisans, it seemed freedom must lie around a single diplomatic bend; but Harry Truman made no atomic ultimatum, there was no rollback of the Soviet armies. In the words of an interested Lithuanian: "Reality methodically and pitilessly destroyed whatever hopes remained."

Stalin garrisoned Lithuania with strong forces, eight divisions plus air force units—over eighty thousand men. But the brunt of the struggle was borne by the Soviet secret police, then called the NKVD, which required army assistance only in extraordinary circumstances. Such was the case in February 1946, when the army sent tanks to help the NKVD assault on a hilltop rebel strongpoint, an event that suggests the heightened intensity of the partisan war.

The Soviet control measures confronted a people in turmoil at the end of the war. Over half the Lithuanians who had survived forced labor in Germany or service in the German army stayed in the West. About 50,000 more fled to the West as refugees and another 150,000 emigrated to Poland. Russian deportations and executions in 1944–1945 accounted for as many people as had left. The country gained additional population, of German extraction and similarly opposed to the Russians, with Stalin's absorption of the East Prussian port of Memel, renamed Klaipéda, into Lithuania.

National upheaval produced a wave of recruits for the "forest brotherhood." The estimated number of partisans in the field rose to almost forty thousand by the spring of 1946. Unlike the other Baltic States, the Lithuanians managed to form a national command during 1946. This was the United Democratic Resistance Movement, or BDPS (Bendras Demokratinio Pasipriesinimo Sajudas). A report by BDPS officers in the summer of 1946 cited six major battles fought against the Russians since the end of World War II. These each involved about two hundred Russians against half as many partisans and ended with the vast majority of the Russians being killed by the "forest brotherhood."

Mikhail Suslov, chief in Lithuania and later prominent communist theoretician, thought the situation so serious that in early 1946 the Organization Bureau offered the first of a succession of amnesties to partisans who turned themselves in. The Soviets reneged on the offer by arresting numbers of the defectors some months later. An NKVD unit under a Major Sokolov also began in 1946 to organize Soviet security units posing as authentic bands of freedom fighters, using captured uniforms and unit insignia. At first the "false flag" units tried to demoralize the Lithuanian people through atrocities carried out in the name of the resistance. Lithuanian sources claim the subterfuge was seldom successful and that the BDPS command was more concerned about the threat of the Soviet amnesty than the effects of the "false flag" operations.

Partisan resistance reached a plateau of sorts in 1947, with strength eroded to perhaps 25,000, facing 50,000 Soviet security troops. Suslov was gone by now, but the Russians offered more amnesties, followed by yet another wave of deportation in the summer and fall. That November a Lithuanian liberation committee in the West complained about Soviet behavior to the United Nations. Meanwhile, inside the country, BDPS held a formal training course during the summer of 1947 for seventy-two newly selected noncommissioned officers, camping in the woods at sites that were shifted constantly. This course was followed by a second in September 1948. Soviet security units found this second training camp, but the partisans shot their way out after a day-long gun battle. The strength of the "forest brotherhood" benefited from the resentments triggered by the Soviet drive for agricultural collectivization, and climbed back to 30,000, but Stalin called in one hundred thousand troops and security police to fight them.

In February 1948 the Lithuanians made their largest recorded attack, against a Soviet garrison of 250 men. This is quite small by "real war" standards, and there was an even smaller attacking force of 120 partisans from two different units. But the "forest brotherhood" could not prevent the Lithuanian communist party from tripling in size between 1946 and 1949.

Soviet control brought production "norms" to Lithuanian farmers. The norm was a tax in kind imposed on the farmers, and making the norm was the farmers' main consideration. The Organization Bureau simultaneously controlled credit and the prices for use of farm machinery. In fact, the State Land Fund contained over a third of all farm implements in the country. The effect was to pauperize farmers, who became peasants working their own land for the state. This process assumed military importance since the partisans relied upon the farmers for food, farmers who now had to deduct that food from what they had left after meeting the "norm."

Collectivization also hurt the partisans because it relocated the farmers in defended localities under close Soviet supervision. In Mao Tse-tung's analogy, collectivization dried up the sea in which the partisan fish needed to swim. The partisans resorted to armed raids in pursuit of food, but attacks on state farms meant stealing from other Lithuanians, who were left behind to meet their "norms." Partisan resistance substantially slowed the rate of collectivization in Lithuania, which was held to 62 percent by the end of 1949. But the cost was high: Partisan strength fell rapidly to a level estimated to be only five thousand by 1950. Against them the Russians deployed the 2nd and 4th Special Task Divisions of the NKVD.

There was no question that the Baltic resistance groups could have benefited from outside help. Before the end of 1945 the Lithuanian partisans had contacts among displaced persons in Sweden, Germany, France, and Britain. Some of those contacts were themselves in touch with Western intelligence. The Lithuanians had a regular courier service, mostly by land, across Poland and East Germany. Little is thought to have come immediately from these relations, though arms dealing is known to have been going on in the Baltic. When, in 1947, the Swedish police set out to investigate a ring of rum runners, they wound up instead with a gun-smuggling operation involving deserters from the Soviet army. That August, the Russian newspaper *Pravda* accused the Estonian government-in-exile in Sweden of being a mere front for American espionage.

The Americans were not ignorant of conditions in the Baltic States. President Truman himself, in a dramatic gesture near the end of 1946, congratulated a group of Estonian refugees who crossed the Atlantic in an old wooden sailing vessel, and ordered the Immigration Service to ignore their lack of visas. Senator Millard E. Tydings of Maryland actively worked to publicize conditions in the Baltic States. Over twelve thousand Estonians in the displaced persons camps in Germany signed a petition appealing for the freedom of their nation and sent it to Truman. Before his death in 1948, Dr. Alfred Bilmanis, formerly Latvian Minister to the United States, wrote almost a half-dozen books and pamphlets on the history, politics, and urgent needs of his country. The Lithuanian-American Council, a prominent émigré group in the United States, made a public appeal for independence to the Allied Council of Foreign Ministers in January 1947. The council attempted to meet with President Truman but was told that he was unavailable.

In 1948 the Lithuanians sent to the West a partisan leader with the special mission of trying to get outside support. Juozas Luksa-Daumantas appeared first in Britain and then moved on to America, where he wrote an account of partisan action behind the iron curtain aimed at the Lithuanian émigré community. He received little more than expressions of interest.

In May 1948 a study group submitted to President Truman an interim report that reflected keen interest in these partisan actions. The report observed that "secret operations, particularly through support of resistance groups, provide one of the most important sources of secret intelligence." That August, Army staff officers expressed interest in forming a small planning group to fashion a war plan especially designed to "cause the people of Soviet Russia to overthrow their present totalitarian government and to render them all practicable assistance in this undertaking." But the Army staff initiative went nowhere.

However, both the CIA and the British Secret Intelligence Service (SIS) became involved in the Baltic partisan struggle. The Americans used Frank Wisner's OPC, and Wisner in turn put great trust in the Gehlen organization. The three organizations began a joint effort that continued at least into the mid-1950s. Operations were mounted from the western zone of Germany, although certain training and preparations were carried out in England and the United States.

The role of the Gehlen organization was vital from the start. In the displaced persons camps and among the Balt émigrés who had settled in Germany, Gehlen's agents recruited on behalf of OPC. The Org, as it was nicknamed, conducted screening and evaluation of the recruits and made recommendations to the Americans about hiring. Preliminary training was accomplished in Germany, with recruits taking such special courses as parachute jumping in the United States.

There was a fairly large pool of potential recruits for the missions. In western Germany alone the influx of postwar settlers included 4,000 Estonians, 11,000 Latvians, and 5,000 Lithuanians. There was also some direct recruitment by the CIA among émigrés living in the United States. One early recruit to the CIA effort was Juozas Luksa, who parachuted back into Lithuania, but soon died at the side of the "forest brotherhood." Between 1949 and 1951 the CIA reportedly parachuted in several more agents to make contact with the Baltic partisans, but the results were poor.

British intelligence had its own methods for recruiting and training the agents for its part of the Baltic operation. The British played a key role since their occupation zone in Germany included the Baltic coast. SIS developed the idea of infiltrating agents by sea from an early date. This method was preferable to air drops, which were noisy and likely to attract the attention of Soviet authorities along the length of the flight path. Landings from boats could be made silently and secretly.

London already had a force that was perfect for infiltration by sea. This was the Baltic fisheries patrol maintained by the Royal Navy beginning in 1949. The patrol was designed to protect local fishermen from interference from Soviet naval vessels and also to recover and disarm the numerous mines strewn throughout the Baltic Sea during the course of the war. The minesweepers were converted E-boats taken over from the German navy in 1945, and they were manned by locally recruited Germans. The ships were unarmed but the British allowed them to wear the Royal Navy ensign.

The SIS notion was that additional boats could be converted to carry infiltrating agents, and run in the Baltic using the cover of the fisheries patrol. There were protracted negotiations among SIS, the

Royal Navy, and the British Foreign Office—eight months of discussion before consensus emerged. A real problem for SIS was that the British budget was tight, and for covert operations especially it was spread very thin.

Here was where the CIA could be really useful. Frank Wisner's outfit had money to spend. More talking followed, this time between SIS and CIA, and OPC agreed to fund the Baltic boat service. The British agreed to facilitate the activities of the unit provided parties of their own agents were also aboard the boats. As a result the Gehlen organization was instructed to form the secret boat unit, with E-Boats to be furnished by the British.

Gehlen sent out his talent scouts and they came up with an officer who had commanded a German motor torpedo boat flotilla in the Baltic during the war. Hans Helmut Klose was hired, and he promptly approached some of his old shipmates and brought them into the operation.

By the time the crews had been filled and the boats refitted, the Balt agents were completing their training. Working for the Americans, they were under a contract that paid them in German marks during the initial selection phase, $125 a week for three months of training in the United States, then $100 a day for each day spent in the "denied areas," with a bonus of $1,000 should the mission be judged successful. Accounts assert that about half the agents sent in survived their missions. Those cases that are known, however, mostly encountered trouble of one sort or another.

One of the earliest landings was along the coast of Latvia on September 30, 1951. On that occasion the E-boat was sighted while in Soviet territorial waters. Two Russian destroyers, a half-dozen frigates, and eight smaller craft gave chase, but Hans Klose maneuvered his ship to safety—the unarmed, unloaded E-boat outran its pursuers. The agent who landed during this escapade subsequently defected to the Russians.

A more successful mission was the landing of an early OPC team on the Estonian coast in the spring of 1952. Agents Zigurd Krumins and Janis Plos had orders to contact the "forest brotherhood" and then make for Riga, where they were to set up a network to furnish information about Russian naval movements. Their orders did not include fighting alongside the partisans or furnishing them with arms or assistance, except in the event of a future war among the great powers.

From Kurland in October 1952 the agents reported they had made contact with a band of Lettish partisans. The fate of Plos is unknown, but Krumins worked with different partisan bands for a year and a half, until the day when the Soviets captured him, with a radio strapped to his back, as he was trying to hide during a search of a Latvian farm. The agent went before a Soviet court in Riga and was sentenced to fifteen years in prison. In 1960, when CIA pilot Francis Gary Powers went down over Russia in a U-2 spy plane, and was also captured, he was sent to the prison at Vladimir, where for seventeen months he shared a cell with Zigurd Krumins.

Unfortunately, the partisan war sputtered to a futile end just as the CIA-SIS Baltic operation reached its stride. The last battle in Latvia was recorded in February 1950. By that time the partisans in Estonia had been worn down to isolated bands and those in Lithuania reduced to a strength of five thousand. Although the Voice of America began broadcasting in Lithuanian in 1952, it became apparent to the partisans that the British and American agents were intent on intelligence missions and not guerrilla warfare. Estonian appeals for arms brought just a few crates of pistols and submachine guns from the Gehlen organization along with two more agents. In Lithuania the national partisan army decided to disband in 1952. A few partisans continued to fight the Soviets—there are reports of partisans captured as late as 1960 and of deaths in actions against Russians as late as 1964.

The CIA-SIS operation also petered out. Agent teams were sent up the Baltic by boat until 1956, while the boat operations briefly expanded to the Black Sea as well in 1954. But after 1954 the Soviet secret service succeeded in planting a spy within the boat service, while toward the end of 1955 the Royal Navy withdrew its permission for German ships to use British naval ensigns, thereby removing the boat service's cover. Then the new government of West Germany absorbed the Gehlen organization, and ordered it to halt missions into Russia.

Baltic partisan warfare was not only futile but cost dearly in terms of human life. Direct civilian casualties in the three states have been estimated at 75,000. Soviet losses are not known. In Lithuania the partisans claim to have eliminated 80,000 Russian soldiers and somewhere between 4,000 and 12,000 communist officials and local collaborators, while admitting losses of 30,000, including 90 percent of their trained cadres. The Soviets admit to losses of only

20,000 in Lithuania and claim only an equal number of partisans killed.

American intelligence had followed these developments from its operational bases in Germany, and the monitoring station in Stockholm run by the Gehlen organization. From April 1951 Frank Wisner's outfit had direct representation in Stockholm in the form of a field station established there by William E. Colby, who had worked in Scandinavia for OSS after the end of World War II. He dropped a private law practice to work for the CIA and was given the primary mission of organizing stay-behind networks in the region. These groups of agents would only be activated if the Soviets took over the country. The OPC station chief met many Eastern European and Balt émigrés, and talked for many hours about conditions in their homelands, mainly, Colby recalls, to boost their morale and encourage them to maintain links with the opposition movements. A few were steered toward "the correct channels in Europe through which they could get support for anti-Communist activities." Bill Colby was particularly upset by the Baltic partisan failure and its implications for his own attempts to create prospective resistance groups.

·III·

"WE'LL GET IT RIGHT NEXT TIME"

In the end it was not the Baltic coastal plain but the rugged Balkans that became the scene of the first big CIA paramilitary operation. It was a plan to unseat the communist government of Albania, a small state on the eastern littoral of the Adriatic Sea. Geography was a key element in making this campaign possible: Bases were available within a short distance, while Albania bordered on only two other nations, Greece and Yugoslavia, both hostile to Stalin by 1949. So Albania's "iron curtain" was isolated from the rest of the Soviet bloc.

The destabilization of Albania was to be a spoiling action in the cold war, a rollback of the iron curtain and the elimination of Russian influence on the Adriatic coast. To the degree that there was a strategic rationale for this campaign, it lay in preventing Soviet access to warm-water ports, especially on the Adriatic, which is crucial to naval control of the central Mediterranean. The plan was to create internal opposition to depose Enver Hoxha, a wartime resistance leader who had risen to communist dictator. Small bands of commandos were to be infiltrated to set up local guerrilla groups, which could be coordinated and supported from the outside.

The plan, evidently called Operation Valuable, was discussed internally at British government meetings in late 1948 and approved at the end of that year. British difficulties with Albania had started in 1946 with incidents in which British warships were fired upon. Later two destroyers were mined and sunk in the three-mile-wide Corfu Channel on the Albanian coast. Although the British had armed and advised Enver Hoxha with their SOE during the war, by 1949 they were prepared to overthrow him. In February 1949 British foreign secretary Ernest Bevin agreed on the plan to "detach" Albania from the Soviet bloc. The Hoxha government, meanwhile, further encouraged British hostility by refusing to accept an International Court of Justice decision against Albania in the Corfu Channel case.

Despite their own determination the British wanted American help, especially financial backing and the use of certain facilities. In March, William Hayter, a senior British intelligence officer, led a delegation of Secret Intelligence Service (SIS) and Foreign Office officials to Washington to argue for American support of Operation Valuable, as well as to present a full range of alternatives for the prosecution of the cold war. The Americans responded with alacrity and the DCI consulted with the 10/2 Panel.

Operation Valuable was coordinated by a joint committee in Washington. British representatives were the SIS liaison man and their Balkan expert at the embassy. Americans included Robert Joyce, representing the State Department and its Policy Planning Staff, and James McCargar, a detached foreign service officer, for the Office of Policy Coordination. In typical fashion Wisner charged his deputy, Franklin Lindsay, with a leadership role in the Albania campaign. The first OPC field officer assigned was Robert Low, a veteran of the OSS in Cairo, who had recently served as a correspondent in the Balkans. Still the British initially provided almost all of the manpower.

There were high hopes in Washington. Albania was, Frank Wisner exclaimed to Bob Joyce, "a clinical experiment to see whether larger rollback operations would be feasible elsewhere."

That April, Wisner returned the British visit and conferred with SIS officials in London. He suggested the use of Wheelus Field, a United States air base in Libya, as the place from which to mount the campaign. The British pointed out that the island of Malta, a British possession, was much closer to the objective. So Malta became the training and boat base, although some supplies were brought in through Wheelus. Wisner ruefully told an SIS officer, "Whenever we want to subvert any place, we find that the British own an island within easy reach." An old castle on Malta, Fort Bin Jema, was activated as a training center, a boat was procured for agent landings, and SIS rented a villa on Corfu as a monitoring station. A number of paramilitary experts from wartime days were induced to participate in Operation Valuable, including Harold Perkins, who ran the operation, and David Smiley, who supervised training.

Feelers were put out in other directions, as well. Yugoslavia, which had halted its aid to Greek leftist guerrillas and broken with Stalin in 1948, was asked to participate. Though the Yugoslavs had approached the United States through CIA channels for military aid, and were depending on this assistance to forestall any intervention by Russia, they did not want to increase Soviet hostility by acting against Albania. Exhausted by its civil war, Greece also wanted no part of Operation Valuable, though certain Greek generals tacitly assisted the CIA.

The most important collaborators were Albanian émigrés. SIS called upon Julian Amery and Neil McLean, who had worked in Albania for SOE during the war, to sound out their old contacts in Rome, Athens, and Cairo. The politics of Operation Valuable were indeed byzantine.

The most accessible Albanian leaders were those of the Balli Kombetar, or "National Front," centered in Rome and Athens. This group was republican but had collaborated with the Germans and Italians in the war in addition to waging partisan warfare against them. One leader had been interior minister under the Germans and was directly involved in a massacre of demonstrators that occurred in February 1944. Another had been justice minister for the Italian occupation government. After meetings with SIS and OPC representatives in Rome, Balli was brought into the operation in late June and early July 1949.

Immediately following these meetings, the Western representatives flew to Cairo to call on the exiled King Zog. Originally the monarch had been a tribal potentate in central Albania. He had seized power in a 1924 coup and made himself king in 1927 of a country that was truly sovereign only between 1912 and 1939. Zog now led his own Legaliteti political movement, and when he learned that the West had dealt first with the Balli Kombetar he was so furious he asked the Western delegates to leave the room.

Julian Amery saved the day, arguing that the time was not ripe to reestablish the monarchy and that King Zog needed allies if he wished to attain that goal.

"He was like Talleyrand," recalled Frank Wisner's representative, OPC officer Robert Low, "I've never seen such diplomacy in my life."

King Zog relented.

In Paris on August 26 a number of Albanian exile leaders held a press conference to announce the formation of an Albanian National Committee. This group of leaders then secretly toured Britain, and more openly visited the United States, where it was sponsored by the OPC-funded Committee for a Free Europe. Acquiring American entry visas for some of the leaders was especially problematic given their lack of passports and history of collaboration with the Nazis. Many of the same individuals previously had been denied entry by State. But OPC stepped in and argued that visas were in the national interest. The CIA did not want to be too closely involved, however; State liaison man Bob Joyce reported back, "My friends state that they would prefer not to approach the visa division directly in this case."

Eventually the Albanians got their documents, survived further misadventures with United States immigration officials in Canada, and made it to the United States, where they made appearances in New York and Washington, and were received by deputy assistant secretary of state Llewelyn E. Thompson on September 19, 1949. Two of the Albanians went to New York to open an office for the national committee. There, on October 3, a senior Balli Kombetar politician, the seventy-year-old Midhat Frasheri, suddenly died of a heart attack at the Lexington Hotel. OPC officer Low was called in by the police to identify the dead Albanian and explain his connection to Frasheri.

By coincidence, that same night in the Adriatic the British boat *Stormie Seas* took two parties, totaling twenty Albanian partisans, across the channel from Corfu. The pixies, as SIS called the Albanians, had received training on Malta since July. This first foray met disaster: Four of the paramilitary men were killed, the others escaped into Greece. Albanian government security forces had evidently known the time and locations of the landings and they were waiting.

One big problem with Operation Valuable was that one of its top men was a Soviet spy. That officer was H.A.R. "Kim" Philby, then beginning his tour as SIS liaison in Washington, and one of the two British representatives on the joint coordination committee.

American and British leaders discussed Operation Valuable at the highest levels during Ernest Bevin's September 1949 visit to Washington. A CIA report prepared at that time concluded that "a purely internal Albanian uprising at this time is not indicated, and, if undertaken, would have little chance of success." Although presumably CIA analysts were not aware of Operation Valuable, they nevertheless noted nine weaknesses of the Hoxha government. Their report also highlighted greatly strengthened Soviet control measures along with the continued improvement of Hoxha's sixty-five-thousand-man army and fifteen thousand security forces.

Significantly, the report concluded, "the possibility of foreign intervention, in conjunction with widespread popular unrest and antigovernment hostility . . . represents a serious threat to the regime."

An Albanian campaign fit squarely with United States policy objectives in force since 1948, which included the intent to "place the maximum strain on the Soviet structure of power and control, particularly on the relationships between Moscow and the satellite countries." The general objective was given concrete expression in NSC-58, the basic policy paper on Eastern Europe, which was available in draft form to Secretary of State Dean Acheson during the Bevin talks. Approved with modifications by President Truman that December, NSC-58 provided for an ideological offensive on all fronts that "should be maintained not only on the overt but on the covert plane." In particular, "we should increase the support and refuge we may be able to offer to leaders and groups in these countries who are western-oriented."

In his conversation with Acheson on Balkan policy, Ernest Bevin inquired whether the United States basically agreed with the overthrow of the Hoxha government. Acheson replied in the affirmative.

"Are there," wondered British Foreign Secretary Bevin, "any kings around that could be put in?"

The picture seemed less bright in the wake of the failed October landings. This is evident in a December 1949 CIA report, ORE 71-49, which worried that loyalty to King Zog might be eclipsed by other differences among the nationalist factions.

> The settlement of differences among the exiled Albanians to provide leadership and coordination is a prerequisite for any effective Albanian resistance against the Hoxha government. Not

even this turn of affairs, however, would assure the achievement
of any successful resistance without material aid from an outside
power. This combination of factors necessary for the overthrow
of the Hoxha regime is, as yet, lacking.

Political differences would ultimately limit recruiting to strict
quotas; 40 percent from the Balli Kombetar, 40 percent from the
Legaliteti, the rest from other factions.

After its disappointing start, Operation Valuable sputtered on for
months, then years, with increasing levels of resources. The Americans became directly involved in 1950, when they began to mount
their own "pixie" expeditions, formed a recruit unit in Germany,
and set up bases there and in Greece. Seven Poles with wartime experience in Royal Air Force partisan support units were hired to fly
transport aircraft and parachute the Albanians. An OPC office using
the cover of a movie producer opened in Rome. The first fully
American "pixie" insertion occurred by air drop in late November
1950.

Kim Philby retained his post in Washington through the summer
of 1951, when he at last fell under suspicion and was recalled. In the
interim there had been a dozen infiltrations with almost fifty
"pixies." Virtually all those staged by sea or air had failed. In a
spectacular failure in July 1951, after Philby was already under investigation, three groups were parachuted in by OPC—one was
wiped out on landing, one surrounded in a house and burned alive,
while two "pixies" of the last group of four were killed and the
other two captured.

Only overland infiltrations seemed to have any success. One
group in September 1950 managed to survive for two months inside
Albania but could not raise any resistance. The most successful
"pixie" was Hamit Matjani, a CIA favorite called the Tiger, who
made fifteen incursions into Albania. His habit was to move overland and secretly. Matjani's sixteenth mission, a parachute drop,
was his last. The Tiger and his party were ambushed by Hoxha security forces.

Matjani's last mission had actually been set up by Hoxha's own
security men with Soviet advice. After managing to capture a radio
and two officers of King Zog's bodyguard sent in during the spring
of 1952, they forced the captives to use their radio to mislead Matjani with glowing reports of a growing resistance and requests for

more aid. It was the same kind of deception with which the Soviets had succeeded in Poland, where they received CIA aid in weapons and gold by creating a spurious partisan movement at the end of 1952. At that time the SIS, frustrated by more boat-landing failures in the summer, withdrew completely from the Albania campaign. The Americans carried on, to drop Matjani to his death in May 1953.

The Hoxha government retained captives who were paraded for a week-long show trial in April 1954. Not even the Americans could continue after this. Frank Wisner had simply been wrong when he insisted, to Philby at an early stage of Operation Valuable, that "We'll get it right next time!"

Widespread disillusionment resulted from the Albanian experience, not least among the former "pixies." Halil Nerguti complains, "We were used as an experiment. We were a small part of a big game, pawns that could be sacrificed." There had never been much chance of success. Michael Burke, OPC station chief in Rome until 1951, voiced a general opinion when he observed, in 1982, that "in the end it was not possible to do without overt air and military support from England and the United States or somewhere. You couldn't do it just with the locals."

British officer David Smiley moved on to the elite military Special Air Service, then became a soldier of fortune. CIA manager Franklin Lindsay left for the Ford Foundation, while Washington subordinate E. Howard Hunt "welcomed" his orders for transfer to the Latin America Division. Michael Burke was himself transferred to Germany, where he ran agent drops directly into the Soviet Union.

It fell to the Southeast Europe Division chief, John H. Richardson, to liquidate Operation Valuable. A wartime veteran of the Counter-Intelligence Corps in Italy, Richardson had been renowned for his skill, tact, and the apparent ease with which he got Italian townspeople to accept Allied military governments. Flying to Rome after the Matjani disaster, Richardson had the most delicate of missions. Joseph Leib, the Rome CIA station chief, still believed in the Albanian adventure.

Richardson sat down over drinks with the station chief, and got right to the point. Albanian activities would end immediately.

"Then," asked Leib, "it's all over?"

"All over."

"I don't know what they'll say about it in London." An aide accompanying Richardson noted that tears glistened amid the stubble
on the overworked man's face.

Richardson responded gently, "London already knows."

Russia itself was the heart of the "denied areas." Even before
there was a CIA, the Central Intelligence Group had orders to collect data about Russia as quietly and extensively as possible. There
was a rush to make contacts among Russian exiles and others with
knowledge of the Soviet Union, and thus a great incentive for the
émigrés to produce lots of information for American consumption,
both real and false. Pandering became so widespread that the term
"paper mills" was applied to shops that produced bogus intelligence. One émigré told the Gehlen people that nine tenths of the
material the Americans were buying had been manufactured.

Still the CIA had no alternative except to deal with the exiles. A
big wave of emigration had occurred during and after the Russian
civil war. By the 1940s these people were well entrenched, especially in France, Britain, and China. They had their own network of
political factions and social clubs. When the CIA and the British
began looking for information on the Soviet Union, it was natural
that they should turn to these people. Some of the political groups
functioned as an underground, with their own contacts in, and courier services to, the Soviet Union. The principal ones were OUN
and the NTS.

The Ukrayinska Viyskova Orhaniztsiya (UVO)—better known by
its English-language rendering OUN, the Organization of Ukrainian
Nationalists—was a creature of the Ukrainian nationalists. This organization was founded in Paris in the early 1920s by refugees.
From the beginning, the Soviets recognized the OUN as a threat;
the organization responded by infiltrating Russia. The Soviets
scored telling blows in 1926, when OUN leader Symon Petlyura was
shot seven times on a Paris street, and in 1938, when original OUN
founder Eyhen Konovalets was handed a bomb in a Rotterdam café.

Back in the Ukraine, OUN established resistance groups and carried out occasional sabotage until World War II intervened. At that
time nationalist Stepan Bandera was serving a life sentence for his
murder of the Polish minister of the interior. Bandera escaped during the Germans' 1939 invasion of Poland and was elected head of
OUN. Two years later the Germans invaded Russia and Bandera

and other OUN leaders associated themselves with the occupation authorities. Bandera became disillusioned with the Germans and was imprisoned by them, but when he agreed to resume cooperation toward the end of the war, he was released. In mid-1944, Bandera and other Ukrainians formed a Supreme Liberation Council to fight the Soviets.

During the Russo-German war OUN was armed by the Germans. Many Ukrainians fought in the auxiliaries. Whole units of them, with German officers included, later formed the core of the OUN paramilitary army. Ukrainians claimed a strength of fifty thousand by September 1944, scattered across the Ukraine, southern Poland, and eastern Czechoslovakia. From that summer, when the last German troops were driven from south Russia, OUN fought on its own. This was partisan warfare on a grand scale, and it did not end with V-E Day. Courier links reportedly broke down after May 1946, but in 1947 OUN leaders still claimed as many as one hundred thousand partisans under arms in eight large formations.

In 1946 Soviet military officials repeatedly demanded the extradition of Stepan Bandera from the American occupation zone of Germany as a war criminal. Bandera, who had fled to the American zone at the end of the war, was warned to hide even though the CIC did have information possibly involving him in war crimes. American authorities informed the Soviets that they had no knowledge of Bandera's whereabouts.

On the ground, the partisan struggle continued for the liberation of the Ukraine, including those parts of it relocated within Poland and Czechoslovakia by border changes. Ukrainians had suffered terribly in the Great Patriotic War—three million sent to Germany as forced labor, half that number still missing, two and a half million killed. There were plenty of reasons for them to support OUN and very few to welcome the return of Stalin. Among the Hutzul, who inhabit the foothills of the Carpathian Mountains, OUN feeling ran especially strong. This eased difficulties of filtering partisan bands and couriers back and forth across the Czech, Polish, and Soviet borders.

Stalin's response was vigorous and sustained. Large Red Army forces were posted to the Ukraine. Communist party activists sent to the Ukraine and Moldavia included Nikita Khrushchev, Leonid Brezhnev, and Konstantin Chernenko. Postwar work in south Russia was clearly a stepping-stone to power for many Soviet leaders.

A military appointment that is worth noting was that of Marshal Georgi K. Zhukov who was sent to command the Odessa Military District in July 1946. Zhukov had distinguished himself in virtually every battle of the Great Patriotic War and was considered perhaps Stalin's best general. Speculation at the time centered on the possibility that he was being demoted. But State Department intelligence reports, in 1947, observed the possibility that he was being used to stabilize the situation in the Ukraine. In fact, the local CPSU headquarters in Odessa had been burned down during riots there the preceding winter.

After Zhukov took command, military operations assumed major proportions. Soviet and Eastern European reports in 1946 several times claimed the "liquidation" of some hundreds of partisans, whom the Soviets typically tried to associate with the Nazis by claiming the bands were led by German officers. In the spring of 1947, the Polish army, itself officered by Russians, began evacuating local populations in southern Poland. There were also coordinated operations in the triborder region by Polish, Czech, and Soviet forces. But OUN was still powerful. The partisans struck back on March 28 when they machine-gunned the Polish vice-minister of defense.

While the Czech army made strenuous efforts to seal off their border, they were unable to prevent the infiltration of several Ukrainian bands. After campaigning all summer and into the fall, Czech defense minister, General Ludvík Svoboda estimated that 100 or 200 partisans were still at large. For their part, the Poles claimed to have eliminated six "brigade groups" of Ukrainians in the Lublin and Cracow districts, with 2,000 partisans killed or captured. As for the Soviets, in a January 1948 speech reported by *Pravda*, Nikita Khrushchev declared, "The Ukrainian people have destroyed an insignificant bunch of Ukrainian nationalists and will annihilate the remnants of them."

Khrushchev probably made these remarks with some satisfaction. Four years before, while accompanying Soviet armies advancing across the Ukraine, he had been forced to take extraordinary measures to protect himself while traveling from town to town. Partisans then were known to be organizing large units around Rovno under a leader called "Taras Bulba," after Gogol's hero. Referring to the partisans in his memoirs, Khrushchev concedes that the "flare-ups" of fighting "sometimes amounted to war," and that partisan activity "became so serious that the Polish forces had to conduct full-scale military operations."

But Khrushchev's January 1948 speech was intended for public consumption. In fact, the Ukrainian partisan struggle was far from over. Members of the unit that escaped to Germany in 1947, Company 95 of the Ukrainian Insurgent Army, variously estimated OUN armed strength at between 50,000 and 200,000 soldiers. They also revealed details of the structure of the partisan forces: units administratively organized into "regiments," with fighting units of platoon (40 men), company (150 men), and battalion (500 to 800 men) size. Most combat units were of company size and each one had six to eight machine guns, an equal number of mortars, and small arms.

This information about OUN capabilities did not prevent State Department intelligence reports from concluding that resistance in the Ukraine was probably no longer serious. But it also did not prevent Ukrainian appeals for aid. A conference of émigrés meeting in New York adopted a resolution to this effect, and sent a telegram to President Truman on August 31, 1947, in which they observed that the "Ukraine is fighting for its freedom by means of its powerful insurgent army. We endorse her fight for freedom on the grounds of the Atlantic Charter. We believe that Russian aggressiveness would lose its power if [the] Ukraine were liberated and acquired self-rule."

Although no American aid was immediately forthcoming, toward the end of 1948 United States military planners reduced the priority assigned to Ukrainian cities, so that these urban areas would no longer be attacked during the initial air offensive of an atomic war. This was seen as a measure that could be exploited for purposes of psychological warfare against Russia.

At the same time, there was growing interest in operations in the "denied areas." The 1948 intelligence study NSC-50 advocated relations with anti-Soviet resistance groups as a prime means of acquiring information. Such views were translated into pressure on OPC in 1949, and resulting pressure by Wisner on the Gehlen organization in 1950, to get agents into Russia. Pentagon wish lists briefed to CIA included up to two thousand agents on the ground to monitor Soviet ports, air bases, and other targets.

However, the hour was very late in the Ukraine. Many partisan companies were down to cadre strength. Though one such unit conducted a daring five-week raid into Romania, Brigadier General

Roman Shuchewycz, commander of the insurgent army, ordered the deactivation of the army and its transformation into an underground, on September 3, 1949. The CIA's Ukraine operation began only two days later, with a team of two agents dropped by parachute after a flight from Germany across Central Europe.

Like some others, the CIA's Russian effort was a joint operation with SIS. As with the others, OPC differed with the British over which émigré factions to back. SIS chose OUN. Officers at OPC believed the tide of history was running against the partisans and preferred to collaborate with a Russian social democratic group named the National Labor Alliance or NTS (Natsionalno Trudovoi Soyuz).

NTS had formed along émigrés of the first wave who opposed both Soviet and czarist rule. It had been founded in Belgrade in 1930 and espoused parliamentary democracy. Like OUN, the NTS maintained courier services into Russia and tried to establish networks there. Like Stepan Bandera, the NTS had collaborated in the early days with the German wartime administration in Russia. But unlike OUN, NTS made no effort to create partisan forces. Rather, under Dr. Georgi S. Okolovich, NTS ideologist Vladimir Poremski developed the celebrated "molecular theory," in which widening sectors of Russian society would come to oppose the communists and ultimately combine to overthrow Soviet rule.

These views were advanced in pamphlets, in the NTS newspaper *Posev,* and on the broadcasts of the affiliated station Radio Free Russia. There was an administrative headquarters in Paris and a field center at Frankfurt with more than two hundred personnel. NTS actually recruited its own agents among the émigrés and trained them in the Bavarian hills at Bad Homburg. The Russian émigrés already had relations with the Counter-Intelligence Corps and with Army G-2, as well as the Gehlen organization and SIS. So it was easy for the NTS to make contact with OPC.

Soon the Russian operation was in full swing. Frank Wisner's boys, with the Gehlen organization, did preliminary screening and training, recruiting Russian émigrés under the same terms offered the Balts. Published estimates of the number of "special forces" agents trained before 1954 range up to five thousand. The number who received training in the United States was much lower but included, during the years 1948 to 1950, at least two hundred men with Nazi connections, whom the State Department was asked to admit on grounds of national security.

The SIS took the lead in actual infiltration. British intelligence had worked with the Ukrainian OUN before the war, and saw no reason to give up the relationship afterward. British experts also felt that OPC had misplaced confidence in the NTS.

According to Kim Philby, Anglo-American cooperation on both Soviet "denied area" schemes—in the Baltic and the Ukraine—was chilly. On the Ukrainian situation, Philby recalls the CIA arguing that Stepan Bandera was anti-American, that OUN represented extreme nationalism with fascist overtones, and that anyway its roots were among the first wave, now "old," emigration. On the Baltic, there was a meeting in Washington, Philby asserts, between the responsible CIA officers and the SIS chief for northern Europe, Henry Carr, which ended with the sides openly accusing each other of "wholesale lying."

Philby claims the accusations were justified, on both sides!

A conference at the highest level between the CIA and SIS was held in London in April 1951. The occasion was a European tour by Allen W. Dulles, recently hired by the CIA as deputy director for plans to manage the activities of both Wisner's OPC and the competing Office of Special Operations. Dulles's subordinates had encouraged SIS to abandon Bandera and OUN. At the London conference SIS officials flatly refused, even though they were in a weakened position because the two SIS missions sent into Russia during 1950 had both disappeared without a trace.

The CIA and the British remained deadlocked, with the practical result that support continued for both the Ukrainians and the NTS. In 1951 the British dropped three parties of six men each into the Ukraine, the foothills of the Carpathians, and southern Poland. None of the teams was heard from again. A CIA four-man team that infiltrated along the Baltic coast was unproductive, as were three missions involving five agents dispatched to the Ukraine and Moldavia. Planes to drop these agents into the "denied areas" were flown by the British through Cyprus and by the CIA through Greece and western Germany.

Intelligence agents operated at grave disadvantages in the Soviet Union. The population was closely controlled and state security was everywhere. (It was only in 1951, apparently, that the CIA learned the details of the printing processes the Russians used to produce their internal passports and other documents.) The power of the partisans was broken by the time agent teams began to arrive.

Remnants of OUN and Bandera forces held out among the Hutzul in the Carpathians until 1952, but the bands were slowly tracked down by the Soviets. There was no longer much chance of finding them no matter how many teams were infiltrated by Western intelligence.

Another sixteen agents were lost by the Americans in at least five missions mounted during 1952 and 1953. British losses are still unknown, as are those of the Office of Special Operations, which ran its own agent missions into the "denied areas." Whatever the figures, it was clear that losses were mounting and that there was very little to show for it.

Until 1951 the Soviets had the advantage of information from Philby, but he was not their only intelligence resource. Beginning in 1950 they received reports from Heinz Felfe, a senior officer of the Gehlen organization and from Canadian spy Gordon Lonsdale.

The flow of refugees and displaced persons, which was a main source of recruits for OPC and the SIS, could also be used by the Russian secret service to insert their own spies into the Western operations. One of the most valuable Soviet spies was Captain Nikita Khorunshy, who defected from East Berlin in 1948 and told the CIC his reason was he had fallen in love with a German girl.

Like many émigrés, Khorunshy moved to Frankfurt. There he joined Russian social clubs and soon became associated with NTS. The émigrés relied on his recent knowledge of conditions in Russia, and hired Khorunshy for their agent training school at Bad Homburg. Thus the Soviets had their own spy at the very center of the operation being run against them. Using intelligence from Khorunshy, the Russians were able to insert into the refugee camps more agents with the specific qualifications sought by the Western services, agents who were recruited, sent back to Russia, and compromised their individual missions. Khorunshy meanwhile supplied the Soviets, beginning in 1951, with a constant stream of information on all the agents trained through the NTS–Gehlen organization–OPC network. He also suggested and supplied the information necessary for an assassination attempt against NTS chief Dr. Okolovich. Khorunshy was discovered after the betrayal of a 1953 team he had trained at Bad Homburg. Though he was arrested in 1954, that year the Soviets captured a solo agent and another team being infiltrated by the CIA.

For their part, the Russians did adopt Khorunshy's recommendation for the murder of Okolovich. In February 1954 they sent to Frankfurt a team of two East Germans plus Captain Nikolai I. Khoklov to execute the NTS leader. Operation Rhine miscarried, however, when Khoklov repented and made a personal confession to Okolovich. The extent to which NTS by this time had become subordinated to the CIA is suggested by the ease with which the Americans then took Khoklov away from NTS.

The "Khoklov affair" was the first of a series of similar Soviet measures against émigré figures. Okolovich was beaten during an abortive kidnapping. NTS ideologist Poremski was the subject of another abortive murder attempt. The Russians were more successful with Ukrainian leader Lev Rebet, whom they assassinated in 1957. Also killed were a couple of senior Eastern European broadcasters for Radio Free Europe. This campaign climaxed on October 15, 1959, when Stepan Bandera was killed outside his Munich apartment building with a dose of cyanide fired from an ingeniously constructed gun.

Secret warfare against Russia ground to a halt. The British were frustrated with the failure of OUN and considered NTS an ineffective organization. They broke off relations with Okolovich's network in 1956. Officials of the CIA took a different view of the "denied areas" programs. They admitted the failures but persisted for a long time, as if mere repetition could ensure success.

On a trip from Munich to Washington in 1953, Allen Dulles told one of his senior specialists on Soviet affairs, "At least we're getting the kind of experience we need for the next war."

One day in April 1954, Dulles was at Frank Wisner's Georgetown home for a lunch with Michael Burke, the Munich station chief who was making the go/no go decisions on the agent airdrops. Burke was most concerned about the Washington perspective on the overflights, since he had no notion of the political implications when making his overflight decisions. Wisner and the DCI made some appropriate remarks—Washington would always stop the mission if there were problems. Soon afterward a plane returning from one of the Soviet drop missions encountered two fighter interceptors over Hungary. The crew managed to elude the planes in cloud cover, but greater difficulties clearly faced any further missions. The CIA's Soviet program finally ended.

Michael Burke had had enough. After working for OSS, for OPC on Albania, and now on the Soviet campaign, he felt it was time to move on. Burke left the CIA to become manager of the Ringling Brothers Barnum and Bailey Circus, and later president of the New York Yankees. Burke, at least, *could* move on. Not so for many of the émigrés recruited by the CIA. Reflecting on this period some three decades later, State Department Balkans expert John C. Campbell commented: "What did we offer these people? We did not have any means really of supporting a revolt which might break out. I think we were responsible for the loss of some good, patriotic people from those countries because we gave them money and instructions."

·IV·
ADVENTURES IN ASIA

C hoosing sides may have been a dilemma for people in Europe, but in the Far East that dilemma was multiplied a thousandfold. In China cooperation between nationalist and communist parties broke down soon after the defeat of Japan; Chiang Kai-shek and Mao Tse-tung merely resumed their interrupted struggle for leadership. All over Asia the cold war was especially pernicious in that nationalist and religious movements were recast as members of a global ideological struggle. With China, India, and Southeast Asia in the cold war, the potential for enormous power hung in the balance.

The United States was involved in the struggle for Asia from the beginning. There were abortive efforts to mediate between the contending factions in China, after which President Truman aligned himself with Chiang Kai-shek against the Chinese communists. Mao Tse-tung's field armies nevertheless swept through mainland China. The nationalist collapse climaxed in 1949 when the Chinese communists overran Peking and southern China. This happened despite American military and economic aid to Chiang, and at precisely the time when American covert action capabilities were coalescing within the CIA and the Pentagon.

Proposals were soon afoot in Washington to exploit the still-tenuous communist control of the mainland, by using a new nationalist base on the islands off the China coast. The Korean War injected tremendous momentum into the program; in turn, this expansion eventually created a dilemma for the controllers of secret warfare. But, aside from their policy implications, as we shall see, the secret campaigns against China had only indifferent success. More important, the intelligence buildup that occurred during the Korean War greatly expanded our capability for, and interest in, covert actions of all sorts.

After being driven from the Chinese mainland, Chiang Kai-shek's nationalist forces succeeded in establishing themselves on the islands offshore. Taiwan was the biggest, with room for an entire nation, the nationalists later decided. Hainan, off southern China, was next, with smaller island garrisons off the provinces of Fukien and Chekiang. There were also remnants of the nationalists on the mainland in Kwangtung and Yunnan—in early 1950 they were driven across the borders of Indochina and Burma, respectively.

Coastal islands were a different matter. The Chinese communists had no navy to speak of and no experience with amphibious war. Only small vessels, mostly junks, were even available to be commandeered. Mao's armies made one big effort, in early 1950, to fight their way onto Hainan, which they accomplished after ten invasions and considerable casualties when, as so often had happened in China, the morale of the nationalist forces broke. Superior force was no guarantee against defeat; Chiang ordered the nationalist survivors back to Taiwan. Although there were fears the communists would follow, an invasion of Taiwan was a much more difficult proposition and was not then attempted.

So, after about $2.2 billion in economic and military aid and surplus military equipment had been poured into China, American policy had few successes to show.

Proposals for covert action actually predated nationalist defeat in the civil war. Chiang had gone to Taiwan in early 1949, resigning the presidency in favor of his vice-president, General Li Tsung-jen, who was left to try to negotiate a settlement with Mao. That spring Claire Chennault, a retired American officer who had commanded the Flying Tigers during the Sino-Japanese war, the Fourteenth Air Force in China in World War II, and afterward organized a private airline called Civil Air Transport that operated in China, went to Washington with a proposal for United States military aid for a nationalist bastion in southern China plus covert aid to guerrilla forces loyal to Li Tsung-jen.

The State Department was not much interested in the Chennault plan, so the former general went to his business partner in Civil Air

Transport, Thomas G. Corcoran, well connected with government. Corcoran put Chennault in contact with CIA officers, culminating in a series of meetings during the summer of 1949. By August, Chennault was talking to Colonel Richard G. Stilwell, chief of the Far East Division of OPC, who was not only interested in military assistance but thought an airline like Civil Air Transport could provide CIA with an important covert asset. President Truman simultaneously directed the State Department to reexamine the feasibility of Chennault's plan.

Before these deliberations could be completed, however, nationalist military resistance disintegrated on the mainland, forcing a shift in emphasis to those operations that could be mounted from outside China. Civil Air Transport became even more important as a potential asset, but the airline was in financial trouble. In early October the CIA received an analysis of the Chennault plan from George Kennan, head of State's Policy Planning Staff, which took no position on the project, but was nevertheless used by Frank Wisner as if State had approved it. Civil Air Transport (CAT) was enlisted in the secret war, flying its first mission for the CIA on October 10, 1949. Tommy Corcoran, on behalf of CAT and Emmet D. Echols of CIA's Office of Finances, signed a formal agreement on the first of November.

In the Pentagon, meanwhile, on October 28, 1949, a detailed proposal for covert operations in China was sent to the secretary of defense by General John Magruder. Magruder endorsed the proposal, citing his experience as chief of the Strategic Services Unit. Secretary of Defense Louis Johnson forwarded both the proposal and an accompanying memorandum from Wisner at OPC to the President. Harry Truman expressed some interest in November 1949, but the final collapse of the nationalists on the mainland temporarily halted the effort.

United States government interest came at an opportune moment for Civil Air Transport. Founded in 1946 by Chennault and Whiting Willauer, CAT was essentially a paramilitary operation from the beginning, making its living flying troops, supplies, and dignitaries back and forth in the Chinese civil war. The airline's performance in 1948 was impressive: 34 million ton-miles; 223,700 passengers carried; and 88,238 tons of cargo consigned. By mid-1949, however, runaway Chinese inflation and the nationalist disintegration meant CAT faced disaster. The CIA arrangement brought in a half-million dollars in a hard currency, $200,000 of it up front. The airline was able to relocate its base facilities to Taiwan and corporate headquarters to Hong Kong, ending the chaos of existence on the mainland. (Chennault's friendship with Chiang Kai-shek and his exclusive alliance with the nationalists meant the end of demand for domestic air transport once the communists had taken over.) The CIA money did not resolve the underlying market problems for the private company, and Civil Air Transport was forced to go back to the CIA again and again until the intelligence agency virtually owned the airline.

Access to a fleet of transport aircraft proved a great boon to the OPC. In Europe air missions had to be run through the American or British air forces. Missions required delicate interagency discussions, sometimes a little horse trading, too. In Asia with CAT, OPC could dispense with politics. Sometimes there was a question whether CAT crews would volunteer for the flights, but since Willauer's pilots flaunted their skills and can-do attitudes, this was rarely a problem.

The earliest arms request was from General Ma Pu-fang, a Muslim leader in northwest China, who was thought to have fifty thousand troops plus a trained reserve four times as large. Aid to Muslims in the northwest was the sole covert action known to have been specifically mentioned by President Truman, at a November 1949 meeting on assistance to anticommunist Chinese. But before shipments could be organized, General Ma was defeated. Gathering his fortune of $1.5 million in gold bars, Ma Pu-fang escaped on a CAT plane and then departed China on a pilgrimage to Mecca.

Recruits willing to undertake missions to the mainland had to be found. This was not difficult because the nationalists ardently wished to return; Chiang sounded the keynote in a speech in which he promised to go "back to the Mainland," a theme he dwelt on repeatedly throughout the 1950s and which was adopted as a slogan by the pronationalist "China lobby" in the United States.

Yet there were difficulties in Asia, not unlike those the CIA was encountering in Europe. There were factions among the nationalists, all of whom hoped to corner prospective United States aid. Alfred T. Cox, the OPC officer sent to Hong Kong, to represent CIA at the headquarters of Civil Air Transport, found himself beoming a sort of broker between the United States and the squabbling factions.

Chinese politics embarrassed the United States from the earliest stages of the operation. Immediately after leaving the mainland in December 1949, sixty-year-old acting president Li Tsung-jen went to New York for medical treatment. There, the general was invited to Washington by President Truman for an official visit. Li claimed to have 175,000 guerrilla troops loyal to him, mostly in southwest China. In a memorandum of February 22, 1950, he proposed a four-point program to President Truman, including organization of guerrilla warfare; underground activities; penetration of overseas Chinese; and mobilization of liberal elements dissatisfied with both the communists and the nationalists.

As acting president of China, Li Tsung-jen stayed at the official Blair House residence during his visit to Washington. President Truman planned a formal reception for him as a head of state, at a luncheon to be held on March 2. But on March 1, in Taiwan, Chiang Kai-shek suddenly and unilaterally declared himself the lawful ruler of China and reassumed the presidency. Li was instantly deprived of power and remained in the United States, where he competed with Chiang for influence among ethnic Chinese in this country.

Despite the internal political struggle among the nationalists, some intelligence officers at OPC continued to believe Li Tsung-jen offered a viable alternative, a "third force" in China untainted by either communism or the excesses and corruption of the nationalist government. But because Chiang Kai-shek controlled the offshore islands, the potential bases for the secret war, there was ultimately no choice but to support the Taiwan authorities.

The China campaign was masterminded by the Far East Division of OPC. The chief of that division was an officer on detached service from the Army who had fought with OSS Detachment 101 in Burma during the war. His deputy, Desmond FitzGerald, was another former officer who had been in Burma, as an adviser to the nationalist army. Both officers were enthusiastic about the possibilities.

As early as May 1949 the director of central intelligence, Rear Admiral Roscoe H. Hillenkoetter, had asked the Pentagon to form a staff of service representatives to help the CIA establish a paramilitary training program. Two months later the secretary of the army approved assistance to the OPC in the area of guerrilla warfare, and space for a CIA training facility was set aside at Fort Benning. The

Pentagon went on to establish a staff to coordinate military arrangements for psychological warfare and covert operations with CIA that November. Despite this military cooperation, the OPC Far East Division chief refused to commit the CIA to any explicit command arrangement with the Pentagon. Richard Stilwell would only say he was "reasonably certain" that military theater commanders would be informed of and could approve covert operations carried out in their areas.

Having kept its options open, the CIA began to put in place the elements necessary for a secret war against China. An office under commercial cover called Western Enterprises was opened on Taiwan in 1950; it was called Western Auto by agents. Training and operational bases followed in southern Taiwan and the other offshore islands.

After promises of action against the mainland from the beginning of 1950, a small raid occurred near Nanhwei in April and a larger one at Shihpu the next month. The port of Canton was momentarily cut off from the interior by the actions of thirty thousand guerrillas. Deep inside China, in Sinkiang province, American money was reportedly funneled to tribal minorities and some White Russians who formed a cavalry unit to resist the communists. Peking radio broadcasts several times charged D. C. MacKiernan, the American vice-consul in this area, with providing the aid. Before the end of the year, Taiwan leaders would claim to have more than a million active guerrillas on the mainland. United States intelligence estimates at the time carried the more conservative figure of 600,000 or 650,000, only half of whom could be considered loyal to Taiwan.

The Chinese communists openly admitted the existence of a resistance movement and conducted "bandit suppression" operations against the guerrillas. Reporting to a party congress in June 1950, Mao Tse-tung mentioned a figure of 400,000 "bandits," an estimate cut in half by Premier Chou En-lai that October, shortly before Peking claimed the arrests of an astonishing 20,000 agents of "U.S. military intelligence" since the beginning of 1949. During the course of 1950 the People's Liberation Army (PLA) mobilized some 1,157,000 men in central and southern China, an effort that may have been related to other military operations, but was explicitly linked to meeting the "bandit" threat. That November there were even reports that the PLA had had to shift troops from Fukien province (opposite Taiwan) to Chekiang to counter guerrilla activity.

Much of the initial guerrilla threat had more to do with the communists' incomplete consolidation of power than the impact of early CIA operations. In many places in China there were nationalist remnants, local warlords, even actual gangs of bandits. The fact is that the guerrillas did not hinder Peking from withdrawing from southern China the field armies it used to intervene in the Korean War. Thus the military impact of the anticommunist guerrilla movement must be judged as minimal.

A new phase of the secret war began with the outbreak of hostilities in Korea in June 1950. The end of World War II had left Korea, like Germany, divided into occupation zones, making reunification a national political issue. The Soviets in North Korea and the Americans in the south each proceeded to organize governments in their areas. Unlike Germany, in Korea the occupation forces of the superpowers were withdrawn, leaving the Koreans to settle their own quarrels. Sharpening rhetoric and hyperbole, threats from both North and South Korea to achieve reunification by force, ended in a North Korean invasion of the south. Within days President Truman decided to oppose the North Korean invasion, committing the United States to the war. The United States sought and obtained a United Nations mandate to halt the aggression in Korea and fought the war under the UN flag.

The Korean hostilities created a demand for covert operations against North Korea. The China programs, if anything, were reinvigorated, especially after the November 1950 PLA intervention in Korea. At first the American resources for paramilitary and commando actions were quite limited. The CIA's main strength was assigned to clandestine intelligence missions by the Office of Special Operations (OSO) operating out of Yokosuka. The OPC, by contrast, was just getting into action. A new chief of station for Wisner arrived in Tokyo to discover that his total strength consisted of six men living out of a hotel room.

One impediment to a rapid expansion of OPC operations in Korea was General Douglas MacArthur. Wearing the various hats of Far East area commander, UN theater commander, and American force commander, MacArthur had a primary interest in special operations conducted within his zone. During World War II the general had prohibited OSS operations in his area; in 1950 there were fears MacArthur might do the same for Korea. The CIA could be considered especially vulnerable, as it had avoided making any explicit promises regarding the primacy of military commands.

Far East Command (FECOM) did not refuse to allow the CIA into Korea. But MacArthur remained a reluctant player in the secret warfare; FECOM allowed access but did little to encourage special operations, and did as much as possible to preserve command authority. MacArthur also continued to entrust special operations to the staff of an officer with whom he had close personal ties, his director of intelligence, even though responsibility for these activities in the U.S. Army had been transferred to the staff division for psychological warfare.

Initially the military had by far the greater resources for paramilitary operations anyway. Air Force transports stood ready at several bases in Japan. The Navy sent out from San Diego the fast transport *Horace A. Bass,* a ship equipped with four landing craft and modified to carry 162 commandos. Some Marine reconnaissance troops and Navy underwater demolition teams joined with the ship in a Special Operations Group (SOG) by August 6, 1950. Only two days later the capability was augmented with the addition of a submarine transport, *Perch,* converted to carry up to 160 troops. The British also contributed a squad of Royal Marines to the SOG force.

The CIA had CAT for its air arm, but had a long way to go to match this military capability. The new OPC commander was Hans Tofte, son of a sea captain. He was fluent in Chinese, having worked for ten years as a shipping company official in Peking and Manchuria before the war—another of that band of flamboyant OSS veterans. Tofte's World War II experience had been in organizing arms shipments to guerrillas across the Adriatic Sea from Bari, Italy, and later parachute drops of agents from Dijon, France. At one time in his little Adriatic fleet, Tofte had managed as many as forty-four vessels.

A Danish citizen, Tofte returned to Copenhagen after the war as the local manager for Pan American Airlines. Later he married an American woman and moved to Iowa where he remained active as an officer in the Army reserves. When the OPC began China operations, they tried to recruit Tofte, with fervent pleas from Far East Division chief Richard G. Stilwell and his deputy Desmond Fitz-

Gerald during a December 1949 meeting in Washington. The forty-three-year-old Tofte was on summer active duty with the reserve when he learned of the fighting in Korea. Two days later he showed up at the CIA's E Street headquarters. Frank Wisner saw in him a well-qualified former comrade who could speak six languages including Chinese. Hans Tofte was hired and assigned to Japan.

Tofte quickly began creating an infrastructure for CIA operations. At the Atsugi air base, he and deputy Colwell Beers found a fifty-acre tract of land isolated at one corner of the base. The men paced off building locations and within a week engineers and construction troops were building the facilities for a CIA contingent that would number over a thousand personnel. On Yong-do island in Pusan bay they established an installation to train Koreans for behind-the-lines missions. Tofte recruited an energetic Marine officer, Lieutenant Colonel "Dutch" Kraemer, to run the base. The military's SOG coordinated sea transport for agents while Civil Air Transport provided a fleet of forty aircraft for the clandestine air effort.

One early result of OPC's Korean War expansion was Operation Bluebell, an attempt to gather intelligence on North Korean and Chinese troop movements. Literally thousands of Korean refugees were dispatched behind enemy lines and told to make their way back as best they could. Returning refugees were then debriefed on what they had learned. The quality of the information garnered from Operation Bluebell is demonstrated by CIA's conclusion that *children* had provided the best intelligence.

Another project was a movie begun in late 1950, based on a diary kept by a Japanese colonel imprisoned after the war in a Siberian labor camp. The film opened in twenty Japanese theaters and played in over seven hundred during a brief commercial run. When OPC officers added up the figures, a profit of $104,000 went to the U.S. Treasury, a bonus to the anti-Soviet propaganda value of the project.

A paramilitary operation, Stole, was a covert attempt to block Indian medical aid from being given to Mao's China for humanitarian reasons. Medical supplies including makings for three full field hospitals were aboard a Norwegian freighter en route for China. Operation Stole was to stop the shipment at all costs; CIA approved a million dollars for the action. Hans Tofte met in Tokyo with other OPC Far East station chiefs to plan the operation. At one point, Al

Cox in Hong Kong made preparations for sabotage under the noses of British authorities in case the Norwegian ship docked there. When the freighter bypassed Hong Kong, a more discrete plan evolved—Tofte simply approached Chiang Kai-shek, who was happy to lend his patrol boats to a scheme for stopping the ship on the high seas and commandeering its cargo. Cox and other CIA agents were present, though hidden belowdecks, when nationalist gunboats pirated the cargo.

The general expansion of covert operations naturally exacerbated the command problem. In Tokyo, FECOM set up a Far East Command Liaison Group under the intelligence staff to supervise all military and CIA activities. A CIA officer controlled the innocuously titled Documents Research Division, which planned operations. The Joint Advisory Commission Korea (JACK) actually ran the activities, its head a military officer detailed to CIA. An additional management organization, Covert Clandestine and Related Activities Korea (CCRAK) was formed in December 1951 in a further unsuccessful effort to resolve the overlapping roles of military and CIA paramilitary efforts.

Decisions in Washington sharpened the command problem by expanding the scope of covert activities. In the first week of the war, President Truman gave orders to protect Taiwan with naval patrols by the Seventh Fleet in the Taiwan Strait. By late 1951 he was asking what additional actions could be taken to hurt the Chinese communists. In early 1951 National Security Council policy paper NSC-101 approved support for a vigorous program of covert operations to aid anticommunist guerrilla forces. Disruption of Chinese communist supply lines was under explicit consideration in NSC-118, and President Truman approved this at the end of the year.

In early 1952 the Joint Chiefs issued orders for the Navy to provide the CIA with ships and facilities for coastal landings, on the mainland in addition to Korea. Joint planners at the Pentagon, in deference to the loyalties commanded by Li Tsung-jen and others, were arguing that the United States should support *all* the anticommunist Chinese. That February the Joint Strategic Planning Committee recommended a $300 million budget for covert operations onto the mainland. Regarding CIA's association with Chiang Kai-shek's faction, the military planners warned, "Covert activity within China would be unlikely to overthrow the Chinese communist regime in the absence of an effective counter-revolutionary movement, a political program, a clear-cut organization and competent leadership—none of which the Chinese Nationalists appear capable of providing at this time."

In the summer of 1952, when it merged the OPC and OSO into a unified Directorate of Plans, the CIA established a North Asia Command to consolidate control over its various operations against the Chinese run from Japan, the offshore islands, and Thailand. By then Wisner had created an international network including elements in Singapore and in Burma, bases in Japan, Korea, and on the Pacific island of Saipan, all serviced by CAT, with cooperation from the Navy on sea transport.

The CIA facilities primarily existed to support paramilitary operations. Koreans were mainly recruited in that country and Japan and trained on Yong-do island. Chinese were recruited whenever possible but mostly on Taiwan, where they also received training.

Advanced training for recruits of both nationalities was provided by the CIA at a secret base located in the mid-Pacific on the island of Saipan. Actually, by using the island, the United States violated international law, since Saipan was technically a United Nations dependency, part of the Trust Territory of the Pacific Islands, which was merely administered by the United States. When supervision of the trust was transferred from military to civilian hands in 1951–1952, the Navy successfully fought a Department of the Interior plan to place the trust territory headquarters on Saipan, and security was preserved.

The CIA facility used a military designation, Naval Technical Training Unit, for its cover. Recruits were flown in at night by C-47 aircraft like those of Civil Air Transport. New arrivals were blindfolded on the ground en route to the base. But the CIA facility had been built on the highest mountain on the island, with surroundings plainly visible to the trainees. The standard of living and style of construction on the rest of the island bore little relation to the concrete barracks and tract houses of the CIA base, and there were periodic emergencies for the base personnel when the "Naval Technical Training Unit" had to be quickly sanitized and closed down for the visits of United Nations trusteeship commissioners.

After training, the recruits were returned to the hands of the operating stations for their missions. These included commando raids and sabotage strikes at selected targets. In Korea intelligence-gathering patrols were landed on both coasts; in China, liaison with local anticommunist resistance groups was established. Over twelve hundred Koreans were trained at Yong-do, formed into strike teams, and used on the secret missions. The estimate of Chinese recruits is less firm—only some "hundreds" are cited.

The military's special operations effort became even larger. Under several cover designations that finally ended with Far East Command Liaison Detachment (Korea), 8240th Army Unit, FECOM ran a vigorous paramilitary program. Section Baker furnished air support with C-46's and C-47's; Sections Leopard, Kirkland, and Wolfpack were the field forces. Wolfpack, for example, was set up in March 1952 with a total strength of four thousand Koreans and 7 Americans (basically the commander, his senior staff, and communications specialists). Each of six battalions had its base on a different island off the Korean coast. Raids frequently involved naval gunfire support and bombing to back battalions of up to 800 men. By late 1952, Wolfpack had grown to eight battalions with 6,800 men and an American contingent of 12. At that time Leopard was reporting a strength of 5,500. When, in early 1953, FECOM took cadre from Wolfpack and the 8240th Unit to form the United Nations Partisan Forces in Korea (UNPFK), it expected to obtain a force of 20,000 troops within a few months. The UNPFK organization was even copied by French special warfare officers from Indochina for an expansion of the French paramilitary effort there to be made with United States military assistance funds. As an example of partisan effectiveness, for the period of November 15 to 21, 1952, FECOM reported a total of sixty-three raids and twenty-five patrols, claiming 1,382 enemy casualties.

The CIA's operations against the mainland were generally smaller, but more widespread and diverse in nature. Advice, training, and supplies were given to Chiang Kai-shek's forces, who claimed in early 1952 to have made fifteen raids on the mainland during the preceding seven months. Strength of the CIA station on Taiwan already exceeded six hundred, with the station undertaking a huge range of activities. Airdrops of propaganda leaflets over the mainland were numerous; there were up to thirty flights a month, which dropped some three hundred million leaflets in 1953, according to one account. Many of the leaflet drops were flown by Civil Air Transport, others by the nationalist air force.

A separate program of aid to guerrillas in Manchuria who were not loyal to Chiang was also carried out by CIA. This operation, known as Tropic to CAT pilots, used CAT crews flying out of Japan at night in unmarked C-47's. The Yale class of 1951 was heavily recruited for the program, recalls John T. Downey, who joined the CIA that year after graduation. Assigned to set up resistance in Kirin province, Downey visited Saipan in 1952 to select a four-man team who were dropped in July. In November, Downey and Richard G. Fecteau, who had been with CIA only five months, and a CAT flight crew, were forced down in China when attempting to recover an agent parachuted into Kirin to observe the team at work. The failure of this November 29 flight and capture of Downey and Fecteau by the Chinese communists essentially brought a halt to the Manchuria program. The twenty-two-year-old Downey remained imprisoned in China until 1973 and his colleague Fecteau until 1971.

One of the biggest CIA operations in China was known to CAT pilots by the code name Paper. It began in early February 1951. Operation Paper was nothing less than an invasion of China by nationalist guerrillas based in the Shan states of northern Burma. This paramilitary effort was carried out in the face of the Burmese government, and created an unnecessary international controversy. It also led to organized nationalist Chinese involvement in heroin traffic that continues to this day.

Project Paper began with Li Mi, another of Chiang Kai-shek's many generals. As an army commander in central China, Li had not been above executing some of his subordinates to inspire obedience from the others. Clever as well as ruthless, Li escaped in disguise when his army disintegrated during the Yangtze River campaign. He made his way to Yunnan province, where he was placed in command of a nationalist unit at K'un-ming. When the provincial governor left K'un-ming in December 1949, virtually handing the administration over to the communists, Li Mi called out his troops and took over the city. During the early months of 1950 he slowly retreated toward the Chinese border as the PLA approached, and then entered, Yunnan.

About 1,500 of Li Mi's troops withdrew into Indochina where the French interned them after disarming the lot. But the French had an army in Indochina, while Burma had little in the way of a military force and that was fully occupied by a revolt among Keren tribesmen. In these chaotic conditions, General Li Mi was easily able to cross the Burmese border with an organized force of 2,200 from the nationalist 97th and 193rd divisions. Once in the country, the Chinese drafted Burman tribesmen for labor and to fill their own ranks. Despite some clashes with the Burmese army, Li increased his strength to 4,000 soldiers before the end of 1950.

Project Paper was intended to reinforce and reequip Li Mi's band for a return to Yunnan. It was made possible by Civil Air Transport's airplanes, which could parachute instructors and weapons to the Chinese in remote northern Burma. Airplanes flew from a CAT detachment set up at Bangkok, with personnel shuttled down from Taiwan and weapons from the CIA depot on Okinawa. The whole operation was coordinated by Alfred Cox, OPC's chief of station at Hong Kong, and Sherman B. Joost in Bangkok.

Cover for the Li Mi arms flow was ingeniously provided through a parallel operation carried out with the Thai government to train and equip paramilitary forces for that country. In Miami the CIA chartered a company, the Overseas Southeast Asia Supply Company—Sea Supply, as it was familiarly known—with a $38-million government contract to support the Thai. Its cable address, "Hachet," gave commercial cover to CIA officers working with both the Thais and Chinese. Before the end of 1953 there were about 200 employees at Sea Supply plus another 76 Americans in the embassy working overtly as advisers; some 4,500 Thai soldiers had been trained and equipped. Whatever happened to Li Mi, the Thai came out of the bargain very well. Indeed, the assistance to Li Mi and the existence of Sea Supply were open secrets in Bangkok. Sherman B. Joost, experienced as a team leader with the OSS in Burma during the war, did not much mind the attention.

Operation Paper began with three CAT planes picking up equipment on Okinawa, and air-dropping it to Li Mi's partisans. Soon there was a regular supply flow. The Burmese government evidently first learned of this outside support for Li Mi when its own intelligence officers observing the Chinese witnessed five of the supply drops.

Meanwhile, Li Mi began calling his forces the Yunnan Province Anti-Communist National Salvation Army. A first invasion of Yunnan, in two columns with two thousand men and accompanied by CIA officers and regular supply drops, was made in April 1951. The nationalists advanced into Yunnan but were driven out again within one week. In July, Li Mi sent his subordinate Liu Kuo-chuan on a second incursion, which was also defeated by PLA local units.

This failure should have occasioned a critical review of the Li Mi operation. Indeed, David M. Key, the United States ambassador to Burma, reported from Rangoon that the Burmese government had knowledge of Americans in the area and of the use of United States equipment by the nationalists. He concluded that "this adventure has cost us heavily in terms of Burmese goodwill and trust." Nevertheless, the reaction in Washington was to decide that the support for Li Mi had been insufficient.

The CIA brought in a new logistics support director, James A. Garrison, to manage the now-substantial arms flow to Taiwan, Thailand, and Burma. American engineers were sent in to supervise the reopening of an old World War II airstrip at Mong Hsat. Then CAT began an even larger airlift that was no longer confined to parachute drops. Some seven hundred nationalist troops from Taiwan reinforced Li Mi, whose strength by 1952 had grown to twelve thousand.

Open controversy erupted after the Chinese communists, in late December 1951, publicly charged that the United States was ferrying nationalist soldiers from Taiwan to Thailand and Burma. These charges were then made by Soviet diplomats in a United Nations political committee. The controversy bubbled despite several State Department denials, including one by Secretary Dean Acheson, and a statement by an American delegate to the UN that the nationalists had simply failed to honor a pledge to remove their troops from Burma. The Burmese UN delegate agreed with the charges that Li Mi was receiving outside aid; nationalist denials were countered by the evidence of copies of actual orders from Chiang Kai-shek to Li Mi that had been captured by the Burmese army. In the middle of the controversy, *The New York Times* reported, on February 11, 1952, that witnesses in Burma had seen Li Mi's soldiers sporting brand-new American weapons. This was followed in April by reports from Burmese sources that Americans, including ex-military fliers, were smuggling the arms to Li Mi.

The United States persisted in its policy of denials. To lessen the visibility of the issue, Chiang prevailed upon Li Mi to return to Taiwan. To explain the nationalists' ability to acquire arms, reports were leaked that Li Mi's men had been selling opium to finance their operations. It is not clear whether the United States at this stage encouraged the drug trafficking to preserve the cover of the CIA operation, but the selling of drugs by the nationalists from Burma has been an important source of cash for them ever since, a pernicious practice that has cost America far more than it gained from the military activities of Li Mi.

No matter how threadbare the cover story, the American denials continued. The true facts were so closely held within the OPC that the chief of the CIA's analysis branch was not told of them. Nor, by and large, was the State Department. The United States ambassador to India, Chester Bowles, asked for and received assurances that there was no American aid to Li Mi. As Asian governments increasingly refused to accept these claims, Bowles was reduced to arguing that no American administration could affort to halt the arms flow to Chiang during an election year, for fear of being accused of coddling communism.

Passing through Washington en route to his new assignment as ambassador in Rangoon, diplomat William J. Sebald received similar assurances. When Sebald attempted to repeat the disclaimer at a diplomatic reception, Burmese army chief of staff Ne Win replied, "Mr. Ambassador, I have it cold. If I were you, I'd just keep quiet."

In the summer of 1952, Li Mi returned to Burma to lead a second invasion of Yunnan. That August twenty-one hundred nationalists marched sixty miles into China before being driven out again. This was the last of the series of remarkably ineffective invasions. Instead the nationalists turned even more actively against the Burmese government. Li Mi had always been careful to shield his Burma base, guarding it with more troops than he used in the Yunnan incursions. Now he forged links with the antigovernment Keren tribesmen and even with the Burmese communist party. In the fall of 1952, Li crossed the Salween River in a major offensive against the Burmese army.

Not only was the Li Mi operation against the Chinese communists ineffective, it led to the ruin of United States relations with Burma for most of the 1950s. Whereas in 1952 the Burmese refused to demand any UN investigation, feeling that neither superpower was likely to accept its conclusions, the next year Rangoon proposed a resolution branding the nationalist Chinese presence an act of aggression against the Burmese nation. When the United States refused to support the motion, Prime Minister U Nu unilaterally terminated all United States aid programs in his country.

The Li Mi operation had been dear to some CIA officers. It was a special favorite of Desmond FitzGerald, deputy chief of OPC's Far East Division. FitzGerald was another member of the wartime Burma contingent, having served as adviser to the nationalist Sixth Army. Educated at private schools and Harvard College, the forty-two-year-old FitzGerald often served as a conduit for project proposals within OPC. He pursued the cold war confrontation with an almost romantic fervor and he played an important role in preventing the cancellation of Operation Paper following Li Mi's 1951 debacle. With nothing but failure to show by 1952, plus an international uproar over the intervention, FitzGerald now had little alternative but to go along with dismantling the operation.

This evaluation of the Li Mi operation was given to Chester Bowles by an Indonesian cabinet minister in April 1953:

> What could be more ridiculous than to allow American arms to be used to build up the power of a renegade group totally incapable of inflicting any damage on the Communist Chinese, but fully capable of thwarting the democratic Burman government's effort to crush her own communist rebellion and bring order to a troubled nation?

Seven years later, in May 1959, intelligence officers would tell a U.S. President that the Chinese nationalists in Burma caused "nothing but difficulty." They embarrassed a government which Washington by then considered more favorably, and gave the Chinese communists a pretext for intervention in Burma. "In short," according to the synopsis furnished by President Eisenhower, "they make trouble for our friends but do not have sufficient capability to even tie down significant ChiCom forces."

In the space of a few short years, the CIA created massive paramilitary operations in Asia while the military undertook large programs as well. Bases opened during this period, plus the acquisition of the proprietary Civil Air Transport, would give the CIA an infrastructure for Asian operations conducted throughout the 1950s.

Apart from the creation of the support network, however, the results of paramilitary operations conducted were paltry. There was some military impact in Korea, although this was limited because the activation of the large paramilitary units in 1952 occurred after the most active, mobile phase of the war. Operations conducted by the CIA in Manchuria and Yunnan were almost totally ineffective. Moreover, they prompted more stringent communist security measures, so may even have impeded the CIA in developing intelligence information sources on the mainland. Finally, as in the Burma effort, some CIA operations actually proved detrimental to larger United States foreign policy interests.

The Korean-era expansion of covert activities and organizations in the Far East nevertheless mirrored a more general United States government effort to establish and standardize procedures and means in this area. The result would be a covert operations establishment that has carried the United States through the succeeding decades.

·V·

THE COVERT LEGIONS

The Washington center of the secret wars was awash with studies, proposals, and plans. Such operations as the Albanian and China campaigns were only the tip of the iceberg. During the Truman administration, more precisely during the Korean War, the organizations and procedures for paramilitary operations were created and standardized.

There was swirling controversy among the White House, the CIA, and the Pentagon. For President Truman the problem was to stimulate covert operations while maintaining their secrecy, and preserving sufficient control over them. At CIA the question was who would direct covert actions within the agency and how the director of central intelligence could command them. Over in the Pentagon the military was concerned about how they should relate to CIA and what military resources should be devoted to paramilitary operations.

President Truman's problem was simplest at the beginning of the covert era. At the time he approved NSC-10/2 in 1948, it seemed natural to oversee closely such a sensitive endeavor. That summer there were three NSC meetings that specifically dealt with the Office of Special Projects, forerunner of the OPC, including the nomination of Frank Wisner as director.

But a President could not plausibly deny knowledge of supposedly secret activities if they were too often openly discussed at council. Truman resorted to a special panel for NSC-10/2 activities composed of the DCI plus representatives of the secretaries of state and defense. Only disagreements among the panel were to be referred to the full NSC. The first departmental representatives were George Kennan for State and Colonel Ivan D. Yeaton for the Pentagon. The degree of cooperation achieved by this panel is suggested by the lack of any record of NSC-10/2 matters being referred to the council. Yet this cooperation also meant a lack of opportunities for the President to decide on covert intelligence activities. Eighty-one covert actions were initiated during Truman's tenure by the DCI on his own authority after consultation with the 10/2 Panel or its successor 10/5 Panel.

Without frequent discussions with the NSC, President Truman was forced to rely directly on his DCI, but that official himself had only indirect control over the OPC. During an earlier era, when the Central Intelligence Group was run out of a three-room office next door to the White House, some sort of indirect administration might have been possible. Amid the burgeoning organizational growth of the Korean War era, it no longer was.

On E Street in Washington, there were some temporary construction office buildings, erected during the Depression, that had housed the OSS during the war. After the formation of the CIA, its headquarters were placed at the same location. From there, Rear Admiral Roscoe H. Hillenkoetter as DCI, presided over the inception of American covert operations.

If there was anyone who could have been expected to be aware of the danger of another Pearl Harbor, it was Roscoe Hillenkoetter, an old-line Annapolis man. He had been executive officer aboard the U.S.S. *West Virginia* that fateful Sunday morning. Dressing in his cabin when the attack began, Hillenkoetter could not even reach the quarterdeck of his ship before it was already sinking. He returned to the Pacific later in the war to create a functioning joint intelligence center for the theater commander in only six months' time.

Hillenkoetter had been appointed DCI in May 1948. It did not harm his chances that he was fluent in three languages, and had served as naval attaché in Paris. Hillenkoetter was also an associate of Admiral William D. Leahy, who at the time was advising President Truman on intelligence questions and may have recommended him. Hillenkoetter's appearance coincided with the appointment of Frank Wisner to what quickly became the OPC.

There were many conflicts between Hillenkoetter in the main office and Wisner, who ran his fiefdom from Building L. Intelligence authorities like Ray Cline argue that Hillenkoetter lacked the rank, prestige, or political clout to "lead the CIA into high-gear performance." But NSC-10/2 created an ambiguous administrative situation for OPC. With his authority from the NSC and his policy directives from the 10/2 Panel, the OPC chief could draw expenses from the CIA while shielding his activities from the DCI's supervision—hiding behind either the State or Defense departments when necessary. Moreover, as one of the old OSS hands, Frank Wisner drew on knowledge and support from friends throughout the Agency. Hillenkoetter had no equivalent network of contacts.

The DCI was a minority on the 10/2 Panel, had only general supervisory jurisdiction over OPC, and in addition, had his hands full just in endowing the CIA with a first-class staff of intelligence analysts. Hillenkoetter, who had done that kind of work during the war, was naturally more interested in his intelligence staff and had less understanding of covert operators.

Wisner thus had many advantages in the contest for bureaucratic power within the CIA. The foremost among them was White House interest in aggressive prosecution of the cold war. Both NSC-4/A and NSC-10/2 were, in part, exhortations to move faster, as was the Dulles-Jackson-Correa Report, which reviewed all aspects of intelligence for President Truman in 1949. Approving the report's conclusions, Truman made a consistent effort to implement them through his NSC, and also brought into government two of the report's authors as deputy directors of the CIA.

OPC field stations increased from seven to forty-seven, personnel to about 6,000 by 1952, slightly more than half of them overseas contract personnel. About half of the OPC people worked for the Far East Division. German operations employed another 1,200. Just between fiscal 1950 and 1951, OPC multiplied from 584 to 1,531, with most of the growth in paramilitary personnel. Some observers believe the publicized budget figure of $82 million in 1952 is too low, that OPC was spending that much in Eastern Europe alone. In any case, clandestine collection and covert operations were by then absorbing 60 percent of CIA's personnel and 74 percent of its budget. The tail had truly grown big enough to wag the dog.

By then Roscoe Hillenkoetter was gone. He turned to a sea command, a cruiser division in the Pacific, and reached Korean waters soon enough to lead the ships giving gunfire support to the U.S. Marines in the evacuation of Hŭngnam after the Chinese communist intervention.

The new DCI was General Walter Bedell Smith, who assumed office on October 7, 1950. "Beetle" Smith had the prestige and contacts Hillenkoetter lacked, and was pugnacious enough to intimidate anyone, Frank Wisner included. General Smith had been General Dwight Eisenhower's chief of staff during the war, a field commander afterward, and ambassador to Moscow during the first, formative years of the cold war.

Having stood up to Joseph Stalin in the bear's own lair, Smith made mincemeat of CIA bureaucracy. Less than a week after he came on board, the new DCI announced he was unilaterally assuming direct administrative control over OPC, a change reluctantly accepted by representatives of State, Defense, and the Joint Chiefs of Staff on October 12, 1950. A couple of months later, when Smith learned that a subordinate actually controlled communications between headquarters and the field stations, so that the DCI did not see all the cable traffic, he threw a fit. "The operators are not going to decide what secret information I will see or not see," the DCI exclaimed, and promptly set up a personal cable secretariat.

Beetle Smith's next move came in January 1951 when he got Allen Dulles appointed as deputy director for plans (DDP) at CIA. The DDP was supposed to manage both the OPC and the Office of Special Operations (OSO), which gathered clandestine intelligence. Dulles was perhaps the best known OSS spy, famous for his work in Switzerland in the war and his role in arranging the surrender of German armies in northern Italy at the end of it. A lawyer by trade, Dulles had been active in politics and government since the Versailles Peace Conference in 1919, and had authored books on his exploits and other espionage topics. He was an author of the NSC-50 study, in which he had recommended merger of OPC with OSO. Smith's feeling was that Allen Dulles would be able to knock heads together and *make* things work between OPC and OSO.

The merger idea was known as the "fusion" project. Both Wisner and the OSO director, General Willard G. Wyman, were known to be in favor of it. So was Lyman B. Kirkpatrick, the executive assistant to the DCI. Bedell Smith had been approached regarding the subject by CIA legal counsel Lawrence Houston even before he took over. But there were many differences over how "fusion" ought to be accomplished. While the talk continued, OPC grew constantly larger, surpassing OSO in both size and budget. The Western Hemisphere divisions of both offices were united on a trial basis in August 1951. At that point, Dulles was promoted to deputy DCI and his place taken by a detached Army officer. "Fusion" stalled.

The last straw came in early 1952 as a by-product of the Li Mi partisan operation. The OPC station in Bangkok tried to recruit a senior CIA officer away from OSO, leading to open dissension in the ranks among agents fearful of bureaucratic "poaching." Lyman Kirkpatrick went out to Thailand to cool the hot heads, while Bedell Smith decreed final "fusion" would occur in August. The CIA established a new Directorate of Plans, known by the same acronym as its chief, the DDP. And the covert operators had their moment of triumph: Frank G. Wisner became DDP.

As the "Wurlitzer" (jukebox) appelation implied, Wisner was quite interested in propaganda and psychological warfare. "Secret," or "black," propaganda activities, as well as partially attributable "gray" ones, were the particular mission of OPC by order of the President under the NSC-4/A directive. The same support that Wisner had lent to the Committee for a Free Europe, the balloon leaflet efforts, and other programs was now extended to the Asian hemisphere. An Asian analogue to Radio Free Europe was set up on Taiwan to beam programs onto the mainland. There is evidence of CIA complicity in subsidizing publications, labor movements, and youth and public interest groups, including the Committee of One Million Against the Admission of Communist China to the United Nations. The propaganda effort was nothing if not global in scope.

In pursuing these programs, Wisner was simply following orders from Harry Truman, a President deeply interested in psychological warfare. Truman held to the belief, common in the United States at that time, that psychological warfare was an insufficiently appreciated resource. Developed in World War II, it had a special role to play in the cold war. Truman's interest continued after his promulgation of NSC-4/A. He returned to the subject repeatedly during his time in the White House. In February 1949 he ordered the creation of a State Department psychological warfare office.

The President actually rescinded the NSC-4 series of directives in March 1950, when he adopted NSC-59, a comprehensive program for foreign information and psychological warfare planning. NSC-59 established a staff for this purpose within the State Department and apportioned responsibilities to State and the Pentagon. Truman approved orders for "A Plan for National Psychological Warfare" in NSC-74. He also asked Rear Admiral Sidney W. Souers to return as a consultant and review nonmilitary cold war activities, with a view toward further improvements in coordination. Souers learned that suggestions were afloat for the creation of an interagency group in this area, responsible directly to the President and the NSC.

The former DCI supported the recommendation, to which Truman responded by setting up a Psychological Strategy Board (PSB) under the NSC in the spring of 1951. That fall, in approving NSC-10/5, the President gave PSB membership on the 10/5 Panel that approved covert operations.

Creation of the PSB marked a significant milestone in the escalation of the secret war. Formerly there had been much propaganda, of course, some of it "black" stuff coming from OPC. But these operations were conducted on a more or less ad hoc basis with little formal interagency coordination or appraisal. Now the PSB would be brainstorming comprehensive propaganda plans, to cover both peacetime and war, for many specific countries and contingencies.

Planning for propaganda and psychological warfare, and later monitoring national efforts in this regard, was the job of a PSB staff office. As its first staff director, President Truman chose Gordon Gray, who had previously sat with the President on the NSC while serving as secretary of the Army. Gray was also well known to Frank Wisner and to CIA deputy director William H. Jackson: All of them had worked for the Wall Street law firm Carter, Ledyard and Milburn before World War II, as had the man Gray hired as his PSB assistant, Tracy Barnes.

The first comprehensive plan was for Germany. It was completed and sent to the PSB in the summer of 1952. Plans for other psychological operations aimed at reducing communist party electoral power in France and Italy, at encouraging "Soviet orbit escapees," at influencing negotiations for a Korean cease-fire, at creating a pro-American disposition on the part of Japanese, and for "Doctrinal (Ideological) Warfare Against the USSR."

Despite, or perhaps because of, its ambitious aims, the PSB encountered bureaucratic opposition in its endeavor to centralize psychological-warfare planning. Much like the State Department mechanism Truman had previously established, PSB often found it difficult to get the interagency cooperation it needed. Pentagon and CIA documents and input were not forthcoming. Gordon Gray may have been a friend of Wisner's, but the CIA man was a seasoned bureaucratic infighter and guarded his prerogatives jealously. By December 1951, Gray was forced to appeal to DCI Walter Bedell Smith to send CIA representatives to PSB office meetings. Gray also sent Smith copies of his information briefings on PSB organization and objectives in hopes that the CIA would stop seeing PSB as a threat. By mid-1952, DCI Smith was still reacting angrily to continued claims that CIA support for PSB remained inadequate. In particular, some PSB planners felt the CIA had not developed sufficient information on political differences among Soviet leaders and considered requesting a special national intelligence estimate on the subject, in order to prepare a PSB plan to be put into operation upon the death of Stalin.

All of the high-level interest, the encouragement of President Truman, and the advice of psychological warfare experts like Paul Linebarger had not heretofore raised the techniques above a relatively crude stage of development. An early plan for a "psychological offensive" against Russia, for example, is studded with moralistic rhetoric that sounds like a collection of homilies and themes. The three objectives in this plan were: to emphasize to Soviet rulers and peoples the reckless nature of their policy, to establish goodwill between the peoples of the two nations, and to widen the schism thought to exist between the Soviet people and their rulers. The propaganda themes suggested to reach these objectives included the following:

> The attempts of all tyrants to conquer the world have always failed. . . . Truth, mercy, pity, charity, love of family, hospitality, are some of the basic values which have always been dear to the Soviet peoples and . . . are held in common with the people of the free world, but in contempt by the Soviet rulers. . . . The U.S. is peace-loving and honors the sovereignty and integrity of peoples and nations [while, by contrast, Soviet] statements of possibility of peaceful co-existence have been made only for the purpose of deceiving Soviet and other peoples. . . . [In Russia] first freedom of speech was lost, now freedom of silence.

The close relationship between psychological warfare and covert operations is further demonstrated by the composition of the strategy boards. An early representative of the Secretary of Defense was John Magruder, who had managed many covert operations for OSS and the Pentagon's SSU. The DCI was CIA's delegate, Frank Wisner the alternate. Representing the Joint Chiefs of Staff was Rear-Admiral Leslie Stevens, who also handled military participation in covert operations at the Pentagon's highest levels. Rather than restraining and coordinating propaganda activities, the Psychological Strategy Board Harry Truman created instead became a stimulant for an intensification of the cold war.

Gordon Gray's appointment to the PSB came unexpectedly. Son of a president of the R. J. Reynolds Tobacco Company, Gray had the luxury of being able to devote himself to selfless public service. A North Carolina state senator both before and after the war, an assistant secretary at the Pentagon, and then secretary of the army, Gray left government service in 1950 to preside over the University of North Carolina.

A few short months after his arrival at Capitol Hill, Walter Bedell Smith and William H. Jackson came down from CIA to extend Truman's offer to head PSB. Smith said he wanted Gray to succeed him as DCI, and working at PSB would make him a logical choice for the post.

Besides, said Smith, "the President is serious about setting up this board and we think that you are well-equipped to do it."

Gordon Gray was in fact a logical choice for director of the Board. During the war he had worked in the broadcast section of the European high command and in Luxembourg setting up a network for shortwave communication with the United States. Because of guilt pangs over leaving his university post so quickly, Gray began to spend half his work weeks in the capital. PSB started as one desk at the CIA's E Street headquarters, and Gray shared an office and secretary with a CIA man. Using funds drawn from Pentagon and CIA accounts, Gray was later able to get for PSB the three buildings at the end of the block on Jackson Place, around the corner from Blair House and just a short walk from the NSC offices at the Old Executive Office Building.

Service at PSB was the beginning of over three decades of association with the intelligence field for Gordon Gray. His discretion and ability were legion, but in this early period they could not shield him from buffeting in the interagency struggle for control of psychological warfare. Gray thought PSB had a charter to put together a plan for the cold war. So did the Soviet press, judging from their denunciations of him. But Gray's friend Frank Wisner refused, while PSB was still at E Street, to make the short walk from K Building to attend staff meetings.

As for the State Department, Paul H. Nitze, chief of the Policy Planning Staff, told Gray, "Look, you just forget about policy, that's not your business; we'll make the policy and then you can put it on your damn radio."

Others had an easier time of it, namely the military experts on unconventional warfare, for whom Gray had toiled while still at the Pentagon. In the early postwar years, there was little support for these methods in the armed forces. Army Ranger units and Merrill's Marauders of Burma fame were disbanded, as were the Air Force's air commandos. Psychological warfare capabilities existed only residually within the intelligence staffs of the various services. At first, even the interest of senior generals like Dwight D. Eisenhower was insufficient to galvanize action to re-create such capabilities. Some senior officers felt covert "psywar" operations would not be accepted by the American people, and that a military "psywar" effort was precluded by the political structure of the United States.

The advocates of military "psywar" were then assisted by the appearance of NSC-4/A, which demonstrated presidential interest in the area of psychological warfare. The Army began a staff study in January 1948 that led to the adoption that fall of a plan for establishing standardized units plus "psywar" staffs at theater, army, and corps levels.

Army proponents also attempted to carve out greater roles for themselves. General Albert C. Wedemeyer, chief of the Army's Plans and Operations Division, felt that the assignment of all "black" propaganda to the CIA was basically unsound. General Robert McClure, a prime mover in the Army's effort to enter the "psywar" field, argued that the Army possessed a greater capability for propaganda, in the form of outlets and audience, than even the State Department. As assistant secretary of the Army, Gordon Gray also encouraged the development of a "psywar" capability.

At first, paramilitary covert operations were considered part of the "psywar" function, which was the province of the Army's intelligence (G-2) staff. The paramilitary side had been viewed with some distaste by Army Secretary Kenneth Royall who said at a June 1948 meeting that he wished his service to know nothing about covert operations. Prodded by Gray and others, Royall soon began to allow participation in overt and later even in covert propaganda. By March 1949, Gray was forced to admit to his boss that "we are actually participating in Europe." Royall then designated Gray as the civilian official to whom all covert matters would be taken.

Meanwhile, the Army planning staff acquired a "special warfare" section within its "psywar" area. Manned by veterans of Merrill's Marauders, OSS, and guerrilla commanders in the Philippines, the "special warfare" section laid down contingency plans for paramilitary actions, including one to obstruct westward movement of Soviet reinforcements by activating a partisan force in Eastern Europe. This was one Army response to the Joint Chiefs' JCS 1807/1, an August 1948 memorandum to the Secretary of Defense recommending that the United States should support guerrilla warfare under the policy direction of the NSC, acquire means to carry it out, and assign primary interest to the CIA during peace and the military in war.

Carrying out covert operations naturally would require real units and troops. JCS 1807/1 recommended against any sort of "special warfare" corps; instead it favored individual training within the services of specialists who could be on call to lead native guerrillas. For its part, the Army consulted with former OSS Detachment 101 commander Colonel Ray Peers on the formation of a "Ranger Group," planned in early 1949 to include about 115 officers and 135 enlisted men. These "airborne reconnaissance agents" would be assigned temporarily to theaters, army groups, and armies to execute specified missions. This was a step toward a "special warfare" corps, not away from it.

While the Army continued planning, the Air Force moved ahead with the first actual "special warfare" units. Called Air Re-Supply and Communications (ARC) wings, five of these units were formed and stationed at such forward bases as Great Britain, Libya, Okinawa, and Clark in the Philippines. The ARC wings operated a wide variety of transport aircraft in exactly the same fashion as the

CIA's Civil Air Transport. The ARC wings engaged in disaster relief, frequent maneuvers, and training flights in an attempt to disguise their actual covert purpose.

A further impetus to the creation of actual military units for "special warfare" was an action of the Congress in 1950. Building on America's traditional commitment to freedom and interest in the "captive nations," a bill was proposed that set aside funds for a legion of Eastern European émigrés who might be sent back into their countries. This Lodge Bill became Public Law 587, passed by the 81st Congress in June 1950, on the eve of the Korean War. It led the Army to propose formation of a "Special Forces Regiment" of three battalions with a total of 2,481 men, 1,300 of whom might be foreign recruits.

The Lodge Bill also provided for up to 2,500 alien enlistments in the United States Army. The Army itself raised the ceiling to 12,500; however, by August 1952 only 5,272 foreigners had applied for enlistment; of those, 411 received the required security clearances, 211 actually enlisted and, by November 1952, only 22 wound up assigned to the new Special Forces.

While the émigré dream perhaps did not come to fruition, the Special Forces themselves did; once again it was the Korean War that furnished the specific impetus. At Army headquarters in Washington, the increased need for coordination arising from the war, combined with the continuing interest in the possibilities of "psywar," led to formal establishment of an Office of the Chief of Psychological Warfare, under the experienced leadership of General Robert McClure. This office also was charged with "special warfare" planning. Although in 1950 only 7 active Army officers had specializations in "psywar," by 1952 there were whole radio and leaflet propaganda units, and the Army had set aside 2,500 personnel spaces for the covert warriors in a new unit, the 10th Special Forces Group. By April 1953 the group had reached an actual strength of 1,700 officers and men.

The early months of 1953 were a time of change for the covert warriors. The Korean War was winding down, to end in a stalemate with the armistice signed at P'anmunjŏm on July 27, 1953. By then, after repeated failures, the paramilitary operations in China had been discontinued. Those in Korea ground to a halt more slowly but just as certainly, with mixed results. Reports from the Korean partisan units claimed substantial accomplishments, but some veterans recall a much less effective effort.

The Korean era still witnessed a substantial buildup of means to carry out psychological warfare and covert operations, plus mechanisms to plan and manage them. Before the end of the conflict, both the CIA and the military possessed paramilitary resources. Veritable covert legions were ready to undertake operations on command. Operators like Frank Wisner and managers like Gordon Gray were equipped to make the most of the available resources.

Through his unflagging enthusiasm for psychological warfare, President Harry Truman played a major role in this buildup. It occurred in secret while, in public, the political perception developed that the Truman foreign policy of "containment" stood helpless in the face of the global challenges of the cold war. The way was open for someone to offer a different direction and General Dwight D. Eisenhower, the Republican party's candidate in the 1952 presidential election, did just that.

Eisenhower spoke often of the ideological struggle against communism; a recurrent theme of the 1952 electoral campaign was that the Truman administration had failed to wage this struggle. The Republican party platform offered to "roll back" the iron curtain, while Eisenhower, though he pledged to end the Korean War, promised to intensify the cold war, through such measures as removing the restrictions on Chiang Kai-shek, unleashing him against the mainland, and strengthening propaganda efforts in Europe.

It was Dwight Eisenhower who won the 1952 election. His victory rang in a new atmosphere at the CIA, where at least one intelligence officer felt the Republican platform read like the proposals he used to write at the OPC. The morning after the election, one of the senior paramilitary officers, home from Bangkok, pranced through the Directorate of Plans rooms shouting, "Now we'll finish off the goddamned Commie bastards!"

·VI·

BITTER FRUITS

The jangling telephone most often brought new problems, the minor crises that made up a routine day for the President's appointments secretary. No doubt this was what was expected that early spring day in 1955 when John Earman, a special assistant to the director of central intelligence, came on the line. But Earman had a question, not a problem. It concerned an appointment with the President set for 9:50 A.M. on March 24. The meeting had been arranged to award the National Security Medal, the highest decoration given by the United States for intelligence work. A few months earlier, on December 15, 1954, President Eisenhower had signed a memorandum awarding the medal to CIA officer Kermit Roosevelt, for the latter's role in a prime covert operation, the toppling of a legally constituted government in Iran.

Everything about the ceremony was very closely held. The National Security Medal itself was secret, awarded by the President at his discretion, unlike the military Medal of Honor, which is approved by Congress. Award citations and the medals themselves are secret, kept in CIA vaults for the duration of an intelligence officer's career. The National Security Medal was not only secret, it was special—Kermit Roosevelt was only the fourth person to receive it.

The award ceremony came off without a hitch. Roosevelt, his wife, and his two children entered the White House through a side entrance, to avoid speculation by the press about why a grandson of Theodore Roosevelt (and cousin of FDR), should be received by a

Republican President. The appointment itself was not on the record and was set just ten minutes before a session of the NSC making it convenient for DCI Allen Dulles, Secretary of State John Foster Dulles, and Ambassador Loy Henderson to be present as well. The presentation by President Eisenhower was a clear indication of the esteem in which he held the intelligence community.

Iran was a covert action writ large, solving a problem Eisenhower inherited from the Truman administration. The Iran problem had a cold war overlay and it arose from oil, specifically from British interest in Iranian oil. The CIA covert action was the end result of an Anglo-Iranian oil crisis that had endured for over two years, drawing in the British government, the Royal Navy, the SIS, and then the United States.

The problem initially grew from an action that had been applauded in the United States at the time: the Iranian lower house of parliament, or Majlis, had enacted legislation rejecting a Soviet oil concession for northern Iran. The same law contained a provision that all oil concessions would be reviewed within a certain time, and in 1950 the British oil activities in the south were brought up for renegotiation.

The British had an arrangement that gave them total control over pumping, refining, and shipping oil in southern Iran through the Anglo-Iranian Oil Company (AIOC). Under an agreement binding until 1993, AIOC paid Iran rents, taxes, and salaries of Iranian employees. The money accounted for half of Iran's budget, but in fact AIOC was paying more in taxes to the *British* government than to the nation whose oil it pumped, and AIOC itself was earning ten times as much as it paid to Iran.

AIOC's wealth and power were visible in the palatial homes of its managers, sustained by the influence of the British embassy, itself occupying an expanse of nineteen blocks in the crowded capital of Teheran. Sure of their position, the British offered only cosmetic changes when the oil agreement was up for review. They also contrived to have an official parliamentary commission report that an Iranian nationalization of AIOC was completely infeasible. The prime minister who presented this conclusion to the Majlis read a statement that had clearly been inadequately translated from English into the Iranian language *Farsi*, and this linked him to British interests. He was shouted down in the Majlis and, on February

19, 1951, shot dead as he knelt to pray in a mosque. His successor was a popular nationalist leader, Dr. Mohammad Mossadegh, who immediately presented a bill providing for government absorption of Anglo-Iranian. The bill became law and AIOC was taken over on May 2.

That summer the crisis sharpened as AIOC refused any settlement under which they would not continue to refine and ship the Iranian oil. The British government sided with AIOC and at one stage alerted their 16th Parachute Brigade on Cyprus to be ready for action. The cruiser H.M.S. *Mauritius* was sent to Ābādān to evacuate British nationals who worked for AIOC. The Truman administration interceded, however, and convinced the British to abandon military action, although they went ahead to organize a global boycott of Iranian oil. AIOC assisted with the boycott by filing suits against any ship that carried Iranian oil whenever it touched at ports in favorable legal jurisdictions.

The impasse in Anglo-Iranian relations that developed out of the oil crisis persisted through the advent of the Eisenhower administration. American mediators W. Averell Harriman and Paul H. Nitze made no headway in either Teheran or London. Mossadegh insisted Iran had a perfect right to nationalize AIOC, and that it *had* offered compensation. The oil company, on the other hand, was equally unyielding in its insistence on restoration of most of its previous status in Iran.

Because of its global interests and activities in oil production, AIOC had a working relationship with the SIS and was soon demanding political action in Teheran, to bring about a change in government to one willing to settle on terms favorable to the company. This proposal came to the attention of the CIA at the end of 1951 when an SIS delegation lobbied for such an operation during a visit to Washington. In 1952, British intelligence again showed the proposal to Kim Roosevelt in London and renewed the offer as a project for a joint operation shortly after the 1952 elections in the United States.

While the Truman administration was in office, the official policy favored amicable resolution of the AIOC matter and nothing happened with the British proposal for covert action. The DCI, Walter Bedell Smith, knew of British interest but was careful not to become officially involved. Smith had been Eisenhower's chief of staff during the war, and was selected to serve as undersecretary of state after Ike won the election, most likely to be the President's eyes and ears at the State Department. John Foster Dulles was chosen secretary of state and his brother, Allen Welsh Dulles, the new director of central intelligence. The Iran covert action project began to move ahead.

Though Gordon Gray may have been disappointed that he wasn't asked to be DCI, the truth was that Allen had the inside track for that position in the Eisenhower administration. As the brother of the secretary of state, Dulles would be able to avoid the squabbles endemic to new Washington bureaucrats establishing a pecking order. Allen also had impeccable credentials in both diplomacy and intelligence, having served with State from 1916 to 1926 and with OSS during World War II. He had already contributed to the CIA with his participation in the Dulles-Jackson-Correa investigation and his support for the Committee for a Free Europe, plus service as CIA's deputy director, in which position he had presided over the final "fusion" of OPC and OSO. With his ever-present pipe and professorial air, Dulles projected the perfect image for America's chief spy.

Allen Dulles's era at the CIA began on February 23, 1953. Another SIS delegation, this one headed by British intelligence chief Sir John Sinclair, was in Washington at the same time. Its mission was actually to plan a joint operation against Iran. Allen Dulles was by no means ignorant of the issues, having headed the Near East Division during his time at State. Dulles had also been a partner, along with John Foster, in the Wall Street law firm of Sullivan and Cromwell, which represented AIOC's parent firm in the United States. The new DCI had not shied away from secret activities while he was with OSS; he worked from Switzerland with anti-Hitler Germans, a native resistance movement about which Dulles wrote in his 1947 book *Germany's Underground*. Though he maintained a casual and noncommittal posture in front of the British, Dulles favored the idea of a joint operation in Iran.

In the meantime, the situation in Iran worsened with the continuing boycott. When Dr. Mossadegh, in mid-1952, sought the power to rule by decree, the constitutional monarch Mohammad Reza Pahlavi attempted to dismiss him. This effort collapsed within a few days in the face of rioting in Teheran. Mossadegh received the powers he sought, and these were extended for a full year in January 1953.

Mossadegh appealed to the incoming Eisenhower administration for foreign aid, not so much to settle with the "former oil company" as to develop Iran's other resources. The United States previously had provided technical assistance as well as, in fiscal 1952, $23.4 million in economic aid. But President Eisenhower's official response, sent on June 29, 1953, was that "it would be unfair to the American taxpayers for the United States government to extend any considerable amount of economic aid to Iran so long as Iran could have access to funds derived from the sale of its oil and oil products if a reasonable settlement were reached." Only technical assistance and military funds were offered.

In fact, however, the American response went even further. Four days before Ike's letter, Kim Roosevelt carried a twenty-two-page paper, outlining objectives for an operation in Iran, to a meeting in the office of the secretary of state. The paper was a rewrite of the much more detailed British plan left by SIS chief Sinclair and his deputy George Young. John Foster Dulles read the paper and asked a few questions. Some State Department officers, for instance, the American ambassador to Iran, Loy Henderson, opposed the plan, but they remained silent or made pro forma comments. CIA officers opposing the plan were not present and their views were not presented by Allen Dulles. Secretary of Defense Charles Wilson, who knew only those parts of the plan that concerned the Iranian military, was "appropriately enthusiastic."

The plan was approved and dubbed Operation Ajax. Kermit Roosevelt was put in charge. Here was the real response to Mossadegh's pleas for foreign assistance.

Compared to the protracted period of planning and gaining approval for Ajax, its organization and execution occurred with considerable dispatch. Kim Roosevelt entered Iran under a false identity, met with the Shah, and assured him of personal support from both Eisenhower and Winston Churchill, if he tried once again to dismiss Mossadegh. Working with a core of only four or five CIA agents, Roosevelt activated networks of agents created by the SIS, and used SIS communications through Cyprus for his cables to Washington. Operation Ajax focused on getting the Iranian army to back the Shah against Mossadegh.

It was the struggle for control of the 200,000-man armed forces and 50,000-man police force that triggered the actual Iranian coup.

Mossadegh had assumed the position of defense minister in his own cabinet, and moved in the spring of 1953 to supplant the Shah as commander in chief. He appointed his own candidates as head of the police and chief of staff of the army.

It is quite likely that the Shah, who had failed to act decisively throughout the AIOC crisis, was steeled in his determination to rid himself of Mossadegh after the latter's effort to become commander in chief. In this case, the Majlis refused Mossadegh's request for the powers, leading the premier to dissolve parliament on July 19. When Kermit Roosevelt met with the Shah, some days later, the Iranian potentate was more than ready to be convinced, and his decision was enthusiastically supported by his sister, Princess Ashraf.

Mossadegh's own schemes were running into trouble. His candidate for chief of police bragged on his first day at headquarters that he had a list of all the British spies on the force. By the next morning the man had been gunned down. In desperation Mossadegh, who was a populist nationalist and in no sense a communist, opened trade talks with the Soviet Union on August 8. This news in turn led President Eisenhower to issue the final go-ahead for Operation Ajax.

Kermit Roosevelt had prepared the ground carefully, using his long experience in the Middle East. Roosevelt had worked there for OSS during the war, coming to it from academic study at the California Institute of Technology. As an early CIA man, he was on hand in Egypt to forge a relationship with Gamal Abdel Nasser, when he emerged at the top of a national revolution, which overthrew a corrupt monarchy. Roosevelt had seen crowd tactics firsthand and now, in Teheran, he used CIA money and SIS agents to arrange for some. Roosevelt also used the military and police contacts of General H. Norman Schwartzkopf, an American who had trained Iranian police from 1942 to 1948, to recruit a prominent Iranian former commander, General Fazollah Zahedi, to the anti-Mossadegh plot.

The Shah of Iran evidently had some last-minute qualms about Ajax. It was arranged that the first move would be a decree from the Shah that dismissed Mossadegh. To prepare for this, as a cover, Allen Dulles left on August 10 for a "vacation" at a ski resort in the Swiss Alps. The vacation story began to strain credulity when, shortly thereafter, Princess Ashraf and the United States ambassador, Loy Henderson, turned up at the same resort. But the Shah's decree was late and the impatient Americans sent Henderson back to Teheran.

The Shah fired Mossadegh, and appointed Zahedi as premier, in decrees that were left with a subordinate, as the Shah himself departed with Queen Soraya for the Caspian seacoast town of Ramsar. The subordinate was then arrested while attempting to present the first decree to Mossadegh. There were street protests by nationalists, and by the Iranian communist party, or Tudeh. Up to six thousand of the pro-Shah rioters recruited by the CIA then took to the streets as well.

Eisenhower perceived Mossadegh's failure to put down the Tudeh demonstrations as coddling of communists. He professed to see a move into the Soviet orbit. Loy Henderson was ordered to make a demarche to Mossadegh who then called out the police. Full-scale rioting broke out on August 18 and 19. On the second day pro-Shah tank units, informed by *New York Times* reporter Kennett Love of weak guard forces at the premier's house, attacked Mossadegh's residence. The Shah returned from Italy, whence he had fled after issuing his decrees, and paraded in triumph through the streets of Teheran.

So ended Operation Ajax, the first apparent United States paramilitary victory. Kim Roosevelt received personal thanks from both Churchill and Eisenhower, as well as the medal already mentioned. Aside from its direct cost, estimated at $10 million to $20 million—far more than the $100,000 or $200,000 originally estimated—Operation Ajax had unfolded in a controlled fashion following a scenario if not a precise plan.

The big winners were the Shah and his men, who gained absolute power, which they held for twenty-six years, until themselves swept away by a religious conservatism even more potent than the populism of Mossadegh. Through support of the Shah, the United States committed itself to his regime in an irrevocable way that blinded it later when it should have recognized the growth of opposition. As for the cost to American taxpayers in foreign aid, Eisenhower approved $45 million in new funds soon after the Zahedi cabinet took office, and the flow neared a billion dollars before the end of his administration. The losers were Mohammad Mossadegh, who was eventually captured and put on trial, and, ironically, AIOC—although Iranian oil production resumed in August 1954 under an international agreement, the "former oil company's" claims were never fully resolved.

Kim Roosevelt returned to Washington as an assistant director in the Directorate of Plans. Under Wisner, Roosevelt directed the political action staff and supervised that component's field operations. He tried to use a White House debriefing to critique Operation Ajax.

"If we, the CIA, are ever going to try something like this again, we must be absolutely sure that the people and army want what we want.

"If not, you had better give the job to the Marines."

Roosevelt wrote later that John Foster Dulles did not want to hear such advice. Indeed this was true, for within weeks of that occasion, Roosevelt was offered command of a similar covert action being planned for Central America.

Kim Roosevelt declined the offer after his inquiries showed that the criteria he had cited at the White House were not likely to be met in Guatemala. The government there was of social democratic bent, elected in November 1950 with over 50 percent of the vote in a free election. President Jacobo Arbenz Guzmán thereafter acquired even greater popularity among the peasantry through his ardent efforts to reform Guatemala's agriculture and economy.

Like the Iranian affair, the Guatemalan operation also had its economic angle. This time an American firm, United Fruit, was involved. It too had negotiated with the law firm Sullivan and Cromwell. United Fruit was the largest landowner in Guatemala, holding some 550,000 acres on which it grew bananas, and also a controlling interest in the country's only railroad. Beginning in February 1953 the Arbenz government expropriated almost 400,000 acres of this land to parcel out to the peasants. The Guatemalans offered compensation, however—twenty-five-year term bonds at 3-percent guaranteed interest for the exact book value of the assets claimed by United Fruit to the Guatemalan government for tax purposes. This settlement was rejected out of hand by *la frutera*, the fruit company, which, like AIOC, went to its home government for relief.

Lawyer Thomas G. Corcoran was not only a counsel for Civil Air Transport, but also for United Fruit. Tommy Corcoran acted as intermediary in 1953, selling *la frutera*'s scheme for action to the

CIA. He met with Undersecretary of State Walter Bedell Smith that summer and that conversation is recalled by CIA officers as the clear starting point of the plan.

Although one account of the Guatemala operation alleges it was approved by an NSC special group review in August 1953, in fact it is probable that ad hoc procedures were used, like those for Operation Ajax. By the fall, however, definite action was in the wind since the CIA had already begun to form a task force.

The timing of the decision to undertake the Guatemala operation reveals a link between Guatemala and Iran. At the time the Guatemala situation was under consideration, the short-term success of Operation Ajax was most impressive. Kim Roosevelt noticed a twinkle in John Foster Dulles's eyes at his White House debriefing, and surmised that something similar was up his sleeve. Even the code word people seemed to allude to Iran when they designated the Guatemala effort, Operation Success. In this case, the CIA saw no possibility of foreign intervention, yet there were definite advantages to be had in cooperating with United Fruit, which by itself had already made advances toward some anti-Arbenz political figures.

Allen Dulles was the executive agent for Operation Success. He kept in close touch with the planning and execution through two personal assistants, Tracy Barnes and Richard E. Bissell, Jr. Barnes had been with the OSS in Switzerland under Dulles, and later worked for Gordon Gray on the Psychological Strategy Board, whence he had moved over to CIA as an aide to the DCI. Bissell had been an economist by trade and came to CIA from the Ford Foundation. Together they coordinated the Washington end of planning and logistics for the Guatemala operation.

Frank Wisner's task as deputy director for plans was to select the field commander for Operation Success. Once Roosevelt turned the job down, Wisner got Allen Dulles to recall the Korea station chief, former Army colonel Albert Haney. In Korea, Haney had done a first-rate job setting up CIA guerrilla units, and Guatemala was expected to have a paramilitary component. Briefed in late October, Haney accepted on the spot and was posted to a CIA forward base established at Opa-Locka, Florida. He exercised general supervision over CIA station chiefs in all the nations surrounding Guatemala, plus direct control over the forces assembled for Operation Success.

One of Haney's problems was the CIA's own Western Hemisphere Division. Its director, like Haney, was a counterintelligence man, but from FBI, not Army. Joseph Caldwell King's FBI experience dated to when that agency had had official responsibility for all intelligence operations in Latin America. Within the Directorate of Plans, the Western Hemisphere Division still had formal control over the stations Haney was supposed to use. King, who was less affectionately known as "Jesus Christ," for his arrogance, privately thought Operation Success was not going to work, and anyway did not want some interdepartmental task force on his turf.

More familiar with the area than Haney, who had a Far East background, King called the task force chief into his office to suggest a meeting with Tommy Corcoran. *La frutera* had plans and weapons CIA could use.

Haney did not like the idea and was blunt about it.

"If you think you can run this operation without United Fruit," King rasped, "you're crazy!"

Wisner and Allen Dulles, however, backed Haney and gave him a free hand.

In the end, United Fruit itself decided not to go in on Operation Success. If the operation failed, the company would be grievously damaged, not only in Guatemala but globally. It did want to be informed, though, and Tommy Corcoran retained his go-between role, keeping *frutera* executives up to date on the latest developments in planning.

Despite Haney's, and United Fruit's own preferences, in at least one respect the CIA *was* carrying on with United Fruit's program. That is, there had *already been* one CIA paramilitary effort aimed at Guatemala, and that one had involved *la frutera.* Under a plan with the code name Fortune, in the waning months of the Truman administration CIA passed weapons to United Fruit intended for anti-Arbenz rebels. Operation Fortune proved abortive and was halted, but the cast of characters involved with Operation Success—"Tacho" Somoza in Nicaragua, Honduran officials, and so forth—was almost identical.

Al Haney soon had his task force and a plan to go with it. The chief of political action—the CIA euphemism for psychological warfare—was E. Howard Hunt, who had worked previously on Albania. Under Hunt, Haney brought in David Atlee Phillips, an amateur actor and journalist, recruited in Chile four years before, to run a "black" propaganda radio station. On the paramilitary side,

Haney also brought in William A. Robertson, Jr., a CIA trainer on Saipan, who had been Haney's deputy in Korea and enjoyed going along on the behind-the-lines missions with the CIA guerrillas, in violation of standing orders from Washington. Also on the team was the former Berlin station chief, Henry Hecksher, whose professionalism and skill were already legendary at CIA, and who would operate under cover in Guatemala to supply front-line reports.

The plan itself was a carefully concocted mix of military and psychological strategies. A rebel "liberation army" would be formed and trained in neighboring Nicaragua; supported by a covert air force contingent, the rebels would invade Guatemala. Intervention by United States armed forces was ruled out, but the rebel invasion would be preceded and accompanied by a meticulously arranged propaganda campaign from the "black" radio station in the hopes that the Arbenz government might panic in the face of doctored news bulletins. The United States embassy in Guatemala City would contribute unremitting diplomatic pressure on Arbenz throughout the process. The military plan, such as it was, had to be changed at the last moment when Salvadoran officials refused to allow the invasion to be mounted from their country. The final plan based the rebels in Honduras. From there the main force would march overland and capture the railroad station at Zacapa while several boatloads of men would make for the Caribbean port of Puerto Barrios. Both places, plus Guatemala City, would be bombed by the CIA air force.

The groundwork was prepared as quietly as possible. An unenthusiastic station chief in Guatemala was replaced in early 1954 by John Doherty. Appointed ambassador to Honduras in late 1953, in a move that may have been encouraged by Tommy Corcoran, was Whiting Willauer, until then a senior manager with Civil Air Transport. Willauer, as he reported in a letter to Claire Chennault, worked day and night to arrange training sites and instructors plus air crews for the rebel air force, and to keep the Honduran government "in line so they would allow this revolutionary activity to continue." Later, participants would acknowledge that if some of the Guatemalan rebel aircraft had been shot down, the surviving pilots would have been found—speaking Chinese. A total of about a dozen aircraft were assembled, including three bombers plus P-47 and P-51 fighter-bombers.

Operation Success entered the execution phase in early 1954

when the political action campaign kicked off. Dave Phillips checked material for the radio broadcast during a visit with Henry Hecksher, who posed as a German businessman. American ambassador John Puerifoy set the tone in January 1954 when he told a reporter for *Time* magazine that "public opinion" in the United States might "force" actions "to prevent Guatemala from falling into the lap of international Communism."

The Arbenz government was not without its own resources. In recruiting a rebel leader, the CIA went first to the candidate who was defeated in the 1950 elections, Miguel Ydigoras Fuentes. He had already been approached by United Fruit and was not interested. Americans then turned to former Colonel Carlos Castillo Armas. He had been in exile since the failure of a revolt he had staged in 1949. Joining with the CIA, Castillo Armas issued a declaration from Honduras in December 1953, stating his intention to liberate Guatemala from Arbenz. When Guatemalan police began an investigation, they came across correspondence among Castillo Armas, Ydigoras, and Somoza about their plans and referring to "friends" who could only have been the CIA. This material was released to the Guatemalan press at the end of January.

The charge that Americans had a role in the Castillo Armas plans was termed "ridiculous" by the State Department, at the very moment that a dilapidated barn, in rural Honduras, was being converted to serve as the site for the clandestine radio "Voice of Liberation." Concurrently, a force of about 170 Guatemalan exiles, assorted Latin Americans, and American soldiers of fortune was training in CIA camps in Nicaragua and the Panama Canal Zone. Whiting Willauer was in the last stages of arranging for the rebel "air force."

Later, Guatemalan police made arrests based on what they learned from the Castillo Armas documents. Eisenhower refers to these actions in his memoirs as mass arrests, a "reign of terror," and government killings among the opposition. Eisenhower recalls "agents of international Communism in Guatemala [who] continued their efforts to penetrate and subvert their neighboring Central American states, using consular agents for their political purposes and fomenting political assassinations and strikes." Aside from individual arrests of opposition figures, it is worth noting that there is little evidence to sustain the charges leveled by the President.

One action by the Arbenz government *did* threaten to derail all the preparations for Success. The Guatemalans turned to Czecho-slovakia to buy two thousand tons of arms from the Skoda works. Washington learned of the move when an agent in Poland reported the loading of weapons aboard a freighter at Szczecin. The ship turned out to be the 4,900 ton Swedish vessel *Alfhem,* which eluded several attempts at interception and reached Puerto Barrios on May 15, 1954.

The "*Alfhem* affair" led to the first military action of Operation Success. CIA paramilitary man William "Rip" Robertson wanted to go into Puerto Barrios with frogmen and sink the Swedish ship with explosives but Washington turned him down. Instead, he was told to send a party from Castillo Armas's "liberation army" to blow up the railroad tracks outside the port. Robertson led the team himself and laid explosive charges on the track, but they fizzled when the detonators got drenched in a downpour. The CIA team then opened fire on one of the trains, but did not stop the ten-train convoy leaving Puerto Barrios. One anti-Arbenz soldier died in the ambush.

After all this trouble, the Czech weapons proved of little use to the Guatemalan army. They included large-caliber cannon designed to be mounted on railway carriages, of limited value on Guatemala's nominal railroad network, with seven hundred miles of track. *Alfhem* had carried antitank guns though there were no tanks in Central American armies. Only a small fraction of the World War II-vintage British and German small arms arrived in working order. Eisenhower might think Arbenz a communist, but clearly the real communists were no friends of Guatemala—the Czechs had taken the government's hard currency and delivered useless weapons.

In what was a supreme irony, the useless weapons from Czecho-slovakia enabled Eisenhower to state at a press conference that Guatemala had become an "outpost" of "the Communist dictatorship" on the American continent.

On May 23 the Navy received orders to conduct surveillance of shipping near Guatemalan ports. The next day, Ike told a party of congressional leaders he was ordering the Navy to actually stop "suspicious" foreign-flag vessels on the high seas. *Alfhem* herself was intercepted on the return voyage and escorted to Key West for a thorough search. The Dutch government lodged an official protest after a Dutch ship was boarded at San Juan, Puerto Rico, on June 4. Later it was decided no more ships would be boarded without specific State Department authorization. James Hagerty, Eisenhower's press secretary, wrote in his diary on June 19 that "I think the State Department made a bad mistake, particularly with the British, in attempting to search ships going to Guatemala. . . . As a matter of fact, we were at war with the British in 1812 over the same principle."

Operation Success was already in its final phase. The "black" radio began broadcasting on May 1; there were also cartoons, posters, pamphlets, and over two hundred articles based on CIA materials placed in the Latin press by the United States Information Agency. Castillo Armas made his invasion on June 18 riding in an old station wagon with a few trucks. Only about 140 soldiers were with him. Castillo Armas advanced to a church six miles into Guatemala, then halted to await the popular revolution that would support him.

But there was no popular uprising. Castillo Armas could not advance even the few more miles to his assigned objective, Zacapa. The seaborne force sent to capture Puerto Barrios also failed. The CIA was myopically optimistic when it reported to President Eisenhower, on June 20, that Castillo Armas had taken in three hundred soldiers and been joined by the same number for a total of over six hundred armed men.

All now depended on Whiting Willauer's rebel air force. It had run a number of bombing and leafleting missions since the first day of the invasion. A raid that caused some damage at Puerto Barrios involved a hand grenade and a stick of dynamite. Another pilot missed his target and then ran out of gas, crash-landing over the Mexican border where he was held by authorities. The CIA operation could have been exposed right there, as it was an American national, William Beall, who had been taken into custody. But the Agency managed to get him released quietly and Operation Success survived the flap. Two other planes were hit by small arms fire from the ground and could not be repaired. The rebel air force seemed no more effective than the "liberation army."

Allen Dulles got the bad news in an afternoon phone call from Al Haney on June 20. The rebel air force could not operate more than four of its planes at any one time. Losses made the difficulty greater; the supply of high explosive bombs was limited, so pilots had resorted to dropping smoke bombs, leaflets, or empty Coca-Cola bottles, which made a noise very much like the explosion of a bomb.

Haney reported that Nicaraguan dictator Tacho Somoza had offered two of his own P-51 fighter-bombers to replace the rebel losses, but only if the United States would itself replace Nicaragua's aircraft. This sounded like a simple expedient until State's assistant secretary for Latin America insisted upon a presidential decision in the matter.

Eisenhower met with Allen and Foster Dulles at the White House on the afternoon of June 22. Henry F. Holland, the State assistant secretary, entered the office carrying several legal tomes. But legality was not the issue.

The President turned to Allen Dulles. "What do you think Castillo's chances would be without the aircraft?"

Dulles replied without hesitation. "About zero."

"Suppose we supply the aircraft," Eisenhower pressed, "what would be the chances then?"

"About twenty percent."

Mainly because of the important psychological impact of air support, Ike agreed to the request. The planes from Somoza were in action the next day, and air attacks became the main activity of the rebels.

The bombing itself led to the worst scare involving Operation Success. This happened at a delicate moment in Washington—a summit conference of the President with Prime Minister Sir Winston Churchill and Foreign Minister Anthony Eden of Great Britain. Anglo-American relations had just grown very cold, because of differences over how to respond to a crisis in Indochina, where the French had lost the Battle of Dien Bien Phu. The situation was not helped by the fact that Eden and John Foster Dulles held each other in low regard. President Eisenhower hoped to repair the Anglo-American "special relationship" at the June summit. But the British were already concerned over American boarding and search of ships at sea. Then the CIA bombed and sank a *British* merchant vessel.

The ship was the *Springfjord*, which had sailed from the Pacific port of San José. Tacho Somoza feared the vessel carried gasoline, with which the Guatemalans might fuel their trucks and airplanes to attack Nicaragua and exact retribution for the assistance Somoza was giving the CIA.

The Nicaraguan dictator turned to Rip Robertson, the top CIA officer at the airfield, and demanded that the ship be stopped. Robertson asked Opa Locka for orders but his cable arrived at two in the morning of Sunday, June 27: Al Haney and Tracy Barnes refused permission and told Robertson to use some other method—frogmen or a commando raid.

This reply infuriated Somoza, who thundered at Robertson, "If you use my airfields, you take my orders!"

Robertson, who had also been disappointed by the orders to desist, gave in and ordered up one of the fighter-bombers. Fifteen minutes out of base, the plane found *Springfjord* and hit her with a five-hundred-pound bomb on the second pass. Fortunately, no one was killed or wounded by the bomb and the ship sank slowly enough for everyone to abandon ship. *Springfjord*, it was later learned, had carried only coffee and cotton.

When news of the sinking reached Washington later that day, it destroyed the cordial atmosphere Eisenhower had been seeking to create at the summit. Frank Wisner left immediately for the British embassy to offer personal apologies. The British leaders allowed themselves to be mollified and the CIA later quietly reimbursed Lloyd's of London, insurers of the *Springfjord*, the $1.5 million they had paid out on the ship.

However, *Springfjord*'s sinking did achieve a significant psychological impact on the Guatemalan crisis. The Guatemalans finally felt pushed to the point where the army began to consider ousting Arbenz. The president was given an ultimatum and he resigned before the day was out, taking refuge in the Mexican embassy where he asked for political asylum. So Operation Success had achieved its aim after all.

Despite the success of this unintended strike, the *Springfjord* incident had a rather different effect at CIA. It convinced Eisenhower of the necessity for more rigorous control over covert action, soon leading to establishment of a senior review group similar to Truman's 10/2 Panel. Rip Robertson was branded as a "cowboy," and Allen Dulles fired him. In a 1966 interview with *New York Times* reporters, Richard Bissell conceded that the action "went beyond the established limits of policy."

The CIA thought it had done rather well on the Iranian and Guatemalan operations, so well, in fact, that within months the agency was deliberately leaking certain details of both operations to the writers Richard and Gladys Harkness for a series of favorable articles. Eisenhower's memoirs employ only the thinnest of linguistic disguises in discussing these two crises, calling CIA agents in Teheran "representatives" of the United States government, and saying of Guatemala that the United States had to do something. Allen Dulles is even more forthright in his book *The Craft of Intelligence:*

> In Iran, a Mossadegh, and in Guatemala, an Arbenz had come to power through the usual processes of government and not by any Communist coup as in Czechoslovakia. Neither man at the time disclosed the intention of creating a Communist state. When this purpose became clear, support from outside was given to loyal anti-Communist elements in the respective countries—in the one case to the Shah's supporters; in the other, to a group of Guatemalan patriots. In each case the danger was successfully met.

But was the danger met, or was it really there in the first place? In the cold war vision of a two-camp world, there was apparently little room for indigenous nationalisms. Not only did the United States readily act against countries like Iran and Guatemala, but the actions were initiated regardless of the nations' efforts to maintain friendly relations with the United States. The operations made a mockery of the oft-reiterated American principle of nonintervention in the internal affairs of other states.

The CIA was unleashed in the name of democracy, but democracy as defined by American foreign policy came to mean governments that followed pro-American policies. No elections occurred in Iran between the 1953 CIA operation and 1960, and thereafter parliament existed at the pleasure of the Shah. In Guatemala after 1954 the republic was abolished. A new constitution was adopted only in 1965, but that was soon suspended by military rulers. In fact, the excesses of the ruling oligarchy became such that the Americans themselves, in the time of the Carter administration, finally halted virtually all foreign aid to the country.

In both the cases of Iran and Guatemala, the United States received credit from world public opinion for creating dictatorships, not democracies. In the short term these covert operations seemed to be shining successes. So while the fruit might prove bitter in the long run, the Eisenhower administration was encouraged to try more of the same.

·VII·

"CREATE AND EXPLOIT TROUBLESOME PROBLEMS"

Even more than Harry Truman, President Eisenhower took an active role in defining policies and erecting mechanisms for conducting covert operations. Ike was also, as a general with long military experience behind him, better equipped than his predecessor to make judgments concerning the feasibility of covert actions. Although he managed intelligence better than most American presidents before or since, Eisenhower, like most politicians of his era, believed completely the rationale for the cold war, and he encouraged covert operations.

It is important today, when Eisenhower's presidency is being reevaluated by American historians, to examine this role in crises and covert operations, the concrete military expressions of the cold war. As the emerging "hidden hand" interpretation might lead one to expect, the covert record shows President Eisenhower to have been intimately involved in the operations of the secret war. The story of how Dwight Eisenhower managed to do this while preserving his options for "plausible denial" shows a masterful ability to command ponderous organizations. The key lay in Ike's use of his staff, a habit he no doubt acquired in the military.

At the strategic nuclear level, Eisenhower did his best to resist a stampeding arms race and avoid war with the Soviet Union. But, as the man who institutionalized covert operations, Eisenhower does not appear the moderate, even liberal, Republican who seems to be emerging from historical reappraisal.

Ike institutionalized covert operations precisely by creating a staff and mechanism to manage them. The President did this even

108

as Operation Success was in motion. He sustained this effort through the end of 1955, by which time he was satisfied. In the process, the President created a central command for global operations.

Ike began to consolidate control over covert operations during the heady days of both the crises in Guatemala and in Dien Bien Phu. On March 15, 1954, the President approved a directive to replace NSC-10/5. This was titled "National Security Council Directive on Covert Operations" and numbered NSC-5412. The top-secret order gave a rationale for continued activity, described a range of operations for which it assigned responsibility, and prescribed a procedure for getting approval of such projects.

Truman's 10/5 Panel had approved covert actions informally, but the NSC directives merely gave it authority to regulate the OPC. These procedures were dismantled anyway when the Eisenhower administration took office. Gone also, after the Solarium study, was the Psychological Strategy Board, with Gordon Gray, who far from becoming the DCI, was exiled to serve on the review board that sat in judgment of the nuclear physicist J. Robert Oppenheimer. Without Truman's established procedures, Operation Ajax was approved on an ad hoc basis and probably Operation Success was as well.

With NSC-5412, President Eisenhower was, for the first time, investing the mechanism for managing the secret war with formal powers.

But within three short months, in the waters off San José, Guatemala, the CIA was sinking a ship against orders; moreover the vessel was chartered to an American ally.

Eisenhower openly expressed satisfaction to returning members of the Success task force, but privately he determined to get an independent review of covert operations. NSC staff members approached retired Air Force lieutenant general James H. Doolittle, who agreed to head a four-man study group. The final secret instructions to Doolittle were contained in a letter from the President dated July 26, 1954. Ike wanted a comprehensive review of the factors of personnel, security, cost, and efficiency of covert operations, as well as an assessment as to how to "equate the costs of the overall efforts to the results achieved." The panel was to report to Eisenhower personally with its recommendations on how "to improve the conduct of these operations."

Jimmy Doolittle was a good choice. The dynamic leader of the airmen who bombed Japan in 1942, immortalized in the movie *30 Seconds Over Tokyo*, Doolittle had participated in wartime special operations, and had a solid understanding of such activities. He also was aware of technological developments since. He was known to Ike from the time when both were commanders in Britain in 1944. Doolittle got his basic instructions in a conversation with Ike in early July, then sat down with William B. Franke, Morris Hadley, and William B. Pawley to perform the review.

Doolittle's committee had its first meeting at CIA headquarters on July 14. They were extensively briefed by the Agency, State, the Office of the Secretary of Defense, the armed services, the FBI, and the Bureau of the Budget. By July 29 a staff had been assembled and the review was in full swing. After meetings with both Allen Dulles and Frank Wisner, Doolittle and consultant J. Patrick Coyne made a field trip in mid-September to inspect CIA installations in Western Europe. The "Report of the Special Study Group on Covert Activities" went to the President on September 30.

The Doolittle Report gave solid support to the rationale for the secret war. The second paragraph of the report stated quite baldly:

> As long as it remains national policy, another important requirement is an aggressive covert psychological, political and paramilitary organization more effective, more unique and, if necessary, more ruthless than that employed by the enemy. No one should be permitted to stand in the way of the prompt, efficient and secure accomplishment of this mission.

So serious was the conflict with communism that "there are no rules in such a game. Hitherto acceptable norms of human conduct do not apply." The secret warriors could have asked for no better.

But the report was also critical of CIA performance in several areas. It concluded that the staff of five thousand could be reduced by 10 percent with no adverse effect. The "fusion" of the old OPC and OSO was termed a "shotgun marriage." The report warned that the "Cold War functions" of Directorate of Plans (DDP) had come to overshadow its clandestine espionage role, and the committee recommended that the DDP be completely reorganized into a viable "Cold War shop." The DCI should himself be given more staff support in important covert action projects, with this staff to be provided from the President's NSC apparatus, leading to better implementation of NSC-5412.

These results were controversial enough for President Eisenhower to ask Doolittle to discuss them personally with Allen Dulles. Doolittle reported back to Ike in person on October 19, 1954, that his study was in no sense a whitewash, but a constructive criticism of the CIA. He thought Dulles's basic problem was organizational—the CIA had grown "like topsy"—but neither the DCI nor Frank Wisner was an especially good organizer.

Doolittle remarked that Allen Dulles had taken criticism of himself pretty well but that he fought for his staff people "to the point of becoming emotional." Doolittle cited their mutual comrade, Walter Bedell Smith, who had said at one time that Allen was "too emotional to be in this critical spot" and that "his emotionalism was far worse than it appeared on the surface."

Eisenhower replied, "We must remember that here is one of the most peculiar types of operation any government can have, and it probably takes a strange kind of genius to run it."

The President also defended his DCI: He had not seen Allen "show the slightest disturbance." Furthermore, their purpose was to improve the CIA itself, and Allen had important contacts throughout the world.

Having enforced reasonably good security at the NSC, "it was completely frustrating," Ike felt, "to find always evidence that people are talking."

Doolittle tried one other tack, referring to the relationship between the DCI and the secretary of state. Having brothers in these two posts entailed problems that "it would be better not to have exist."

Eisenhower resisted that argument strenuously. He had appointed Allen in full knowledge of the relationship, Ike said. It did not disturb him at all, because CIA's work was partly an extension of State's job, and because a confidential relationship between the two brothers "is a good thing."

Ike never wavered. "I'm not going to be able to change Allen," observed the President. "I have two alternatives, either to get rid of him and appoint someone who will assert more authority or keep him with his limitations. I'd rather have Allen as my chief intelligence officer with his limitations than anyone else I know."

What the President did instead was work hard at implementing

NSC-5412. At first he tried to do this through the Operations Coordinating Board (OCB), an interagency subgroup under the NSC that was supposed to focus specifically on implementation. Authority over the covert operations was given to the OCB in the presidential directive. Composed of designated representatives from the various agencies, OCB was really a rather junior group to be making decisions on covert operations. So, a more senior element of OCB was created called the Planning Coordination Group, and on March 12, 1955, in a revised NSC-5412/1, Eisenhower ordered that this group be advised in advance of all major covert operations and that it "shall be the normal channel for giving policy approval for such programs as well as for securing coordination of support therefor."

This still proved inadequate. The directive talked about "need-to-know" in its statement of the CIA's responsibility to seek approval of operations; the agency interpreted this to mean that not all elements of a plan had to be briefed or approved. When the agency insisted it had been completely forthcoming, Eisenhower reacted by establishing a panel of direct designees of the President, State, and the Pentagon, plus the DCI. Ike's designee was his special assistant for national security affairs. This body was so senior there could be no question of its "need-to-know." It became known as the 5412 Group after the directive that established it, NSC-5412/2 of December 28, 1955.

Any problems with an operation would be taken directly to the President by his special assistant, who would speak at meetings as the voice of his boss. Eisenhower preserved his "deniability" by not actually participating in the 5412 Group, but he was in constant contact with each of its members. The President also held White House postmortems, like those after Iran and Guatemala, along with semiannual reviews of ongoing and planned operations presented to the full NSC by the DCI.

Eisenhower's commitment to the cold war is clearly demonstrated in NSC-5412/2. The directive provided the secret warriors with the broadest possible charter, the breadth of which is worth quoting in its entirety:

3. The NSC has determined that such covert operations shall to the greatest extent practicable, in the light of U.S. and Soviet capabilities and taking into account the risk of war, be designed to:

a. Create and exploit troublesome problems for International Communism, impair relations between the USSR and Communist China and between them and their satellites, complicate control within the USSR, Communist China and their satellites, and retard the growth of the military and economic potential of the Soviet bloc.

b. Discredit the prestige and ideology of International Communism, and reduce the strength of its parties and other elements.

c. Counter any threat of a party or individuals directly or indirectly responsive to Communist control to achieve dominant power in a free world country.

d. Reduce International Communist control over any areas of the world.

e. Strengthen the orientation toward the United States of the peoples and nations of the free world, accentuate, wherever possible, the identity of interest between such peoples and nations and the United States as well as favoring, where appropriate, those groups genuinely advocating or believing in the advancement of such mutual interests, and increase the capacity and will of such peoples and nations to resist International Communism.

f. In accordance with established policies and to the extent practicable in areas dominated or threatened by International Communism, develop underground resistance and facilitate covert and guerrilla operations and ensure availability of those forces in the event of war, including wherever practicable provision of a base upon which the military may expand these forces in time of war within active theaters of operations as well as provide for stay-behind assets and escape and evasion facilities.

This turgid bureaucratic prose encompassed a multitude of possibilities for covert operations. The CIA would spend the remainder of the 1950s exploring them.

While President Eisenhower pondered the problems of managing covert action, secret wars continued in the field. At the same time Operation Success was unfolding, another set of operations was being carried out in the Far East.

One was supervised by William J. Donovan, wartime chief of

OSS and now ambassador to Thailand. This was repatriation of the Chinese nationalists in northern Burma in accordance with the express wishes of the Burmese government. General Li Mi himself returned to Taiwan in October 1952 but his soldiers were still in Burma. A four-power military conference including Burma, Thailand, Nationalist China, and the United States, held in Bangkok in 1953, agreed to repatriate the remaining Chinese forces. This in turn led to Operation Repat, a Civil Air Transport airlift of Chinese who crossed from northern Burma to Thailand and were then flown to Taiwan.

An initial group of 50 Chinese troops crossed the border on November 8, 1953, bearing no weapons but carrying a seven-foot-tall portrait of Chiang Kai-shek. Flights began the next day; CAT used eight C-46 aircraft for the lift, modified with extra fuel tanks yet still flying at the limit of their range. In the first phase, which lasted into December, some 1,925 nationalist troops and 335 dependents returned to Taiwan. In the second phase, in February and March 1954, another 2,962 troops and 513 dependents were airlifted out. Additional people flown out later brought the final total to 5,583 soldiers and 1,040 dependents, for each of whom CAT was paid $128 from U.S. foreign aid accounts.

Operation Repat was something of a farce, however. Some of the evacuees were Shan and Lahu tribesmen, not Chinese, and the flow of dependents swelled the numbers of evacuees without ameliorating the Burmese security problem. In later years many of them would contrive to return to Burma. In addition, the 5,600 troops brought out only a thousand rifles, sixty-nine machine guns, and twenty-two mortars, some of these antique pieces dating from 1907, not the modern weapons with which the CIA had supplied Li Mi. The Chinese maintained forces in Burma, no longer under CIA control, that later increased to a strength of twelve thousand, with continued involvement in the drug trade.

There were significant changes in the Taiwan Strait. The Seventh Fleet had had orders during the Korean War to bar the strait to forces of both sides. Eisenhower changed the order to block only Peking, freeing Chiang Kai-shek to raid the mainland. In early 1953 the United States gave the nationalists their first jet aircraft (F-84 fighters), and sanctioned an expansion of the nationalist marine corps to three brigades, a tripling of Chiang's amphibious force.

In connection with the jet deal, the nationalists agreed not to use their American weapons, particularly aircraft, on offensive missions without prior consultation with the U.S. military advisory group on Taiwan. But Chiang did not seek prior American approval three months later, in July 1953, when aircraft were committed for tactical air support of a nationalist force raiding Tungshan on the mainland. The nationalist chief of staff apologized, claiming dire emergency—the KMT raiders were being driven into the sea and needed to buy time for an orderly evacuation. The nationalists promised it would not happen again, but in June 1954 Chiang's navy used its American-supplied destroyer escorts to seize a Soviet tanker on the high seas between Luzon and Taiwan. Eisenhower's administration assumed a posture of studied neutrality in this later incident.

Another nationalist operation was propaganda, including both radio and leaflet programs, the latter delivered over the mainland principally by aircraft, but also by balloons, in bottles, and in bamboo canisters. Nationalist sources claimed dispersal of 300 million leaflets on the mainland during 1953, with an average of fifteen aircraft overflights a month, some as far distant as Szechuan province.

The CIA's early involvement in global operations by Civil Air Transport also included a second airlift program, in French Indochina. This CAT action resulted from the military aid program, which had loaned France C-119 "Flying Boxcar" transports instead of the C-47s the French requested. The first CAT flight in Indochina was a supply lift to an entrenched camp in Laos on May 6, 1953. Within a year a detachment of twenty-four CAT pilots would be caught up in the French debacle at Dien Bien Phu. Twenty-one Civil Air Transport pilots had familiarized themselves with the C-119 at the Far East Air Force base at Ashiya, Japan. The whole class went to Indochina. These personnel actually outnumbered the French aircrews given C-119 orientations in two groups at Clark Air Force Base.

Squaw II was Civil Air Transport's project name for the Dien Bien Phu airlift (Squaw I having been the Laotian lift in the spring of 1953). The CAT crew brought everything they needed, down to their own refrigerator and supply of bottled beer. In all, the CIA proprietary flew 684 sorties to Dien Bien Phu. The pilot who flew most frequently was A. L. Judkins with sixty-four flights; next was

Steve A. Kusak with fifty-nine. The original chief pilot, Paul R. Holden, was on his fifth mission to Dien Bien Phu when he was wounded by antiaircraft fire. Pilots recall the flak over the entrenched camp as being as heavy as anything they encountered over Germany in World War II. Kusak himself was flying a mission alongside James B. McGovern on May 6, 1954 when the latter was shot down in his C-119. Nicknamed "Earthquake McGoon" after a popular comic-strip character, McGovern died just hours before the final collapse of the French at Dien Bien Phu, one year to the day after CAT had flown its first mission in Indochina.

At one point in the Dien Bien Phu crisis the French asked the U.S. for the loan of some B-29 bombers. In the United States there was discussion of encouraging the French to add an air component to their Foreign Legion, which could then be given B-29s, and which American crews could then be encouraged to join. But the option was impractical given the immediacy of the crisis.

The Eisenhower administration was nevertheless so impressed with CAT performance that it considered forming a proprietary that would operate combat aircraft to help the French. At the request of the NSC Operations Coordinating Board, a plan was prepared by the staff of General Graves B. Erskine, assistant to the secretary of defense for special operations. The concept provided for an International Volunteer Air Group (IVAG) that could be "sponsored" by France or some Asian government. The unit would fly several squadrons of F-86 jet fighters, and there was some talk of giving it B-29s as well. It was expected IVAG could be set up within eight months, at an initial cost of $130 million and an annual operating cost of $200 million.

Though first discussed by an NSC subcommittee meeting on Indochina, IVAG could possibly have had much wider covert applications, and this potential was clearly perceived by the Pentagon special warfare planners: "such a unit will always be useful as a ready striking force in the event of renewed aggression in any part of the Far East. Without it no air striking force exists which can be employed on short notice in circumstances where it is undesirable to employ official U.S. air power."

In the event of a declared war the IVAG could be "officially inducted into the U.S. Air Force as an additional wing."

Pentagon planners believed that "creation of an IVAG is consonant with and within the framework of U.S. national policy," but felt the project required "NSC affirmation" and an opinion from the attorney general that confirmed the legality of enlistment by U.S. civilian and military volunteers.

The original plan called for creation of the unit before the end of the 1954 rainy season in Indochina, but the crisis receded and no NSC action was forthcoming. The United States did consider a private firm, Aviation International Limited, to recruit American aircraft mechanics to assist the French air force in Indochina, but military personnel were used over the short term and the first Indochina war ended soon afterward.

The OCB recommendation to form an International Volunteer Air Group was nevertheless finally taken up that summer. The recommendation was approved by the NSC at its 211th meeting on August 18, 1954. Because the Indochina war had already ended, the IVAG plan was shelved as a contingency option, but the planning exercise was significant in establishing an NSC-approved role for the kind of illegitimate air force the CIA had just used in Guatemala and would soon resort to in the Far East.

Aside from the air effort, Indochina was also the locale for a widening paramilitary effort by the United States, which began with secret discussions in 1953. Strapped for money, and facing the escalating cost of their war in Indochina, the French asked for military aid in the area of "special warfare" and the Eisenhower administration agreed.

The main French special-warfare activity was running certain auxiliary forces in southern Vietnam, plus partisan units behind enemy lines in the north. In the south there were two syncretistic religious movements—the Cao Dai, and Hoa Hao—and also a band of river pirates, the Binh Xuyen, whose private armies were financed by French intelligence. There is evidence that a senior CIA officer, briefed in Saigon in December 1953 regarding French special-warfare actions, was offered a role in control over the three bands in return for additional aid money. The briefing was repeated for another CIA man in March 1954, but the offer was rejected three months later. There were nevertheless rumors in Saigon of American contacts with the private armies, especially after, late in 1953, two women connected with the United States embassy were found dead in a jeep, on a rubber plantation close to Cao Dai headquarters. In another incident, also hushed up for diplomatic reasons, a consul at the embassy was arrested on a bridge when he was stopped for an identity check, and was found to have plastic explosives in his car trunk.

American special-warfare experts were also active in northern Vietnam. In the north, the French had about ten thousand partisans in nineteen separate bands, operating behind the lines of the Vietnamese revolutionaries. This was an increase over previous levels and it was encouraged by the Americans. Beginning in 1953 two U.S. Army officers were permanently stationed with the French special-warfare command in the north to service all requests for equipment. Major Roger Trinquier, the French commander, visited Korea that year to observe how Americans organized partisan forces there. By February 15, 1954, the American ambassador to Vietnam was reporting that "we are already making [a] contribution to increased French practice of 'unconventional warfare.'"

President Eisenhower himself was not satisfied with progress. In a June 1954 letter to friend and fellow general, Alfred M. Gruenther, who was then serving in France with NATO, Ike complained that the French had rebuffed most American offers of the kind "that would tend to keep our participation in the background, but could nevertheless be very effective. I refer to our efforts to get a good guerrilla organization going in the region."

But the French lost at Dien Bien Phu, negotiated a settlement at Geneva, and were soon withdrawing from Indochina. The partisan groups in the north ended up being taken over by the Americans, who managed to smuggle in a few shipments of weapons and explosives under cover of the French evacuation. There was no base or capability for long-term support, however, and by 1956 the last of the partisans had been eliminated.

The Americans were more successful in South Vietnam, the southern "regroupment zone" established by the 1954 Geneva agreement. A unit called the Saigon Military Mission was set up there in July 1954 as cover for intelligence operations. It was headed by political action specialist Edward G. Lansdale, an Air Force colonel, who had received the National Security Medal for work in the Philippines in the early 1950s. Initially with only ten officers and a few men, the Saigon Military Mission soon acquired much greater importance, because Lansdale established a close friendship with politician Ngo Dinh Diem, who became the leader of South Vietnam.

France's settlement at Geneva provided for elections throughout

Vietnam by 1956 and reunification of the country. The Eisenhower administration refused to associate itself with the agreement and eventually encouraged South Vietnam to abrogate it. Lansdale was instrumental in convincing Diem to claim nation status for South Vietnam and to become its president.

While Diem was casting the die for a second Indochinese war, in which both "special warfare" and the CIA would play a much greater part, the United States conceived of its new Southeast Asian ally in terms of the "two camp" world conflict. Thus the Vietnamese army was designed by American planners to meet a conventional military threat. In a vision embodied in the 1955 war plans, the CIA was supposed to retard the advance of any such enemy by operations in Laos. Meanwhile, the U.S. Pacific Fleet would make coastal raids to harry any advance through North Vietnam. The fleet had three teams of SEALS, Sea Air Land Soldiers, commando units for special warfare, which developed from the frogman teams of World War II. Reinforcing its force after D Day up to twelve SEAL teams, the Pacific Fleet felt it had the strength to carry out the mission. But war, when it returned to Vietnam, took the form of guerrilla warfare against Ngo Dinh Diem. The Americans and South Vietnamese had prepared themselves for the wrong threat.

The mid-1950s were a high point of sorts for the secret warriors in Europe, especially in the use of pure psychological warfare intended to create and exploit problems for the Soviets and to complicate their control over Eastern Europe. The Americans took advantage of spontaneous outbursts of resistance within the Soviet satellites, the closest the Eisenhower administration ever came to implementing its commitment to "rollback" of the Iron Curtain.

More than propaganda could have been involved if some had had their way. The CIA and the British, it will be recalled, had espionage and liaison operations in place behind the iron curtain using Russians and Ukrainians. There were also the Eastern Europeans in the Army's 10th Special Forces, whose entry had been facilitated by the 1950 Lodge Bill, and an amendment to the 1951 Mutual Security Act, which set aside specific funds for an Army unit of Eastern Europeans. It might have been an American Foreign Legion.

Aside from the specialists it integrated into Special Forces, the Army did nothing with this mandate with which it had been saddled. The Russian propagandists had a field day even so. Frank

Wisner told Tracy Barnes in the winter of 1951 that the United States was taking a propaganda beating on this question. Congress nevertheless appropriated money, which the Army did not use, in several annual budgets.

When Eisenhower became President, he tried to get the Army to cooperate on the formation of an Eastern European unit. Instead, his Army general friends told him the many reasons why they thought the unit could not function effectively.

"Fellows, tell me this," Ike countered, "just how high does a fellow have to go in this outfit before he can call the shots?"

But, Army leaders continued to balk at the organization of an Eastern European unit, devoting the bulk of their efforts to the still-modest Special Forces program.

Ike's interest was also piqued by the concrete evidence of dissatisfaction with Soviet rule in East Berlin, which erupted into riots in June 1953. Thousands took to the streets beginning on June 16 to demand a reduction of recently imposed production "norms" and, before it was over, elections by secret ballot. The news was beamed across East Germany with sympathy by the United States military outlet Radio in the American Sector (RIAS). That night Henry Hecksher, then the CIA's Berlin station chief, asked for but was refused permission to arm the rioters. Demonstrations throughout East Germany were soon countered by Soviet military forces called out of their camps. The United States' only official action, after a late June NSC decision, was to offer limited food aid, through Moscow, to the East Germans.

It was not possible for the United States to make any military moves in support of the Easterners because of the risk of touching off a major war with the Soviets.

Over the summer and fall the administration conducted a major review of its overall strategy, dubbed the "Solarium" study for the White House indoor garden where the panelists often met and the final report was presented. Three task forces of planners were assembled, each to argue for a particular line of strategy. The "rollback" approach was subsumed in Solarium's "Alternative C" designed "to increase efforts to disturb and weaken the Soviet bloc," overtly and covertly attacking the "Communist apparatus" worldwide, and missing no opportunities "to confuse and unbalance our enemy."

The Task Force C program foresaw detailed preparations for

atomic warfare, expediting development of cadres of European émigré fighters in the Volunteer Freedom Corps, and the employment of Chinese nationalist troops, first against Hainan island, then the mainland. Planners estimated costs at about $60 billion for the first two years, declining to $45 billion in subsequent fiscal years, with perhaps another $5 billion required if the program led to the resumption of hostilities in Korea.

George Kennan, chief of the Task Force A panel, argued eloquently for the alternative of "containment" as offering lower costs and less risk of war with Russia.

Eisenhower took Kennan's point. When the presenters had finished, the President jumped up and said he wished to summarize. Rollback, Ike said, would strain American alliances and represented "a departure from our traditional concepts of war and peace." President Eisenhower chose to restrict military spending and avoid greater risk of atomic war.

Few have noticed that in the case of the Solarium study the President did not select a pure strategy. Containment, Kennan's option "A," was *mixed* with elements of the Task Force C program, in particular covert action. That this was the case is evident from the record of the NSC meeting on July 30, 1953, where participants discussing the Solarium results explicitly raised the possibilities for action in Guatemala, Iran, and Albania.

Allen Dulles remarked that a CIA paper on Albania had already been sent to the Psychological Strategy Board. The DCI also asserted that the National Security Council needed to make new policy decisions, presumably for unilateral U.S. action, on Guatemala.

Only in the case of Albania did President Eisenhower interject a cautionary note, "because of the question of who gets it and who gets hurt."

Strategy was strictly prescribed during the Eisenhower administration by a series of NSC decision documents. For Eastern Europe there was the NSC-143 series and the NSC-158, "U.S. Objectives and Actions to Exploit the Unrest in the Satellite States," both contemporaneous with Solarium. In February 1955 there followed NSC-5505/1, "Exploitation of Soviet and European Satellite Vulnerabilities." A report on progress achieving the objectives of NSC-5505/1 was submitted on December 14, 1955. Thereafter, a revised policy was accepted in NSC-5608/1, "U.S. Policy Toward the Soviet Satellites in Eastern Europe," approved on July 18, 1956. By then a train of events was already in motion that led to renewed crisis in Eastern Europe.

The events of 1956 were triggered not in Washington but in Moscow, where Nikita Khrushchev was consolidating power as the successor to Stalin. Addressing the Twentieth Party Congress, Khrushchev laid bare many of the corruptions and rigidities of Stalinism in an effort to discredit competitors in the Politburo. He was successful in this political maneuver, but a copy of the secret speech reached the CIA from a contact with a European communist. The text was in Wisner's hands in L Building by April 1956.

Khrushchev's speech was an immensely important lever for the cold war. Here was the leader of Russia, admitting that party practices and leadership had been gravely flawed. The speech even discussed Stalin's personal interventions in the affairs of satellites like Hungary and Yugoslavia, which eventually resulted in an open split with the Yugoslavs, who were driven into the hands of Washington. Khrushchev claimed to offer an alternative "socialist legality." Clearly the speech was political dynamite.

The text materialized after Allen Dulles ordered a specific search for it, which, he writes, "I have always regarded as one of the major coups of my tour of duty." Authentication was undertaken carefully, both with trusted academic specialists on Russia and with CIA officers. Ray Cline, then chief of the Office of Current Intelligence, which specialized in analysis, was called in and judged it a reliable source.

Use of the Khrushchev speech quickly became a point of contention, however. Cline recommended publicizing it as a move in the psychological war to discredit Soviet rule. Frank Wisner favored selective secret use of the document to mobilize an active Eastern European resistance. The CIA began recruiting a force similar to earlier concepts for émigré units. The question of what to do with the speech was decided at a very high level.

Ray Cline recalls working with Dulles over a speech the DCI was to deliver. It was a Saturday, June 2, 1956. Dulles interrupted this other work suddenly, swung his chair around, and looked intently at the intelligence analyst.

"Wisner says you think we ought to release the secret Khrushchev speech."

Cline related his reasons for thinking this. He writes that "the old man" had a twinkle in his eye when he answered, "By golly, I am going to make a policy decision!" Allen Dulles phoned the DDP and told Wisner he had given the matter great thought and had decided the speech should be printed.

This version is suitably romantic but the fact is that, three days earlier, on May 31, Dulles had given a copy of the speech to NSC adviser Dillon Anderson with the special request that secrecy be kept "pending a decision as to what, if any, public use should be made of this document." It is inconceivable that Anderson did not go to the President on a matter of this importance. If Cline is accurately quoting Allen Dulles, the possibility exists that the DCI was amused at hoodwinking his own OCI chief, about a decision he was not making.

The Khrushchev speech was published in the press on June 4, 1956, beginning a hot summer and fall in Eastern Europe.

The revelation occurred during an ongoing political action campaign by CIA's "radios." In 1953, Radio Free Europe had introduced a technique of "saturation broadcasting" to counter Soviet jamming efforts. Once reception was assured, RFE moved ahead to specially targeted propaganda campaigns. Operation Veto was inaugurated in early 1954 to encourage long-term resistance, especially in Hungary. It was succeeded by Operation Focus. Radio broadcasting was supplemented by balloon leafleting, which peaked in 1954–1955 and played a major role in Focus. By this time RFE had studios in Munich and offices in New York with a staff of 1,400, among them 400 to 500 émigrés and 150 Americans. It had a substantial capability to exploit Khrushchev's secret speech.

Concentrating on broadcasting back the news from the east, RFE found quite a lot to say. There were riots in Poznań, Poland, in reaction to the news of Khrushchev's "destalinization" program. With these riots came the return to power of the communist faction of Wladyslaw Gomulka, a leader previously purged for his belief in the existence of more than one road toward socialism. Soviet troops were momentarily deployed, but Gomulka succeeded in getting Khrushchev to back down with a threat to break openly with the Warsaw Pact.

This news electrified Budapest. On October 23 young party demonstrators swept through the streets demanding installation of a new government under Imre Nagy, a Hungarian communist who similarly had previously been purged. Nagy became premier, but the opposing wing of the Hungarian communists continued to control the party. The government invited Soviet forces to restore order.

Arrests by Hungarian secret police brought widening circles of revolt. A secret-police detachment in the village of Magyarovar was murdered by outraged citizens. But then ten thousand Russian troops appeared in Budapest. Within three days, there was street fighting in the capital and resistance in the provinces. RFE reported all of these events. Some of the Hungarian exiles on its staff could not resist making vague statements about Western support, inflating Hungarian hopes of aid from the Americans.

Assistance to the rebels was an immediate question at the CIA, as it had been in the East Berlin episode. But the military risk to Western Europe from an intervention had not changed since 1953, and Eisenhower's answer had to be the same. On two separate occasions in the Hungarian crisis, the President rejected proposals to airdrop arms to the Hungarians. The second came after the Hungarians themselves went on the air with a "Free Hungary" radio that appealed for CIA help. Ike ended the debate with an assertion that Hungary was "as inaccessible to us as Tibet."

Anyway the crisis had caught the Directorate of Plans without a prepared force for operations in Hungary. Wisner's émigré unit was far from ready. The Russians moved in, on November 4, with more than 200,000 troops and over twenty-five hundred armored vehicles, reconquering Budapest by November 8 and the rest of the country before the end of the month. The Eisenhower administration, meanwhile, had been largely diverted by the unfolding Anglo-French intervention at Suez, and was unable to spend much time considering the Hungarian situation.

Frank Wisner, however, was impatient to be on the scene. Wisner's Mississippi drawl was soon heard at the CIA station in Vienna, instructing subordinates but especially talking with new refugees arrived from Hungary. There were over 190,000 refugees following the collapse of the revolt. Vice-President Richard Nixon and former OSS chief Wild Bill Donovan also came to Vienna to receive some of the fugitives. Casualty estimates in Hungary range up to 30,000 dead and 50,000 injured.

Eisenhower's decisions affected morale among the secret warriors. The DDP officers saw in Hungary "exactly the end for which the Agency's paramilitary capability was designed." Some of them thought intervention could have been carried out without triggering a war with the Russians. In passing up intervention, Bill Colby recollects, "we demonstrated that 'liberation' was not our policy when the chips were down in Eastern Europe." Similarly, writes Harry Rositzke, a CIA man who had spent his entire postwar intelligence career in Soviet operations, "it was clear that the steady barrage of assurances that the West was firmly opposed to the continuing Communist exploitation of subject peoples could not fail to give RFE's listeners the hope that the United States would come to their aid."

Wisner, too, in a way was broken on the Hungarian anvil. One night he spent on the border, watching the wink of machine-gun fire, as Soviet security forces tried to halt the flow of helpless refugees. Bitter, he left Austria, and stopped in Rome, where station chief Bill Colby thought him close to a nervous breakdown. In fact, the DDP could not continue with his trip, which involved visits to England, France, Germany, and Greece as well; he contracted hepatitis and went into hospital with a 106-degree fever. Deputy Richard Helms filled in during Wisner's recovery.

Allen Dulles received White House instructions to produce a formal postmortem analysis of the part played by Radio Free Europe in the Hungarian business. This task was assigned to Cord Meyer, who since 1954 had been handling CIA contacts with the "radios." His office, with the assistance of two Hungarian-speaking analysts, made a full survey of RFE broadcasts during the period. Meyer's conclusion, based on the survey and on the day-to-day events of the crisis, was: "I am satisfied that RFE did not plan, direct, or attempt to provoke the Hungarian rebellion."

Vice-President Nixon, too, had gone from Vienna to the border one night. There he had asked Budapest students whether they felt RFE and the Voice of America had had any effect in encouraging their rebellion. They had answered with a simple yes.

Nixon's account was not yet available when Allen Dulles forwarded the four-page report of his political action staff to the White House on November 20. The highlighted passage on the White House copy, among the paragraphs of justification for RFE, read, "A few of the scripts reviewed do indicate that RFE occasionally went beyond the authorized factual broadcasting of the demands of the patriot radio stations within Hungary to identify itself with these demands and to urge their achievement." Further, "there was some evidence of attempts by RFE to provide tactical advice to the patriots as to the course the rebellion should take and the individuals best qualified to lead it." The RFE broadcasts, said one conclusion, "went beyond specific guidances" although the uprising itself resulted from Soviet repression rather than RFE broadcasts or Free Europe leaflets.

The administration discontinued blunderbuss propaganda campaigns like Operation Focus, tightened central corporate control over RFE broadcasting decisions, and ordered an end to the balloon leaflet program.

The last loose end was the émigré "liberation army" set up by the CIA. Never used, the unit was disbanded. Some of the recruits joined the Army, where they ended up with Special Forces and soon found themselves in places as distant as Laos. Others returned to Europe, where the NTS and OUN-R plots still boiled. In Germany, 1958 was the high point for a mysterious organization called the Battlegroup Against Inhumanity (Kampfgruppe gegen Unmenschlichkeit). Drawing funding from the Crusade for Freedom, the conduit that had been established to finance RFE, the "battlegroup" was linked in 1958 with several commando-style raids in East Germany, including a failed attempt to blow up the six-span bridge over the Elbe at Weimar. These and earlier actions by the group aroused such controversy in Germany that it disbanded in 1959.

The legacy of Hungary was bitterness all around. At the CIA, as Bill Colby put it, "whatever doubt may have existed in the Agency about Washington's policy in matters like this vanished." Among the Eastern Europeans the realization began to dawn that American claims to support resistance to the Soviets were mainly rhetorical. In the White House, growing awareness of the sensitivity of these types of activities led to a reduced emphasis on psychological warfare. Hungary demonstrated that the mere existence of certain types of capabilities can create controversy, even in the absence of any effort to do so.

Eisenhower worried about control, but pursued his cold war as well. The very rush of events made it difficult to go back over old ground, to check the implementation of orders previously given. The mechanism for decision, the 5412 Group plus the semiannual presentations of the program for the President, made it impossible to exercise day-to-day control. The initiative shown by the 5412 Group then became crucial to protecting the President's interests; but, like many bureaucracies, 5412 reacted to recommendations rather than exerting positive leadership. The real initiative lay in the hands of the CIA which, in fulfillment of the 5412/2 objectives, launched more cold war adventures around the world.

·VIII·

ARCHIPELAGO

Although some elements of the CIA regretted not being able to act in the Hungarian crisis, there were a variety of other jobs to which they could turn: an array of operations from the Middle East to the China coast to the islands of Southeast Asia. These included both political action and covert operations, but unlike the easy victories in Iran and Guatemala, success proved much more difficult to achieve.

Paltry results did not dampen their ardor, however. While the President monitored the overall program, his secretary of state, John Foster Dulles, with his brother Allen, oversaw execution. John Foster Dulles pursued the secret war with the same zeal and energy with which he covered distances, en route to diplomatic meetings, to become the most-traveled secretary of state in American history. Of course, Foster kept close tabs on the operations through Allen, the DCI.

Foster Dulles was abrasive and rigid in an administration that accented pragmatism. His advantage was mainly the common outlook he shared with President Eisenhower. But the secretary of state was already in physical decline—he would die of cancer in January 1959—and the continuing crises that followed Hungary took a great toll on his remaining strength. Not least among these were several that involved CIA operations.

One of the new plans originated in the months before Suez. A CIA contract officer, assigned for purposes of cover to the Operations Coordinating Board, heard the code name Straggle used at an

Anglo-American intelligence conference. It had been dropped by George K. Young, deputy to the SIS chief, in connection with a Middle East plan. When the CIA man returned to Washington, he discovered that a planning task force called Omega had already been formed at State.

Unfamiliar with the chain of command the CIA man, Wilbur C. Eveland, thought

> that plans to undertake a coup in Syria were centered in the Department of State struck me as highly unusual. I'd expected to see papers referring to NSC policy decisions and instructions that the OCB coordinate carrying them out. Instead, it seemed, the decision had been made by the Secretary of State, and the Omega planners were in charge of following through.

Foster Dulles held a meeting on May 23, 1956, to consider the final Omega paper. Shortly thereafter Eveland, an experienced Middle East hand, was directed to scout the possibilities on the ground. He was given two months. In July, Kermit Roosevelt went out to Jordan on another assignment related to the mission's planning.

Operation Straggle, known to the Americans as Wakeful, led to a complete disaster. The basic idea was to bring about a coup by Syrian officers to forestall the leftist Ba'ath party. In fact, however, the British seem to have manipulated CIA into timing the operation for precisely the beginning of the Anglo-French-Israeli action against Suez. The coup project collapsed as key Syrians and Iraqis became convinced the Americans were only assisting the other action against Nasser's Egypt.

The coup was resurrected in 1957 as Operation Wappen, with the CIA in Beirut coordinating a covert working group composed of representatives of SIS plus Iraqi, Jordanian, and Lebanese intelligence services. The station chief in Damascus also had his own version of Operation Wakeful, for which he brought up from Khartoum political action specialist Howard "Rocky" Stone, one of the officers who had worked with Kim Roosevelt in Iran. The agency got in touch with former Syrian president Adib Shishakli, who had been considered unacceptable as an ally in the 1956 coup planning. This time Syrian officers who had been re-

cruited simply walked into the office of intelligence chief Lieutenant Colonel Abdul Hamid Sarraj, named the CIA officers, and
turned in the money they had been given. American agents Rocky
Stone and Frank Jetton were caught red-handed, exposed in the
Syrian press, and expelled from the country. In its August 26, 1957,
issue, *Time* magazine nevertheless dismissed reports of the United
States–sponsored coup as Soviet propaganda.

One novelty for the CIA during 1956 was a global inspection tour
by the DCI. Allen Dulles took along analyst Ray Cline as senior
aide, and the group covered over thirty thousand miles in fifty-
seven days. They used the director's personal plane, a specially
modified military version of the DC-6 called the C-118. Dulles in-
spected the stations in Europe, Turkey, Pakistan, India, Thailand,
South Vietnam, Singapore, Australia, the Philippines, Taiwan,
South Korea, and Japan. After the whirlwind tour, Dulles paused a
few days in Hawaii, to write a report and recommendations on the
stations.

Dulles's world tour was a token of Washington's recognition of
the CIA's global role, but not a portent of changing fortunes in the
secret war. For the warriors a more accurate sign lay in the fate of
Allen Dulles's airplane—in 1958, through a chain of coincidences
and misfortunes, the C-118 blundered into the Soviet Union, then
was shot down with the loss of four of the nine occupants. This set
the tone for an operation being prepared in Indonesia.

Dwight Eisenhower, in his own recollections of the presidency
mentions Achmed Sukarno of Indonesia exactly once: Eisenhower
remarks that he had not seen Sukarno in some years. This comment
was made in the context of a discussion of why Ike felt justified, in
rejecting a 1960 plea by Sukarno and four other national leaders, for
summit talks between the United States and the Soviet Union.

Ike's general dissatisfaction with Indonesia led to a major paramilitary operation in the late 1950s designed to overthrow the existing government, much as in Iran or Guatemala. In the 1960
appeal for superpower detente, Sukarno was in fact speaking from
the experience of having been caught between the adversaries.

Sukarno's unpardonable offense in the eyes of the Eisenhower
administration was to reject division of the world into two camps.
Sukarno espoused a third way, neutralism, taking neither side in the
cold war. As did certain other leaders of the era—U Nu of Burma,

Nasser of Egypt, Nehru of India—Sukarno advocated a new association of "nonaligned" nations. The Indonesians hosted a major international conference at Bandung in the winter of 1955 for this coalition, and the People's Republic of China played a major role in these meetings and garnered additional international recognition.

Throughout his stewardship of the State Department, John Foster Dulles remained a steadfast opponent of nonalignment. Son of a minister, Dulles behaved as if choosing one of the cold war camps was a moral duty for other nations. It was especially galling to him when the Chinese communists were able to emerge from diplomatic isolation through the neutralist movement. At the Geneva conference in 1954, Dulles had refused even to shake hands with Chinese foreign minister Chou En-lai.

This disposition blinded Dulles to certain real opportunities for improving relations. In 1957, for example, Burmese Prime Minister U Nu offered to intercede for the Americans during an official visit to Peking. He did so and the Chinese agreed to release the captured CIA agents John T. Downey and Richard Fecteau in exchange for nothing more than American agreement to allow a few journalists to visit the People's Republic and report on the "new China." Dulles refused and the CIA men languished in prison into the 1970s.

Because of Chinese involvement in the nonaligned movement, Dulles feared the Soviets would be able to manipulate the neutralists for propaganda gains in the cold war. Sukarno was an object of particular opprobrium for organizing the movement and hosting the Bandung conference. Dulles was thus open to suggestions for a covert operation against Sukarno.

The Indonesian president appeared vulnerable because of the cultural and geographic nature of his country. A Dutch colony for almost four centuries, Indonesia was a mélange of Muslim, tribal animistic, and Buddhist influences. The different social groups were naturally isolated from each other due to geography—Indonesia was a vast archipelago of six major and about three thousand minor islands in an arc from the tip of the Malay Peninsula to the Philippines. Independence came in the rush of decolonization after World War II. For the Indonesians the problem lay in transforming the kaleidoscopic society into a unified nation-state.

Achmed Sukarno had been a prominent wartime nationalist, and active in the postwar resistance against the Dutch. He was the natural choice for president of an independent Indonesia. Pragmatist and visionary at the same time, Sukarno was in no sense a communist. Indeed he outlawed the Indonesian communist party in 1949 following an abortive coup attempt. After cooperating with the armed forces, Sukarno then turned away from them after an attempt to play politics by army leader Colonel Abdul Haris Nasution in 1952. Sukarno walked a tightrope among the many political factions.

Economic chaos reigned amid the political struggle. Rubber, tin, and oil were the main export products but prices for the first two fluctuated widely in the early 1950s, while oil production was falling. By the mid-1950s the small budget surplus of 1951 had become a deficit almost five times larger. Factionalism was so rampant that in 1956 the parliament had yet to ratify the government budgets for 1950, 1951, and 1952.

The first CIA operation was a political action. Elections were to be held on September 29, 1955, and the Americans wished to influence them. Kermit Roosevelt approved a program memorandum requesting a million dollars for the effort. The memorandum was only a few paragraphs long, and completely lacked the detail of need, plan, and expected results usually required of political action programs. The project sailed through the bureaucracy, received all necessary approvals, and the money was spent to benefit the progressive Muslim Masjumi party. Exchanging the dollars for Indonesian *rupiah* on the Hong Kong black market, the CIA was able to parlay its approved budget into the equivalent of four million United States dollars. But in the elections the Masjumi were far outshown by the communists, who received over 6 million of the 34.5 million votes cast. Sukarno then appeared to confirm American fears by making official visits during 1956 to China, Russia, and other Eastern European countries. The Americans began to cast around for ideas.

Again it was Frank Wisner who set the pace. One day toward the end of 1956, he said to the chief of DDP's Far East Division, "I think it's time we held Sukarno's feet to the fire."

Wisner's subordinate returned to the Far East Division with the word that new arrangements for Sukarno were a priority. One officer with the Indonesia branch, FE/5, recalls being told that "if some plan for doing this were not forthcoming, Santa might fill our stockings with assignments to far worse jobs." The Far East Division was the biggest in DDP at the time, so the division chief had plenty of choices in the matter.

As it happened, the division chief, Alfred C. Ulmer, Jr., knew about paramilitary operations, but very little about Asia. He had been transferred from European operations under a CIA policy of providing executives with experience in regions remote from their own specialties. Ulmer had begun with the Navy, was transferred to OSS, earned the Bronze Star, and stayed on with SSU even before the CIA was created. He had served in Vienna (under Counter-Intelligence Corps cover) and Madrid, and had been station chief in Athens. His work in Greece impressed Wisner, who brought Ulmer to headquarters in 1955 as chief of the Far East Division.

Ulmer depended on FE/5 to develop a plan for Indonesia. It was at just this juncture that an opportunity seemed to blossom in that country. Indonesian local area commanders in western and north ern Sumatra, frustrated by command changes in the army and other factors, declared themselves independent and not bound to the national military command. The Indonesian colonels who began this revolt in December 1956 then used their own troops and government-provided equipment to smuggle goods on a large scale through Singapore. The revolt widened in March 1957 when the colonel commanding at Menado, in South Sulawesi province, declared a state of emergency and replaced the civilian government. There, on Celebes Island, was issued a Charter of Common Struggle (Piagam Perjuangan Semesta) or, in the Indonesian acronym, PE-MESTA. This term soon was used to identify the entire rebellious movement. PEMESTA became an open rebellion after April 6, 1957, when twenty-nine soldiers of the national army were killed in a clash on Celebes.

The CIA had several avenues for contacting the Indonesian plotters. Richard Bissell, then a special assistant to Allen Dulles, recalls that Indonesians had approached the Agency at least two years before the operation. He observes, "I think it's fair to say [that] all the people the Agency dealt with eventually ended up as opponents of Sukarno." These contacts may have come through the Indonesian military attaché in Washington, who later defected. In addition, a CIA agent was in contact with a representative of the colonels. Finally, the United States conducted a training program for the Indonesian national police, in the course of which CIA officers made quiet attempts to recruit promising Indonesian candidates.

An approach came in April 1957 through the local channel from two of the most prominent colonels—Achmed Hussein of central Sumatra, and Maludin Simbolon, who had been passed over for army chief of staff in favor of Nasution in 1954 and now commanded northern Sumatra. The officers wished to meet personally with a CIA man. Al Ulmer saw the request at home on a Sunday morning, when the desk officer brought him the cable from Djakarta. Top security was immediately imposed by Ulmer, who restricted knowledge to only nine men at CIA.

With some trepidation, since there had as yet been no 5412 Group approval of an Indonesian operation, Ulmer got Allen Dulles and Wisner to let him follow up on the contact. A meeting took place; the Indonesian colonels wanted modern American weapons; this left FE/5 in a quandary, since it still lacked presidential approval. After an unsuccessful try at arranging a private arms deal, it was determined to seek appropriate authority to move ahead in Indonesia.

Sukarno himself helped the Eisenhower administration decide to support PEMESTA. In February 1957 the Indonesian president gave a speech in which he prescribed "guided democracy" for his country. Asserting that "Western style" democracy had proved inadequate in Indonesia, Sukarno declared that political parties should disband themselves in the interest of the nation, leaving a system of authoritarian rule by the president, assisted by an advisory council Sukarno himself would appoint. The speech came after Sukarno's extended tour of the communist states; it was read in Washington as a thinly disguised initiative to bring the communist party into association with the president of Indonesia. To top it all, Sukarno then welcomed Soviet President Kliment Voroshilov to Indonesia for a stay of over two months. In May the United States flatly rejected a request by Sukarno to make a visit to Washington. In the fall of 1957, as it turned out, there would be little opposition to putting Indonesia on the CIA agenda as a major operation. When Frank Wisner hand-carried to the DCI's office a simple voucher that would enable him to draw $10 million for the operation, Allen Dulles, it is reported, signed the chit with a little flourish.

The active phase of the Indonesia operation occasioned some resentment in the FE/5 branch. It was difficult for the DDP officers to give up control to the CIA task force. Allen Dulles kept in close touch, although he delegated the supervisory role mainly to his deputy, Air Force lieutenant general Charles Pearre Cabell. Bissell was brought into the planning, despite his usual job of managing aerial reconnaissance programs—because U-2 aircraft were to be used over Indonesia to gather tactical intelligence in support of the operation. Cabell began to rely on Bissell's organizational skill for some of the operational planning.

The mood was ecstatic in DDP's Far East Division. Ulmer exclaimed, "We'll drive Lebanon off the front page!" FE/5 felt that official approval meant they could use the Pacific Fleet for arms shipments delivered the right way. The State Department did impose certain restrictions—there was to be only one team of Americans on the ground, one agent plus his radio operator to maintain contact with the colonels in Celebes. Ulmer's deputy, Desmond FitzGerald, thought such a penny-packet commitment would lead to failure. Such doubts were not to be ignored since, as the top man with real Far East experience, FitzGerald carried much of the load in arranging the planning.

The Indonesia project is unique in that it shows very clearly the command role of John Foster Dulles in the secret war. The secretary of state was in New York for a meeting of the United Nations General Assembly when he received word from brother Allen, on September 16, 1957, of the final go-ahead. Only his side of the conversation was recorded by the official notetaker:

"Then you got the green light otherwise?"

"Is this the West and not the East end?"

"Nearer us?"

"OK."

The first item of business at the NSC meeting of September 22 was an interdepartmental committee report on Indonesia. Its recommendation was "to continue the present pattern of our formal relations, but so to adjust our programs and activities as to give greater emphasis to support of non-Communist forces in the outer islands, while continuing attempts to produce action by non-Communist elements on Java." Before the end of September a formal policy was in place that logically entailed execution of the CIA's covert operation.

From that moment, the secretary of state was in frequent contact with Allen Dulles regarding the Indonesia operation. Foster Dulles overruled his own ambassador in Djakarta, John Allison, who had learned of American contact with the colonels and argued against CIA support for PEMESTA. As was the case with the American ambassador during the Li Mi business in Burma, Allison was then deliberately misinformed regarding the extent of CIA involvement.

Foster Dulles called Allen on November 29, though, to tell the DCI of an "extremely significant" cable from Allison that involved a "complete reversal," in that the ambassador was now advising action. Foster said, "What was happening there was that one by one they were gradually being eliminated. Our assets were gradually shrinking. Today we have substantial assets with which to deal. We will, however, have only half those assets six months from now."

The degree of Foster Dulles's involvement was again demonstrated the very next day when, in an assassination attempt carried out by Darul Islam fanatics, and unrelated to the PEMESTA revolt, five hand grenades were thrown at Sukarno as he left a school fund-raising bazaar in the company of two of the older children. Though Sukarno escaped, ten persons were killed and forty-eight children injured. The immediate question was whether to send condolences on the deaths and congratulate Sukarno on his escape. Foster thought it a wise thing to do. He told Allen, "Probably the failure to do it would look suspicious, but the Sec[retary] said he wanted to be sure it was handled in a routine way."

During early December difficulties arose with the British. At Singapore the CIA had maintained liaison with British intelligence for many years, but for the Indonesia operation it was thought desirable to expand the local station and put it on an operational footing. Singapore was the ideal conduit for arms shipments. But the British blocked these CIA efforts.

Allen went to Foster while senior British Foreign Office officials were visiting Washington for discussions. The secretary remarked, "If this thing goes on the way it is we will have something across there which will be pretty bad." A few minutes later Foster was on the phone to his undersecretary, Christian Herter, and said, "what he would like to do is see things get to a point where we could plausibly withdraw our recognition of the Sukarno government and give it to the dissident elements on Sumatra and land forces to protect the life and property of Americans; use this as an excuse to bring about a major shift there ... we may never have a better opportunity." On December 12, State's intelligence director, Hugh S. Cumming, Jr., told Foster he hoped the secretary "will get the British with us in Indonesia. MI-6 [SIS] wants to move and cooperate with CIA."

Allen Dulles remained optimistic. In mid-January the DCI told his brother, "Everything is going all right on the other matter on the other side of the world."

This view was echoed in a last-minute official appraisal sent by the CIA over Dulles's signature on January 31. The fourteen-page paper argued that the "Padang group" of military men seemed assured of the support of at least one of the four major political movements, that the group believed that Sukarno's grip had been weakened, and felt that it could obtain "Western, particularly US support."

Intelligence reported that "the group, in present circumstances, believes it could successfully resist any military action by forces loyal to the central government." The CIA had advanced knowledge of the rebel ultimatum, which it predicted would be delivered "on or about 5 February," but critically miscalculated in its assessment that Sukarno would not attempt to put pressure on the outer islands in the short run; CIA assumed the Padang group would be in a better position on the outer islands and that "at a minimum," PEMESTA could launch "fairly widespread guerrilla warfare" on Java. The Agency hedged only in its statement that "we are unable to estimate the outcome of an effort by the Padang group to defeat the central government on Java," and its observation that the conclusions applied only until Sukarno received substantial Soviet military aid.

At the State Department, Hugh Cumming was called into the secretary's office. Foster Dulles told him, "This is my own feeling: as between a territorially united Indonesia which in leaning toward Communism and a break-up of that country into geographical units, I prefer the latter." Later Cumming was briefed in more detail by two senior State officials at Foster Dulles's direction. Though he claims to have stopped them before they could broach the CIA operation, Cumming necessarily had knowledge of the plan as he was State's intelligence chief. Indeed, we have seen that Foster Dulles discussed operational aspects with Cumming as early as December 1957.

The Far East Division at DDP expected that 5412 Group approval would bring cooperation throughout government on arms shipments to the Padang group, but the Navy continued to drag its feet. Admiral Arleigh Burke, the chief of naval operations, simply did not press the matter within his service. Both Allen Dulles and Christian Herter raised this with him in late February.

At about this time, aerial reconnaissance disclosed Indonesian site preparations for a bomber-size airstrip on the island of Natuna Besar, north of Sumatra. At the Pacific Command, Admiral Felix Stump began to fear that Sukarno might allow Soviet bombers to use the facility. Navy reticence suddenly melted away, and submarine shipments, expected to take three days each, were quickly arranged.

When word of the arms shipments was sent to the American embassy at Djakarta, it embarrassed John Allison, who continued to advocate accommodation with the Indonesian central government, an option that had now been clearly rejected. Accounts differ on whether Allison asked for an immediate transfer or was simply ordered out of the country.

Foster Dulles sent Allison, a career diplomat, to Czechoslovakia to represent the United States there. The former ambassador in Djakarta could only speculate, in retrospect, that Sukarno "disgusted" John Foster Dulles.

Allison had his moment while passing through Washington en route to Prague. He stopped for a debriefing at the CIA, where the intelligence officers listened carefully and were very polite.

Afterward, as a senior CIA man conducted the ambassador to his car, the officer remarked, "You should know that several of us here agreed with your reports and recommendations from Djakarta. I think you will be proved right in the end."

Maintaining the secrecy of the operation became difficult in the face of the open political crisis in Indonesia. CIA's plan was similar to that used for Guatemala, containing a prolonged "stalling period" during which psychological pressures would be brought to bear on the Sukarno government. Foster had some doubt about this, as he told Allen on February 4, since "during the stalling period the present regime is going to get a lot of stuff."

It is not surprising that, in another telephone conversation between the DCI and John Foster Dulles the next day, "the subject of Archipelago came up." In fact that country was a topic of discussion at fourteen of the seventeen NSC meetings held between November 1957 and March 1958; keeping discussion of it out of the NSC proved almost impossible.

In at least one instance, the NSC meeting of February 27, discussion at the council came very close to the thin line separating the overt and covert tracks. The notes on a telephone call Foster made to Allen Dulles at 4:20 P.M. that afternoon are worth quoting at length:

> The Secretary said he does not know whether the talk this a.m. about the area should lead to greater activity. Allen said he is talking about it now. You reach a point where it is extremely difficult to do much more without showing your hand. The Secretary thinks if it is going to work we should take some risk of showing our hand. They agreed it is the last chance. The Secretary mentioned buying stuff in the Philippines. Allen said the question of delivery is difficult. They can get it in only the way we do it. Allen said they are going ahead. We are ready to give them a bird as soon as they can eat it. We are pushing ahead as daringly as we can. It is a vigorous program and they are very happy with it and cooperate very well. The Secretary just wanted him to know he has the feeling we can't play too safely here and we have to take some risk because it looks to him it is the best chance we have. Allen is glad to hear it.

At any rate, United States government plausible deniability was beginning to evaporate. In the field it finally did.

While Washington schemed, in Indonesia events moved inexorably toward a climax. To distract popular attention from the PEMESTA colonels, Sukarno revived a territorial dispute with the Netherlands, which had lain dormant for six years, over the part of New Guinea called West Irian. Sukarno then left the achipelago to travel. While Sukarno was in Ōsaka, Japan, the colonels came into the open, by sending him an emissary who presented an ultimatum to dismiss his cabinet and turn away from "guided democracy." PEMESTA presented an alternate list of acceptable cabinet ministers, and promised to support Sukarno if he agreed to appoint them.

The Indonesian leader refused. On February 15, PEMESTA proclaimed a rebel government composed of representatives from Sumatra, Celebes, and Java, though there was little rebel support on the last island. This move was a signal for Frank Wisner, who loved to be at the scene of the action, to leave for Singapore, there to command the archipelago operation in the field.

In Singapore the CIA station had been augmented for the project. The Navy also quietly moved two destroyers there so as to be able to intervene to save American citizens in Indonesia. The complete list of assets at Singapore, along with the full extent of British and Australian collaboration, are as yet unknown. Another prime base for "Archipelago" was the Philippines. Navy submarines left from Subic Bay while airdrops of supplies to Celebes were staged from a CIA compound at Clark Air Force Base. The Agency enlisted the services of 300 to 400 Americans, Filipinos, and nationalist Chinese to service and fly a small fleet of transport aircraft and fifteen B-26 bombers, modified by the Air Force for ground support missions with the addition of nose assemblies carrying eight .50-caliber machine guns. Some of these planes and crews later moved forward to Menado on Celebes, where PEMESTA had reactivated a World War II air base. It was the International Volunteer Air Group concept in action.

Meanwhile, the Indonesian government had begun to take strong measures against the rebels. Chief of Staff Nasution dismissed six of the rebel colonels, and more discharges were to follow. Nasution declared force would be used if necessary, and a week later a warship maneuvered ostentatiously off Padang, a stronghold of the Sumatran rebels. On February 21, PEMESTA radio stations at Padang and the rebel capital of Bukittinggi were bombed and strafed by government aircraft. The radios were put out of action for over a week, dealing a serious blow to the psychological warfare plans of the rebels.

John Foster Dulles made a concerted effort to prevent the American role in the rebellion from becoming public knowledge. In appearances before congressional committees in early March and the beginning of April, Dulles insisted that the United States was following a correct course in accordance with international law and that it was not intervening. At press conferences he told reporters that the PEMESTA rebellion was an internal matter, that the United States would not allow arms sales to either side, and that the revolt should be dealt with by Indonesians "without intrusion from without."

The second week of March government troops, reinforced by drops of paratroops, made landings on the Sumatran coast. Nasution personally coordinated three columns converging on Padang for an overwhelming attack. Progress was slow owing to the torrid jungle, not PEMESTA opposition. Some rebel officers deserted, rebel units changed sides; more often the PEMESTA forces simply ran away. A real battle was fought for Padang, which fell on April 18 after three days of resistance, to a combined airborne and amphibious assault.

As Wisner agonized in Singapore, the CIA did what it could to stiffen PEMESTA resistance. The original limitation of one agent team with the rebels was lifted, two more were landed from submarines in April and May. But white faces were not enough—the rebels simply lacked morale. Anthony Poshepny, who landed with one team, had already seen fierce partisan action in Tibet and found the Indonesians quite tame. Another CIA paramilitary adviser recounted a distressing episode that was all too typical. A PEMESTA band was sent to recover weapons from a scheduled CIA airdrop; the rebels marked the drop zone and knew the plane's time of arrival and approximate flight path, but still ran away at the first sound of aircraft engines.

A major mistake in the Indonesia plan was its reliance upon a rebel movement that was not cohesive or unified. The PEMESTA colonels were opposing central rule from Java, but one needed to go no further than their political program to realize that personal gain was the most significant motivation. The program envisioned a loose federation of regions, essentially major islands and groups of islands in the archipelago. The regions were to retain most of their income, giving only limited amounts to a central government. It was a plan that would have served well in warlord China.

The same separatism exploited by the CIA to create the operation ensured that the rebel movement could not function as an effective alliance. Difficulties were increased by the geographic dispersion of the islands, which precluded joint military actions. There was also a mismatch between the ideological commitment of the CIA's secret warriors and the less lofty aims of the rebel colonels. This kind of mistake had also been made in Guatemala, but that time Arbenz had panicked. Sukarno stood his ground, with able assistance from Abdul Haris Nasution.

Another significant problem was simply the disparity in means between PEMESTA and the Indonesian government. Sukarno had a navy, an air force, marines, and paratroops. As former area commanders, the rebel colonels had their local forces but not much more. The kinds of light weapons and ammunition the Americans could deliver by submarine or airdrop could not make up for the difference in forces. Even so, the efforts to supply PEMESTA threatened to reveal the CIA's hand in the rebellion. On April 8 the *Chicago Daily News* printed a report detailing American airdrops to PEMESTA, triggering a flap in Washington. General Cabell was sent to Pearl Harbor to prevent further leaks, but security was preserved only because the press did not pick up the *Daily News* story.

Still casting about for some means of strengthening PEMESTA, the Americans considered according recognition to the rebels. Foster Dulles seems to have favored this course, which was mentioned at one press conference and discussed with the President on April 15. But Hugh Cumming's people assembled a paper that showed the United States would have only very weak legal grounds for doing this.

Then came the battle of Padang and PEMESTA defeat. Allen Dulles gave his brother details in a lunchtime phone conversation on April 17. Foster remarked that Nasution's invasion "has happened with far greater efficiency, speed and precision than he had expected." Allen, who was not surprised at the defeat, warned, "We have to be careful not to get too far out on a limb." A few days later the DCI told the secretary he thought the defeat *had* surprised the PEMESTA leaders and that "there is no fight in them." When Foster brought up the possibility of recognition for a Sumatran state, Allen advised waiting another week. Sure enough, on April 28 the word was that "the East is boiling," and the rebel capital on Sumatra, Bukittinggi, fell on May 4. With the end on Sumatra the rebel capital moved to Menado on Celebes.

A most conspicuous facet of the covert assistance to PEMESTA was the rebel air force. The Indonesian air force remained loyal to the Sukarno government, which made it difficult to explain how a rebel air force materialized almost overnight. The first rebel raid was against Bandung in late March. About a dozen more occurred later; targets included Makassar, Morotai, Balikpapan, and Ambon. In the April 28 bombing of the oil port at Balikpapan, a British tanker was hit along with an Indonesian gunboat. On other occasions ships were attacked at sea.

The danger of American exposure was again very high. On March 23 there was another flap in Washington when a U.S. Navy plane, which may have been on a reconnaissance mission, was shot up by the Indonesian air force. Catastrophe was avoided when the aircraft managed to land at a friendly base and the pilot cooperated with an appropriate cover story. Later in the campaign two of the rebel B-26 bombers were shot down, while the government claimed to have destroyed six more on the ground in raids on Menado.

Through its own intelligence the Indonesian government learned a fair amount about the air operations and used this information to discredit the purported nationalist motivation of PEMESTA. Airdrops of weapons to the rebels were reported on several occasions, and the Australian air force was linked with the mission at least once. The government accused American and Chinese "adventurers" of operating the rebel air force, and later announced it was sending a list to Washington identifying these individuals.

In response, President Eisenhower commented publicly for the first time, at his news conference on April 30. Ike repeated the line that the United States was neutral in the struggle and added, "Now on the other hand, every rebellion that I have ever heard of has its soldiers of fortune." The President felt he had done so well with the press that he called up Foster Dulles afterward to brag about it, the only time during the entire operation that the two discussed Indonesia on the telephone. Foster Dulles followed up with the press the next day, saying the United States had no legal obligation to control the activities of American soldiers of fortune.

The soldier of fortune argument turned out to be disastrous. On May 18 one of the rebel B-26 bombers raided Ambon, hitting a crowded village marketplace, where people were on their way to church. The plane was hit over its intended target, an airfield, and its right wing caught fire. The crew bailed out and were captured by the Indonesians. The bombardier was Indonesian, but the pilot was an American, Allen Lawrence Pope. Within a day, Washington knew Pope had been captured, as Cabell confirmed for Foster Dulles, but CIA had "a lot of confidence in the man." Pope had flown in Korea and for Civil Air Transport, including fifty-seven missions to Dien Bien Phu. He had been recruited for the Indonesia operation in Saigon in December 1957. His first Indonesian mission took place in March 1958.

It was at this point, on May 20, that John Foster Dulles stood before the press to say the Indonesian rebellion should be resolved without intrusion. What the Americans did not know was that Sukarno could prove that Pope had an official relationship. The CIA was certain that Pope could stand up to torture. The B-26 planes had been "sanitized" to prevent being linked with United States government inventories, and the pilots had to undergo strip searches before each mission to ensure that no incriminating evidence was carried. But Pope concealed his papers aboard the aircraft. The Indonesians captured Air Force and Civil Air Transport identification cards, Pope's contract for the operation, plus a post exchange privilege card for Clark Air Force Base. The papers, and Pope, were displayed for the world press at Djakarta on May 27. Both the United States President and secretary of state had been caught in an open lie.

This was the end for "Archipelago." An officer at FE/5 heard Allen Dulles explicitly use the phrase "we must disengage" as the DCI ordered a stand-down for CIA's field forces. Some of the paramilitary adviser teams had to make arduous jungle treks to coastal areas where they could be taken out by submarine. One British sub was even sighted and attacked from the air off Celebes. The PEMESTA revolt was crushed with the capture of Menado, on June 26, by government forces. The final result of the rebellion was to strengthen the hand of the central government on Java; in the words of historian Brian May: "The American intervention was a gift to Sukarno."

The "Archipelago" catastrophe strained relations with the British and Australian intelligence services, but no one at the CIA was cashiered. The CIA man who had made the original contact with the colonels was given his choice of new posts and took London. A prime undercover agent went on to Algeria. Even Allen Pope, who was tried in December 1959 and sentenced to life in prison, would fly again for CIA. The disaster did finally sap the strength of Frank Wisner. The DDP chief went to London as chief of station to be replaced in Washington by Richard Bissell. Al Ulmer went to Paris as station chief, his place at Far East Division being taken by Desmond FitzGerald.

What happened next in Washington had less to do with Indonesia than the President's desire to fine-tune his staff organization. Ike was angry about the "Archipelago" fiasco, but the administrative changes that occurred had been in the works for some time, anyway. The changes concerned the 5412 Group, the Directorate of

Plans within the CIA, and the lines of contact between CIA and the Pentagon.

A major source of the proposals was the President's Board of Consultants on Foreign Intelligence Activities (PBCFIA), also known as the Hull Board, after its chairman, General John E. Hull. The board consisted of a group of Americans chosen by the President who met monthly in Washington, were briefed by the intelligence agencies, and reported to the President once or twice a year. Ike had established the board in 1956 to head off an initiative that would have created a joint congressional committee for intelligence oversight.

At its first meeting the members of PBCFIA endured a briefing of eight hours by the CIA, densely packed with details of intelligence reporting, analysis, and covert operations. Lyman Kirkpatrick, the inspector general of CIA, who had responsibility for all dealings with the board, recalled that first briefing as "brutal" and writes that it "was in truth a saturation effort." Later, as the arrangement became more routine, there was time for reflection. PBCFIA developed its own recommendations for President Eisenhower.

The board began to argue in December 1956 that the approvals for CIA's cold war activities were made by "extremely informal and somewhat exclusive methods." Moreover, "projects become almost too exclusively the responsibility of the Central Intelligence Agency." The board felt State and Defense should be in closer touch with implementation as well as approval, and that ambassadors should be told of operations in their areas to the extent to which they wished to be informed, except by unanimous decision of the 5412 Group.

By 1958 the Hull Board had developed additional views, expressed in their report of October 30, and personally to the President at a meeting on the morning of December 16. As spokesman for his board, General Hull made covert operations the second-highest priority on his list of topics. He pointed out that the initial evaluations of proposals were made by a staff within the Directorate of Plans itself and objected that "it [is] undesirable for a group of this type to have responsibility for evaluating its own work."

The CIA did act on this administrative question. Lyman Kirkpatrick and the new DDP, Bissell, instituted a broad inquiry on the DDP mission. By February 1959 the internal inspection and review staff in DDP had been abolished. Still, Allen Dulles argued, in a memo submitted February 16, 1959, that the CIA took into account all available intelligence before beginning a cold war operation, that the Agency was always on guard against self-serving intelligence, and that the Hull Board had an exaggerated idea of the autonomy enjoyed by DDP. The last argument is interesting in that one of the PBCFIA members was Jimmy Doolittle, who had expressly studied covert operations for Eisenhower in 1954.

In fact, executive control was a more important issue than ever. Rather than shrinking after the Korean War, the Directorate of Plans had grown. Between 1953 and 1961 it added a thousand personnel slots directly, plus an equal number in DDP support functions elsewhere within the CIA. The cold war directorate absorbed 54 percent of the Agency's budget.

By 1958 there were also seven thousand *military* personnel *outside* of CIA giving direct support to the Agency's operations throughout the world.

Such operations as "Archipelago" required a high degree of cooperation between the military and the CIA, making the nature of their formal relationship an important matter. The Pentagon-CIA link ran through the 5412 Group, the staff of which was provided by CIA. One proposal backed by the Hull Board in 1958 was to substitute a joint staff with representatives from the Pentagon and State. At the December meeting, President Eisenhower made clear his view that the 5412 Group should meet as a "court" with minimal staff assistance from their own agencies.

Everything depended on the 5412 Group.

One man working for the President made the 5412 Group his special concern. He was Gordon Gray.

Gray had once hoped to become the DCI, but any chance he may have had for the job expired with the Truman administration. He was held over as a hearing board member, however, to help judge the Oppenheimer case, and impressed Eisenhower tremendously with his calm demeanor. Gray's efficiency and discretion also pleased the President when he was brought in to run the Office of Defense Mobilization. When Robert Cutler, Ike's special assistant for national security affairs, left the White House to return to his Boston bank, the President turned to Gray, though a Democrat, to fill this important post. Thus Gordon Gray was finally catapulted over the DCI. Now he would help Eisenhower run the CIA.

As the President's special assistant, Gordon Gray was Eisenhower's representative on the 5412 Group. He spent most of 1958 observing CIA oversight in action. Though the DCI was officially only an adviser to the group, Gray found that the committee exercised virtually no initiative, which left the field largely to Allen Dulles. The special assistant raised his doubts openly at the December 1958 meeting, with Hull and Doolittle, and was then assigned to study the entire relationship between the 5412 Group and CIA, with an eye toward possible revision of NSC-5412/2.

After Christmas, President Eisenhower met directly with Allen Dulles and Gray. Ike laid great stress on his arrangements for executive management of intelligence and clandestine operations, with the Hull Board and the 5412 Group reporting directly to him. The system *had* to be made to work because it was intended "to obviate any tendency for Congressional groups and their staffs to get into these activities."

Allen Dulles no doubt made appropriately conciliatory comments, but Gordon Gray was not satisfied. The semiannual 5412 review for the President was presented on January 15, 1959. Four days later, Gray sent a memorandum to Allen Dulles, the secretary of state, and the Pentagon representative on the 5412 Group with what he called "random thoughts" on procedure. But Gray's criticisms were not random at all. They included these issues: Only four or five of the items covered in the review had been discussed in the 5412 Group within the preceding six months; a better understanding of the mission of the group was necessary; "the criteria with respect to what matters shall come before the Group are ill-defined and fuzzy"; the committee needed to develop procedures to evaluate operations in addition to approving them; and, "I strongly believe that the President would expect some initiative" from the group.

Eisenhower agreed. In an effort to force 5412 to deal with these problems, on December 26, 1958, the President requested that the group hold regular weekly meetings in place of the occasional ones that had been the rule. The problems nevertheless persisted. When Gray gave one of his regular briefings to Eisenhower somewhat later, on June 22, 1959, "the President then referred to one particular activity which he was disturbed about but said that he assumed it had been approved by the 5412 Group. I [Gray] reported that it had not been approved by the Group within the last eleven months."

Finally, the relations between the Pentagon and CIA were a continuing point of controversy in the management of intelligence. The CIA actually dealt with three different parts of the Pentagon—International Security Affairs represented the secretary of defense; the Joint Chiefs of Staff provided military input; while direct coordination of joint execution, as well as military "cover" support, was in the hands of an assistant to the secretary of defense for special operations. Throughout the Eisenhower period this officer was Marine Lieutenant General Graves B. Erskine, in whom Secretary of Defense Neil H. McElroy had complete confidence. McElroy's successor, Thomas S. Gates Jr. who took office in December 1959 and served throughout the remainder of the administration, had been a naval reserve staff officer off Iwo Jima in 1945, where Graves Erskine had commanded the 3rd Marine Division. Gates, too, allowed total freedom of action for the assistant for special operations. Erskine also had direct access to President Eisenhower when necessary.

The Hull Board criticized the many different facets of Pentagon involvement, and raised the possibility of a single focal point, preferably some office under the Joint Chiefs. Eisenhower retorted that this was letting the military into political matters, while letting the 5412 Group get into the actual implementation of covert operations would be a mistake. So, in effect, Ike defended his existing command arrangements for covert action.

President Eisenhower continued to wrestle with the dilemma of control versus security and plausible deniability. The problem was difficult and Ike could not ultimately solve it, though failures like those in Syria and Indonesia must have spurred him on, as did the recurrent political pressures for congressional oversight mechanisms in the intelligence field. But the 5412 Group could not seem to exercise initiative—there was no one, really, to *question* covert operations. So long as policymakers shared a belief in the efficacy of cold war activities, approvals would be secured easily, no matter what the structure of the policy machinery. This unquestioning belief had already led to the most difficult paramilitary action yet mounted by the secret warriors, a partisan war on the high plains of Asia.

·IX·

THE WAR FOR THE ROOF OF THE WORLD

Nestled in the foothills of the Himalayas lies the Indian village of Kalimpong. A dot on a map within the triangle formed by the conjunction of the borders of Nepal, Sikkim, and Bhutan, Kalimpong was virtually unknown to outsiders. Tourists who came to see the mountains would visit the Nepalese capital of Katmandu. If they ventured near Kalimpong, it was usually to see another Indian town, the tea center Darjeeling. Typically, those tourists who did reach Kalimpong were interested in yet another country, for the village was a main point on the trail to Tibet.

It was in the guise of a tourist that an American came to Kalimpong in the spring of 1955. The man was not what he seemed, but an unnamed official of an unnamed United States government agency. Indeed, perhaps Kalimpong was not what it seemed either. For several years already the village had been at the center of a dispute between India and the People's Republic of China—Peking complained repeatedly that Kalimpong was being utilized as a base for fomenting resistance to Chinese communist rule. Whether or not this was true, Indian prime minister Jawaharlal Nehru did tell the Indian parliament, as early as September 1953, that Kalimpong was "a nest of spies." Agents came from every country, said the prime minister. "Sometimes I begin to doubt whether the greater part of the population of Kalimpong does not consist of foreign spies."

The American who came in 1955 may have been a diplomat but he was most probably a spy. He is not further identified by the man

149

who tells the story, George N. Patterson, a Scottish missionary who had worked in eastern Tibet, spoke the language, wrote several books about the country, and resided in Kalimpong. Patterson was one of the small group of Westerners who knew anything about Tibet; enchanted with the country, he was well known in Tibetan political circles, including those of the Dalai Lama, the religious ruler of this semifeudal theocracy atop the Himalayas.

As Patterson tells the story, the American came to him. It was not the first time. The previous year an Indian intelligence official had also appeared, asking Patterson if he could contact prominent Tibetans willing to discuss resistance to the Chinese. It was exactly for such a contact that the American came. Patterson acted as translator in several meetings over four days.

The Tibetan had outlined his difficulties for the Indian official, much as he now did for the American. The American expressed sympathy but stressed the problems inherent in supplying people or equipment over the mountains, and said the cooperation of the Indian government was essential. According to Patterson, the American went on to draw up a ten-year assistance program designed to overthrow the Chinese after the first five. The American said a special United States agent would be appointed who had no contact with the embassy but would be assigned to handle Tibetan affairs. Rapgya Pandatsang, a moderate politician and the Tibetan representative at this meeting, nodded in understanding.

Tibet was another of those situations in which the secret warriors were able to use a local resistance movement to American advantage. The resistance sprang up as the Chinese communists attempted to consolidate their rule. Traditionally conservative, the Tibetans were both politically and culturally distinct from the lowland, or "Han," Chinese, of whom the communists were only the latest political shading. Although Tibet had served for several centuries as a Chinese vassal state, the reins had been very loose since the downfall of the Manchu dynasty in 1911. This had permitted the emergence of warlords in China, local potentates with powers similar to those of the Dalai Lama in Tibet. In addition, India lay immediately to the south of Tibet, leading to a certain competition for influence in Lhasa between the regional powers. To some degree the Tibetans were able to play the powers against each other in an effort to preserve independence, or at least a large degree of autonomy.

The tragedy for Tibetan independence lay in the relative strengths of the Chinese communists and nationalists. Whereas Chiang Kai-shek lacked the power to be more than a first among equals, Mao Tse-tung's movement was unified and also more determined to impose central control over every corner of China. The new mandarins had a program, tremendous energy, and the People's Liberation Army (PLA). There was ultimately no way the lowlanders could have been kept out of Tibet. Once the Han arrived, moreover, the primitive Tibetans would have to face an enemy with modern implements of war—planes, tanks, and guns.

Tibet was hardly prepared for modernization. The "roof of the world" was a land of monasteries, over three thousand of them, nomads, and small towns, ruled by a hierarchy of monks who were advised by a small commercial elite. The Dalai Lama was nothing less than the godhead, the incarnation of Buddha, chosen as a child by wise monks, after tests, signs, and meditation. In this land policy followed portent.

Signs in Lhasa were ominous. A sacred object, a gilded wooden dragon, began to drip water from its mouth. The PLA was known to be approaching Yunnan; then, in the summer of 1950, Tibet itself. A belated effort to create an effective army with military aid from India never had the time to succeed. In August 1950 the PLA Eighteenth Army defeated a tiny Tibetan army that could only be described as feudal in nature: a handful of ancient guns, the Dalai Lama's personal guard, and armed monks and farmers. After briefly fleeing his capital, the Dalai Lama agreed to subordinate himself to a Chinese administration.

Communist rule was wrenching for Tibetan society. Economic development, industrial production, even the introduction of money, required fundamental changes in a society that had used barter as a primary form of exchange.

Friction developed rapidly between the Chinese communists and the Tibetan theocracy. The Chinese soon alienated the Tibetan people with the establishment of work "norms"; attempts to divide Tibet by placing portions within other provinces; and their forcible induction of several thousand Tibetan children, to be educated as party cadres in the lowlands and returned to work for the Chinese administration. Tibetan resistance was inevitable.

A major difficulty for the Chinese in Tibet was the utter lack of a communications infrastructure. There were no railroads, roads, or even airfields, a condition that not only precluded rapid economic development but also prohibited any extensive military operations using modern equipment. The Chinese set out to remedy this with two massive construction efforts—a road from Lake Koko Nor across the ancient Tibetan province of Amdo to Lhasa, and another across Kham from Kangting to Lhasa. These roads represented a tremendous feat of engineering; the Kanting road, for example, was built at an average altitude of thirteen thousand feet; it crossed fourteen mountain ranges and seven large rivers, including the headwaters of the Mekong and Yangtze. When the road reached Lhasa, in 1954, the price of tea declined 30 percent while a box of matches, previously dear enough to command a whole sheep, fell to only two pounds of raw wool. But these effects further demonstrated to Tibetans an unwanted transformation of their society.

In 1953, Chinese road surveyors in Kham began to talk reform. The Tibetan governor of one district, Rapgya Pangdatsang, resigned his post but could find no support in Lhasa, where the Dalai Lama earnestly wished to avoid confrontation with the Chinese. The following year, when the Chinese began to establish cooperative farms in the Kantse and Litang areas, fighting began with the Khampa, fierce and skillful horsemen who became very effective partisans.

Early in 1955 the Chinese arrested Lobsang Tsewong, an Amdo leader who had spoken out against the new inequities, sparking a series of local uprisings and demonstrations. When a unit of 200 PLA troops arrived to restore order in the mountainous Golok district, the tribesmen captured and disarmed them, cut off their noses, then sent them back to the PLA as a warning. The Goloks joined forces with Dorji Pasang, a chieftain of over 100,000 families who had been fighting for several years already. The PLA responded by sending large detachments to eastern Tibet. One force of three regiments met and was defeated by the united Amdo rebels, losing 7,000 or 8,000 troops before they retreated.

The Chinese situation also worsened in Kham. There the PLA threatened the main livelihood of the Khampa, by levying taxes on traders and smugglers. It was said the Litang monastery, with five thousand monks and 113 satellite monasteries, literally thrived on such trade and smuggling. Fearing the worst, the PLA garrison at Litang tried to disarm the populace but were themselves overwhelmed instead. Even at Batang, a town known for its Tibetan collaborators, the people rose up against the lowland Chinese.

Khampa partisans managed to block the Kangting road at three points, further limiting the PLA's ability to react to the rebellion.

Kham and Amdo were the provinces the Chinese attempted to split off from Tibet, calling them Inner Tibet and incorporating them into the Chinese provinces of Sikang and Tsinghai. But by 1956 unrest was spreading, affecting even the Dalai Lama, who previously had cooperated by consenting to head a 51-member "preparatory commission" to oversee the integration of the state into China. It happened that 1956 was a special occasion for Buddhism—the 2,500th year since the birth of Buddha, marked by a "Jayanti" celebration in India. The Dalai Lama naturally attended, bringing with him 50 persons in his immediate party plus a retinue of 150 monks and officials. Once in India, the Tibetan leader asked Nehru for political asylum. Nehru informed the Chinese of this development, and communist foreign minister Chou En-lai made a sudden visit to India where he met secretly with the Dalai Lama, who was convinced to return to Tibet only by promises of changes in Chinese policy. Such changes as did occur were merely cosmetic, leaving the Dalai Lama virtually a prisoner of the Chinese in his Lhasa monastery, the Potala.

George Patterson's story is only one version of the origins of the CIA's paramilitary operation in Tibet. Another account has it that the activity was simply an expansion of an espionage network set up by the Dalai Lama's second-eldest brother, Gyalo Thondup. Based in Darjeeling, where Thondup lived, the Tibetan network supposedly had had connections with the CIA since 1951. The meetings at which Patterson interpreted may have represented CIA's final decision to deal itself a hand in Tibet, so both versions may be correct.

It is impossible at this writing to give a detailed analysis of the Washington decision making for Tibet. The appropriate records remain security classified. If not for the courts, in fact, the entire discussion of Tibet in the Marchetti and Marks book, *The CIA and the Cult of Intelligence,* would have been deleted by Agency censors. Tibet is "buried in the lore of the CIA as one of those successes that are not talked about," according to Fletcher Prouty, an Air Force colonel who managed secret air missions for General Erskine's Office of Special Operations.

This reluctance to discuss Tibet is undoubtedly related to the subsequent improvement of United States relations with the People's Republic of China. Today it is thought indelicate to draw attention to an explicit paramilitary effort to stir up trouble for that very nation. Refusal to open the record on Tibet is ironic, given the many failures that pepper the CIA's paramilitary record, since the war for "the roof of the world" was one of the more profitable operations run, at least in intelligence terms. Despite CIA reticence, a fair description of the overall dimensions of the Tibet operation is possible from the public record.

Developments in the rebellion suggest that the beginning of effective cooperation between the CIA and the partisans dates from 1956. That February simultaneous attacks occurred at several points in eastern Tibet, so widely separated that coordination seems clearly to have been necessary. More pointedly, in a revealing cultural change, beginning in 1956 clothing made of parachute material began to appear in Tibet, supplementing scarce cotton as a fabric. The first airdrop is said to have occurred in 1956, south of Batang, on a drop zone lit by flares, carried out by a plane that flew over Burma to reach Tibet. In addition, in 1956 the American Society for a Free Asia, the ostensibly private lobby group that, like its European counterpart, had been set up with CIA help, sponsored a United States lecture tour by Thubten Norbu, an ex-abbot and the Dalai Lama's eldest brother. Speaking in support of the rebellion, Norbu would make several similar visits over the course of the next few years.

Complementing airdrops was CIA training. Recruits often took a month to negotiate the trails down to India, either to Kalimpong or to Assam and thence through India. The Pangda brothers had made a fortune using these trails during World War II to smuggle arms to Chiang Kai-shek. They had a well-established support net, including a warehouse at Kalimpong that was now reopened. Recruits traveled in groups to Calcutta by train, where the next link was a contact address. Chartered planes then flew the recruits to Taiwan, with refueling stops at Bangkok and Hong Kong where the planes' blinds remained drawn.

In camp, the recruits from Kham and Amdo were shown a new world, a world of sophisticated weapons and communications unknown to Tibet. The Tibetans became very proficient soldiers; their cavalry were universally feared by the PLA. Yet the Tibetan language had no word for "cavalry." Skilled horsemen, the

Tibetans had thirty different words for parts of a horse's harness but none for the harness as a whole. The language had different words for specific species but none for "tree"; there were scores of terms for depths of trance or meditation but none for "sleep." The new military objects Tibetans were encountering led to the words "sky-boat" for airplane and "sky cloth" for parachute.

Some recruits transcended their lack of experience with Western technology to become radio specialists. Others became weapons experts or air-ground coordinators who could mark drop zones for supply missions. On Taiwan the recruits were eventually divided into three groups: one to retrace its steps to Tibet, and become unit leaders with the partisans; one to remain in the training camp as instructors and translators; a last group selected for special missions and given further training. The special-mission training during the early years was given on another island, very probably at the CIA facility on Saipan.

The initial training on Taiwan squarely places the Tibet operation within the larger framework of the secret war against the People's Republic of China. Taipei was a very important CIA station with a broad range of activities run from Taiwan. Its importance was reemphasized after the Taiwan Strait crises of 1954–1955 and 1958. Chiang Kai-shek still nursed his dreams of a return to the mainland. During the 1958 crisis, Rear Admiral Roland N. Smoot, commander of the United States military mission on Taiwan, was taken to see Chinese nationalist training of special forces, some five thousand of them. Chiang Ching-kuo, Chiang's son and deputy for intelligence matters, described an ambitious plan to land the special forces along the coast. While the Americans refused assistance for such a large effort, they did support boat or midget submarine landings of commando parties of from a dozen to twenty men until 1962. Boat groups usually left from Quemoy, the submarines from Taiwan.

The CIA station from early 1958 to June 1962 was under Ray Cline, who became a close personal friend of Chiang Ching-kuo. Through this channel the CIA had some contact with nationalist special forces, and there were also joint agent and propaganda activities. The use of agents was largely replaced in about 1960 with overhead reconnaissance—nationalist pilots were trained to fly U-2's given to Taiwan under the military assistance program. The photographic evidence came back to CIA for interpretation. The station's Tibetan involvement was restricted to training even though that state was considered part of China, and the Tibetan operation seems to have been under the direct control of the station in India.

Though the rebellion was confined to eastern Tibet in its early years, Chinese actions in 1956 virtually ensured it would spread more widely. One of these was the reduction of Litang monastery. In late February, during the third week of Tibetan new year celebrations, PLA forces suddenly surrounded and laid siege to the monastery. Litang was crowded with its 4,000 house monks, 2,000 more in for the celebrations, and 2,000 or more merchants and townspeople. The Chinese besieged the place for sixty-four days, culminating in a strike by Chinese jet bombers, the first use of such aircraft in the Tibetan war. A group of Tibetans charged the PLA lines and broke through; about 1,600 got away and 2,000 more escaped that night. The next day the PLA occupied Litang. Many of the prisoners they captured would be cruelly put to death. It was the beginning of a Chinese scorched earth strategy designed to break the power of the theocracy. Instead, it actually had the effect of uniting Tibetans in resistance.

Another PLA action that proved counterproductive came that summer, when a PLA commander in Kham attempted to coerce over two hundred prominent Tibetan leaders to agree to the Chinese social reforms. The Tibetans refused, escaped, and had little alternative but to join the resistance. This provided CIA recruiters with a pool of prospects who were leaders in their own society, strengthening the resistance in an especially useful way.

For the Chinese communists, the Tibet war was a conflict for roads. In these early years the roads were the substance as well as the symbol of the arrival of Mao's party in Tibet. The roads were defended by surveillance and maintenance stations at twenty-mile intervals throughout Kham and Amdo. Just manning this system of posts required forty thousand PLA troops and half that number of local militia.

Because the roads were the only Han lifeline, they controlled the military capabilities of the PLA. These roads quickly became the main target for the *ten dzong ma mi,* Tibet's "soldiers of the fortress of the faith." Raids and ambushes continued on a large scale in Kham and Amdo. By 1957 it was estimated that eighty thousand Tibetans were fighting with the main partisan group, with another ten thousand bandits or local tribesmen also arrayed against the Chinese.

One of Chou En-lai's promises to the Dalai Lama in India had been Chinese withdrawal from Tibet. Some party cadres were pulled out, but many more Han specialists and farmers were resettled into Tibet in a sort of colonization program. The most significant withdrawal was of the PLA, which removed most of its forces from central Tibet, but instead of transporting them to China proper, committed the units as reinforcements in Kham and Amdo, to a level of over a hundred thousand troops. Soon the PLA had some fourteen divisions combatting the partisans. The supply system was strengthened by the opening in Lhasa of a major truck maintenance shop in 1957.

Not even these measures stemmed the success of the partisans, especially the Khampa, who by 1958 claimed to have ejected the Han Chinese from all of southeastern Tibet. A partisan leader visiting Kalimpong reported that forty thousand PLA soldiers had been killed in battle since 1956. In central Tibet a partisan unit under Amdo Leshe, which reportedly had received some of the earliest American airdrops of weapons and radios, fought in the Lhoka district and essentially kept clear the pack trail from Kalimpong, upon which the rebels depended for the bulk of their ammunition. Leshe was said to be in direct radio contact with Taiwan. In Amdo and Kham the partisans cut the Chinese roads.

Warfare brought about splits in Tibetan society. There was also the moral problem for traditionally nonviolent Buddhist Tibetans choosing to war against the Han. The PLA helped resolve these problems by bombing monasteries, beginning with Litang in 1956. Ultimately, even the monks took sides. The Panchen Lama, Tibet's second religious leader, went with the Chinese, eventually to become the Chinese-recognized religious leader of the country. But most of the lamas took the rebel side. This was the case at the Drepung monastery, one of Tibet's largest, with seven hundred subsidiaries in Lhasa alone, which sheltered a delegation from Kham after the Litang siege. At the Drepung, a monk remembers, "I saw the [rebel] weapons, guns and rifles, come in by night. Night after night."

For the Americans, getting those cases of weapons into Tibet became much easier after 1956. At the time of the Hungarian crisis,

President Eisenhower had remarked that that nation was as inaccessible as Tibet. Ike was right—at that time the United States lacked a long-range transport aircraft capable of carrying heavy payloads. But in December 1956 the C-130 Hercules, produced by Lockheed, began to join the U.S. Air Force, and that, more than anything else, made possible an expansion of the secret war in Tibet. This remarkable plane had the range to make the extended flights (more than twenty-four hundred miles, flying from Bangkok) and still carry significant loads—up to twenty-two tons for the C-130E.

Civil Air Transport did not own any C-130's and is not known to have leased any before its March 1959 reorganization into Air America. Among its two hundred missions over the Chinese mainland carried out before 1961, it is credited with flights to Tibet, but these very probably utilized four-engine C-54 or PBY5A aircraft. Such C-130's as flew in the Far East belonged to the Air Force's 315th Air Division based in Korea and Okinawa. Their use was controlled by General Erskine's office in Washington. Clandestine work did consume Air Force resources, not only for Tibet but for Thailand, Laos, and Vietnam. The Air Force was clearly responding to this work load when, in March 1961 on Okinawa, it established an E Flight within the 21st Troop Carrier Squadron, equipped with C-130's and specially selected personnel for top-secret missions.

Highly qualified aircrews were vital for the Tibet flights. These had to be made at night at low altitudes, and needed to ascend the Himalayas, and find remote drop zones without benefit of radio navigation beacons, which were not dependable at such distances. Navigators had to rely on star fixes instead. A typical flight would carry palletized cargo for drop, perhaps some Tibetans to be parachuted, and a CIA control party of four officers. Fortunately, emergency landings in India were possible because the CIA had achieved a degree of cooperation with the Indian services.

The CIA ignominious failure with the PEMESTA colonels in Indonesia was a perverse boon for the Tibetan secret war. For Indonesia, the CIA had assembled stocks of weapons and equipment that, by the summer of 1958, had suddenly become superfluous, at least for Indonesia. These stocks constituted an important addition to those available for the Tibetan resistance, which had just become a unified national movement. The flag of the new force was first raised before the eyes of five thousand cheering cavalrymen, drawn up on an open plain less than a hundred miles from Lhasa, before a portrait of the Dalai Lama. The date was June 16, 1958. The force was called the Tensung Tangla Magar, the National Volunteer Defense Army (NVDA). Its formation ushered in the most intense phase of the Tibetan war.

Although the NVDA was a unified resistance army, national resistance to the Han had yet to become universal in Tibet. The NVDA fighters were still mostly drawn from Kham and Amdo. While resistance was stirring in central Tibet, it was largely held in check by one man—the Dalai Lama. The new phase of the secret war began with a struggle for the heart and mind of that one man.

Tenzin Gyatso, the fourteenth Dalai Lama, was the embodiment of the spirit and wisdom of his people. According to tradition the Dalai Lama, as well as his colleague the Panchen Lama, are venerated as incarnations of the disciples of Tsong Khapa, who founded lamaism in Tibet in about A.D. 1400. He had been discovered in his home village at age two and a half on the basis of oracles, visions, and tests administered by the searchers. In a peculiar twist of fate, the new Dalai Lama, in 1939, had had to be ransomed from the Chinese Muslim warlord Ma Pu-fang, the same man who had been the intended recipient of aid in one of the CIA's earliest paramilitary efforts in China.

In the developing struggle in Kham and Amdo, Tenzin Gyatso was one lama who tried not to take sides. He worked with the Chinese to the extent that was necessary, but at least three times refused to call out the Tibetan army in support of the PLA. In India he had forced concessions from Chou En-lai. On the other hand, the Dalai Lama denounced the resistance and advised Tibetans not to become involved. He also allowed the dismissal of his own cabinet in favor of a group more acceptable to the Han. The NVDA leadership knew that the Dalai Lama *had* to be enlisted if there was to be an effective national resistance and, by early 1959, many of the lamas also believed that Tenzin Gyatso was a virtual prisoner of the PLA in Lhasa. Many Tibetans determined to save him.

In late 1958 the NVDA began an offensive into central Tibet. Eschewing their usual marauding tactics, the partisans began to make direct attacks against PLA garrisons. By December, PLA posts within twenty-five miles of Lhasa were raided by the NVDA. In late January or early February of 1959, the PLA garrison at Tsetang, only thirty miles from Lhasa, was overrun by the Tibetans. For the first time, there was an NVDA presence very close to the capital.

The Chinese evidently thought they could take the Dalai Lama hostage. The Tibetan leader was invited to what was billed as a dramatic presentation at the compound of the PLA Tibet Military Area Command, headed by General Tan Kuan-san. Senior Tibetan advisers to the Dalai Lama, some of whom had been secretly supporting the NVDA, interpreted this as a PLA bid to capture and hold the political-religious leader. They urged the Dalai Lama to make excuses and not to attend.

The Dalai Lama did not attend the Chinese presentation—the Norbulinka palace at which he was staying at the moment was surrounded after dawn on March 10, 1959, by a crowd of thirty thousand who demonstrated against the Chinese and shouted that their religious leader must be protected. One Chinese collaborator who appeared in the street was stoned to death. Tension mounted with mass demonstrations over the following days. The PLA garrison of perhaps forty thousand troops were observed strengthening their fortifications around the city. Tenzin Gyatso later would write, "I felt as if I were standing between two volcanoes, each likely to erupt at any moment."

On March 15 some PLA troops appeared outside the Dalai Lama's abode and his guards had to be restrained from firing on them. On the seventeenth, as the Tibetan leader sat with his cabinet, two mortar shells exploded in a nearby garden. That fateful Tuesday the decision was hastily made to flee Lhasa. The Dalai Lama abandoned his stand against a confrontation between Tibetans and Chinese. That night, in three groups, the Dalai Lama, his immediate family and senior advisers escaped from Lhasa. Tenzin Gyatso was disguised as a common soldier of the guard. The group carried nothing with them in order to avoid attracting attention. In subsequent days between 8,000 and 13,000 of its citizens left Lhasa, including 500 of the 7,000 monks at the Drepung monastery. This exodus received powerful stimulation on March 20 when PLA General Tan ordered open hostilities. Only then did the Chinese command realize that the Dalai Lama was gone.

French explorer and scholar Michel Peissel describes these events as "one of the strangest and most ill-understood coups of recent times." Under its top leader, General Gompo Tashi Andrugtsang, the NVDA offensive drove to within miles of the capital, precisely timed to place a protective force near Lhasa just as the Dalai Lama fled. Units of NVDA partisans formed a rear guard behind the Dalai Lama's party throughout its trek south to the Indian border region known as the North East Frontier Agency, and also created a decoy northeast of Lhasa to confuse Chinese searchers.

On November 1, 1958, Gordon Gray sent a note to NSC executive secretary James Lay. It read, "if, as a result of the new social experiment in Communist China, there should be some sort of revolt, is our policy clear as to what course of action we would follow?"

In fact Washington had anticipated only limited potential from the Tibetan rebellion, as indeed from any operations against the People's Republic of China. This was made clear in a secret survey of the possibilities for uprisings in China that Eisenhower received in the summer of 1959 from Assistant Secretary of State for Far Eastern Affairs J. Graham Parsons. Regarding Tibet the survey predicted that

> if the Tibetans are able to maintain their resistance movement in the face of large-scale Chinese Communist suppression efforts, other border area minorities might be emboldened to carry out dissident activities. However, the Chinese Communists probably have the capability of preventing prolonged rebellion, except in the most isolated areas, and of containing it.

At the same time peasant uprisings in central China were also deemed unlikely. Further, the survey judged that the nationalists greatly exaggerated their capacity to intervene upon the mainland, although the State Department believed it "by no means suicidal" of Chiang Kai-shek to contemplate such raids.

In the meantime, despite the small chances for success, the 5412 Group considered in secret deliberations its answer to the policy question posed by Gordon Gray. Memoranda that remain classified, from Allen Dulles to President Eisenhower dated January 22 and March 3, 1959, concerned Tibet; these possibly included a request for formal approval of this project. On March 23 there was a further letter from Allen Dulles, while the President's staff secretary reported from the CIA and State intelligence reports that "the Tibetan uprisings apparently have resulted in a considerable loss of prestige for Communist China in India."

India's opinion was crucial, since Nehru had turned aside the Dalai Lama's request for political asylum in 1956. In July 1958 the Chinese had also protested in a diplomatic note to New Delhi that Kalimpong was a center of the resistance. But by then Nehru, too, had chosen sides, and the Chinese charges were rejected. In the Indian parliamentary debates ignited by the Dalai Lama's journey, the prime minister went out of his way several times to defend the Tibetans living at Kalimpong from charges of participating in the rebellion and to deny that the village was a "command center" of the NVDA effort.

One exchange, which occurred in a parliamentary debate on April 2, 1959, is especially revealing. After a Nehru statement regarding Kalimpong, member Nath Pai asked, "What is the Home Ministry doing about it? It seems to be absolutely ineffective."

Nehru replied, "The Home Ministry or the External Affairs Ministry are not at all worried about the situation."

Member Hem Barua then asked incredulously, "They allow the spies to [conduct] espionage?"

"Absolutely yes," said Jawaharlal Nehru.

In another debate, Nehru explained that India's first news of the events at Lhasa was a message on March 10 from the consul general, which had arrived the next day. But the New Delhi journal *Statesman* reported in its issue of March 2, 1959, before anything had happened in Lhasa, that there would be a coup in Lhasa and that the Dalai Lama would flee that city on March 17.

American ambassador Ellsworth Bunker kept Washington apprised of developments, but the best information came from the CIA. Deputy director General Charles Cabell or Desmond Fitz-Gerald, the DDP's Far East Division chief, were in almost daily telephone contact with Gordon Gray during this period.

The CIA was so well informed because it had furnished an American radio operator, who traveled with the Dalai Lama's party. The agent was able to set up repeated airdrops of supplies (which was crucial because the party had left Lhasa without anything), to communicate with nearby NVDA units, and to furnish daily reports to CIA headquarters. There may have been other CIA agents with the party as well. Although the Agency's "denied areas" specialist Stephen Meade, and paramilitary expert Anthony Poshepny, have been credited with entering Tibet to bring out NVDA recruits, it is believed that the mission to rescue Dalai Lama represented a departure from past practice.

On April 1, just as the Dalai Lama's party was entering India, Eisenhower in Washington was told, "We have informed Embassy New Delhi we think the US should take no action with respect to Tibetan refugees which would diminish the effect the revolt appears to be having in India."

A message from the Tibetans, received on April 2, confirmed success and contained an important plea: "You must help us as soon as possible and send us weapons for 30,000 men by airplane." It is likely that that message sparked additional action in Washington. The NSC, which had not discussed Tibet since June 20, 1957, suddenly met on the subject in March, twice in April, and again in June 1959. A thirteen-page classified CIA report, a letter from Allen Dulles to the President, and a cable reporting the Dalai Lama's views were sent over before the NSC meeting on April 23. The DCI's letter concerned the Dalai Lama's resolution to continue to resist the Chinese. Meanwhile, on April 21, in the face of a strong offensive by PLA forces, field commander Gompo Tashi issued orders for the NVDA to abandon its headquarters in the Lhoka district, which had been defended to permit the escape of the Dalai Lama.

Tibetan sources maintain that the Eisenhower administration made an important decision in May 1959. The outcome was an expansion of the program and a determination to begin training Tibetans within the continental United States. Five groups totaling almost five hundred men were to be given instruction and then sent back to their native regions. The recruits were selected to represent all three provinces—Amdo, Kham, and central Tibet.

The American site for training was located at Camp Hale, Colorado, near the town of Leadville, about a hundred miles southwest of Denver. Tibetans were flown into Peterson Field, six miles east of Colorado Springs, and moved by buses with blacked-out windows to the base, which was situated at an altitude of over ten thousand feet, about the closest the United States could come to the rarefied atmosphere of Tibet. Camp Hale had been used in World War II to train mountain troops for service in Alaska and Italy and also the 99th Ski Battalion, which furnished some personnel that OSS sent to Norway. Most of the base was dismantled later by German prisoners, but what was left was used by the Army for winter maneuvers until it was closed in 1956. Camp Hale seemed an ideal location for a CIA facility. The Tibetans, who were never told they were in the United States, came from the Far East aboard huge C-124 Globemaster transports with a single refueling stop in Hawaii.

To discourage curiosity among American citizens, a cover story was put out that unspecified "atomic tests," though not explosions, were to be conducted at the reopened base. A story to this effect was given to the *Denver Post* and printed on July 16, 1959. The telephone and utility companies were asked to give a day's notice before sending linemen to service poles in the vicinity of Camp Hale. Finally, the military guards and recruits themselves were given orders to shoot to kill if unauthorized persons were encountered on the grounds.

While the secret training program proceeded, the Dalai Lama took his cause to the United Nations, where it had not been discussed since 1950. Ireland offered a resolution that condemned the Chinese for genocide. Despite its support of the Tibetans against the Chinese, the United States wished to avoid drawing attention to a region in which it was involved, and wanted to stay in the background in this UN debate, as Secretary of State Herter told Ambassador Henry Cabot Lodge. The rate at which the diplomatic initiative gained momentum surprised the State Department. Herter feared the resolution would fail to pass and that defeat would be a serious setback. He opposed "a resolution recognizing [Tibet's] independence or sovereignty," instead suggesting "a slap on the wrist" for the Chinese. Secretary Herter told Lodge he had declared to a British diplomat that "all we wanted to do was to have this thing come in as mild a resolution as possible." American interests were not identical to those of the Tibetans. British support for the UN resolution was also lukewarm, expressing doubts regarding Tibet's status as an independent nation. Overtures were made to a brother of the Dalai Lama, then in New York representing the Tibetans, to accept a less strident UN resolution.

On October 21, 1959, the United Nations General Assembly passed a resolution expressing concern that human rights were being suppressed in Tibet. The vote was 45 to 9, with 26 abstentions, among them the British. The Soviet bloc voted solidly against the resolution.

There was not a word about independence or sovereignty, the primary aims of the Tibetans.

Inside Tibet the fighting continued without pause. In Lhasa alone during 1959, according to documents captured later from the PLA, the number of Tibetans killed was put at 87,000. That year, the Tibetan year of the Earth-Pig, the PLA determined once and for all to cut the supply trails north from Kalimpong. The Chinese deployed 100,000 troops in Lhoka in a powerful pacification effort that ultimately required two and a half years. Toward the end of 1959, for the first time, 200 to 300 Soviet advisers were claimed to be active in Tibet.

Dwight Eisenhower made a state visit to India in late 1959, but deemed it inexpedient to meet with the Dalai Lama, who was living in India at the time. Tibetan requests for such a meeting were rebuffed. (The following year, the United States also discouraged a visa request by the Dalai Lama to visit this country.) However, in New Dehli, Ike did accept certain gifts that were bestowed upon him through CIA channels by NVDA commander Gompo Tashi. Along with a Khampa knife, charm box, and articles of Tibetan clothing, came a letter from Tashi summarizing the origins of the revolt and ending on this note:

> We Tibetans have determined to fight to the last against the Chinese Communists with full weapons of modern warfare as there is no alternative left to us except to fight. We see no other Powers other than the United States which is [sic] capable of giving us help in every respects [sic] to free Tibet from the domination of Red China. The situation has become very serious like a patient about to die. Under the circumstances as stated above, with a heavy heart, we appeal to your Excellency to impart necessary instructions about the best possible course for us to follow.

The gifts were acknowledged orally, but because Gompo Tashi had not used "channels considered by the Embassy to give him official status," no other reply was thought necessary. Dwight Eisenhower continued to preserve his plausible deniability.

Despite the refusal to associate with the Tibetans openly, secret plans continued. Before his NSC meeting of February 4, 1960, the President met to discuss Tibet with a group including Gordon Gray, Herter, Allen Dulles, Cabell, and Desmond FitzGerald. Two weeks later there was another discussion of 5412 Group matters.

In May and June 1960 mass defections and mutinies among PLA troops were reported. There was stiff resistance in southern Tibet. In one battle, the PLA claimed to have killed eight hundred of an NVDA force of three thousand men. Just then, another event affecting the intelligence world brought United States air support for

the Tibetans to a complete halt. On May 1, 1960, a CIA U-2 reconnaissance plane was shot down deep inside the Soviet Union, its
pilot, Francis Gary Powers, turned in by Russian farmers to the
Soviet authorities. This incident led to the collapse of a summit
conference with the Russians in Paris, and caused President Eisenhower to issue orders for the immediate suspension of all intrusions
into the airspace of communist nations. Included in the stand-down
were the C-130 flights into Tibet.

The secret war in Tibet was passed on from the Eisenhower administration to President John F. Kennedy's. It was up to Kennedy
to decide what to do with the NVDA partisans. Ike's ban on overflights continued through the remainder of his term, while NVDA
commanders made increasingly desperate pleas for supplies. When
John Kennedy took the oath of office, on January 20, 1961, the CIA
had already prepared proposals for changes in the Tibet operation,
for alternate routes of delivery overland.

Eisenhower's suspension of overflights left the CIA with stores in
Okinawa, Taiwan, Thailand, and Laos. One estimate is that the CIA
had already equipped fourteen thousand "soldiers of the fortress of
the faith," almost all the active male population still fighting in the
high Himalayas. Supplying the NVDA without C-130's seemed to
be an impossible task, but the CIA attacked it with some efficiency,
especially Des FitzGerald, who is reported to have been keen on
the matter.

In the summer of 1960 an International Jurists Commission established by the United Nations released its conclusions that genocide had been attempted in Tibet, lending momentum to CIA
proposals that fall. On September 15, 1960, a 5412 Group meeting
was held immediately prior to the convening of the Security Council, so it would be convenient for Secretary of Defense Gates to attend for the Pentagon. According to a brief record note, "As a result
of the discussion the DCI said he would reorient his thinking to
some extent," and would come back with an alternative proposal.
About two months later, DDCI Charles Cabell briefed the 5412
Group on Tibet and Cuba.

The evidence suggests that the Tibet matter was specifically
handed over to the Kennedy transition team in late November
1960, several weeks after the election, though Eisenhower himself
did not sit down with the President-elect until December 6. In ref-

erence to that meeting, Ike specifically recalls that JFK had already been briefed a number of times by Allen Dulles on international matters including the Far East. In fact, in a discussion with Gray and Eisenhower on the morning of November 25, "Mr. Dulles reported to the President on certain consultations he had had with respect to projected undertakings in Tibet and received further guidance from the President."

The Tibet effort was being run through the embassy in New Delhi, and John Kennedy's man for India was Harvard economist John Kenneth Galbraith. Before leaving for his post, on March 27, 1961, Galbraith was briefed on CIA operations in India by Richard Bissell. There was an element of irony in this meeting of two economists, one perhaps the foremost American Keynesian, the other a man who had long resisted Keynesian arguments but ended up administering Keynesian-style foreign and military aid, first for the Marshall Plan, then for the CIA. Bissell showed Galbraith the list of projects, many of which distressed the ambassador.

Galbraith determined to stop some of the "spooky activities" he did not like. One of them was Tibet, whose partisan fighters he calls "deeply unhygienic tribesmen." One of Galbraith's first orders to the country team in New Delhi was to make a full investigation of CIA operations. He recalls that CIA station chief Harry Rositzke made no special effort to defend the operations in progress. As for himself, the economist writes, "I was not troubled by an open mind. I was convinced that most of the projects proposed would be useless for their own anticommunist purposes and were capable, when known, of doing us great damage as well."

The ambassador carried his views back to Washington in May 1961, where he found the administration subdued by other CIA failures. Galbraith argued his position energetically with the President, Robert Kennedy, and McGeorge Bundy, the new NSC adviser. He then put his arguments in a memorandum he showed to Allen Dulles, Bissell, and other senior CIA officials. Galbraith told them he had gone directly to the President and that Kennedy had been sympathetic.

Ambassador Galbraith was not wholly successful, however; he could not get the Tibet operation canceled. The partisans had achieved the status of a United States ally and had to be supported. When the CIA did end its network inside India, the operation was merely reorganized to work from Nepal, while Indian intelligence picked up some of the remaining Tibetans for a special border activity after the Sino-Indian war of 1962.

The NVDA resistance rapidly relocated its main camp to the tiny area of Mustang, a high mountain stronghold almost 150 miles northwest of the Nepalese capital Katmandu, where the "soldiers of the fortress of the faith" began arriving in late 1960. To Katmandu the CIA sent its political action specialist Howard Stone as chief of a beefed-up station, while the Agency also created a new proprietary airline, Air Nepal, for air assistance. Long flights from Bangkok over India to Mustang were made with this cover while light aircraft did short-range work around Katmandu. Of this operation Galbraith comments, "I was especially disturbed by [this] particularly insane enterprise."

Galbraith believes that later, in conjunction with Robert Kennedy, he succeeded in cutting the Nepalese connection, but an incident that occurred in December 1961 demonstrated beyond the shadow of a doubt that it was still in progress. In the early morning of December 7, a convoy of the Tibetans from Camp Hale were delayed in reaching Peterson Field by deep snow and icy road conditions. Instead of getting away in their C-124 at night, the Tibetans arrived after dawn. Sitting on the apron at Peterson, the C-124 was observed by airfield employees. To preserve the secrecy of the operation, Army soldiers held forty-seven American citizens at gunpoint in the name of a dubious national security, and then told them it would be a federal offense to talk about it. The story was in the *Colorado Springs Gazette* the next day, and was kept out of *The New York Times* only by means of the personal intercession of Secretary of Defense Robert McNamara.

Snafus like the one at Peterson Field had shut down other covert operations, the Indonesia fiasco being one case in point. In its way, the Peterson incident was even more serious in that the CIA was proscribed by law from operating inside the United States, and there is no authority for such preventive detention as holding citizens at gunpoint to protect the secrecy of a CIA operation.

It was at about this time that the "soldiers of the fortress of the faith" achieved one of their greatest successes in the field. A small party sent to disrupt traffic along the Amdo road wiped out a PLA convoy. Among the corpses, they found the commander of the PLA's western region and his entire staff. The bags of documents included reports on the 1959 Lhasa uprising, material bearing on the Sino-Soviet rift, and a file of issues of the *Bulletin of Activities* (*Kung-tso T'ung-hsun*), which was a secret journal providing guidance for PLA political commissars, that covered the period January to August 1961. The political journal was actually translated and released to American scholars by the State Department in August 1963. This windfall is the reason Ray Cline records that Tibet "resulted in a bonanza of valuable substantive intelligence."

In any case, the pattern of Tibetan operations changed completely after 1960. With the end of direct airdrops and the PLA's domination of the trails above Kalimpong, it was no longer possible to wage an actual partisan war. The NVDA reestablished itself at Mustang, but that base was so remote that only raids, not sustained operations, were possible. Gompo Tashi was replaced by Baba Yeshi, whose clumsy methods annoyed the second generation of Camp Hale-trained NVDA leaders. But the resistance, its numbers reduced to less than seven thousand, sputtered on for years. There was a communications center with two special antennas at Orissa, and an NVDA headquarters in New Delhi. Joint meetings among the NVDA, CIA, and Indian intelligence representatives were held weekly.

Complaints against Baba Yeshi eventually resulted in his replacement by a nephew of the late Gompo Tashi Andrugtsang, Gyato Wangdu. He was by this time the sole survivor of the original cadres trained by CIA in the mid-1950s. By then the camp at Mustang had attained the look of a permanent base, with a three-story command center and twenty-five other buildings. There were staff sections for supply, transport, ammunition, intelligence, and internal discipline. It was a far cry from the ordeal of the first arrivals at Mustang, four thousand strong, who had almost starved before supplies had got to them.

The Tibetans maintained their presence at Mustang into the 1970s, mounting occasional raids that were generally successful, but there was not a chance of liberating Tibet. Baba Yeshi turned against the NVDA after his dismissal, while the United States also abandoned them following its rapprochement with China. Mao Tse-tung demanded the end of the charade when the king of Nepal visited him in Peking in November 1973. The next year the Nepalese, with information gleaned from Baba Yeshi, and prior arrangements with the PLA to patrol their side of the border, put ten thousand royal troops up against Mustang, including Gurkha who were just as fierce as any Khampa. Wangdu escaped with the NVDA archives and a small Khampa escort, only to be killed in a later ambush. Seven other Tibetan leaders who surrendered at Mustang sat in jail at Katmandu until pardoned by the king in 1981. It was the end of the Khampa rebellion.

From the beginning it had been clear in Washington that Tibet could never be more than a large-scale harassment of the People's Republic of China. To achieve this effect, the CIA had promised liberation to the Tibetans, who were caught up in their hopes and dreams, but whose agony was extended by the war. Tibet was also a searing experience for the CIA paramilitary experts, who had learned the language and customs of the country, become emotionally attached to its struggle, only to have to close down the operation later on. They saw the darker side of the CIA's intelligence "bonanza."

For the Tibetans, over 100,000 of whom are now refugees from their country, there was just one mitigating factor—their defeat took many years, so they could adjust gradually to the trauma. In Cuba, the CIA's next paramilitary disaster, trauma would be a matter of a mere seventy-two hours of hell.

·X·

CUBA I: "ANOTHER BLACK HOLE OF CALCUTTA"

This New Year's party was quite subdued, not the usual boisterous festivity that Fulgencio Batista y Zaldívar hosted on this holiday. Some of the sixty guests ate *arroz con pollo*, rice with chicken, served by military aides in dress uniforms, a few drank champagne, most coffee. Until that day, the guests had been the rich and powerful of Cuba. Batista, the host, was Cuba's dictator, though he called himself "President." The date at this party, December 31, 1959, was significant because it would be Batista's last day in power. Some of the guests knew or suspected as much, in particular Batista's military commanders, who were determined to convince him to give up his posts.

The Batista government was tottering because of a revolution, a seemingly irresistible force coming down from the mountains, the Sierra Maestra, where it had begun two years earlier. At first the guerrillas, led by young Fidel Castro, had been contained in the Sierra Maestra by the Cuban army. But Batista's dictatorship was corrupt, and oppressive, and increasingly had lost its support among Cubans, who flocked to Castro's Twenty-sixth of July Movement (M-26, or Movimiento del Veintiseis de Julio), which took its name from the date of an unsuccessful revolt Castro had previously led. By 1958 the M-26 guerrillas had come down from the Sierra to create fronts in several parts of Cuba, defeating Batista's army in battle. The handwriting was on the wall.

Batista was no fool, he knew what was coming. The dictator made only a brief appearance, around midnight. He did relinquish the reins of power at a meeting with his military commanders.

171

Then, with his family and closest supporters, Batista left for the airport. There the group boarded two airplanes, which took off for Miami from the Camp Columbia base at 2:40 in the morning on January 1, 1959.

The M-26 unit closest to Havana at that moment was 150 miles away—a column fighting at Santa Clara under the Argentinian *commandante* Ernesto "Che" Guevara. Seven hours after Batista's departure, Che was asleep atop the hood of his jeep. He was awakened by M-26 officers and given the news. Guevara immediately organized his column for a road march to Havana. The force left at dusk and drove on through the night. They arrived in the capital the next morning and went directly to the fortress La Cabaña, whose garrison of fifteen thousand men dwarfed the small M-26 column.

The M-26 *commandante* walked up to La Cabaña's iron drawbridge. There he shouted, "I am the Che Guevara. I want to talk to your chief."

A few moments later a government jeep came out of the fortress and crossed the bridge. The occupant, an army major, unholstered his pistol and handed it to Guevara.

"We are not interested in fighting. It is not necessary now."

The Cuban civil war was over.

Throughout his time in power, the United States backed Batista. The change in government on January 2, 1959, brought a new beginning for Cubans but also a new opportunity for Washington in its relations with Havana. That the United States failed to grasp this opportunity was due both to the policies of Fidel's revolutionaries once in power and to a certain impatience on the part of the Eisenhower administration. These would lead to one of the most spectacular covert operations disasters of the postwar period.

The origins of the hostility that persists today between the United States and Cuba is shrouded by the mists of time. It is therefore important to note that in 1959 Fidel Castro was *not* a communist nor was his Twenty-sixth of July Movement a communist party. Nor were the communists brought into government at the time M-26 took power. According to a 1958 CIA report the Cuban communist party favored general-strike tactics rather than the armed insurgency carried out by M-26. Cuba's communist party numbered twelve thousand. Argentina, Brazil, Chile, and Mexico all had communist parties four or more times as large as Cuba's. Castro's own M-26 was also many times larger than the Cuban communist party.

Fidel Castro himself was not at first a communist either, but rather a scion of the upper classes. His social standing, it is true, was blemished: He was born out of wedlock to his father's housekeeper. She eventually bore Angel Castro five children before his first wife left him and he married the former servant. Angel Castro had a 23,300-acre farm in Oriente province; his estate later was estimated to be worth a half-million dollars. Fidel was the fourth of the seven children (two by the first wife), and he was born in 1926. He studied in Jesuit schools and later took up law at the University of Havana, where he began politics as a student leader. Fidel acquired his progressive politics in Colombia and Mexico, and he was able to temper them in jail for almost two years after the failure of the Moncada Barracks revolt. Castro was freed from prison on the Isle of Pines in May 1955, in an amnesty granted by Batista, but within a year had begun his guerrilla career in the Sierra Maestra. Once in power, Castro espoused *"fidelismo,"* as opposed to Marxism, and soon styled himself "the Maximum Leader." Castro may have begun a new dictatorship, but in this respect he was no different from Batista and no less worthy of American support.

In its relations with the Castro government, the Eisenhower administration began with a wait-and-see attitude, which soon underwent subtle changes. At the CIA, for example, the initial assessment of the Cuban situation explained Batista's fall in terms of the corruption of his regime and the consequent lack of public support for it. Allen Dulles is said to have taken this report and personally rewritten it. A paper that Dulles *did* forward, to State in February 1959, was not at all complimentary to the Castro government. Calling the situation "far from stable," the paper asserted the M-26 organization was "lacking [in] dynamic positive leadership," its government "floundering," and its difficulties magnified by "the relative youth and inexperience of a great many top leaders." Thus, "the glamour of the Sierra Maestra and the straggly beards is rapidly wearing off as the realities of the situation daily become more apparent."

Fidel visited Washington in April to give a speech at the annual meeting of the American Society of Newspaper Editors. He did not meet Ike but spoke with State Department officials and had a three-hour discussion with Vice-President Richard Nixon. The

Vice-President thought Fidel sincere but reported, "He is either incredibly naive about communism or under communist discipline." The State Department analysis read:

> With regard to his position on communism and the cold war struggle, Castro cautiously indicated that Cuba would remain in the western camp. However his position here must still be regarded as uncertain. He did go sufficiently far in his declarations to be vulnerable to the criticism of radicals among his supporters.

On his own copy of the State Department analysis President Eisenhower wrote, "We will check in a year!"

Castro did have a problem, but it was with the conservatives not the radicals in Cuba. By and large, the landed and monied families in Cuba had maintained ties with the Batista forces. Fearful of the revolution, they were soon leaving in large numbers, taking their dollars with them. By December 1959 there were 100,000 Cuban émigrés in the United States alone. Without these skilled workers—technicians, doctors, and lawyers and their money—there was little private or public capital to diversify the Cuban economy away from sugar production, the market for which was concentrated in the United States and strictly regulated by the American government through a quota system. At the same time, the Mafia, which had had large gambling concessions at the Havana hotels under Batista, left Cuba after the prohibition of this kind of activity, drying up another potential source of capital.

The *fidelista* solution was expropriation, as had been tried by Mossadegh in Iran and Arbenz in Guatemala. There was an element of irony in this since Castro's father had once worked for United Fruit. In any case, a decree allowing nationalization was promulgated in the fall of 1959. In December the first American concern, a local subsidiary of Otis Elevator, was "intervened," as the Cubans called expropriation. During 1960 the sugar plantations and Havana hotels followed. The Cubans added to the injuries by not offering compensation to owners of the "intervened" companies.

A second fear was that the Cubans would attempt to export their revolution throughout Latin America. There were reports of a "legion" created for this purpose. During 1959 and 1960 small armed groups invaded Panama, Guatemala, and the Dominican Republic, much as Castro himself had sailed to Cuba in a boat to establish a base in the Sierra Maestra. These rebels were nationals of their own countries and, while some did receive Cuban assistance, the movements were in no sense fomented by Castro. In fact, the "invasion" of the Dominican Republic was carried out from Puerto Rico, a territory of the United States. In any case, the evidence indicates that expropriation was more important than support of revolutions in turning the United States against Cuba.

There was at least some recognition of these factors in the United States government, even at the CIA. On November 5, 1959, its deputy director, General Charles Cabell, testified to a Senate Judiciary subcommittee that neither the Cuban communist party nor the CIA considered Castro a communist, that the Cuban communist party did not control Castro's government, but that it was seeking to influence him. Cabell also downplayed Cuban participation in Latin American revolutionary expeditions, pointing out that they had not been organized or dominated by the Cubans. Significantly, Cabell conceded that "anti-Communists have an interest in rumors which will increase our alarm over the Communist influence in Cuba."

As Cabell spoke on Capitol Hill, at Foggy Bottom Secretary of State Christian Herter was putting finishing touches on a memorandum he sent to Eisenhower that same day, November 5. The paper contained four recommendations for more forceful action on Cuba. These included: doing nothing to assist Castro's consolidation of power; a propaganda campaign in Latin America to promote the United States' conception of democracy; encouragement both within Cuba and elsewhere of opposition to the course of the Castro government while avoiding the impression that the United States was pressuring Cuba; and preserving mutual Cuban-American interests for the United States and a "reformed" Cuban government.

The secretary of state ended on a note that is quite revealing: "In view of the special sensitivity of Latin America to United States 'intervention,' I would propose that the existence and substance of this current policy statement be held on a very strict 'need to know' basis."

Dwight Eisenhower accepted both the policy proposals and the recommendation for secrecy. On November 9 Andrew Goodpaster informed Herter of the approval. At the White House, knowledge of the action was to be restricted to Goodpaster himself, Ike's son John S. D. Eisenhower, and one confidential secretary. In April 1959 the President had been willing to wait a year to see how Castro dealt with Cuba's problems; now, long before that time was up, Eisenhower had approved the policy that led directly to a secret war against Cuba.

From their offices around the Reflecting Pool, CIA officials quickly fell into line behind the new policy. The DCI asserted in a public speech on December 4 that Latin American communists had instructions to use nationalism as a slogan to justify breaking ties of friendship with the United States. Just one week later, Allen Dulles received a memorandum from the chief of DDP's Western Hemisphere (WH) Division, Joseph Caldwell King, which insisted Castro's " 'far left' dictatorship" could not be permitted to stand, because it could encourage expropriations of American property in other Latin countries. King advocated four actions, among them that "thorough consideration be given to the elimination of Fidel Castro . . . [which] would greatly accelerate the fall of the present government."

Allen Dulles carried the idea of an anti-Castro project to the 5412 Group meeting of January 13, 1960. There the State representative questioned any effort to move against Castro in the absence of a solid Cuban opposition. Dulles acknowledged this criticism but emphasized the CIA actions would be aimed at allowing opposition leaders to gain a foothold, rather than any quick move against Castro. Yet "over the long run," Dulles observed, "the U.S. will not be able to tolerate the Castro regime in Cuba."

The 5412 Group gave its conditional approval to the project. On January 18 a dozen officers met with J. C. King to organize a Cuba task force within the CIA. The task force became the fourth branch of King's division, WH/4 in CIA usage.

Selected for chief of the task force was a man who is pseudonymously called by existing accounts either "Cliff" or "Jake Engler." Another Burma OSS veteran, Engler was graduated from the University of Pennsylvania. He remained in intelligence, was a veteran of Operation Success, and had commanded the CIA training facility at Fort Benning. At the time he was picked for WH/4, Engler was serving as chief of station in Caracas.

Early planning for the Cuban project focused upon several separate components. One was an initiative to train twenty to thirty Cubans who could return to the island and become local guerrilla leaders, much as the CIA had previously done with the Tibetans. A second element was a plan to disrupt the Cuban economy through sabotage of such major targets as sugar refineries. A third possibility was direct action to eliminate Cuban leaders Fidel and Raúl Castro and Che Guevara.

On March 9 the WH/4 task force learned that the DCI had prepared a special policy paper to be presented at the next meeting of the 5412 Group. The plan envisioned a Cuban exile force to be trained over a period of six or seven months. Allen Dulles feared that in the interim there might be a Cuban attack against the American-leased base at Guantánamo Bay, while J. C. King pointed out that, unless the top Cuban leaders could be eliminated in one "package," the operation might be a drawn-out affair, in which the Castro government would be overthrown only through the use of force.

A White House meeting the next day touched upon these themes again. The Cuba item was ninth on a long NSC agenda. In the discussion, the chief of naval operations, Admiral Arleigh Burke, opined that what was needed was a Cuban leader to unite anti-Castro factions. Many of the Cubans around Castro were worse than the "Maximum Leader" himself, Burke felt, and therefore "any plan for removal of Cuban leaders should be a package deal."

Allen Dulles observed that there were anti-Castro leaders but most of them were no longer in Cuba; he noted that the CIA was preparing a plan to deal with the Cuban situation.

The DCI's remark came in reply to President Eisenhower wondering what could be done:

Ike had said, "We might have another Black Hole of Calcutta in Cuba."

In fact, the main action on the Cuba plan occurred outside the NSC deliberations, in accord with Ike's December 1958 instructions, to Gordon Gray, that he did not wish the specifics of covert operations presented "at Council." Indeed, Allen Dulles had already met with Eisenhower and Gray on the Cuba matter. Accompanied by aides Dulles went armed with schematic, color drawings of sugar refineries and explained how CIA proposed to disrupt Cuban sugar production. The DCI presented the basic harassment plan.

Dwight Eisenhower listened patiently. "Allen, this is fine," Ike finally interjected, "but if you're going to make any move against Castro, don't just fool around with sugar refineries. Let's get a program that will really do something about Castro."

"Yes, sir!" the DCI responded crisply.

Dulles was back within weeks with a new plan, a scheme he unveiled on March 14, 1960, after the annual review of 5412 activities. Three days later, at 2:30 P.M. on Thursday the seventeenth, the President took the unusual step of himself convening a meeting of the 5412 Group in the Oval Office. The subject was the Cuba plan, and Dwight Eisenhower accepted it.

The CIA plan was embodied in a memorandum titled "A Program of Covert Action Against the Castro Regime" dated March 16, 1960. Its stated objective was "to bring about the replacement of the Castro regime with one more devoted to the true interests of the Cuban people and more acceptable to the U.S. in such a manner as to avoid any appearance of U.S. intervention." The essence of the program would be "to induce, support, and so far as possible direct action, both inside and outside of Cuba, by selected groups of Cubans." The plan envisioned that "since a crisis inevitably entailing drastic action in or toward Cuba could be provoked by circumstances beyond the control of the U.S. before the covert action program has accomplished its objective, every effort will be made to carry it out in such a way as progressively to improve the capability of the U.S. to act in a crisis."

Allen Dulles's subordinates at CIA's WH Division felt they would be able to create "a responsible, appealing and unified Cuban opposition" located outside Cuba, after which "a powerful propaganda offensive can be initiated in the name of the declared opposition." To undermine the base of Castro's popular support and spread the opposition message, a semicovert "gray" radio station would be established. The facility would broadcast on long- and shortwave bands and, in the original proposal memorandum, would probably be located on Swan Island. The CIA reported that work was already in progress toward the creation of a covert intelligence and action organization inside Cuba. It would be "responsive to the orders and directions of the 'exile' opposition."

Although the parmilitary staff presented the concept in fairly great detail, most of which remains classified, the CIA's budget estimate did not provide for the size the force eventually attained. The concept received the code name Pluto.

The paragraph on military action from the Pluto concept memorandum is worth quoting in full, as a later investigating committee chose to do:

Preparations have already been made for the development of an adequate paramilitary force outside of Cuba, together with mechanisms for the necessary logistical support of covert military operations on the island. Initially a cadre of leaders will be recruited after careful screening and trained as paramilitary instructors. In a second phase a number of paramilitary cadres will be trained at secure locations outside of the United States so as to be available for immediate deployment into Cuba to organize, train, and lead resistance forces recruited there after the establishment of one or more centers of resistance.

Preparations were expected to take six to eight months, although the CIA reported that a limited air capability "already exists under CIA control" and could easily be expanded. Within two months the Agency planned to supplement this with a similar capability under deep cover in another country.

Having approved the initial concept, the President settled back to await results. The CIA went ahead with propaganda plans as well as certain operations on the island, but no armed insurrection against Castro materialized. The CIA responded by increasing the size of Operation Pluto along with the numbers of cadre anticipated. By August the CIA had refined their plan, and presented it in a new memorandum to the President. On August 18 there was another White House meeting with Allen Dulles, 5412 Group officials, the chairman of the Joint Chiefs of Staff, and Treasury Secretary Robert Anderson, who headed an administration committee to coordinate trade policy on Cuba. This time the President approved measures for the implementation of the planning ordered in March.

Among those measures was a budget for Operation Pluto, which has been estimated at $13 million or $15 million. One day that summer Allen Dulles visited Maurice Stans, director of Eisenhower's Bureau of the Budget, to ask that the money be included in the CIA request for fiscal year 1962.

"It is needed," explained the DCI, "to supply and train somewhere in central America a group of exile Cubans who are preparing for a guerrilla invasion to overthrow Castro."

Stans questioned the expenditure, but the DCI refused to provide any CIA documentation in support of it. When Stans protested, Allen Dulles retorted angrily, "It's none of your damn business! If you question my authority go to the President and ask him."

Stans did exactly that but Dwight Eisenhower soothed his budget director with an explanation: "I authorized Dulles to spend that money but I did not authorize any specific military action by the anti-Castro Cubans. That will have to come later and I won't give it an OK unless I'm convinced it is essential and I'm convinced it won't fail." Stans went back to his office and wrote the Operation Pluto money into the budget request.

Ike probably rued the day in later years, but at a Cabinet meeting on August 18, 1960, the President confirmed his approval of Pluto funding and instructed the Pentagon to cooperate with the CIA in training Cubans, though he prohibited any use of American military personnel in combat. The Cuban operation clearly had support at the highest levels of the United States government.

Approval at the White House brought almost immediate action at CIA headquarters. In the offices of WH/4 the task force listened while Allen Dulles laid down the parameters for Operation Pluto and Dick Bissell supplied the details. Tracy Barnes, chief of DDP's functional Psychological and Paramilitary Staff, would be Bissell's man supervising the Cuba task force. He too did a lot of talking. Richard Helms sat quietly—rather out of character for him—frequently looking down at his fingernails. Soon Helms stopped coming to Pluto meetings altogether.

The silence of the DDP's chief of operations was attributed to his distaste for and opposition to the plan. Helms increasingly focused on running CIA's clandestine intelligence missions, leaving Cuba entirely to Bissell. But unlike Helms, Bissell had complete faith in Operation Pluto. So did Barnes and the WH/4 task force, which as yet comprised only ten officers. Jake Engler ran the unit and made day-to-day decisions that did not require policy choices. David Atlee Phillips, a veteran of Operation Success plus three years of service under journalistic cover in Batista's Cuba, headed psychological warfare. The two chiefs of political action were E. Howard Hunt, who had done the same during Guatemala, and Gerry Droller, an officer of European extraction who had no Latin America experience and did not speak Spanish.

The first component of Pluto to get under way was psychological warfare. Phillips met with Bissell about setting up a "black" radio station to beam unattributable anti-Castro programs into Cuba. The psychological action chief wanted six months of propaganda to prepare the ground in Cuba before any paramilitary operation. Bissell gave him a month to get the broadcasts going. Luckily the "psyops" people found in West Germany a surplus U.S. Army 50-kilowatt transmitter, which was about to be given to the Voice of America. The Agency managed to take over the medium-wave radio transmitter—three railroad cars worth of equipment. It was shipped to Swan Island in the Caribbean, where the Navy built a pier just to land the thing. Initial broadcasts were made on May 17, exactly thirty days after Bissell's orders.

Political action was more problematical. Operation Pluto was predicated on an active opposition to Castro. As will be seen, opposition within the island was mostly eradicated during the same months the CIA was creating its infrastructure for Operation Pluto. Among the exiles, meanwhile, it was possible to choose only between those who had had ties with Batista or those who had opposed him by aligning themselves with the Twenty-sixth of July Movement. President Eisenhower understood when he approved Operation Pluto that Batista supporters were not to be used in the operation; certain senior CIA officials also believed in this concept of a "third force," which in the Cuban context meant moderate M-26 adherents who had split with the *fidelistas* as the organization moved to the left. It so happened, however, that WH/4's political action chiefs held different views.

Howard Hunt was known within the Agency for his extreme conservatism. For Operation Pluto that meant that Hunt was largely unwilling to cooperate with any of the moderate former M-26 elements. Gerry Droller, on the other hand, was an opportunist who did not much care about the political coloration of his recruits. There would be continual friction on the subject of which Cubans to enlist, and, in addition, a personal antipathy quickly developed between Hunt and Droller.

The search for a surrogate Cuban political movement centered in Miami, where the CIA soon established a task force forward command post. The cover was an electronics firm that worked on government contracts, in order to explain the building's tight security and extensive communications equipment. Hunt became the Miami action officer while Droller worked out of Washington, posing as a steel tycoon on his visits to the forward base. By the end of May the CIA had forged sufficient political links to back the formation of a Cuban Democratic Revolutionary Front (FRD, or Frente Revolucionario Democrático) uniting five exile leaders and their groups. Later critics of the Cuban fiasco point out that this selection excluded fully 116 other Cuban political factions. Even so, the FRD proved to be an acrimonious alliance, hardly less contentious than that of Hunt and Droller.

By this time paramilitary preparations had also begun. Training for radio operators, who could be landed in Cuba to work with insurgents, began with a group of about twenty in May, on Useppa Island, off Fort Myers, Florida. At about that time, Bissell made a visit to the Panama Canal Zone, to inspect facilities that would be used for training a similarly sized cadre of guerrilla leaders. The first group of guerrilla recruits left on June 2 for Useppa Island, then went on to Panama for eight weeks at the CIA's secluded compound inside Fort Gulick. This group included José Perez San Roman, Manuel Artíme, and José Blanco, who would become leaders among the Cuban exiles.

Already it was becoming apparent that the original guerrilla concept would not work. The CIA decided to expand the exile force to several hundred men, but this required a much larger training facility. A logical choice for a location was Guatemala, where the Agency had turned out a government so easily in 1954. Robert K. Davis, now the station chief in Guatemala City, was told to find something suitable. Davis had good contacts in the local business community; finding a base turned out to be as easy as having lunch. Roberto Alejos, brother of the Guatemalan ambassador in Washington, volunteered his coffee plantation, named Helvetia, esconced in the Sierra Madre, Guatemala's Pacific coastal range. Alejos thought that all he would need for the Cubans to use the place was a few extra refrigerators. The CIA gladly provided them.

The changes of plan confused some officials outside the CIA, not least of them the President. On June 29, Ike told Gordon Gray he did not quite remember the details of the 5412 Group deliberations that had taken place on March 17. Gray reminded the President of the program Allen Dulles had presented and then reported "the current thinking as to the timetable of various events." Several weeks later, during Eisenhower's sojourn at Newport, Rhode Island, Gray further informed him of a new CIA proposal to expand training of exiles, use Guatemalan bases, and enlarge the budget to go with them.

Before the end of August the Guatemalan facility was ready, and on the twenty-second the cadre trainees were flown up from Fort Gulick. The radio operators had already been in place for over a month. Recruits for the rebel air force arrived on August 29, the first Cuban doctor for the exiles about a week later. The Helvetia base was called Camp Trax.

Training could not begin immediately. Alejos had just agreed to CIA use of his coffee plantation when the Agency determined to expand the exile force. Thus the first arrivals spent much time constructing barracks for those to follow. The first night a large number of Cubans were at Trax was August 27; soon afterward there were 160 recruits. In late September weapons arrived, training was provided by a group of twenty CIA contract personnel, including some Eastern Europeans, Mexicans, Chinese, and even a Filipino, José Valeriano, who had begun his CIA work with Ed Lansdale years before.

With the growing numbers of exiles and trainers involved in Operation Pluto, the CIA's cover story broke down. The early recruits had dealt with Americans who insisted they were working privately and had no government connections. The scale of Trax, the activities there, and the close cooperation with United States officials in Panama and Guatemala made it impossible to deny an official connection with the exile preparations. The Cubans knew better by late August and *New York Times* reporter Tad Szulc, in Costa Rica covering a conference of foreign ministers of the Organization of American States (OAS), learned of Operation Pluto from Cuban friends. Szulc checked with the State Department and was dissuaded from writing any story at that time.

Another potential leak was plugged in Florida. Local residents near Homestead had seen Cubans drilling and heard their loudspeakers at a farm. As a joke some firecrackers were thrown into the compound; the exiles thought they were under attack and poured from their quarters with guns blazing. A prankster was wounded, several Cubans arrested, and only a confidential request from federal authorities convinced local officials to drop charges. But a Miami newspaper got wind of the story, including the CIA connection with the exiles. In Washington, Allen Dulles received the reporter and his bureau chief and was able to convince them to kill the story.

Air power was a crucial element of the Pluto program. Transport between Florida and Guatemala was vital, but secrecy could not be maintained if United States military aircraft were used. On July 15, 1960, Allen Dulles approved a proposal to create a new CIA proprietary. In early August the Agency acquired cheaply—for exactly $307,506.10—all outstanding shares in the faltering Southern Air Transport. The air cargo line had a four-acre property, owned one C-46, and leased one other. Planes and crews from Air America quickly beefed up the Miami line, which carried recruits from a former Navy base at Opa-Locka to Guatemala.

The Florida run was used strictly for purposes of logistics. For Operation Pluto there had to be an actual rebel air force to fly supply missions to Cuba and provide air support for the exiles. This aspect of the program was held very closely by Dick Bissell, who set up an air staff of fourteen officers. It was supervised by Air Force colonel Stanley Beerli, who had previously run the U-2 program for the DDP. Recently, the whole U-2 effort had ground to a halt with the shooting down of Francis Gary Powers, but Bissell and Beerli were not held responsible and were able to concentrate on Operation Pluto. Bissell directed Guatemala station chief Bob Davis to set up an air base for the operation in that nation.

Bissell told Davis to have his airstrip functional within a month. The chief of station did his best, contracting an American construction firm already active in Guatemala, but construction was slowed by rain through much of the summer. The work also ran heavily over budget estimates, eventually costing $1.8 million, almost twice what had been provided for it. The airstrip was at Retalhuleu, about thirty miles from Camp Trax. There the CIA assembled an air force of fifteen B-26 bombers, five C-46 transports, plus 7 C-54's. Retalhuleu base was called the Hilton by the less comfortable exiles at Trax. The facilities there had to serve a much smaller contingent—among the exiles only five C-46 and seventeen B-26 crews plus mechanics. There were two American advisers, both former naval pilots. Retalhuleu was ready by late September.

In Washington the CIA's air staff soon decided that there were not enough aircraft crews. Some ninety-two Cuban exiles had been screened in Miami but not all could be accepted. This time the solution was to go against the President's express orders not to use Americans in combat roles—CIA officials approached the Alabama Air National Guard and asked its commander, Major General George R. Doster, to recruit crews who could be used in Operation Pluto. Within forty-five days of the October request, Doster had succeeded in recruiting a contingent of eighty Americans with experience in B-26 and C-54 aircraft. "Poppa" Doster and his men then joined the Cubans at Retalhuleu.

As for the component of the Cuba plan that involved a possible assassination of Fidel Castro, the CIA evidently made certain inquiries, and its Technical Services Division some preparations, but not much came of them. There were contacts between the Agency and the Mafia on an idea for the latter to execute the mission in the CIA's behalf. There was also a cable to the station in Havana, in July, advising that the action was being considered. Tracy Barnes, who had sent this cable, and Bissell, evidently kept the matter entirely in their own hands—Allen Dulles was not briefed until the fall of 1960, by which time the initiative had been sidetracked in favor of the more extensive combat option.

For Operation Pluto to work the exiles also needed a navy. Airdrops were fine as far as they went, but there were not enough aircraft to move or supply the large Cuban ground force being organized at Camp Trax. There was also a requirement to infiltrate guerrilla cadres before the landing. Acquiring another defunct company in the Florida Keys, which it called Mineral Carriers, the CIA got two large vessels and another base. The ships were converted landing craft infantry (LCI) left over from World War II, each displacing about 250 tons and capable of carrying two hundred men. Two CIA contract officers controlled this facet of Operation Pluto. One, Grayston Lynch, was a former Army Special Forces officer with service in Laos. The other was Rip Robertson, the CIA man who had been cashiered for allowing the bombing of the British freighter during Operation Success. Robertson apparently had been sneaked back onto the CIA payroll.

President Eisenhower's alleged motive for approving Operation Pluto was to counter a leftist or communist Fidel Castro. Despite this reasoning, at the time the go-ahead was given, Cuba did not even have diplomatic relations with the Soviet Union. Castro had accepted a visit from Soviet foreign minister Anastas Mikoyan, with a $100 million long-term loan, in February 1960, after the United States had refused credit to the Cubans. Actual exchanges of diplomats only occurred the following summer, after the CIA operation was already in motion.

Several strange incidents occurred in Cuba at this time. On February 19 a plane piloted by an American blew up while flying over the España refinery in Matanzas province. A month later, near Matanzas town, a second plane was shot down and two Americans captured. The captives, William L. Schergales and Howard Rundquist, were injured and hospitalized; one of them issued a statement that the Cuban government itself had hired them for the flight. The story could have been true or, just as likely, a bit of propaganda disinformation repeated by the American press.

There was also an incident in Havana harbor. The Pan American dock in the harbor, already nationalized by the government, was in use on March 4 for unloading of the French motor vessel *La Coubre*, which was carrying general cargo plus ammunition purchased by the Cubans from Belgium. Suddenly and without warning there was a blast, which blew away the ship's stern and most of its superstructure. Secondary explosions followed as the stacked munitions were engulfed in the flames that quickly spread. All the firefighting equipment in Havana was brought up to contain the blaze before it could reach the nearby Tallapiedra electric plant. Over a hundred people were killed or injured. Castro blamed the Americans; Washington denied it. The only sure fact was that the Compagnie Trans-Atlantique Française had lost a merchantman. A week later the Cubans expropriated their first three sugar mills.

As was previously noted, whatever opposition existed inside Cuba was extinguished before Operation Pluto got under way. Perhaps the strongest was Huber Matos, one of Fidel's original *commandantes* in the Sierra Maestra. Matos resigned in October 1959 to protest excesses of the revolution; he was arrested at home the next day by Fidel himself. Iginio "Nino" Diaz claimed to have a band in the hills outside Guantánamo until the spring of 1960, but the force never had a battle with *fidelistas* and Diaz, claiming a shortage of partisan recruits, soon turned up in Miami to make cause with the other exiles. In Oriente province an underground formed under Dr. Manuel Francisco Artíme, but when the industrial manager's letter of resignation appeared on the front page of a Havana newspaper, Artíme had to go into hiding and get the Americans to smuggle him off the island. Cuban engineer Manuel Ray, who had been M-26's underground chief for Havana and then Castro's minister of public works, also claimed to be organizing a network and wanted CIA help.

Political action people at the Agency gave all their assistance to the *frente*, the FRD. This made control of the united front group a critical issue for the Cuban exiles and led to the same divisiveness the committee was intended to avoid. Howard Hunt had a low opinion of "Manolo" Ray and did what he could to ensure that CIA support for Ray's own political group remained halfhearted. Hunt, also waging his bureaucratic battle against Gerry Droller, got the WH/4 political action chief proscribed from visiting Miami without permission. With CIA pouring at least $115,000 a month into the *frente* alone, there was plenty to fight over.

While the politicians argued, the little resistance inside Cuba was worn down. Ray did at least have a real group; the failure to cooperate with him at an earlier date proved a crucial mistake in Operation Pluto. There was another guerrilla band in the Escambray mountains of Oriente, led by Sierra Maestra veteran Captain Manuel Beaton. With estimated guerrilla strength at up to three hundred men, Beaton's band was denigrated by some as no more than a collection of his relatives. The first CIA supply drop into the Escambray came by a C-54 in early October. This plane was hit, lost an engine, and barely made a crash landing in Mexico. Pluto's cover again came close to being blown.

Airdrops into the Escambray became a substantial part of the activity of the base at Retalhuleu. Before Operation Pluto came to its end there would be sixty-eight supply missions flown, only seven of which were rated as successful. There were also more emergency landings in Jamaica and the Cayman Islands. By the spring of 1961 the meager supply drops and the blockade of the Escambray initiated by Castro's Fuerzas Armadas Revolucionarias (FAR) were starving out the guerrillas.

Seaborne expeditions were the other main means of infiltration into Cuba, the purpose of the *Barbara J* and *Blagar*, as the CIA called its two converted LCIs. The two craft were intended to work as mother ships, remaining in international waters as much as possible, while Cubans went in either on fast motorboats or quiet rubber rafts. Bissell recalls that there were quite a few infiltrations across beaches along the north coast, but that the agent teams were usually arrested after only a day or two ashore. In early 1961 the Cubans imported fast patrol ships and coastal radars from Russia, enabling them to blunt the seaborne maneuvers of the slower (14 knot) LCIs.

These failures were of prime importance to the paramilitary officers at WH/4. The final facet of Pluto to be nailed down was selecting leaders for the paramilitary component of the operation. A Marine colonel on detached service handled straight military matters, while the CIA side was placed under Richard Drain, recently returned from a posting as deputy chief of station in Athens. Drain was appointed only on October 1.

Assessing the situation, these paramilitary chiefs concluded that another expansion of Operation Pluto was in order. The exile unit would be increased to battalion size, a force of some 800 men. Recruiting lagged, however, and by November 20 the complement in Guatemala numbered only 420. The WH/4 paramilitary section also supervised the creation of training sites for exile landing craft crews at Lake Pontchartrain, Louisiana, and for frogmen at Vieques Island off Puerto Rico. These activities continued in the face of the failure of activities inside Cuba.

Meanwhile, the analytical component of CIA, the Directorate of Intelligence, had been cut completely out of the action on Operation Pluto. The analysts did not "need to know" about the planned uprising. As a result, they could not furnish effective intelligence support to the paramilitary planners. The chief analyst, DDI Robert Amory, Jr., was not even told in confidence about Pluto.

On October 30 the Guatemala City daily *La Hora* published an article revealing the existence of Camp Trax and the Cuban exile training there. This report was picked up by *Hispanic American Report*, a regional studies newsletter published by Dr. Ronald Hilton of Stanford University. The Stanford piece, in turn, led to an editorial in the November 19, 1960, issue of *The Nation*.

To cap it all, the Cuban force at Trax was then deliberately used to intervene in Guatemalan politics. On November 14 some army officers revolted against President Miguel Ydigoras Fuentes, who was responsible for allowing the CIA to operate in Guatemala. Cuban exile units from Trax were deployed to Guatemala City and to Puerto Barrios to disarm the rebels. The U.S. Navy also responded, dispatching Amphibious Squadron 10 to the Caribbean with the helicopter carrier *Boxer*, five destroyers, and a contingent of two thousand Marines. Ydigoras was saved and with him CIA's privileges in the country. As a by-product of the intervention, however, the existence of the Cuban unit was inevitably revealed.

Further, the CIA itself contributed to rupturing the secrecy of

Pluto. In an effort to stimulate recruitment among Cuban exiles in Miami, Howard Hunt conceived the idea of taking pictures of Trax. This was done, the pictures were distributed widely, and soon found their way to publication in the *Miami Herald*. Sets of the photos even reached the Cuban government—the Ministry of Information released them to a Havana newspaper.

In Eisenhower's councils after November 1960, it was no longer possible to argue that Operation Pluto was a secret. The most that could be claimed was that the details of the operation remained secret. Total surprise would be impossible.

President Eisenhower had good reason for being frustrated with the repeated recasting of Pluto, as well as with leaks about the operation. Ike was also unsuccessful in rallying hemispheric support for sanctions against Cuba. The President had been keen on this during his state visit to South America in the spring of 1960, but the Latin heads of state were decidedly unenthusiastic. That August the Organization of American States (OAS) also failed to pass the kind of tough resolution sought by the administration to back its Cuba endeavor.

Economic relations were the one area in which the administration pretty much had its way, once the cycle of expropriation by the Cubans and American retaliation had become firmly established. Ike continued to be pleased by the performance of Bob Anderson, who coordinated United States trade actions. In mid-March the United States revoked an export license already issued for a sale of helicopters to Havana. Two months later all existing aid programs were terminated. In July the quota for Cuban sugar was drastically reduced after congressional amendment of the law permitted such revisions. On his side, Fidel had nationalized the entire Cuban sugar industry by October 14. The administration answered with an embargo on almost all trade to Cuba, decreed on October 19, 1960.

Political relations deteriorated with the evaporation of trade. Twice during 1960 the United States ambassador, Phillip Bonsal, was recalled from Havana for "consultations" to punish the Cubans. After Castro demanded withdrawal of half the embassy personnel, the United States, on January 3, 1961, ended all diplomatic relations with Cuba.

Termination of relations occurred after Operation Pluto had expanded yet again. The new concept was aired at a full-scale briefing in Allen Dulles's office the week after the 1960 presidential election: guerrilla infiltration was to be abandoned in favor of a conventional amphibious landing. The Cuban exiles would establish a beachhead, fly in their FRD executive committee to declare a provisional government, and then request United States assistance. Action on the plan had already begun—on November 4, Trax had been instructed to switch from guerrilla to conventional training for all but sixty of the Cuban recruits.

The plan for a conventional invasion went to the 5412 Group on November 16, to President-elect John F. Kennedy on the twenty-seventh, and was presented to Eisenhower two days later. Ike instructed his subordinates to expedite preparations but did not make any final decision on the conventional-invasion option.

At the November 29 meeting, President Eisenhower questioned whether Pluto was sufficiently imaginative and bold, given the need for plausible deniability, and whether things were being done effectively. Ike repeated the concerns of William D. Pawley, a well-informed businessman who had complained to the President about the size of the operation and political character of the *frente* (too far to the left, Pawley felt). The President said he was unhappy about the general situation. Referring to the transition of administrations, Ike also commented he did not want to be "in the position of turning over the government in the midst of a developing emergency."

Most officials present agreed that the size of Operation Pluto should be expanded to two thousand or even three thousand exiles, though Allen Dulles warned this would require training bases other than Trax. As for the *frente*, the DCI defended the CIA's choice among the Cubans.

On December 8 the 5412 Group met again to go over much of the same ground. The CIA briefed the group on the conventional-invasion option, including the latest planning developments. The Agency also complained that the Pentagon was dragging its feet in assisting Pluto, specifically by refusing to release Special Forces personnel for temporary duty training the exiles.

It was true. Since August the Office of Special Operations, which advised the secretary of defense on covert operations, had been registering objections to Pluto; both Graves Erskine and Ed Lansdale had voiced criticisms. Lansdale was especially acerbic in his comments to Undersecretary James H. Douglas, who was representing the Pentagon at these Cuba meetings. In the discussion on December 8, Douglas agreed to recommend the release of twenty-seven Special Forces advisers but made it clear the Pentagon in no way supported the CIA plan.

For his part, Eisenhower worried that there was not enough synchronization among different agencies on Operation Pluto. On December 7 the President approved the selection of special representatives at CIA and State who would serve as focal points in the bureaucracy for all matters related to the Cuba operation. Dick Bissell chose Tracy Barnes as his representative; State's man was Whiting Willauer, who had done so well during Operation Success in maintaining the Honduras base for the CIA's Guatemala coup.

The leaders of the secret war gathered again on January 3, 1961, to discuss both ending diplomatic relations and the progress of Pluto. Dick Bissell reported that Ydigoras of Guatemala had asked for the Cubans to be removed from his country by March 1, and that the exiles' own morale would suffer if they did not see action by that time. Willauer agreed that there was also a time problem with the OAS and that the only suitable alternative to Guatemala would be training on American bases, a suggestion that had been repeatedly rejected already. There was, however, considerable confidence in the exile troops—Gordon Gray mentioned an observer's report that called the Cubans the best army in Latin America. Although he warned of some equipment shortages, General Lyman D. Lemnitzer agreed.

President Eisenhower summarized: The only two reasonable alternatives were supporting the Cubans to go in March or abandoning the operation.

Exactly one week later a detailed account of the Cuban training in Guatemala by Tad Szulc was on the front page of *The New York Times.*

Did the President bequeath his successor a "developing emergency"?

President Eisenhower's administration ended with the Cuban operation in mid-course. Only two days before the inauguration of John F. Kennedy, Ike's councils were still uncovering problems with Pluto that could only be passed along. It was left to Jack Kennedy to choose between the alternatives that Ike had summarized on January 3. It was a tough choice for a novice President.

By not confronting that choice himself, Eisenhower has left questions history has yet to resolve. The consequent CIA failure at the Bay of Pigs has usually been cast as the fault of the Kennedy people, who came in implicitly trusting the secret warriors. Eisenhower had been sitting at the apex of the secret war for eight years; he knew better. He knew the difficulties with the 5412 Group, the CIA's penchant for keeping implementation issues out once approvals had been given, and the conflicts between military and civilian intelligence agencies. Ike also knew the current status of Pluto and the specific problems of the Cuban operation. On January 3, or up until the time that JFK stood to take his oath of office, President Eisenhower could have shut down the Cuba operation with just a few words. But he didn't.

The recently declassified memoranda of the Operation Pluto meetings in December 1960 and January 1961 reveal that the arguments Kennedy was given to continue the operation were well rehearsed. Before JFK assumed office, many in high places were aware there were significant weaknesses in the CIA's operation plan. It was clear that Castro's FAR forces were much more powerful than any force the exiles could raise. Moreover, the point had also been raised, by State on January 3, that American forces would have to back up an invasion force. The conditions necessary for success simply had not been created.

On the morning of the inauguration, as they left for the ceremonial motorcade to the site, Ike advised JFK to do whatever was needed to ensure the success of the Cuba operation.

Eisenhower believed in the secret war. His administration had consistently made efforts to improve the efficiency and range of covert operations while protecting both presidential control and plausible deniability. These aims were just too ambitious. In the operations themselves, failures were as common as gains, while leaks routinely occurred. Mechanisms designed to preserve plausible deniability had deteriorated to such a degree that the President allowed himself to become a principal participant in special group discussions of the Cuba operation.

Control of covert action would seem to imply the imposition of some discipline in the costs of these activities. But, such spending data as are available indicate that *no* major operation of this period was accomplished within the original budget estimated. Operation Ajax in Iran was estimated as low as $100,000 or $200,000, but cost

$10 million. Operation Success cost twice as much as the $10 million allotted to it. Before the last failure of a Cuba operation, the $13 million or $15 million estimated for Operation Pluto would mushroom to something over $100 million. It seems that once the aim of a covert operation was accepted, the controls were thrown away.

The question of direct American involvement in Operation Pluto also illustrates that the control system had gone awry. That no Americans were to be involved in combat was one of the fundamental assumptions. After the fiasco in Indonesia it is doubtful whether Ike would have accepted any direct American involvement. But, before the end of his administration, Americans were flying with the Cuban rebel air force, and CIA agents were commanding the rebel LCI mother ships.

Two years after President Kennedy's tragic death, Dwight Eisenhower would maintain, in interviews and in his memoir *Waging Peace*, that he had never approved a specific invasion plan because the exiles had never had a unified political leadership. According to Ike there had been a "program" but no plan. This recollection is supported by Ike's son and some others from the White House staff. Yet the date on the CIA's plan for a conventional invasion around Trinidad, Cuba, is December 6, 1960. There was a date for the invasion, too—March 1961—as well as a specific timetable for invasion-related events.

Ike's memory is correct only in a technical sense: Approval was withheld from *the* invasion plan because the President's counselors found problems with it. Eisenhower nevertheless had approved *an* invasion plan, and he knew that John Kennedy was entering office without the detailed understanding of the evolution of Operation Pluto that would have facilitated a decision. Not acting to halt the operation was tantamount to an approval—the only real question remaining was the landing site.

At numerous meetings on Pluto, Gordon Gray remembers, the President repeated one conclusion he had reached. "Now boys," Ike would say, "if you don't intend to go through with this, let's stop talking about it."

·XI·

CUBA II: FROM PLUTO TO MONGOOSE

John Fitzgerald Kennedy swept into office with a confidence that belied the narrow margin of his victory in the 1960 elections. Though President Kennedy's "New Frontier" offered fresh visions of America's role, actual policies on questions like Cuba changed not a whit. Though the President dismantled much of the NSC structure created by his predecessor, no doubt with the notion of moving away from a certain fancied passivity with which critics had tarred the Eisenhower administration, Kennedy made no changes whatever in the leadership of the CIA.

The secret war went on much as before, with the sole difference that the mechanisms established to control it temporarily disappeared. Later we shall see continuities in the operations that both administrations carried out in Southeast Asia, but the most obvious continuity was in Cuba. That disaster decisively demonstrated the fallacy of abolishing controls over the intelligence community.

Problems with the Cuban exile force seemed to be growing daily. Besides discussions in the Miami and Havana newspapers and revelations in *The New York Times,* there were difficulties at Camp Trax itself. Officials at CIA expressed concern that the Pentagon was still dragging its feet with respect to cooperation. Without Special Forces trainers, they believed, the Cubans could not be ready before late 1961.

The exiles themselves posed the biggest problem. At Retalhuleu the Cuban pilots resented the handling of air operations and being excluded from the base's little social club. A number of them staged a strike to protest working conditions. At Camp Trax the Cubans also resented their living conditions, compared to those of the American trainers, who lived in Roberto Alejos's plantation hacienda at the top of the hill. Further, when the Cubans attempted to elect their own leaders, the Americans insisted on selecting the commanders for the expanded unit. These conditions resulted in a virtual mutiny in January 1961.

So serious was the situation that José San Roman, the Americans' candidate for the top command, resigned the post to reenlist as a private. During the crisis the Americans asked the Cubans to turn in their weapons. Some 230 of the exiles, including the entire 2nd and 3rd "battalions," also tried to resign and 100 of them remained adamant even after a solution to the crisis was patched together. Howard Hunt and several of the FRD political leaders flew to the base and exhorted the men in speeches. For the moment, the crisis passed, but the troops clearly had to be sent into action soon.

Meanwhile, the Cubans suffered their first training casualty. He was Carlos Rodriguez Santana, recruit number 2,506, who died in a mountain fall. In memory of him the Cubans adopted the unit designation Brigade 2506. San Roman remained in command of a force that eventually totaled about 1,400 men. The brigade was organized into six small "battalions" and a heavy-weapons group. Men of the 1st Battalion were trained as paratroopers; those of the 4th constituted a small armored force with five M-41A2 tanks plus trucks that mounted .50-caliber machine guns. The weapons unit contained 4.2-inch mortars, 3.5-inch bazookas, and 57- and 75-millimeter recoilless rifles. The "battalions" ranged in strength from 167 to 185 men, somewhat fewer than standard rifle companies in the U.S. Army. There was also a commando force of 168 men intended to make a diversion at another point on the Cuban coast while the main landing was in progress.

Richard Bissell expected to be able to send reinforcements into the Brigade 2506 beachhead once the invasion began. An additional 300 recruits were gathered in the Miami area, of whom some 162 actually would be moved to the Central American bases. Total reinforcements available were later put at about 500. Arms for 4,000 Cubans would also be landed.

Finally, there was the exile air force under the nominal command of Major Manuel Villafaña. The air group numbered over 150 Cubans, with an equal number of Americans, both as aircrew and in support roles. The combat element consisted of sixteen B-26 bombers, the air transport unit of eight C-46's and six C-54's. In yet another demonstration of the rapidly eroding secrecy surrounding Operation Pluto, in its January 27, 1961, issue, *Time* magazine printed a photograph of Cuban rebel aircraft sitting on the ground at the Retalhuleu base.

In Washington on the day the *Time* photo appeared, President Kennedy attended his first full-scale presentation on the Cuba project. During the presidential campaign, JFK had twice been briefed by Allen Dulles on international matters in general, including the Cuba situation; but Kennedy had not been made privy to the covert plan. Because Jack Kennedy had not been "witting" on Operation Pluto, there had been something of a flap in late October within Richard Nixon's entourage. Kennedy declared in a speech that the United States should train and aid Cuban "freedom fighters" against Castro. Not only was this precisely what was being done under Pluto, but "freedom fighters" was exactly what the exiles were being called in Ike's secret councils.

But Kennedy did not know of Operation Pluto—the reference in his speech was selected innocently by writer Richard Goodwin to inject a note of dynamism into the candidate's pronouncement. Pluto was first broached with JFK when Allen Dulles and Bissell visited him at Palm Beach on November 27, 1960. Bissell briefly outlined the plans, after which the pipe-toting DCI took Kennedy into the back garden for a private conversation, presumably to secure the President-elect's approval. Although the substance of that discussion is unknown, shortly afterward Howard Hunt learned from Tracy Barnes that JFK had given a "qualified go-ahead" to Pluto, leading to various actions during the last days of the Eisenhower administration that have already been described.

While the Palm Beach discussion had been general and exploratory, the White House meeting on January 27 was specific and detailed. It focused not so much on the conventional-invasion plan as on a comparison of that option with six other alternatives, including economic warfare and blockade. An intelligence report from the Office of National Estimates, which also had been kept in ignorance of Pluto, concluded that Castro was successfully consolidating his power. The new President ordered an accentuation of political action, sabotage, and overflights by the CIA; a review of CIA plans by the Joint Chiefs of Staff; and preparation of an anti-Castro propaganda plan by the State Department that could be implemented throughout Latin America.

Though the President's initial orders seemed restrained, Kennedy proceeded to rob himself of the machinery Eisenhower had created to exercise close control. The oversight device of the 5412 Group was superseded by meetings at which JFK himself presided. More than ever before business was transacted directly with the new NSC staff, yet Kennedy showed little interest in consulting Ike's White House staff secretary, Andrew Goodpaster, who had most of the relevant information at his fingertips. Kennedy also abolished the President's Board of Consultants on Foreign Intelligence Activities, the only mechanism specifically intended for intelligence oversight. Finally, in an action that had special impact on interagency coordination for Operation Pluto, on February 8 the State-CIA group headed by Whiting Willauer and Tracy Barnes passed out of existence.

In this fashion President Kennedy satisfied his desire for direct leadership, eliminating the levels of staff offices within the NSC that he thought had stifled government under his predecessor. What the new President did not see was the positive value of these institutions. Unlike Ike, JFK would have no interagency staffs senior enough to get things done on their own, and no council of officials capable of providing a second opinion on what the President heard from his advisers.

Events now began to move swiftly toward their disastrous conclusion. A few days after Kennedy's orders, the Joint Chiefs of Staff were officially briefed on the CIA's plan for the conventional invasion. This provided for a landing on the south coast, near the town of Trinidad and the Escambray mountains. The Joint Chiefs' official opinion, after a few days of study, was tendered in the paper numbered JCSM 57-61 and titled "Military Evaluation of the CIA Paramilitary Plan—Cuba."

The seventeen conclusions in the JCS paper indicated continuing divisions of opinion regarding Pluto. On the one hand, the military judged that the airborne drop should be successful, that it would take several days for Castro to assemble large FAR forces against the landing, and that, despite its shortcomings, the CIA plan had a fair chance of success. On the other hand, they observed that the Cuban army could eventually reduce the beachhead.

The military's warning about the beachhead implied that a rapid breakout from the landing site was necessary. But the CIA's own view, contained in a January 4, 1961, report to Gerry Droller, "Policy Decisions Required for Conduct of Strike Operations Against Government of Cuba," was quite the opposite: Brigade 2,506 should try to survive in the beachhead and not break out until the time was opportune or the United States intervened openly. Indeed, the CIA political action specialists had plans to fly in the Cuban politicians to form a provisional government while the logistics people made careful arrangements for supply landings throughout the first month on the beachhead. The conflicting views of military and CIA were not reconciled, and President Kennedy now lacked the supervisory staffs to tell him this was the case.

American intervention was clearly a sensitive matter. CIA paramilitary officers understood the necessity for disabling the FAR naval and air forces that could intercept the exile landing. Although a fairly extensive program of exile air strikes had been laid on, it was known in advance that Castro possessed some jet fighters. The exiles had no comparable aircraft. Support by American jets was the most obvious form intervention might take, and it had been mentioned both by CIA officers and Whiting Willauer. Yet the President took a different stand.

On February 9 clarification was sought by Admiral Robert L. Dennison, commander of the Navy's Atlantic Fleet. At a discussion with Kennedy the admiral asked, "Am I likely to be involved in a bail-out operation?"

"No," replied the President; if there were any problems, the exiles would fade into the hinterland; American forces would not become overtly involved.

The next day Dennison received a directive from Joint Chiefs chairman General Lyman Lemnitzer defining the scope of and restrictions on U.S. Navy support for the invasion, which was clearly to be minimal.

By mid-February it was apparent that Operation Pluto could not make the planned invasion date of March 5; the operation was delayed for a month. The Guatemalans had to be asked to accommodate the exile force during the delay. The military took advantage of the extra time to dispatch three colonels on an inspection tour of Camp Trax and Retalhuleu. Their assessment was that the brigade seemed to be in good shape but that the odds against achieving surprise were something like 17 to 3. The air evaluation stated that one Castro plane with .50-caliber machine guns could sink most or all the invasion fleet—so if surprise was not achieved the operation would fail.

How could the President interpret the conflicting reports that reached him? He turned to Allen Dulles one day in the Oval Office and questioned him about the odds. The DCI alluded to his own discussion with President Eisenhower on the eve of the Guatemalan project, Operation Success. "I stood right here at Ike's desk," said Dulles, "and told him I was certain our Guatemalan operation would succeed, and, Mr. President, the prospects for this plan are even better than they were for that one."

Despite his doubts, Kennedy, in the retrospective opinion of his NSC staff chief, McGeorge Bundy, now kept looking for ways to make Pluto work. At a full-dress presentation of the Trinidad plan by Bissell on March 11, the President rejected this kind of "spectacular" invasion and asked for an alternative, but nevertheless then approved National Security Action Memorandum (NSAM) 31, which stated that he expected to approve the invasion.

Over the next few days a flurry of activity at WH/4 produced a new plan for a landing around the Bay of Pigs, about eighty miles west of Trinidad. In just two days the paramilitary planners were able to present the Bay of Pigs option to the Joint Chiefs of Staff, and the Joint Chiefs met on it on March 15. Later that day both options were outlined again for JFK at the White House. The President rejected Trinidad again as a "World War II assault operation" unsuitable as a paramilitary plan; he also directed that the Bay of Pigs plan itself be reoriented to provide for a night as opposed to a dawn landing. Again there was no one to tell the President that the United States had never carried out a major nighttime invasion. Final approval followed on March 16. Only then was an interdepartmental working group established to oversee implementation of Operation Pluto.

The President was infected with the enthusiasm of his CIA paramilitary specialists. He thought the military approved, but was not aware how little they had actually had to do with the plans. There were some voices in opposition to Pluto, notably Arthur Schlesinger, then a Latin American policy adviser and sort of court historian; Chester Bowles, Undersecretary of State in the new administration; Truman's former secretary of state, Dean Acheson; and

JFK's recent Senate colleague William J. Fulbright. But their warnings were dismissed by a President who wanted to look tough.

One important issue that remained to be considered was the image of the United States in world public opinion. Plausible deniability was necessary for covert actions precisely so that leaders might deny American involvement. An important forum for world opinion was the United Nations General Assembly, then in session in New York City, where a Cuba debate was already on the agenda. Kennedy had appointed Adlai Stevenson his ambassador to the UN and felt Adlai's integrity was a vital asset in the world forum. Kennedy ordered Arthur Schlesinger to brief the ambassador together with CIA and State Department people.

Unfortunately, Schlesinger arrived late for the meeting in Stevenson's suite at the Waldorf-Astoria Hotel on the morning of Saturday, April 8, so Tracy Barnes, CIA's man on the team, carried out most of the briefing. Steeped in the Agency's "need to know" tradition, Barnes provided only the most cursory of overviews, shorn of the details that could have enabled the ambassador to play his role effectively. Barnes's reticence was probably encouraged by the ambassador's reaction—Stevenson doubted that Kennedy had thought through the problem in approving the invasion. Within days the effect of Tracy Barnes's inadequate description would become painfully apparent.

Meanwhile, the implementation of Pluto was accelerating. Two final postponements resulted in an invasion set for April 17. On April 1, Admiral Dennison got his basic marching orders in JCSM 365-61. The Navy would reinforce Guantánamo in case Castro moved against it, and provide a task force built around the carrier *Essex* that could furnish air cover if required. The destroyers *Eaton* and *Murray* with their superior navigation equipment would convey the invasion fleet from a rendezvous point to the Bay of Pigs, while the amphibious ship *San Marcos* carried landing craft for the Cubans with their vehicles and some supplies. A submarine would carry out a diversion at another point on the Cuban coast. Dennison's major task force was instructed to avoid overt association with the exile fleet.

The invasion itself was not mounted from Guatemala but from Puerto Cabezas in Nicaragua, codenamed *trampoline*. The rebel navy began to assemble there at the beginning of April, starting with the CIA's two LCIs, the *Blagar* and *Barbara J.* Five merchant ships of the Garcia Shipping Company had also been chartered by CIA to carry the bulk of Brigade 2,506. On April 10 the exile force began to move from Trax and the other bases to Trampoline, where a base force of 316, including 159 Americans, assisted in loading. The first ship sailed on April 11, the fastest vessels on the thirteenth. The next day, Tracy Barnes and a senior paramilitary man went to New York again to inform the Cuban exile politicians.

President Kennedy was still reserving his final decision, and had the option to cancel Operation Pluto up to twenty-four hours before the action began. Although a military man sent down to observe loading operations reported back that the situation was chaos and the shipping inadequate, the President's last qualms were evidently resolved by another cable from a Marine colonel:

> My observations have increased my confidence in the ability of this force to accomplish not only initial combat missions but also the ultimate objective, the overthrow of Castro. The Brigade and battalion commanders now know all details of the plan and are very enthusiastic. These officers are young, vigorous, intelligent, and motivated with a fanatical urge to begin battle. . . . They say they know their people and believe after they have inflicted one serious defeat upon the opposition forces, the latter will melt away from Castro. . . . I share their confidence.
>
> The Brigade is . . . more heavily armed and better equipped in some respects than U.S. infantry units. The men have received . . . more firing experience than U.S. troops would normally receive. I was impressed with the serious attitude of the men.

The President gave his go-ahead. When it was all over and the Brigade leaders had returned from captivity, this cable was shown to them by a reporter researching the battle. They insisted unanimously that, until the final moment of embarkation, they had been told nothing about the actual plan.

The crucial first action of Pluto was the effort to destroy the FAR air force. If Castro's airplanes were not eliminated, they would pose a tremendous threat to the invasion fleet. The FAR inventory included six B-26 bombers, four T-33 jet trainers modified to be fighters, and two to four British-made Sea Fury fighters. Principal bases were at Havana and Santiago. Under the plan a surprise air attack was scheduled for two days before the invasion, and any of Castro's planes remaining would be bombed at dawn following the landing. That was the plan, but reality turned out somewhat differently.

It was hoped to conceal the exiles' hand in the bombing by claiming the air strikes were being carried out by pilots defecting from Castro's forces. To this end the CIA acquired two extra B-26 bombers whose missions were simply to fly from Nicaragua to Florida where the pilots would give out this cover story. The real strike would be conducted by eleven bombers that would hit six Cuban air bases. This was then scaled back to three main fields hit by six bombers.

Bombing and strafing of the airfields was successful as far as it went. The exile planes achieved surprise, about half of Castro's air force was in fact destroyed shortly after dawn on April 15, 1961.

But almost immediately the plans started unraveling because the CIA cover story fell apart. The exile planes detailed for this purpose reached Florida as planned. One landed at Opa-Locka, the other at Miami International Airport where its pilot, Mario Zuñiga, recited the prearranged story that disaffected FAR crews were responsible. His B-26 was photographed by the press and the pictures were flashed almost immediately to New York where the United Nations session had turned to Cuba.

The pictures clearly showed FAR markings, which the CIA had thoughtfully painted on the aircraft. Adlai Stevenson exhibited them in the debate and used them as the basis for a strong statement denying any American complicity in the action. But the photos showed too much—the Miami B-26 had one of those special nose assemblies with machine guns, which had been devised in 1958 for the Indonesia operation; Castro's B-26's had plastic noses for a bombardier's work space. An enterprising reporter discovered that the Miami bomber's machine guns were taped up and thus could not have been fired. It also strained credulity that a bunch of spontaneous defectors could have launched a coordinated strike that appeared simultaneously over several different bases. In addition, Henry Raymont, the UPI reporter then in Havana, had seen the strike planes and saw no markings on them. Adlai Stevenson's statement was exposed as a fabrication, and the ambassador himself quickly realized he had been poorly informed by Tracy Barnes.

President Kennedy was embarrassed at this turn of events. He determined to send McGeorge Bundy up to New York to give a fuller account to Stevenson but could do little about the next portion of the CIA plan—a diversionary landing was scheduled for Oriente province that night and the last minute to cancel it had already passed.

This diversion, however, failed of its own accord. The Garcia lines ship *La Plata* was carrying 168 men of a group under Nino Diaz who were supposed to make Castro think theirs was the real invasion. The week before, the team of specially trained exiles that was supposed to guide the men to the beach had been wiped out in an accident with a hand grenade. A new group detailed for this mission approached the shore, thirty miles east of Guantanamo, only to see some Cuban troops guarding the beach, a rocky one that would complicate landing. Another try the next night also failed; heavy seas were blamed.

Meanwhile, Colonel Stanley Beerli at the CIA's Air Operations Center was laying the groundwork for a follow-up air strike to neutralize the remainder of the FAR air force. Beerli and his assistants were selecting targets from the latest U-2 photographs when fate again intervened, in the person of the deputy director of CIA, General Charles P. Cabell.

Cabell was in charge that weekend because Allen Dulles, as part of the cover, had decided to go ahead with a speaking engagement in Puerto Rico he had accepted some time previously. Returning from a golfing date in sport shirt and slacks, Cabell learned of the latest bombing plan and asked if it had been approved. He was clearly aware of the administration's embarrassment at the United Nations, and though Beerli insisted everything was fine, Cabell wanted to check with Secretary of State Dean Rusk. Within a few minutes, McGeorge Bundy, alerted by Rusk, called in to report that the President had decided that no strikes could be launched until Brigade 2,506 had captured an airstrip inside Cuba, which could be claimed as the base for the exile bombers.

At this point, Richard Bissell was called in, and he and Cabell appealed directly to Rusk, who rejected their entreaties. Both CIA officials protested vigorously; Rusk finally agreed to phone the President and put their arguments before him. JFK again rejected the air strike and Cabell refused an offer to speak to the President directly. Air missions were restricted to direct support over the beaches. There would be thirteen B-26 sorties on the day of the invasion but none of them against the FAR bases. Castro's air force would have its chance.

Now it was all up to Brigade 2,506. The fleet of four ships and two LCIs arrived off the Bay of Pigs on schedule. Except for three large landing craft with the vehicles and four for personnel, all brought by the American amphibious ship, the Cubans were dependent on small fiber-glass boats with outboard motors. These would slow down the operation. At least the beaches were marked—against orders that no Americans were to be directly involved, Rip Robertson and Grayston Lynch led frogman teams onto the shore to accomplish this.

The parachute drop of the 1st Battalion was successful as well. These men took up positions to block Castro's reinforcements near Covadonga and the sugar plantation Central Australia. The main landing occurred at the resort Girón, called Blue Beach, where the CIA's experienced photo interpreters had failed to detect the offshore reefs, in fact, agency men even repudiated the observations of exiles who had vacationed at Girón and knew the reefs well. As a result, some of the landing boats were destroyed on the reefs while, as the tide fell, unloading came to a halt.

Dawn found most of the Cubans ashore, but with far less than the planned seventy-two tons of supplies. In addition, the invasion fleet, which was to have withdrawn, was still in place off the beaches. That was when Castro's air force made its contribution: In two strikes, at six-thirty and at nine A.M., Sea Fury aircraft sank the ships *Houston* and *Rio Escondido*, the former still containing many supplies and 130 men of the 5th Battalion. The survivors had to swim ashore without equipment, into the salt marshes of the Zapata Peninsula, across the bay from the Brigade positions. *Rio Escondido* went down with the Brigade's communications van and aviation gasoline intended for use at the Girón airstrip.

One major landing point was at Playa Larga, called Red Beach, at the head of the Bay of Pigs and almost thirty miles by road from Girón. There, the troops of the 2nd Battalion got ashore in good order. With Brigade 2,506's impaired communications, however, it was hours before Red Beach was able to get in touch with exile commander "Pepe" San Roman at Girón. The battalion at Playa Larga was in good position to move north and reinforce the paratroops landed near Central Australia but they got no orders. By the time San Roman had established radio contact, yet another CIA error was becoming evident.

One of the big assumptions throughout the planning stages was that Castro would need days to react to the landings. Exile officers had specifically been told just before embarkation that there would be no resistance forces at the Bay of Pigs, that FAR would require until D plus two, the second day after the invasion, to mount significant opposition. Bissell and the other planners repeatedly used this estimate, yet their confidence in it was striking given their considerable ignorance of conditions in Cuba. Admiral Dennison in his own planning had submitted a list of ninety specific questions on Castro forces, and twenty-nine on the Cuban resistance, as early as December 1960; less than a dozen were answered.

The paramilitary specialists had been wrong about the reefs at Girón; they were also wrong in believing that no Castro forces would be in the landing area. About a hundred militia guarded Girón and its vicinity and a larger force, the FAR 339th Militia Battalion was at Central Australia where they were already putting pressure on the paratroops north of Playa Larga.

At the time of the first invasion scare in December, FAR mobilization orders had created great confusion. Repeated subsequent scares created a highly efficient system, however, plus Castro had had two days since the surprise air attacks to set his forces in motion. This time there were no mistakes; large forces, including armor, were deployed against the exile brigade from the very first day. By early morning of the second day, April 18, the exiles had been driven back from Central Australia and Playa Larga, and FAR tanks were moving down the road to Girón. The paratroop roadblocks near Covadonga on the opposite flank of the bridgehead were also in retreat.

Yet another mistaken estimate on the part of the Directorate of Plans was that large numbers of Cubans would join Brigade 2,506. The DDP's reports spoke of 3,000 to 5,000 active guerrillas at a time when the estimates prepared by the Office of National Estimates and the Directorate of Intelligence showed no such large-scale resistance. A few bands did exist; their only significant accomplishment in this period was the burning, on April 14, of El Encanto, Cuba's largest department store, and the sabotage of two "intervened" Woolworth stores and the Hershey sugar mill warehouse. Put on guard by these incidents and the surprise bombing,

Castro's police arrested anyone who might have any reason to oppose the government—20,000 people by some accounts. In any case, there was no mass uprising. Only about 50 Cubans joined the exiles.

Brigade 2506 had no real chance. On the second day, Pepe San Roman's troops were driven back on all fronts. The Cuban pilots of Major Villafaña's air force were also demoralized after losing two of their planes on D day. To shore them up, Bissell now authorized combat missions by the American contract crews. The biggest success of April 18 was a strike against the Castro column advancing from Playa Larga, but the nine sorties carried out that day and night, each of which could spend only about twenty minutes over the Bay of Pigs, was a severely limited capability. In addition, two American-crewed B-26's were shot down by Castro's jets with the loss of Riley Shamburger, Wade C. Gray, Willard Ray, and Leo F. Baker. They were American casualties in a war that, according to President Kennedy, as recently as his April 12 news conference, was strictly between Cubans with no United States participation.

By the third day, April 19, Brigade 2506 had virtually exhausted its ammunition. The ships of the invasion fleet, carrying the supplies, had become demoralized and scattered. They had to be rounded up by Dennison's naval vessels. *Blagar* and *Barbara J* with their CIA commanders maintained better discipline, but they carried little. Amid frantic appeals from Pepe San Roman and the CIA chain of command, President Kennedy came closer than ever to intervention. There were intermittent overflights by American jets from the *Essex,* and on Wednesday the nineteenth the destroyers *Eaton and Murray* closed in toward shore with orders to take off survivors; 26 were found. Twenty-two more survived a sailboat odyssey to land in Mexico. The remnants of Brigade 2506 including San Roman, political adviser Manuel Artíme and Erneido Oliva, who had been the best combat commander, scattered into the swamps and were rounded up one by one. Castro's forces captured 1,214 Brigade soldiers, and themselves suffered perhaps 1,700 dead and 2,000 wounded.

At one of the numerous Washington discussions of how to limit the damage caused by the defeat, the Joint Chiefs were amazed to hear Bissell say, after all the talk of how an uprising was going to overthrow Castro, that the brigade was not prepared to switch to guerrilla-style fighting. President Kennedy finally conceded, raising his hand up just under his nose, "We're already in it up to here."

Two persons with a special interest in the outcome of the Cuban operation were former officials Richard M. Nixon and Dwight D. Eisenhower. The man who had lost the 1960 election, Nixon was planning a foreign policy address in Chicago, and had arranged for a CIA briefing through Kennedy. Allen Dulles was to make the presentation at Nixon's home in Washington on April 19. That evening the DCI appeared an hour and half late. Dulles was nervous and shaken.

Asked if he wanted a drink, Allen said, "I certainly would—I really need one. This is the worst day of my life!"

When Nixon asked what was wrong, Dulles blurted out, "Everything is lost, the Cuban invasion is a total failure."

In a rush the DCI sketched in the latest developments in Cuba and blamed Kennedy's "nervous aides" for getting JFK to make compromises with the plan like dropping the air strikes. "I should have told him," said Dulles, "that we must not fail." Allen stared at the floor. "I came close to doing so but I didn't."

"It was the greatest mistake of my life!"

Nixon heard President Kennedy's version directly, in a telephone call and an afternoon meeting at the White House.

Allen Dulles faced the music with Eisenhower on Friday, April 21. Ike was conciliatory and tried to reassure the shattered DCI. The briefing was a prelude to the weekend, which the Eisenhowers had been invited to spend with their successors at Camp David. The next day, Ike and Mamie Eisenhower helicoptered over from Gettysburg anticipating a social visit, but JFK opened with business, and walked the former President over to the terrace at Aspen Lodge to talk.

President Kennedy did not quibble over the CIA's responsibility in the fiasco. "The chief apparent causes of failure," JFK told Ike, "were gaps in our intelligence, plus what may have been some errors in shiploading, timing, and tactics."

By their own accounts, Nixon and Eisenhower encouraged Kennedy, in his moment of disaster, to pursue Fidel Castro. Richard Nixon advised the President to find a "proper legal cover" and then "go in" against Castro. Eisenhower told Kennedy he would support "anything that had as its objective the prevention of communist entry and solidification of bases in the Western hemisphere."

Neither the old administration nor the new one appeared to understand that implacable American hostility was having precisely the wrong effect on Cuba, driving Castro right into the arms of the Russians.

Six weeks later, Ike was given a detailed account of the Bay of Pigs by his business friend William D. Pawley, who had received the information from one of Brigade 2506's escapees. Pawley also recounted what he had learned of meetings at the White House during the invasion. In an allusion to John Kennedy's 1956 book *Profiles in Courage*, Ike wrote in his diary that "if true, this story could be called a 'Profile in Timidity and Indecision.'"

Ike then sealed up these notes and an accompanying map in an envelope that was only opened some years later by archivists working on his papers.

One thing that John Kennedy had also told Eisenhower was that there would be an investigation. Indeed, given the scope of the fiasco, an investigation could not be avoided. The committee, which called itself the Green Board, was chaired by General Maxwell D. Taylor. Robert F. Kennedy represented his brother, the President. Allen Dulles guarded the interests of the Central Intelligence Agency. Admiral Arleigh Burke watched out for the Navy. The board held twenty hearings with witnesses that included the principal CIA and military participants, from Bissell on down, plus Cuban escapees and politicians.

The declassified transcripts of this testimony reveal an oddly circumspect investigation. It could hardly have been otherwise. The details of the air strikes, the plans for Trinidad versus those for the Bay of Pigs, the military's consideration of the CIA plans, were examined over and again. Yet some of the central questions were not squarely confronted at all.

Failure was attributed to the belief this large operation could be conducted with plausible deniability within the meaning of NSC-5412/2; to lack of coordination among United States agencies; to the attempt to command the operation from a distance, with headquarters at Washington. The panel concluded that the guerrilla option had not in fact been available to the exiles, and that the Operation Pluto plan itself had had "a marginal character . . .

which increased with each additional limitation." By not actually rejecting the CIA plan, the Joint Chiefs seemed to have approved it, and thus bore a measure of responsibility. All United States agencies were at fault in failing to do everything possible to ensure the success of the plan.

The CIA came out looking much better than it should have. Nothing was said of the absurdity of mounting an invasion planned in only two days, a month before actual implementation, and very little about the military feasibility of committing fifteen hundred Cuban exiles in a beachhead area thirty-six miles wide. The report even observed, "We do not feel that any failure of intelligence contributed significantly to the defeat," though it conceded that the intelligence had not been perfect and that the effectiveness of Castro's military forces "was not entirely anticipated or foreseen."

In its recommendations, the Taylor Report discussed possible establishment of a "Strategic Resources Group," consisting of a chairman, the DCI, and the undersecretaries of state and defense—this was nothing less than the old 5412 Group, resuscitated. The report also recommended that the military be given primary responsibility for paramilitary operations, with the Joint Chiefs of Staff as the normal avenue for presidential advice, and that an inventory of the United States' paramilitary assets be conducted.

President Kennedy responded to the recommendations with his National Security Action Memoranda 55 and 56 in late June. NSAM-55 in fact appointed the chairman of the Joint Chiefs as his main adviser for "military-type" actions in time of peace as well as of war; NSAM-56 ordered the recommended inventory of American assets for covert warfare. This instruction led to an interagency study directed by Richard Bissell, with Walt W. Rostow of the NSC staff as a prime moving force. The study provided impetus for the administration's emphasis on counterinsurgency techniques. Kennedy also revived one oversight unit—not the 5412 Group but the President's Foreign Intelligence Advisory Board (PFIAB). The prominent citizens group, to which Clark Clifford and Gordon Gray were soon appointed, met no less than twenty-five times between May and December 1961; PFIAB submitted some 180 recommendations, some of which developed out of the board's own postmortem of the Bay of Pigs. Ninety percent of them are said to have been implemented.

Though the CIA might not have looked so bad in the Taylor Report, there is no question that the debacle stripped away its luster, especially that of the Directorate of Plans. Kennedy had considered Allen Dulles a master spy and an asset to the administration. At lunch with Arthur Schlesinger and James Reston during the last days of the Pluto operation, the President instead opined, "Dulles is a legendary figure and it's hard to work with legendary figures." He kept Dulles on for a time, until the completion of the new CIA headquarters building in Langley, Virginia, the construction of which had been one of the DCI's great dreams, then let him go.

Dulles retired to write a book, *The Craft of Intelligence*, in which the passage explaining away the Bay of Pigs contained only a few lines. Later Dulles reacted angrily to the publication of the Schlesinger and Theodore Sorensen memoirs on Kennedy and wrote several drafts of a reply, never published, that came to hundreds of pages. The rebuttal demonstrates, according to an analysis by political scientist Lucien S. Vandenbroucke, that CIA officers consciously allowed President Kennedy to remain ignorant of weaknesses in the Pluto plan in the expectation that, when the chips were down, JFK would have to go along with whatever was necessary to save the exiles.

Thenceforth, Kennedy kept the Agency at arm's length. He told aides of his desire to "splinter" the CIA "into a thousand pieces and scatter [it] to the winds." But the actual Agency shake-up was much less extreme. Richard Bissell had been considered the leading candidate to succeed Dulles as the DCI; now he was asked to resign instead. When Bissell resisted, he was offered an inferior job. At the end of 1961 he left to head the Institute for Defense Analysis. Tracy Barnes was moved over to division chief of the newly created Domestic Operations Division, with subordinates like E. Howard Hunt and Hans Tofte and not much to do. On the other hand, Gerry Droller was promoted to special assistant for political action for the Western Hemisphere Division, while Jake Engler became its chief of operations. Only a few dozen officers retired and almost no one was cashiered.

While there were plenty of complaints about the handling of this covert operation, the Bay of Pigs did not bring an end to the secret war against Castro. If anything, the administration seems to have redoubled its efforts. An ad hoc subcommittee of the NSC, prodded by Robert Kennedy, directly monitored the action. The new operation was dubbed Mongoose and has been called "the Kennedy vendetta."

Although NSC directives following the Bay of Pigs made the Department of Defense primarily responsible for advice on special activities, its operational role remained minimal. Edward Lansdale served as the Pentagon contact man for matters concerning Operation Mongoose, coordinating military support as well as arranging the agendas for and keeping the records of the NSC Special Group, which effectively replaced the former 5412 Group in overseeing the covert action program.

For its part in Operation Mongoose the Central Intelligence Agency greatly expanded the Miami station, which retained its location in a colonial-style building on the south campus of the University of Miami and its cover as an electronics firm. From Berlin the Agency brought in a new station chief, Theodore G. Shackley, who was soon running one of the CIA's largest operations, with an annual budget of more than $50 million, over a hundred leased vehicles, several thousand Cuban agents and over three hundred American employees. Zenith Technical Enterprises, as it was called, or JM/WAVE by its Agency designator, in fact grew larger than the organization established to support the Bay of Pigs invasion. The CIA's LCI mother ships remained in service and were soon supplemented by a fleet of hundreds of motorboats based in Miami and throughout the Florida Keys.

The paramilitary activities of the anti-Castro Cubans were more or less openly conducted, cloaked only by the array of political groups centered in Miami. Because the operations were being run out of the United States, the CIA was compelled to create liaison ties with a variety of federal, state, and local authorities, such as the police and customs service. Conduct of Operation Mongoose from within the United States inevitably involved daily violations of laws ranging from the CIA's National Security Act charter to the Neutrality Act to statutes involving firearms possession and perjury. A frequent occupation of the JM/WAVE staff was bailing out or otherwise rescuing CIA or Cuban personnel who had run afoul of the law.

Use of the anti-Castro political groups proved to be a double-edged sword. As paramilitary operations succeeded one another, most of them clearly beyond the exiles' capacity, cover became increasingly threadbare. The Cuban groups enjoyed the cachet of their secret ties with the United States government, but in the longer run, exposure of their CIA connections made it difficult for them to claim political legitimacy as independent groups. "CIA front" was a charge later used to discredit many Cuban groups, not least by the Castro government itself.

A more immediate problem was that the CIA's relations with and assistance to the Cuban groups loosened the Agency's control of the covert war. Some attacks were carried out independently by Cubans striving to attain credibility with CIA. Some operations canceled by CIA were carried out anyway by Cubans angry at being denied their chance to strike at Castro. It was sometimes hard to tell if an action that occurred had been authorized by CIA or not. Many raids by Cuban groups like the Second Naval Guerrilla and Alpha 66 were not. Yet once the CIA had provided training and equipment, the Castro government had some justification for its charges that the anti-Castro raids, independent or not, were backed by the United States.

Operation Mongoose peaked in the eighteen months that separated the Bay of Pigs from the Cuban missile crisis. There were numerous attempts to infiltrate agents into Cuba, most of them failures. There were several more schemes aimed at assassinating Fidel Castro, all abortive and some involving CIA links with the Mafia. Cargoes of Cuban sugar were contaminated with chemicals in San Juan, Puerto Rico, and other ports. Shipments of machinery and spare parts en route to Cuba were sabotaged. There were commando raids against Cuban railroads, oil and sugar refineries, and factories.

The covert program helped exacerbate tensions between the United States and the Soviet Union as well. The Bay of Pigs invasion was followed by an expansion of Soviet military aid to Cuba and an attempt by Khrushchev to extend a Soviet nuclear umbrella over the Caribbean island. The Soviet military buildup in Cuba that resulted in the missile crisis was motivated primarily by Soviet strategic considerations, but Castro probably would not have accepted the emplacement of Soviet nuclear weapons on Cuban soil had it not been for the American threat.

President Kennedy kept his distance from the paramilitary offensive. But his brother Robert was in the forefront of the operation, prodding the planners to get moving, encouraging action within the NSC Special Group, even making field trips to visit the CIA facilities in Florida. His enthusiasm fueled the secret war and won support from many who had been disgruntled by the Operation Pluto fiasco. Typical of them was Rip Robertson, the CIA "cowboy" who thought little of politicians. He met RFK during the Taylor committee investigation and returned to tell the exiles that Kennedy was all right. Robertson went on to serve throughout the covert operations against Cuba.

Operation Mongoose formally evolved from a list of thirty-two planning tasks assigned by Edward Lansdale on January 30, 1962. By February 20 there was a detailed six-phase timetable intended to culminate in an open revolt against Castro before the end of the year. Lansdale became chief of the Washington task force running the operation, with a CIA group under him called Task Force W and headed by William K. Harvey. From the new CIA headquarters at Langley, Harvey supervised the activities of Ted Shackley's Miami station. With the pressures of organization, progress was slow—by September Mongoose was still mired in its first phase—intelligence gathering.

In a way, the administration's hand was then forced by one of those freelance strikes by the Cuban exiles. Acting on information that Czech and Soviet officers gathered on Friday nights, for parties at Havana's Blanquita Hotel, exiles determined to make a raid; six Cubans crammed a speedboat with two .50-caliber machine guns, a 20-millimeter cannon, and a recoilless rifle. On August 24 the exiles entered the suburban harbor of Miramar, got close enough to the Blanquita to see the lights in the ballroom and the uniforms, and shelled the place.

Once exiles were mounting such missions on their own, it became even more difficult for the CIA to restrain those Cubans working for Task Force W. In early September the NSC Special Group approved escalation to phase two, raids against Cuba. One commando strike at a power plant was evidently considered but discouraged. Sharp argument erupted at a Mongoose meeting on October 4 when John McCone, the new director of central intelligence, charged that the NSC had been holding back the forces. Bobby Kennedy retorted that, to the contrary, the Special Group had "urged and insisted upon action by the Lansdale operating organization" and that no specified action had ever been rejected at the NSC level. The October 4 meeting concluded that "more dynamic action was indicated."

Just ten days later a CIA U-2 reconnaissance plane flying over Cuba returned with photographs that showed equipment associated with Soviet nuclear missiles. Operation Mongoose was swept away in the heat of the Cuban missile crisis. Robert Kennedy sat with his brother and other officials through an almost continuous series of meetings of an ad hoc "executive committee" of the National Security Council. The officials considered diplomatic approaches to the Russians, an invasion of Cuba, blockade or bombing of the missiles.

The secret warriors had their own brands of solutions for the new Cuban crisis. At the State Department, Robert A. Hurwitch, who was special assistant for Cuban affairs, recommended having exile pilots bomb the missiles, using unmarked planes for the ostensible purpose of attacks on oil refineries. At the CIA, Task Force W actually moved, very probably in response to the Mongoose directive for "more dynamic action" to place ten commando teams of six men each within Cuba. Bill Harvey thought the teams could guide United States invasion forces when they landed. Three teams had already left for points on the north coast of Cuba when one Cuban, who wanted assurances that the cause was good, phoned Robert Kennedy. The attorney general, now facing the horrifying prospect of a potential nuclear war, was not the gung ho advocate of covert action he once had been. On October 30 the NSC ordered a halt to all Mongoose operations. Lansdale was sent to Miami to close down the CIA station. There was no more talk, as there had been on October 4, of a plan to mine Cuban harbors.

The missile crisis was eventually resolved at a high level between the two superpowers. The Soviets removed their offensive weapons from Cuba; the Americans later dismantled similarly threatening forward-based systems in Turkey. As for the covert forces in play, the CIA was ordered to reorganize yet again. William Harvey was removed from command of Task Force W, to be replaced by Desmond FitzGerald, an Asian expert, but an officer with far more paramilitary experience. While Langley cut back on the Cuban operations for a time, that situation changed again in early 1963.

During these events, the exile prisoners from the Bay of Pigs languished in Cuban prisons. Hurt by the trade embargo in place since January 1961, Castro offered to trade the prisoners for medicines, tractors, spare parts, and other such items. Desultory exchanges on the matter occurred repeatedly through 1961 and 1962. After the missile crisis, Castro's price came down while the administration threw its weight behind an effort to raise the required $53-million worth of medical equipment, drugs, and baby food. The exchange was negotiated by lawyer James A. Donovan, who had arranged the trade of Soviet spy Rudolf Abel for CIA U-2 pilot Francis Gary Powers, which was consummated during the summer of 1962.

The final agreement on the prisoner exchange was made on December 22, 1962. Some 1,179 veterans of Brigade 2,506 returned to the United States. In a covert twist within this game, CIA assassination planners bought a scuba diving suit to be presented to Castro as a gift by Donovan. At Langley's Technical Services Division, Agency scientists impregnated the suit with fungus to cause a chronic skin disease and the breathing apparatus with a tubercule bacillus. The suit was carried to Donovan by an unwitting lawyer, John Nolan, who learned of the ploy years later during the assassination investigations of the 1970s.

"Can you imagine," recalls Nolan, "I mean, can you imagine? Here is Jim Donovan—the guy who has already done his stuff once, a guy the Other Side trusts—down in Cuba, trying to cut a deal, very tough negotiations, very delicate discussions, everything has got to be above-board because Fidel holds all the cards, and the Company is setting Donovan up—not even telling him, keeping him unwitting—to hand Fidel Castro this nice big germ bag."

Fortunately, the American lawyer, witting or not, took the precaution of replacing the diving suit with one he bought himself.

Castro returned the prisoners, including twenty non-Brigade agents of the CIA. Cuban government statements pointedly feared a new invasion by a larger, better-equipped exile brigade, however. The United States denied any such plan but, in fact, there *was* another exile brigade organized by the American military, which had been trained under a special Cuban volunteer program since July 1961. In early 1963 the program was handling a weekly influx of two hundred Cuban exiles. What to do with the brigade was a key topic of the NSC meeting of January 25, 1963. As the issues were summarized, for Vice President Lyndon Johnson by his military adviser, "the basic decision must be made as to whether an invasion of Cuba, directly or indirectly, is to be supported, or whether, in a lesser sense, serious provocations or incidents should be a part of the basic policy. When this decision is made, the disposition of the Cuban Brigade can more easily be determined."

The basic decision was to restrict post-Mongoose actions to harassment of the Cubans; the raison d'être for the brigade disappeared. Only 128 Cubans volunteered for the special program between the beginning of 1964 and the end of April 1965, by which time 2,947 had entered the program and 2,659 had completed their training. The anti-Castro aim of these Cubans was clearly demonstrated when only 61 of them continued in United States military service after their training. The program was phased out in November 1965.

Raids against Cuban targets continued through 1963. Independent raids also remained a problem, subject only to rather haphazard controls. In 1962, for example, despite the existence of hundreds of boats that very probably carried out thousands of cruises, U.S. customs, Coast Guard, and other authorities apprehended exactly four boats and fifty Cubans. It is very likely that these seizures were intended as lessons to the exiles to follow the orders of their CIA controllers. Independent raids in March 1963 caused serious damage to Soviet merchant ships off Oriente province, leading to diplomatic protests. Secretary of State Dean Rusk declared, in a letter discussed at an NSC meeting on March 29, "I am concerned that hit and run raids by Cuban exiles may create incidents which work to the disadvantage of our national interest. Increased frequency of these forays could raise a host of problems over which we would not have control."

The Cuban operation began to die away as sensitivity to the problems of control increased. Continuing official support by the United States only served to encourage the exiles. There were periodic strikes, and NSC discussions as late as 1965, but the government's attention was increasingly drawn to Southeast Asia and Cuba was left behind. The CIA bases in Miami and the Florida Keys closed down one by one.

Ending the CIA secret war did not in this case end the paramilitary activities. Exile groups continued on their own with sporadic attempts at harassment of Castro's Cuba. In the mid-1960s one mission was even financed by an American magazine just for the journalistic scoop it could achieve. Exile groups merged, split, renewed their memberships, and conducted their own training. In the 1970s a newer group, called Omega 7, carried out assassinations of opponents and of Cuban diplomats assigned to the United Nations in New York.

As a result of the Cuban operations the secret warriors succeeded in creating a cadre with military skills, a cadre that far outlasted the operations themselves. Cuban pilots later flew B-26 bombers for the CIA in the Congo, and for the Portuguese elsewhere in Africa. Cubans enlisted in an abortive invasion of Haiti launched from Florida in the late 1960s. Cubans were available to be recruited by Republican campaign officials in the 1972 political intelligence effort that led to the Watergate scandal and the downfall of President Richard Nixon. One of the Cubans arrested at the Watergate Hotel that June was Bernard Barker, Howard Hunt's lieutenant during Operation Pluto. Another was Rolando Martinez, who had participated in 354 CIA missions during the Cuban operations. As recently as the early 1980s, Bay of Pigs veterans filed lawsuits against the United States government seeking military veterans benefits.

Most recently, Cuban Americans have been a major private funding source for the effort by Nicaraguan *contras* to overthrow the Sandinista government of that country. Cubans have provided paramilitary training for some Nicaraguans, and it is very likely that some Cubans worked with the CIA during the 1983–1984 campaign of mining Nicaraguan ports.

·XII·

COLD WAR AND COUNTERINSURGENCY

The Cuban operations represented a peak for a certain kind of paramilitary action. The frantic era of the OPC and the early days of the CIA were gone, their passing symbolized perhaps by the 1961 retirement of Frank Wisner, who had grown weary of the increasingly ceremonial role of chief of station in London. Paramilitary plans in Wisner's era had frequently involved grand schemes carried out against foreign governments. Kennedy's administration brought a marked shift toward operations carried out in collaboration with established governments instead of against them.

The failures in Cuba contributed to the change of emphasis, demonstrating anew the resilience of target governments. Yet the shift was in the wind before the first parties of frogmen stepped ashore at Girón. It was propelled by the alteration in views held at the top levels of the executive branch. President Kennedy had responded to an argument about military strategy when he developed his interest in guerrilla warfare. But this interest would have important implications for CIA operations and for the balance between CIA and the military capabilities in the paramilitary field. Sustained by Kennedy's support, and given greater responsibilities after the CIA's failure in Cuba, the military moved quickly to expand its special-warfare forces.

National security policy during the Eisenhower administration had combined an active paramilitary campaign waged by the CIA with a "New Look" military policy that was radical in a different way. Ike's military policy rested upon the enormous power of nuclear weapons, the assumption that future wars would be nuclear ones, and a strong desire to maintain the strength of the American economy, which Eisenhower felt could not be preserved over the "long haul" in the face of large military budgets. Thus rigid ceilings had been placed on defense spending. With the atomic forces emphasized, the ceilings required reductions somewhere in the military, and these cuts could only come in the area of conventional forces. The Eisenhower period therefore witnessed manpower reductions in the Army and Marine Corps.

There was substantial opposition to the Eisenhower policy, not least from within the Army itself. One chief of staff resigned over the issue in 1955. With some notable exceptions, other Army generals also opposed the New Look policy, but the President carefully kept the Navy and Air Force satisfied, and appointed chairmen of the Joint Chiefs of Staff who supported him. The Army argued in isolation through much of the Eisenhower administration.

The CIA was the one shop with an interest in common with the Army—limited war capability. Paramilitary operations were limited wars, with possible contingencies for employment of conventional forces. As early as 1955 the CIA had commissioned a detailed study, Project Brushfire, of the political, psychological, economic, and sociological factors that led to "peripheral wars." The study was conducted by a research institute, the Center for International Studies, under economist Max Millikan at the Massachusetts Institute of Technology (MIT). Brushfire was one among a continuing series of contracts for research reports that CIA gave to the MIT institute, although it appears to have been their first big study of limited war.

On his copy of an information memo regarding Brushfire, Eisenhower's Joint Chiefs chairman commented, "I think the answers [to the causes of wars] are so plain that it is a waste of money."

The CIA wanted to be involved in early 1958, when Eisenhower himself ordered an interagency policy review on limited war versus full-scale conflict. Then John Foster Dulles sought to discourage his brother Allen from participating, saying the CIA should be concerned with the intelligence questions, not the "operational" ones. Allen Dulles allowed himself to be mollified by the promise that the CIA would be allowed to get into "operational" aspects on some later occasion.

While further limited war studies were done, and the CIA did participate in them, its interests were hardly known outside government, while Army officials trumpeted their opposition to the New Look to whoever would listen. The most prominent Army spokesman was chief of staff General Maxwell D. Taylor. Specifically, Taylor asserted that a strategy of massive nuclear retaliation could not counter "brushfire" wars, and that the United States should adopt a strategy of "flexible response" to be able to conduct conflict at any level. At CIA, where paramilitary action was conceived as a rung on the ladder of conflict, they were undoubtedly cheering silently from the sidelines.

The most important individual affected by the limited war debate of the 1950s was John Fitzgerald Kennedy, then a senator from Massachusetts. Kennedy clearly aligned himself with the opponents of the "New Look." In the early stages of his presidential campaign, on October 16, 1959, Kennedy gave a speech at Lake Charles, Louisiana, in which he declared, "Our nuclear power . . . cannot deter Communist aggression which is too limited to justify atomic war. It cannot protect uncommitted nations against a Communist takeover using local or guerrilla forces. It cannot be used in so-called 'brushfire' peripheral wars." JFK was determined to change this approach to limited war.

John Kennedy's vision was different from the military's, however. The Army thought of a limited war as something like Korea, a familiar type of conflict on a less than major scale. The young President was much more impressed by guerrilla warfare and its supposed antidote, the tactics of counterinsurgency. On February 1, 1961, at one of his first NSC meetings, JFK ordered the national security bureaucracy to examine putting more emphasis on the development of "counter-guerrilla forces." Kennedy's intention was reiterated in one of the first National Security Action Memoranda of his administration, NSAM-3, issued only two days later. As the instrument to effect change within the military, JFK selected Max Taylor as his personal representative.

Maxwell Davenport Taylor came to the Kennedy administration after a brief engagement as president of Lincoln Center for the Performing Arts, in New York, which was then in its final stages of construction. This employment seemed to make Taylor even more attractive to JFK's Camelot crowd. Here was a general who was cultured, who had written a book, and who had stood up against

Eisenhower's military policy. Moreover, Taylor was a World War II hero, a paratrooper who had participated in several major assault airdrops, including divisional command in two of them. Later he had been the last wartime commander of the U.S. Eighth Army in Korea, as well as superintendent at West Point. Having adopted Taylor's "flexible response" argument, Kennedy could not help but be impressed with the man.

As Taylor recalls it, within a few days of the inauguration he refused an offer to be ambassador to France—his family had moved too many times during his career, and had just endured yet another move, from Mexico City to New York. Taylor himself had just signed a five-year contract with Lincoln Center. He remained for the moment in New York, where he read confused reports about the Bay of Pigs in the newspapers. Two days after the fall of Girón, President Kennedy called and personally asked Taylor to head his inquiry into the Bay of Pigs operation, and the general began commuting to Washington.

Several times during the course of the investigation, Robert Kennedy privately talked to Taylor about serving in the administration. He continued to resist all blandishments, but softened to Bobby Kennedy's wit and his skill as an interrogator, and appreciated RFK's work when the time came to assemble his presentation for President Kennedy, the NSC, and the principals involved in the Cuban operation. Taylor paid Bobby Kennedy the compliment of saying he would have made his unit, the elite 101st Airborne Division, during the big war. As the investigation neared its end, Bobby Kennedy told the general that the President was going to replace Allen Dulles at CIA and offered Taylor the job.

While still considering the offer, on June 23, 1961, Max Taylor helicoptered up to Gettysburg with Allen Dulles to brief Dwight Eisenhower on the results of the Bay of Pigs inquiry. The last time the general had seen Eisenhower, the two were bitterly divided over defense policy and service budgets. Max wondered if he should ask Dulles to test the waters ahead of him and see how Ike reacted.

Allen was in no position to do favors that day; he himself was in the woodshed with the former President as a result of the botched up Bay of Pigs.

Neither man need have worried, Ike was extremely cordial. Eisenhower disagreed with a few points, and complained in particular about Kennedy's dismantling of the 5412 Group machinery for monitoring covert operations. But one of the main recommendations of the Taylor Report was to establish just such an entity, which the report had called a "Strategic Resources Group."

General Taylor returned to Washington where he declined the offer to serve as the DCI. Yet he did not escape from intelligence—President Kennedy immediately offered Taylor a position in the White House as special military representative. Only three days after Taylor's visit to Gettysburg, President Kennedy signed a charter letter appointing Taylor to advise and assist on military matters plus provide "an analogous advisory function in the fields of intelligence and of Cold War planning, with particular attention to Berlin and Southeast Asia."

With these general duties, Kennedy in fact put Taylor in charge of the NSC Special Group. Early ad hoc procedures were formalized by a directive drafted by Taylor, which JFK approved on January 18, 1962. This established the Special Group (CI)—the abbreviation for "counterinsurgency"—to formulate plans, subject to the President's approval, on both cold war and counterinsurgency matters.

Military men who worked on Operation Mongoose remember that Taylor insisted on action as strongly as did Bobby Kennedy.

General Maxwell Taylor had been a paratrooper. In the Army at that time, paratroopers were thought of not only as a military elite, but as thoroughly modern, flexible officers. Solidly cast in this "Airborne" mold, Max Taylor was not typical of the officer corps. The more conventional Army officers were the men who, throughout the 1950s, hindered the development of Special Forces.

The 10th Special Forces Group had been in place at Fort Bragg, North Carolina, since June 1952. In September 1953 it was supplemented by the 77th Special Forces Group, which remained in the United States while 782 men of the 10th were deployed to West Germany, where they have ever since occupied a former German army base at Bad Tölz in Bavaria. This early expansion coincided with the repatriation of the Korean War partisan veterans.

Subsequently, Special Forces expansion slowed to a snail's pace, as anxious Army generals preserved their conventional units as best they could within the New Look budgets. The brass was preoccupied with adjusting to nuclear warfare and had little time for advocates of unconventional warfare.

Progress, however, was steady, if slow. A big step was the deployment of the 10th Group to Germany. There, Special Forces teams planned for partisan campaigns in Eastern Europe and began to show what they could do in NATO military maneuvers. At home, in 1956 maneuvers, Special Forces troops caused enormous disruption to the other team, even penetrating the opponents' tactical command radio network. Detachments were sent to foreign nations to train their armies, while a permanent presence was established in the Far East with provisional teams sent to Hawaii in 1956 and Okinawa the next year. This provisional detachment became the nucleus of the 1st Special Forces Group, established on Okinawa on June 24, 1957. Men from Special Forces conducted certain missions in Laos as early as 1959, and were included in the assistance command in South Vietnam in May 1960, when they began to train Vietnamese rangers at the invitation of President Ngo Dinh Diem.

A Special Forces "group" was a novel organization, as military units go. One component was an administrative base that served the needs of all the teams, technically called "operational detachments." From group headquarters a C Team provided intelligence and control support for all the regions of a country, while B Teams would do the same within regions.

The basic field unit was the A Team, at the lowest level, small units of Americans who could command or advise large irregular formations. To perform technical and medical services and furnish support, the A Teams had to have a wide range of skilled experts, for which Special Forces recruited experienced officers and noncommissioned officers (NCOs), selected only the best of them, and then cross-trained the team members in several of the required skills. Originally authorized for two officers plus thirteen NCOs per team, many operational detachments were down to eight men or even six during the lean years of the late 1950s. Cross-training was expected to allow the A Teams to function effectively despite their small size.

The notion of Special Forces command levels for regions and countries, with A Teams for the field forces, was clearly oriented for organizing resistance to an enemy. Because of the expertise of the A Team members, however, these units were also well suited to train friendly forces, and to command friendly irregular units within friendly territory. By adopting these counterinsurgency methods,

Special Forces at last found the role that sustained it through the Vietnam era.

This was not evident at first. There was a wave of disillusionment among Special Forces, as at the CIA, after Eisenhower took no action in response to the Hungarian revolt. The unconventional-warfare experts were also smarting from an encounter with the Army bureaucracy, which banned the wearing of Special Forces' semiofficial headgear, the green beret. Dedication was a valued attribute in a Special Forces man, but a man had to have a good deal of it to stay in Special Forces at that time. By 1960, Special Forces groups had increased threefold but still totaled only about two thousand men. This was fewer than the number of personnel spaces the Army had allocated in its 1952 decision to maintain an unconventional-warfare unit.

Good fortune came to Special Forces with the election of John F. Kennedy. Within days of JFK's inauguration one of the President's NSC staff, Walt W. Rostow, was questioning the adequacy of Army training for war against guerrillas. Special Forces was already adopting counterinsurgency courses at Fort Bragg. These emphasized the economic, social, political, and psychological origins of war. Special Forces seemed to be on top of the subject, and President Kennedy saw a major role for Special Forces' knowledge in "brushfire" wars.

A few months later, Rostow was at Fort Bragg to address the students of the Special Warfare Center, in a speech cleared personally by Kennedy. Rostow had completed his own inquiry, which JFK encouraged, and found that the core of Special Forces was estimated to be only a few hundred men. Just two weeks before Jack Kennedy's inauguration, Khrushchev had declared Soviet support for "wars of national liberation." Now it seemed important to prepare for a global struggle.

Rostow's speech placed guerrilla war in the context of global underdevelopment, a sort of crisis of modernization that could be exploited. Although Rostow commended the students for reading Lenin, Guevara, and Mao Tse-tung, he insisted that guerrilla wars had been fought long before the Russian Revolution. "Guerrilla warfare," as Rostow put it, "is not a form of military and psychological magic created by the Communist." Rather, "we confront in guerrilla warfare in the underdeveloped areas a systematic attempt by the Communists to impose a serious disease on those societies attempting the transition to modernization." America's central task was "to protect the independence of the revolutionary process now going forward." Guerrilla warfare "is powerful and effective only when we do not put our minds clearly to work on how to deal with it."

Special Forces was perceived in Washington to have done just that. Rostow was back at Bragg in late 1961, this time accompanying Jack Kennedy on the President's own personal tour of the Special Warfare Center. Its commander, Brigadier General William Yardborough, took a calculated risk and greeted Kennedy wearing the proscribed green beret. The President came and saw, spoke supportive words, and helped quietly from the White House as Special Forces were given new impetus. On April 11, 1962, the President released an official message to the Army; the message called the green beret "a symbol of excellence, a badge of courage, a mark of distinction in the fight for freedom." Henceforth, Special Forces would be called the Green Berets and there would be official regulations governing the size and color of the berets and how they should be worn.

From the beginning of the Kennedy administration, there followed a rapid expansion of Special Forces. In March 1961 the Army doubled the number of units. The different groups would specialize geographically—the 10th Group covered Europe; the 1st, Asia; a new 8th Group, Latin America; and 3rd and 6th groups were planned to take on Africa and Middle East assignments. The 77th Special Forces Group was redesignated the 7th Group. Authorized strength doubled to 1,500 men per group, including thirty-six A Teams, nine B Teams, and three C Teams. Psychological warfare units were also increased, in early 1965, to three battalions and two companies plus detachments. By November 30, 1964, the actual strength of Army special-warfare forces stood at 11,343.

In Germany the 10th Group retained its mission of infiltrating the Soviet bloc. The theater war plan, OPLAN 10-1, according to revelations in the British press, provided in 1962 for six subversive activities and forty-nine guerrilla warfare zones throughout Eastern Europe where the 10th Group would be dispersed. Its A Teams were each credited with the ability to mobilize one 500-man partisan battalion every month, for a total field force of 74,500 within six months, according to the estimates of the Special Operations Task Force Europe.

In its focus on behind-the-lines wartime activity, the 10th Group became an exception within Special Forces. Green Berets working in other areas of the world concentrated more on questions of counterinsurgency and military assistance. The future looked bright. "For the first time in United States history," said Army spokesmen in an informational publication, "this [guerrilla-organizing and psychological warfare] capability has been made available before it is needed. Through it the Army now has one more weapon which can be applied with discrimination in any kind of warfare."

There were Air Force special forces, too. These provided support, especially airlift, in the form of the ARC wings. The Air Force called its approach to special forces the "air commando" concept. Such units had actually been formed and used in Burma in World War II; they had been responsible for supporting the Kachin and OSS field agents. An "air commando" unit contained a little bit of everything—medium and light transport aircraft plus fighter-bombers. The same unit could supply partisans, make air strikes in their support, and maintain physical contact by flying light planes onto small airstrips. The OSS paramilitary men benefited greatly from air commando support in Burma. Had the Khampa partisans had such capabilities in Tibet, the PLA might never have been able to overcome them.

Air commandos were eclipsed in Eisenhower's budget-conscious Air Force. Faced with expensive bomber and missile programs and adjustment to the nuclear age, there was little interest in counterinsurgency. Tactical air commanders were preoccupied by their transition to supersonic jet fighters. Even the air transport commanders had bigger-ticket programs like the C-130 Hercules or the large jet C-141 Starlifter. The air commando concept fell nebulously somewhere among the functional responsibilities of the various Air Force commands.

Despite all obstacles a start was made in the late 1950s with the formation of a small, secret organization within the service; and, as was the Army, the Air Force was galvanized by the advent of Kennedy. In March 1961, responding to JFK's instructions that each of the services examine how best it could contribute to counterinsurgency, U.S. Air Force headquarters ordered the Tactical Air Command to create an experimental counterinsurgency unit along air commando lines.

Very soon thereafter, on April 14, 1961, the Air Force activated the 4400th Combat Crew Training Squadron under Colonel Benjamin H. King at Eglin Air Force Base, Florida. The unit based its planes at nearby Hurlbut Field. Initially, there were sixteen C-47's, eight B-26's, and eight T-28 "Texans," propeller-driven training aircraft converted to carry bombs or rockets and machine guns. Nicknamed the "Jungle Jim" unit, the 4400th began with 124 officers and 228 airmen, with the dual mission of training indigenous aircrews and participating in combat.

Meanwhile, for top-secret airlift missions over longer distances, the Military Airlift Command established special E Flights in certain of its C-130 squadrons. The unit for the Far East, for example, was E Flight of the 21st Troop Carrier Squadron on Okinawa, formed in late 1961 with four or five C-130's. When necessary these planes would be loaned to the CIA and flown by Agency contract aircrews.

In April 1962 the Air Force dispensed with euphemisms and reactivated its 1st Air Commando Squadron, a formation that traced its lineage directly back to Burma in March 1944. The squadron was later expanded to a wing, supplemented by more combat crew training squadrons, a combat support group, and at Eglin, the Special Air Warfare School. All these capabilities were controlled by a Special Warfare Division at USAF headquarters; it was subordinate to the deputy chief of staff for plans and operations. Long before this stage arrived, the original Jungle Jim unit had been sent into action in Southeast Asia.

There were also changes within the office of the secretary of defense. The Office of Special Operations (OSO) was abolished after the Bay of Pigs. Although such OSO representatives as Ed Lansdale had consistently raised objections to Operation Pluto, the Joint Chiefs were apportioned some of the blame for the failure and Secretary of Defense Robert McNamara was none too happy with the existing institutions. Graves Erskine had run a tight ship, but perhaps there was just too much work for a single office to handle.

At that time the OSO was truly an intelligence focal point. Not only did it handle liaison on covert operations, but everything else from military personnel for detached service to cover arrangements to Pentagon participation in reconnaissance satellite development, as well. McNamara had been advised that he did not really need a special assistant for these matters. In a sudden move the day after the final defeat of the Cuban exiles at the Bay of Pigs, most of the OSO personnel were reassigned to other military tasks.

According to some officers, at the time there were fears in OSO that Lansdale might succeed in taking over the special assistant's functions. After all, Lansdale was already deputy to Graves Erskine and one of the foremost proponents of counterinsurgency techniques. But there were questions as to whether Lansdale was as knowledgeable about satellites and other technical-intelligence issues.

The OSO officers need not have worried. When the office was abolished, its technical responsibilities were assigned by McNamara to the director of defense research and engineering. Deception responsibilities went to a special planning office on the Navy staff. Lansdale retained a small staff to handle special activities only. Some credit Erskine with accomplishing this division of tasks. In any case, Lansdale did not succeed to the OSO empire. Rather, what finally emerged was a new office of the special assistant for counterinsurgency and special activities (SACSA).

A Marine general had headed OSO, and now another Marine was assigned to SACSA. Perhaps with an eye cocked toward the White House, the Marine Corps gave the post to an officer who had served in the South Pacific with John F. Kennedy during World War II. The officer was Major General Victor "Brute" Krulak. His assistant was Colonel Jack L. Hawkins. Both maintain they were skeptical of such covert operations as Mongoose, but on counterinsurgency the SACSA office proved to be very active, especially in regard to Southeast Asia.

Despite the Cuban setback, the CIA retained solid and growing capabilities for paramilitary action. Interagency cooperation with the military was now regulated by a Pentagon-CIA memorandum of understanding signed in 1957. The Directorate of Plans remained the largest component of CIA, a thousand stronger than when Ike took office, accounting for 54 percent of the Agency's budget. Field stations in Africa increased by 55 percent between 1959 and 1963, while personnel in DDP's Western Hemisphere Division increased 40 percent from 1961 to 1965. Afterward, the emphasis shifted to Southeast Asia.

Dick Bissell was an enthusiastic exponent of counterinsurgency, having led the 1961 summer study that included Walt Rostow, but his sins were too many and he passed on. His replacement was Richard McGarrah Helms, a professional's professional and a man selected from among the espionage specialists in CIA. Passed over for DDP in 1958, when he had expected the job, Helms now began a meteoric rise that took him to the top of the CIA. In the process, he presided over the peak of the secret war, the years from the Kennedy administration to Nixon-Kissinger era.

Helms was one of the few senior officers untouched by the Bay of Pigs. Though chief of operations for DDP, Wisner's, and later Bissell's second-in-command, Helms attended few of the Bay of Pigs planning sessions and had nothing to do with its implementation. He had been ideally positioned for a decade to take over the DDP. Starting out as a naval reserve lieutenant, Helms served successively with OSS, the Strategic Services Unit, then Central Intelligence Group, and the CIA, with Central European espionage as a specialty. In the early CIA, Dick Helms had been with the espionage unit that had been outshone by Wisner's "Wurlitzer." Now he had his chance.

When Helms took over the DDP, it was expanding, but infected with self-doubts. A few weeks before Helms became DDP, CIA general counsel Lawrence Houston noted for the record his opinion regarding the legal basis for cold war activities. The CIA's own lawyers admitted that "there is no statutory authorization to any agency for the conduct of such activities." Houston added that there was no explicit prohibition either, and that "some of the covert cold-war operations are related to intelligence within a broad interpretation" of the National Security Act of 1947.

In examining the language of the 1947 law, the CIA lawyer specifically conceded its failure to cover paramilitary operations—the clause that read "such other duties and functions" in the act was explicitly tied to "*intelligence* affecting the national security." Thus, wrote Houston in his January 15, 1962, memorandum, "it would be stretching that section too far to include a Guatemala or a Cuba even though intelligence and counterintelligence are essential to such activities."

Houston's conclusion was: "Therefore, the Executive Branch under the direction of the President was acting without specific statutory authorization, and CIA was the agent selected for their conduct."

Defending the government's conduct in these paramilitary operations, the CIA general counsel was reduced to arguing that "it can be said that the Congress as a whole knows that money is appropriated to CIA and knows that generally a portion of it goes for clandestine activities. To this extent we can say that we have Congressional approval of these activities." Thus, according to the CIA's own legal staff, there was no general congressional approval for paramilitary operations, there was no specific authorization, there was only the weak argument that Congress had approved the policy through the act of appropriating money. It is worth noting that a parallel argument—that Congress had, in effect, approved a declaration of war by appropriating money for the Vietnam War—was later ruled invalid by the courts.

Larry Houston believed that it was for the administration to decide the nature and extent of its cold war activities. Prodded by Bobby Kennedy and Max Taylor, it did—the NSC Special Group approved 163 covert operations between January 1961 and November 1963, compared to 104 approved in the eight years of the Eisenhower administration. Even so, an internal audit later found, in 1961–1962 the Special Group considered only about 16 percent of the covert operations actually initiated by the United States.

Helms had another difficulty in that the autonomy enjoyed by CIA stations was being cut back. The degree of control an ambassador should have over CIA operations in his country had been a touchy issue throughout the Eisenhower years. The experiences of Chester Bowles in India, William Sebald in Burma, and John Allison in Indonesia highlighted the difficulties. After an interagency study in 1958, Eisenhower gave the CIA virtually total autonomy with instructions that the ambassador's writ stopped short of intelligence activities.

This policy was reversed by the Kennedy administration when State Department official U. Alexis Johnson drafted a letter, above presidential signature, to ambassadors. Dispatched as a circular cable in May 1961, the Kennedy letter established a "country team" concept. CIA and other departments could sit on embassy senior councils but the ambassador was the authority. Yet John Kenneth Galbraith's troubles with the CIA in India showed that State's authority still had a long way to go.

A third problem for the new DCI was managing the hidden components of what was fast becoming an intelligence empire. The covers and contacts staff had placed people in journalism, broadcasting, business, and academe. Within the Pentagon itself there were between seven hundred and a thousand "units" that supported or provided cover for the CIA, ranging from post boxes and telephones to full-scale formations of men and equipment. Even elsewhere in CIA, by 1961 there were about a thousand more employees working in support of the DDP than there had been in the beginning of the Dulles era.

A singular headache was the array of CIA proprietaries. When John McCone succeeded Allen Dulles as DCI in November 1961, preparations were already in place for the latest addition to the proprietaries, what became a complex of insurance and investment companies, formed in the Domestic Operations Division of DDP to handle contract agents' and survivors' benefits arising from the Cuban operations.

Then there was Civil Air Transport, reorganized in 1959 after aviation law changes by the Taiwan government. The CIA incorporated a holding company in Delaware, Pacific Corporation, to act as top-level management with corporate headquarters in Washington and field offices at Taipei. The CIA airlift force was renamed Air America, an ostensibly private air charter firm. Massive maintenance facilities on Taiwan were spun off as the subsidiary firm Air Asia. Both subsidiaries performed contract work for the United States government. A rump CAT remained on Taiwan as a Chinese domestic airline with the Pacific Corporation holding residual interests. This proprietary group was nothing if not massive—Pacific Corporation employed over 20,000 people at its height. Air America alone directly employed 5,600, up to 8,000 if support personnel in the corporation are counted, and owned or operated 167 aircraft.

Much smaller but still significant was Southern Air Transport, which grew large enough to have semiautonomous corporate divisions for Atlantic and Pacific operations. This company both owned and leased DC-6 prop four-engine transports, Boeing 727 jets, and the civilian version of Lockheed's C-130 aircraft. Southern Air Transport soon won a $3.7-million Air Force contract to move cargo and passengers on interisland routes in the Far East.

Managing the far-flung proprietaries, including many more than the ones mentioned here, constituted a formidable task. The CIA used a combination of interlocking boards of directors and Agency personnel working under cover in the companies. On February 5, 1963, the DCI ordered establishment of an Executive Committee for Air Proprietary Operations, to oversee at least part of the hidden empire. The EXCOMAIR, as it was called, was chaired by Lawrence Houston and included representatives of the DDP and the comptroller's office. Houston had already, in the summer of 1954, headed a management study of the air proprietaries, and argued in 1956 that CAT should be retained, as a contingency asset, when the Special Group considered liquidating it.

As DCI, John McCone, a California businessman, made no pretense at micromanagement of the CIA. Such experts as Houston and Richard Helms knew their jobs better than the DCI could hope to. The general counsel, the DDP, and the other component chiefs were given a relatively free hand, much more so than under Allen Dulles. In his turn as DDP, though he endeavored to emphasize espionage, Helms recognized the increased interest in counterinsurgency and encouraged DDP efforts in Africa, Latin America, and southeast Asia. By the mid-1960s, Helms had almost as many people working in DDP as the entire Department of State, and it constituted more than a third of the CIA's personnel strength. Former CIA officers estimate that about 1,800 covert action officers served in DDP, as against 4,200 working on espionage or counterespionage. The bulk of the paramilitary officers worked for the Special Operations Division, while about 4,800 DDP officers were assigned to the area divisions, of which Far East was the largest with about 1,500 and Africa the smallest with only 300 officers assigned. The Directorate of Plans alone spent almost 60 percent of the CIA's budget (aside from the DCI's contingency fund) and furnished most of the approximately 5,000 CIA personnel stationed overseas.

One illustration of how the system worked when the military and CIA cooperated is provided by a tragic page from the history of Africa, the arrival of independence for the former colony Belgian Congo, today the nation of Zaire. The Congo was another of those crises that began in the twilight of the Eisenhower administration and lingered long into Kennedy's. The American operation occurred against a backdrop of intense political strife and residual colonial ambition among the Belgians.

Trouble swiftly followed independence day, June 30, 1960. The Belgians had done as little as possible to prepare the Congo for independence, to the extent that, for example, there were a mere *thirteen* Congolese college graduates, and no African officers in the

Congolese army. The Europeans' basic strategy was to concede independence but to ensure that Belgians would be required to *operate* all the institutions of the Congo. The Belgian commander of the Congolese army, General Emile Janssens, is reported to have hammered home the point at a meeting with African soldiers where he wrote on a blackboard *"avant indépendance = après indépendance."* The colonial relationship would endure.

Five days after independence the Congolese army began to revolt against their Belgian officers at Thysville, ninety miles from the capital. There, at Camp Hardy, a main base of the Force Publique, as the army was officially known, the Belgians were locked up. There were frantic stories of rapes and looting, and unrest in army units in Elizabethville and the capital, Leopoldville. A day of panic in Leopoldville followed on July 8, when both the British and the French embassies ordered evacuation of nonessential personnel. Several thousand Europeans fled across the Congo River to Brazzaville in the Congo Republic before rebel armed boats blocked the river.

The revolt naturally triggered a response by the infant government of the Congo. Prime Minister Patrice Lumumba attempted to deal with the mutineers and restore order. He dismissed General Janssens, then all 1,135 Belgian officers in the Force Publique, and gave promotions to many native soldiers.

Lumumba, the chief of the Mouvement National Congolais, was a young radical black with Pan-African sentiments; he was one of the Congo's thirteen college graduates. In May 1960 elections, Lumumba's party had garnered thirty-five seats to become the largest in the legislature and the only party with deputies elected in five of the Congo's six provinces. The Belgians would have liked to avoid a Lumumba cabinet, but the government inevitably coalesced around the biggest parliamentary party.

While the charismatic Lumumba possessed a popular following, the army revolt allowed the Belgians to claim that the Congolese government was ineffective and intervene with Belgian paratroop units on July 10, 1960. In various attempts to obtain countervailing assistance, Lumumba and Congolese President Joseph Kasavubu appealed for United Nations protection, the cabinet asked for American help, and Lumumba as prime minister requested Soviet assistance. The United Nations did pass a resolution to assist the Congo, with United States support. A United Nations security force that would eventually amount to nineteen thousand troops from thirty different European, Asian, and African nations was dispatched to the Congo.

The maneuvers for foreign support drew the United States and Soviet Union into the local situation, in effect bringing the cold war to Africa.

The Eisenhower administration did not favor Lumumba and did what it could to encourage opposition, especially from the more moderate President Kasavubu. American diplomats in Leopoldville reported negatively on Lumumba's initiatives, and policy hardened rapidly after the CIA station chief, Lawrence Devlin, cabled on August 18, 1960, that both the embassy and the station believed the Congo was experiencing a "classic Communist effort takeover government."

While the Americans made up their minds on Lumumba, the Belgians continued to occupy parts of the Congo, notably Katanga province where many of the country's most valuable mineral resources were located. Urged by the Belgians, Katangese politician Moise Tshombe attempted to secede the province, further complicating the internal problem. The slow formation and arrival of the United Nations force allowed the Katanga secession to bring the nation to the brink of civil war.

Political cleavages deepened in September 1960, when President Kasavubu, using the continued national crisis as justification, dismissed the Lumumba cabinet. The Americans had made their choice—there is evidence that the 5412 Group approved financial support for Kasavubu days before the constitutional coup. Lumumba, however, reacted by attempting to dismiss the president, creating an impasse that was resolved by parliament annulling the actions of both officials.

Joseph Mobutu was the wild card in all this. Twenty-nine years old, a former journalist, Army NCO, and member of Lumumba's party, Mobutu had been made an instant "colonel" after the army revolt and Lumumba installed him as chief of staff of the new independence army. He was then cultivated for weeks by American diplomats and CIA officers, including station chief Devlin. On September 14, Mobutu launched a military coup and declared he was "neutralizing" Kasavubu, Lumumba, and *all* the politicians for the rest of the year.

The prime target was Lumumba, whom Mobutu hoped to supplant with the help of the Americans. Allen Dulles was amenable to any solution that excluded Lumumba, whom he regarded as a figure with a "harrowing" background who had undoubtedly been "bought" by the communists. At the CIA a small office formerly responsible for DDP activities in several African lands was suddenly elevated to become the Congo Task Force. The sudden importance of Africa was revealed to Lawrence Devlin in late September, when the top CIA scientist descended on Leopoldville with exotic poisons and a plan to assassinate Lumumba. While, as with the plots against Castro, senior participants have steadfastly denied any presidential approval, the Senate investigation of the 1970s amply demonstrates that, approved or not, such CIA operations as this one against Lumumba actually occurred.

Dealing with Lumumba took months, exorcising his ghost required years of fighting in the Congo. Lumumba was incarcerated for a while, then freed by friendly UN peacekeeping soldiers. He made for Stanleyville in Orientale province, where supporters had set up yet another separatist government. Surveillance reports from the CIA were evidently instrumental in the capture of Lumumba by Mobutu troops on December 1. The degree of the CIA's complicity in the consequent murder of Lumumba, which occurred on January 17, 1961, remains in dispute.

Four days later John F. Kennedy was sworn in as thirty-fifth President of the United States. For almost a month the Congolese leader's fate remained the best-kept secret in Katanga. JFK reacted with shock and anguish when he learned of Lamumba's death on February 13. Still, the President's advisers had already proposed an activist role, and Kennedy had approved the recommendation.

Mobutu's ban on political activity in the Congo expired with the new year. Soon Kasavubu announced his appointment of a new prime minister and cabinet, while Mobutu remained the strong man of the armed forces. This uneasy coalition in Leopoldville prevailed for five years, until Mobutu returned from the shadows with a military coup that established his political domination in the Congo for over two decades.

Although the Americans had what they wanted—an allied government in Leopoldville—the price was the disintegration of the country. With the formation of yet another secessionist government in southern Kasai province, there were no less than four "nations" in the Congo. The United States' role became one of reinforcing

Leopoldville until Mobutu's army could reunite the nation by force. The United Nations peacekeeping force also sustained some criticism for acting so often in the American interest.

The scale of the Congo program necessitated close cooperation between the CIA and United States military. The program was massive: By May 1961 the Air Force had lifted 20,460 United Nations troops and 5,953 tons of equipment to the Congo, while the Navy had brought in another 5,096 UN troops and repatriated some 2,655. Direct military assistance to the Congolese included eighteen helicopters, ten C-47 aircraft, and five of the bigger C-119's. There were small arms, ammunition, and military advisers. In the fall of 1961, United Nations troops moved against Moise Tshombe's Katangese secessionists, who had hired European mercenaries, and fought a pitched battle for Elizabethville.

A political gambit in late 1961 was the formation of a government under Cyrille Adoula, who received substantial CIA support. Political action specialists assisted and financed a new political party. Paramilitary operators provided more C-47 aircraft and hired Cuban exile pilots, the first of a succession of Cuban contract employees to work for the CIA in the Congo. With this assistance Mobutu's army began the reconquest of Orientale in late 1961.

The secession dragged on for months. Barely had the Congo been reunified when, in the summer of 1963, a new rebellion commenced. This timing was the worst possible for Leopoldville—the United Nations force was withdrawing while Mobutu's army remained far from combat-effective. The best elements of the Congolese army were now units of white soldiers of fortune, principally of Belgian and English extraction, who were proud to call themselves mercenaries.

It was the mercenaries combined with the CIA air force who spearheaded operations against insurgents for another five years. There was a brief intervention by Belgian paratroops flown in by the U.S. Air Force in late 1964, when Europeans in Orientale were held hostage for over three months. Use of American Special Forces was considered but rejected on this occasion, and even the Belgians were considered unnecessary by Colonel Mike Hoare, whose 5 Commando unit of mercenaries was close to reaching Stanleyville at the moment of the airborne drop. Over two thousand foreign nationals were rescued and evacuated to Leopoldville, renamed Kinshasa after Mobutu's 1965 coup. The Congo itself was renamed Zaire.

Through all of this, the CIA air unit remained in place as an absolutely vital resource. Mobutu had no pilots of his own. American Special Forces provided advisers and temporarily deployed teams in the mid-1960s, when it was believed that Che Guevara was in Zaire helping the insurgents. At one point, station chief Benjamin Hilton Cushing volunteered CIA financing for Zaire's entire mercenary recruiting effort, though this offer was refused.

The CIA air force would indeed have been familiar to any veteran of the Bay of Pigs, or, for that matter, to any American airman from "Jungle Jim." There were ten C-47 transports, eight or nine B-26 bombers, and eight of the light T-28 fighter-bombers. Belgian pilots and maintenance crews worked the transport planes; the combat aircraft were repaired by the Western International Ground Maintenance Organization (WIGMO), a corporation chartered in Lichtenstein, which employed fifty to a hundred mechanics. When additional mercenaries were hired later to man a boat patrol on Lake Tangkanyika, WIGMO also maintained the naval vessels. The Cuban pilots were hired by another of those ubiquitous Miami corporations. The pilot group on rotation in early 1965 has been described by Mike Hoare as the best crop of Cubans yet. In mid-1966 there were only a dozen Cuban pilots, but they accounted for the vast majority of the combat air support in Zaire.

According to Cyrus Vance, an official on the Special Group during this period, the decision to wind down the Congo operation was made in early 1966. Actual withdrawal took eighteen months. This did not end DDP activities in Africa, however. The station in Ghana is informally credited with assisting the overthrow of Kwame Nkrumah during 1966. Some of the Cuban mercenary pilots from Zaire also went on to fly for the Portuguese in other African colonial wars. The hypothesis that these were private adventures is cast into doubt by the indictment of Intermountain Aviation, another CIA proprietary, for illegally exporting B-26 bombers to Portuguese Africa. General counsel Lawrence Houston, who was required to give testimony at the trial, denied any CIA connection with the arms shipments, while admitting that the Agency had known of the B-26 transfer flights five days in advance.

The Congo shows the secret warriors at full stride—created under Truman, enhanced by Eisenhower, built up by Kennedy, enthused by the potential of counterinsurgency strategy. By the 1960s the capabilities were in place and the contingencies existed to use them. The Congo was but one front in a global competition, Cuba a second. Two such campaigns conducted simultaneously was quite an achievement, but even more impressive is that both campaigns were conducted simultaneously with a third sustained effort in Vietnam. That would be the biggest of them all, counterinsurgency writ large.

·XIII·
VIETNAM

Though not cut from the same mold as Maxwell Taylor, Edward Geary Lansdale also considered himself something of a theorist. Managing Operation Mongoose and backstopping covert action at the Pentagon had taken Lansdale away from his primary interest, which was counterinsurgency. For a decade after his tour in the Philippines, during the Huk rebellion there, Lansdale remained a prominent advocate of psychological warfare and other CI methods. He expounded what he calls the "demotic" strategy, an approach especially aimed at the popular will with a goal essentially similar to what would come to be called "winning hearts and minds."

Amid his other work at the Pentagon's Office of Special Operations, Lansdale occasionally got the chance to expound his views. One such occasion occurred in 1959, after Eisenhower authorized Air Force C-130's to fly special-aid supplies of construction equipment to certain upland villages in Laos. Lansdale then made a tour, adding the Philippines and Vietnam to the itinerary, and came back to write a long report on the potential of "civic action" as a tool in counterinsurgency. A skilled harmonica player, he could easily believe in the armed patrol with a guitarist, helping to build a village dispensary and school, giving medical help to the villagers—and any other tactics to gain popular sympathies.

Lansdale argued his case with great zeal. He also had special credibility in this case, as author of the successful anti-Huk campaign, for which he had been awarded the National Security Medal; and as the American behind the apparent success of South Vietnamese President Ngo Dinh Diem. Despite his fervor, Lansdale's strategy was controversial in a pre-Vietnam era bureaucracy. Even within CIA, where political action was a more widely accepted technique, there were those who favored direct responses. John Kennedy's election had the effect of giving Lansdale another opportunity to make his case.

At the beginning of 1961, just a few weeks before Kennedy's inauguration, Lansdale was ordered to South Vietnam to make a fresh assessment. Briefly, he found that the government was increasingly ineffective in the countryside and had lost its dynamism, while guerrilla warfare was becoming more widespread and the army seemed unable to cope with it. Civilian control over the armed forces was such that Diem had barely survived a military coup attempted two months before by a popular paratroop colonel. The United States military advisory group, with which Lansdale himself had served from 1954 to 1956, was too small and too hampered by restrictions to have much impact on the South Vietnamese army.

Lansdale spent a little over two weeks in Vietnam. He spoke with Diem and other political and military figures, as well as personnel from the United States embassy. Compiling his report on the plane ride back, Lansdale was able to submit it on January 17, 1961. In exhortatory fashion the report presented a vision of an operation "changed sufficiently to free these Americans to do the job that needs doing."

In Saigon, Lansdale found American and Vietnamese officials whose attitudes reminded him of those of French and Vietnamese in Hanoi in 1953–1954. He believed Vietnam was undergoing an "intense psychological attack," that 1961 would be a fateful year, and that "Vietnam is in a critical condition and [we] should treat it as a combat area of the cold war, as an area requiring emergency treatment."

The answer was to pick "the best people you have," in Lansdale's opinion, "a hard core of experienced Americans who know and really like Asia and the Asians," who were given freedom of action. A new United States ambassador should be sent immediately, as well as "a mature American" to conduct "political operations to start creating a Vietnamese-style foundation for more democratic government."

This report created some stir in Washington. Walt Rostow

showed it to Kennedy on the afternoon of February 2. The President was busy and didn't want to read it all. Rostow told him he should. Kennedy looked up when he had finished.

"This is the worst one we've got, isn't it?" asked JFK curiously. "You know, Eisenhower never mentioned it. He talked at length about Laos, but never uttered the word Vietnam."

The secretary of defense wanted to hear from the author himself. Robert McNamara asked Lansdale around to his office to explain the recommendations. Casting about for some means of dramatizing the Vietnam situation, Lansdale scooped up an armful of rebel weapons—punji stakes and such, still caked with blood and mud—which he had gathered to encourage the Special Forces to open a weapons museum. He literally dumped the stuff on McNamara's mahogany desk, explaining that the United States-equipped South Vietnamese were being beaten by rebels with such instruments. Lansdale figured this was the best way to use his five minutes with the secretary of defense.

"Somehow I found him very hard to talk to," recalled Lansdale later. "Watching his face as I talked, I got the feeling that he didn't understand me."

It was the Pentagon that derailed President Kennedy's plan to appoint Lansdale ambassador to South Vietnam, reportedly with threats of McNamara's resignation. Several more attempts to assign Lansdale to Vietnam in one capacity or another were also blocked, until 1965 when ambassador Henry Cabot Lodge overrode all opposition. In the meantime, Ed Lansdale retired in 1963 with the rank of major general. In Vietnam, psychological warfare would function strictly as an adjunct to conventional military force.

One recommendation of the Lansdale Report that made it through the bureaucracy was an effort to improve Washington-level handling of Vietnam matters. President Kennedy formed a committee to canvass the alternatives and present him with a list of options. Given the Pentagon's status as the biggest player in Vietnam, it was not surprising that McNamara deputy Roswell Gilpatric chaired the group. A Lansdale fan in the White House, Walt Rostow, favored nominating the Air Force general to serve on the Gilpatric committee, but the Pentagon again brought in someone else.

The Gilpatric committee faced a difficult task; many of the members had entered with the new administration and were just finding their balance. Gilpatric's own recollection is that "none of us ... who were charged with the responsibility for this area, had any preparation for this problem. What we didn't comprehend was the inability of the Vietnamese to absorb our doctrine, to think and to organize the way we did." Nevertheless, the Gilpatric group came back to President Kennedy on May 6, 1961, with a menu of more than forty options.

Kennedy's decisions in this initial case conditioned much of the subsequent United States experience in Vietnam. Between doing nothing on one end of the scale or committing United States forces on the other, JFK chose to make a graduated expansion of the American effort, beginning a cycle that would be repeated many times. In the case of the Gilpatric recommendations, President Kennedy approved some of them in the NSAM-52 directive, which he signed on May 11. The United States would expand the military advisory group, and pay for a thirty-thousand-man increase in South Vietnamese forces. Of particular importance for the secret warriors, the NSAM-52 program included deployment to Vietnam of a provisional Special Forces group of four hundred Green Berets plus a mandate to "expand present operations in the field of intelligence, unconventional warfare, and political-psychological activities."

Kennedy also searched for a strategic concept he could use to manage the growing conflict. Counterinsurgency theory suggested population resettlement, leading to the "strategic hamlet" program and many subsequent variants. Geography suggested the possibility of sealing off South Vietnamese borders, thus preventing the infiltration of weapons or men from the north or through Laos. The border control approach was being touted as early as May 1961 by Robert Komer, a CIA analyst on detached duty with the NSC staff. The twin pillars of pacification and isolation of the battlefield provided the foundations for United States strategy throughout the Vietnam War.

In the summer and fall of 1961, Kennedy briefly flirted with sending combat forces to Southeast Asia. The possibility arose in the context of the Laos situation, but it was desirable also from the Vietnamese standpoint: An American occupation of the Laotian panhandle might have had the effect of blocking the Ho Chi Minh Trail, which the North Vietnamese had built in 1959 to send men and supplies south.

That November, Kennedy again faced a recommendation for regular American troops, this time from Maxwell Taylor and Walt Rostow who had just returned from a personal-evaluation mission on behalf of the President. Rostow had taken Ed Lansdale along to perform the special assignment of compiling a survey of resources for unconventional warfare. The Taylor-Rostow Report also included recommendations for a "radical" increase in numbers of Green Berets, along with "increased covert offensive operations in the North as well as in Laos and South Vietnam."

Once more President Kennedy rejected the troop request while approving almost everything else, including the increase in covert action.

Indeed, more secret warriors were reaching South Vietnam. The same day he sent Taylor and Rostow to Saigon, JFK had ordered out an Air Force combat detachment to bomb the supply lines of the rebels, called the Vietcong. The unit sent was the 4400th Combat Crew Training Squadron, the special air warfare "Jungle Jim" unit, which became operational on November 16, 1961. It flew secret air missions under the code name Farm Gate.

This deployment was part of a much wider expansion of American forces. The size of the assistance group rose from less than 700 when JFK took office to over 12,000 by mid-1962. There were many more military advisers, United States supply units to support the Vietnamese, United States helicopter units to fly them into battle, the Special Forces, plus Navy, Air Force, and Marine Corps detachments. Farm Gate retained its clandestine status, while semi-clandestine Air Force units followed: Mule Team to fly short-range air transports, and Ranch Hand (at first called Hades), which dropped toxic chemicals for the purpose of defoliation. The Vietnam contingent could hardly be called a "group" any more; it was redesignated the Military Assistance Command, Vietnam (MACV), continuing to expand to 15,000 in 1963 and about 22,000 a year later.

Conditions in South Vietnam deteriorated despite this plentiful support, however. The Vietnamese army never seemed able to catch the elusive Vietcong. Government officials were increasingly vulnerable to danger in the countryside. It was evident by 1963 that President Diem had lost most of his remaining political support, in particular when his brother, Ngo Dinh Nhu, began using force to quell demonstrations sponsored by Buddhists. The feeling in the Vietnamese army was that the political crisis was making it impossible to prosecute the war against the Vietcong. In Saigon, talk of a coup was in the air.

Those early days in Vietnam were an adventure for Americans, much as Korea had been a few years earlier. In the first days of South Vietnam it had been Lansdale who had established a close relationship with Diem and the Vietnamese authorities. When Lansdale left at the end of 1956, the liaison role remained the major activity of the CIA station at Saigon.

Later that role grew somewhat larger. In addition to liaison reporting, the CIA wished to have its own sources among South Vietnamese politicians and interest groups. By 1960 the Agency was supplying the best information outside the presidential palace, save perhaps for the Vietcong intelligence networks. Indeed, in a 1960 coup attempt, CIA officers had been in contact with the plotters throughout the proceedings. This caused some difficulty for the CIA station chief, William E. Colby, when Diem's brother Nhu found out about it.

Another task put on the CIA's list at this time was assistance for a program to infiltrate North Vietnam, using Vietnamese special forces (formed in 1958) or else paramilitary teams set up by CIA. Army colonel Gilbert Layton was detailed to the CIA station to supervise this effort. By 1961 the Agency had set up four teams of eight men each, but the units conducted operations only inside South Vietnam. Suggestions for commando raids in the north were resisted by intelligence specialists, who preferred to implant agent networks before making attacks that would encourage the North Vietnamese to tighten their security. As late as 1963, when President Kennedy asked for plans to land paramilitary teams in the north, NSC adviser McGeorge Bundy warned him that operations against North Vietnam presented many of the same difficulties as other "denied areas."

Colonel Layton, Colby, and other CIA officers had far more success with a paramilitary effort in South Vietnam. They began experimenting with the creation of armed forces among the tribal minorities in the Central Highlands. At first the purpose was self-defense, an upland counterpart for the "strategic hamlets," but as the strategy of border control gained acceptance the tribal units came to be seen as the basis for a striking force that could prevent Vietcong supplies from entering the south.

One result of the Taylor-Rostow Report was approval of an initiative to put the tribal program on a more formal footing. The tribal units would be called Civilian Irregular Defense Groups (CIDGs), with fortified base camps and leadership from the Green Berets. From 1961 to 1965 some eighty base camps or area development centers were established. Special Forces participation increased dramatically—from one medic on temporary duty in late 1961, to the first A Team deployed from Okinawa in February 1962, to a peak authorized strength of 3,480 by 1968. Until November 1962 the CIDG program was entirely a CIA responsibility; thereafter operational command was gradually transferred to MACV by the summer of 1963. All responsibility went to the military in a 1963 phase-out of CIA known as Operation Switchback.

By then, Colby had left Saigon for Washington, succeeding Desmond FitzGerald as chief of the DDP's Far East Division when the latter moved over to handle Cuba. Colby's place as chief of station at Saigon was taken by John H. Richardson, an officer from the Army Counter-Intelligence Corps. Richardson was an authentic espionage hero in Italy during 1944–1945, when he was instrumental in helping to capture the notorious German agent Carla Rossi. "Jocko" Richardson stayed on at CIC after the war, switched to the Central Intelligence Group, then the CIA. He had been assigned to Italy, Vienna, and Trieste, and moved to Saigon from Manila, where he had been chief of station. A veteran secret warrior, it was Richardson who, in the denouement of the Albania campaign, had been given the job of closing down the operating bases.

Richardson's style was not unlike that of DCI John McCone, who let his subordinates carve out empires so long as they did not cross the boss. There were different empires, too, in the Saigon station, no longer the homogeneous unit of forty that Bill Colby encountered in 1959. The paramilitary crowd made up one circle, the espionage crew another. Since 1961 there had been a communications intelligence circle also, while the demands of the Vietnam conflict swelled the station with a growing group of analyst types. Then there were the political action people.

One of the CIA political action men played a major role in the demise of President Diem. He was Lucien Conein, whose cover was as a lieutenant colonel assigned to the Vietnamese Interior Ministry, but whose real function involved contacts with the Vietnamese generals. Familiarly called Lulu or Black Luigi, Conein, who was born in France, had entered the OSS in the same training class as Bill Colby, and had run agent operations in Eastern Europe after the war. He had been a "Jedburgh" and a veteran of French commando operations in northern Indochina in 1945. Conein had also been a member of Lansdale's 1954–1956 intelligence mission, when links with the Vietnamese army were first forged.

Of course the biggest empire within the CIA station was Richardson's own. It was customary for station chiefs to maintain certain relationships themselves, in particular with the chiefs of the host countries' intelligence services. Thus Colby handed over to Richardson his relationship with Ngo Dinh Nhu, now the chief of Vietnamese intelligence and special forces. A gregarious man who spoke four or five languages including French, indispensable in Vietnam, Richardson had been a classmate of Richard Nixon at Whittier College in California. He got along with Nhu quite well.

Richardson's problem was not the Vietnamese but the United States government. Convinced that Diem's time had run out, the United States was desperately trying to get the Vietnamese president to make concessions and broaden the base of his government. Prime movers in this effort were the assistant secretary of state for Far Eastern affairs, Roger Hilsman, and the American ambassador, Henry Cabot Lodge. In August 1963 a notorious incident occurred when Hilsman, evidently with preliminary authorization, but while President Kennedy was out of town, drafted a cable insisting that Nhu must go. If Diem would not fire his brother, then the United States would have to look for alternatives. Nhu's special forces had just carried out a series of bloody attacks on Buddhist pagodas that was widely condemned. This was regarded as the last straw.

Lodge was enthusiastic about the cable though he advised against any ultimatum. Jocko Richardson, however, reported back through CIA channels that the ambassador had regarded the cable as an order to support a coup d'etat. Richardson opposed this. At Langley, Bill Colby backed him up. John McCone was on vacation but was quickly informed and also opposed any coup, although a cable from the DCI, on August 26, instructed Conein and CIA officer Alphonso G. Spero to tell the Vietnamese generals the substance of the Hilsman cable and say the United States would not oppose a coup if it had a good chance of succeeding and American forces were not involved.

McCone went on to oppose the coup initiative, and he was soon joined by Taylor, McNamara, and Vice-President Lyndon Johnson. The Hilsman cable was scuttled.

Lodge considered that he had been undermined by John Richardson. He insisted on the transfer of the station chief; Richardson was abruptly recalled on October 5 after little more than a year in Saigon. For a time the Vietnamese generals backed down, but two days before Richardson's hurried recall, Conein was told by the Vietnamese that a coup was being planned. That coup was carried out on November 1, 1963. Diem and Nhu, and the latter's equally hated wife, died in custody of the plotters the next day. Thanks to Conein, the CIA had had a front row seat to the coup planning if not its precise timing, of which the embassy got only four minutes' warning. Assassination seemed epidemic in November 1963. Just three weeks later, President Kennedy was killed by a sniper's rifle in Dallas, Texas.

Asked for his opinion of the United States' support for the Diem coup almost two decades later, Edward Lansdale replied, "I think we should never have done it. We destroyed the Vietnamese Constitution, not we, but the people we were working with, threw it in the waste basket." There would be several more coups before 1967, when General Nguyen Van Thieu and Air Marshal Nguyen Cao Ky consolidated their power to control the Saigon government.

Soon after the Diem coup, Bill Colby went out to Saigon to pick up the pieces. He had Jocko Richardson to dinner the evening before he left Washington. The top priority was to replace the station chief; Colby called in Peer de Silva, recently sent to Hong Kong after a long tour as CIA chief in Korea, where he too had seen a coup up close. De Silva had a strong background in espionage against "denied areas," particularly the Soviet Union, and had been the officer in charge of security for the atomic-bomb project. In Vietnam he was called on to preside over a significant escalation in paramilitary activities.

Escalation was mandated by President Lyndon Baines Johnson, Kennedy's sudden replacement in the Oval Office. If anything, LBJ was even more receptive than had been Kennedy to arguments favoring "graduated" military force, like the "Plan Six" strikes against North Vietnam for which Walt Rostow had argued in 1961. Within four days of assuming office, LBJ approved NSAM-273, which called for studies of different levels of increased activity, including statements of the resulting damage to the north and the plausibility of denial. The directive also called for plans to conduct military operations up to fifty kilometers into Laos and other measures to help the South Vietnamese. In response, Pentagon planners came up with OPLAN 34-A, which Johnson approved in January 1964.

A requirement for deniability immediately involved the CIA. De Silva's station was ordered to redouble efforts to infiltrate agents into the north, which began with airdrops in April. McNamara had the mistaken impression that the CIA drops proceeded at a rate of one a week. Instead, McGeorge Bundy told Johnson on July 24, there had been a total of eight CIA drops so far; they had been moderately successful, as radio contact had been preserved with about half the parties.

Another secret-warfare program under the CIA was a more ambitious effort to make coastal raids on targets in the north. The CIA procured and armed a number of very fast motorboats, called Swift boats, built in Norway. There were also slower but heavily armed Nasty boats. Commando units of Vietnamese special forces used the Swift boats for raids, often accompanied by American advisers. The need for Green Beret and SEAL expertise in operations of this kind led MACV to organize a Studies and Observation Group (SOG) as an unconventional-warfare task force, in January 1964.

Among the 34-A operations, which were carried out by air or by sea, were the delivery of propaganda leaflets and "gift kits"; the airdrop of teams to conduct sabotage along North Vietnamese roads; and the drop of another team targeted against the Red River valley railroad from Yen Bay to Lao Kay. By late July only three seaborne missions had occurred that were considered successful: the demolition of a bridge on Highway 1, the partial destruction of a storage area, and the temporary interdiction of a water-pumping station. On the last night of July, there was another Swift boat raid to shell the North Vietnamese radar station and other facilities on the islands of Hon Me and Hon Ngu in the gulf of Tonkin.

The Hon Me raid, inadvertently or otherwise, coincided with another United States intelligence operation, a "De Soto" patrol into the Gulf of Tonkin. De Soto patrols were made by U.S. Navy ships and were intended to collect communications intercepts. Ships carrying out these operations had enhanced equipment for radio intercept, direction finding, and traffic analysis. De Soto patrols had long been carried out off the coasts of China, the Soviet Union, and

North Korea; President Kennedy had approved a similar program for North Vietnam in 1962, when the first such patrol was carried out. There was a second De Soto mission in 1963, and the destroyer *Craig* made an intercept cruise in the Gulf of Tonkin in March 1964. There is some evidence of a futher De Soto patrol that July. In any case, the destroyer *Maddox* was on a De Soto patrol when it arrived off the North Vietnamese coast, to find four Swift boats passing her on a southerly heading, the 34-A raiders returning to base. That evening the *Maddox* was off the shores of the islands so recently shelled.

In response, the North Vietnamese sent torpedo boats, which attacked the *Maddox* in international waters the next afternoon. They were driven off after one of their torpedo boats was sunk and the others damaged. President Johnson deliberately ordered the *Maddox* back into the Gulf of Tonkin, accompanied by another destroyer, *C. Turner Joy*.

The two destroyers together, two nights later, mistook instrument readings for a second attack.

President Johnson retaliated by ordering carrier air strikes on North Vietnam. The early reports, which mistakenly cited as many as six enemy craft and nine or ten torpedoes, impelled Johnson to go to Congress for a resolution supporting his action. Congress approved the Gulf of Tonkin Resolution on August 7, 1964. This resolution was then used by the President in place of a declaration of war to commit United States troops to combat in South Vietnam.

McGeorge Bundy's immediate problem was what to do with De Soto. As a reconnaissance project, De Soto patrols were approved by the Special Group, renamed the 303 Committee by President Johnson in his NSAM-303. Bundy was chairman of the group that should have made the decision. Because of LBJ's extreme sensitivity to developments in Vietnam, this question was taken up directly by the President.

Both De Soto patrols and 34-A operations were temporarily halted while Washington debated policy. The Joint Chiefs of Staff argued for open military action, bombing North Vietnam and relaxing rules of engagement for American forces. Maxwell Taylor, who had become ambassador to South Vietnam in July, favored action but only after waiting until December to see if the Vietnamese political situation stabilized. Like Kennedy before him, LBJ accepted other recommendations involving less than the maximum option: Resume De Soto patrols and 34-A operations; reinforce Farm Gate with heavier B-57 jet bombers. Thus operations like De Soto and 34-A, which could be considered provocative, were suddenly approved not on their merits but as alternatives to even greater provocation.

President Johnson specifically approved resumption of naval patrols on September 10 in NSAM-314. The 34-A operations were to resume as soon as the first De Soto patrol had been completed.

McGeorge Bundy was in his office at 9:15 A.M. on a Friday morning, September 18, when De Soto had another false alarm. The new patrol in the Tonkin Gulf consisted of the United States destroyers *Morton* and *Parsons*, which reported they had opened fire on four radar contacts they had believed to be torpedo boats making a night attack. The initial response of the Joint Chiefs was that the United States should immediately attack North Vietnamese air bases and oil facilities in the Hanoi-Haiphong area. Cooler heads prevailed for the moment. Information that afternoon and the next day made it increasingly clear that there had been no premeditated attack, though North Vietnamese boats may have been at sea.

Early in October, when two more destroyers were designated to conduct another De Soto patrol, the ships were specially equipped with star shells—photographic and sound-recording equipment to provide tangible records. These ships were also sent on an exercise patrol in friendly waters, and underwent mock attacks by day and night using some of the Nasty boats from Da Nang.

Had the original De Soto patrol made such preparations, there might never have been an incident in the Gulf of Tonkin. As such precautions were in the purview of the 303 Committee, one wonders just how much attention was being given to them by the Special Group, not only for De Soto but on all kinds of covert operations.

The CIA, at least, felt itself to be under tight control. According to a February 1967 memorandum:

> The policy arbiters have questioned CIA presentations, amended them and, on occasion, denied them outright. The record shows that the Group/Committee, in some instances, has overridden objections from the DCI and instructed the Agency to carry out certain activities. . . . Objections by State have resulted in amendment or rejection of election proposals, sugges-

tions for air proprietaries, and support plans for foreign governments. . . . The Committee has suggested areas where covert action is needed, has decided that another element of government should undertake a proposed action, imposed caveats and turned down specific proposals for CIA action from Ambassadors in the field.

State Department participants on the 303 Committee like U. Alexis Johnson also felt that Special Group monitoring was rather strict. Johnson himself earned the sobriquet Dr. No for the frequency with which State cast vetoes on proposed operations. Yet in the period November 1963 to February 1967, the 303 Committee approved 142 covert action projects. This averages out to 5.25 approvals per month, compared to 4.8 during the Kennedy administration. Considering that the 303 Committee normally met only once a week, and that proposals were submitted in advance for discussion within the departments, a lot more work must have gone into approval than implementation.

The gains from all this were strictly limited, but the lessons learned by President Kennedy were lost. Bundy recalls:

> In 1961, I listened with a beginner's credulity to the arguments of the eager operatives who promoted what became the Bay of Pigs. . . . Through the next two years and more, I watched with increasing skepticism as the Kennedy Administration kept the pressure on the CIA for more and better—if smaller—covert operations.
>
> I think that eventually I played a small part—his own learning from experience was much more important—in President Kennedy's growing recognition that covert action simply did not work and caused more trouble than it was worth.

Kennedy's demise and replacement by Johnson ended the potential for a change in policy on covert action. Certainly the 303 Committee approval figures cited above demonstrate that Bundy was unsuccessful in stemming the tide of covert action proposals, many of which would be executed in Vietnam.

In the Central Highlands of South Vietnam, it did not much matter what the policymakers were saying in Washington. Here the war effort progressed slowly while Special Forces attempted to seal the border and cut the Vietcong supply trails. Unlike many other facets of MACV's work, the CIDG program involved Americans directly rather than as advisers to the Vietnamese. In fact, the lowland Vietnamese had little affinity for the many tribes of *montagnards* (French for mountaineers; the American colloquial expression was "yards"), and were at first willing to give the CIA and Special Forces a free hand.

The program began in October 1961 among the Rhadé, one of the eighteen major *montagnard* tribal groups. The villagers of Buon Enao agreed to accept American arms and training. Men from the Vietnamese special forces, officially called the Luc Luong Dac Biet (LLDB), were included in these missions from the beginning, even, in theory, commanding them, but often functioning more as observers. At Buon Enao there were more LLDB than Americans, but the Rhadé deferred to the Green Berets. By December 1961, radiating out from Buon Enao, the *montagnards* had cleared out an enclave containing forty villages and 14,000 tribesmen. The Americans had armed 975 Rhadé as village defenders and 300 more as a mobile strike force, known as Mike Forces. A year later there were two hundred villages and 60,000 Rhadé in the cleared area, with 10,600 self-defense forces and 1,500 in the Mike Forces. The method was repeated with other tribes, including the Sedang and Hré, who were regarded as superb fighters; the Bahnar and Bru, who were rated as effective; and the Jeh and Ma, considered merely capable. By December 1963 there were 43,376 village militia and 18,000 strike forces. Green Berets assigned to the CIDG numbered 951 in October 1964.

Nha Trang, a port town on the central Vietnamese coast, was the hub of this tribal war against the Vietcong. Farm Gate aircraft stationed there flew supplies to the villages and CIDG camps and provided some air support. When MACV wanted to give Special Forces their own air unit for support, the Air Force opposed this. The command countered it would hire Air America for the job, so the Air Force then stationed more planes at Nha Trang. The base grew wildly. Vietnamese commandos trained there, the shallow-water port was deepened, major logistics facilities and airfield expansion were undertaken. Special Forces headquarters, redesignated the 5th Special Forces Group in October 1964, had already moved there twenty months before.

One major boon to the 5th Group was CIA funding, because its procurement system, unlike the Army's, allowed for easy local and specialized buying of what Special Forces needed, at all levels of the unit. Under an accounting arrangement known as "Parasol-Switchback," 5th Special Forces continued to use CIA accounting methods for nine more years after the Agency passed control of the *montagnard* program to MACV in 1963. Resources of the 5th Group were far greater than those available to other components of MACV.

As late as March 1965 Nha Trang had one of the only two stockpiles of U.S. Army ammunition in South Vietnam and it belonged to 5th Special Forces. The group's stockpile eventually was deemed sufficient to supply forty thousand people for sixty days.

Supporting the CIDG camps, and actually getting the supplies to them, was not so easy as stockpiling. In many cases the camps were not even on the road network. When they were, the road itself would often be in disrepair or blocked by the Vietcong. The Vietnamese army was thinly scattered in the Central Highlands and in no position to support the CIDG camps. The Vietnamese corps command and base was also at Nha Trang, subject to the same geographic obstacles as 5th Special Forces.

Military support for the CIDG camps became critical in the case of enemy attacks. This was the basic reason for the Mike Force units. Unless a reserve was poised for immediate counterattack, it was usually too late to affect the outcome of an attack on a CIDG camp. It was not long before the National Liberation Front (NLF) realized the potential of the border control strategy and began to contest the issue in the Central Highlands. Two Special Forces officers were captured in an ambush as early as 1963. In 1964 the NLF overran Polei Krong. That July they just failed to capture another camp whose CIDG "strikers" and Green Beret team held out by sheer determination. Captain Roger Donlon earned the first Medal of Honor awarded in Vietnam for this action at Nam Dong, and two of his Special Forces sergeants received posthumous Distinguished Service Crosses.

Heroism was not enough for Colonel John H. Spears, commander of 5th Special Forces Group. Spears needed to count on certain capabilities in planning the defense of the CIDG camps. Mike Force was the obvious answer, but they expanded far more slowly than the CIDGs as a whole: 30,400 strike forces to 1,800 Mike

Force in October 1965; 34,800 to 3,200 in late 1966. The peak was 34,346 strike forces to 5,733 Mike Force in 1967. Thereafter, total numbers fell, although Mike Force continued to expand, reaching 9,326 native "strikers" in October 1969.

In the early days the Mike Forces were just not big enough or mobile enough to be everywhere at once. Colonel Spears met the problem by designating a portion of Mike Forces as "Eagle Flight," which could be airlifted to any CIDG camp under attack. With a dozen Green Berets and 149 "strikers" in each Mike Force unit, airlift was possible with a reasonable-sized helicopter force. Such tactics were still in use in 1966, when Colonel Francis J. Kelly commanded 5th Group. Kelly told a newly assigned deputy, as the man had just stepped off the plane at Nha Trang and was still unshaven, that if any CIDG camp appeared threatened he would order in the Nha Trang Mike Forces by parachute and the deputy would lead the mission.

Reaction forces were supplemented with certain special-capability units. The earliest of these was Project Delta, formerly Leaping Lena, jointly run by 5th Group and the LLDB. Delta provided small reconnaissance patrols that could spot NLF units for attack by artillery and air bombardment or ground troops. At a later stage a Vietnamese army ranger battalion was added to Delta to provide small combat units and fix the NLF in place while the other forces were being called in. The project was run by Special Forces Detachment B-52, whipped into shape by Captain Charlie Beckwith. Delta ultimately numbered 93 Green Berets, 187 "strikers," 185 LLDB, and 816 Vietnamese rangers.

Colonel Kelly also added two other special units, Projects Sigma and Omega, run respectively by the B-50 and B-56 detachments of 5th Group. Each project consisted of 127 Green Berets and 894 CIDG fighters and was paid, trained, and commanded by Americans. These units fielded "Roadrunner" teams of four to six "strikers" and Berets, identical to those of Delta, which furnished the United States a unilateral capability for long-range ground reconnaissance.

Air power was a key requirement of Special Forces strategy. Planes and helicopters were necessary to supply the CIDG camps, reinforce them, attack the enemy, and insert the Roadrunner teams or reinforcements for them. Nha Trang base was like a cauldron, filled with the special-warfare types, "spooks" in the idiom of the era, both Green Berets and air commandos. In 1962, the Army put twelve UH-1 Iroquois helicopters into Nha Trang plus the 23rd Special Warfare Aviation Detachment (Surveillance), whose real mission was air strikes using armed light planes. In 1964 the Air Force added Project Duck Hook, a unit of six specially equipped C-123 transports. These increased until reaching the strength of two squadrons and were then consolidated into the 1st Air Commando Wing. The 14th Air Commando Squadron, the first gunship aircraft unit in Vietnam, with its 32 AC-47 "Puff the Magic Dragon" aircraft, was also based at Nha Trang. To complete the picture, Nha Trang was used to stage top-secret missions into North Vietnam and Laos, about which more will be said shortly.

With the growing importance of Nha Trang came expansion of the base. Over an extended period of time, in this tightly constricted area were built a port, a major airfield, the supply depots, and the Special Forces cantonments. Coordination was not always satisfactory between U.S. Army Engineers and the Filipino construction crews hired by Special Forces and the Air Force. In 1965, Army engineers spent weeks digging deep drainage ditches for a supply depot in anticipation of the rainy season. Then Air Force contractors installed ditches to drain the airfield that rendered completely ineffective the depot drainage system. A study concluded that "only the crash allocation of equipment and manpower to relocate the drainage facilities prevented a major disaster from flooding." The work had to be done on the very eve of the rainy season.

For all of its difficulties the special-warfare campaign in the Central Highlands was one of the most successful of the Vietam War. Despite this, or perhaps because of it, the Special Forces were always viewed with some suspicion by other Americans assigned to MACV.

Their relationship with the South Vietnamese was also most sensitive. As the CIDG program started to show successes, the Vietnamese wanted to take it over. In fact, Vietnamese actions led to a political crisis in the highlands in September 1964, when the Vietnamese army tried to integrate the CIDG units into its own forces. The Rhadé tribe and others rebelled at six CIDG camps; some of them marched on the provincial capital Banmethuot and took it over for a night. Over sixty Vietnamese soldiers were killed; others were saved only by the intercession of the American advisers. At some camps the Green Berets themselves were locked in their quarters, while in at least one instance the Americans sided with the *montagnards*.

The *montagnards* who occupied Banmethuot briefly marched under the three-starred flag of FULRO, the French language acronym for a *montagnard* independence movement. The South Vietnamese made political concessions, in a March 1965 proclamation, giving the tribes increased autonomy, but its terms were largely honored in the breach. In September 1965 there was another rebellion by Mike Force "strikers." When it collapsed, FULRO leader Y Bham fled to Cambodia where he set up his own *montagnard* underground, considered an enemy by the South Vietnamese government. Even so, there is some evidence of CIA support to FULRO in Cambodia.

In 1969, when the United States began to withdraw and "Vietnamize" the war, 5th Special Forces began to be reduced. The numbers of CIDG "strikers" were also reduced. Beginning in June 1970 the CIDG elements, particularly the Mike Forces, were converted into South Vietnamese ranger units. In the end the Vietnamese got their way.

Neither cleavages between Vietnamese ethnic groups nor coups in Saigon interrupted the Johnson administration's slide into deepening commitment. Farm Gate was augmented by more powerful B-57 jet bombers after the Tonkin Gulf incident, while 34-A operations resumed that winter. The NLF helped accelerate the involvement with its own actions. Apparently in retaliation for the Tonkin Gulf air strikes, in November 1964 the Vietcong executed a very damaging mortar attack against the Farm Gate B-57 bombers on the ground at Bien Hoa. That Christmas Eve, the NLF bombed the American bachelor officers' quarters at Saigon, followed in early February by another destructive mortar and rocket attack on the United States air base at Pleiku. McGeorge Bundy happened to be in Saigon at that moment, and joined the chorus advising President Johnson to respond by bombing the north.

Although he had rejected a similar recommendation only a month before, LBJ now ordered the first strikes on a "tit for tat" basis, and this soon became a concerted bombing campaign against North Vietnam. To protect the air bases, American combat forces were then committed to Vietnam beginning on March 8, 1965.

In turn, the NLF set off a car bomb outside the United States embassy in Saigon on March 30. Among the many badly injured in the blast was CIA station chief Peer de Silva.

Open American actions continued to be supplemented by secret 34-A operations. In the period from January 19 to February 2 alone, the "spooks" attempted three air and nine naval missions against the north. A plane dropped four agents and four bundles for team Remus on the night of January 20; one agent was killed on landing, while another broke a leg. One naval mission aborted because of engine trouble; two heavily armed Nasty boats, intending to shell a coastal observation post, collided, aborting another mission on January 26. Still, five targets were shelled, one of them twice.

By this time the CIA had built an extensive network in Vietnam. With four hundred officers, Saigon had surpassed Miami as the largest CIA station. There was also a training center for pacification teams at Vung Tau; the boat base for 34-A at Da Nang; plus a force of fierce Nung for the raids who were armed and trained by the CIA.

In March 1965, as part of LBJ's search for Vietnam options, DCI John McCone presented a twelve-point program for political action developed under Richard Helms at the DDP. Breaking with the image of a CIA that did not advocate policy, Helms's memorandum to McCone argued that key activities "should be intensified or initiated in the general field of covert political action." Further, "some of these actions are covert in the traditional sense of secrecy and non-attributable sponsorship. Others are on the overt side, but are properly undertaken by CIA because of our flexibility and capability to move into situations quickly, bypassing cumbersome governmental mechanisms."

Seven of the twelve CIA initiatives remain classified two decades after this program was adopted. The other points were recommendations to expand political action teams working in disputed areas, to organize *montagnard* "strikers" in a "highly flexible" manner, to provide assistance to local partisan groups willing to fight the National Liberation Front, to expand harassment teams working in NLF areas, and to develop small irregular elements to track down, infiltrate, and capture enemy communications centers.

The CIA naturally considered such techniques as these to be more subtle than blunt military force. This view was not completely shared within the administration, especially at the Pentagon, where Secretary of Defense Robert McNamara liked his options quantified and analyzed. A veteran by this time of a half-dozen inspection visits and command conferences at Honolulu, McNamara was also periodically briefed by CIA. At about this time Dick Helms was promoted to deputy DCI while Desmond Fitz-Gerald succeeded him as director of plans, thus becoming responsible for the McNamara briefings.

In one of their encounters, McNamara told Des FitzGerald, "You know, it's hard to make sense of this war."

"Mr. Secretary, facts and figures are useful," FitzGerald replied, but you can't judge a war by them. You have to have an instinct, a feel. My instinct is that we're in for a much rougher time than your facts and figures indicate."

McNamara questioned, "You really think that?"

"Yes, I do."

But when the secretary of defense pressed for some basis for the statement, the DDP simply repeated, "It's just an instinct, a feeling."

FitzGerald later told Stewart Alsop, a journalist friend, about this conversation. When Alsop then printed a piece that said McNamara had a fixation with quantifying this war, the secretary of defense decided FitzGerald had been the source. There were no more briefings by the DDP.

Elements of the CIA plan were adopted, but the ones we know about were carried out by Special Forces not the Agency. Shortly afterward John McCone left government.

Through MACV-SOG, the euphemistically named Studies and Observation Group, the military had already taken over the effort to place agents in North Vietnam. The CIA had come to believe this program was futile but nevertheless turned over the five teams it had managed to place. SOG succeeded in infiltrating another. All, in the opinion of senior Special Forces veteran Charles Simpson, were probably being controlled by the North Vietnamese in much the same way the Albanians and Russians had "turned" teams in the fiascos of the 1950s.

In Vietnam, SOG increased to a peak strength of two thousand Americans and eight thousand Vietnamese. It had its own air support from the 90th Special Operations Wing and Project Duck Hook, based at Nha Trang. Of five missions assigned Duck Hook in October 1964, only one had been successfully accomplished by the end of November.

There were other efforts as well. Another air operation was called Buttercup; it reportedly included at least one drop into China, and featured U.S. C-130's registered in foreign countries. Maritime operations included Timberlake coastal raids and Fascination, an attempt to disrupt the north's fishing industry. There were also plenty of operations across the border into Laos and Cambodia.

The South Vietnamese participated in these efforts. Two helicopters managed to insert team Romeo just north of the demilitarized zone in late 1965. However, Vietnamese C-47's failed to complete *any* of their twelve assigned missions in the first quarter of 1966. After that, responsibility was shifted to the Vietnamese pilots of A-1 Skyraider strike aircraft, which completed five resupply missions that year. An American reinforcement-resupply mission was also completed on December 25, 1966, using a Duck Hook C-123.

The peak of the secret war waged by MACV-SOG came in 1967–1968. Seven successful Duck Hook flights occurred in the first quarter of 1967; afterward another ten were completed before the halt of American bombing in November 1968 brought an end to overflights. For the two-year period the completion rate was about one in every three missions. Of six SOG teams scheduled for insertion in September–October 1967, only three were landed successfully. One C-130 was lost on the ground in November, while another with eleven men aboard disappeared on December 29, 1967.

Another special air warfare unit based in Thailand, with the code name Pony Express, carried out missions over North Vietnam beginning in January 1967. That year Pony Express completed eight of thirty-seven missions assigned. It successfully recovered a SOG team in September 1967. Meanwhile, Vietnamese efficiency declined even further. During 1968 the Vietnamese completed only three of thirty-two scheduled missions. Finally, the U.S. Air Force used sophisticated F-4 jet fighters from Da Nang to resupply SOG teams in the Red River delta region of North Vietnam. Fifteen of these missions were completed between 1966 and 1968, a success rate of about 20 percent.

The overall effort in the north consumed great resources for gains of very little in intelligence or propaganda value. Except in Laos, which will be dealt with at length, throughout the war North Vietnamese troops were never significantly hampered by unconventional warfare or other threats on home ground. The military value of MACV-SOG is to be found, not among the close-knit cadres and villagers of North Vietnam, but in Laos, Cambodia, and the south, where their special-mission capability was prized. In those places the "projects" and the SOG, with plentiful support and a sort of private air force, plus the weight of MACV backing them up, had a tremendous raid and reconnaissance potential. Nowhere did this become more evident than in one theater of the Indochina war, where the CIA and the Green Berets virtually ran the whole show.

·XIV·
THE HIGH PLATEAU

The secret war reached its climax among the rugged mountains and high plains of Laos, Vietnam's landlocked neighbor. In Laos paramilitary action and political manipulation attained heights never achieved before or since. In previous paramilitary efforts the CIA had always been hampered in one way or another: Actions had been impeded by the United States' reluctance to show its hand, as in Cuba or Albania, or by a lack of truly popular indigenous groups to recruit, as in Indonesia or the People's Republic of China, or by the lack of suitable support bases, as in Tibet. In South Vietnam, there were other agencies like the Pentagon with a better claim to exercise command. Even such CIA successes as Iran and Guatemala had been achieved in the short term—as coups rather than extended paramilitary campaigns.

Laos would be different. There was no difficulty in defining a mission for the secret warriors—insurgency was increasing in South Vietnam and the north was using Laos to move its supplies to the battle area. Thus Laos was the front line in the struggle to seal off South Vietnam's borders. Bases were plentiful both in the south and in neighboring Thailand, another American ally. At the same time, American military command was excluded by the terms of the 1954 Geneva agreement on Indochina, which allowed only French military personnel in Laos to advise the Royal Laotian Government (RLG). In Laos the CIA had the field all to itself, with the military supporting its actions, rather than the other way around, as had been the case in the Korean War, and was now the case in Vietnam.

* * *

After the 1954 agreement, Laos had a good chance to reach its goal of independence with stability. It was a small country with a small political elite; leaders of all persuasions were well known to each other, many of them related. Prime examples were two princes of the royal blood, Souphanouvong, a leader of the communist movement, and his brother Souvanna Phouma, a proponent of neutralism between East and West. The French had some residual influence, while an American presence was established after Geneva and slowly grew throughout the 1950s.

Of course, the Eisenhower administration had no mind to accept a neutralist solution. Much as he did with Sukarno, Nehru, and Nasser, Ike insisted that Laos side with the Western camp in the cold war. Ambassador J. Graham Parsons spent two years discouraging formation of a coalition government. American aid began in 1955. By 1960 the United States had provided Laos with over $250 million in assistance, two thirds of it to pay the entire costs of maintaining RLG armed forces.

The CIA station played a critical role in political action. Showing anew their predilection for "third force" political options, the secret warriors backed Laotians who formed a pro-American Committee for the Defense of National Interests (CDNI) after a 1958 electoral upset in which Souphanouvong's party and its allies gained the majority of the seats contested, while the prince himself was elected by the largest margin of victory in every district of the country. The young people who formed CDNI were called *les jeunes*. In the Laotian political capital, Vientiane, many of them had risen through the Junior Chamber of Commerce, and they were reformist, anticommunist, and had the rare advantage of being united across traditional clan and party lines. It quickly became an open secret in Vientiane that the American special services were supporting the conservative CDNI.

Elections in 1958 were supposed to complete a formal process of reintegration for Laos, which was under military control of the different factions, just as in warlord China. The socialist Lao People's Front (Neo Lao Hak Xat, or NLHX) and especially its parent, the Laotian communists, or Pathet Lao, dominated in the provinces Phong Saly and Sam Neua. In November 1958, Prince Souphanouvong accepted the king's authority within these provinces and Pathet Lao troops were integrated into the Royal Lao Armed

Forces (RLAF), while the NLHX was to be represented on a neutralist coalition cabinet to form under Souvanna Phouma. In a ceremony in February 1958, some 1,500 Pathet Lao soldiers joined the RLAF while 4,284 more were discharged. But the accord disintegrated when the Souvanna cabinet fell in July 1958.

Suddenly *les jeunes* took center stage, gaining seats in a cabinet formed in August even though some of the four CDNI ministers had lost in the elections. At the same time, two Pathet Lao ministers were dismissed. Trouble quickly followed within the RLAF as the two battalions that consisted of Pathet Lao troops revolted, rekindling the Laotian civil war.

The Eisenhower administration cut back aid to Laos for fiscal 1959, when it appeared that a neutralist government was emerging. But aid was increased when fighting resumed with the Pathet Lao, and increased again in 1960 as the conflict deepened. As the American conduit to the CDNI, the CIA station in the United States embassy grew especially important.

In Vientiane, however, all was not well at the embassy. Ambassador Horace Smith initially argued for supporting Souvanna's neutralist solution and considered his policy had been undermined by CIA. Station chief Henry Hecksher refused to tell his boss about some Agency activities. Ambassador Smith took his grievance to Allen Dulles early in 1959, demanding that Hecksher be transferred elsewhere. The DCI knew of Hecksher's arrogance, but he knew as well of the station chief's resourcefulness. Hecksher had worked against the Russians, and turned in a fine performance in the Guatemala operation. Dulles backed up his station chief; and at the end of his normal tour, he was even assigned to northeast Thailand, where he continued to control some cross-border operations into Laos. Taking that into consideration, Hecksher outlasted his ambassador, for Smith was replaced in the summer of 1960 by Winthrop G. Brown, a former Wall Street lawyer and ambassador to New Delhi.

Only three weeks after Brown's arrival, the pro-American government in Vientiane was overthrown in a coup by the paratroop forces of Captain Kong Le. A veteran of the French campaign for Dien Bien Phu, Kong Le remained inscrutable to most of the Americans, who seemed unwilling to believe his declarations for neutralism, and harbored the theory that Kong Le was a communist, or so-called "fellow traveler." American perceptions aside,

Kong Le became the strong man in Laos and asked Souvanna Phouma to form a new government. Like his predecessor, Ambassador Brown counseled Washington to cooperate with Souvanna as the most pro-Western leader sustainable in Laos. Brown believed that the new CIA station chief, Gordon L. Jorgensen, agreed with him.

In the fall of 1960 the die was cast for the secret war. Washington still wanted no part of neutralism. Their solution was Colonel Phoumi Nosavan, a *jeune* from the RLAF who had used the CDNI as a springboard to power, eventually becoming a general and minister of defense. Phoumi had been cultivated by the CIA from an early date and had his own personal adviser assigned by the Agency, John Hazey. A veteran of OSS and the French Foreign Legion, Hazey had a personal back-channel for communicating with Washington without going through the local station. Hazey argued for increasing support for Phoumi, instead of the government in Vientiane, as the pro-American alternative.

Washington decided to take the Vientiane position on the surface, but to secretly support Phoumi. The Hazey link was strengthened. That October, J. Graham Parsons, now risen to assistant secretary of state for Far Eastern affairs, returned to Vientiane to demand of Souvanna Phouma the renunciation of all ties with the Pathet Lao, in effect the abandonment of neutralism.

Souvanna refused.

Shortly thereafter, 5412 Group member John N. Irwin, who represented the Pentagon as assistant secretary of defense for international security affairs, visited southern Laos for direct talks with Phoumi Nosavan. A second Irwin trip occurred before Kennedy took office. The Americans began to channel their military assistance directly to Phoumi's forces, bypassing the Vientiane government. Reports of a North Vietnamese invasion of Laos, which grew from a trumped-up border incident, were used to justify further military aid increases.

Phoumi denounced the Souvanna coalition, resigned his cabinet post, and ordered his forces to take the capital. The Kong Le forces inflicted several ignominious defeats on Phoumi's men before they retreated from Vientiane in mid-December. By that time the neutralists had virtually been driven into the arms of the Pathet Lao. Souvanna Phouma and Souphanouvong formed their own coalition, excluding Phoumi, on November 18, 1960. A little over two weeks later, on December 4, the Soviet Union began an airlift of military supplies to the Kong Le-Pathet Lao forces, and the Pathet Lao began a military offensive of their own.

Political intrigue had turned Laos, the Land of a Million Elephants, into a battleground of the cold war.

The Americans had been able to act very quickly in Laos, once the decision was taken to support Phoumi, because the apparatus had been carefully put in place over the preceding years. By the summer of 1960, when Washington briefly considered evacuation of Americans in the face of the Laotian crisis, there were over six hundred Americans in the country, mostly working for the United States mission or private relief groups like International Voluntary Service.

One special feature of the United States' operating mission in Laos was that military representation was not restricted to the attaché. There was a military advisory group in all but name, headed by a United States general officer. In deference to the Geneva agreement, the advisory group was called a Program Evaluation Office (PEO) and had the ostensible task of monitoring the effects of American programs in the country. The PEO had its beginnings in December 1955, with the installation of a six-man staff at Vientiane. By early 1956, PEO was dispatching small teams of advisers to RLAF units, usually with Thai interpreters who translated English to Lao.

The Eisenhower administration added 107 Green Berets to PEO beginning in the summer of 1959 for Project White Star. This was the assignment of mobile training teams to each of the twelve battalions of the RLAF. White Star teams trained, but were also prepared to command, the Laotian infantry. The Special Forces men came from the 7th Group at Fort Bragg; they were flown in from Bangkok aboard Air America planes.

Green Berets in Laos wore civilian clothes and used PEO cover. Lieutenant Colonel Arthur D. "Bull" Simons was the first White Star commander, and he had a tough job satisfying so many bosses—the PEO chief, the CIA chief of station, the ambassador, the Laotian government, even the French military mission, which had sole responsibility for Laos under the Geneva accord. Early White Star veterans include Grayston Lynch, later a CIA boat man at the Bay of Pigs; and Charlie Beckwith, who later trained with the elite British Special Air Service and then went to Vietnam where he commanded Project Delta. The White Star officers were in a delicate and dangerous position. On more than one occasion teams of Americans were exposed in the field when the Laotian soldiers they accompanied ran away from impending battles.

Another facet of the Laotian program, one that preceded and prefigured the CIDG effort in Vietnam, was the creation of armed paramilitary units among the hill tribes. This program was given high priority after August 1960, when a CIA special national intelligence estimate found that North Vietnamese senior cadres and supplies were finding their way south through the panhandle of Laos. Throughout this region hill tribes were perched atop the Annamite Mountains, which separate Vietnam from Laos. Living on the Bolovens Plateau in the southernmost part of the panhandle, opposite the South Vietnamese and Cambodian borders, were the Kha. White Star was soon extended to them.

The biggest tribal mobilization of all, and the very foundation of the CIA's secret war in Laos, was that of the Hmong, or, as they were then known, the Meo. The alliance with the Meo came about in the fall of 1960, when the tribe began to draw military supplies from Phoumi Nosavan. These could only have been moved by CIA. When Phoumi's forces succeeded in capturing Vientiane, the Meo openly declared their allegiance to the general.

Alliance with the Meo momentarily averted a crisis for the United States-backed Phoumi. That general's own troops were of poor quality, while the Meo were stout fighters. The Meo held and even gained ground in the face of the Pathet Lao-Kong Le forces, now augmented by a North Vietnamese 105-millimeter artillery battery, flown in by the Soviets. Phoumi's forces, in contrast, abandoned a strategic base in the Plain of Jars (so named for its use as a burial ground by ancient Lao peoples) at the first hint of a challenge. The White Star advisers had to be extracted by three Air American planes, one of which was hit by antiaircraft fire; two other PEO teams also were evacuated under less extreme circumstances. The contract flight crews reported sighting seven Russian aircraft, presumably those in the Soviet airlift to the Pathet Lao.

It was not surprising that the White Star advisers were exposed by the open combat. Although the deputy chief of the PEO and thirty Americans served with Phoumi's headquarters, most of the PEO men were with units at the front. The Green Berets disdained desk work and wanted to be in the heat of battle. One RLAF colonel, to whom Phoumi gave command of Mobile Group 15, had been in charge for several days before he accidentally encountered his Green Beret "advisers," not at his command post, but with the forwardmost detachments. When the surprised colonel asked his superiors about the Americans, he was told they were with White Star. As for the ostensible "mobile training" mission, the RLAF colonel recounts that he had almost no contact with the Americans.

Green Beret Captain Moon, who died fighting with Mobile Group 15, and the passengers and crew of an Air America plane that was shot down, may well have been the first American casualties in a war that officially did not exist.

President Eisenhower not only approved the White Star project but made certain other decisions that clearly indicate his concept of the conflict in Laos as a secret war. He approved the movement of B-26 bombers to Thailand; but these were not initially used in Laos because of the difficulty of assembling crews of appropriate nationalities. Lighter T-6 strike aircraft were also approved for use with Laotian pilots, but initially without bombs, only machine guns. The aircraft themselves were to be given by the Thai. United States military aid to Thailand would include an equal number of more modern aircraft as compensation. By January 4, 1961, Air America was laying plans to put mechanics into Vientiane to service the Laotian T-6 fleet.

The indirect provision of ten strike aircraft to the RLAF was in motion before John Kennedy took office. These were the first strikeplanes in the Laotian air force, and thus a qualitative improvement of RLAF capabilities. Eisenhower also ordered a task force with Marines into position for intervention in Laos. Naval units were placed on DEFCON 3 alert status.

Laos was one of Ike's main topics of discussion with Kennedy in their preinauguration White House meetings; he authorized warnings to Khrushchev that the United States intended to ensure the "legitimate government" of Laos remained in power. At a morning meeting on December 31, 1960, Ike joked, in a Laos discussion, that perhaps the time had come to use the plans that had been drawn up for airborne alert of the Strategic Air Command. In parting he insisted to the group, which included Allen Dulles, Gordon Gray, and J. Graham Parsons, "We must not allow Laos to fall to the Communists, even if it involves war."

In Laos the effect of the United States' actions was to undermine the delicate political balance. Kong Le in league with the Pathet Lao represented one of the worst conceivable possibilities, even from the American standpoint. Souvanna Phouma, recently forced to flee to Thailand but harboring no illusions, said of Graham Parsons, and by extension of American policy, that he "understood nothing about Asia and nothing about Laos."

At least Phoumi Nosavan's forces did manage to capture and jail prominent Pathet Lao leader Prince Souphanouvong, but only for a time. In a feat of Laotian derring-do, Souphanouvong converted his guards and walked from jail a free man.

President Kennedy did not feel Laos was the place for a major war. In office, he used United States military forces, briefly converting the PEO into an open military advisory group, but he aimed for an international accord to neutralize the place. With the help of Averell Harriman, Roger Hilsman, and Dean Rusk, Kennedy achieved his aim in a 1962 Geneva agreement. When Phoumi Nosavan stood in the way, his American assistance evaporated and his CIA link, Jack Hazey, was pulled out—reportedly despite opposition from Desmond FitzGerald and Bill Colby.

It was Harriman who engineered the cutoff of Phoumi. A loyal Democrat and senior statesman, Harriman carried some weight with John Kennedy, and he went to some length to set up a credible Laotian neutralization agreement. Harriman also knew what he wanted—when CIA officers briefed him in Vientiane on their assessment of Laotian politics and the extent of popular support for *les jeunes*, the President's irascible envoy turned off his hearing aid in the middle of the meeting.

Diplomacy eventually led Harriman to Geneva, where there was another international conference. Harriman got the agreement, but in the end neither side kept it. The United States laughed with scorn at North Vietnamese assertions that all their forces had withdrawn: Only *forty* enemy soliders passed the international commission's border checkpoints. But the United States violated the agreement just as blatantly—by continuing to arm and command the Meo tribesmen.

Meo is a bastardization of the Chinese name *Miao* used for this mountain people, who are also known as *Hmong*. The tribes respect no borders and Hmong are found in Laos, China, and North Vietnam. Generations of French and American secret warriors knew them as Meo, a people who practiced slash-and-burn farming, proud but friendly, raising poppies for opium, with villages in the mountain valleys.

It was probably inevitable that the Meo would be dragged into the American war. Their poppies had had hidden effects on war in Indochina since the anti-French resistance, when both sides had used the money, though the Meo mostly sided with the French, under the leadership of Touby Lyfoung, a pro-French notable and the first of his tribe to graduate from a college. Touby's Meo formed an important auxiliary force for the French, in 1954, for example, making up the bulk of the manpower in a vain overland relief attempt to save Dien Bien Phu.

One veteran of the Dien Bien Phu debacle was a young officer named Vang Pao, who had led a French commando unit on that fruitless expedition. Vang Pao had first gone to war in 1945, at the age of thirteen, as an interpreter for French soliders who parachuted into the Plain of Jars. He joined the fighting forces in 1947 and became an officer in the Royal Laotian army when that was formed in 1950. Vang stayed on in the army after the Geneva agreement, rising to command the RLAF 10th Battalion, which was composed mostly of Meo. Where Touby Lyfoung was mainly a potentate and tribal politician, Vang was a military commander.

Choosing sides was of some importance to the Meo in the new Laotian war. Feeling too old for another war, Touby restricted himself to acting as a sort of Meo elder statesman, leaving the main leadership role to Vang Pao. While some Meo sided with the Pathet Lao (clan leader Fay Dang becoming a member of the NLHX central committee), Touby and Vang Pao made their alliance with the CIA, not directly supporting Phoumi but waging a parallel war.

From the fall of 1960, Vang Pao's forces began to receive a portion of the military aid flowing to Laos. There were then fifteen Air America C-46's and C-47's based at Bangkok moving a thousand tons of supplies a month to Phoumi at Savannakhet. The Meo force, calling itself the Armée Clandestine, the Secret Army, harrassed Pathet Lao positions and made some raids into Phong Saly and Sam Neua provinces. Eight White Star Green Beret teams reportedly accompanied the Vang Pao forces.

At this point, the Kong Le neutralist forces, retreating from Vientiane, made straight for the Meo area of the Plain of Jars. Vang

Pao lost his own village and was forced to retreat into the surrounding mountains. Worst of all, the Plain of Jars airfield was lost, endangering the supply flow to the Meo. The Pathet Lao joined in the Plain of Jars offensive, to threaten the entire Meo tribal area on the high plateau.

The spring and summer of 1961 witnessed a mass exodus from the Plain of Jars by the Meo. Whole villages moved. Over seventy thousand Meo trekked into the mountains to make new homes. Without a crop already in the ground, the Meo were threatened with starvation in their new homes.

Total disaster was averted in large part because of the work of two Americans, who organized the system that would revictual the Armée Clandestine for the next eleven years. One of these men, Edgar M. Buell of the U.S. Agency for International Development (USAID), became a legend in Laos. Buell started airdrops of rice into the mountains, indiscriminate "blind" drops at first, because the whereabouts of the Meo was unknown for over three months. "Pop" Buell left his embassy desk to parachute into the mountains himself, walking the forests and personally contacting Meo village bands. Villages that agreed to give loyalty to Vang Pao were scheduled for regular rice drops, supplies of seeds and tools, medicine, and so forth.

The second American of crucial importance was an Air Force major named Harry C. Aderholt. In 1959–1960, Aderholt was the commander of the Air Force's small unconventional-warfare detachment on Okinawa. One of his duties was to advise the CIA on air operations in Southeast Asia. Aderholt went to Vientiane in early 1960 to set up a light-plane service from the Laotian capital to Phong Saly town, where a tiny six-hundred-foot landing strip was carved into a mountain at an altitude of six thousand feet. Working with Vang Pao, "Heinie" Aderholt surveyed much of northern Laos for a network of airstrips, which came to be called Lima Sites, then stayed in Laos two years to oversee their construction.

In the Laotian highlands the United States supply network, serviced by Air America, had the immediate effect of increasing the adherents to Vang Pao's forces. Secretly drawing unit leaders from the nucleus of six Meo battalions in the RLAF, a practice that enraged Royal army officers when they learned of it, the Armée Clandestine grew from about 1,000 soldiers at the end of 1960 to 8,000 in the spring of 1961 and 9,000 that summer. A memorandum written by Lansdale at that time explicitly noted that the Vientiane CIA station chief controlled the Meo troops. Assigned to work with them were nine CIA specialists, nine Green Berets, and ninety-nine Thai contract agents, from the so-called Police Aerial Resupply Unit (PARU), which the CIA had been training since the days of the Li Mi operation in Burma.

With his retreat from the Plain of Jars, Vang Pao established a new Meo center at the foot of Phu Bia, the tallest mountain south of the plateau. Pop Buell set out on a fifty-eight-day march around the circumference of the Plain of Jars to bring in the Meo villagers. In December 1961 the Meo opened two new bases farther west, at Long Tieng (LS-30/98) and Sam Thong (LS-20), which became the main centers of the Meo movement. Long Tieng served as Vang Pao's headquarters for over a decade, became a major mountain commercial center, and a rallying point for the Meo. Sam Thong became an administrative, medical, and education center.

Consolidation of this new Meo refuge continued for about five years. The Geneva agreement of 1962 had little effect on CIA support to the Meo. Ingeniously, the CIA met the requirement for "withdrawal" of foreign troops by pulling its people back to bases in Thailand, from which they would simply fly to jobs in Laos with the first Air America flights in the morning. Repeated Pathet Lao warnings before the cease-fire date were ignored; it is not surprising that the Laotian conflict continued virtually unabated after the 1962 negotiations. A neutralist solution was still fundamentally unacceptable to the United States, and became increasingly unacceptable to the North Vietnamese as well.

Known by its radio "handle," Sky, Long Tieng became the nerve center of the CIA secret war. The Lima Site airstrip and landing techniques were perfected to the point that C-130's could disgorge entire palletized cargoes in quick flybys. Smaller Air America planes would relay the cargo to the outlying Lima Sites. Every morning, Sky handed out assignments to the fleet of transports as they entered Laotian airspace. Sometimes Air America came laden with passengers, often with fuel for the stocks at the Lima Sites, or with additional cargo for distribution. Sky frequently assigned as many as four or five successive flight missions a day to the light transports.

Secret warfare in Laos assumed the dynamic, freewheeling style of Sky air operations. The epitome of that style was embodied by another American who attained legendary stature in the war. Identified by the CIA acronym UPIN, he was Anthony Poshepny. A figure solidly cast in the CIA "cowboy" mold, Tony Po, as Poshepny called himself, went everywhere with a boxer's mouthguard in his pocket, always ready for a fight. Tony flew in from the big CIA Thailand base Takhli in 1963, and was assigned as the senior adviser to Vang Pao, or Sky chief. He had been transferred up from the Cambodian border, where he had been working with antigovernment rebels in that country. An alumnus of CIA training with the Camp Peary class of 1953, he had been one of the paramilitary officers landed in Indonesia during the PEMESTA affair, and had worked extensively on the Tibet operation, including missions into the Chinese hinterland.

At Long Tieng, Tony Po presided over an intensification of the Armée Clandestine struggle. Vang Pao struck his greatest blow yet in 1963, in a commando raid that destroyed a Pathet Lao supply road, by dynamiting a full kilometer, sending some sections tumbling down a mountainside.

The Armée Clandestine was significantly stronger now, up to a strength of thirty thousand soliders. Vang Pao and Tony Po worked out a program to increase Meo striking power with units patterned like the Mike Forces within the CIDG in South Vietnam. Some ten thousand Meo were formed into Special Guerrilla Units (SGUs), regular partisan battalions with three companies and a headquarters, supported by bazookas and a few heavy mortars. These became the regular forces in Vang Pao's Armée Clandestine. They were later supplied with 75- and even 105-millimeter mountain guns, the latter usually lifted from mountaintop to mountaintop by Air America helicopters, and used to fire down into posts under attack.

Such growth was not instantaneous nor was it achieved without difficulty. Throughout the 1963–1965 buildup period the USAID program was instrumental in increasing support for Vang Pao. Rice was dropped to villages whose men were away fighting and a modern hospital was established at Sam Thong, which also became the site of the first junior high school expressly created for the Meo. At the same time, a Meo trading company was set up at Long Tieng, which thus became a market center. Gradually, Vang Pao acquired the image of the man who was leading his tribe into the modern era.

For the CIA the Meo program became a model of "nation building," the political action approach that fosters civic institutions in hopes that grateful clients would then cooperate with American policies. In the 1950s the tactic had seemed successful when practiced by Ed Lansdale in the Philippines and with Diem in South Vietnam. But "nation building" among the Meo, as indeed with the *montagnards* in Vietnam, carried with it a new political problem. In the Central Highlands and around the Plain of Jars, the CIA was in effect creating nations within nations. Activities like those at Long Tieng and Sam Thong were possible only to the degree that the central government was willing to extend autonomy to the tribal peoples. Saigon triggered the *montagnard* political crisis of 1964–1965 precisely by moving to reduce the autonomy accorded tribes in the Central Highlands. The CIA's relative success with Vang Pao was the result of the Royal Laotian Government being too weak to assert similar authority over the Meo. From the Americans' strategic standpoint in the Indochina war, however, the need to keep the Vientiane government weak, and to give free rein to the Meo Secret Army, flew in the face of fostering the type of national government that could defeat the Pathet Lao. Rather, in recognition of Meo autonomy, Vang Pao received repeated promotions of his original RLAF rank, was treated as the commander of an RLAF military region, and Touby Lyfoung became a minister in the Royal Laotian Government. Despite such tokens the lowland Lao never fully trusted the Meo.

The Armée Clandestine mobilization was greatly facilitated by its status as a CIA project. Military supplies were hidden in the assistance flows to Thailand and the RLAF. Air America provided much of the airlift under contract to USAID. Funds were hidden in military assistance, USAID, and CIA budget requests.

In fact, the only remaining obstacle proved to be funding. The expansion of the Armée Clandestine after 1964 could not be accomplished without noticeable increases in funding. Although the CIA budget was secret, the small CIA subcommittees of the Congress had to be induced to approve the higher budget requests.

To obtain congressional approval, the CIA relied on its recognized role in counterinsurgency doctrine plus the vital contacts it had acquired in Laos and Thailand. The Agency also was not above exaggerating a little to spice up its presentation. Langley desk officer Ralph McGehee, who handled Thai matters at headquarters after a tour in the field, recalls being flattered one day when Far East Division chief Colby invited him to present parts of the CIA case. The briefing was eventually approved by DDP Des Fitz-Gerald, and went to Congress with a request to fund over a hundred Secret Army units. Vang Pao actually had only a couple dozen platoon-size units at the time, but at Langley McGehee and other DDP officers performed a paper reorganization of the Armée Clandestine, endowing it overnight with the required number of units, each with a strength of only a few men. Desk officer McGehee felt remorse over such falsification, but Congress was impressed with CIA's apparent success in the Meo mobilization and approved the secret budget, which was unknown to senators and congressmen outside those on the small CIA subcommittees of the armed services committees. Congress as a whole never explicitly considered the Laos request; it passed on the budgets of those agencies that were involved. The Central Intelligence Agency settled down to fight a real war in Laos. The only question was for how long it could remain a secret.

William H. Sullivan almost missed his assignment to Laos as ambassador because Maxwell Taylor wanted him to serve as chief of staff for a new mission to South Vietnam. Taylor, as ambassador there, directed all aspects of United States operations, including MACV. President Johnson had prevailed on Taylor to assume the ambassadorship at Saigon, leaving his post as chairman of the Joint Chiefs, to direct the Vietnam War. LBJ saw it as putting his first team in play.

Bill Sullivan could hardly refuse the summons. Taylor was the President's man, for LBJ much as for JFK, while Sullivan was the State Department officer chairing the Washington interagency committee managing the Vietnam War. Sullivan went to Saigon, but got Max to agree his posting there would be temporary. He moved on to Vientiane in December 1964, though he returned to Vietnam at intervals for several months thereafter.

Sullivan was no doubt anxious to get into the action in Vientiane. As leader of the "country team" in Laos, Ambassador Sullivan could command the CIA station and would be responsible for implementing the second of the two basic decisions made in Washington on Laos. The first had come in the wake of the Geneva agreement, when Colby had convinced Averell Harriman, known to Washington bureaucrats as the Crocodile, to support continued assistance to the Meo. The second decision was to intensify the

Laotian war, and this was made by President Johnson on the basis of recommendations assembled by the Sullivan committee in the spring of 1964. The program included "protective reaction" air strikes in the Laotian panhandle, cross-border raids from South Vietnam, and more support for the Meo.

As boss in Vientiane, Sullivan could be certain that the American mission would pursue the program with vigor. This might not have been the case with Leonard Unger, whom Sullivan replaced as ambassador. Unger had been dubious about the value of a large-scale tribal army and had made sure that the Meo operation was reversible in its early years. Sullivan by contrast threw himself headlong into the project. Thinking Unger "a most reluctant militarist," Sullivan recalls that "direction of this war effort was a tremendously absorbing and enervating task. I eventually came to live with that task on a twenty-four hour a day basis."

The ambassador's lieutenant and deputy for action missions was the CIA chief of station in Vientiane. In the mid-1960s this was Theodore Shackley, a hard-driving thirty-seven-year-old former chief of the Miami station who was transferred before the final demise of the anti-Castro opposition, which Shackley himself dates in 1966. Ted Shackley used Laos to devise his own brand of counterinsurgency theory, which emphasized CIA as opposed to military action, and squarely embraced the "nation building" formula. In Laos under Shackley, the CIA developed fishponds, established pig-breeding centers and cooperative retail stores, and managed vocational training schools. The stores, Shackley notes, were particularly well received by the Meo who "were quick to recognize that one does not eat rhetoric and propaganda."

The first of the pig-breeding centers, dreamed up by two CIA officers in the mountains, completely transformed a deteriorating military situation by gaining the loyalty of the Meo in one district.

As Richard Helms puts it, "The agency . . . was flat out in its effort to keep the tribes viable militarily in that Plain of Jars area."

Working "flat out" meant a contingent of about 250 Americans either in Laos or commuting to their assignments; Air Force personnel permanently assigned to help the intelligence staffs at Long Tieng; and a budget that grew to $300 million a year. In keeping with covert operations etiquette, Sullivan issued strict orders for Americans to keep out of combat and says that "when I found those orders were willfully disobeyed, I peremptorily removed [offenders] from the country." Despite Sullivan's orders, however, the CIA station appears to have taken no action against such "cowboys" as Tony Po, who reportedly suffered more than a dozen wounds in assorted firefights, and once made a fantastic thirty-mile march to safety carrying a wounded native comrade. Tony went on to further assignments to lead another tribal strike force, the Yao, in northernmost Laos, where he sent missions into Burma and the People's Republic of China.

In large part, Air America made it all work. This CIA proprietary's role in Southeast Asia is far more extensive than generally realized. In South Vietnam alone, by late 1965 Air America was moving 1,650 tons of cargo a month with a fleet of over fifty planes, among them two dozen C-45's, C-46's, and C-47's. This increased to 2,500 tons a month in 1967 and 1968.

Of primary importance for Laos was Thailand, where Air America had facilities at Bangkok, Takhli, and Udorn. Maintenance was available at Vientiane and Udon, the site of a major base for the proprietary. It was there, with the transfer of sixteen Air Force H-34's in March 1961, that the Air America helicopter fleet originated. By mid-1966 the proprietary's aircraft based in Thailand included twenty-one helicopters, along with twelve Helio U-10 light planes, and twenty medium transports. The helicopters were vital for air-rescue services in addition to their general aviation role. During the first two years of the United States bombing, Air America rescued four times as many downed air crews as the Air Force.

Air America pilots were supposed to be flying during their time off from service on the regular flight routes. They were paid bonuses, given tax advantages, and could clear upward of $40,000 a year, a huge sum at that time. The flying was hazardous, often with clouds, sudden mists, and rain. The destinations were frequently tiny, tricky airfields.

An especially sensitive base in Thailand was Takhli. Bearing the code name "Pepper Grinder," Takhli had a "spook" compound where top-secret projects were housed, including U-2 and SR-71 reconnaissance missions and quiet C-130 transport flights into Laos. Because Air America owned no C-130's, the Air Force lent it some from the special air-warfare E Flight on Okinawa. Of four Air America crews trained on C-130's in the mid-1960s, only one was left by 1970.

The hub of the Meo war was Long Tieng, code-named "Sky." Situated in a high mountain valley, Sky boasted an increasingly well-developed air base: a long paved runway, good radio navigation beacons, an all-weather landing system, and air-traffic controllers. Planes landed or took off every few seconds. There were flight lines on both sides of the concrete strip, one to handle planes, the other helicopters. Sky also had a sophisticated telecommunications center and an air-conditioned officers' club for the Americans. Rescue helicopters and RLAF T-28 fighters used Long Tieng as a forward base.

Surrounding the base was a Meo town that grew to a population of 40,000. There were no paved streets or street lights but there was an incredibly well-stocked market. When Vang Pao imported a shiny Cadillac, a road was built up the ridge to connect Sky with Sam Thong. Vang Pao had his headquarters at Long Tieng together with a propaganda outlet, the "Radio of the Union of the Lao Races."

With the intensification of the secret war went the growth of the CIA proprietary that fed it. Flying Tiger, by way of comparison, had been the largest private air charter airline in the world when Air America was formed. By 1968, Flying Tiger had only twenty-eight aircraft and 2,068 employees, whereas Air America had almost two hundred planes and four times as many workers. In February 1969 the Air America fleet in Thailand consisted of twenty-nine helicopters, twenty light planes, and nineteen medium transports. This unit alone was larger than Flying Tiger.

The demand for air tonnage in the Laotian operations led to an anomaly in secret warfare—competition from a private company. An Air America manager was hired away by Continental Air Services, which then sought some of the same USAID contracts. Because any legal action against the Air America monopoly would threaten to reveal the real ownership of Air America, Continental Air got some of the Laotian work. The company built up a fleet of twenty-one aircraft in Thailand by 1966, rising to twenty-five three years later, including ten medium C-46 and C-47 transports. In addition, some contract work was carried out by Bangkok-based Bird Air, and beginning in late 1967, the CIA and USAID got together to buy Vang Pao two old C-47's, so the Meo leader had a private air service of his own.

"Air America did a magnificent job," comments division chief Bill Colby, "but it was not a combat air force." The attacks in support of the Meo were also carried out from Thailand, by Air Force

T-28's in "Jungle Jim" type units. A few of these planes were given to the RLAF to lend credence to the cover. The T-28 force eventually attained a strength of a hundred fighter-bombers in the 56th Special Operations Wing. This was supplemented by wide use of U.S. Air Force gunships, first the AC-47, later the improved AC-119 and AC-130 models.

In all of these activities, Thailand played a vital role, one established at the very beginning of the 1960s. Chief of the CIA station there at that time was Robert Jantzen, whom Desmond FitzGerald once called "the greatest single asset the US has in Southeast Asia." With help from ambassadors U. Alexis Johnson and Kenneth T. Young, Jantzen encouraged the Thai to assume a cooperative attitude. The Thai responded not only with supply ports and air bases, but pilots for the T-28's and contract agents for CIA on the ground. Soon, as will be seen, the Thais were even providing recruits for the Armée Clandestine. Jantzen was given a medal.

In 1964, Meo SGUs cooperated with the RLAF in an ambitious counteroffensive during the rainy season, attacking the eastern flank of the Pathet Lao on the Plain of Jars. Called Operation Triangle, the offensive was possible only because of an American airlift that was so substantial it had to be approved at a very high level in the Johnson administration. With Air America and T-28 combat air support, the RLAF regained critical positions on the Plain of Jars before the rainy season ended in November. Retreating Pathet Lao and North Vietnamese troops were repeatedly ambushed by Meo SGUs.

Operation Triangle set the pattern for the remainder of the war in Laos. In the dry season the Pathet Lao would attack. When the rains came, the RLAF would use American planes and helicopters to leapfrog combat units into key positions and force back the Pathet Lao and their North Vietnamese allies. American support was coordinated by the embassy's shadowy Requirements Office, a CIA unit that replaced the military PEO after the 1962 Geneva agreement. RLAF units participating in the attacks would first be sent to Thailand for special training, to circumvent Geneva prohibitions against foreign military training in Laos. For their part, the North Vietnamese soon were permanently maintaining two full divisions in northern Laos.

Apparent success in 1964–1965 greatly pleased Washington. The Meo program was something of a showcase. To show his appreciation of the Laotian effort, in August 1964, President Lyndon Johnson ostentatiously received Pop Buell at the White House. By the end of 1965, USAID was reporting that, on its $1.6-million budget for the Village Health Program, it was funding 140 hospitals and dispensaries, serving 150,000 patients a month, and had trained 268 medics in the last fiscal year. Training work was contracted out to the Filipino health organization Operation Brotherhood, whose work in Laos was paid for by USAID.

One aspect of the Laotian war that was not going so well was the attempt to seal off the borders of South Vietnam. There were three components to this effort: aerial reconnaissance missions known as Yankee Team; a bombing campaign; and cross-border scouting and raiding expeditions launched by MACV-SOG.

The Yankee Team missions were a failure. North Vietnamese antiaircraft fire against the planes led to the first bombing, so-called protective-reaction strikes by aircraft accompanying the reconnaissance planes. Even with this support, the results of observation were indifferent. In June 1965, Ambassador Sullivan spent a full day with the general commanding the Laotian air force, being briefed in detail on the parts of the Ho Chi Minh Trail recently used to infiltrate the first North Vietnamese regular division into the south. In his report to Washington, Sullivan dryly noted, "All our Yankee Team photo reconnaissance missions over this area have failed to turn up a decent trace of a route."

Yankee Team was soon subsumed into the regular air effort over Laos. The air campaign began in December 1964 when United States aircraft were authorized to add "armed reconnaissance" strikes to their Yankee Team support mission. The number of aircraft flights, or sorties, allowed daily was increased in the spring of 1965, coincident with the introduction of combat troops in South Vietnam. In March 1965 the air campaign was split into two components, with strikes in the panhandle against the trails called Steel Tiger, and air support for Vang Pao in northern Laos called Barrel Roll. Between 1965 and 1971 it is estimated that 1,150,000 *tons* of bombs had been dropped in the Steel Tiger operation plus another 494,000 tons in Barrel Roll. By the time a peace agreement was signed in Paris in early 1973, the weight of bombs dropped on Laos exceeded the tonnage of all munitions used by the United States in World War II.

Cross-border operations from South Vietnam were the bread and butter of MACV's Studies and Observation Group (SOG). This effort gathered momentum in 1964 when Vietnamese officers, acting for the Americans, and senior Laotian generals, reached an agreement allowing these missions, which had been recommended in Washington policy memorandums for over a year.

The earliest cross-border missions were for scouting and were organized along the same lines as the attempts to put agent teams into North Vietnam. Eight-man agent teams were inserted at night across the Laotian border by South Vietnamese helicopters. An early reevaluation of the project occurred when four teams provided by Special Forces Project Leaping Lena were almost completely destroyed, with only four survivors escaping to South Vietnam. A fifth team inserted after a renewed go-ahead returned with meager intelligence results.

Other participants in the early cross-border operations were teams of CIA Nung. This was not the first time Nung had fought in Laos—in 1961–1962 the CIA had secretly reinforced RLAF forces with an obscure unit called the 111th Special Battalion. The soldiers, identified as "Chinese," were the CIA's Nung partisans.

For Project Shining Brass, which was MACV-SOG's code name for the cross-border patrols, the Nung were given final training by the Vietnamese LLDG center at Nha Trang. The patrols became more extensive in 1965, when the MACV-SOG code name was changed to Prairie Fire, now including overland infiltrations from Special Forces-CIDG camps in the Vietnamese border region. The patrols identified Ho Chi Minh Trail routes and marked them for bombing by Steel Tiger. This effort was supplemented by a "Roadwatch" program in which the patrols scouted for specific North Vietnamese movements and then called in air strikes on them. In Thailand the Air Force deployed a special air warfare helicopter detachment, with the code name Pony Express, to help move the Roadwatch teams. Prairie Fire executed over 250 missions in 1967, including patrols penetrating as far as twelve miles into Laos. By 1968, in addition to the Green Berets serving with the 5th Special Forces Group, there were another 598 Americans assigned to Prairie Fire.

Ambassador Sullivan's biggest problem with the cross-border operations was MACV commander General William C. Westmoreland. Saigon wanted a lot more military action in the Laotian panhandle, either an occupation by friendly forces or an invasion by the Vietnamese army to cut the Ho Chi Minh Trail. MACV prepared plans for such an invasion in September 1966 and again in

1968. But Sullivan repeatedly advised against such a step. "The biggest job Bill Sullivan had," observed one American official, "was to keep Westmoreland's paws off Laos."

In 1971, when both Sullivan and Westmoreland had returned to Washington, the Vietnamese army went ahead with an invasion of the panhandle. Using the code name Lam Son 719, the operation turned into a major military debacle.

Warfare on the ground continued in northern Laos. Strong Pathet Lao attacks on a Lima Site in early 1966 resulted in stationing AC-47 gunships in Thailand for the first time; by mid-1966 three had gone down over Laos. Americans in Laos began to collect "hostile fire" pay beginning in January 1966. That was also a peak of sorts for the Meo, whose New Year's celebration that month was attended by the king of Laos and the diplomatic corps. The Pathet Lao dry-season offensive that year cleared Sam Neua province, but Meo and some RLAF irregulars took to the nearby hills and began guerrilla resistance in the countryside. Later that year the CIA quietly shifted its support for the neutralist military unit to a deputy who promptly ousted Kong Le, who was finally forced to seek refuge in Thailand. Another coup was attempted in Vientiane but failed. Toward the end of 1966 press reports of Americans in the field with Laotian forces further eroded the plausible deniability of the secret war in Laos.

A good measure of relative war effort of the Americans and the Royal Laotian Government is the monthly tonnage hauled by airlift. The Laotian air force averaged four hundred tons a month in 1966; through Air America, the CIA was moving six thousand tons a month plus sixteen thousand passengers. That year the Air Force also contributed 7,316 strike sorties.

The campaign against the Ho Chi Minh Trail furnished the Armée Clandestine with a new mission in support of the air war. Accurate bombing required accurate navigation, leading the Air Force to put a radio beacon atop Phu Pha Thi, a Meo sacred place in Sam Neua province. Later a radar was added and helicopters were based in forward areas for rescue and recovery missions. Phu Pha Thi, called Project 404, became Lima Site 85. Pony Express lifted 150 tons of equipment to the site for the radar installation and a dozen Americans were required to run the equipment. Vang Pao's Meo were asked to defend the facility.

Sam Neua was not a backwater but rather the front line in Laos.

Pony Express was still helicoptering in equipment to LS-85 when Pathet Lao preparations for the 1968 dry-season offensive made clear it would be aimed at clearing Sam Neua. A Pony Express CH-3 was shot down during its approach for landing in December 1967. Within months government forces had been ejected from most of Sam Neua.

Nor did Phu Pha Thi escape the adversary's attention. The North Vietnamese made a concerted effort to knock out this installation. In one of the few recorded instances of North Vietnamese bombing, in January 1968, two Soviet-built AN-2 transports, modified to carry bombs, were actually shot down attempting to bomb LS-85. On the night of March 11, 1968, a major ground attack overwhelmed the Meo defenders of the fifty-six-hundred-foot-high mesa. Thirteen Americans died in combat.

Government forces came back to Sam Neua in their rainy-season rollback and regained parts of the province. The Americans selected a new radio beacon site to replace LS-85, which they built in July 1968. But the new site was lost when they again retreated.

Vang Pao's Secret Army reached its peak strength during this period. There were 40,000 soldiers, mostly local defense forces, but about 15,000 grouped in Special Guerrilla Units. Yet the additional strength was matched by the North Vietnamese who staged a buildup of their own.

The spooks had Laos wired for sound and filled its air with photo reconnaissance planes. In at least one case, according to Ted Shackley, CIA even had radio beacons planted on a Pathet Lao unit and could completely monitor its movements. MACV intelligence estimates show that between December 1967 and August 1968 the combined strength of NVA and Pathet Lao forces increased from about 51,000 to over 110,000. The North Vietnamese contingent comprised an estimated 34,000 combat troops, 6,000 advisers, and 18,000 support troops. A major program of road building employed over 13,000 engineers and porters, setting the stage for an even more massive dry-season offensive in 1968–1969.

The results of the campaign were ominous. Within three months the RLAF and Meo were driven once and for all from Sam Neua, and from points around the Plain of Jars. Between January 10 and 15, Air America and Pony Express helicopters joined hands to lift over five thousand people cut off near Sam Neua. Another evacuation reduced losses in the fall of Lima Site 36. Thirty-four airfield sites were lost in the operations.

Air power was the American response, more specifically constant support from the AC-47 gunships of the 14th Special Operations Wing. The unit's operations officer, Colonel William H. Ginn, Jr., met with Vang Pao to explain the air support system and promise that no more Lima Sites would be lost. The Meo were given strobe lights to identify their own positions at night, enabling the gunships to suppress surrounding areas on call. North Vietnamese attacks failed in May, but again in June Lima Site 108 was overrun, necessitating another Air America–U.S. Air Force emergency evacuation, by helicopter to Long Tieng. Still, Vang Pao did not lose many more positions and even managed to recapture a few of the lost Lima Sites.

Even Bill Sullivan's powers were taxed by the demands of meeting the 1969 dry-season offensive. "There wasn't a bag of rice dropped in Laos he didn't know about," said William P. Bundy of Sullivan. But Vientiane was a trying post at the best of times and Sullivan had been four years on the job. In the spring of 1969 the new Nixon administration recalled the ambassador. Sullivan was disappointed to learn he would go back to the same Vietnam interagency committee he had left in Washington, but had little choice except to return.

In Vientiane the embassy team was not quite the same as before. Ted Shackley moved over to Saigon as chief of station there. His place was taken by Lawrence Devlin, one of a number of Congo veterans whose assignment to Laos was specially requested by G. McMurtrie Godley, formerly ambassador to the Congo and now Richard Nixon's choice for the same task in Laos. Godley proved, if anything, to be even more involved than his predecessor in the day-to-day management of the war, earning the nickname "field marshal."

Richard Nixon backed up the ambassador's authority, as had Kennedy before him, with a letter confirming the primacy of the State Department's official representative.

There were sea changes in Washington as well as Laos, not least of all at the Central Intelligence Agency. An era passed unheralded when a deeply depressed Frank Wisner put a shotgun to his head in the spring of 1965. It was Dick Helms, the professional espionage specialist, who became director of central intelligence in mid-1966.

The paramilitary club at Langley suffered another real blow in February 1967, when Desmond FitzGerald collapsed while playing tennis on his home court. The DDP was awarded a posthumous National Security Medal, but his replacement was Thomas Karamessines, a Helms protégé from the espionage crowd. The secret warriors could no longer count on the same support from top levels at CIA.

According to CIA officer Victor Marchetti, rank-and-file CIA people were also becoming less enamored with the Laos operation, not because they objected to the involvement in Indochina, but because the effort was unwieldy and obvious rather than sophisticated and secret.

A few in the military were becoming concerned with increasing losses. Until 1969 the Air Force had been lucky—only three helicopters had been shot down in Laos and fourteen of the fifteen aircrewmen were rescued. Now luck ran out. In one year six large Air Force CH-3 helicopters were downed and a seventh lost on the ground, half the total of helicopters of this type lost in Laos during the entire war.

Perhaps the sudden spate of losses had something to do with the change of heart, a most important one, that occurred in the United States Congress. Political support for the Indochina war was waning in Congress, support for Laos especially.

One case in point was Senator Stuart Symington of Missouri, whose support was especially important given his membership in the restricted CIA subcommittee.

Symington had backed the Laotian war. On a visit to Laos and Thailand in 1966, the senator had had good things to say, to pilots and embassy people, about the efficacy of the secret war. He encouraged the CIA to tell its story, and watched in the Armed Services Committee on October 5, 1967, when Theodore Shackley presented the assembled senators with a two-hour briefing about how and where the war was being fought and for how much money. The CIA was putting soliders on Laotian battlefields for many times less dollars per man than were the military in South Vietnam.

Two years later, Stuart Symington was taking a different tack. He demanded an explanation at hearings on United States worldwide commitments, asserting that the United States was "waging war" in Laos and had been for years. Said Symington, "It is time the American people were told more of the facts."

At this October 1969 hearing, Senator Symington succeeded in drawing from William H. Sullivan the admission that there was no formal obligation by the United States to the Meo.

In his own testimony, DCI Helms refused to be drawn out on the authority for this covert "war," restricting himself to reiteration of the "such other functions" language in the 1947 National Security Act. In an October 30, 1969, memorandum to Helms, general counsel Lawrence Houston argued that CIA had "no combatants as such" in Laos, and that "I know of no definition . . . which would consider our activities in Laos as 'waging war.'" Although the CIA lawyer carefully noted that "from 1947 on my position has been that this is a rather doubtful statutory authority on which to hang our paramilitary activities," he advised Helms, "I think you were exactly right to stick to the language of the National Security Act."

Clearly Symington had some reason to be exasperated with the Agency's disingenuousness. As the senator put it at his hearing, "I have never seen a country engage in so many devious undertakings as this."

Helms, for his part, fastened on Symington's change of heart as dishonesty. In a 1981 interview, Helms said, "When Senator Stuart Symington got up and started talking about a 'secret war,' he knew far better than that."

One element that may have helped sour key figures in Washington was the drug traffic. It has already been noted that the Meo raised poppies and had done so for decades. Processed in laboratories, those poppies could become opium, heroin, morphine, or other powerful drugs, some of them hallucinogenic, many addictive. The drug trade was lucrative and as pervasive in northern Laos as it was in upper Burma and Thailand. The area, indeed, is known as the Golden Triangle for precisely this reason.

When the CIA decided to run a war in northern Laos, the drugs came with it; there was no way to avoid them. The Chinese from Burma, the old Li Mi band, bought some of the poppies and moved them across the border in caravans. Lowland Lao and Thai bought more. But when the CIA came with Air America, they brought an incomparably more efficient means of transportation.

By the mid-1960s, CIA officers were reporting intelligence on the movement of drugs as a supplement to their regular activities. The information was passed on to drug enforcement authorities but not much else was done about it. Even this was too much for some. On one occasion, Helms told Senator John Stennis, chairman of the Armed Services Committee, of this CIA reporting.

Stennis paused, shook his head, and said, "I'm not sure you people ought to be getting involved in things like that. I don't know that that's a proper activity for you."

"Well, Mr. Chairman," replied the DCI, "how could we possibly not help the United States government when we've got such a hideous drug problem in this country?"

Helms maintains that the CIA did help, but its attitude was ambivalent at best. Tony Po, for example, threatened to throw out of his plane anyone carrying drugs, but he did nothing about caravan traffic or drug laboratories in the sectors where he was in charge. Nor could the CIA do anything to prevent the Meo's own use of drugs, which was widely accepted in their culture. There were a few attempts to encourage the Meo to raise other cash crops in place of poppies, but the return on growing potatoes was so meager in comparison with poppies that the substitution was absurd. There are unconfirmed but persistent reports that CIA officers were disciplined when they did take such actions as destroying drug labs in their areas.

Air America had had a policy against smuggling on its aircraft since 1957. But security against drug running was dependent on the pilot. The only sanction provided for passengers found with drugs was to land at the nearest airfield and put them off the plane. When the Air America crews themselves were running the drugs, there was nothing to stop them. Not until early 1972 did the CIA proprietary set up a Security Inspection Service.

Moreover, here too there was competition. Some of the people involved in moving drugs are said to have been among the most senior officers in the Royal Lao Armed Forces. Drugs were moved by RLAF and by other private Laotian air carriers. Air America crews faced the daily temptation of huge profits for smuggling small packages.

In the summer and fall of 1972, the CIA inspector general undertook a formal investigation of the drug traffic, spurred on by the detailed revelations that had appeared in a book the Agency had made some effort to suppress, *The Politics of Heroin in Southeast Asia*. The charges were so serious there was little alternative to an official investigation. A team of officers began in Hong Kong and spent over two weeks at eleven Agency facilities, interviewing over a hundred CIA, State, USAID, Pentagon, Air America, and other employees. The resulting report, "Investigation of the Drug Situation in Southeast Asia," found no evidence that the CIA or any of its senior officers had ever permitted drug traffic "as a matter of policy." There had been individual cases of smuggling but the individuals involved were found to have been disciplined promptly.

Despite the denials, drugs were moving. This points directly to a key weakness of covert operations: Making alliances with indigenous groups inevitably involves buying into the less wholesome features of such groups. Even if only through guilt by association, this in turn may discredit CIA programs as well as the larger aims of American policy.

In turning against the Laotian secret war, Senator Symington and others in Washington were reacting, in part, to factors other than the basic military situation. Drugs were a major problem in the United States, however, and had real military implications in South Vietnam, where American soldiers were becoming addicted in increasing numbers. Officials who believed the military situation in Laos could be divorced from every other factor were simply wrong.

The North Vietnamese dry-season offensive of 1969 climaxed with the loss in late June of Muong Soui (LS-108), the largest airfield in northern Laos, which the Royal Government had held since the days of Operation Triangle. Seven battalions backed by light tanks and powerful artillery spearheaded the attack over several nights; not even heavy support from sophisticated AC-130 Spectre gunships could stop them. Several times the forces on the ground requested strikes on enemy tanks but the gunships were unable to spot any. Government troops finally broke and ran away. One unit was saved by three U.S. Air Force and eleven Air America helicopters flying out of Sky at Long Tieng. The next morning several large fires burning out of control were all that was left of the defenses at Muong Soui.

There were two reactions to the loss of Muong Soui. One was propaganda: The government's Ministry of Foreign Affairs issued a white paper charging North Vietnamese violations of the 1962 Geneva agreement. The paper described instances of North Vietnamese involvement in combat, named prisoners of Vietnamese nationality, and estimated the size and composition of Vietnamese forces in Laos. This was a departure from the practice of pretending the 1962 agreement still held.

But the propaganda was designed to justify a further intensification of the war. Planning for the counteroffensive was ordered by Ambassador Godley as one of his earliest actions in Laos. At Godley's urging the United States, which had been refusing to furnish supplies and air cover for operations into the Plain of Jars since Operation Triangle, now agreed to provide such support. Several of the largest towns on the plain, targeting of which had been resisted by William H. Sullivan, were now destroyed by bombing.

The offensive onto the high plateau was to be carried out by Vang Pao's Armée Clandestine. Vang visited Vientiane to coordinate plans for the attack, which drew the code name About Face. In August the Secret Army moved north, Air America helicopters lifting Meo Special Guerrilla Units to key points.

Vang Pao was chosen because the Royal Lao army, though comprising fifty thousand troops, lacked initiative and offensive capability. Vang was, moreover, a character whom the CIA trusted and that trust was mutual. In 1968, as a gift, Vang Pao gave President Johnson an ornate flintlock musket of Meo antiquity. On two occasions the Americans rewarded Vang with secret visits to the United States. On one of these trips VP, as Americans affectionately called the Meo commander, toured the Green Beret training center at Fort Bragg. During the other trip, Vang was taken to see colonial Williamsburg and Disneyland. With six wives installed at Long Tieng, the Meo chief had a lot of shopping to do as well. At Disneyland the CIA reciprocated Vang's gift with a replica Zorro costume.

A few months later, Vang Pao was back in uniform leading the Meo in Operation About Face. The Secret Army spilled onto the Plain of Jars from the mountains, with about fifteen thousand men in the SGUs. According to Lao sources, the CIA was backing VP with a command team of 3 officers at Long Tieng, about 30 more Americans in training programs, and a couple of dozen men with the SGUs. The CIA teams with the Special Guerrilla Units varied from 4 to 12 men, most with Green Beret backgrounds. Aside from Long Tieng, there were three other CIA training bases in Laos, and at least one major training facility in Thailand. Estimates of the total number of CIA officers involved ranged from 50 to several hundred. Officially the Laos embassy had only some 70 "assistant military attachés." There were also 73 Americans with Continental Air Services and 207 with Air America.

The Meo army with its American support was fabulously successful. By the end of September the SGUs had advanced practically to the border of North Vietnam, recapturing Muong Soui along the way. At a critical juncture of the campaign, the short, wiry Vang Pao dressed up in his Zorro suit to visit the plain.

But the success was deceptive. Operation About Face proved to be the high-water mark of the Meo in the secret war. In their next dry-season offensive, the Pathet Lao and North Vietnamese went straight for the Armée Clandestine bases. Both the Plain of Jars and the mountain strongholds were threatened. The Secret Army was not what it used to be, increasingly employing Thai mercenaries contracted by the CIA; they did not have the same commitment to fight as the Meo. By 1970 whole SGUs were composed of Thai, while Vang Pao was drafting Meo children of thirteen or fourteen years of age.

First to go was the Plain of Jars. Vang Pao himself, with 1,500 troops backed by artillery, was forced out of Xieng Khouang. This loss was an important indicator of sagging Meo morale: although the government claimed 6,000 North Vietnamese troops had attacked the town, most of them had in fact been diverted to carrying supplies. Actually the Meo had retreated before a force led by only 400 Vietnamese. Equipment left behind included two cannon, thirteen recoilless rifles, five Russian-made tanks, and seven trucks. An Air America helicopter pilot, J. C. Maerki of Fort Worth, Texas, was killed by sniper fire on a supply ferry flight into the plain.

In Vientiane and Washington the situation looked quite serious indeed. Ambassador Godley requested massive air strikes by B-52 bombers in late January. By this time, however, Washington was at loggerheads over the "secrecy" of the Laotian war. Senator Symington was pressing for release of the full transcript of the hearing on Laos. The Nixon administration sanitized the transcript so heavily as to make it misleading, whereupon Symington refused to issue it. Thus Godley's request for air strikes came in the midst of a charged political situation.

Fearing leaks from the Pentagon about B-52's in Laos, Secretary of Defense Melvin Laird instructed his representative to *oppose* the B-52's in order to create a record of rejecting the option. Secretary of State William P. Rogers also opposed the plan. But according to

Henry Kissinger, national security adviser to President Nixon, Laird wanted the strikes, but within the purview of a super-secret program, in which the usual official records would be falsified. Similar B-52 missions had already been carried out in Cambodia.

The growing congressional opposition and increasing enemy successes sharpened Washington's problem. "We were caught," recounts Kissinger of the Washington policymakers, "between officials seeking to protect the American forces for which they felt a responsibility and a merciless Congressional onslaught that rattled those officials."

The Royal Laotian Government made the first of several appeals for B-52 strikes toward the middle of February. Kissinger recommended the option at a meeting with the President, Laird, Dick Helms, and the Joint Chiefs' acting chairman. Richard Nixon approved strikes if the Pathet Lao advanced beyond Muong Soui. Within twenty-four hours these conditions had been met; an attack with three B-52 bombers, a typical "cell" strike, was carried out on the night of February 17–18. More followed, yet a few days later Vang Pao relinquished his last positions on the Plain of Jars.

Strikes by the B-52's were enough, in Kissinger's phrase, "to trigger the domestic outcry." Senators Eugene McCarthy and Frank Church, along with Senate majority leader Mike Mansfield, depored the escalation. By February 25 Symington, with Mansfield and Senators Charles Mathias, Albert Gore, John Sherman Cooper, and Charles Percy, were demanding full release of the Laos hearing transcripts.

Within hours the Laos war was secret no more. The story broke not in Washington but at Long Tieng, and on press tickers the world over. Making the scoop was as simple was walking down a mountain. Journalists, with embassy cooperation, chartered an Air America plane to Sam Thong, the USAID center. The secret warriors were proud of their civic action programs and wanted to show off the place. Over a thousand Laotian nurses and medics had trained there; Sam Thong had a two-hundred-bed hospital, a junior high, and a high school. Its facilities were certainly impressive for a mountain tribal culture.

But three journalists were much more interested in Long Tieng, the main base of the Armée Clandestine. The three reporters walked out of Sam Thong, then down the trail to Long Tieng, leaving behind the larger party on the official tour. One of the reporters,

Tom Allman, a stringer for *The New York Times* and the *Bangkok Post*, actually walked into the Secret Army's main base and watched for two hours before being challenged by a Laotian colonel, then questioned by an American. The other reporters, Max Coffait of Agence France-Presse, and John Saar of Time-Life, were taken into custody and all were placed on a plane to Vientiane.

Ambassador Godley was furious. He declared, "The American mission has lost any interest in helping out the press whatsoever because of what happened this afternoon."

It was too late to halt the revelation, however. Allman filed a dispatch to the *Los Angeles Times*. For the first time, Long Tieng had been observed by outsiders. Landings and takeoffs from the Lima Site were clocked at one a minute. On the apron were about a dozen transport planes, ten light planes, a dozen or more unmarked T-28 strike aircraft, three observation planes, and three large helicopters. Air traffic was so intense that planes and copters had to form a holding pattern before they could land. The reporters, wandering at will through Long Tieng, counted scores of windowless buildings sprouting numerous radio aerials, and tall men wearing civilian clothes but carrying automatic weapons. Allman became convinced of their nationality when he discovered the base had an air-conditioned, American-style officers club with panoramic glass windows.

The Long Tieng report broke the dam and led to a flood of revelations. The White House, in an effort to manage the breaking story, immediately announced that Nixon would be releasing some information on the United States in Laos. A statement admitted that Americans had fought there. Three days later a State Department spokesman asserted that American war deaths in Laos totaled 25 contractor personnel and 1 dependent. A reporter then wrote of a military fatality, Army Captain Joseph Bush, killed at Muong Soui on February 10, 1969. In rapid succession the press revealed several other incidents where Americans had been killed, including the radar station battle at Phu Pha Thi. The Nixon administration countered with a new statement, after a search of the records, that 200 Americans had died and 193 were missing. Numbers of Americans in the country were put at 228 military men, 388 government employees, and 424 contractor personnel.

In the Senate, Symington asked the administration to bring McMurtrie Godley back to testify before the committee. Foreign

Relations committee chairman J. William Fulbright went ahead and put on the record some information the administration had been trying to keep secret: that DCI Helms had admitted in testimony that CIA used USAID cover in Laos. Fulbright added that recruiting and training of partisan soldiers and native agents was handled by the embassy's Rural Development Annex, while the mysterious Special Requirements Office handled logistics and military aid. Further details were added to the record in April 1970, when continuing political pressures forced the administration to relent and release the 1969 congressional testimony.

Any chance of limiting the damage was lost when Nixon ordered an invasion of Cambodia. Further Laos hearings were scheduled by the Senate Foreign Relations Committee. Angry senators ruled out allowing Nixon's officials to testify in executive session. This record would be in the open. These political events plus the military developments in Laos marked the final shift in tide of the secret war.

Nowhere was the deterioration situation more apparent in the Meo uplands, where the refugee flow was suddenly tripled. The North Vietnamese seemed to be everywhere, to be capable of anything. On the Plain of Jars, Vang Pao's SGUs had panicked when faced with two to four enemy tanks. Now there were rumors of North Vietnamese tanks in the mountains. Both Long Tieng and Sam Thong seemed threatened.

An evacuation was hastily ordered. Some 110,000 Meo sought refuge, carrying out whatever they could. Sam Thong was abandoned with most of the civic improvements the Meo had gained in a decade of war. A large new refugee center was improvised at Ban Son (LS-272) to the southwest. At Long Tieng, for the first time in the Meo war, the base had to be prepared for defense. Vang Pao reduced his headquarters by sending the administrative elements to other Meo sites. Certain Meo valuables and many fearful tribesmen left there, too.

Air America was at the center of action. From Sam Thong it flew out sixteen Americans, two hundred hospital patients, and over two thousand Meo and Lao. The CIA proprietary also brought reinforcements in to Vang Pao at Long Tieng, two battalions of Thai contract troops fresh from training. The U.S. Air Force itself began daily flights from Pepper Grinder to Sky with the "spook" C-130's of the special air warfare E-Flight, this an exception to the usual rule that Air Force planes should be flown by Air America crews.

One of the Air Force Hercules transports went down in April with thirteen Americans aboard, the only aircraft of this type to be lost in the Laotian war.

In fact, the North Vietnamese threat was less than had been perceived. Of their 12,000 troops, fully 10,000 were working to move supplies forward. The assault force of 2,000 soldiers did not attack Long Tieng, but occupied Sam Thong. The Vietnamese dynamited the houses used by some of the Americans, burned the hospital and USAID warehouse, then withdrew. After a few weeks the Meo reoccupied the place. That summer, in Operation Leapfrog, the Secret Army regained some lost territory, but the pendulum had swung in Laos. Vang Pao was no more successful defending the territory he gained in Leapfrog than he had been with About Face in 1969. With their new supply roads the Vietnamese, meanwhile, were stronger than ever. They forced the permanent abandonment of Sam Thong in the 1971 dry-season offensive. Long Tieng was threatened again, as it was a third time in the 1972 offensive.

Meo forces had begun an irreversible decline. An army with a strength of 27,000 sounded formidable, but the proportion of Meo in the SGUs had fallen to only 20 percent. Thai mercenaries, amounting to about 12,000 in the Armée Clandestine, had become the largest group in the force. Lao officers described the SGU Thais as drifters, unemployed and uneducated men with brief training and no motivation. By 1974, when the remaining Thai mercenaries were withdrawn, their numbers had swelled to 17,000. The withdrawal left Vang Pao with but 6,000 men.

Naturally the Americans did not stand by idly through all of this. The CIA did everything it could to shore up the partisan force. By this time the Vientiane station was under the command of Hugh Tovar, Devlin having returned to Langley as chief of the Africa Division of DDP. Another OSS veteran, Tovar had been parachuted into Laos once already, at the end of World War II. The kind of activist that the CIA seemed to prefer in Laos, Tovar had been chief of station in Indonesia in 1965, when a successful military coup overthrew President Sukarno. Tovar helped maintain the warm relationship between the CIA and the Indonesian military, which was responsible for giving the United States access to a wide range of information on and samples of Soviet equipment. In Laos, Tovar's problem was of a different sort.

Together with Ambassador Godley, Tovar had at his disposal more resources than had yet been devoted to Laos. Disclosure of the secret war had led Nixon to put Laotian military aid back in the Pentagon budget, thus openly funding the war, and increasing the amount. In fiscal 1971, United States expenditures amounted to $162 million for military aid, $52 million for USAID, and reportedly $70 million for local CIA costs. The Agency and the Pentagon probably spent at least as much to fund the Thailand side of the Laotian war, while the budget for the air war no doubt amounted to billions.

All the money could not make up for flagging Meo support. The CIA further contributed to Vang Pao's political difficulties by sanctioning the use of herbicides against Meo poppy fields after a 1971 government law prohibiting these flowers. Enraged Meo blamed Vang Pao, and Armée Clandestine impressment gangs had to threaten *Meo* villages with destruction in order to raise recruits for Vang Pao's forces.

In late 1971, Senator Symington sponsored an amendment to the appropriations bill that set a ceiling of $350 million for all United States funds spent in Laos. This level prevailed in 1972, though it was increased to $375 million for fiscal 1973. By that time, Indochina peace negotiations were in full swing, leading to agreements signed in Paris in January 1973. For Laos the agreements provided a coalition government, like that intended in 1958 except that the Pathet Lao were incomparably stronger. Fourteen years of warfare accomplished none of the original United States policy goals.

Vang Pao was one of the big losers in the negotiated settlement, which ended American air support for the Secret Army. The cease-fire was to go into effect at noon on February 22, 1973, a time when Vang was facing a renewed North Vietnamese offensive and defending Long Tieng yet again. Several of his outposts were under attack as the cease-fire neared.

The Meo general made a last appeal to the CIA to continue the American air support. In reply he was handed a message from the chief of unit at Sky: "As we discussed previously, USAF support would cease as of 1200, 22 February. I confirmed this . . . today by talking with CRICKET, the [airborne command plane] in this area. USAF were under instructions to clear Lao air space."

Disgusted, Vang Pao kicked the dirt and showed the message to reporters nearby.

Leaving Laos, one of the last shifts of American command planes radioed back, "Good-bye and see you next war."

One of Long Tieng's outposts fell two and a half hours later. The last CIA advisers left aboard Air America. Vang Pao was on his own, on a road that could lead only to exile.

The secret war brought the Meo no nationhood, only three unhappy migrations. Far from uniting them, the effect of the Laotian war was to scatter the Meo to the winds. Some thirty thousand live in refugee camps in Thailand, their numbers periodically increased by new migrations from home. About fifty-five thousand Meo have been resettled in the United States. Vang Pao himself has become a farmer in Montana; there are pockets of Meo in places as diverse as Philadelphia, Minneapolis, and Fresno.

Direct losses of the war in Laos are still not known with certainty. Over a million Laotians were made refugees at one time or another, a third of the country's entire population. Destruction from the bombing was immense. Only a handful of CIA battle deaths are admitted by Agency and State Department officials. The Pentagon maintains that about half its losses resulted from the air war but lists over 400 deaths and 556 servicemen still missing in action. Deaths in plane wrecks or in combat for Air America totaled 17 Americans plus an equal number of locals for the years 1970–1973 alone. From the scattered data it appears that about 1,000 Americans perished.

Beginning in 1973 the new Royal Laotian Government pressured Air America to cease its operations. The CIA proprietary did halt flights to some 350 airfields and turned a dozen C-123 transports over to the Laotian air force. Many employees of the Air America base at Udon were laid off. Americans working there had numbered 250 including 100 pilots, 42 of whom left in 1973. After a Laotian prohibition on its operations, Air America closed up shop in June 1974. The Udon facilities were taken over by Thai Airways Aircraft Maintenance Company.

The results of the CIA's postmortems on Laos are not known. One view has been furnished, however, by Douglas Blaufarb, a senior CIA official with long service in both Laos and Vietnam. Blaufarb, who defended the Meo against press criticism when he served at the embassy in 1971, continues to believe that the tribe had a right to fight for its future, and that their struggle was misunderstood in the United States, in part, precisely because of its secrecy. In mobilizing the Meo, the United States incurred an "undoubted moral obligation," which it could do little to meet. Blaufarb also believes the war effort was hampered by the predominance of the

American military in Southeast Asia, which constantly menaced the independence of the ambassador and his staff in Vientiane. Finally, argues this former CIA officer, the improvised nature of the secret war led to an open-ended campaign without clear aims other than the general United States objectives in Indochina.

The secret war in Laos represented many things to many people. To some it was a laboratory to test counterinsurgency techniques, to others a political morass at the edge of the Vietnam imbroglio. To some Americans, Laos symbolized government secrecy used to cloak activities of doubtful legality. To Anthony Poshepny, one who didn't come back, Laos was a supreme adventure. Tony Po lost his heart to a Yao princess and stayed in northeast Thailand to become a gentleman farmer.

·XV·

GLOBAL REACH

Lyndon Baines Johnson was a President with a passion for domestic policy. Proud of instituting a variety of social programs he collectively called the Great Society, LBJ viewed foreign affairs as problems that came with his job. President Johnson was keenly disappointed with the Indochina war, which absorbed ever greater amounts of time, energy, and the economic resources he wished to devote to the Great Society—not to mention the idealism of American youth, which might have transformed the nation.

The growth of controversy and opposition to the war ultimately cast a pall over Johnson's own political future. In the spring of 1968 the President decided he would not run for reelection. The strongest candidate in the resulting free-for-all, and victor in the November elections, was Richard Milhous Nixon.

Like Johnson, Nixon was prepared to use the full powers of his office, even to seize powers for it. This has led political analysts to term the Nixon years the era of "the imperial presidency." Unlike his predecessor, Nixon was primarily interested in foreign policy. He was also suspicious of the bureaucracy, and wanted to center policy-making in the White House.

Paradoxically, Nixon was personally bored with the details of policy. This made the choice of his staff a crucial decision, especially the assistant for national security affairs and his NSC staff. For his purposes, Nixon's selection of Henry A. Kissinger for NSC adviser proved to be an inspired choice. Formerly a professor at Harvard, Kissinger proved adept at bureaucratic maneuvers and at fighting in the political alleyways of Washington.

Nixon's dominance of American foreign policy would be out-lasted by Kissinger's, by two and a half years in the end. At the out-set of his administration, however, there was no question as to Richard Nixon's power and authority. The remarkable political comeback was the prelude to an increased global role on the part of the United States.

From his eight years as Vice-President under President Eisen-hower, Nixon had acquired a broad understanding of the techniques of covert action and their potential. Nixon now took command of ongoing projects in Southeast Asia, and initiated new actions there, and in the Near East and Latin America.

One of Nixon's earliest coercive actions was not really a paramil-itary operation but rather a secret escalation of ongoing cross-bor-der operations from Vietnam to Cambodia.

American activities in Cambodia were not new. According to Prince Norodom Sihanouk, erstwhile king, prime minister, and re-sistance leader, relations with the United States had been de-teriorating steadily since the days when Nixon served as Vice-President. Nixon himself knew of these developments, having visited Sihanouk in Phnom Penh as early as 1953.

Soon after the 1954 Geneva agreements, the United States had been instrumental in setting up a regional alliance, the Southeast Asia Treaty Organization (SEATO). Cambodia was encouraged to join by John Foster Dulles, who did not take kindly to Sihanouk's refusal. Allen Dulles repeated the offer during a 1955 visit, again to be rejected. The Americans did not seem to care that the Geneva accords explicitly prohibited Cambodia and the other states that had succeeded French Indochina from joining any multilateral alli-ance.

Sihanouk remained head of state throughout the 1950s and 1960s. He remained committed to neutrality despite increasing pressures to take sides. The Americans gave some foreign aid but linked any substantial assistance to alignment with SEATO. Sihanouk was ada-mant in resisting and came to regard the desire for dollars as a per-nicious disease among Cambodians. In 1965 he rejected further American aid and diplomatic relations between the countries were broken off.

American efforts to change this basic situation went beyond dip-lomatic exchanges, so much so that Sihanouk entitled his memoir of this period *My War with the CIA*. Before the break in diplomatic relations, the tally of United States embassy personnel identified as CIA officers by Khmer intelligence had reached twenty-seven. Sihanouk believes this list was incomplete. He also believes that Robert McClintock, the American ambassador in the mid to late 1950s, was from the Agency. Though McClintock had served in Indochina during the French war, and had long had an abiding interest in special warfare and military operations, there is little other evidence to suggest he was a CIA man. However, Eisenhower did appoint John Puerifoy, the supervisor of the Guatemalan Operation Success, as American ambassador to the adjoining country of Thailand.

It was in Thailand and in South Vietnam that Americans quietly began supporting Cambodian resistance to Sihanouk, specifically through the Khmer Serei and Khmer Krom. By the late 1950s these groups were making raids into Cambodia. The fact that the Khmer Serei and Khmer Krom were incorporated into the CIA/Green Beret Mike Forces, during the American war in Vietnam, made obvious the existence of some complicity, but the origins of this support are still shrouded in the murky history of secret operations.

A more clearly attributable plot arose in 1958–1959, when the Americans attempted to forge a direct relationship with a Cambodian army regional commander named Dap Chhuon. It was hoped that, in a reincarnation of the strategy that had failed in Indonesia, the Cambodian general would mount a coup to overthrow Sihanouk, or, failing that, form a separatist regime, which the United States could recognize and assist.

Sihanouk's suspicions were aroused by Dap Chhuon's sudden popularity among very senior American visitors who had no time for the Cambodian head of state. The stream included Edward Lansdale, another general who was the United States ambassador to South Vietnam, the United States Pacific theater commander and the Pacific Fleet commander. Activity was coordinated by an American at the Phnom Penh embassy, Victor Matsui, a former Marine identified as CIA by Sihanouk, who is said to have had over a million dollars to dispense on the operation.

The Dap Chhuon plot was broken in the spring of 1959 when Sihanouk dispatched his army chief of staff, Lon Nol, to arrest the errant commander. Lon Nol killed him instead. At Dap Chhuon's villa, Khmer authorities found two South Vietnamese radio operators with their equipment, posing as Chinese filmmakers.

Victor Matsui went on to work for a time in CIA's efforts to penetrate North Vietnam, and then for the Agency in Pakistan, from which he was expelled for espionage activities in 1966.

Meanwhile, the Vietnam War had escalated from small-scale guerrilla activity to regular forces on both sides. Cambodia became increasingly vital to the North Vietnamese as an extension of the Ho Chin Minh Trail. Sihanouk continued to maintain a strictly neutral position between the warring sides.

Beginning in mid-1967 the Americans countered with cross-border patrols into Cambodia just like those into Laos. Patrols typically comprised three Americans and nine indigenous personnel, were inserted by helicopter, and walked out. This project was run by MACV-SOG under the code name Daniel Boone. At Banmethuot at the foot of the Central Highlands, MACV-SOG established an element called Command and Control South in November 1967 to regularize Daniel Boone. The unit contained reconnaissance teams, larger "Hachet" patrol units, plus four strike force companies. When the Daniel Boone missions were revealed in the American press, the code name was changed to Salem House. The SOG unit also made efforts to install agent networks in the Cambodian border regions. There were four hundred operations into that nation in 1967–1968, and over a thousand during the next two years.

Cross-border operations were still in progress when Richard Nixon was inaugurated as President in January 1969. A month later there was an upsurge of fighting in South Vietnam. Nixon determined to retaliate by secretly bombing Cambodia while officially continuing to respect its neutrality. Salem House missions would be used to find targets and assess the results of the bombing.

The Cambodian effort utilized B-52 bombers, some of the most powerful weapons in the United States' arsenal. To carry out this bombing campaign known as Operation Menu, in a nation with which the United States was at peace, Nixon ordered unprecedented levels of secrecy. The regular Pentagon records, themselves classified and supposedly secure, were falsified to indicate that the bombing missions were hitting South Vietnam. Pilots were briefed for flights over Vietnam and diverted at the last moment. Within a little over a year, B-52's flew 3,060 sorties over Cambodia, dropping more than 100,000 tons of bombs.

Far from wiping out North Vietnamese based areas, the Operation Menu bombing had little apparent effect. Salem House teams found the enemy infuriated, not dazed. One bombing assessment patrol under Special Forces captain Bill Orthman was practically wiped out. When another team was ordered out on the same mission, the men rebelled and refused to go. Several were arrested but MACV could hardly court-martial soldiers publicly for refusing to violate the neutrality of Cambodia. No action was taken.

Green Beret morale was affected, however, by other courts-martial that did take place. An intelligence activity in Cambodia, Project Cherry, ended in January 1968 with charges against its commander, Captain John J. McCarthy, Jr., in the killing of a Cambodian interpreter suspected as an enemy double agent. The most celebrated trial occurred in 1969 when eight Green Berets, including Colonel Robert B. Rheault, commander of the 5th Special Forces Group, were accused of murder in the death of another suspected double agent. This agent had been acting as part of Project Blackbeard, a set of networks in Cambodia controlled by Captain Robert F. Marasco. The agent's murder evidently followed Marasco's discovery that his sources in Cambodia were drying up. Army charges in the case were dropped after CIA officers refused to testify at the court-martial. The "Green Beret affair" resulted, in Washington, in one of the few meetings ever held by the top-level United States Intelligence Board at which all subordinates were excluded and no notes were taken.

With crippled agent networks and ineffective Salem House missions, Nixon nevertheless forged ahead in Cambodia. The apparent willingness of the United States to act encouraged those Khmer who opposed Sihanouk's neutrality. This was especially true for Prime Minister Lon Nol, his lieutenant Sirik Matak, and Khmer Serei chief Son Ngoc Thanh. On March 18, 1970, while Sihanouk was abroad, Lon Nol launched a coup d'état, overthrew the chief of state, and plunged Cambodia squarely into the Indochina war.

The extent of American complicity in the Lon Nol coup has long been in dispute. The official version is that there was no involvement whatsoever. Sihanouk believes the CIA was a prime instigator. The truth probably lies somewhere in between. Doubts on the official version arise from three factors: the behavior of the Khmer Serei; United States and Vietnamese contacts with Lon Nol; and CIA foreknowledge of the Phnom Penh coup.

Whatever is said about Lon Nol, there is no doubt that the

Khmer Serei owed their status to the CIA. Sources ranging from Si-hanouk to Lon Nol's own army commanders agree on this point. Funding for the organization in Thailand was more or less covert, but Khmer Serei in Vietnam were openly recruited for CIA's Mike Forces. Most peculiarly, through 1969 there was a wave of "desertions" from the Khmer Serei in Thailand with entire units going over to the Cambodians; two hundred in January, three hundred in May; three full battalions at the end of the year. As prime minister and army commander under Sihanouk, Lon Nol incorporated some of these Khmer Serei into the national police and others into the Phnom Penh garrison.

As soon as he launched the coup, Lon Nol appealed for American assistance. Within two weeks there were eighteen hundred Mike Force Khmer Serei in Cambodia. Some of them had been airlifted to the border. Before the end of the year, four thousand Khmer Serei and Khmer Krom had joined Lon Nol.

"What we knew at the time," recalls Cambodian General Sak Sutsakhan, "was that these 'Special Forces' were under direct U. S. command in South Vietnam."

As early as mid-February 1970 the Special Forces captain in charge of the camp at Tieu Atar in South Vietnam was ordered to send two companies of *montagnard* strikers to Bu Prang camp to replace Khmer Serei, who would be moving into Cambodia when Sihanouk was ousted.

Henry Kissinger presses the official version in his memoirs. He argues that "we neither encouraged Sihanouk's overthrow nor knew about it in advance. We did not even grasp its significance for many weeks." Not until the very day of the coup, reports Kissinger, did a CIA report circulate in Washington predicting that such an event might occur.

In the first days of March, however, an Air Force pilot flew a party of about sixty American diplomats and military officers to Phnom Penh for secret talks. He believed the purpose of this highly classified mission was to negotiate Cambodian neutrality, but afterward he met spooky types from the embassy, at a Saigon bar, and they knew all about the Phnom Penh flight. The pilot was told he was stupid—the Americans had been talking to a Cambodian general willing to move against Sihanouk, who would soon be overthrown.

During this same period, Khmer Serei leader Son Ngoc Thanh

also met with Lon Nol, a fact confirmed by Secretary of Defense Melvin Laird. Regarding this contact Bill Colby of the CIA told journalist William Shawcross that "Lon Nol may well have been encouraged by the fact that the U. S. was working with Son Ngoc Thanh. I don't know of any specific assurances he was given but the obvious conclusion for him, given the political situation in South Vietnam and Laos, was that he would be given United States support."

In other interviews for his study on Cambodia, Shawcross was told, by MACV deputy commander General William Rosson, that the United States military had several days' notice of the coup and a request for American assistance. Saigon CIA analyst Frank Snepp also told of contact with Lon Nol by the Defense Intelligence Agency.

Perhaps the most telling indicator was inadvertently supplied by Henry Kissinger himself. The date of Kissinger's memorandum to Richard Nixon, reporting Lon Nol's plans for expanding the Cambodian army, is March 17, 1970—the day *before* the coup.

Nixon, of course, was amenable to helping Lon Nol. In his own memoir he expresses surprise at the coup, quoting himself asking Secretary of State William Rogers, "What the hell do those clowns do out there in Langley?" But on Kissinger's memo, according to the NSC adviser, Nixon wrote, "Let's get a plan to aid the new government." A few days later, Nixon instructed Kissinger, "I want (DCI) Helms to develop and implement a plan for maximum assistance to pro-U. S. elements in Cambodia." Kissinger was ordered to say nothing about this to the bureaucracy or the NSC Special Group monitoring covert operations. The aid matter would be handled like the Operation Menu air strikes.

Prepackaged shipments of unattributable CIA weapons were en route to Phnom Penh before the United States formally considered arms aid to Cambodia.

Nixon followed up, in the last days of April, with a full-fledged MACV invasion, with the South Vietnamese, of the Cambodian border regions. The invasion ignited a political firestorm in the United States.

Although Richard Nixon learned much of what he knew about leadership from President Eisenhower, there were fundamental differences between the two men. Ike tried to be subtle, to work with a hidden hand. Nixon preferred to think in terms of dramatic decisions yielding reliable results. One such was conceived in the early days of the Cambodian invasion and taken to the President for approval.

The spectacular mission was nothing less than an attempt to liberate American prisoners from a camp in the heart of North Vietnam, a camp only two dozen miles from downtown Hanoi. There had been other attempts to rescue prisoners, in South Vietnam, Cambodia, and Laos, since 1966. The raid on the Sontay prisoner camp would be the ninety-first rescue mission, but one of the most ambitious and the first in North Vietnam. Only twenty of the previous rescue missions had been successful, freeing 318 South Vietnamese soldiers and 60 civilians. Only 1 American, an Army enlisted man, had ever been rescued, and he had died of wounds inflicted at the last moment by his captors. Still, the Pentagon began considering a rescue mission at Sontay almost as soon as the prisoner camp was discovered.

The Sontay raid was the brainchild of Brigadier General Donald D. Blackburn, one of the Army's premier special-warfare enthusiasts, who by 1970 was head of Laird's office of special assistant for counterinsurgency and special activities (SACSA). Blackburn had been a paratrooper fighting the Japanese during World War II, from which he emerged at twenty-nine years of age as a full colonel. He taught at West Point, was an adviser in Vietnam, and commanded a Special Forces group at Fort Bragg. In 1960 it was Blackburn who got the assignment of setting up White Star in Laos. After a tour with SACSA he returned to Vietnam in 1965 as commander of MACV-SOG. Blackburn had worked North Vietnam before, with SOG, whose Bearcat base prepared agent teams for infiltration, and he felt a raid at Sontay might work.

After receiving intelligence of the existence of the prisoner camp, SACSA and DIA began a feasibility study for a rescue mission. A proposal was accepted by the Joint Chiefs on July 10, 1970, and chairman Admiral Thomas Moorer gave Blackburn the green light for planning and preparation. On August 8 a joint contingency task force was created under Air Force brigadier general Leroy J. Manor to carry out the raid. As chief of the ground element, Blackburn handpicked Special Forces Colonel Arthur D. "Bull" Simons, who had run White Star for him a decade earlier. Like Blackburn, Bull Simons was a legendary figure, with two tours in charge of White

Star, one with SOG, service at MACV, where he helped develop contingency plans for an invasion of Laos, and command of the Special Forces group oriented toward Latin America. Blackburn worried about a heart condition Bull had recently developed in Korea, but was reassured when Simons told him he was back up to 250 push-ups a day.

Planning reached an advanced stage by the late summer. Practice exercises had begun when Laird took the basic idea to Richard Nixon for approval, which was promptly forthcoming. The Sontay operation was christened Ivory Coast.

This spectacular mission was planned down to the last detail, including exercises against a mock village set up at Eglin Air Force Base in Florida. So great was the secrecy that the mock village was disassembled and concealed each time a Soviet reconnaissance satellite was expected overhead. There were more than 100 exercises, while the HH-53 helicopters, intended to fly in the raiding party and extract the prisoners, made some 368 practice flights totaling 1,107 hours in the air. General Manor held a full dress rehearsal at night on October 7.

The following day, Blackburn, Manor, Simons, and Air Force general John Vogt, director of the joint staff, presented a detailed status report to Kissinger at the White House, recommending that Operation Ivory Coast be carried out late that month. The Joint Chiefs, Laird, and DCI Richard Helms had already been apprised of progress. For reasons apparently connected with the Vietnam peace negotiations, however, the raid was postponed another month.

Admiral Thomas Moorer was the presenter on November 18, when the Operation Ivory Coast plan was again briefed at the White House, this time directly to Nixon, Laird, Kissinger, Helms, and Secretary of State William P. Rogers. The President was told he had to make a decision within twenty-four hours or postpone the raid at least until the spring of 1971. Nixon kept the briefing book to examine it, but gave his approval in time. Ivory Coast went forward.

Word was flashed by cable to Pepper Grinder, the "spook" base at Takhli, Thailand, where by now Bull Simons, the fifty-eight-man assault force, and the helicopters were standing by. From there the force moved up to Udon. Ivory Coast was executed during the night of November 21–22. The air assault, search, and recovery aboard the HH-53's took just twenty-seven minutes. None of the Green Berets were killed; the worst casualty was a sprained ankle. Even the Air Force crew of another helicopter, which deliberately crashed inside the compound as a diversion, got out. Only two things marred the perfect performance.

One amounted to an intelligence failure of some proportions—*there were no prisoners* at Sontay. It had indeed been an active camp when the rescue mission was first conceived, but during the summer the camp was threatened by flood waters from the nearby Red River and had been evacuated. Washington had aerial photography that confirmed as much—pictures taken by a high-altitude SR-71 spy plane that covered the camp on October 3. But more photos from SR-71 overflights in early November showed the camp back in use. Crops had been planted in the complex. Additional SR-71 flights the week before the raid, and in the days immediately preceding it, confirmed Sontay's renewed employment. Reconnaissance drone flights scheduled for the day before the raid were canceled because of adverse weather.

Though the Sontay complex was back in use, it was not a prisoner camp. That name did not appear on the prisoner head count and list of camps passed to the Americans by an agent in Hanoi about a week before the raid. A new camp was listed near the city of Dong Hoi. This information became known to the DIA, whose director in Washington told Admiral Moorer and General Blackburn. SACSA challenged the information throughout a late-night session at DIA. He thought the agent report ambiguous, while the three most recent SR-71 flights had returned marginal photography or none at all.

"That crazy Blackburn," another officer remembers thinking, "is going to invade North Vietnam so Bull Simons can land in an empty prison camp."

At a six A.M. meeting, Blackburn indeed recommended to Admiral Moorer that the raid go ahead.

Moorer took the decision to Melvin Laird, who let stand the execute order, which had already gone out. Simons and General Manor were left to discover for themselves whether Americans still inhabited Sontay.

Simons's raiders found no prisoners, but they ran into someone else, and that was the second thing that went wrong at Sontay. One of the HH-53 assault helicopters mistakenly landed at a secondary school about six hundred meters from the objective. The school had been converted into a barracks and there was a short, sharp firefight in which the Green Berets killed an estimated 100 or 200 enemy. These soldiers, however, were too tall for Vietnamese, and are thought to have been either Chinese or Russian. Operation Ivory Coast could have turned into a major international incident. The Nixon administration had made no preparations to deal with this kind of eventuality. Fortunately, the other side made no discernible reaction.

The last part of the Sontay story is the deception of Congress and the American public that was inadvertently revealed by Nixon himself. Air strikes were made against North Vietnamese targets that night to divert attention from Operation Ivory Coast. These became known, but Laird at first denied the bombing, then claimed the strikes were in "protective reaction" for the downing of a Marine reconnaissance plane two weeks before.

For his part, Richard Nixon had arranged to host Thanksgiving dinner for disabled veterans drawn from military hospitals in the Washington area. Nixon had also planned on having the freed prisoners at this White House dinner, but there were none. Thanksgiving came, and the President sat down to table with a small group of servicemen. Busy autographing White House matchbooks, Nixon began talking about Sontay, including the air raids made to pin down North Vietnamese defenses. This story got back to a junior reporter covering the city desk of *The Washington Post* that Thanksgiving.

Secretary Laird's careful obfuscations were blown by his boss. As for Henry Kissinger, the former NSC adviser maintains he learned of the intelligence that Sontay had been closed only after the failure of the raid.

There would be 28 more rescue missions attempted before the end of the war. Of the total 119 missions undertaken between 1966 and 1973, fully 98 were raids. Only one American prisoner was ever recovered. Raids might be spectacular but they were not going to determine the outcome of the Vietnam War. That could only be done on the ground, in the south.

In the south there were two wars really, the war of posts and combat divisions, and the pacification war, the contest for the loyalty of the Vietnamese people. The second was the business of the CIA, and had been since Operation Switchback took the Agency out of paramilitary action in South Vietnam. A comprehensive pacification program had been proposed by the Agency in 1965, and the CIA was involved in planning and expert assistance for many of the pacification activities that followed.

President Johnson wrestled repeatedly with pacification, which he did not want to leave entirely to the military. At conferences in Honolulu and Manila, in decisional documents, and in innumerable telephone conversations, LBJ pressed the theme that the "other war" was the real war. Johnson's interest owed much to a White House staff that gave sustained attention to pacification issues, in particular to a CIA officer on detached duty with the NSC, Robert W. Komer. LBJ thought so much of Komer's work that he was soon a White House troubleshooter. In 1966, Komer served for a few months as acting NSC adviser. When LBJ decided he needed a Washington coordinator for pacification programs, Komer was the man.

A year later, President Johnson decided that a top-level Saigon command for pacification was necessary. Again LBJ chose Komer, and promised him anything he needed to get the job done. The Saigon unit was called the Civil Operations and Revolutionary Development Staff (CORDS), and "Blowtorch Bob" (as Ambassador Cabot Lodge called the impatient but brilliant CIA man) swung into action to energize the programs already in place.

Langley soon learned just how much influence Komer had in the White House. By late 1967, Richard Helms felt that the time had come for a change at the top of the DDP's Far East Division. The DCI called in division chief William E. Colby and offered him the plum posting of chief of the Soviet Russia Division. Bill Colby naturally accepted, and was already getting his first briefings when Komer asked instead for Colby's assignment to Saigon as deputy chief of CORDS. At one of the President's regular "Tuesday Lunch" decision meetings, LBJ turned to Helms and out of the blue ordered the DCI to send Colby out to help Komer. Helms, who had known nothing of the CORDS chief's request, apologetically told Colby of the reassignment. "Bob Komer, [Helms] said, had put a fast one over on him."

The CORDS era led to one of the most controversial pacification programs of the Vietnam War. This resulted from Komer's thinking about how to specifically target the Vietcong cadres and leadership in the villages. Komer settled on a massive intelligence program to collect information on suspected Vietcong, who could then be "neutralized" by South Vietnamese security forces. At first called ICEX, for Intelligence Coordination and Exploitation, the program was put into place in 1968. Its name was changed to Phoenix in 1969, when the South Vietnamese set up a parallel program they called Phung Hoang, after a mythical bird with the magical powers to bring news of peace (Phoenix was a loose translation of the Vietnamese term).

Phoenix grew into a major effort, with interrogation centers in every one of South Vietnam's 235 districts and 44 provinces, card files, and computerized indexes. There were special 50- to-100-man strike forces called Provincial Reconnaissance Units (PRUs), special security in the Vietnamese National Police Field Force. The regular police force was beefed up, and some responsibilities given to the more than 500,000 local militia troops. About 600 Americans were assigned to support the program, mostly military but some State Department and 20 to 40 CIA specialists.

By the time Phoenix was in place, Komer was gone, sent to Turkey as ambassador. Bill Colby succeeded him as CORDS director. United States funding for Phoenix increased throughout his term at CORDS. Though Phoenix was formally a CORDS program, not a CIA project, the Agency provided weapons for the local militias, paid for the Saigon computer files, funded and trained the PRUs, and passed intelligence to the Phoenix organization.

This program piled up some impressive statistics. During 1969 alone, Phoenix "neutralized" 19,534 Vietcong suspects, of whom 6,187 were killed. In 1971, Colby told a Senate hearing that 20,587 had been killed, 28,978 imprisoned, and 17,717 converted into agents for Saigon. Not to be outdone, the South Vietnamese government itself claimed that over 40,000 had been killed. However, when questions arose regarding the legality of some of these operations, even under Vietnamese law, the authorities rapidly retreated into an admission that 87 percent of the supposed Vietcong cadres had been killed in the course of regular military actions.

A major controversy surrounding Phoenix concerned whether it was an assassination program. Directors deny that it ever was, but a number of American veterans of Phoenix assert the opposite. Whatever the truth may be, Colby himself felt compelled to issue a directive in 1969 that prohibited assassinations and other violations of the laws of war. Early in 1970, moreover, two Army lieutenants assigned to Phoenix, Francis T. Reitemeyer and Michael J. Cohn, were able to secure honorable discharges as conscientious objectors, after convincing a federal judge that they were being ordered to maintain a "kill quota" of fifty Vietcong a month.

Phoenix operations greatly swelled the flow of detainees into South Vietnamese prisons, and prison conditions were so deplorable that they became a separate issue to the antiwar opposition in the United States. This was another CORDS area of responsibility: It was, as Colby writes in retrospect, "one situation we obviously missed."

The worst abuse of the Phoenix program was the use of hearsay, even malicious gossip in a deliberate effort to suppress a segment of the population. Often feuds, political maneuvers, even gangster-style "protection" rackets, fueled the tips to Phoenix operatives. Vietnamese military courts often acted solely on the basis of confessions extracted under interrogation. Phoenix-approved guidelines for prison sentences had only limited meaning in a world where terms could be extended indefinitely beyond the court-mandated sentences. Innocent people suffered under Phoenix and some of them died.

There can be no doubt that the pacification effort had some impact. North Vietnamese diplomats and officers have said as much in interviews since the war. Their forces were increasingly forced into base areas in Cambodia and Laos, and they were clearly forced to resort to regular military tactics for the 1972 Easter offensive. That Phoenix was so successful is the favorite argument of those who defend its methods. An anecdote Bill Colby has told many times is how he twice weekly would stay overnight somewhere in the "boonies," and how, by 1972, the evenings could be spent in pleasant surroundings rather than buttoned up in some bunker. Colby fondly recalls traveling alone, at night, on motorbikes or boats, with the legendary Vietnam hand John Paul Vann.

Perhaps the program's success had more to do with the strategic choices made by the North Vietnamese. It was the enemy himself who, by frittering away so many cadres and local forces in the 1968 Tet offensive, decisively weakened the infrastructure. This effect occurred independently of any Phoenix action.

Attributing the North Vietnamese concentration of forces in sanctuaries solely to pacification is a long leap of faith. Once the Nixon administration adopted a policy of American withdrawals combined with "Vietnamization," the other side had a clear military incentive to avoid combat until the United States troops were gone. Moreover, the North Vietnamese obviously made certain redeployments with an eye toward the Paris peace negotiations. Phoenix may have facilitated the adversary's choices but it probably did not determine them. It is worth noting in this connection that overall size of North Vietnamese forces hardly varied between 1968 and 1972 despite the supposed weakened infrastructure, which theoretically should have reduced the adversary's ability to maintain forces. It is also hard to believe that pacification was the sole factor obliging the North Vietnamese to shift to regular warfare. The sophistication and technical means of American military forces, no doubt compelled the adversary to use equivalent capabilities to win on the ground.

Finally, the political control measures applied in Phoenix further disrupted any remaining possibilities for developing a "third force" movement in South Vietnam. A "third force" might have given political legitimacy to the Saigon government—in time for it to combat the North Vietnamese more effectively.

Despite the apparent success of the pacification program, the invasions of Cambodia and Laos, the bombing and Secret Army operations in Laos, and all the rest, the North Vietnamese were poised for a major conventional offensive by 1972. Nixon responded with huge increases in air power, not only in the south but renewed bombing of North Vietnam, including the mining of Haiphong harbor and fierce Christmas bombing of Hanoi with B-52's. North Vietnamese attacks were halted, and the offensive led to the Paris agreements of 1973, which took the last United States combat forces out of the war. Saigon was left with residual military aid plus advice from American attachés and civilian contractors.

The Vietnam War continued for two more years. To Saigon, Nixon sent a new ambassador, Graham Martin, who had already seen the middle of the war, from Thailand. Martin and CIA station chief Thomas Polgar ignored growing indications of Saigon's deterioration and North Vietnamese strength. The end came in 1975 with another North Vietnamese offensive, before which the Saigon forces simply crumbled. The CIA and the other American services were forced into a frantic evacuation that ended with helicopters atop the United States embassy. Many Vietnamese employees and agents were left behind, with key documents identifying them, for the northerners to capture.

In 1968, before Nixon hired him to work in the administration,

Henry Kissinger wrote an article that advocated a settlement providing a "decent interval" for United States withdrawal. Thinking with shame of the Americans' final abandonment of their Vietnamese allies, senior Saigon CIA analyst Frank Snepp could find no better title for the book giving his account of the debacle.

On the afternoon of March 7, 1969, Richard Nixon helicoptered out to Langley, with Richard Helms, to address senior officials of the CIA in the Agency's large auditorium. As is common in such ceremonial pep talks, the President painted the role of CIA in the most glowing terms. "I look upon this organization," Nixon said, "as not one which is necessary for the conduct of conflict or war, or call it what you may, but in the final analysis . . . one of the great instruments of our Government for the preservation of peace, for the avoidance of war, and for the development of a society in which this kind of thing would not be as necessary, if necessary at all."

Fine words these, but they did not prevent the White House from ordering a string of covert operations, carried out around the world. The President was probably referring, in that comment at Langley, to the CIA's role in supplying intelligence reports and estimates, leaving in the background the "call it what you may" war.

Referring to that, Nixon said: "I think the American people need to understand the need for this foreign policy option."

But there was little hope in 1969 that the public attitude toward covert operations would ever be as permissive as when Nixon had been Vice-President, before the Bay of Pigs and Vietnam. Controversy sharpened in 1967 with the revelation of CIA funding for Radio Free Europe, Radio Liberty, and a variety of other youth, labor, media, non-profit, and public interest groups. In Nixon's first moments in office, the generous termination grants CIA gave RFE and RL began to run out.

Nixon supported continuing funds for them, and new funds were openly appropriated by Congress for two years, but in January 1971 the late Senator Clifford P. Case of New Jersey detailed the secret CIA funding of RFE and RL and announced legislation to make them independent units funded directly. Both Nixon and Kissinger worked on the legislation, which passed Congress on March 30, 1972, providing the radios with $36 million for that fiscal year. The funds are administered by the Secretary of State and all CIA conec tions were cut. Indirect connections remain in that RFE and RL retain relationships with many of the same émigré organizations and individuals who associate with the CIA.

One nation to feel the weight of Nixon's covert option was Iraq, and even more so the Kurds in Kurdistan. This secret war involved, basically, the United States doing a favor for the Shah of Iran.

The Kurds were a nomadic people, a loose confederation of some forty tribes who earnestly desired nationhood. They were spread out across the borders of five countries: Iraq, Iran, Syria, Turkey, and the Soviet Union. As early as 1948 a CIA estimate observed, "The mountain tribes known as the Kurds are now and will continue to be a factor of some importance in any strategic estimate of Near East affairs." Periodically, Kurds had fought the Turks, Iraqis, and Iranians in quest of their freedom—*sarbasti* in the Kurdish tongue. Shortly after World War II, Kurds had cooperated with the Russians in setting up a short-lived tribal "republic" in northern Iran. After a 1958 coup in Baghdad, Kurdish autonomy seemed threatened by the Iraqis. The tribes took the field again in a partisan war in which long campaigns alternated with several cease-fires. Mullah Mustapha Barzani, a tribal potentate since 1945, led the main forces. Finally, from sheer exhaustion, the Iraqis and Kurds reached agreement on a fifteen-point settlement in early 1970.

Peace might have reigned except for Iran. The Iranians had several border disputes with Iraq including an acrimonious one over the demarcation line in the Tigris River, which had changed course in such a fashion as to put the main shipping channel used by the Iraqis into an area claimed by Iran. No friend of Baghdad, the Shah feared the end of the Kurdish war would bring more direct confrontation between Iran and Iraq. He was not averse to stirring up trouble.

The Shah offered the Kurds money and weapons to resume their fight. Dissatisfied with Iraqi implementation of the 1970 settlement, the Kurds were tempted but they did not trust the Shah either. Barzani countered that he would consider the offer only if the United States guaranteed that the Shah would not be allowed to suddenly cut off the Kurds.

Teheran passed the Kurdish request on to the United States. Nixon and Kissinger made an official visit to Iran in May 1972, immediately after the Moscow summit at which the first SALT agreements were reached. In Teheran, John B. Connolly, a close political associate of Nixon's, told the Shah that the United States was willing to help the Kurds. The CIA handled the American side through its station in Teheran.

Kissinger set up the Washington apparatus for the Kurdish secret war. His military aide, Colonel Richard Kennedy, met with one of Barzani's sons, and with the CIA, on the Kurds' requests. A staff assistant, Alfred L. Atherton, Jr., became the NSC focal point.

At first the CIA provided $1 million worth of captured Soviet weapons and ammunition. Later aid was raised to $5 million and ultimately to $16 million. The Israelis were also helping the Kurds, and had been since 1965. These involvements were dwarfed by the Shah's, which reportedly ran to several hundreds of millions. Armed with this assistance, which began in August 1972, the Kurds raised 100,000 partisan troops, a larger force than Mustapha Barzani had ever fielded before. The Kurds engaged large Iraqi forces, including over 65,000 regular troops, with five hundred tanks and two hundred guns, plus auxiliaries.

Fourteen months later the Iraqis were allied with other Arab states in the October War with Israel. Two Iraqi armored divisions and parts of two infantry divisions were deployed into Syria, almost half of Baghdad's total armed forces. Seeking to take pressure off their own front in Syria, Israeli paramilitary advisers suggested to the Kurds that now was the time for a big offensive against Iraq. Barzani thought this a good idea; the White House did not. On October 16, 1973, Kissinger instructed the DCI to tell the Kurds not to make the attack. Barzani relented.

For the Shah the Kurds were but a card to play in his dealings with Iraq. After the October War, Teheran and Baghdad bridged some of their differences, leading to a *modus vivendi* in March 1975. Simultaneously, the Shah halted his aid to the Kurds, stopped free passage for CIA arms shipments, and closed his borders to Barzani's men. The next day the Iraqis began a large-scale offensive into Kurdistan.

On March 10 the Kurds sent an anguished appeal through CIA channels: "Our people's fate in unprecedented danger. Complete destruction hanging over our head. No explanation for all this. We appeal you [sic] and U. S. Government intervene according to your promises." Barzani also sent a personal letter to Kissinger, who was by now secretary of state in addition to NSC adviser: "We feel ... that the United States has a moral and political responsibility toward our people who have committed themselves to your country's policy."

The CIA station chief in Teheran, forwarding the Kurdish appeals, asked if Langley had been in touch with Kissinger's office on this matter. Further, he warned, "If [the United States] does not handle this situation deftly in a way which will avoid giving the Kurds the impression that we are abandoning them they are likely to go public. Iran's action has not only shattered their political hopes; it endangers [the] lives of thousands." Kissinger made no reply to Barzani's appeals. The CIA station chief, who had offered options for ameliorating actions, and advised "it would be the right thing ... to do," was left holding the bag.

Pressed on the abandonment of the Kurds, a senior United States official retorted, to a congressional investigating committee staff, "Covert action should not be confused with missionary work."

Columnist William Safire slyly hints that the callous official was Henry Kissinger.

Ironically, a decade later, in the 1980s, the United States has switched sides and discreetly favors Iraq in a war against Iran. The Kurds, who survived their crisis of 1975, as well as military campaigns by Turkey and Iran, are still firmly emplaced in northern Iraq, a greater threat than ever to Baghdad, and now a people who have little reason to respect American interests. Mullah Barzani died in 1979 but his sons and their allies carry on, and have long memories.

Another nation to experience the CIA covert option was Chile, in the southern cone of Latin America. An American ally for many years, proud of its tradition of over a century of democracy, Chile had not had a coup since 1925. A Marxist candidate, Salvador Allende Gossens, succeeded in his third try for the presidency and attained the plurality in the Chilean elections of September 4, 1970. To Nixon, Allende became something like what Castro seemed to Kennedy.

The election of Allende occurred despite the best efforts of United States operatives, both official and corporate. Four million dollars had been funneled to supporters of Christian Democrat candidate Eduardo Frei by the CIA in the 1964 elections, which Allende lost. Looking ahead to the 1970 campaigns, the NSC Special Group approved $700,000 in CIA funds during 1969–1970. John McCone, now representing private interests as chairman of International Telephone and Telegraph (ITT), increased the secret election fund to defeat Allende to over a million dollars. ITT also coordinated its election plans with the CIA, including meetings between top company officials and Western Hemisphere Division chief William V. Broe. Anaconda and Kennecott corporations, fearful of the expropriation of their copper mines in Chile, also contributed to the united election fund, which was supervised on the spot by CIA station chief Henry Hecksher and Ambassador Edward Korry. While there were tactical differences on how the fund should be spent, all agreed on the objective of preventing an Allende administration.

The common thread that links the action in Chile with many other covert operations is the threat of nationalization of American-owned local subsidiaries of multinational corporations. Expropriation or the fear of it also figured in the operations in Cuba, Guatemala, and Iran.

Allende insisted on a "peaceful road" to socialism and arrived at victory through a completely democratic election. His Unidad Popular (UP) movement was a leftist united front.

The Chilean communists themselves were arrayed in a variety of factions variously favoring Havana, Peking, or Moscow. The CIA's intelligence estimates before and during the election projected that Allende had a fifty-fifty chance of winning. But they agreed that an Allende victory would have no effect on the global balance of power or strategic situation.

None of the developments in Chile came as a surprise to Washington. The NSC Special Group considered strategy for Chile four times between Nixon's inauguration and Allende's election, meetings that in fact approved the monies spent by the United States during the campaign. As in too many other instances, Kissinger blames the bureaucracy—State for allegedly opposing intervention, while Ambassador Korry was consistently warning of the Allende candidacy; and the CIA for being complacent, though Dick Helms had told the Special Group, as early as the spring of 1969, that action had to be prepared soon if the United States was going to take sides in the Chilean election. Kissinger defends himself with this curious statement:

Had I believed in the spring and summer of 1970 that there was a significant likelihood of an Allende victory, I would have had an obligation to the President to give him an opportunity to consider a covert program of 1964 proportions, including the backing of a single candidate. I was resentful that this option had been foreclosed without even being discussed.

In fact, according to Special Group minutes, Kissinger told the covert action managers, more than two months before the Chilean elections, "I don't see why we need to stand by and watch a country go Communist due to the irresponsibility of its own people."

Allende's victory in the September election was not a sweep. His Popular Unity movement achieved a plurality but not an absolute majority, throwing the election into the Chilean congress, where the final vote was set for October 24, 1970. But the first-round election result threw Washington into a frantic effort to head off the feared result. Kissinger now goaded the CIA and State for action even though he had remarked to Chilean diplomats, the year before, "I am not interested in, nor do I know anything about, the southern portion of the world from the Pyrenees on down."

The NSC adviser acted in response to Nixon, who was distraught at the specter of a second Marxist nation in the Western Hemisphere, democratic or not. It did not matter that Allende was not a communist. Some years later, in a celebrated television interview with David Frost, Nixon rationalized that the addition of Chile to Cuba would have made Latin America a "Red Sandwich," a sort of variant on the domino theory alleged to apply to Southeast Asia.

On September 15, Nixon met with Augustin Edwards, publisher of the conservative Chilean newspaper *El Mercurio*, an associate of Nixon's friend Donald Kendall, chief executive of Pepsi Cola. Edwards's dark forebodings were such that Nixon felt driven to act, and DCI Helms, with Kissinger, were called in to discuss the possibilities that very day. Nixon was going to "play hardball." Results were all that counted. The CIA could have $10 million if needed, risks were not to be considered, the Agency should put its best men on the job and act without reference to the United States embassy in Santiago. Nixon ordered Helms to "make the economy scream." He wanted a CIA plan within forty-eight hours.

"The President came down very hard," Helms related to Senate investigators in July 1975. "If I ever carried a marshall's [*sic*] baton in my knapsack out of the Oval Office, it was that day."

On September 18, Helms was back in the Oval Office with the plan and his DDP, Thomas Karamessines. The Special Group had considered, on September 8 and 14, a concept for political maneuvers to affect the Chilean congressional vote. Helms did not believe this would work, but Ambassador Korry and the embassy could be left to try that approach, called "the Rube Goldberg gambit" or Track I. The secret CIA program would be an effort to induce a military coup and was called Track II. Nixon approved. Karamessines would be the CIA liaison with the White House; he met with Kissinger six to ten times over the next month.

Track II was very closely held at Langley. A special Chile Task Force was set up at CIA. There was talk of running it directly out of Karamessines's office but that would have been a tip-off in the Agency that something was up and the task force was put in a mail room instead. A propaganda expert and Chile specialist, David Atlee Phillips, was called back from Rio de Janeiro to head the task force. Hecksher was informed and Santiago military attaché Colonel Paul Wimert was used as a go-between, but otherwise the twelve-man CIA station was bypassed. Instead, the Agency sent four deep-cover officers into Chile to handle the direct action. Ambassador Korry was left to believe that Track I was all the United States was doing in Chile. Helms, Karamessines, and Phillips all testified later that there had been intense pressure from the White House for results.

Track II did not lead to any military coup, however. The CIA contacts encouraged certain Chilean officers to assassinate the commander of the Chilean armed forces, General René Schneider, on October 22. This action created a backlash in Santiago, and Salvador Allende was confirmed as president of Chile two days later.

The Schneider assassination occurred about a week after the White House ordered a halt to any planning for this type of action. Kissinger would like the public to believe that this order ended the covert action in Chile but that is simply false. Karamessines testified: "As far as I was concerned . . . what we were told to do was to continue our efforts. Stay alert, and to do what we could to contribute to the eventual achievement of the objectives and purposes of Track II. . . . I don't think it is proper to say that Track II was ended."

The CIA's Chile Task Force remained in place. Covert action funds approved by the NSC Special Group afterward dwarfed anything spent on elections before, including the expensive and successful campaign in 1964: $2.8 million in fiscal 1971, $2.9 million in 1972, and $1.68 million in 1973. The CIA actually spent $7.5 million in that period. For fiscal year 1974 the Special Group approved $1.1 million but the CIA had expended only $231,000 of that money at the time Allende was overthrown, on September 11, 1973. To get some idea of the relative increase of these amounts, consider the case of *El Mercurio*, the Santiago newspaper. Long considered a friendly source by CIA, whose task force leader Dave Phillips had worked for it in his earliest days in Chile, *El Mercurio*'s subsidies from the Agency quadrupled during the Allende years of covert action.

Hecksher, who was against Allende but had also warned against using the Chilean military, was replaced at the Santiago station by Ray Warren. Ambassador Korry was also replaced by another career diplomat, Nathaniel Davis. Economic assistance was halted; U.S. AID funds dried up; the United States prevented loans to Chile by multilateral government-backed sources like the World Bank and even discouraged them from private sources. Funds for the Chilean military, on the other hand, were continued and increased, a none-too-subtle hint to the officers.

American actions polarized the political situation in Chile, turning the middle class against Allende and eroding the traditional political neutrality of the armed forces. President Allende did his best against enormous difficulties, but he inevitably made mistakes, and sharpened American hostility by proceeding with plans for the nationalization of industries. A cutoff of United States exports halted the flow of spare parts, with serious consequences for the Chilean economy. Unrest began to reach a fever pitch in the fall of 1972, when the truckers union began a series of national strikes, halting virtually all transportation in Chile for months on end.

The trucker strikes were the catalyst for the last act of the drama that had begun with Track II. A decade afterward it is still impossible to say how the truckers were able to sustain a year-long strike forsaking their own livelihoods. Rumors current at the time were that the truckers were being financed by the Americans or the Brazilians. State Department and CIA officials denied to Congress that the United States had had anything to do with the strike. David A.

Phillips, who was back in Washington in 1973, following service in Venezuela, as Western Hemisphere Division chief, also denies CIA complicity in the strike. But the truckers union did not collect large dues and had no appreciable strike fund.

Despite the widespread chaos, Allende's Popular Unity scored major gains in Chile's March 1973 elections—eight more seats in Congress on a plurality of 43.4 percent. Allende's own share of the vote in 1970 had been 36.3 percent.

Until 1973 the armed forces remained quiescent, under the strict constitutionalist leadership of chief of staff General Carlos Prats. Loyalist forces crushed a coup that was attempted on June 29. Two months later discontent within the armed forces surfaced in the form of a demonstration outside Prats's home by officers' wives. Prats resigned. He was succeeded by General Augusto Pinochet, who led the military coup of September 11, 1973, and became chief of the junta that wrested control from the Chilean government. Salvador Allende died in his office at the La Moneda presidential palace, which was bombed and attacked in the coup.

Kissinger and Nathaniel Davis assert that Allende created the opposition himself. While it is true that the social changes introduced by the Popular Unity government over a short period of time triggered Chilean fear and doubts, such assertions beg the question of American involvement. American money fueled a drum roll of Chilean press criticism, and made possible the coalescing of right-wing opposition groups, like Patria y Libertad (Fatherland and Liberty), which spearheaded the anti-Allende forces. Former ambassador Korry estimates that Track II led to *nine* different assassination plots, including one against Allende himself.

Moreover, the outcome in Chile ultimately hinged on the attitude of the armed forces, and it was made abundantly clear to the Chilean military that United States' friendship was not to be had by supporting the constitutional government. Nor, apparently, was the United States military innocent of involvement in the coup itself. American military attachés were in the field with Chilean army units participating in the coup. Several naval vessels were off the Chilean coast for UNITAS (an annual naval exercise participated in by the United States and Latin American nations), and one of these ships is reported to have landed a Navy SEAL commando team in Chile. As part of the same maneuver, the United States had deployed thirty-two aircraft to the nearby Argentine base at Mendoza. Finally, on the day of the coup, a United States electronic intelligence aircraft was over the Andes Mountains. It was variously reported to have been relaying communications among the coup plotters or recording them for United States intelligence. This last action, in particular, would have been impossible without some forewarning.

The Pinochet junta immediately declared a state of siege and began a tremendous campaign of repression. At least two American citizens, Charles E. Horman and Frank Teruggi, died at the hands of the Chilean military, along with Chilean citizens unofficially reported at 5,000 to 25,000 against the junta's bland claim of a mere 1,000 dead. The United States government made little effort to seek explanations, apologies, or compensation to the families of the dead Americans before recognizing Pinochet's junta on September 29, 1973. Three years later, on September 21, 1976, Pinochet reached directly into the United States to assassinate Chilean exile Orlando Letelier, former defense minister and ambassador to the United States, with a car bomb on the streets of Washington, D.C. Riding in the car with Letelier, another American citizen, Ronnie K. Moffitt, was also killed in the blast. Similarly, General Carlos Prats and his wife were gunned down in Buenos Aires in 1974.

After his 1972 reelection, Nixon appointed Helms as ambassador to Iran, effectively getting the former DCI out of the way, for failing to take drastic action in the first place to stop Allende.

Nevertheless, Helms was obliged to testify several times in early 1973 to the Subcommittee on Multinational Corporations of the Senate Foreign Relations Committee chaired by Frank Church, which was exploring United States actions in Chile. Always loyal to the chain of command, Helms prided himself on learning to get along with Presidents, and denied in sworn testimony that the CIA had tried to overthrow the government of Chile. Four years later, Richard Helms was indicted for perjury in this testimony. He pleaded no contest to the charges, was pronounced guilty, and was let off with a two-year suspended sentence and a fine of $2,000.

It is instructive that, forced to acknowledge the CIA involvement to later congressional investigators, Kissinger, in his memoirs, continues to castigate the bureaucracy for inadequately implementing orders that he initially refused to admit had been given.

*　　*　　*

For more than two decades, since the inception of covert operations in the Truman administration, it had been assumed that a certain duplicity went with the territory. This was the very essence of the concept of "plausible deniability." But the rationale for deniability was to prevent knowledge of covert actions from becoming available to those nations that figured as targets of such actions; it was never intended to deny information to decision makers in the United States government. The Nixon administration elevated duplicity to a virtual management principle.

Since the inception of covert operations, the problem of controlling them had been a thorny one. We have seen the efforts of Truman, Eisenhower, Kennedy, and Johnson. Nixon too made his changes. One participant at a 1968 Council of Foreign Relations symposium had described the 303 Committee as "moribund." According to Kissinger, change came not for this reason but because the 303 Committee was identified in a 1969 news story.

Again, Kissinger's account is less than straightforward. In fact, the reconstituted NSC Special Group was expanded to include the attorney general. John N. Mitchell, Nixon's attorney general, was a close friend of the President, and it is highly likely that he was added to the Special Group as the President's personal representative to keep an eye on Kissinger, whom Nixon did not entirely trust. Other Special Group members saw little reason for the inclusion of Mitchell, who rarely spoke at meetings, and played with his pipe instead.

The change was formalized on February 17, 1970, in Nixon's National Security Decision Memorandum (NSDM) 40. The Special Group thus became the 40 Committee. The NSDM also rescinded NSC-5412/2 with its anti-Soviet rationale for covert operations. Instead, Nixon's directive stated, "I have determined that it is essential to the defense and security of the United States and its efforts for world peace that the overt foreign activities of the U. S. Government continue to be supplemented by covert action operations."

Under NSDM-40 the Special Group was reponsible for policy approval of "all" major and politically sensitive covert action programs, including those suggested by departments other than the CIA, for the joint reconnaissance schedule, and for annual review of covert programs. To fulfill its role in planning, at CIA the DDP's Missions and Programs Staff was to develop the justification and objective memoranda for 40 Committee approval. A new Covert Action Staff also replaced the previous Psychological and Paramilitary Operations Staff in that functional area.

Having carefully set up this framework, Nixon and Kissinger proceeded to ignore it often. U. Alexis Johnson, a 40 Committee member who represented the State Department, writes, "It is true that during the Nixon administration the President and CIA bypassed the Committee on sensitive topics." When Nixon gave his first go-ahead on Cambodia, he ordered Kissinger to say nothing about it to the 40 Committee. Everyone from the Special Group to the secretary of state was deliberately cut out of Track II. Similarly, the 40 Committee was not consulted on the matter of the Kurds.

Among the decisions that *can* be traced to the 40 Committee, those on intelligence collection figure prominently. Overhead and satellite reconnaissance missions, and the *Glomar Explorer's* attempt to raise a Soviet missile submarine from the floor of the Pacific Ocean, were discussed by the 40 Committee. One actual covert action decision was to spend $10 million to influence the Italian elections in 1972, which was much like the budgets approved for Chile. A good many of the 40 Committee's meetings were taken up by six-month or annual status reports about ongoing activities. The 40 Committee appears to have been used for everyday decisions but not on the big plays.

Kissinger was the chairman of the 40 Committee. He set up the meetings and the agendas, assisted by a single staff man supplied by the CIA. Only principals were allowed to attend. Henry was the ultimate arbiter. The first official manual on covert operations, prepared by the CIA in 1972, observed that only about a quarter of them would be considered by the 40 Committee. Excluded were not only many minor, unimportant operations, but virtually all the big, sensitive ones.

One technique used by Kissinger to minimize the committee's impact was to have as few meetings as possible. He liked to poll the members by telephone for decisions, on the dubious theory that they had better uses for their valuable time. Beyond the question of what could be more important to national security executives than running the nation's covert action program, it cannot have escaped notice in the Kissinger NSC that phone calls permitted fewer records being kept. Avoiding meetings also prevented the kind of give-and-take among members that could have allowed the bureaucracy to realize more of what was going on. During 1973 and 1974 the Special Group adopted forty decisions without once meeting for discussion of an actual covert action program.

The Special Group has never been so moribund as during the Nixon-Kissinger years.

Richard Nixon lost his ability to wield power even as he concentrated it in the Oval Office. "Watergate" is an ugly name from the Nixon years, a product of his 1972 reelection campaign.

Watergate is important to the CIA because the break-in team was composed of Bay of Pigs veterans, not only Cuban exiles (contract agents) like Bernard Barker, but CIA officers like Howard Hunt. Agency security specialist James W. McCord, Jr., was also caught in the break-in. When it was revealed that the CIA had furnished material assistance to Hunt, had prepared certain psychological profiles of Americans at the request of the White House, and that virtually the same Watergate cast had carried out other illegal break-ins on White House instructions, the CIA knew it had a major political problem. General Vernon A. Walters, who held the post of DCI from 1972 to 1976, spent a great deal of his time in the intelligence community coordinating the defense of the CIA in the Watergate investigation and the others that succeeded it.

This period was also a time of change for the secret warriors. The man chosen to replace Helms was James R. Schlesinger, a defense analyst with no intelligence experience other than his work on a management study for Nixon in 1970. Schlesinger was shifted to secretary of defense after only five months at Langley, but in that short time he presided over some important changes.

Within the Agency itself, Schlesinger was convinced that much of the dead wood lay in the Directorate of Plans. Personnel figures began to fall as about a thousand officers were retired, asked to resign, or fired. Many of these men had been paramilitary specialists. The covert action budget was already tumbling, and had been since the Laos funding was taken away from the CIA and given to the Pentagon. DDP itself was retitled, becoming, more appropriately, the Directorate of Operations (DDO). Tom Karamessines was replaced as DDO by Bill Colby, back from Vietnam, and then by William Nelson, a Colby protégé.

Another change initiated by Helms was continued under Schlesinger, and consummated by his successor as DCI, William E.

Colby. This concerned the major air proprietaries. A DCI directive in 1972 ordered that Air America be retained only until the end of the Indochina war and that Southern Air Transport be sold off. A former owner of this freight line negotiated for the purchase and offered $5.6 million. The purchase was approved by Helms during his last month as DCI and confirmed by the Southern Air Transport board of directors. Other air freight companies objected, however, and one of them offered $7.5 million for Southern Air Transport. This offer, made during Schlesinger's last days at Langley, was rejected. As acting DCI, Colby ordered the proprietary liquidated on July 31, 1973, but the former owner then made a further counteroffer to buy Southern. The sale was closed on the last day of 1973. There were some later repercussions when the former owner himself proceeded to liquidate Southern Air Transport, violating the contract provision against windfall profits. In the course of its subsequent lawsuit, the CIA officially admitted ownership of Southern Air Transport and was awarded a judgment of $1.3 million, for a total of $6.9 million on the transaction. The losers in all of this were the CIA's contract employees at Southern, whose jobs evaporated.

The Central Intelligence Agency liquidated Air America all by itself. By 1975 the parent Pacific Corporation had been reduced from 11,200 employees to 1,100. Air Asia, the massive Taiwan aircraft maintenance facility, was sold to E-Systems, a Texas corporation. The proprietary's planes and other assets were sold off individually. The Church committee was informed that the liquidation would be completed by June 30, 1976, and was expected to realize a total of $20 million in proceeds.

These changes progressed under William Colby, the acting DCI. Later Colby was appointed and then confirmed as director of central intelligence. During his confirmation hearings at the Senate, Old West–style "wanted" posters sprouted overnight on walls all over Washington. It was an adaptation of a technique widely used in the Phoenix program. The posters featured an ace of spades— used by Americans in Vietnam to connote death or killing—within which was a sketch of Colby's face. The DCI made sure that CIA's Office of Security did nothing about the posters. Colby's agency still had a global reach but its grip was no longer so strong.

·XVI·

"ROGUE ELEPHANT"
TO RESURRECTION

The Watergate investigations affected Bill Colby far more than he expected. Watergate revelations of Central Intelligence Agency aid to White House domestic political operations stripped away much of the cold war mystique that had helped protect the Agency. Congress was a major locus of dissatisfaction, and was propelled not only by revulsion at CIA domestic involvement, but by growing fears concerning the general quality of intelligence oversight. Concern over the disingenuous handling by the administration of explanations for United States actions in Laos and Chile was fueled by Watergate. Colby became DCI just in time to deal with the resulting explosion.

The Agency was in the midst of its secret war in Iraq then, and would even be dispatched on another adventure in Africa during the very height of intense congressional investigations. Colby and his successor would be forced to rein in the American secret warriors, although later the paramilitary capabilities were resurrected. The political controversy ushered in a decade of turmoil for the CIA.

A simple telephone call triggered the tempest. The call, on December 18, 1974, was to Colby from journalist Seymour Hersh, who worked for *The New York Times*. Hersh was a noted investigative reporter who had won the Pulitzer Prize for earlier writing on Vietnam. Now, he told Colby, he had it from several sources that the CIA had carried out a massive intelligence operation against American opponents of the Vietnam War that had included break-ins, mail intercepts, wiretapping, and surveillance.

The DCI met with Hersh and tried to explain that the information uncovered really reflected distorted elements of several different affairs that were individually within the Agency's charter. In any case, Colby maintained, such activities had ceased and a 1973 set of directives had made plain that CIA would stay within the strict letter of the law. Colby insisted that Hersh's information had been blown out of proportion.

Seymour Hersh did not see it that way. The article he wrote was splashed across three columns of the front page of the Sunday *Times* on December 22. The headline read: HUGE CIA OPERATION REPORTED IN U.S. AGAINST ANTI-WAR FORCES, OTHER DISSIDENTS IN NIXON YEARS.

The immediate consequence of these revelations, as Colby himself concedes, was "a press and political firestorm." Colby remembers these events as "ruining not only the Christmas season for me but nearly all of the next year as well."

The problem was so great because the Presidents, in all the years since 1947, had avoided so successfully further legal codification of intelligence duties, responsibilities, and restrictions. The Presidents preferred ambiguity because it gave them more freedom of action. But each time the White House successfully avoided intelligence reforms, the pressure built a little in Congress, until by 1974 the pot was boiling and indeed red hot. Bill Colby's bad year had as much to do with the White House as with the press.

One critical component of the controversy concerned legislative oversight of the intelligence function. The executive branch itself had once posed the issue—in 1955 an intelligence study group under the Hoover Commission, mandated by President Eisenhower, had recommended creation of a congressional joint committee on intelligence similar to the joint panel that exercised oversight over the atomic energy program. Soon there were a score of bills before Congress proposing to regulate the intelligence community, including one submitted by Senator Mike Mansfield (D-Montana) with no less than thirty-four cosponsors.

Though he had initially requested the Hoover Commission's report, President Eisenhower did not agree with its recommendation, and moved to head off the Mansfield Bill. Ike's dual response was to set up the PBCFIA, a citizen oversight group later known as the President's Foreign Intelligence Advisory Board (PFIAB), and to support an arrangement for secret subcommittees of the congressional armed services panels to approve United States intelligence budgets. Previously such approvals had been made only on an ad hoc basis by individual congressmen and senators. The Mansfield Bill was defeated in the Senate by a vote of 59 to 27. Fourteen of the senator's cosponsors turned against him on the floor, as well as all the members of the Armed Services Intelligence Subcommittee. For some years afterward, similar bills were introduced at every session of Congress, but were repeatedly tabled or defeated.

Despite the more formal structure, this arrangement could not be called oversight. The intelligence community had no responsibility to cooperate with PFIAB, which was strictly an advisory group to the President, or to keep the congressional subcommittees "fully and currently informed" on intelligence activities. The DCIs would appear with their budget requests, and the CIA would answer specific questions if they were put, but no one would volunteer any information.

Contacts were kept to a minimum where intelligence programs were concerned, as opposed to briefings on substantive questions of intelligence analysis. According to official records, in 1955 and 1956 there was but a single briefing provided for the Senate's Armed Services intelligence subcommittee, with none at all in 1957. The average for the decade from 1955 to 1964 works out to less than two a year. During the months of planning for the Bay of Pigs in 1960, neither the Senate Appropriations nor the Armed Services committees had any meetings at all with CIA officials.

Such briefings as occurred were hampered by the CIA's obsession with protecting itself, and its "sources and methods," on security grounds. Real reasons were sometimes quite different. On one occasion in the early 1950s, when Allen Dulles expected some hard questioning, as a result of successful Soviet penetration of one of CIA's covert operations, the DCI told his assembled DDP division chiefs, "Well, I guess I'll have to fudge the truth a little." With a twinkle in his eye, the DCI averred that he *would* admit the full truth to the subcommittee chairman, "that is, if [he] wants to know." On another occasion, Dulles commented to his assistants, "I'll just tell them a few war stories."

If anything, the legislators made it easy for the intelligence officers. The senior senators and congressmen who made up these subcommittees appreciated their access to the secret world and had no wish to rock the boat. A typical attitude was expressed by Republican senator Leverett Saltonstall of Massachusetts, who once commented: "It is not a question of reluctance on the part of CIA officials to speak to us. Instead it is a question of our reluctance, if you will, to seek information and knowledge on subjects which I personally, as a Member of Congress and as a citizen, would rather not have."

By 1965 the subcommittees had expanded to include both the Armed Services and Appropriations panels, but the CIA's reticence was unchanged. That year the DCI refused to answer certain questions in testimony before the Senate Foreign Relations Committee, though he stated he would answer the same questions if posed by the secret subcommittees or PFIAB. The Foreign Relations Committee chairman, Senator J. William Fulbright (D-Arkansas), was incensed that CIA would provide information to private citizens that it would deny to elected senators. Fulbright became a strong supporter of a bill offered by Senator Eugene McCarthy (D-Minnesota) calling for an investigation of the CIA by a panel of the Foreign Relations Committee. The bill was approved by the committee and went to the Senate floor.

The McCarthy Bill posed a challenge to the existing minimal legislative oversight, and now Mike Mansfield was majority leader in the Senate. Lyndon Johnson, as majority leader in 1956, had helped oppose Mansfield's original joint committee bill, but he was now in the White House. As majority leader, Mansfield was willing to support a compromise, but as an individual senator the Montana Democrat stood behind McCarthy's legislation. Mansfield met with Armed Services Committee chairman Senator Richard B. Russell (D-Louisiana), who also headed the intelligence subcommittee, and with Fulbright, to make it clear that if a compromise were avoided, he would back the McCarthy Bill.

President Johnson was advised to steer clear of this legislative issue, but LBJ, like Ike, worked behind the scenes to preserve the status quo. As early as the fall of 1965, a presidential directive reaffirming the role of PFIAB had been prepared, which, as McGeorge Bundy put it, "we plan to use . . . as appropriate with Congressional leaders when there is any question about our effective supervision of the Intelligence Community." The paper was useless when the issue actually arose, because Fulbright and others were angry precisely because PFIAB was being given material denied to Congress.

When NSC aide Walt Rostow, who had replaced Bundy, reported to LBJ that Fulbright was unhappy and did not understand why the Foreign Relations Committee should be denied access, the President scrawled across the bottom of his copy of the report, "Because they leak!"

Far from steering clear, LBJ played an active role in what followed, backing up the strong opposition of DCI William F. Raborn. On June 2, 1966, the day after Mansfield met with other principals to seek a compromise, the President in turn met with Mansfield and the Senate minority leader, Illinois Republican Everett F. Dirksen. The President opposed broadening CIA reporting to the Senate. Significantly, LBJ assigned his political aide Harry C. McPherson, Jr., to handle the matter, not NSC adviser Rostow or the NSC staff man on intelligence, Peter Jessup. A few weeks later, when Dick Helms took over as DCI, advice continued to come from the White House, now via political assistant Bill Moyers.

The strategy was worked out in meetings and phone calls between McPherson and Senator Russell. They compromised in order to water down the McCarthy resolution, which lost its provisions for a staff and a budget and a report by a certain date, and became just an addition to the existing secret subcommittee. In response to a further letter from Fulbright, the CIA again refused to provide information to the Foreign Relations Committee. Russell came out strongly against the bill, and when Russell and McPherson determined that they had the votes to defeat it, they resisted any attempt to table or postpone consideration of the resolution, which was defeated by a vote of 61 to 28 in July 1966. To mollify proponents of the legislation, Fulbright, and the ranking Republican member of his committee, were then invited by Russell to sit with the secret subcommittee the following year, while the CIA went up to Capitol Hill for a detailed presentation to the Foreign Relations Committee on Laos. Eugene McCarthy later became a close friend of Richard Helms.

Following this episode, the CIA's relations with Congress remained much as they had been before. Meetings increased somewhat: Between 1965 and 1974, on the average, the Senate Armed Services Committee was briefed three times a year; the Senate Appropriations Committee, four times a year; and the House Armed Services Committee, four times a year. Congressional attitudes continued to be lackadaisical. The House unit held no meetings at all in 1971 or 1972, while in 1967 the CIA appropriation was approved by both House and Senate after a single congressman went out to Langley to observe a rehearsal of the budget presentation.

The CIA continued to take advantage of this situation. In 1966, Helms went up to Capitol Hill with his deputy director for science and technology and a collection of fancy spy gadgets, to successfully deflect discussion of real issues. Similarly, Helms gave the following advice to his special assistant on Vietnam affairs, George Carver, before Carver's first appearance on the Hill: "Don't waffle, don't ramble and don't guess. When you're getting into an area you feel you can't discuss, you tell them. But you also tell them as succinctly as possible the answer to the question they asked. Not the question they should have asked." It is not surprising that Helms felt confident deliberately misleading Congress on Chile in his 1973 testimony.

The attitude began to change in this late period of the Nixon administration. Opposition to the Vietnam War led to questioning many policies, including those in intelligence matters. The revelations of United States involvement in Laos from Senator Stuart Symington and others brought another close call for the CIA. This time the issue was war powers. Attempting to lock the barn door, after the Vietnam War had been initiated and conducted without congressional declaration, Senate Republican Jacob Javits of New York, and Democrats Thomas F. Eagleton of Missouri and John Stennis of Mississippi introduced bipartisan legislation in 1973, the latest of a series of such proposals, that would restrict the power of the President to conduct military operations without congressional approval. Earlier attempts had failed to pass one of the houses or had not cleared conference committees, but in 1973 the votes were definitely there. The War Powers Bill, numbered S.440 in the Senate, had so many cosponsors that passage was assured and there were almost enough to override a presidential veto.

While most of the senators focused on the aspect of regular military operation, Tom Eagleton believed that modern wars did not necessarily start with big invasions. He was concerned about the CIA and covert wars becoming overt ones, with Vietnam and Laos as object lessons. Senator Eagleton offered an amendment to extend the restrictions of S.440 to civilian employeees of the United States government—clearly targeting the CIA. Eagleton believed he could find support for this provision in July 1973, a time when Fulbright's Foreign Relations Committee took the unprecedented step of rejecting Nixon's nomination of Ambassador G. McMurtrie Godley for the post of assistant secretary of state for Far Eastern affairs. Godley's role in running the Laos "secret war" was an important factor in gathering the opposition to his new nomination.

Eagleton nevertheless met disappointment in his effort to include the CIA under the War Powers Act. As soon as the Missouri senator offered his amendment, John Stennis, now Armed Services Committee chairman and in charge of the CIA subcommittee on intelligence, asked Eagleton to withdraw it. Stennis favored restrictions as part of comprehensive CIA charter legislation separate from the War Powers Act. Javits also opposed CIA inclusion, as did the Senate floor manager for the bill, Maine Democrat Edmund S. Muskie. Muskie's reading of a Stennis letter during the Senate floor debate was instrumental in the defeat of the Eagleton amendment by a vote of 53 to 34. This, plus a certain lack of definition in the bill, turned Eagleton from one of its original proponents into an active opponent of the legislation. The bill nevertheless passed, as did a similar measure in the House, was vetoed by Nixon, and Congress then overrode the President's veto. The War Powers Act became law but did not restrict the secret warriors.

The Central Intelligence Agency had been very lucky for a long time. None of the more than two hundred legislative measures intended to oversee or restrict it that were introduced before 1974 had passed. By 1974, however, there was a lot of bad feeling in Congress on the issue. Some legislation was tentatively considered that year by the Senate Committee on Government Operations. Before anything emerged from the effort, Bill Colby got the aforementioned telephone call from Seymour Hersh.

President Gerald R. Ford was en route to a skiing vacation at Vail, Colorado, when Colby called to warn him of the imminent appearance of the Hersh story on CIA domestic activities. Ford immediately asked for a report; later that day, responding to a growing number of press inquiries, the President issued a public statement that he had asked Henry Kissinger, acting as NSC adviser, to obtain the report from William Colby. In their discussion the DCI had had to be most circumspect with the President, who was aboard Air Force One when Colby called—the two had spoken over an open line, in a radio patch to the White House switchboard.

Bill Colby's bad year got off to a rousing start that Christmas Eve.

That evening he crossed the Potomac from Langley to visit Kissinger at the State Department. In the two days since the Hersh article had appeared, the DCI had assembled a memorandum describing how *The New York Times* report was exaggerated. But there was fire behind the smoke, as Colby was obliged to admit—in fact, Hersh had succeeded in uncovering some of the major CIA abuses exposed internally in a report ordered by Jim Schlesinger in response to Watergate. The CIA inspector general's report contained almost seven hundred allegations filed by the CIA's own employees and was so sensitive it was sardonically referred to as "The Family Jewels."

It happened that Kissinger had never been briefed on "The Family Jewels," a compendium completed during the transition in which Colby replaced Schlesinger as DCI at Langley. One can imagine the outburst Colby now endured from Kissinger.

At last Colby proceeded with his briefing, then handed Kissinger a copy of the report. It contained allegations of CIA assassination efforts against such foreign political leaders as Castro, Ngo Dinh Diem, and Dominican dictator Rafael Trujillo. Kissinger flipped quickly through the various allegations, but slowed down when he came to the part about assassinations. He stopped and looked up at Colby.

"Well Bill, when Hersh's story first came out I thought you should have flatly denied it as totally wrong," said Kissinger, "but now I see why you couldn't."

Kissinger took Colby's thirty-page report to Vail to show President Ford. There were no White House denials, and Ford made no statements in support of the CIA. There were also no denials by Colby or official statements from the CIA.

The only denial of the Hersh story came on Christmas Day from Richard Helms, a source who increasingly lacked credibility. Colby himself wanted to save the CIA but was not prepared to lie or do anything illegal. That was going to mean sitting tight for the inevitable investigations.

On January 4, 1975, Gerald Ford declared his administration would not tolerate illegal activities by intelligence agencies, said he had been assured by Colby that no such activities were in progress, and announced formation of a commission to investigate domestic abuses under the chairmanship of Vice-President Nelson Rockefeller.

Very swiftly Congress established its own investigative committees. The Senate approved its resolution S.21 on January 27, by a
vote of 82 to 4, naming a Select Committee to Study Governmental
Operations with Respect to Intelligence Activities. The fourteen-
member panel would be chaired by Idaho Democrat Frank Church.
The House of Representatives established a ten-member panel in
February but this became embroiled in disputes and was replaced
five months later by a slightly larger Select Committee on Intelligence led by New York Democrat Otis G. Pike. So began what has
since been known as "the Year of Intelligence."

In his memoir, *A Time to Heal,* President Gerald Ford writes as if
the blame for "the Year of Intelligence" should be put on "investigative journalists" like Seymour Hersh, and congressional committees who wanted to look at *"everything* in the files." Ford is correct
that the atmosphere created by the Watergate scandal contributed
to the intensity of the investigations, but the CIA abuses were
hardly incidental.

From the instant of his first exposure to "The Family Jewels,"
President Ford's major concern was leaks. This fear is the one point
he returns to repeatedly in his memoir, and it was certainly on his
mind while in office. In fact, the terms of reference for the Rockefeller Commission were carefully drawn in a futile effort to avoid
investigation of the most sensitive areas, like assassinations. It was,
however, an idle hope that this presidential commission would head
off congressional investigations.

Obviously, it would not be possible for the commission and committees to investigate without collecting data, or for them to report
without revealing such information. Withholding documents and
witnesses or restricting testimony by officials was sure to arouse the
ire of the investigators, only encouraging leaks. Moreover, refusals
to supply information occurred in the open and were openly reported in the press without any need for investigative journalism.
One of the worst examples happened with Henry Kissinger and the
Pike committee, which was forced to go to the full House of Representatives to secure subpoenas. The subpoenas were voted but Kissinger surrendered the materials only when he was about to be cited
for contempt of Congress. Before "the Year of Intelligence" was
over the House voted seven subpoenas but the government surrendered the materials for only four of the cases. Three it rejected, including one addressed by name to Kissinger ordering him to supply

copies of all State Department recommendations to the NSC on covert operations since January 30, 1961. The second subpoena also concerned covert action, while the third related to intelligence reporting on the Strategic Arms Limitation agreements.

Ford's opinion is that the Pike committee was out "to stick it to Kissinger." After consultation with the attorney general, President Ford intervened on November 19, 1975, writing Otis Pike that the subpoenaed documents had been legitimately withheld. The committee responded by voting to cite Kissinger for contempt of Congress, a measure that would go to the full House in December. But the White House compromised by releasing some of the material.

Counterattack came in early January 1976, when White House aides told the congressional committees that if they hoped to obtain intelligence materials in the future as oversight panels, staffs would have to be reduced plus stiff penalties for leaks adopted, penalties to include expulsion from Congress. For its part, the CIA recommended numerous deletions from the Pike Report for reasons of national security. A number of these were accepted but about 150 deletions were rejected despite prior agreements guaranteeing confidentiality. The Ford administration was able to prevail upon the full House of Representatives not to release the Pike Report. Some 246 representatives voted to suppress the report, against 124 for its release.

When television reporter Daniel Schorr asked for his reaction, Speaker of the House Thomas P. "Tip" O'Neill, Jr., said, "This is an election year, and they're getting a lot of flak about leaks, and they're going to vote their American Legion posts."

But, counter to President Ford's wishes, the Pike Report was leaked and major portions were printed in two installments in a New York weekly, *The Village Voice.* Subsequent investigation established that over two hundred copies of the report had been delivered to an assortment of congressional and executive offices at the time of the leak. No culprit was ever found, though it was discovered that the initial leak had been to Daniel Schorr.

Ironically, Gerald Ford might have done better with the initial House committee leadership. The original choice for chairman of the Select Committee on Intelligence had been Congressman Lucien Nedzi (D-Michigan). Not only was Nedzi from the President's home state, but he had been chairman of the intelligence subcommittee. Nedzi's leadership of the House investigation began to disintegrate, in fact, when it became known that the Michigan congressman had been briefed by Bill Colby on that portion of the "Family Jewels" report concerning assassination attempts. Nedzi told none of his colleagues what he had learned, and he was forced to resign, to be succeeded by Pike.

Frank Church was a liberal Democrat with presidential aspirations. Some observers believe that Church wanted to ride the intelligence investigations to national prominence, positioning himself as a dark horse for 1976, with a solid bid for the presidency possible in 1980. Be this as it may, the Senate investigation was conducted quietly and systematically, with little of the acrimony that characterized relations between the Ford administration and the Pike committee.

Though there have been repeated if unconfirmed allegations that material was also withheld from the Senate committee, Frank Church had been around and he knew where to look. The Idaho Democrat had been a member of the Foreign Relations Committee when that body was spurned by the CIA in 1966. He participated in the Laos hearings of 1967 and 1969. Church was also chairman of the Subcommittee on Multinational Corporations to which Richard Helms lied about CIA involvement in Chile. Ambitious or not, Church was determined to follow up on several of these subjects.

Like the others, the Church investigation went into domestic abuses. It examined intelligence analysis, as did the Pike committee, and the history of the intelligence community. Intelligence organization and budgets figured in the mix. But some of its best work concerned covert operations, the nine hundred major and several thousand minor clandestine actions that had been carried out since 1961.

The investigation was nothing if not thorough. For its interim report on alleged assassination plots, the Church committee conducted numerous interviews, held sixty days of hearings, and accumulated over 8,000 pages of sworn testimony. Some witnesses were reinterviewed on the basis of information uncovered later in the investigation. For its general review of covert operations, the committee got 14 CIA briefings and conducted staff interviews with 120 people, including 13 former ambassadors and a dozen CIA chiefs of station. The investigation lasted past its original September 1975 deadline, eventually to hold over 250 executive session hearings, plus 800 interviews and gather more than 110,000 pages of documentation. Sixty professional staff assisted the senators in the effort. A final report was approved and released in April 1976.

This report ran to six volumes, including detailed staff studies. There were also seven volumes of hearings, an interim report on the assassination plots, and a case study of covert action in Chile. Six additional case studies on covert operations remained classified at the request of the CIA.

One significant conclusion was drawn from all this: There had been a failure to provide the necessary statutes to conduct intelligence operations within a constitutional framework. Presidents had made excessive and sometimes self-defeating use of covert operations, while inadequate legislative attention had been given to intelligence budgets. The fundamental issue was to balance the requirements for secrecy with those of American democracy.

From all the millions of words in the hearings, findings, and recommendations of the Church committee, one phrase in particular stuck in the mind of Gerald Ford and the many others who heard it. One day at the hearings, Frank Church wondered out loud whether the Central Intelligence Agency had not become a "rogue elephant." Government officials have spent years trying to live down that damning epithet.

Frank Church's opinion after the investigation by his committee was that United States government capabilities for covert action should be very sharply circumscribed. The majority of his colleagues were not willing to go so far.

Referring to the secret warriors, in comments appended to the committee report, Church noted his conclusion: "Certainly we do not need a regiment of cloak-and-dagger men, earning their campaign ribbons—and, indeed, their promotions—by planning new exploits throughout the world. Theirs is a self-generating enterprise." With the capability in place, pressures on Presidents to use it, the senator believed, were immense. For this activism, Frank Church wrote, "I must lay the blame, in large measure, to the fantasy that it lay within our power to control other countries through the covert manipulation of their affairs. It formed part of a greater illusion that entrapped and enthralled our Presidents—the illusion of American omnipotence."

This viewpoint was undoubtedly reinforced by yet another CIA adventure, a covert action in Africa being carried out even as the investigations in Washington wound toward their finales. This African adventure was called Operation Feature. Like the earlier effort in the Congo, Feature was intended to change the apparent flow of events in an African colony headed for independence. This time the target was the Portuguese colony of Angola immediately to the south of Zaire.

The Angola affair really began in Portugal, the colonial power, with the April 1974 leftist military coup that overthrew a long-standing dictatorship. Portugal had been waging counterinsurgency warfare against indigenous independence movements in Angola and other African colonies. The new Portuguese government had no stomach for such warfare, and Portugal announced its withdrawal from Africa. Angola would become independent, the Portuguese decided, on November 11, 1975. Until independence day, under an agreement the Portuguese negotiated with the three rebel movements in January 1975, there would be a coalition government preparing for elections.

Angola was a classic case of colonial underdevelopment. The situation was complicated by the fact that few of the Portuguese settlers intended to stay on past independence. Each of the rebel groups had built its own armed forces and political organization, and the three groups were left to fight it out among themselves. The groups were tribally based, so the political competition had ethnic aspects as well. The Popular Movement for the Liberation of Angola (MPLA by its Portuguese initials), the National Front for the Liberation of Angola (FNLA), and the National Union for the Total Independence of Angola (UNITA) all espoused vaguely socialist ideologies, all were left of center, and all had accepted money and weapons from communist nations. MPLA was comprised mostly of the Mbundu tribe; founded in 1956, it had the best political organization and was an offshoot of the Angolan communist party. FNLA was made up of the Bakongo tribe, of about 700,000, more than half of whom had fled to Zaire early in the anti-Portuguese war. Holden Roberto, an educated Christian of peasant stock, had founded FNLA in 1954. Roberto's chief lieutenant, Jonas Savimbi, broke away from FNLA in 1966 to form UNITA among the Ovimbundo, the largest tribe, two million of whom inhabit the Benguela plateau in southern Angola. The groups had waged parallel wars against the Portuguese but were not allied in any way.

Except for the cold war, Angola would have reached independence without anyone taking much notice. During the period of the revolution, the CIA had played both sides, funding Holden Roberto as an intelligence source, while selling the Portuguese B-26 bombers and permitting them to recruit Cuban exile pilots for the planes. When the Portuguese coup occurred, the CIA formed a special task force, but its purpose was to influence events in Portugal, not Angola. The connection with Roberto had been maintained, but FNLA's main support came from the People's Republic of China, which was arming Roberto's troops and training them in Zaire, with a unit of over a hundred military advisers in camps that Joseph Mobutu had permitted Roberto to establish. The MPLA was receiving some support from the Soviet Union.

Within days of the Angolan agreement on a coalition, the 40 Committee approved a recommendation to increase the subsidy to Holden Roberto by $300,000, but rejected a suggestion for another $100,000 to Savimbi. President Ford quickly confirmed both decisions. Buoyed by the additional aid, Roberto took a hard line and, in February, ordered his FNLA troops to attack MPLA cadres in the capital, Luanda, and in northern Angola. In one instance in early March, fifty unarmed MPLA activists were gunned down. These attacks ended any possibility of a coalition.

At this juncture the Soviets took a hand by resuming aid to the MPLA, which they had previously terminated in 1973. The assistance included an airlift of weapons to Luanda. MPLA had long maintained friendly relations with Castro, and the Soviet airlift was followed by the dispatch of a small contingent of Cuban advisers.

The Soviet bloc aid seemed to make Angola a cold war battlefield in Washington's eyes, and posed the immediate question of what to do about it. An interagency task force was formed, under Nathaniel Davis, newly appointed as assistant secretary of state for African affairs, to study the problem. Davis, according to his own account, had already advised Kissinger against covert support to Savimbi, who was soliciting arms everywhere. UNITA had been receiving some from the Chinese since 1974, and had had ties to Mao Tsetung for a decade before that. Davis warned that the United States would have to reckon with "probable disclosure," and argued that "at most we would be in a position to commit limited resources, and buy marginal influence."

The recommendation of the interagency group chaired by Davis was against intervention; instead the group held out for diplomatic efforts to encourage a political settlement among the three factions. This reflected a basic understanding that Angola was an African, not a cold war, problem. Military intervention carried a high risk of exposure with the possibility of negative effects in Angola, across Africa, and in relations with Portugal; it offered only limited results and potentially contributed to increased involvement by the Soviet Union and other foreign powers.

According to the Pike committee, which studied the Angola covert operation in some detail, the Davis group's recommendation was removed from their report "at the direction of National Security Council aides" and presented to the NSC as merely one policy option, the others being to do nothing or to make a substantial intervention. The June 13 report of the interagency group was thus used to frame a stark choice for President Ford, who selected the intervention option.

Action then returned to the 40 Committee, dominated in 1975, as before, by Henry Kissinger. Meeting on July 14, the Special Group directed the CIA to propose a covert action program within forty-eight hours. Operation Feature was the result. Although the evidence is not yet clear, it appears that the top leadership at Langley may have opposed this intervention—the CIA came back to warn of the risk of exposure as well as to estimate a $100 million price tag for the effort, an amount that was not available in the DCI's contingency fund. Nevertheless, the 40 Committee gave the go-ahead and on July 17 President Ford approved an expenditure of $14 million. The CIA, which had advised against Track II in Chile and the Kurdish operation, was again given marching orders, for which it was lukewarm. That a plan was proposed at all was used by Kissinger, in 1976 Senate testimony, to argue that "the CIA recommended the operation and supported it."

One reason Bill Colby might have been lukewarm was that he probably knew the difficulties involved. Langley simply was not prepared. The Africa Division of the DDO was still the smallest in the Agency and had its hands full watching some fifty nations. James Potts, who had replaced Lawrence Devlin as division chief, was, paradoxically, one of the strongest advocates of Operation Feature. On the other hand, the Special Operations Group of paramilitary experts had been reduced under DCI Schlesinger and also lacked recent African experience. Moreover, Feature was being ordered just a few months after the final denouement in Vietnam, where the CIA had been squarely caught up in the debacle, and the Agency was still licking its wounds.

Operation Feature went forward under a very high priority. The operation was so urgent, in fact, that a first planeload of weapons was on its way to the FNLA, via Zaire, before Langley even formed its task force to manage the program. By August 9 two more loads had been sent aboard Air Force C-141 transports, while a shipload of supplies was being assembled.

The Angola task force was a little different from the usual CIA arrangement. Appointed as chief was John Stockwell, a twelve-year Agency veteran and old Africa hand who had also served in Southeast Asia. Stockwell, the Agency's equivalent of a colonel, was relatively junior for the job, which was a slot normally reserved for generals. Judging from Stockwell's account of Operation Feature, it was then run by Potts, the division chief, rather than directly by the DDO, William Nelson, which it would have been under normal CIA procedures.

Jim Potts, his assistants, and Stockwell labored to prepare detailed plans, right up to the last minute before DCI Colby carried them to a 40 Committee meeting on August 8, where the planning received top-level approval. Nathaniel Davis resigned when he learned that the Angola effort was to proceed despite his objections.

CIA principals gathered in the DDO's office for a review of the plans and the interagency working group. When Potts's deputy suggested that the moment had come to determine exactly how involved the CIA should become, DDO William Nelson spoke up: "Gentlemen, we've been given a job to do. Let's not sit around wringing our hands."

John Stockwell was then dispatched on a two-week fact-finding mission to Zaire and Angola, visiting both Roberto and Savimbi. It emerged that Savimbi was by far the more credible opponent for the MPLA, which, in July, had succeeded in driving both the other factions out of Luanda. On August 20, while Stockwell was observing the FNLA and UNITA, President Ford authorized an additional $10.7 million in expenditures.

By the time Stockwell reappeared at Langley, Operation Feature was in motion. Mobutu was critical to the operation since CIA arms shipments were technically supposed to replace Zaire's arsenal, while Mobutu forwarded weapons from his own army to Holden Roberto. Relations with the FNLA and Mobutu were handled by the chief of station in Kinshasa. The station chief in Lusaka dealt with UNITA. Theoretically, no Americans were supposed to work inside Angola.

The Americans acquired 2 Swift boats for the FNLA, and solved the quandary of how to get an air force by the simple expedient of offering a reward for would-be defectors who brought airplanes in with them. Eight assorted light planes were contracted, commandeered, or diverted. The Swift boats, 140 trucks, 300 radios, and 70 mortars sailed from Charlestown for Africa on August 30 aboard the freighter *American Champion*. Operation Feature deliveries to Zaire also included a dozen M-113 armored personnel carriers and over 17,000 modern automatic rifles. Zairian shipments to UNITA and FNLA, however, included no APCs, only 7,000 automatic rifles, and more than 12,000 old M-1 .30-caliber carbines. Mobutu successfully used the opportunity to reequip his armed forces, and when Holden Roberto's troops failed to show any striking power in northern Angola, Mobutu was willing to commit two of his para-commando battalions and a detachment of 10 Panhard armored cars, in return for more CIA arms shipments.

Not only the Americans had got themselves involved—China continued to provide assistance to FNLA almost until independence day. Even more ominous was South Africa, both through its armed forces (SADF) and its intelligence service, the Bureau of State Security (BOSS). After BOSS quietly provided money, arms, and training to UNITA, South Africa escalated in the summer of 1975, committing a unit of armored cars plus associated logistics. These forces provided Savimbi's spearhead in a UNITA offensive that was the most successful military action taken against the MPLA.

Langley coordinated war strategy with BOSS, permitted high-level intelligence negotiations by BOSS officials in Washington, and sent some of its UNITA arms through South African channels. The CIA also funded gasoline necessary to move the SADF armored cars that were helping Savimbi. There were plans to procure a C-130 transport and some helicopters, to be given directly to SADF for its UNITA supply flights. In October the South Africans asked for CIA help in procuring 155-millimeter artillery shells they claimed were needed in Angola.

Stockwell's account maintains that Africa Division chief Potts entertained thoughts of even wider cooperation with the South Africans. Any such thoughts were stifled by staunch opposition from the State Department. The diplomats upheld the Kennedy administration's arms embargo on South Africa and quashed suggestions for major collaboration. The diplomats were proved right in the fall, when journalists in Africa confirmed the presence of South African troops with UNITA. There was an instant wave of public revulsion toward the Western-supported factions in Angola that dealt Operation Feature's political action component an irreparable blow.

Ironically, one of the diplomats closely questioning CIA plans for Angola was Frank Wisner, Jr., the son of the legendary secret warrior who had done so much to establish covert action. Another cautious diplomat was Edward Mulcahy, State's representative on the interagency implementation committee group, who quietly threatened to resign in protest if Potts went ahead with certain measures with the South Africans.

On the ground in Angola, the South Africans were good fighters. Their operation, under the code name Zulu, provided strong backing for UNITA, and also easily occupied certain hydroelectric facilities that furnished power to South Africa in Namibia. Savimbi proved to have the strongest movement. A captivating speaker and inspiring leader, Savimbi led a competent political organization that had grass roots. Much of Roberto's support, in contrast, resided in Kinshasa and refugee camps in Zaire. With the South Africans of the Zulu force, UNITA regained much of Benguela province and threatened the important port at Lobito and the Benguela railroad, one of Angola's few major transport systems.

Thus threatened, the MPLA turned to *its* Soviet and Cuban allies. Moscow increased the scale of its shipments, allowing MPLA's troops to introduce potent 122-millimeter rockets during the summer and fall. Another shipload of Cuban advisers entered in August. Upon independence the MPLA government asked Cuba for major assistance. By then there were 2,600 Cubans in Angola, but in an emergency airlift and sealift apparently called Carlotta, Cuban regular units were introduced in large numbers, about 5,000 in December, up to 15,000 by the spring of 1976. Soviet aid was estimated at $100 million by December 1975, and four times that amount by March. Weapons sent in early 1976 included T-54 tanks and MIG jet fighters. The Soviets had always had the capacity for such a large flow but had delayed intervention to this degree until its client appeared truly menaced.

These developments had been anticipated in the original June interagency intervention study, and had now come to pass. In northern Angola the FNLA failed to capture the isolated enclave of Cabinda, seat of the nation's oil production. Cuban units with MPLA forces then began to push back the FNLA. Holden Roberto tried to raise a mercenary force to stiffen his army. Roberto offered a million dollars for a "parachute regiment." Soldier of fortune John Banks was given an advance on this money to recruit in England. In the United States the recruiter was David Floyd Bufkin, a former pilot and California crop duster, who is variously reported to have received his money from either Roberto or the CIA directly.

Mercenary recruiting used the grapevine plus ads in newspapers. Bufkin also appeared on television and advertised in the action magazine *Soldier of Fortune*. Roberto's "parachute regiment" ultimately received 140 British and 7 American recruits, some with no military experience, some as volunteers for noncombat duty only. Twenty-three arrived too late and were sent home. Another group was rejected as unsuitable.

The Central Intelligence Agency had a parallel effort going to recruit mercenaries in Portugal. This yielded about 300 men who were sent to FNLA. Through French intelligence, which also contributed ammunition, four helicopters, and its own agents, the CIA made contact with longtime soldier of fortune Robert Denard, who recruited twenty mercenaries for UNITA. Another forty were sent to UNITA by BOSS. Instructions supposedly prohibiting Americans from working inside Angola were disregarded by an Army mobile training team at FNLA headquarters in Ambriz, and by CIA communications instructors and observers with both FNLA and UNITA.

The worsening situation was viewed with alarm in Washington. In late November, Langley prepared a menu of options for the 40 Committee featuring programs alternatively costed at $30 million, $60 million, or $100 million. Deputy Assistant Secretary Mulcahy personally carried the options paper to Kissinger before he left on a ten-day diplomatic mission.

Later Mulcahy was unable to tell the interagency working group just what Kissinger had decided. "He read it," Mulcahy reported. "Then he grunted and walked out of his office."

"Grunted?" asked Potts incredulously.

"Yeah, like, unnph!"

The working group was reduced to trying to figure out what a positive "unnph" might sound like.

Ultimately, for the moment, they decided not to allow the CIA advisers in combat. President Ford approved another $7 million in military aid, exhausting the DCI's contingency fund; further money would have to come from Congress.

In "the Year of Intelligence," Congress was no longer the rubber stamp it had once been. It also knew a lot more about Operation Feature than it had about earlier secret-war efforts as a result of new reporting requirements instituted in 1974. In an amendment to the foreign aid bill that year (Public Law 93-559, Section 32), Senator Harold Hughes (D-Iowa) and Congressman Leo B. Ryan (D-California) successfully sponsored legislation to require reporting of significant covert operations to relevant committees of Congress. In practice, this worked out to eight committees with 163 members and their senior staffs. In commenting on the Hughes-Ryan Amendment, President Ford again focused on the dangers of leaks rather than the advantages of oversight.

In any case, because of Hughes-Ryan, Congress was informed about Operation Feature. In particular, Senator Dick Clark (D-Iowa) was briefed by Colby on the Angola program shortly before a fact-finding trip to Africa in August 1975. The senator was chairman of the African Affairs subcommittee of the Foreign Relations panel, and was suspicious of the intentions behind Feature. The information Clark gathered in his visit led him to suspect United States collusion with South Africa. He returned determined to do something about Angola.

The revelation of the issue to the public was delayed for a time by the secret classification of Colby's CIA briefings. Congressmen swore not to reveal what they learned in the thirty-five briefings the DCI gave them in 1975–1976. Press revelations of the South African involvement opened up the issue. In early December, Senator Clark proposed legislation terminating aid for Angola. It was just at this time that the executive branch was coming to Congress to ask for more Angola money.

At this critical moment the cover of Operation Feature disintegrated. The first press revelations on Feature appeared in *The Washington Post* and *The New York Times* in late September. Even afterward, in his congressional appearances, Colby continued to maintain that no CIA weapons were going directly to the guerrillas and that no Americans were involved inside Angola. The government subterfuge was revealed by a coincidence. On December 5 diplomat Ed Mulcahy was late to a hearing at Senator Clark's subcommittee. The CIA witness, DDO William Nelson, went up first and admitted the truth about United States involvement. Bill Nelson was a Colby protégé; as the DCI had suddenly been called in by President Ford about a month before and asked for his resignation, Nelson probably feared that his own days at CIA were numbered. In any case, when Mulcahy arrived late and began to testify, he laid out the agreed-on version that minimized United States actions. Senator Clark confronted Mulcahy with DDO Nelson's testimony, trapping the administration in a lie. The predictable result was legislation to terminate covert action in Angola.

The Clark Amendment technically prohibited expenditure of CIA funds in Angola, except for intelligence gathering, as well as reprogramming of funds from one government account to another. The amendment also precluded Pentagon funding of Operation Feature, sealing the fate of the program. The Clark Amendment passed the Senate by a vote of 54 to 22 on December 19, 1975. Two days later there was another provocative article on the front page of *The New York Times*. This time Seymour Hersh had details of Feature plus the story of Ambassador Davis's resignation.

Dick Clark's amendment passed the House of Representatives in late January 1976, as Kissinger failed in Moscow to inject the Angola issue into a superpower meeting on arms control. The legislation was signed into law on February 9, 1976, by President Ford, with considerable misgivings. For the first time a covert action had been halted by congressional order.

The last calamity was reserved for the FNLA mercenaries. Generally an undisciplined lot, the mercenaries were under a self-styled "colonel," an enlisted veteran of the real British Parachute Regiment, who called himself Costas Gheorghiu. The man was unbalanced in the opinion of some of his mercenary colleagues. The FNLA mercenary campaign had cut a swath of murder and rampage across northern Angola, culminating in a military-style execution of more than a dozen of the soldiers of fortune by their own comrades for alleged desertion and misconduct.

Other mercenaries were killed on patrols against the Cubans and MPLA. Among the latter was a real paramilitary expert, who had been well regarded by the officers at Langley—George Bacon III, a Green Beret who had served with MACV-SOG in 1968–1969 and gone on to a tour for CIA with the Meo, using the Agency code name Kayak, during 1972–1973. Bacon had received an intelligence medal for his work in Laos, and got further CIA training, but quit in disgust at what he perceived as the American "betrayal" of South Vietnam. Bacon was a "cowboy" in the CIA tradition and had been enthusiastic about Angola.

The demise of the mercenaries came when a big patrol was captured by the Angolans. This group included Gheorghiu and three Americans. In Luanda, the Angolan MPLA government tried the mercenaries. The self-styled colonel, American Daniel Gearhart, and two others were condemned to death. Three soldiers of fortune got sentences of thirty years, three got sentences of twenty-four years, and three more got sixteen years, including the Americans Gustavo Grillo, a Marine Corps veteran of the Battle of Hue, and Gary Acker, also a Vietnam veteran. Subsequently the State Department barely acknowledged the status of these American prisoners and provided little assistance in their families' efforts to secure their release. Grillo and Acker were finally released in a 1982 prisoner exchange arranged between Angola and South Africa.

Surviving mercenaries voiced plenty of complaints about their CIA severance pay. Mobutu simply pocketed final CIA payments given to him for Roberto and Savimbi. The South Africans continued to play with UNITA to destabilize Angola. Thoroughly disillusioned, CIA officer John Stockwell resigned and went public with the details of the Angola adventure. With this fiasco so recently revealed, it is not so surprising that Senator Church would have such strong remarks to make on covert action in his committee's final report.

These events of "the Year of Intelligence" touched off a struggle to regulate the intelligence agencies that has ebbed and flowed ever since. "Oversight" is the name of the game, a game that the executive branch, generally claiming there is too much of it, has been much more successful at playing than Congress. The legislators on Capitol Hill first moved to create reporting requirements through Hughes-Ryan, then strengthened the monitoring process by replacing the secret CIA subcommittees with permanent select intelligence committees in both houses of Congress.

Oversight did not mean the end of covert action. On February 15, 1976, days after President Ford signed the Clark Amendment (Public Law 94-329) into law, and a month after replacing the dismissed Bill Colby as DCI, George Bush refused to say whether

United States aid to Angola had halted. During the Ford administration there were also covert actions in Portugal and, reportedly, in Madagascar, where an American ambassador who had been a career CIA officer was expelled following a puzzling series of musical-chairs military coups. Oversight simply meant that such operations were reported to Congress and backed by a "Presidential Finding" that justified the action. Hughes-Ryan specified that all significant or anticipated actions by the CIA that were not for intelligence-gathering purposes be covered.

The executive branch tried to limit oversight as much as it could, especially where covert operations were concerned. A detailed explanation of its position, in which the CIA construed the statutory basis for its activities, was furnished to the House intelligence committee by CIA special counsel Mitchell Rogovin in December 1975. The legal argument was that intelligence activities were within the "inherent powers" of the President; they had been conducted by Presidents long before a CIA was created, and thus did not represent any attempt to assert new powers for the presidency. Rogovin also referred to the "such other functions" provision in the 1947 National Security Act, and argued that Congress had never objected to intelligence practices before, and had always approved the budgets.

These arguments by the CIA were undercut, however, by the legal opinions of the CIA general counsel rendered on several occasions since 1947. The congressional committees obtained a copy of a paper prepared in 1974 for the general counsel's office, which took much the same position as had general counsel Lawrence Houston: The National Security Act "functions" language restricted itself to intelligence gathering; extending it to covert operations strained the meaning of the law. The paper noted that covert operations were an *implementation* of policy, a power shared by Congress and the President under the Constitution.

Paradoxically, by setting down reporting requirements for covert operations, the Hughes-Ryan Amendment could be construed to have authorized them in the name of Congress.

Much of 1976 passed while Congress set up its machinery for intelligence oversight. Legislation containing intelligence charters was considered during the Carter administration in 1978 and 1980 but never made it through Congress. Meanwhile, feeling favoring regulatory action on intelligence peaked in Congress during the middle years of the Carter administration. When charters were considered at hearings, the vast majority of CIA professionals testified against excessive restrictions upon covert action. Witnesses at the various hearings included such figures as George Bush, John McCone, Richard Helms, Bill Colby, E. Henry Knoche, Richard E. Bissell, Jr., Tom Karamessines, David Atlee Phillips, and General Richard G. Stilwell.

Outpacing a slow-moving Congress, the executive was quick to seize the initiative on intelligence reform. In early 1976, President Ford promulgated Executive Order 11905, the first public regulations ever to describe the function of intelligence and restrictions on it. Ford's executive order prohibited assassinations, a reiteration of internal directives Colby issued in 1973. It replaced the 40 Committee with a panel called the Operations Advisory Group, placing covert action decisions in the hands of Cabinet-level officers rather than their deputies. The attorney general continued as a member while the director of the Office of Management and Budget was added as an observer. Covert operations were defined as those intended to further United States policies abroad.

President Jimmy Carter continued the practice of intelligence regulation through Executive Order 12036, which he signed in 1978. Assassinations continued to be prohibited. The covert action decision-making body became the Special Coordinating Committee of the NSC, with essentially the same membership. Covert actions were defined somewhat more narrowly as those "conducted abroad" in support of national foreign policy objectives. Typical activities approved by the decision-making machinery during that period included the provision of special communications equipment for personal security to the presidents of Egypt and the Sudan, and an anti-Cuba propaganda campaign to be conducted in the Horn of Africa.

The Carter administration proved to have no great appetite for covert action, thus postponing the day of reckoning between congressional oversight and executive power. President Carter nevertheless defended executive primacy in covert action. He supported legislation during 1980 to reduce CIA reporting to the two specialized intelligence committees of Congress. Carter also made use of a gambit first resorted to by Kissinger and Ford—blanket Presidential Findings issued to the intelligence committees justifying in advance all covert operations concerning terrorism, narcotics, or counterintelligence. From the oversight standpoint the danger was that other areas would then be included by future Presidential Findings once the device had become established.

As in many things during his years in the White House, President Carter was frustrated in his first selection of a DCI. He originally choose Theodore Sorensen, but Sorensen had to withdraw after the nomination ran into strident congressional opposition. Next, Carter turned to Admiral Stansfield Turner, a regular naval officer who then held a top command position in Italy. Turner and the President had been classmates at Annapolis. Though forced by regulations to retire from the Navy in order to accept Carter's offer, Turner took the DCI job and went to Langley. A novice at intelligence work, Stansfield Turner still provided strong and thoughtful leadership for the community.

An outsider among the tribes at Langley, Turner was not popular at CIA despite being an able director. Any chance he had of being accepted by CIA insiders evaporated with the manpower reductions Turner was obliged to make as a result of budget limits. The former DCI recounts that although the actual reduction in force (RIF) was minimal, with most coming from early retirement and attrition, the paperwork and notification within the Agency were handled in such a way that the DCI appeared most callous. Inexperienced at Langley, Turner did not know to keep a sharp eye on the implementation of his instructions in this matter.

It is to Stansfield Turner's credit that he persisted through the controversy and did the best he could to make the intelligence community responsive and responsible. In the DDO, Turner brought forward William Wells and John N. McMahon, officers he considered highly dependable. Everywhere, Turner sought to manage the colossus. Still, the former DCI recalls, "Being confident that the organization was not *out* of control was not the same as feeling that it was adequately *under* control."

The RIFs at the CIA, familiarly remembered at Langley as the Halloween Massacre, further reduced paramilitary capability but, in DCI Turner's opinion, actually improved espionage resources. Turner also believed in technical collection programs, machine spies in an era in which professionals were rededicating themselves to improving human intelligence—HUMINT in the jargon. As for congressional oversight, Stansfield Turner believed it was a positive benefit for the CIA—a view that was decidedly unconventional at Langley.

Still, Turner strongly resisted any suggestion that prior notification be given Congress. Turner also advocated restricting the reporting requirement to the intelligence committees, and adopting harsh strictures against leaks. Most of this Congress yielded in its Intelligence Oversight Act of 1980, passed as an amendment to the fiscal 1981 intelligence budget, which supplanted the Hughes-Ryan Amendment. Congress did insist on being "fully and currently informed," and got some definition of the elements that should go into a proper Presidential Finding. Senators favoring legislation of a comprehensive intelligence charter were forced to give up on the project. By 1980 the pendulum had swung from restraining the "rogue elephant" to "unleashing" the CIA.

International events account for a good deal of the impetus for the shift in public opinion. Three developments especially affected the debate over the role of covert operations and controls over them: the rising incidence of terrorism, the fall of the Shah of Iran, and the Soviet invasion of Afghanistan. The rise of terrorism, on which the Carter administration took a hard line, led to renewed attention to military special-warfare activities. This ended the post-Vietnam retrenchment of Special Forces, which resulted in a force of only thirty-six hundred, in three groups all deployed in the United States, and with detachments only in Europe and the Far East, plus one battalion in Panama. Reserve and National Guard units had assumed the bulk of the special-warfare capability, with manpower of fifty-eight hundred. Antiterrorism provided a new rationale for the organization, much as counterinsurgency had under Kennedy. With the support of chief of staff General Edward C. "Shy" Meyer, and despite opposition from officers favoring a more traditional role for Special Forces, the Army formed two elite commando units, called respectively Blue Light and Delta. These initiatives against terrorism received personal attention and support from Zbigniew Brzezinski, President Carter's assistant for national security affairs.

The second development that elicited a covert action response from the United States was the fall of the Shah of Iran, along with what followed. Policymakers and intelligence analysts in Washington either refused to recognize the growing vulnerability of the Shah or could not agree on what to do. Carter was left to complain to Turner, Brzezinski, and Secretary of State Cyrus Vance about the poor quality of political intelligence he was receiving. Similarly, more detailed criticisms were made publicly by a House intelligence committee study, and repeated extensively in the press and by opinion leaders. Pressure for better reporting translated somehow into more covert operations.

The Iranian crisis of 1978–1980 ended by calling into question the United States special-warfare capability. The diplomats proved unable to forge a friendly relationship with the Islamic Republic formed in Iran under the Ayatollah Khomeini. Iranian student militants took over the United States embassy on November 4, 1979, capturing the mission records and sixty-three American diplomats. Three others, including Chargé d'Affaires Bruce Laingen, happened to be at the Iranian Foreign Ministry when the embassy takeover occurred, and were detained there. The next day, NSC adviser Brzezinski ordered preparation of a contingency plan for a rescue mission; he wished to present President Carter with a military option in addition to diplomatic means. Secretary of State Vance strongly resisted any resort to force in resolving the Iranian crisis.

While Vance explored a variety of diplomatic avenues, Carter wrestled with the delicate question of what to do with the Shah, whose admission into the United States originally triggered the embassy takeover. The military busied itself planning a rescue mission along lines similar to the Sontay raid. General Meyer gave the task top priority and selected Special Forces Operational Detachment Delta as the strike force. Formed and trained by Colonel Charlie Beckwith, who had led Project Delta of the 5th Special Forces Group in Vietnam, Delta trained intensively to take over the embassy plus a nearby soccer stadium and free the American hostages. A joint task force formed under control of the Joint Chiefs to provide C-130 and helicopter lift for the rescue.

In Teheran the Iranian militants released thirteen black and women hostages a couple weeks after the takeover. Otherwise, diplomatic efforts were of no avail, except for a quasi-covert action carried out by the Canadians on behalf of six Americans who had taken refuge in the Canadian embassy at the time of the November seizure. On January 29, 1980, the six Americans were smuggled out of Teheran under Canadian passports. This was reportedly one of the few instances during the Carter administration in which DCI Turner did not give prior notice to at least some members of the congressional intelligence committees, who were briefed only five hours after the Americans escaped from Teheran.

For the most part, the CIA worked to facilitate Operation Eagle

Claw, as the rescue was named. Former Air America experts from Laos solved some of the logistics headaches. An Agency plane actually landed at night on the Iran desert to take soil samples at the site of a planned secret air base called Desert One. The DDO's paramilitary division furnished and installed precise navigational systems for the Marine Corps helicopters scheduled to carry Delta. According to press reports, at least seven agents worked in Iran in the months before the rescue, obtaining a fleet of local trucks to shuttle the commandos from their hiding place to the embassy.

Special-warfare forces had the main role in Operation Eagle Claw. Under Major General James Vaught of the Army, the joint task force endlessly practiced segments of the mission and held at least six major exercises. The White House was periodically brought up to date on preparations. In early April, frustrated at the continued failure of diplomatic efforts, President Carter turned to the military option. A key decision to finalize the mission planning was made while Secretary Vance was on vacation, enraging the secretary of state, who felt he had no alternative except to resign.

Vance made one last effort to dissuade his colleagues from the military option, at a full session of the NSC on April 16. He failed to sway any opinions, after which Vaught and Beckwith were called in to brief on the raid. President Carter gave final approval. Over the next week, the Eagle Claw forces moved to staging bases in Egypt and aboard an aircraft carrier in the Indian Ocean. The rescue mission began on the night of April 24–25, when a flight of eight RH-53 helicopters launched from the carrier *Nimitz.*

Operation Eagle Claw proved to be an abortive mission. Three of the helicopters had mechanical failures and either returned to the *Nimitz* or were abandoned. At Desert One after the third abort, there were not enough helicopters left to provide confident airlift for the remainder of the mission. Beckwith, Vaught, and the other joint task force leaders reluctantly canceled the rest of the plan. As the withdrawal at Desert One began, there was a collision on the ground between a helicopter and one of the C-130's, killing seven Americans.

The losses at Desert One obliged Carter, through Secretary of Defense Harold Brown and the Joint Chiefs, to reveal the existence of the mission. The Carter administration faced criticism and ridicule from many quarters. Cyrus Vance, who perhaps had earned the right to criticize, remained charitably silent. Nevertheless, the

Carter administration continued to maintain a military option as part of its search for a way out of the hostage crisis.

Jim Vaught continued to command the joint task force, which went ahead with a larger-scale plan. Vaught had some of the best covert operations people around. His air component commander was Brigadier General Richard V. Secord, who worked on the air supply missions to the Kurds in Iraq and had special-operations experience going back to "Jungle Jim," plus specific experience in Iran as air advisory group boss there from 1975 to 1978. Vaught's chief operations planner was Colonel Robert C. Dutton, holder of three Distinguished Flying Crosses as a pilot flying out of Thailand in the Vietnam War. Dutton had previously served under Secord in the Iran advisory group. The joint task force staff worked in unison; individual will, a desire to get the hostages out, overcame the crevices of Pentagon politics, in this case the services' demands that each be a component of the task force.

Some criticisms of Eagle Claw centered on inadequate planning of the project. There had not been enough helicopters; the requirement to use a unit precluded a Pentagon-wide search for the best pilots; the many exercises had never included a complete rehearsal of all phases of the operation. General Vaught's new plan was called Honey Badger. It was designed to correct these deficiencies.

Even worse than before, the problem with Honey Badger was intelligence. As soon as the Iranians discovered Desert One, they dispersed the hostages and redoubled their vigilance. In desperation and in hope, the U.S. military turned to the expatriate Iranians, who flocked to volunteer their services and their contacts. One Iranian who did this was Albert Hakim, to the extent of putting his Multitech Corporation, which still operated in Teheran, at the disposal of the Americans. The degree to which this was considered patriotic among Iranians may be gauged from the fact that Hakim offered his services to General Secord despite having been turned down by Secord, when both worked in Iran, for lucrative business contracts. Now Secord put Hakim in touch with Air Force intelligence.

A flood of reports came in from Hakim and the other sources. General Secord remembers hundreds. But intelligence could not pin down the locations of the hostages because there was no way to check the veracity of the reports. This uncertainty continued into the fall, with the joint task force in constant consultation with the CIA. In October, Langley suddenly announced it had new information, then presented an elaborate briefing on the hostages. Secord called this the "Eureka" briefing because of the Agency's abrupt claim that it had all the answers—all this could just be someone's wild idea of what was going on. Joint task force intelligence had no information collaborating the CIA's view. General Secord actually escalated this intelligence dispute up the chain of command to the White House, where Carter administration policymakers were reminded of the unresolvable intelligence problems of the military option.

By comparison the actual military side of the equation was in much better shape. The Honey Badger force was ready to go in August 1980. Whenever there was fair consensus on the intelligence picture, Dutton and the operations staff put together a new plan. General Vaught's forces conducted at least six major exercises rehearsing successive versions of the Honey Badger rescue mission. A start was also made toward filling the void of in-place assets in Teheran with the Army's formation of a Foreign Operations Group (FOG), a unit intended to facilitate deep-cover activities by Americans. Air Force HH-53 helicopters, with better avionics for navigation through sandstorms, were substituted for the Navy ships used in Eagle Claw.

As the preparations continued, costs mounted rapidly. Honey Badger was of such importance, however, that General Vaught's task force spent the money and only then went back to the services to tell each how much it owed. The intention was to go back to Congress later for the funds in a supplemental appropriation. In the event, Honey Badger was never carried out. Instead, diplomatic prospects improved, an accommodation was arranged, and the hostages were released after 444 days of captivity on January 20, 1981. Subsequent debriefing by the joint task force chief of intelligence, incidentally, showed that the "Eureka" information had indeed been mistaken.

Fiasco in the Iran hostage crisis crystallized opinion on the need to strengthen special-warfare capabilities. As Stansfield Turner put it, "The talent necessary for covert action is available in the CIA and it must be preserved."

What Turner wanted was to have capability in reserve, but to avoid squandering it on insignificant activities. Admiral Turner preferred highly directed operations, such as one mounted in an East African country to recover certain equipment from a downed aircraft. Another time the deputy director for central intelligence, Frank Carlucci, reportedly supervised a paramilitary foray into Yemen.

At this juncture, as Washington began to resurrect covert action, another international development intervened to provide a situation in which covert intervention seemed desirable. This event was the Soviet invasion of Afghanistan in December 1979. Langley immediately prepared plans for operations in Afghanistan and gave prior notice of them to the congressional committees. The first known briefings on this subject occurred on January 9, 1980. Langley's representatives were Frank Carlucci and John N. McMahon, the director of operations.

·XVII·

NEW WAVE
COVERT ACTIONS

Jimmy Carter recalls the Soviet invasion of Afghanistan as a shock "to a world which yearned for peace." At the time, President Carter said as much, when he told a reporter on New Year's Eve that the Soviet action affected his thinking more profoundly than anything that had happened in his time in the White House. One of his responses was a covert action to help the Afghans against the Russians. As Carter put it to undergraduate students at Emory University in 1982, a covert program was the best way to punish the Soviets short of "going to war, which wasn't feasible."

Where Carter made one big paramilitary play, his successor Ronald Reagan has used covert techniques widely. President Reagan continued the secret war in Afghanistan, and selected new battlefields ranging from Nicaragua to Chad and Libya. In the process of conducting these protracted campaigns, the CIA regenerated its covert action capabilities and the military its special-warfare forces. The administration has conceded nothing to congressional oversight unless it had to. At the same time, it attempts to use the existence or threat of covert operations openly as an instrument of foreign policy.

The Reagan years have left "plausible deniability" in tatters. The hand of the White House and the NSC have become visible, standing the very definition of covert action on its head. In the process, Reagan's secret wars have revealed new problems of accountability and control, and led to an unprecedented confrontation between Congress and the executive over a specific covert action.

357

* * *

Invasion of Afghanistan by the Soviets represented not so much a blitzkrieg, as was breathlessly written in the news accounts of those days, but a creeping intervention down the path into an unmarked quagmire. This was no surprise in Washington, where Soviet progress there had been closely monitored for several years. American intelligence had a good estimate of the number of Soviet military advisers in Afghanistan, their gradual increase, and their activities. Weeks before the December 1979 invasion, the United States detected the buildup of combat forces; and the introduction of Russian paratroops into the Afghan capital Kabul. As early as the summer before the invasion, NSC adviser Brzezinski warned President Carter to expect the Russians to support a coup that would overthrow the government in Kabul.

The first Soviet airborne units deployed to Bagram, an air base outside Kabul, in the second week of December. More paratroops landed beginning on December 20, but the coup and invasion started on Christmas. Marxist President Hafizullah Amin was killed in a shoot-out with Soviet agents and other Afghans in his own office. Amin had enjoyed complete powers for only a few months since the ouster of his own predecessor, the Marxist Nur Mohammed Taraki. Now Amin in turn lost out to another communist faction headed by Babrak Karmal who assumed the office of president. Karmal immediately asked for major Soviet assistance, an appeal that became the official justification for the Soviet intervention. North of Kabul, the vanguard of an 85,000-man Soviet army began crossing the border, tactically disposed, it may be noted, for a road march, not for combat. Simultaneously, the airlift to Bagram assumed massive proportions, with 215 flights on December 26–27. By then the Russians had 8,000 to 10,000 soldiers around Kabul and were there to stay.

In international political terms, the Soviet "invasion" of Afghanistan made not the slightest difference. No countries switched camps; the Russians gained nothing at the United Nations. Afghanistan had already been a Soviet ally for the better part of a decade, that alliance forged by a parliamentary government long before the Marxist coup of April 1978. The Soviets appear to have made their move in order to avoid losing an ally. This seizure of power had the principal effect of sharpening the enmity among different factions of Afghan communists. Both the government put in power and the one overthrown in December 1979 were communist regimes.

"The invasion of Afghanistan," writes Jimmy Carter, "was direct aggression by the Soviet armed forces against a freedom-loving people." Although the facts are not as simple as Carter suggests, the President's fury was sufficient for him to initate a number of actions that transformed United States-Soviet relations: deep cuts in American grain sales to Russia; a boycott of the 1980 Olympics, scheduled to be held in the Soviet Union; and withdrawal of the SALT II arms control treaty from Senate ratification proceedings. In his State of the Union address in January 1980, the President countered further by enunciating what was called a Carter Doctrine to protect the nations of South Asia, the Middle East, and the Horn of Africa against Soviet encroachments.

Covert action was one component of the United States' response. A tribal resistance movement already existed in Afghanistan, opposing Kabul's control. The Afghan rebels had begun fighting the Marxist government in 1978 and soon dominated much of the rugged mountainous countryside. Despite increased Russian aid—including several thousand military advisers, and an additional 15,000 military and police, giving a total of 140,000 under arms—the Afghan government remained penned up in the large towns and cities. This evident deterioration in the security situation was one of the main factors that led the Soviets down the slope toward their decision to invade.

Russian intervention unloosed towering waves of international condemnation, including resounding defeat at the United Nations on a resolution of censure. In this climate the United States approached Egypt and the People's Republic of China about a joint operation to aid the Afghan rebels. President Anwar Sadat of Egypt confirmed in 1981 that the covert action was suggested immediately after the Soviet invasion. The United States wanted to buy Soviet-type weapons from either or both countries.

Egypt furnished concrete assistance to the Afghan resistance. This ranged from weapons to Egyptian training for some rebels. Sadat considered the Afghans a brother Islamic people fighting against Soviet imperialism, and went out of his way in the spring of 1980 to declare that Egypt would aid the Afghans as long as might be necessary. The scattered reports available on the sources of Afghan arms also indicate that Egypt may have provided bases for some shipments alleged to have gone by air through Oman to Pakistan.

Apparently, the Chinese did not immediately go along on the

Afghanistan project. Secretary of Defense Harold Brown visited Peking a few weeks after the invasion, but his talks centered on military matters and produced no accord on Afghan action. In a series of exchanges over the summer and fall of 1980 the People's Republic modified its stance. The Chinese are believed to have sold Soviet-type weapons to the United States, to have later provided some of their own, and to have sent some training teams to Pakistan to work with the rebels.

Although, according to Zbigniew Brzezinski, there was never an eyeball-to-eyeball confrontation between the United States and Soviet Union over Afghanistan, the Americans were certainly doing what they could to complicate the Russians' situation. Brzezinski notes that one of his main concerns in the weeks after the Christmas intervention was "to make sure that the Soviets paid some price for their invasion." One project dreamed up by the CIA political action experts was to bring some of the Afghan partisans to New York and have them testify at the United Nations. This idea had to be abandoned, it is reported, because of the regulations prohibiting CIA activities inside the United States.

The Russians did pay a price for Afghanistan, a toll exacted in blood and rubles every day of their occupation. Tactical doctrine quickly settled down to routine counterinsurgency—sweeps down the roads, massive attacks in the Kunar and Panshir valleys and near the Khyber Pass, occupation of the cities. The situation, in fact, was not much different than before the Soviet invasion, except that the Afghan regular army disintegrated in the wake of the factional infighting, leaving only about thirty-five thousand soldiers and twenty thousand police to supplement the Russian expeditionary army.

Firepower was a key element in Soviet tactics, as it had been for the United States in Vietnam. In particular, airpower gave the Soviets a very flexible capability that could be used both to help troops on the ground and to bomb rebel strongholds. Villages thought to house rebel bands were bombed so heavily that large numbers of Afghans were obliged to seek refuge in Pakistan to the south, following one or another of the estimated 230 trails that crossed the border. By late 1982 almost one sixth of the population had joined the emigration. These 2.8 million Afghans lived in 339 villages in Pakistan, many of them near the border. There were Soviet shellings across the border and air intrusions into Pakistan, occasionally hitting the refugee villages. Pakistani officials reported sixty-three such incursions during 1984 alone.

The Russians were right to be alarmed about the refugees in Pakistan. Those villages were the very foundation of the Afghan holy war—recruits came from the villages, the bands returned to them to rest in between forays into Afghanistan, and weapons and ammunition are often bought in the village bazaars. Some villages got much larger, like Long Tieng in the Laos war. In Pakistan the camp at Barakai grew to house 140,000, a city in its own right. Many camps dotted the hills around the Pakistani city Peshawar, familiar to earlier generations of intelligence specialists as an electronic-intercept station or a base for the CIA's U-2 program.

The resistance revolves around six major political groupings and many tribal bands. Its structure is that of a loose confederation, not a tight front. The number active at any one time is estimated at between 90,000 and 120,000 out of a total 250,000–300,000 supporters. Usually about one third of the available guerrillas are en route to the combat zones or returning from missions, and a third are resting in the villages. Covert action in Afghanistan amounted to the question of supplies for these large rebel forces.

Afghan resistance has so far stalemated the Russians. The war has ground on for seven years at this writing, hardly the blitzkrieg many feared at the time of the invasion. Soon after their intervention the Soviets were forced to replace their original invasion units, whose soldiers came from ethnic groups with affinities to the Pushtun of Afghanistan. Since then the Russians have rotated their combat divisions through this theater periodically to avoid any unit being in place too long. The strength of the expeditionary army gradually grew to 105,000, perhaps 115,000 by 1984, and 118,000 at the end of 1986. Some estimates put Soviet strength as high as 140,000. Ten motorized rifle divisions form the core of the Russian army in Afghanistan. The cutting edge of the force consists of elements of two airborne divisions plus *spetznaz*, or Soviet-style special forces.

Prolonged warfare has devastated Afghanistan and threatens to spill over into Pakistan. Meanwhile, the Russian casualty list grows longer. By 1985 cumulative Soviet losses were assessed at 40,000 to 60,000, with over 10,000 dead. United States sources at the end of 1986 put Russian losses at 35,000, including 12,000 killed. The pro-Soviet government in Kabul continues unstable, with several coups since the one that occasioned the Russian intervention. Dollar costs of the war are less certain but probably range between $5 billion and $7 billion a year.

Opening the weapons pipeline has given the Afghans just enough extra capability to enable them to exploit their superior knowledge of the terrain to compensate for the Soviets' combat power. President Carter opened the flow in early January 1980; by mid-month rumors of a CIA operation were abroad in Washington. A month later the Egyptian Ministry of Defense announced its training of Afghans. On February 15, *The Washington Post* disclosed that the CIA was involved in the arms shipments. White House officials confirmed that the NSC Special Coordinating Committee had made a decision on Afghanistan.

The early arms aid appears to have been pretty cautious. Soviet weapons only, many of them quite obsolete, were smuggled into Pakistan. There were no really sophisticated weapons like antiaircraft missiles—intelligence officers had some doubt about the proportion of the weapons shipments being diverted to the black market, and had no wish to expose sensitive technology, especially American technology.

At the end of 1980 the members of President-elect Ronald Reagan's transition team who handled intelligence matters encouraged an increase in the Afghanistan program. The transition team unanimously felt more should be done in the way of covert action. William J. Casey, Reagan's 1980 political campaign manager, who was Reagan's choice for DCI, accepted this view, although he largely ignored the transition team report. The new DCI was a friend of the President and member of Reagan's informal "kitchen cabinet." Unlike some other CIA directors, Casey made no bones about offering policy advice to the President; by all indications, he rather enjoyed the role. Afghanistan was one program that would be affected as a result.

In the 1980 campaign, Ronald Reagan already had adopted the rhetoric of aiding Afghanistan. Statements he made advocated more sophisticated weapons, in this case hand-held antitank missiles. Even under Carter the United States moved some distance in the direction of giving more sophisticated weapons—the week before Reagan's inauguration there were reports that, because of rebel weapons, the Soviets had had to relocate all their aircraft and helicopters parked along the runway at Bagram to the side of the base farthest from the surrounding hills. In early 1981 the Russians also reported that the partisans were using caseless mines immune to metal detectors, a relatively sophisticated technology that probably came from the West.

In office, Reagan went further. The President approved repeated and substantial spending increases for the Afghan effort.

The rhetoric of aiding Afghanistan led to a substantial program, the most expensive covert operation the United States has ever conducted. The Carter administration gave perhaps $30 million to the resistance in 1980, reportedly matched by Saudi Arabia with a similar amount. The Reagan administration bettered that amount in 1981 and has since radically increased its support to the resistance. Press disclosures indicate that $625 million, including about $40 million transferred from Pentagon accounts, had been appropriated by 1984. For fiscal 1985 the budget was $280 million, then $470 million in 1986 and $630 million in 1987. Should the war continue, there are predictions of billion-dollar requests for Afghanistan before the end of the decade. The Saudis may have contributed as much as $525 million between 1984 and 1986. In addition the United States had already spent $217 million for refugee assistance in Pakistan by 1982, and was then paying bills at a rate of over a million dollars a day. This expenditure (roughly $2.5 *billion*) makes Afghanistan the most expensive secret war ever waged.

Oddly enough, the Central Intelligence Agency was not that keen on spending all this money. Langley lacked direct control over administration of the aid, which was funneled through a committee of Pakistani generals to avoid offending the sensibilities of that nation. The result was poor accounting and no accountability for the aid, almost an invitation to graft. Under these circumstances, Director of Operations John McMahon told the oversight committees, the CIA could achieve no more than a disruptive effect upon the Soviet occupation forces. McMahon's view was rejected by other administration officials, including Vernon Walters, ambassador to the United Nations, and Fred Ikle, undersecretary of defense for policy. One source was quoted as saying the CIA had "a box score mentality, just like the body-count mentality in Vietnam." William Casey soon promoted McMahon out of DO to be his deputy director for central intelligence. It was a step up but a step away from direct authority for programs like that in Afghanistan. In the meantime the CIA stations at Islamabad and in Cairo, managing the weapons flow, have grown to become two of the agency's largest outposts.

Within the framework of a cold war "spoiling" operation, most of the money should be translated into weapons useful to the Afghans. Sometimes this is not as simple as it sounds. The most glaring example in the case of Afghanistan is the question of antiaircraft capability. The Soviet war effort is heavily dependent on airpower, ranging from about 400 fixed-wing planes flying from bases inside the Soviet Union, to 600–900 planes and helicopters based on Afghan fields, including that nation's air force. From the beginning of the *jihad*, or holy war, it was clear that the ability to do something about Soviet aircraft was what the rebels truly needed.

Improving the rebel antiaircraft capability has nevertheless taken years. For a long time the main antiaircraft weapon was the 12.7-millimeter machine gun, a standard Soviet design that dates from before World War II. A lack of suitable merchandise on the international arms market and desultory talks with the People's Republic of China hampered procurement of small surface-to-air missiles. In the fall of 1983 an amendment to the defense budget bill was proposed by Congressman Charles Wilson (D-Texas) that would have rerouted Pentagon money to purchase new foreign-made heavy antiaircraft cannon. The guns would go to the CIA for the Afghan guerrillas.

The Wilson proposal touched off a flurry of concern within the Reagan administration. The Pentagon's top man on intelligence matters, General Richard G. Stilwell, who had worked for the CIA in the heady days of the OPC adventures and rose to command an Army corps in the Vietnam War, argued that the cannon was the wrong weapon because it required very expensive ammunition. When the House intelligence committee approved the funds but asked CIA for a report on the antiaircraft cannon, it developed that Langley had never tested this kind of cannon and had none of the guns in its warehouses. The Senate intelligence committee then held up action until April 1984, when Casey's deputy, John McMahon, wrote both committees that the CIA favored a field test of the weapon. Senate committee chairman Barry Goldwater, Republican of Arizona, withdrew his objections to the cannon, and a shipment of nine guns by the spring of 1985 was eventually planned for the test.

Results of CIA's field testing are not known, but what is evident is that the rebels have explicitly targeted Soviet airpower. During 1984–1985 there were a series of sabotage, commando, and artillery raids on Soviet and Afghan air force bases, destroying more than two dozen aircraft at major bases like Bagram and Shindand. In 1985 the rebels contrived to capture two of the most modern Soviet gunship helicopters, Mi-24 HIND-D's, which were presented to the United States as an intelligence windfall. There are more frequent reports of rebel use of antiaircraft missiles, and the cannon test may have taken place—in one two-day period in October 1985, according to Kabul sources, the *mujahedeen* shot down two jet fighters and four helicopters. The total of Soviet aircraft lost in Afghanistan was estimated at about seven hundred as of November 1985. Claims of Soviet aircraft losses climbed to nearly one thousand by the end of 1986, followed in early 1987 by repeated clashes between Soviet and Pakistani aircraft in the border area. Pakistan subsequently requested that early warning radar aircraft be sold or leased to it under the military aid program.

The bulk of arms shipments have been less exotic weapons: bolt action and automatic rifles, grenade launchers and bazookas, mortars and recoilless rifles. The flow has been significant—one major band, possessing only 13 machine guns in 1982, had 250 by the spring of 1984—but still limited. According to Washington lobbyists for the Afghans, from 1981 to the summer of 1983, one of the six political movements received a total of only 11,000 small arms, about 130 machine guns, 450 rocket-propelled grenade launchers, and 30 mortars. More than 7,500 of the small arms were obsolete Lee-Enfield rifles. An American reporter accompanying a typical 200-man rebel striking party in January 1985 found the unit armed with one mortar and one machine gun.

Two illustrations of the attrition of aid in the pipeline to the Afghan rebels are relevant because they concern the hotly debated issue of antiaircraft weapons. In January 1985, $50 million in CIA funds was used to buy 40 Swiss-made Oerlikon 20-millimeter antiaircraft cannon; two years later only 11 of the guns had reached the rebels. At about the same time, January 1987, the Afghans exhausted their supply of sophisticated U.S. Stinger surface-to-air missiles (SAMs), which the United States provided (finally releasing the technology) in the summer of 1986. In the case of the Stingers, the rebels received only 100 of 150 programmed SAMs and 28 hand-held launchers rather than 50. Additional SAMs began arriving in February, out of 600 reportedly involved in the 1987 request. There continues to be substantial concern—one of the CIA's original reasons for reticence—that Stingers may be diverted from the Afghan pipeline and appear in the hands of terrorists.

A considerable problem is getting the supplies to where they are needed. Before the end of the line at Peshawar, there are many stages of transit and great opportunities for theft, graft, or other diversion. Pakistan is officially neutral in the conflict and occasionally makes a show of enforcing neutrality. In February 1983, for example, an American science teacher in Pakistan identified as Eugene Ray Clegg, drew a ten-year sentence from a military court for smuggling a consignment of rifles, allegedly for the use of his students. Clegg mysteriously escaped a week after his imprisonment and left the country.

This official neutrality creates a climate of graft on the Afghan supply lines, which amounts to more than just the "cost of doing business." The most optimistic estimates, from CIA sources, are that 20 percent of the aid is skimmed off. Some Afghan groups put that figure as high as 85 percent. The very existence of such a wide range of estimates indicates that there is little real accounting—no one actually knows what has happened to all the covert action money.

That so much money has been approved is partly the result of lobbying efforts by pro-Afghan Americans. An illustration is Andrew Eiva, a West Point-trained officer and Green Beret who gave up his commission in 1980 to aid the Afghans. Eiva claims to have trained Afghans in West Germany and Pakistan, and to have made at least five trips to Pakistan, where he, too, was jailed on suspicion of meddling.

In Washington, Eiva has been a fountain of energy dramatizing Afghan needs and criticizing the aid flow. Almost single-handedly Eiva interested Capitol Hill in an "Afghanistan Effective Support Resolution." This sense of the Congress resolution, passed in October 1984, puts the legislature on record as opposing any program that gives the *mujahedeen* only enough to keep fighting, preventing them from advancing their cause. But the Reagan administration, not wishing to actually preclude the option of a mere spoiling operation in Afghanistan, had the State Department oppose this legislation. Eiva is reported to have been investigated by federal law enforcement officials for violations of United States neutrality laws.

Passage of the congressional motion on effective aid to the Afghans had no program significance, but it put the Reagan administration under political pressure to act more forcefully. Despite continuing opposition from the State Department and the CIA, in April 1985 Reagan approved NSDD-166, which stated a United States policy of driving the Soviet Union out of Afghanistan by all means available. The later decision to supply Stinger SAMs was made pursuant to this decision directive.

With greater resources flowing into the Afghanistan secret war, official attention is beginning to focus on both the covert action and regional policy problems of the project. Pressure built on Capitol Hill through the spring of 1987 for an inquiry into the administration of the aid. On February 25 the House Budget Committee officially asked the General Accounting Office to audit the Afghan aid accounts. Langley resists any such investigation, arguing that GAO knows nothing about covert operations and that its auditors lack the requisite security clearances. Both the House and Senate intelligence committees began related investigations in January 1987 after the disclosure that Iran arms sale money had been passed through CIA accounts in Switzerland set up for Afghan support. Meanwhile, Pakistan's role in the secret war continues to give it leverage over the United States for military aid, despite provisions in American law that bar aid to nations engaged in nuclear weapons programs, which it is widely believed that Pakistan is doing.

Andrew Eiva's case highlights a serious problem, which has garnered attention only recently. What do you do with a *former* secret warrior? The CIA and Special Forces veterans often have difficulties reintegrating themselves into civilian life similar to those faced by the returning Vietnam vets.

In the early years this problem, to the extent that any thought was given to it, was seen as applying to contract agents, not intelligence or military officers. Allen Dulles cited the "disposal" problem to John F. Kennedy as one reason to go ahead with the Bay of Pigs invasion. Far from disposing of the Cuban contract agents, the operation led to almost open-ended CIA involvement with the Cuban exiles. Cubans fought in Operation Mongoose, in Zaire, and in Portuguese Angola, and some of them remained on the Agency payroll at the time of their arrest at the Watergate. Two Cubans are alleged to have been hired by Chilean secret services to participate in the assassination of exile Orlando Letelier. At least five were employed in various capacities, including for alleged assassination plots, by the Libyans in the 1970s and 1980s. Only a few thousand Cubans were employed by the Agency, but other operations brought to America many more exiled peoples. They include fifty-five thousand Meo and perhaps twice as many Cambodians and an equal number of Vietnamese. The future may bring survivors of the Nicaraguan insurgency as well.

What was true of the agents was true for the operators as well.

Retired intelligence and military types have maintained many international connections and work in areas similar to what they did in the service. This is most striking in the case of Special Forces. Bull Simons, in retirement after the Sontay raid, became a security consultant and, in 1979, organized a daring rescue of two American businessmen held prisoner in Iran. The mission exacerbated tensions in the period before the embassy takeover. Relations with Thailand were complicated in 1982 by a free-lance mission launched from there into Laos, in search of evidence of Americans missing in Indochina. The patrol, which may have had some official United States support, was organized by a legendary figure from 5th Special Forces in Vietnam, Captain James G. "Bo" Gritz.

Another legendary figure was Major Richard J. Meadows, veteran of many forays into Laos, a half dozen into North Vietnam, and the man sent into Iran to check, on the ground, the feasibility of the hostage rescue raid. Meadows opened his own security consultant firm, as did the hostage raid commander, "Chargin' Charlie" Beckwith.

Agency people got into the security business as well. The obvious examples are Howard Hunt and James McCord of Watergate fame. More typical were such middle-rank officers as Mike Ackerman and Louis Palombo, who worked a network out of Miami. About twenty former CIA officers are on retainer to many large companies. At a higher level, former DDO William Nelson left the Agency after Angola and became vice-president for security to the Fluor Corporation, a California-based multinational construction engineering conglomerate.

Often the retired intelligence officers tend to get into international finance, which occasionally has its own covert aspects. Richard Helms set up his own company to conduct joint ventures in Iran. After the downfall of the Shah, Helms moved on to other projects. Bill Colby has represented a number of foreign interests through his law firm, and has also done "risk analysis" for multinationals. Africa Division chief Lawrence Devlin returned to his old haunts in Zaire as a personal representative of an American minerals magnate. Vernon Walters earned a $300,000 commission in early 1981 from a Virginia company that wanted assistance making sales in Morocco.

Mercenary action is another option. A conspicuous example occurred in 1978–1979 when, in the last throes of his struggle to hold on to power, Nicaraguan dictator Anastasio Somoza Debayle hired Michael Echanis, Chuck Sanders, and two other former Green Berets to help his National Guard forces. The men trained Somoza's troops, went along on patrols, and there was some talk of assassinations. Echanis also headed the intelligence section on the National Guard staff. Echanis actually received a letter from Secretary of State Cyrus Vance asking him to avoid violations of human rights and refrain from killing noncombatants. In the mercenary's words: "He said I was a disgrace to the United States." Chuck Sanders died in a September 1978 plane crash, with a National Guard general and a Vietnamese mercenary.

Vance may have complained, but no one thought of instituting legal remedies until a far more damaging case was dragged into the open by the press, notably (once again) by Seymour Hersh and *New York Times* reporters Philip Taubman and Jeff Gerth, *Washington Post* reporter Patrick E. Tyler, and columnist Jack Anderson. This was the Wilson-Terpil affair, which grew from the activities of former CIA officers Edwin P. Wilson and Frank E. Terpil.

Using techniques learned in providing cover for CIA activities, Wilson established a number of import-export companies in the United States and Europe. He then made millions of dollars exporting sensitive American technology, even to the Soviets. A hemorrhage of secret-warfare expertise began in 1976 when Wilson made a deal with dictator Muammar Qaddafi to provide training and technical assistance for the Libyan intelligence and military services.

From Wilson the Libyans got training in demolitions and close combat, plus American plastic explosives and timers. Nine former Green Berets, and one on active duty, were enticed into signing up with the training mission. Aircrews were hired to fly Libyan transport planes, and mechanics to service them. Five Cubans were hired to execute special missions for Qaddafi, while one former Green Beret, Eugene A. Tafoya, actually attempted a murder on the Libyans' behalf (he was caught and sent to prison in Colorado). Robert W. Hitchman, a former Air America pilot, acted as Wilson's deputy in Tripoli.

Wilson maintained his contacts with Agency personnel, and his net attracted several active CIA officers. When parts of the story became known to Stansfield Turner, the DCI fired Patry E. Loomis, who had assisted Wilson in recruiting, and William Weisenburger, who had helped design bombs. Turner also discovered that a very senior officer, Theodore G. Shackley, who had risen to deputy to the DDO, was in touch with Wilson and aware of some of his more nefarious activities. Because Shackley informed the Justice Department, he was not fired, but Turner transferred him to a less sensitive job at Langley.

Shackley had first met Wilson when he ran the Miami station for Operation Mongoose and Wilson was a junior officer. Shackley's deputy in Miami, Thomas G. Clines, also in touch with Wilson, served as a go-between, and became a partner in one of Wilson's companies after his mid-1970s retirement. When Shackley in turn retired in 1979, he was hired as a consultant by Clines. Both men had a close brush with criminal indictment as the wheels of justice began to turn against Wilson.

The ultimate ignominy for the United States occurred early in the Reagan administration, when the CIA under William Casey carried out a covert action against a pro-Libyan government in Chad and planned operations against Qaddafi. The Libyans intervened to support their faction in Chad, which resulted in the situation of Wilson's renegade secret operation having furnished support against the CIA's own actions.

The Wilson-Terpil affair proved highly embarrassing and demanded some response. The House intelligence committee held hearings in the fall of 1981 to consider legislation to bar foreign dealings by retired intelligence officers. Vernon Walters told the committee that a ban would be a restriction on individual freedom; at most, he considered, a two-year postretirement moratorium would suffice. Bill Casey moved to head off congressional measures by asking the CIA general counsel to consider how Agency employment contracts might be revised to protect against this kind of activity. No legislation ever emerged, and, for its part, the CIA has never revealed whether protective provisions were added to its contracts.

Some 2,800 intelligence officers retired between 1977 and 1981. Even a tiny percentage of bad apples, as the "Wilson-Terpil affair" vividly demonstrates, can accomplish grave damage, but meanwhile the game goes on. When asked what he intended to do, after his 1982 release from an Angolan jail, American mercenary Gustavo Grillo answered that he intended to go into the import-export business and make money in Angola.

* * *

There has rarely been a closer team of President and DCI than Ronald Reagan and William J. Casey. No director of central intelligence ever spent as much time with a President as did Casey in the first year of the administration. The DCI was perceived as a loyal, tough, and competent adviser, and an effective agent of the President. Reagan appreciated Casey's political campaign work and his outstanding personal achievements.

A Wall Street lawyer, Casey had grown wealthy making investments and dispensing tax advice. An amateur historian, sometime president of the Import-Export Bank, and chairman of the Securities and Exchange Commission, Casey was also one of the original secret warriors. Commissioned as a naval reserve officer in World War II, he had been sent to OSS where he worked as an aide to Wild Bill Donovan. The OSS chief, in turn, dispatched Casey to London, where he helped organize the "Jedburgh" program. In December 1944, Casey replaced his boss as OSS chief of secret intelligence for the European theater. In this capacity he supervised the effort to infiltrate several hundred American agents into Germany and Austria during the last days of the Third Reich. After the war, William Casey was active in OSS veterans associations and would be appointed to PFIAB by President Gerald Ford. To a newly elected Ronald Reagan looking for a DCI, Bill Casey must have seemed a natural for the job.

There was only one big problem, at first. That was Casey's lack of talent for public speaking—which might not impress the senators at a confirmation hearing. Casey could be prepared for his testimony, but that turned out to be the least of his difficulties. One irregularity after another emerged during the confirmation process, until Casey's chances of confirmation appeared threatened.

A political item from the Reagan-Carter election campaign brewed into a significant scandal, which the media pundits began to label "Debategate," a sort of mini-Watergate. Reagan and President Carter had appeared together for several televised debates, formatted as joint press conferences, hosted by the League of Women Voters. Prior to the debate on foreign policy a copy of Carter's White House briefing book was surreptitiously made and given to the Republicans. Reagan's staff used the book to prepare their candidate for things Carter might say. As Reagan campaign manager, Bill Casey had kept the notorious briefing book in his office safe.

Several more items called into question the appointee's judgment or integrity. Casey's personal financial disclosure forms, required by post-Watergate laws, proved to be incomplete and had to be amended. It also developed that Casey had not registered as a foreign agent as required by law during certain periods when he had represented the government of Indonesia. Then it became known that the prospective official intended to continue personally managing his stock portfolio, a situation that might create conflicts of interest for a DCI.

Judgment also became an issue following Casey's confirmation, in the summer of 1981 in what became known as the Hugel affair. This concerned the resignation of a man Casey had personally brought into the Agency as an assistant, following allegations that he had been involved in inside stock transactions. This resignation occurred only two months after Max Hugel had received a further promotion to DDO. Even after the first disclosures, Bill Casey solidly backed his protégé, saying he had known Hugel as an honest man for twenty years. However, after it emerged that there were tape recordings of Hugel giving out business information, Casey admitted to less than two years of a much more distant acquaintance. Max Hugel was jettisoned from the Agency.

Had he not had President Reagan's high regard, Bill Casey himself would probably have been swept away. As it was, Casey mended all the fences he could. He agreed to a blind trust for stocks, listed seventy former clients in financial disclosure statements, and asserted he did not remember anything about Debategate. Inside the Agency, Casey assembled the top CIA leadership in the auditorium to reassure them as well. President Reagan defended Casey with the comment that the criticisms of him were merely personal. In August 1981 the Senate intelligence committee passed a recommendation judging "there is no basis for concluding Mr. Casey is unfit to serve" as DCI.

Casey moved to reassure the professional intelligence officers with his next choice for DDO. Whereas Max Hugel had been a businessman, with little intelligence background, his replacement was the man originally recommended for DDO by the Reagan transition team. John Henry Stein, then assistant to the DDO, was a forty-eight-year-old officer with two decades in the CIA. Stein had been station chief at Phnom Penh during the crucial years 1970 to 1972, and had worked in Zaire and elsewhere in Africa, including a tour as station chief in Tripoli, Libya, in the mid-1970s.

Bill Casey's intentions were reflected in his instructions to his new DDO: Focus on covert paramilitary and political action. Espionage management could be left to the assistant DDO. Instead, the DCI intended to stress the critical role the intelligence community must play, and motivate the best minds to see the profession as necessary for national security. Casey proposed to regenerate the covert action capability of the CIA. He anticipated there might be problems with congressional oversight but believed these could be circumvented.

Langley did its best to follow the director's lead. Greater emphasis on recruitment resulted in a one-third increase in personnel, putting the CIA back to near its Vietnam-era peak manpower. John Stein saved some of the expertise in covert operations by hiring back on short-term contracts eight hundred of the officers let go between 1977 and 1980. Although expenditures for covert operations dropped to only 2 percent of the CIA budget, the base was much larger since the Agency's budget more than doubled and the intelligence community's total budget grew as much as 25 percent over the same 1981–1984 period. Additional spending by other agencies supplemented CIA's budget; in particular, the military undoubtedly contributed to several programs while, by the 1980s, the State Department paid for the radios.

Proprietaries had previously formed one backbone of CIA covert capability. They assumed significance again during Bill Casey's tenure. Evidence has yet to establish whether the United States owns these assets or is relying on a privatized network of corporate entities. These companies carried out a range of activities that were of great assistance to the United States military services and the CIA. As before, aviation companies performed some of the most useful services.

When the CIA liquidated Southern Air Transport (SAT), it was sold to Stanley G. Williams, once an SAT manager for the Agency. Though most of its assets were sold off, SAT continued to do some contract air work, in particular for the Iranian air force, up to 42 percent of Southern Air's private work in 1978. The fall of the Shah hurt SAT badly. Even with the Iranian business, SAT posted a loss of $272,928 in 1978. Without the Shah there was no Iranian account. Williams bailed out in 1979, selling Southern Air to lawyer James H. Bastian, who became its sole proprietor; Bastian had been SAT's legal counsel during its CIA years.

Southern Air Transport maintained its headquarters and operating center in Miami and staged a slow recovery thereafter. Operating revenue in 1982 totaled $9.8 million and profit some $628,700. The following year Bastian brought in William G. Langton as president of the company. Langton had previously worked for two other cargo carriers, Flying Tigers and Evergreen International. In 1984, SAT won $9.1 million in contracts from the Pentagon's Military Airlift Command, a figure that rose in 1985 to $23.4 million out of total revenue of $38.9 million, 60 percent of the company's business.

Southern Air's largest private account was as subcontractor to the Anglo-Irish firm IAS-Guernsey, which had been hired to provide flight services to the Marxist government of Angola. There were 296 flights in Angola between June and December of 1984 alone. Business increased further in 1985 after a competing air charter company left Angola, following the destruction of one of its C-130–type aircraft on the ground in a guerrilla attack. That year SAT flew 579 flights in Angola plus 105 more from the United States to the central Angolan port city Benguela. At one point the State Department warned Southern Air against carrying Cuban soldiers on its flights inside Angola and SAT reportedly ceased doing so.

The charter company also continued its work for the United States government. Through 1986 the Military Airlift Command used eight SAT L-100's daily for shuttle flights among bases in the United States. With the State Department, SAT had contracts for monthly flights to Havana to service the U.S. Interests Section there, plus a subcontracting arrangement to deliver humanitarian assistance to Nicaraguan rebels in Honduras. Even more sensitive SAT flights will be described later in the narrative.

Southern Air Transport remains today a strong company. Its fleet of aircraft has expanded from three in 1983 to eight Boeing 707's plus seventeen L-100's, civilian versions of the C-130, by 1986. At that time the Miami company employed 540 people including 96 pilots. The worst setbacks have been two recent fatal crashes, the first in SAT's history, on October 4, 1986, and April 8, 1987, both of L-100's flying for the Military Airlift Command.

Another possible proprietary is Summit Aviation, which specializes in aircraft brokerage and modification and works out of a field at Middletown, Delaware. Even former employees remain uncertain of the firm's status. During the Nicaraguan revolution in the

late 1970s, Summit reportedly trained half a dozen pilots for dictator Anastasio Somoza Debayle. In the 1980s, Summit Aviation has
been linked with aircraft used by the CIA in El Salvador and Honduras, with planes prepared for Nicaraguan rebels fighting Somoza's successors, and with aircraft modifications done for
Southern Air Transport. In mid-1984, Summit suddenly received a
grant from the Federal Aviation Administration to lengthen the
runway at Middletown, potentially enabling the company to perform work on large multiengine planes.

Yet a third possibility is the Caribbean-based St. Lucia Airways,
which owns or leases two Boeing 707's and an L-100. Attention focused on this charter firm after revelations of secret U.S. arms shipments to Iran, which brought the disclosure that a Boeing 707
making one of these deliveries to Teheran had had St. Lucia markings. The company denies involvement, and the markings could
have been another plane disguised as a St. Lucia aircraft, but press
investigation has uncovered additional details. Another St. Lucia
plane actually flew a cargo of United States weapons to Israel for
transshipment to Iran. There was also a series of four flights between January and April 1986 from an American military base to an
airfield in Zaire identified as a CIA supply point for UNITA rebels
fighting in Angola. Company officials also deny making any flights
to or for Angola, in a carefully worded denial that does not mention
Zaire. Like SAT, St. Lucia performs contract air work for the Military Airlift Command.

With its in-house capabilities plus the privatized or proprietary
network, the CIA went to work on covert action for the Reagan administration. DCI Casey argued in the councils of government for a
vigorous program. In this he was no doubt supported by the President, who publicly declared his support for "freedom fighters" anywhere, and defended United States use of covert action. On several
occasions Casey advocated operations that were talked down in the
corridors at Langley. John Stein as DO reportedly resisted escalation of an operation in Nicaragua; John McMahon, Casey's deputy
director after 1983, was against too large an effort in Afghanistan,
certain Libya plans, and renewed support for UNITA in Angola.
Bill Casey recommended these projects anyway. For the most part
he got his way.

President Ronald Reagan worked to improve the climate within
the executive branch for covert action. The President reestablished

PFIAB, which had been abolished by Carter, and endowed it with an extremely conservative membership who would encourage activism. Mr. Reagan also reorganized the National Security Council (NSC) to create a National Security Planning Group (NSPG), a more restricted subcommittee of the NSC that included Vice-President George Bush, the secretary of state, the secretary of defense, the DCI, the NSC adviser, and top political aides. The attorney general and OMB director, who had been regular members of Carter's NSC Special Group, were relegated to the status of occasional invitees.

The deputy secretaries committee in the Reagan administration, the 40 Committee that was at the center of secret war, was retitled the 208 Committee, for the room in the Old Executive Office Building in which it met weekly. Langley's proposals are advanced in options papers that are passed out at the beginning of a meeting and collected at the end of it. Final decisions are up to the NSPG, and here the Reagan administration parts with its predecessors. Under Ronald Reagan the President himself is a member of the covert action decision Group for the first time, eliminating the traditional role of the Special Group as a screen behind which the chief executive makes his decisions. In this administration, we are told, many of the decisions are made right at the NSPG table.

Mr. Reagan has continued the practice of regulating intelligence activities by executive order. This President's version is Executive Order 12333, issued on December 4, 1981. The executive order contains a somewhat expanded definition of covert action, which it terms "special activities." The order reiterates the existing prohibition on assassinations, and specifically provides that, except in time of war or by specific presidential instruction, the CIA has full responsibility for "special activities." While the domestic intelligence provisions of the order attracted the bulk of public attention at the time, the document clearly specifies the NSC as "the highest Executive Branch entity that provides review of, guidance for and direction to" special activities.

Under existing procedures Mr. Reagan is obliged to sign Presidential Finding statements to justify each covert action, to authorize these actions at the policy level. The President has made some general decisions affecting the CIA's role that are expressed in National Security Decision Directives (NSDDs), the authorization documents of this administration. A covert action against Nicaragua was approved by NSDD-17 in November 1981. About a year later Bill Casey's activist stance was sanctioned by NSDD-75, which ordered global covert operations to keep nations from accepting the "Cuban model" and NSDD-77, which authorized a "public diplomacy" campaign that nevertheless had certain secret aspects.

One place that the Reagan administration inherited a program, or at least a problem, was Iran. The hostages came home on Inauguration Day, but now there were plenty of expatriate Iranians in touch with the CIA, not least of them the Shah, who wished nothing better than to return to Teheran. Reagan administration behavior toward Iran was "extremely schizoid," in the opinion of one Iranian, Mansur Rafizadeh, a former intelligence officer in touch with the CIA until 1983. Rafizadeh believes the American policymakers decided very early on to throw in their lot with Khomeini, in the expectation that Muslim fundamentalism would be the best defense against communism in the Middle East.

Rafizadeh recounts that Bill Casey went to Ronald Reagan in September 1981 with a dual-track program and got approval to try it out for a year. The CIA would contact and fund disparate Iranian exile groups while, simultaneously, the United States would sanction arms shipments to Khomeini. On both tracks the idea was to gather intelligence.

There is no evidence the CIA was successful in selling arms to Iran at this stage, unless Rafizadeh is referring to certain Israeli shipments which the United States is believed to have approved tacitly at about this time. On the other hand, Langley proved quite adept at developing information from the exile groups by placing them in competition with one another. Langley's liaison for the effort was George Cave, a CIA officer fluent in Farsi and former station chief in both Teheran and Saudi Arabia.

There were six or seven main exile circles, and the CIA developed contacts with them all. The German-based group of Admiral Ahmad Madani, former commander of the Imperial Iranian Navy, reportedly received several million dollars, but insisted on complete control of its own operations and was eased out by the CIA as too independent. Many of the exiles were too busy squabbling among themselves to accomplish much, but in 1982 the CIA reportedly began payments of $100,000 a month to the Front for the Liberation of Iran (FLI), under Ali Amini in Paris. This includes $20,000–$30,000 a month for Radio Liberation (Radio Nejat), which broadcasts four hours a day from Egypt with anti-Khomeini programming and has been active from at least October 1982. The Shah's son, Reza Pahlavi, has associated himself with the FLI and appeared on an eleven-minute television broadcast to Iran that disrupted two Iranian domestic TV channels at 9:00 P.M. on September 5, 1986, to date FLI's greatest achievement. The CIA evidently provided miniaturized TV transmission equipment that made this broadcast possible.

At the same time, the CIA was currying favor with Khomeini. In late 1982 a senior Russian agent in Iran defected to the British and was later debriefed by CIA officers. The Russian spy, Vladimir Kuzichkin, provided detailed information on the communist Tudeh party in Iran, including one hundred to two hundred names of party organizers. Langley contrived to pass the list along to the Iranians, who executed most of the Tudeh members before outlawing the party on May 4, 1983. According to Rafizadeh, the CIA did the same thing to many of the exile groups, passing lists of their contacts in Iran to the Khomeini security services. As a result, Rafizadeh reports, over a thousand persons were arrested or executed in Iran.

It is not clear that these different actions represented the purposeful execution of a two-track policy. Mansur Rafizadeh believes such was the case, while an administration source saw United States actions as "groping through a maze," a series of actions but not a policy.

The incoherence of United States policy comes into sharp focus when the question of relations between the United States and Iran is juxtaposed with the Islamic government's support for terrorists in Lebanon. Shiite Muslim militiamen in Beirut began a campaign of terror against the West, particularly the United States, when the Reagan administration abandoned its neutrality in the Lebanese factional infighting. The Shiite militia had close ties with Teheran; as far as can be told from their actions, there was no detente with the "Great Satan," the United States. In a suicide attack on April 18, 1983, fanatics loaded with explosives fought their way into the heavily defended United States embassy in Beirut and blew it up. At that instant a CIA regional conference was going on inside; among the seventeen dead from the bombing was Robert C. Ames, the Agency's chief Middle East analyst, and three other CIA officers. It was a sharp blow to Langley.

This embassy strike by Islamic Jihad was followed by an even more ambitious dual operation, parallel truck bombings of the U.S. Marine and French military compounds in Beirut on October 23, 1983. There the toll mounted with 58 French and 241 American dead plus almost 100 injured, many grievously. There were further bombings, of the United States embassy in Kuwait, an Israeli military headquarters, and, on September 20, 1984, the American embassy in Beirut was hit again, this time with a truck bomb that left another 14 dead. The Shiites also struck directly at the CIA once more, on March 16, 1984, with the kidnapping of William Buckley, recently arrived station chief in this tough Middle Eastern city.

The Agency knew that Beirut was dangerous but it needed to reestablish a presence in Lebanon quickly to stay on top of the tense situation. Buckley had trained security men for Egyptian president Anwar Sadat and could be expected to be careful. He was also single and thus had no family members who could become terrorist targets themselves. Buckley told a friend before his departure that he wasn't too thrilled by the assignment. Despite security measures the station chief was kidnapped off the streets of Beirut and held by his captors for over a year. Buckley became the first of six American hostages taken by the Party of God (Hezbollah) Shiite faction of Mohammed Hussein Fadlallah.

The United States was vitally interested in all of the hostages, and the CIA in Buckley even more. The continued captivity of his station chief was an affront to Bill Casey. It was harder still for Clair E. George, the director of operations, who had himself been station chief in Beirut in 1975–1976, when two American diplomats were held hostage for four months in the course of earlier Lebanese factional warfare.

In Washington the policy response was framed as a policy to counter terrorism, NSDD-138, which President Reagan approved on April 3, 1984. This document did not exclude preemptive attacks on persons presumed to be preparing terrorist attacks. The original language had been even stronger, but the draft assembled in the Political-Military Affairs office of the NSC staff was softened at the insistence of DDCI John McMahon, who feared the order was too broad.

Sometime later that summer Mr. Reagan signed a Presidential Finding directing the CIA to train and support several counterterrorist units. This eventually led to the CIA's training a special unit in one of the Lebanese intelligence services, and that unit in turn detonated a car bomb outside the home of Hezbollah leader Fadlallah on March 8, 1985. The Shiite leader was not at home at the time, but the explosion killed eighty innocent bystanders and demolished people's apartments in the building. This CIA initiative was quickly terminated, with a terse declaration that Langley had had no advance knowledge of Lebanese intelligence activities, after inquiries from the Senate Select Committee on Intelligence.

More and more thoughts in Washington turned toward dealing with Iran and getting Khomeini to influence the Lebanese Shiites. An interagency study completed in October 1984 concluded that a new relationship could be forged only by Khomeini's successors. In April 1985 the NSC adviser learned from a consultant that he had heard in Israel that the Iranians were indeed interested in buying American weapons. The CIA entered the picture in May when Graham Fuller, the National intelligence officer for the Middle East, sent Bill Casey a memo on Iran that argued for "a bolder—and perhaps riskier policy" that would at least ensure a greater United States voice in unfolding events. The Fuller paper, intended for internal circulation at Langley, was later sent to the White House by Casey. But the official position of the CIA, contained in a May 1985 update to the Iran special National intelligence estimate, was more pessimistic: "Improvement of ties to the United States is not currently a policy option."

Two months later Israeli Foreign Ministry official David Kimche approached NSC adviser Robert C. McFarlane on whether the United States was willing to sell weapons to Iran. When McFarlane replied he thought not, the Israeli asked whether the United States would have any objection if Israel sold some of *its* American weapons to Iran, and whether Israel could then replenish its stocks with purchases from the United States. The Kimche request led to an NSPG meeting at the White House on August 8 which, although accounts differ, appears to have given the Israelis a go-ahead.

What followed became a morass of deals with Iran, related both to reopening ties with Teheran and to getting back the American hostages in Lebanon. Most were through Iranian arms dealer Manucher Ghorbanifar, a man with a shadowy past of dealings with intelligence services including Iranian, American, and Israeli. There were two Israeli arms deals, in September and November 1985, and in the second the Israelis bungled their shipment (routing it through

Portugal without appropriate clearances) and came to the United States for help. The United States government became compromised as a result—McFarlane personally intervened with the Portuguese foreign minister, while the CIA was called in to provide an aircraft, which was in fact contracted from Southern Air Transport.

At Langley, DDCI John McMahon objected to use of CIA services without a Presidential Finding. Meanwhile, McFarlane resigned his NSC post in December, to be replaced by Admiral John M. Poindexter, who was in turn asked by the CIA around Christmas for an appropriate finding. Langley's legal counsel, Stanley Sporkin, also requested that the finding retroactively approve the CIA's November involvement. A finding was drafted by the CIA and NSC in collaboration and approved on January 17, 1986. The finding contained a provision that Congress *not be informed* of the operation and that it be carried out by private citizens acting as authorized agents of the United States government. Such a private individual—General Richard V. Secord—was present at a drafting meeting in the White House Situation Room on January 11 to be introduced to Agency principals.

Through 1986, Secord carried out negotiations on arms deals, organized shipments to Iran, and supported the operations in progress. McFarlane was called back to go along on one mission in May 1986 to talk with the Iranians directly in Teheran. A fundamental divergence developed in that the United States officials assumed that all of the hostages would now be released while the Iranians had no such understanding. Secord's team spent the summer of 1986 trying to open a second channel to Iran, bypassing the Ghorbanifar link which was considered completely discredited.

A second channel was opened, one further arms transaction was arranged, but Ghorbanifar learned of the second channel and struck back by revealing the arms trading. The McFarlane visit to Teheran was reported in a leaflet distributed in Teheran, and a few weeks later appeared in the Lebanese magazine *Al Shiraa*. The revelation of the Iran arms deals, together with certain events simultaneously happening in Nicaragua, ignited a firestorm in the United States that threatened the Reagan presidency.

The United States got back three of its hostages, the Reverend Benjamin Weir, Father Lawrence Jenco, and David P. Jacobsen. It sold 2,008 antitank missiles to Iran, plus spare parts and HAWK antiaircraft missiles. But on the streets of Beirut the terrorists grabbed four more American hostages plus the British hostage mediator Terry Waite. The CIA station chief, poor Bill Buckley, was tortured for months to extract information on CIA operations and methods. Buckley expired in the summer of 1986, leaving what is reputed to be a four-hundred-page debriefing. The CIA was grievously wounded. In the meantime the NSC man supervising the arms sales, Marine Lieutenant Colonel Oliver North, had given the Iranians a representative sample of the intelligence that could be available in a cooperative arrangement with the United States.

In Graham Fuller's 1985 paper exploring possible signals the United States could send Iran, he told Bill Casey that an attack on Iran's radical ally Libya could demonstrate United States resolve and possibly remove Libyan dictator Muammar Qaddafi. Fuller's suggestion was but another sally in a little conflict the Reagan administration carried out on the side against Libya, a war that was partly overt, partly covert, and always rather nasty.

The main substantive issue between the two countries concerned law of the sea and airspace. Libya claimed a lot more of the Mediterranean than the seafaring United States was willing to concede. American reconnaissance planes had been overflying Libya since 1972, hoping to detect the successive Soviet weapons shipments to Qaddafi. There were some air incidents during peripheral reconnaissance missions in 1973. There was also the question of Libyan intervention in the civil war in Chad, and threats against the Sudan and Egypt. The Reagan administration intervened in Chad against the Libyans, sent radar aircraft to Sudan, and built a close military relationship with Egypt. It also inaugurated a series of provocative naval cruises into the Gulf of Sidra, the Mediterranean bay disputed by Libya and the United States.

In August 1981 an air incident occurred during one of these naval forays, in which two Libyan interceptors were shot down by Navy fighters when they approached in a hostile manner. Reagan reiterated his position on international waters. Thereafter the Navy's Sixth Fleet conducted one of these deployments off Libya once a year to assert an American naval presence.

The die for conflict was probably cast in late 1981 when there were reports that Qaddafi had sent a five-man assassination squad specifically to murder Ronald Reagan. The reports triggered a spate of security consciousness in the United States capital, where anti-terrorist measures were put into effect at the White House, the

Capitol Building, and other government offices, including the Pentagon, where public spaces under the building were put off limits for the first time in its history. The hit team reports seemed plausible because it was known that Qaddafi *was* behind a terror campaign targeted at his opponents in the Libyan exile community; there had been maybe two dozen incidents since the 1970s. This time the intelligence was wrong, however; it had apparently been willfully fabricated by Iranian arms dealer Manucher Ghorbanifar for unknown reasons. Yet the hit team report was taken at face value because it fit with the Reagan administration preconceptions about "state-sponsored terrorism." How Ghorbanifar managed to get NSC officials in 1986 to take him as a credible intermediary in the Iran arms sales must be a story of great irony.

On the covert side, the CIA, as with the Iranians, was in touch with the pockets of opposition among the Libyan exiles. It is reported that French intelligence took the initiative in 1981 to suggest to the CIA joint action in Libya, and also that the Saudis contributed $7 million to an opposition group the CIA backed. John Stein, who had been station chief in Tripoli from 1972 to 1974, when Qaddafi was consolidating his power, did not think it amiss now to try this project, although McMahon was less enthusiastic over the prospect. The Libyan group, recommended by the Saudis from among approximately twenty opposition coalitions, was called the National Front for the Salvation of Libya; it called for Qaddafi's overthrow in its first public declaration on October 7, 1981. Several years later the group hatched a plan to assassinate Qaddafi and take over the government. The attempt was carried out on May 8, 1984, even though the military leaders of the group had been caught and killed two days before as they tried to cross into Libya from Tunisia. There was a five-hour gun battle in Tripoli, less than a mile from Qaddafi's headquarters, but the rebel group was crushed. Reports are that over twenty thousand Libyans were picked up for interrogation, and that at least two hundred were executed in the aftermath. In all this the CIA had apparently bypassed a more legitimate opposition leader, Abdel Moneim Huni, who had been one of the first dozen members of Colonel Qaddafi's original Revolutionary Command Committee.

The Reagan administration then turned back to more overt methods. An intelligence community vulnerability assessment completed on June 18, 1984, concluded that "no course of action short of stimulating Qaddafi's fall will bring any significant and enduring change in Libyan policies." In the summer of 1985 a special national intelligence estimate warned again of Libyan cooperation with terrorists. A paper at that time by CIA's top intelligence analyst Robert M. Gates observed that a United States–Egyptian operation against Libya would offer an opportunity to "redraw the map of North Africa." Bill Casey subsequently ordered a detailed CIA analysis of targets in Libya. There was then consideration of a project called Flower by the NSC. At the beginning of September, Admiral Poindexter and another senior NSC official went to Egypt to discuss a joint operation with President Hosni Mubarak.

The Egyptians were not forthcoming on this occasion. "Look Admiral," Mubarak is reported to have said, "when we decide to attack Libya it will be our decision and on our timetable."

At the beginning of November it was reported in the American press that Ronald Reagan had approved some sort of plan aimed at Qaddafi. But the military was not happy with Flower. The Joint Chiefs produced an analysis that concluded that ninety thousand troops would be needed to fight Libya, a force that was entirely unattainable. Nevertheless, destructive terrorist attacks at the Rome and Vienna airports toward the end of December renewed President Reagan's insistence on action. In early January 1986 the Sixth Fleet conducted maneuvers in the Gulf of Sidra once more. The following month the Joint Chiefs' senior policy planner, Lieutenant General Dale A. Vesser, was sent again to Egypt and got commitment for joint aeronaval maneuvers off the coast that summer.

Sixth Fleet maneuvers continued in the vicinity of Libya in March. On the twenty-fourth the Libyans fired five antiaircraft missiles, unsuccessfully, at United States planes. The Americans retaliated with strikes on several missile bases and two Libyan patrol boats in the gulf, both of which were sunk. On April 5 there was a terrorist blow in Berlin, where a discotheque frequented by American soldiers was bombed in an action connected with the Libyans. Reagan called for more forceful measures, for striking at the source of terror. Ambassador Vernon Walters was sent on a mission to gather support from European allies. In an operation called El Dorado Canyon, on April 15 Air Force F-111 and Navy A-6E jets struck at three targets around Tripoli, including Qaddafi's headquarters at Aziziyah Barracks, and two other military targets near Benghazi. One F-111 with two crewmen was lost in the raids.

A few days after the Tripoli bombing, Secretary of State George Shultz spoke optimistically about unrest in Libya that might topple Qaddafi. Such speculation struck a responsive chord at Langley if not in Libya, and a campaign of political and psychological pressure was proposed to Casey, who sent his deputy director for intelligence, Richard Kerr, and his Middle East operations chief, Thomas Tweeten, to the White House to propose the concept to Admiral Poindexter. The idea then went to the State Department for further examination from Richard Clarke of the Bureau of Intelligence and Research, and Arnold Raphael and Michael Ussery of State's Near East bureau. They in turn produced a seven-page paper on August 6, 1986, advocating a mix of "real and illusionary events" that would induce Qaddafi to so pressure his military that they might act against him. This plan was discussed the next day at the NSC Crisis Pre-Planning Group where only the military opposed it, and on August 14 by the NSPG with President Reagan in attendance.

The result was a formal disinformation operation against Libya. This involved placing news stories fabricated by the CIA in foreign media, more naval maneuvers by the Sixth Fleet, and another Vernon Walters mission to Europe. The United States also used its joint maneuvers with Egypt to suggest the ease of potential action against Libya. In late August, *The Wall Street Journal* carried a story that noted the United States was on a "collision course" with Libya. As journalists dug for that story, they uncovered the disinformation plan and concluded that the American media was being manipulated by the administration as part of the plot. The latest attempt on Libya collapsed of its own weight while the Reagan administration soon had its hands full defending itself on several fronts.

Angola is one more covert action that deserves brief mention. The United States had been out of that one since the failure of Operation Feature, but the Reagan administration saw itself as the patron of anti-Soviet action worldwide, a stance elevated to the level of the "Reagan Doctrine." Jonas Savimbi and UNITA had gone on fighting the MPLA with support from South Africa and he certainly wished to get the United States back on board. UNITA hired a high-powered Washington firm, Black, Manafort, Stone and Kelly, to do public relations work and Savimbi made a highly publicized visit to the United States in early 1986. Despite the opprobrium of working alongside the South Africans, whose internal problems are even sharper now than in the 1970s, the administration was unable to resist the lure. An initial covert program was set up with $10 million to $15 million, and UNITA was reportedly supplied with fifty Stinger antiaircraft missiles. The materiel is thought to be funneled through an airfield at Kamina in southeastern Zaire.

There can be no doubt that covert action is popular with Ronald Reagan's administration. Projects planned for Surinam and Mauritius were canceled because of congressional opposition or blown cover but there have been plenty of others to occupy Langley. More than fifty covert operations were reportedly in progress by 1984, about half of them in Central or South America, including both paramilitary action and espionage. This number represents a 500-percent increase from the last year of the Carter administration.

Langley was not the only institution to be galvanized by Reagan administration policy. The Pentagon got the dollars for an across-the-board military buildup. Increases toward a "600 ship Navy," larger "multiyear" buys of aircraft, and the addition of Army "light" divisions tailored for counterinsurgency and "low-intensity combat," are among the better-known initiatives in Secretary of Defense Caspar Weinberger's program. Much less known has been the expansion of the special-warfare forces.

Repeated additions to Army forces result from plans laid down early in the administration. In 1981, Secretary Weinberger's Defense Guidance directive instructed each of the armed services to develop special-operations capability. Army Secretary John O. Marsh, Jr., who approved a 1,200-man increase for the Green Berets, gives the largest share of credit for the Defense Guidance initiative to the deputy secretary of defense for policy, General Richard G. Stilwell.

During 1984 the Army, after a decade, reactivated its 1st Special Forces Group at Fort Lewis, Washington, with one battalion deployed forward on Okinawa. Manpower reached 4,000 in four active Army Green Beret groups, with four more in reserve. The Army now has regular Special Forces groups available on both coasts, plus a Special Operations Command at Fort Bragg. There are also the two special-operations battalions (Delta and Blue Light), a civil affairs battalion, and a dozen psychological warfare battalions in four groups. Impressed by the performance of its two elite Ranger battalions in the 1983 invasion of Grenada, moreover, the Army has added a third Ranger battalion along with a regimental headquarters. An additional Special Forces group is slated for activation in fiscal 1989 under current Pentagon planning.

The ground component of Army Special Forces is supported by an aviation detachment of the 101st Air Assault Division, based at Fort Campbell, Kentucky. Nicknamed the "Night Stalkers," men assigned to the unit, Task Force 160, wear civilian clothes on their "black" missions. They fly an assortment of helicopter types like an air-commando unit, ranging from the UH-60 "Black Hawk" to the heavy load CH-47 "Chinook."

Task Force 160 does a lot of night flying and conducts highly classified operations on behalf of the services. In 1983 the unit suffered almost half (seventeen of thirty-five) of all aviation fatalities admitted by the Army for the year. If the USAF had had its way, Task Force 160 would have become even more important. Special air warfare components of the Air Force operate certain helicopters often used in support of the Army unconventional warfare force. As part of an armed forces joint-cooperation program adopted early in 1984, the Air Force wanted to transfer these assets to the Army and divest itself of the function. A transfer of USAF responsibility in this area was blocked in September 1985 by Deputy Secretary of Defense William Howard Taft IV, who directed both services to retain some capabilities for the long-range special-operations function.

Despite a considerable increase in defense spending for aviation special forces, by 1985 there were fewer aircraft available than in 1980, the last year of the Carter administration. Air Force long-range helicopters in the order of battle had declined to only seven HH-53s at Hurlbut in Florida. The service has been ordered to increase this force, while the helicopters are being given added avionics in the "Pave Low" program. The Army is modifying its CH-47s to refuel in the air, an effective "self-deploying" capability. The probable force goal is to give each of the United States theater commanders-in-chief a forward-deployed, heavy-helicopter detachment already integrated with his special-operations command.

Some of this ambitious effort is undoubtedly intended to avoid the kind of ad-hoc patching together of operations among the services that occurred at Sontay and again in Iran. This problem was underlined once more by the United States invasion of Grenada, according to a careful reconstruction by military analyst Richard A.

Gabriel. In fact, operation Urgent Fury, as the Pentagon dubbed its assault on the Caribbean island, may have been something of a debacle for the special-operations forces. Perhaps for this reason Urgent Fury is among the most secret support efforts carried out by Task Force 160.

The Grenada invasion followed a coup attempt in a feud between factions of a political movement considered unfriendly by the Reagan administration. Reminiscent of the Dominican Republic intervention ordered by LBJ in 1965, Urgent Fury had the objective of protecting American citizens, in particular medical-school students attending two colleges on Grenada. This pretext was indispensable given that Grenada, an island of 344 square kilometers and a population of about 112,000 at the time, could hardly be construed as a serious threat to United States interests. Administration strategic arguments centered on the potential for Grenada's use by the Cubans to expand their own influence, and the danger that advanced Soviet or Cuban aircraft might someday base at a large airfield being constructed there.

Whatever its justification, Urgent Fury was planned and mounted in the space of a week, and executed on the night of October 24–25, 1983. It began with a setback for the special-operations forces. For them, at least, Urgent Fury evidently proceeded from one crisis to the next in a tale of mishaps and aborted assaults.

The first step of the landing was a parachute drop by a detachment of Delta Force commandos. The team of thirty-five to forty troopers was supposed to scout and prepare the airfield at Point Salines, where the Americans planned to land a composite Ranger battalion at dawn. The troopers were flown in by an unmarked C-130 from Barbados. The insertion of the Delta team went according to plan, but on the ground the men were discovered during the night, igniting a firefight with Cuban soldiers and construction workers housed near the airfield. Delta was pinned down and could not clear the runway, forcing the Rangers to parachute in. Gabriel estimates that over half the Delta troopers were wounded or killed before Rangers could drive off the Cubans.

Another team from Delta was slated to land from helicopters in the morning to seize the Richmond Prison, on a hillside outside St. Georges, overlooked by the Fort Frederic military facility. By this time the Grenadian defenses had long since been alerted as a result of the engagement with Green Berets at Point Salines. When the helicopters appeared to disgorge their loads of commandos, who had to rappel down ropes as there was no clear terrain for a landing zone, the defenders opened fire on the helicopters from above. Some of the craft aborted their landings and flew away to escape.

The helicopters were from Task Force 160. At least one of them was shot down, recorded on film by an American resident of Grenada. Other photographs taken during the operation clearly showed Hughes 500 helicopters, which had never officially been procured by the Army, as well as another type that had been dropped from the inventory years before. Army spokesmen later admitted to at least one Task Force 160 fatality on Grenada, helicopter pilot Captain Keith Lucas, but continue to insist that the other sixteen deaths incurred by the unit in 1983, all from only two companies of the aviation battalion, occurred during training flights. Discrepancies between the number of helicopters the Army claimed to have lost in the invasion, and the number requested in the next defense budget to replace Grenada losses, suggest that as many as ten losses were not admitted. It is likely that some of these also belonged to Task Force 160.

Mishaps also befell the Navy's Sea-Air-Land groups (SEALs), who had an important role in Urgent Fury. In one instance a party of twenty-two SEALs landed on the grounds of Government House with the intention of evacuating Governor General Paul Scoones to the helicopter carrier *Guam*, which lay offshore. Instead, Cuban and Grenadian troops surrounded the residence, making helicopter evacuation impossible, and besieging the SEALs for two days before Marines reached their position. Up to half the commandos are reported to have been wounded.

Meanwhile, two four-man SEAL teams boated ashore west of Point Salines to disrupt the broadcasts of Radio Free Grenada. One team came under heavy fire, with two killed and the others wounded, the second only succeeded in extricating the survivors and escaping to sea. Two additional four-man SEAL teams, intended to reconnoiter Marine landing zones at Pearls, were completely incapacitated. One team suffered a landing accident and was apparently drowned, while the other team was unable to reach shore after a malfunction of the outboard motor powering their rubber landing boat. These SEALs had to be recovered by a Navy ship hours later. One mission that worked was the seizure of the island's diesel generating plant by another detachment of sixteen SEALs.

All the unconventional warfare elements of Urgent Fury were

coordinated by the Joint Special Operations Command, formed for this purpose after the miscarriage of the Iranian rescue mission. It is worth noting that several months after Urgent Fury the operations staff section of the command was reorganized and many of its personnel transferred. The Pentagon has refused to confirm the presence of the SEALs, Delta, or Task Force 160 on Grenada, although it has never refuted the Gabriel account of the invasion. The death of Captain Lucas was conceded after ABC News showed the film of his helicopter being shot down. Gabriel also reports that Delta personnel had to be dissuaded from filing cowardice charges against another Task Force 160 pilot. The Pentagon is similarly close-mouthed about other reports of activities by Task Force 160 in Central America.

The Department of Defense is somewhat more forthcoming concerning other Special Forces activities in Central America. These are controlled by a unified command, Southern Command, based in the Panama Canal Zone. There the 3rd Battalion, 7th Special Forces run a jungle-warfare training school. Mobile training teams work directly with Salvadoran government forces, training them to deal with the rebellion in that country. Salvadoran and Honduran army units are also trained at camps in Honduras by Green Berets, who have participated in nearly every exercise held there.

Special Operations Battalion Delta remains the highly trained unit it was under "Chargin' Charlie" Beckwith. Elements have deployed for possible counterterrorist action on several occasions, but were not used in earnest until the *Achille Lauro* affair of October 1985, when Palestinian extremists hijacked an Italian cruise ship, killing one American passenger and threatening others. Egyptian officials induced the terrorists to leave the ship with promises of a safe conduct to Tunisia but, determined to bring the Palestinians to justice, President Reagan ordered United States military action. Navy F-15 fighters intercepted the Egyptian airliner carrying the hijackers and forced it to divert to the NATO air base at Sigonella, Sicily.

Meanwhile, a Delta detachment had been moved to Sigonella by an Air Force C-141. When the airliner landed Delta troopers surrounded the plane and prepared to remove the Palestinians. But Italian authorities considered the prisoners theirs since *Achille Lauro* was an Italian ship and Sigonella itself an Italian base. Italian security parked airfield vehicles around the C-141 to block it and brought up troops to surround Delta Force in turn. The soldiers of these NATO allies had an ugly face-off on the tarmac until the Americans let the Italians arrest the terrorists.

Members of Delta have also attracted attention in another less desirable context. Army auditors encountered a number of irregularities in accounting for clandestine funds spent from 1981 to 1983. At one point, over a quarter of Delta's roughly 300-man complement received reprimands. Participants in the secret operations ridicule the investigation for trying to apply standard cost-accounting techniques to covert action. On the other hand, items procured for supposedly clandestine missions included a Rolls-Royce and a hot-air balloon. At least four quiet courts-martial and a civil criminal indictment followed the inquiry.

The civil trial flowed from false statements allegedly made by Lieutenant Colonel Dale E. Duncan, justifying expenses by Business Security International, a private firm that Duncan created and ran in 1983 as a cover for Army clandestine activities. Irregularities amounted to over a third of the $158,000 advanced by the Army over a six-month period to the ostensible civilian security consulting firm. Duncan denies the charges but was convicted by a federal court in February 1986. Duncan's conviction was overturned later by a federal appeals court. He still faces an Army court-martial. Another Business Security International employee, Green Beret Master Sergeant Ramon Barron, was acquitted of court-martial charges in December 1985, while a staffer of the Army's Special Operations Division, Lieutenant Colonel James Longhofer, was also hauled before a military court. In April 1986, Colonel Longhofer was convicted by court-martial and sentenced to two years' confinement.

Some questionable expenditures have clearly been made in behalf of the service covert program by individuals acting privately. There is no way to tell what proportion of the $150 million reported to have passed through Army covert accounts from 1981 to 1983 may be involved. Use of this method of cover on such a scale was evidently encouraged by a new Army entity, the Intelligence Support Activity (ISA). The Duncan company referred to above, for example, had the code name Yellow Fruit and could have been an ISA unit. A Yellow Fruit bank account in Switzerland has been linked with monies used to assist Nicaraguan rebels. Similarly, the phone number listed by a Panamanian company used as a front by individuals working with the Nicaraguan rebels led to a Pentagon security office.

General Richard Stilwell, a sort of *éminence grise* of the Pentagon's intelligence community, greatly stimulated ISA growth. The unit was originally set up by the Army as the Foreign Operations Group (FOG) during the Iran crisis and existed for over a year without the knowledge of the secretary of defense or the justification of a Presidential Finding. It was then made permanent. The ISA has also been connected to operations in the field. These include furnishing intelligence support for a foray into Laos by former Green Beret "Bo" Gritz; an apparent operational role in the January 1982 freeing of General James Dozier, then being held by Italian terrorists; field activities in El Salvador in 1982; and gathering intelligence for Nicaraguan rebels. A number of actions designed to recover American hostages in Lebanon involved ISA. An operational component of ISA may be the Counterterrorist Joint Task Force, of fewer than twenty men, based at Fort Bragg.

The Navy has also increased its capabilities, which reside in two Naval Special Warfare groups. The units operate two Special Boat Squadrons, each with three boat units; three Naval Special Warfare Units, with a total of five SEAL teams and two SEAL delivery vehicle units. A sixth SEAL team was added in 1984, raising the number of actual SEAL platoons (the Navy's equivalent to the Green Beret A Team) from forty-one to about fifty. Future plans include formation of two more of the teams, roughly comparable to Special Forces battalions. Two enlisted SEALs perished in December 1984 in a demolition accident during a training exercise in Honduras.

In 1986 the Navy adopted a special-warfare master plan projecting its activities for the next five years. A force of 1,987 SEALS, set by a 1982 directive, is to be expanded to 2,927, though the number of units is to remain the same. SEAL Team 6, of between 175 and 200 men, is reportedly now specialized in counterterrorist functions. Two other SEAL units, deployed on both coasts, have been reorganized as underwater demolition teams since 1983. Under the new plan smaller SEAL teams will be forward deployed to Puerto Rico, Scotland and Hawaii, and new facilities will be constructed in Antigua, Puerto Rico and Hawaii. The Navy has established a Special Warfare Directorate in its office of the chief of operations.

For underwater insertion there are submarines fitted to attach dry dock well capsules plus submarine delivery vehicles to move SEALS inshore. By 1991 the Navy expects to have seven subs equipped to carry capsules, six of these with shelters, and the first of a generation of advanced submarine delivery vehicles. Surface missions can use short- and medium-range assault boats. The short-range craft was quietly designed and produced in the early 1980s. In May 1984, RMI Inc. of National City, California, received the contract to design the medium-range boat, a ninety-five-foot high-speed craft. The Navy expected to acquire nineteen by the fall of 1990 for $242 million. These plans are now in jeopardy after failure to meet design specifications and irregularities in the program. RMI filed for bankruptcy in August 1986; the Navy took over the prototype air cushion boat, still only 60 percent finished at two and a half times the planned cost. It seems unlikely the Navy can meet its requirements in this area. The Marine Corps, arguing that Marines have natural ability as Special Operations Forces (SOF), provide the teeth and tail that can augment SEAL landing parties.

The Air Force contribution is a Special Operations Wing with five squadrons and a helicopter detachment. Three additional squadrons are in U.S. Air Force Reserve forces, along with two group headquarters. A major Air Force initiative in 1984 was the formation of an Air Division command for the special-warfare people, improving the status and increasing the command span of the force. Major procurement programs include an upgrade of the EC-130E "Volant Solo II" aircraft, and production of twenty-two new MC-130 "Combat Talons" plus a number of HH-60D "Night hawks." The newer aircraft have highly sophisticated avionics systems capable of low-altitude precision navigation at night and in bad weather. In the meantime, however, there were fewer Air Force active aircraft available to SOF in 1984 than in 1980, despite Reagan administration spending increases.

At the Pentagon level an effort is being made to centralize management of the roughly fifteen thousand men and $1.2-billion budget of the SOF. A Joint Special Operations Agency was created under JCS. It was responsible for interservice research and development, joint training and doctrine, and strategic planning, but it had no command powers. Many were not satisfied with this, and SOF reform became attached to the strong congressional initiative for reorganization of the Defense Department. Legislation was enacted in the fiscal 1987 defense budget providing a unified SOF command with status equal to, say, the Strategic Air Command or the rapid deployment force. In April 1987, General James J. Lindsay of the Army was selected as the first commander-in-chief, with headquarters at MacDill Air Force Base in Tampa, Florida.

This selection of MacDill for the SOF command aroused intense dismay from the panel that has been the catalyst for many of the recent changes, the Special Operations Policy Advisory Group (SOPAG). The advisory panel believed the command should be located in the Washington area, because of its sensitive role, to interact with other agencies and the NSC. The panel also protested Secretary of Defense Caspar Weinberger's own failure to nominate an assistant secretary for special operations as required by the reorganization legislation. Six members of the advisory panel sent nearly identical letters in March 1987 while two more went even further.

Weinberger's own office had taken the initiative to form SOPAG in March 1984. This flowed from a panel study of low-intensity warfare done for Fred Ikle, the undersecretary for policy. The panel report recommended a *reduction* in levels of violence used in counterinsurgency, more training to small units, and an emphasis on human rights training. This panel was chaired by General John K. Singlaub, and its report was briefed to President Reagan at a full NSC meeting. The SOPAG panel was formed to follow up the work of Singlaub's group. Its members have included Singlaub himself and Major General Richard Secord. Current SOPAG members are General Robert C. Kingston, General Edward "Shy" Meyer, Lieutenant General Samuel Wilson, Lieutenant General Richard Yarborough; Lieutenant General Leroy D. Manor, Brigadier General Donald D. Blackburn, Professor Richard Shultz, and General Richard G. Stilwell.

The Reagan administration has made key choices for the future development of special warfare. Yet the debate on directions is far from over. Between Pentagon dragging of feet and competition from Langley there is room for many outcomes. Many believe that the national character of covert action demands central control, in effect a new armed service. Others argue that the present arrangements are already effective. Some support giving the special-warfare function entirely to the CIA, or alternately the Pentagon.

While the policy issues remain unsettled, in the Third World the secret wars go on. Perhaps the most visible secret war in progress today, a war mired in discord and abuse of authority, which ultimately led to investigations akin to those of Watergate or the Church committee, is the covert action against Nicaragua.

·XVIII·

BILL CASEY'S
WAR

What is striking about the Nicaragua campaign is the great fervor with which it has been conducted. Here the secret warriors have had their chance to wage an all-out paramilitary campaign in which the special-warfare forces, the regular military, and CIA worked together to put intense pressure on a small Third World country. Green Berets and SEALS provided practical expertise; Langley bought the weapons and provided leadership. The campaign exploited the presence and assistance of other countries and used the classic elements of paramilitary and political action.

The fervor of the Nicaragua campaign is remarkable because there has been little evident consensus at Langley over whether a Nicaragua campaign is either feasible or necessary. The analysts predicted that the Managua government could not be overthrown. The top secret-warrior, Director of Operations John Stein, has been widely reported as opposing the action and its expansion.

Casey's thinking on Nicaragua has been at one with that of President Reagan. Not only has the President made the required decisions, he has lent his personal influence to the operators in covert action. In fact, the covert aspect of the "special activity" was abandoned altogether in an apparent attempt to coerce Nicaragua. White House determination to pursue the campaign ultimately led to a showdown with Congress over intelligence oversight, and international embarrassment of the United States because of the character of its activities. How this came to pass is a story that illustrates many of the dangers of covert action.

The covert action began very soon after President Reagan's inauguration. By March 1981 he had approved a Presidential Finding that an operation was desirable to halt the flow of arms to guerrillas in the neighboring nation of El Salvador, where American military assistance was attempting to shore up the government against another rebellion. The finding went to the National Security Planning Group, which approved detailed preparations. There was support for the concept from both the Pentagon and the State Department.

The first order of business was to assemble like-minded allies. CIA officers opened contacts with antigovernment Nicaraguans but not much could be done without a base. Honduras, bordering Nicaragua to the north, fell into line behind the United States policy, at a minimum turning a blind eye to anti-Nicaragua efforts. Costa Rica, to the south, would come later. A most significant addition was Argentina, which agreed to provide training and some advisers after discussions (which were subsequently denied) with Reagan ambassador-at-large Vernon Walters.

Most of the pieces were in place by the fall of 1981, when Bill Casey came back to the President with a concrete covert action proposal. This plan was discussed by the NSC in mid-November and approved by Reagan in NSDD-17, which he signed on November 23. The plan provided for CIA support and recruiting for a force of five hundred, which it acknowledged could be supplemented by another one thousand Nicaraguan rebels being trained by the Argentines, with an initial budget of $19 million. In an effort not to be restricted to these forces or this funding level, the plan also allowed that the rebels could collect intelligence inside Nicaragua and carry out political action and paramilitary missions. The plan was supposed to rely primarily on non-Americans, though it provided for direct CIA paramilitary action against special targets. The goal was to eliminate an alleged "Cuban presence" and Cuban-Nicaraguan "support structure" in Nicaragua.

The matter of the Cubans must be central to any explanation for the Nicaragua covert action. The Reagan White House was as vehemently anti-Castro as had been John Kennedy's. President Reagan believed the Salvadoran civil war was due to Cuban intervention, and that Nicaragua was the conduit for that support. The President was encouraged in these views by the State Department, then under Alexander Haig. Not able to strike directly at Cuba, the White House wanted to "interdict" aid through Nicaragua. In a way, then, the Nicaragua campaign is a renewed manifestation of the long-standing hostility toward Castro's Cuba.

One indication of American determination to pursue Nicaragua is the extremely harsh rhetoric employed to criticize the government of that Central American country. That government is headed by leftists, specifically the Frente Sandinista de Liberación Nacional (FSLN), which came to power at the head of the popular revolution that deposed Anastasio Somoza. The Nicaraguan dictator did not relinquish the reins of power without a struggle, naturally; Somoza's hillside bunker overlooking Managua had been the nerve center of a counterinsurgency war waged by the national guard under his personal direction. In the vernacular, the revolutionaries became known as Sandinistas; the national guard and its allies, Somocistas. In the CIA's covert action, the support was sent to an opposition with a core of Somocistas who fought a popular Sandinista government. Moreover, the Sandinistas themselves were a coalition of five erstwhile resistance groups, not a monolithic communist, or even Marxist, party. The ideological overlay served to obscure traditional wellsprings of Nicaraguan political conflict that had contributed to the Sandinista revolution.

Langley's operation in Nicaragua made use of existing opposition to FSLN. Managua officials talk hopefully about a "mixed economy," but government control of prices and of much of the supply, plus graft (yet to be eradicated by the revolution), progressively eroded middle-class support for FSLN. The earliest anti-Sandinista groups formed only a little more than a year after the revolution. In Miami, conservative labor leader José Francisco Cardenal and others formed the UDN (Unión Democrática Nicaraguense) and raised enough money to buy two hundred weapons from local gun shops. Volunteers for an armed force trained alongside anti-Castro Cuban enthusiasts at camps in south Florida. Former national guardsmen could join if they accepted civilian leadership. The military chief of staff was a U.S. Air Force veteran.

Another group had closer ties to Somocismo. This was the 15th of September Legion, its name taken from the date of Nicaraguan independence from Spain in 1821. The legion was formed in May 1981 by 308 veterans of the national guard. It was said to be financed by several hundred thousand dollars from Luis Pallais Debayle, a cousin of Somoza. The legion became active just as UDN organizers established themselves in Honduras to coordinate *contra* activities along the Nicaraguan border.

Simultaneously, several *contra* political leaders traveled to Argentina where they met at the Military College with Colonel Mario Davico, an aide to the chief of Argentine intelligence, then called Battalion 601. The Nicaraguans were reportedly given $50,000 in fresh $100 bills, and told that more money and training would follow if the UDN, the Legion, and several smaller anti-Sandinista groups would form an alliance. Further meetings followed in Miami, where Argentine Colonel José Ollas, reportedly using the cover name "Julio Villegas," informed the Nicaraguans that a three-way agreement had been made among the United States, Argentina, and Honduras to help the *contras*. In August 1981 the Nicaraguans proceeded to form a coalition called FDN (Fuerza Democrática Nicaraguense). Fifty *contras* were sent to Argentina for training, subsequently to become instructors at camps in Honduras. Villegas became chief of Argentine logistics; another colonel named Osvaldo Rivera became the chief of operations, supervising a cadre of about fifty advisers in Honduras and Costa Rica.

The man who would emerge as the top *contra* military commander was Enrique V. Bermúdez, a forty-seven-year-old former colonel in the national guard and a principal founder of the Fifteenth of September Legion. Bermúdez became second-in-command of the united FDN forces. A Sandinista spokesman noted at that time that Bermúdez had never been connected to war crimes prior to the revolution; it would have been difficult—Bermúdez was sent to Washington in 1975 for a course at the Inter-American Defense College and had stayed on for three more years as military attaché. When a united army of Sandinistas and national guard was possible for a short while in 1979, as part of a transitional government, Bermúdez was considered to lead it. He traces his own link to the Argentines to late 1980, when, he claims, seventy to eighty Legionnaires received training and were furnished with $300,000.

This question of timing is important as it bears on the initiation of the paramilitary action. The conservative Bermúdez made his claim in conversation with journalist Shirley Christian. Argentine participants, however, clearly date the inception of their activity to mid-1981. It is also at that time, in August 1981, that the United States lost an opportunity for diplomatic accommodation with the Sandinistas, according to former American ambassador Lawrence Pezullo. To Managua the United States' demands appeared both excessive and imperious, with a halt in arms shipments to El Salvador as a precondition to negotiation. In exchange for Nicaraguan concessions in five areas, the United States would have agreed to do no more than strictly enforce its neutrality laws against the *contras*. Sandinista reaction was so negative that no formal response was ever presented.

Most United States aid to Nicaragua was halted in March 1981, coincident with Reagan's Presidential Finding on covert action to halt Nicaraguan arms to El Salvador. All remaining aid was canceled that September. The Sandinistas further infuriated the State Department by their denials of serving as a conduit for arms and by their acceptance of assistance from Cuba. Castro soon sent over two thousand teachers and doctors, and reports of military advisers were current at the time President Reagan approved NSDD-17. The die was cast for action against the Sandinistas in 1981, not before.

Before the program began, the *contras* were merely playing at war. Once it was in place, there was the possibility of some real paramilitary action. Covert aid made all the difference; the transformation was visible on the ground, among the *contra* bands. In the early days, for example, the elite anti-Sandinista unit of the Fifteenth of September Legion, led by Pedro Ortiz Centeno, numbered less than a dozen men armed with shotguns and .22-caliber pistols. As a sergeant with the national guard's "Rattlesnake" Battalion, Ortiz Centeno had taken the *nom de guerre* "Suicide." "Suicide" liked to recount how his legion unit slipped across the border to assassinate selected Nicaraguan officials, but according to some the *contras* had acquired a reputation for robbery and indolence. In the eighteen months prior to July 1982, the Nicaraguan government recorded 45 gun battles, but 234 cases of cattle rustling.

According to the FDN chief of logistics, Captain Armando Lopez, the first CIA weapons arrived early in 1982. This shipment consisted of ninety-two Belgian automatic rifles, four machine guns, and two mortars. "We were all hugging," recalls Lopez, "we forgot about rank. We kissed our weapons. It seemed like a dream."

The first serious strikes occurred in mid-March 1982, when FDN units blew up two road bridges in northern Nicaragua. The next day the Sandinista government declared a state of emergency. By the end of March the government could point to six instances of real or attempted sabotage, including the destruction of a Nicaraguan civilian airliner by bomb in Mexico City during December 1981.

To Managua the threat seemed critical. Problems also proliferated along the Atlantic coast, traditionally inhabited by Indians of the Miskito, Suma, and Rama peoples. The minorities of this region were not effectively integrated into the national polity; FSLN leaders themselves admitted grave errors, including the imprisonment of a number of prominent Indian leaders. In January 1982 the government began to resettle about twenty thousand Indians from villages along the Coco River to camps farther away from the Honduran border. Indian resentment led to new anti-Sandinista forces—Misura (an acronym taken from the first letters of the tribes' names) and a later splinter group Misurasata. A political group originally formed by the Sandinistas themselves, Misura was turned around by Miskito Indian Stedman Fagoth Mueller, who moved to Honduras after revelation of his past service with Somoza's national guard and began to prepare armed bands there.

More headaches for Managua came from the disintegration of the Sandinistas' own united front. A number of Nicaraguan officials and even Sandinista leaders went over to the opposition. One defector was Alfonso Robelo, formerly one of the nine-member Sandinista national directorate. Another was Edén Pastora Gomez, a senior military officer who had become famous fighting Somoza under the name "Commander Zero." Robelo and Pastora moved to Costa Rica where, in April 1982, Pastora announced the formation of a new opposition group called ARDE (Alianza Revolucionaria Democrática). There were other resignations and defections, too, but these were more attributable to Nicaraguan internal politics than to the covert action in progress.

To Washington the Sandinistas must have seemed particularly vulnerable because of the internal dissension, economic weakness, minority dissatisfaction, and presence of *contra* groups across both the northern and southern borders of Nicaragua. Washington organized this campaign within a larger framework of diplomatic and military action. American officials worked to deny international loans to Nicaragua and maneuvered carefully to limit the impact of the "Contadora" group of Latin American countries that attempted to mediate the conflict. United States air, naval, and ground units conducted an extensive series of exercises in Honduras and the waters off Nicaragua. Special Forces participated extensively, as did engineer units, which constructed facilities, including an airfield at El Aguacate that was left behind for use by the CIA program. Military aircraft on a number of occasions, as later documented by a General Accounting Office Report, flew *contra* supplies to this and other fields.

But, as the paramilitary effort gathered steam, the United States lost its Argentine allies. This came as a result of the 1982 Falklands war between Argentina and Great Britain, in which the Reagan administration took the British side following a failed attempt at mediation by Secretary of State Alexander Haig. In May, Argentina announced its withdrawal from Central America, including the Battalion 601 operation with the *contras*. The resulting gap seems to have been filled by other countries, although the evidence is still inadequate to document this involvement. There have been reports of Japanese collaboration with the Miskito, and repeated allegations of Israeli assistance. The Israelis were, at the time, openly selling arms to Honduras, which may also have facilitated Honduran aid to the *contras*. Argentina's involvement was documented toward the end of 1982 when Hector Francés, a Battalion 601 officer in Costa Rica, gave testimony on his country's activities.

With or without other countries, the United States had substantial resources available. The initial CIA stake was repeatedly raised—to $21 million in fiscal 1983, $24 million in fiscal 1984, for a total of about $80 million before funding was interrupted. Ambassador John Negroponte in Honduras, a former Kissinger aide, presided over the United States mission there. The embassy had 149 personnel assigned; there were 176 military men assisting the Honduran armed forces and 50 U.S. Air Force specialists manning an air search radar that overlooked Nicaragua from a site known as Carrot Top on Isopo mountain. Hundreds of U.S. Army troops, especially engineers on construction tasks, passed through during the succession of military maneuvers. Green Berets reportedly numbered 114 in the summer of 1983 and CIA officers about 150 at the end of 1982, with at least as many more stationed in El Salvador, only some of whom worked on the Nicaraguan operation.

Although there were few logistical difficulties with resources, with allies, or base areas—and although Managua still was vulnerable—the *contras* achieved little progress in 1982. They succeeded only in building forces. By the spring of 1983 the FDN claimed 7,000 men in Honduras; others credited it with 5,000. There were also perhaps 2,000 Miskito in Honduras, while Edén Pastora had another 700 in Costa Rica. The troops were divided into "task forces" that rotated their time between sojourns in base camps and forays into Nicaragua. The basic *contra* plan, to seize and hold territory inside Nicaragua then declare a provisional government, never seemed to materialize.

Internal political squabbling was the true obstacle to *contra* progress. Pastora and ARDE refused to accept volunteers who had been members of Somoza's national guard. The FDN had its own national guard problem, in the form of a struggle between factions favoring the leadership of Nicaraguan civilians and those preferring former military men. There were also delicate relations between the FDN and the Miskito groups, who reportedly were being short-changed on supplies in favor of the larger organization. Among the FDN troops in Honduras, Colonel Bermúdez demanded total loyalty and physically intimidated those he thought were not forthcoming. By the end of 1982, though he spent little time in the border camps, Bermúdez was the unquestioned military commander, and any remaining doubt concerned whether he would act independently.

At this stage the CIA stepped in to press harder for a broadened anti-Sandinista coalition. Langley's original marching orders specified use of Nicaraguan nationalists who were both anti-Cuban and anti-Somoza. As a former national guardsman, Colonel Bermúdez failed the second test.

In Miami in November 1982, CIA officers contacted a number of influential Nicaraguan exiles to discuss revitalizing the *contra* leadership. One exile leader, Edgar Chamorro, met with American officers who called themselves "Steve Davis" and "Tony Feldman." Chamorro presented a plan for a sort of congress of perhaps twenty-one leading Nicaraguans, in which Bermúdez would be merely one voice. In early December a new FDN leadership board, of eight civilians and five military men, was announced at a Miami press conference. Chamorro emerged as FDN public relations director, but all the exiles who appeared were primed first by CIA officers in a hotel room. It looked good to the media. *The New York Times* quoted Chamorro saying, "We want to give democracy a chance in Nicaragua."

But in Honduras, the FDN board did not have enough of a presence to exert much control. They succeeded in making only one visit to the camps as a group. More often individuals went to Honduras, but then they appeared as emissaries, with Bermúdez in the role of local potentate. On one occasion three *contra* intelligence officers actually told FDN representatives that Bermúdez and his chief of intelligence, Ricardo "Chino" Lau, who was the colonel's best friend, were plotting to kill them. The FDN directors were unable to do anything to investigate these charges, which Bermúdez simply denied.

Allegations by *contra* officers of human rights abuses inside Nicaragua actually were indicative of the kinds of abuses that became widespread as Bermúdez stepped up the scale of FDN operations, sending in 600- and 800-man units in early 1983. Nicaragua suffered twelve disappearances in 1981, eleven in 1982, and twenty-two in February 1983 alone. Virtually all of these occurred in provinces adjacent to the camps in Honduras. Some say it was a common practice to kill captured Sandinista soldiers and militiamen. There were reports of looting and rapes, of terrorist actions against coffee pickers, teachers, officials, and anyone found in a vehicle. Some observers traced these practices to Argentine advice—holding up Argentina's "dirty war" of the 1970s as the model for the *contras* to follow. Others saw *contra* terrorism as resulting from the predominance of national guardsmen, who had become accustomed to harsh methods during the Somoza-Sandinista civil war.

The *contras* have been sensitive about accusations of associations with the national guard since the birth of the anti-Sandinista opposition. Constantly striving to deny those allegations, they argued that only a small proportion of *contras* were national guardsmen. They were right in that, mathematically, guardsmen could not have made up the FDN force. The FDN troop strength was over 2,000 in 1983, when it was publicly claiming 7,000 men, and about 6,000 in June 1984, when it was claiming as many as 15,000. In the spring of 1987 *contra* leaders were claiming a current strength of 16,000 troops. Somoza's guard peaked at a strength of about 8,000 of whom nearly 5,000 were captured by the Sandinistas before the end of the civil war. There are reports that several thousand of those soldiers remain in Nicaraguan prisons. A generally accepted estimate of the Guard proportion of the FDN forces made up of former guardsmen is 20 percent.

These overall figures obscure the leadership role of the guard, however. Bermúdez is the obvious example but only the tip of an iceberg. When reporter Christopher Dickey was allowed to visit FDN camps in the spring of 1983, four of the five column commanders made available for him to interview were not only national guard veterans but came from the same "Rattlesnake" battalion of the Somoza forces. Column commander "Suicide," who also was a "Rattlesnake" veteran, rose to command two thousand FDN troops while boasting to journalists of his murders and other deeds. Ricardo Lau, the FDN intelligence chief, was notorious for his cruelty on behalf of Somoza while in the national guard. Lau even became an obstacle to *contra* political unity, as Edén Pastora cited him as an example of the worst kind of *Somocista* influence, and refused to incorporate ARDE with any united front in which Lau participated. Months after the FDN announced Lau's resignation, records *contra* propagandist Edgar Chamorro, "Lau was still the last person to talk to Bermúdez at night and the first person to talk to him in the morning." Honduran authorities obliged Lau to leave the country late in 1984. National guard participation remained the Achilles' heel of the *contras*.

Of all the members of the FDN directorate, Edgar Chamorro was the man in a position to know. Many of the directors spent their time raising support for the cause, especially Adolfo Calero Portocarrero, a tower of energy who worked sixteen-hour days on extended fund and consciousness-raising trips to Europe, the United States, and Puerto Rico, and regarded the CIA and the exiles as his constituency. Some of the directors stayed in Miami. But Chamorro set himself up in Tegucigalpa, the capital of Honduras, as the public voice of the FDN. Chamorro wrote the press releases and organized the visits of journalists to FDN camps. Soon his FDN office alone was spending $2,000 a month on creating a democratic image for the *contras*.

One of Chamorro's projects was a manual he called *The Blue and White Book* which discussed the meaning of social justice and democracy. This was distributed to FDN soldiers in the camps. Chamorro felt perhaps that the political education represented by the manual could help counteract the brutality of the military leadership and the excesses of war. But the constant stream of exhortation that the troops received from such other outlets as the FDN radio or the weekly newsletter *Commandos*, which Chamorro also ran, must have limited the impact of his manual.

In the summer of 1983, Chamorro was questioned by a journalist on FDN assassinations. Knowing that the troops in the camps commonly talked about murders and other incidents, the propaganda chief admitted that there had been some excesses. Increased criticism on human rights grounds resulted. Once again the CIA took direct action, after a mid-1983 visit to Honduras by Bill Casey, initiating another manual for use by the *contras*. Meanwhile, FDN tried to clean up its own act by disciplining a number of officers for egregious transgressions.

Contras criticized Chamorro for his admission but the former propaganda chief believes the FDN gained in credibility as a result of his forthrightness. The subsequent CIA manual, however, led to a major setback for Langley. Called *Psychological Operations in Guerrilla Warfare*, the *contra* manual was written by a CIA contract employee with the pseudonym "John Kirkpatrick," who worked with Chamorro several hours a day for a few weeks in Tegucigalpa. "Kirkpatrick" was a former Green Beret, and veteran of Korea and Vietnam who drank too much and denounced the FDN higher-ups while praising the common soldiers. Chamorro thought him not unlike a character out of a Graham Greene novel.

Kirkpatrick's manual relied on his Vietnam experience and postulated classical approaches to insurgency. *Psychological Operations* reprinted verbatim portions of three lesson plans reportedly used at Fort Bragg to train Special Forces in 1968. The manual did not shy away from advocating deliberate terrorism. One section spoke of hiring professional criminals for some activities. Another discussed the creation of "martyrs" to aid the cause, if necessary by arranging the death of the *contras'* own men. Other sections dealt with the selective use of violence, as in assassinating Sandinista officials to cow village populations. Later investigation disclosed that about a dozen low- and mid-level DDO officers reviewed the manual and excised material they thought objectionable. No one objected to the references to assassination, despite the repeated presidential and DCI directives.

Chamorro's doubts about Kirkpatrick were confirmed when, in November 1983, some two thousand printed copies of *Psychological Operations* arrived at his Tegucigalpa office. The FDN propagandist caught the references to hiring criminals and to killing the *contras'* own men. Upset, he locked the manuals in a room and hired two young boys to razor out the offensive pages and replace them by gluing in pages with relatively innocuous material.

In the field the *contra* war continued. From Honduran base camps the FDN mounted forays into Nicaragua with 80-man patrols and 200-man columns. Suicide had become a top combat commander with five columns under his leadership. The Miskitos were also active, while ARDE received its first CIA aid: communications gear, supplies, and 500 AK-47 assault rifles. Edén Pastora and Alfonso Robelo raised nearly 2,000 ARDE troops before the end of the year, while Miskito rebel strength also peaked that year at about 3,000.

Colonel Bermúdez spent most of his time at Tegucigalpa, where FDN had its headquarters, a radio station, and hospital. He planned for a big push through the summer and fall, styled operation Marathon. At Langley, WH Division chief Duane R. Clarridge thought that only two C-47s would be sufficient to resupply the incursions by FDN columns, partisan warfare on the cheap, as it were. Clarridge was close to Casey, the field marshal of the Nicaraguan campaign, but Agency cautions on the thinness of the resources were ignored.

The CIA began a major escalation after mid-1983. It supported an increase in FDN forces toward a target of 12,000 to 15,000. Langley's work on a guerrilla manual for the FDN was another facet of the support. At this time the CIA provided FDN and ARDE with their own air assets and began to prepare an independent campaign to isolate Nicaragua by mining its harbors, cutting off its supplies from abroad.

Contra progress fell short of that anticipated by the planners of Marathon. Just as it should have been gaining momentum, FDN fragmented under the weight of competing interests. In the base camps there was resentment at headquarters' remoteness from the front. There were also internal jealousies. Some of these came to a head in Suicide's camp, where "Krill," one of his top column commanders, openly murdered another unit commander. In the aftermath, Suicide's force, until then the largest operational grouping of FDN troops, splintered into small bands with thir own leaders.

In an effort to restore discipline in the organization, the FDN did appoint a field commander under Bermúdez. Suicide and Krill were brought in, after which both were apparently tried and executed. In the field, meanwhile, Marathon went nowhere. *Contra* emissary Adolfo Calero Portocarrero put the best face on events that September, with a claim that recruits were flocking to the FDN banner at a rate of 300 to 500 a week. A year later, in the fall of 1984, when some claims of FDN strength were as high as 20,000, a similar FDN plan reportedly called Dark Moon produced an equally unsuccessful offensive.

These operations were facilitated by the aircraft the CIA procured through private companies, perhaps a new generation of proprietaries. Five planes were procured by a McLean, Virginia, firm called Investair Leasing, which had a fictitious corporate address at Dulles International Airport. Three of these aircraft were military O-2A's, versions of a Cessna light plane, which were suddenly declared surplus in December 1983 and sent to Elephant Herd, a "multiservice tasking" of the Joint Chiefs of Staff and suitable cover for special activities. Two identical planes—like the O-2A's, also taken from the New York Air National Guard—were simultaneously sold to El Salvador. In February 1984 the planes were armed with rocket pods by Summit Aviation at a Delaware airfield.

A La Jolla, California, company called Armairco had been linked with two light planes that crashed inside Nicaragua—one while raiding Managua in September 1983, and another O-2A shot down during a raid at Santa Clara a year later. Armairco is known to have bought Cessnas direct from the manufacturer. Formed by a former Army major, Armairco has an East Coast branch called Shenandoah Airleasing, which admits that it "may well be" that they do classifed mission work in Central America.

The FDN was also given two venerable C-47 transports, provenance not known, and at least one such plane went to ARDE. Edgar Chamorro was derisive about these planes, telling a fellow FDN director to be sure to visit the National Air and Space Museum while he was in Washington, where he could see the same plane hanging from the ceiling. It is true that the C-47 has been flying for fifty years, but there are still twelve hundred of these planes in service and it is difficult to see how major resupply missions could be flown without medium transports. Still, Chamorro's fears proved somewhat justified in March 1984, when an ARDE C-47 crashed in northern Costa Rica. An unidentified Caucasian who died in that crash may have been a CIA casualty.

There were confirmed CIA casualties in October 1984, when a twin-engine Cessna crashed outside the Salvadoran military airfield of Ilopango. An Agency officer and three CIA contract agents were killed. The plane, crammed with equipment, had been on a night flight to gather intelligence on Sandinista communications and air activity. Other flights are reportedly carried out by Army aviation detachments, and the code name Royal Duke has been associated with similar U.S. Air Force flights using Beechcrafts from Honduran airfields.

The *contra* air campaign was desultory, at best. It was of harrassment value rather than having real interdiction capability. Managua has been raided a few times, Nicaraguan ports on more numerous occasions. There has been little significant damage. At least two FDN planes have been lost. A helicopter was also lost in a raid on Santa Clara on September 1, 1984, along with two more Americans, "free-lance" volunteers Dana H. Parker, Jr., and James Powell III. The Americans were from a private organization called Civilian Military Assistance, which had been active in Honduras since the fall of 1983, organizing shipments of clothing and medical supplies to the *contras*. Some shipments by this and other groups have been carried aboard military aircraft.

The operations against Nicaragua have been indirectly responsible for other American deaths among military men in Honduras. Army warrant officer Jeffrey Schwab was killed on January 11, 1984, when the helicopter he was piloting toward El Aguacate went off course into Nicaragua and was shot up by Sandinista soldiers. The following month, maneuvers led to the death of four Americans, with six others injured, including Green Berets, when their helicopter crashed on a transport flight. Two Navy SEALs perished in a maneuver accident in December 1984. Six American and eight foreign journalists should be added to the military deaths. Casualties inside Nicaragua from 1981 to 1984 totaled over twelve thousand out of a population of three million, while *contra* losses are still unknown.

Nicaragua has been Bill Casey's war as well as President Reagan's. Where Reagan set the policy, the DCI executed it, and William Casey was a very good presidential agent. Supervising the planning at Langley, Casey overrode the objections of the DDO in expanding the operation. In the field, Casey oversaw the arrangements of the case officers under their project director, who identified himself to one of the FDN directors as "Dewey Maroni." The DCI made at least one visit to Tegucigalpa in the early summer of 1982, when the machinery was just getting into gear. There was another trip in this period, to Japan, and about a year later reports began of a mysterious Japanese presence with the Miskito rebels. At the height of the controversy over *contra* human rights violations, in the summer of 1983, Bill Casey was in Honduras again; the guerrilla manual was assembled that fall.

In his determined pursuit of Nicaragua covert actions, Bill Casey ran afoul of the United States Congress in a way unprecedented for a director of central intelligence. Having assured Congress that he would be open to the intelligence committees, Casey as DCI progressively terminated various kinds of reporting that had been routine under the Carter administration. Casey's disdain for the oversight process was no secret at Langley, and it was no doubt reinforced by the painful controversies he endured during confirmation.

After two years of active conflict, the *contras* were unable to achieve any lasting measure of success. A CIA timetable that reportedly called for *contra* "liberated zones" before the end of 1983 had gone badly awry, with FDN failures to capture and hold towns in both years. Casey did his best to gloss the facts, telling Congress in 1983 that the Sandinistas might be overthrown in a year, only to be contradicted, by the American general commanding in Central America and by a leak that no intelligence estimates supported Casey's assertions, which he then claimed had been misunderstood.

The frustration of the secret warriors was mirrored at the highest levels of the United States government. Talk at the National Security Planning Group (NSPG) focused on how to break out of the cycle of *contra* ineffectiveness and military failure. In the discussions, Bill Casey, "Cap" Weinberger, and George Shultz all recognized that Managua was dependent on imports, in particular Soviet weapons and foreign oil. American military maneuvers in Central America had already featured naval task forces off the Nicaraguan coast; now NSPG members, harking back to Kennedy in the Cuban missile crisis, began to talk of a blockade. That involved open use of force, however, and was an act of war; an administration having so much trouble just getting its CIA project funds approved by Congress was not likely to be able to get a declaration of war. Over at least two meetings of the NSPG, Robert McFarlane recalls, attention settled on mining Nicaraguan harbors rather than involving United States military forces.

McFarlane believes it was Bill Casey who suggested the mining option. There was some preparatory work between the NSPG meetings, but the bureaucracy's analytical work was narrowly drawn, not a real risk-cost study. The obvious rejoinder to the mining suggestion—what happens when the mines sink a Soviet ship—surfaced at the NSPG. The decision was to make mines that were not capable of sinking large ships. Of course this robbed the mining of its military rationale. Ronald Reagan made the decision anyway. McFarlane concedes that it was "not one of the happiest episodes" of Reagan administration decision-making.

In the fall of 1983, Casey implemented the plans, attempting to isolate Nicaragua while doubling *contra* forces, creating a southern front, and providing the rebels with air assets. The isolation portion of the plan was carried out directly by the CIA, which was to mine Nicaraguan ports. For this purpose the CIA bought and outfitted an innocent-looking freighter as a mother ship, and assembled simple but effective mines whose prototype was a sewer pipe stuffed with explosives. Tests of the CIA design were held at the Naval Surface Weapons Center and the mines were assembled in Honduras. Reportedly about six hundred mines were produced.

The mother ship itself was leased by the CIA in the summer of 1983 and rapidly modified for its intended role. It was given extra communications and navigation gear and equipment to launch a small flotilla of heavily armed, high-speed motorboats. The mother ship acted as command post and could carry raiding parties to the more distant targets. It also carried an armed helicopter that could support the raids. Commando parties were mostly composed of FDN soldiers, but there was a cadre of other Latins and CIA contract agents, for underwater demolition and other specialized tasks. Contract employees occasionally piloted the helicopter while CIA officers exercised complete command control. The mother ship was first used in a raid on the Pacific coast port Corinto on October 10, 1983.

The assault reinforced a campaign that had already begun. Since the beginning of September there had been two raids at Puerto Sandino, a receiving point for oil deliveries to Nicaragua. There was also an attack on a pier at one town in the Gulf of Fonseca, apparently a suspected transshipping point for supplies to El Salvador.

Edén Pastora took little part in the port campaign, but sponsored an air raid on Managua that occurred on September 8. Two aircraft bombed the airport; one was lost when it flew so low that it was destroyed in the blast from its own bombs. Two ARDE airmen perished. Two United States senators, encouraged by DCI William

Casey to see Nicaragua for themselves, almost fell victims in the Managua bombing. Senators Gary Hart (D-Colorado) and William S. Cohen (R-Maine) were in the air en route to Managua when the attack happened. Their plane was late. Had it been on time, they would have been on the ground at Managua airport. The next day a T-28 aircraft ineffectually bombed the oil storage tanks at the major Pacific port Corinto. About a dozen of these planes were in service in the Honduran air fo. ce. On October 3 an FDN supply flight was shot down by Sandinistas over northern Nicaragua. One man among that crew died but two were taken prisoner; both had been national guardsmen.

A week later the CIA mother ship commanded another attack on Corinto. The raid used two speedboats, which positioned themselves behind an inbound Korean tanker, then peeled off to fire at the shore. Eight large storage tanks containing 3.4 million gallons of oil were set aflame. One freighter with a load of cooking oil suffered slight damage. Soon afterward the Exxon Corporation ordered its own tankers to avoid Nicaraguan waters. On October 21 the port campaign moved to the Atlantic coast with a raid on Puerto Cabezas, known to an earlier generation of spooks as the operational base for the Bay of Pigs.

With the CIA raid the secret war had come full circle for the people of one Nicaraguan village.

In late October the Sandinistas countered by declaring an offshore security zone twenty-five miles wide. Foreign military aircraft and vessels were supposed to secure permission to enter the zone two weeks in advance. While the United States Navy scrupulously observed the limits of territorial waters in conducting repeated De Soto patrols, Air Force SR-71's ostentatiously crossed the sound barrier over Nicaragua, hitting population centers with unnerving sonic booms. In the face of growing shortages, the Sandinistas were indeed forced to increase gasoline rationing by a further 10 to 30 percent. At Corinto twenty-five thousand residents had been temporarily forced from their homes by the oil fires.

The mining was intended to administer the final coup de grace to the Nicaraguan port network, which had handled 11,000 tons of cargo during 1983. It has not yet been established exactly when the mines began to go in, but Managua radio denounced them for the first time on January 3, 1984. Edgar Chamorro recalls being awakened by a CIA officer at two A.M. on the fifth, when he was handed a press release the Americans had prepared, in which the FDN claimed responsibility for the mining. Several days later the FDN went further and declared all ports in Nicaragua to be in a "danger zone."

A Japanese flag ship was mined outside Corinto on January 3 and had to be towed back into port. This was the first of a dozen ships from six different nations to be damaged in the mining campaign. There were also six raids within nine days on the port Potosi on the Gulf of Fonseca, in at least one of which a CIA contract agent piloted an armed Hughes-500 helicopter in combat. Puerto Sandino was attacked by as many as three speedboats supported by three helicopters.

All of these activities were justified by a revised Presidential Finding that the CIA submitted to Congress in September 1983. The finding evoked opposition at the time, with some members of Congress believing it too broad in scope. Bill Casey came back with a paper that, though somewhat narrower, asserted that halting alleged Sandinista export of revolution was the objective.

Throughout these years of the burgeoning Nicaragua operation, Congress had become increasingly uncomfortable with the program. Open-ended support for *contra* actions was difficult to reconcile with the vague and limited aims expressed in the findings. The Senate intelligence committee, chaired by Arizona Republican Barry Goldwater, was not unsympathetic to the aims of the Reagan administration, but its relations with Langley had soured after the controversy over the Casey appointment. The House select committee was even more suspicious. Still dominated by Democrats in consequence of the 1980 election, the House committee initiated legislation in 1982 and 1983 that explicitly prohibited funds being spent by the United States government for the overthrow of the government of Nicaragua. Called the Boland Amendment, after committee chairman Congressman Edward P. Boland, a Massachusetts Democrat who championed the legislation, this restriction passed into law as a secret clause of the fiscal 1983 appropriation (Public Law 97-377, Section 793), and again as an amendment to the 1985 defense budget bill (Public Law 98-473, Section 8066).

In view of the Boland Amendment, the CIA was clearly treading on thin ice in Nicaragua. Indeed, during this period the House of Representatives three times voted to reject paramilitary budgets for Nicaragua, funds that were restored by Senate-House conference committees. The shaky status of this program explains some of Reagan's motives for assuming such an active role, both supporting the *contras* rhetorically and assigning a coordination mission to the NSC staff.

None of this dismayed Bill Casey. Chamorro recounts, significantly, that the first direct approach from CIA to form a united-front came during the debate over the Boland Amendment. When the time came for the port campaign, the CIA was curiously circumspect about the information it gave Congress. Bill Casey personally conducted several of the more important briefings, so there is no doubt that his policy was to provide minimal information to the congressional watchdogs.

Essentially, the CIA used the *contra* connection both as cover for the mining and to mislead Congress. Early in the preparation of the campaign, Langley reported that some *contras* were being trained in mining techniques; then it left Congress to presume that the port campaign was being run by the FDN, Misura, and ARDE, whereas in reality the mining was largely a unilateral CIA operation. To evade the budget limit appropriated by Congress, the mother ship was apparently paid for directly out of the DCI's contingency fund. The presence of the mother ship at the big Corinto raid was not admitted until five months after the fact, while the combat participation of CIA contract pilots in January and March 1984 raids again was not acknowledged for months afterward. Briefings of the Senate committee that winter, at which this information might have emerged, were postponed at CIA request. The House committee received somewhat more information, but only because its staff asked some hard questions. To shield itself, the CIA made reference to the mining but only in a single sentence in a briefing of over two hours' duration.

In addition, the CIA mining project was a flagrant violation of internationl law. Not only did the mining obstruct freedom of the seas, but it was a deed clearly defined as an act of war by the 1856 Treaty of Paris and the Hague conventions of 1899 and 1907. This in turn raised questions regarding the CIA's authority for such an action under the War Powers Act. These considerations were brought to the fore on March 20, when the Soviet tanker *Lugansk* was mined outside Corinto and five Russian seamen wounded in the explosion. In the scramble to contain the flap, FDN leader Chamorro was told, by the same CIA officer who had instructed him to claim credit for the mining, to deny that any *contra* mines could have caused the incident.

Mounting danger to merchant ships sparked an international uproar. Domestic criticism also gained a fierce intensity. Congress overwhelmingly passed a resolution condemning a United States government action. Nicaragua brought suit against the United States in the International Court of Justice. The Reagan administration suddenly felt compelled to reverse the long-standing United States policy of recognizing the jurisdiction of the ICJ, with further adverse effects on world opinion. Among the countries lodging protests, in addition to the Soviet Union, were traditional allies Britain and France, and the French considered sending a minesweeper to help Nicaragua clear its waters.

The mining caused Nicaragua real damage. Toward the end of June, Nicaraguan fisheries minister Alfredo Alaniz announced that five fishermen had been killed, thirty injured, and thirteen fishing boats lost. The volume of imports was temporarily reduced while Nicaragua estimated it had lost $4.3 million in export income. Nicaragua's fishermen took the biggest risks as it was they who swept the mines, typically using two boats in tandem to drag chains across the sea floor. At Corinto by May, over thirty mines had been detonated, with two of the improvised minesweepers sunk. Damage at Corinto alone was estimated at $9 million. At the United Nations, only a veto by United States ambassador Vernon Walters prevented passage of a Security Council resolution condemning the United States.

At this juncture the Senate intelligence committee began to demand explanations of the mining and assert it had not been informed. Subsequent disclosures reveal that the House committee, the better informed of the two, only learned about CIA direction of the mining on March 27, when persistent questioning by two congressmen drove DCI Casey to this admission. Indeed, Bill Casey had been equally circumspect with the Senate committee: a single twenty-seven-word sentence in a March 8 briefing of more than eighty-four pages of text. That one reference merely stated that mines had been placed in Nicaraguan harbors by United States-backed groups—in effect the CIA cover story was given to the oversight committee. Chairman Barry Goldwater resorted to blistering criticism of the CIA; his vice-chairman, Daniel P. Moynihan (D-New York) resigned in protest.

William Casey initially did little to limit the damage. There was a very heated argument between the DCI and the senators on April 2, 1984, and another eight days later, at which the DCI still refused full details although he was supposed to be making formal presentations on the mining. Relations deteriorated so much that DDCI John McMahon had to intercede for his boss. Bill Casey met again with the Senate committee members on April 26, apologized, and promised better. Moynihan was induced to withdraw his resignation. In June, with the approval of the White House, a compromise was negotiated with Congress providing more definition of CIA reporting requirements. Langley agreed to give prior notice of actions that go beyond a Presidential Finding, of anything requiring NSC or presidential approval, and on subjects in which the committee expresses interest.

Because self-serving statements were made, both to the public and to CIA officers in an employee bulletin, confusion has been sown over whether the Agency's notification was adequate. A review of the chronology is necessary here. The House committee was briefed by Casey on January 31 but not explicitly told of the mining for another two months. At the March 27 hearing, the DCI had to be pressed repeatedly on who was directing the mining before Casey admitted, "We are." Senate interest was initially piqued by a Casey letter, of January 12, that said the CIA wanted to draw the entire $24 million from the approved budget immediately, leading staff director Robert R. Simmons to arrange a CIA briefing for early February. Clair George, the DCI's congressional liaison, tried to get a postponement and failed, whereupon Casey himself called committee chairman Goldwater and got the date pushed back to March 8. At that hearing, and again on March 13, Casey focused on the CIA supplemental budget request, making only the minor reference already noted. Much later Bob Simmons saw a March 30 Casey letter to Senator Clairborne Pell (D-Rhode Island) that contained the phrase "unilaterally controlled latino assets." With a decade of experience at Langley in DDO, Simmons immediately saw warning flags and called for a full-scale briefing on April 2, where Bill Casey argued with the senators. Goldwater's official statement after the DCI's second briefing on April 10 noted that the "requirement of the law was not followed in this case by not briefing our committee. . . . I told Mr. Casey that this is no way to run a railroad."

The fracas about the Presidential Finding also led the Reagan administration to work on its general procedures for covert action, finally formalized in January 1985 in NSDD-159. This directive provided that all covert actions be authorized by written findings, that actions in progress be reviewed periodically by senior officials, and that the CIA be responsible for the operational control of any covert action unless specifically provided by the President. As will be seen later, these orders were honored in the breach.

Meanwhile, other aspects of *contra* activity were also running into difficulties. The FDN lost its alliance with the Miskito who were essentially knocked out of the war. Brooklyn Rivera's faction of the Indians reached accommodation with Managua. Stedman Fagoth Mueller lost control over his faction, Misura, which stopped receiving *contra* supplies. Fagoth himself was eventually expelled from Honduras. In the fall of 1984 an angry Congress voted to halt all spending for the CIA project for six months. Then Colonel Bermúdez's air force was set back when one of its two C-47 transports was shot down on a flight out of El Aguacate. All that was left was a C-54 that could not fly for lack of spare parts, and one last C-47 that Edgar Chamorro called the "rusty pelican."

A serious loss was ARDE. Edén Pastora and Alfonso Robelo had the one anti-Sandinista group with revolutionary credentials comparable to the FSLN in Managua. Pastora built his own armed force and refused to work with former national guardsmen. The ARDE facilities in Costa Rica were backed up by a radio station, a factory for making uniforms, several warehouses, and a fleet of about 150 vehicles. But Costa Rica formally took a neutral position in the Nicaraguan war and made some efforts to enforce its stance. Almost a hundred ARDE members were arrested in late 1983, and a shipment of refugee aid from Miami was siezed when guns turned up among the clothing. Seventeen Cuban Americans, thought to be en route to join Pastora, were ordered out of the country instead. Still, ARDE had about three thousand troops and Pastora invaded Nicaragua in early 1984, capturing the small town of San Juan del Norte. "Commander Zero" was ejected from the town, however, after a pause in which the Sandinistas redeployed their forces. On May 30, 1984, Edén had a brush with death—in the form of a bomb built into a tape recorder at a late-night news conference he was holding in the bush. Both the FDN and the Sandinistas had the motive for such an assassination attempt. By the time he recovered, ARDE had lost its steam. About a year later, Pastora was again a victim, this time wounded in a helicopter crash.

Langley could cut off its aid to ARDE, but it could not make the FDN effective. In the aftermath of the mining campaign, DCI Casey carried out a shake-up of the top brass at CIA. Most significantly, it was Clair E. George, his congressional liaison man, whom Casey made DDO. John Stein was moved over to replace the inspector general.

Bill Casey must have thought he was giving Stein a sinecure but it did not turn out that way. In October 1984 came the revelation of the *contra* manual *Psychological Operations in Guerrilla Warfare* with its statements on "neutralization" implying assassination. The manual was denounced by Congressman Edward Boland and a new storm of criticism erupted in the middle of President Reagan's reelection campaign. Reagan was obliged to order immediate investigations by PFIAB and by the CIA inspector general, now John Stein. There was additional investigation by the House intelligence committee, and by the Intelligence Oversight Board. Again Bill Casey's decisions were called into question. Casey tried to escape the heat by reprimanding half a dozen subordinates, including Duane Clarridge's deputy Joe Fernandez and manual supervisor Ray Doty. Clarridge himself was promoted to the DDO's chief of European operations.

At The Hague, the International Court of Justice eventually found in favor of Nicaragua in the harbor mining case. The court also found the United States had no right to seek the overthrow of the Sandinista government. Only the American, British, and Japanese justices dissented from portions of the 11–3 decision rendered on June 27, 1986. The Reagan administration dismissed the ICJ decision and vetoed a resolution in the UN Security Council designed to enforce the court's findings against the United States.

For Congress the last straw was the *contra* manual episode. It voted against a $14-million supplementary request for the paramilitary program and then reenacted the Boland Amendment prohibiting Pentagon or intelligence community assistance to the *contras*. In Honduras the CIA supply lines began to dry up. By June 1984 there was only about $1 million left in CIA project accounts.

The *contras* shifted to a precarious hand-to-mouth existence. Columns remained in the base camps for months at a time awaiting supplies for their next patrol. But Ronald Reagan did not want to give up this secret war. His effort to pursue it led to a covert operation conducted from inside the White House, by the staff of the National Security Council. The result has been a bizarre tale of ideological fervor, greed, and betrayal, and a controversy that eroded the power of the Reagan administration.

·XIX·

PROJECT
DEMOCRACY

The *contras* tried to show optimism following the harbor
mining fiasco. Field commanders asserted that the
FDN had never been in a better position militarily. Political director Adolfo Calero, after defeat of the $14-million para-
military aid request, declared, "I am confident we will pull through
this crisis caused by the Congress."

In fact there had been a real disaster and it had nothing whatever
to do with Congress. Langley expended virtually all of its pro-
grammed funds to conduct the mining, in effect cashing in all of its
chips, for an operation with indifferent military potential once it
had been agreed to use nonlethal mines. The disaffection of the
Miskito and the elimination of Edén Pastora removed FDN political rivals but simultaneously removed the threat to the Sandinistas
from the south. With no *contra* units working from Costa Rica, the
Nicaraguan military was able to focus its effort along the Honduran
border. As the Sandinistas reinforced their militia in the north, the
FDN columns were then running out of supplies from CIA pipe-
lines.

Calero's situation could hardly have looked more bleak. What
reason had he for optimism?

Calero had the expressed intentions of United States officials,
who had met with him in Honduras in April, at the height of the
mining controversy. The Americans were from the CIA and the
National Security Council (NSC) staff. One was CIA task force chief
Duane Clarridge. He introduced Marine Lieutenant Colonel Oliver
L. North from the NSC. North did the talking and his message was

419

reassurance. The administration hoped to win new *contra* funding; the United States would not abandon the *contras*; it was a strong pep talk and gave Calero renewed confidence.

Colonel North's remarks were based on little more than a wish at that time, but the wish was Ronald Reagan's and the President's desires carry great weight in Washington, D.C. North had been called in to see his boss, National Security Adviser Robert C. McFarlane. North and Donald R. Fortier, McFarlane's deputy, were told to do whatever was necessary to ensure passage of the next *contra* aid appropriation. Fortier formed a high-level group that convened from time to time to review the options. North was to concentrate on holding the *contras'* hands, to keep up their faith and spirits.

Adolfo Calero threw himself into private fund-raising efforts in the United States, Puerto Rico, and Europe. One major fund-raising target was the Cuban exile community. *Contra* efforts here got an unexpected boost from Huber Matos, a revolutionary war comrade of Fidel Castro, who visited Honduras to train FDN soldiers following his release from a Cuban prison after two and a half decades as a political prisoner. Many other Cuban exiles volunteered like Matos, but the Nicaraguan rebels could not raise enough money on their own. Calero estimated the FDN needed $1 million a month to sustain itself, $1.5 million to expand. That kind of money was more than the *contras* could raise. Rebel press spokesmen, presumably with Calero's approval, began promising that within forty days *contra* columns would establish an unbroken front line from the Honduran border to that of Costa Rica.

In Washington the United Nicaraguan Opposition (UNO), the umbrella group that masked the FDN, began shopping among high-powered lobbying firms for public relations assistance. Gray and Company actually developed the concept for a public relations campaign, but Calero judged it too expensive while the prestigious Washington firm had misgivings of its own. Though nothing developed from this contact, one Gray and Company employee, Robert Owen, became so dedicated to the *contra* cause that he put together his own version of a support plan. Owen's plan required twin tax-exempt entities, one for tax-exempt educational purposes, the other to raise money and seek influence. Owen decided to show his plan to Lieutenant Colonel Oliver North, whom he had met when Owen was a Senate staffer in 1982. North encouraged Rob Owen to visit

Central America and familiarize himself with conditions there. Owen went to Costa Rica and Honduras in May 1984, spoke to *contra* leaders about their money needs, and reported back to North in his office at the Old Executive Office Building, next door to the White House. It was the beginning of an intense relationship.

Intense is the word for Oliver Laurence North. A hard-driving Marine, North habitually put in twelve- and even sixteen-hour days; once he complained to his boss of getting only two hours' sleep a night. "Ollie" North freely admitted he loved the work. When, in 1984, North was selected for a slot in the student class at the National Defense University, he pulled every string he could to extend his tour of duty at the National Security Council. North could have left after a distinguished tour. He had helped install new NSC crisis management procedures, and toiled on the first-ever United States policy sanctioning preemptive strikes to counter terrorism. Colonel North had also been the NSC focal point in the lightning-fast planning of the Grenada invasion.

A year at the war college would have groomed Ollie North for higher command. He could have looked forward to a battalion to lead, promotion, senior staff and command positions, perhaps a general's stars. Instead, North wanted to stay on the NSC staff. Not even friendly advice from General Richard Secord could convince North to accept the student appointment. North held out and Bob McFarlane kept him on.

Such loyalty to the NSC staff was typical of Ollie, though previously his commitment had been totally to the Marine Corps. North first joined the Marine reserve during the summer of 1961, after his freshman year at college as an English major. Boot camp made Ollie a Marine enthusiast. Later he was able to get into the Naval Academy, where he often spoke of a desire to serve with the Marines. The Annapolis yearbook for North's graduating class notes his intense passion for the Marines. At the academy, North ran track, boxed, and rose to become one of 36 cadet company commanders. One of North's fights was a three-round decision he won against classmate James Webb, highly decorated combat Marine, novelist, and Ronald Reagan's second secretary of the Navy.

Ollie's own hopes were threatened by circumstance. During his first year at Annapolis, North and four other cadets were victims of a head-on crash with a trailer truck while driving home to upstate

New York for a short leave. Ollie suffered serious knee and back injuries that set him back a year at the academy. To resolve lingering doubts among the military selection board at his 1968 graduation, North played a film of his fight with Jim Webb. Ollie won a commission as a second lieutenant in the Marine Corps.

Lieutenant North was sent to Vietnam where he served as a platoon commander in Company K of the 3rd Marines, in Quang Tri province with the Third Marine Division. There, perhaps a legacy of his accident, North invariably used his helmet chin strap, and made his men do so too, though hardly anyone in Vietnam ever did. In February and May 1969, North won two medals for gallantry, a Bronze Star and a Silver Star, and also received two Purple Hearts for combat wounds. He remained in Vietnam until November 1969, finishing with a stint as a junior officer on the division operations staff.

After Vietnam, North served three years as an instructor at the Marine training base at Quantico, Virginia, playing his role with the same intensity he'd shown as a combat leader. In 1973–1974, North went to Okinawa to head the Northern Training Area, which taught survival skills to eight hundred men a month for the 3rd Marine Division. Ollie underwent a still-unexplained hospitalization, some say for "stress," toward the end of 1974. He then spent several years in Washington working on manpower issues at Marine headquarters, followed by a tour as a battalion staff officer at Camp Lejeune, North Carolina.

Ollie met Colonel Robert McFarlane, then also a Marine officer, when both were assigned to headquarters. He met General Secord in 1980, when North was chosen to lead a small Marine unit, sent to eastern Turkey as part of the Iran hostage rescue mission. Then North went to the Naval War College where he wrote a thesis, on the utility of battleships in the modern age, that came to the attention of Reagan's first Navy secretary, John Lehman. It was afterward that North was selected for detached service on the NSC staff. There he worked again with General Secord on weapons sales to Saudi Arabia.

North was the most junior of the military officers sent to the NSC in 1981, but with the exception of Vice-Admiral John Poindexter he outlasted them all. North's work was one reason for this; he went to the political-military affairs section of the staff, where arms deals and crises are the stuff of daily activity. As a Marine officer, North also seemed a logical choice to handle the terrorism issue, where the administration was just beginning to define a policy. Colonel North marched into the vacuum and was soon a truly focal point on the NSC staff.

Another reason for North's longevity on the staff was Robert McFarlane. Drawn first to State as a counselor to Al Haig, McFarlane was brought into the NSC by William Clark in 1982 as deputy national security adviser. When Clark moved on to the Department of the Interior in October 1983, McFarlane succeeded him as chief of the NSC staff. McFarlane had a soft spot for North and thought of him almost like a son. McFarlane gave North primary responsibility for Latin American arms trading, and later the Nicaragua task. North was well suited for these assignments, having concentrated on Latin America in his study of international relations at the Naval Academy.

For all his qualifications and experience, Ollie North remained oddly defensive, as if he constantly felt the need to prove himself, to rise above his short stature (five feet, nine inches) or the lingering effects of his injuries and wounds. Appearing as a character witness at the court-martial of a Marine buddy, North misrepresented himself as a premed in college, where in fact he had scored D grades in geometry and trigonometry. Other times he claimed that during his Okinawa tour he had commanded the "Special Operations Training Detachment," a unit that evidently did not exist. Some colleagues remember North as a chronic name dropper. Others did not mind him so much. One woman who worked with Colonel North, mustering public support for the *contras,* saw him as "the occasional peacock among the roosters . . . with a hint of swagger about him."

For a time Colonel North's swagger seemed justified. He appeared to have a finger in every pie. It was North who orchestrated the aerial interception of the Palestinian hijackers of the cruise ship *Achille Lauro* in 1985. Referring to the World War II interception and shootdown of a Japanese navy commander, North had said, "We can do an Admiral Yamamoto." He was also involved in encouraging Libyan resistance to Qaddafi, and was a central figure in the secret arms sales to Iran. All this was in addition to Colonel North's work for the *contras,* an activity he called Project Democracy.

Ollie's operations did not always come out so perfectly. As a midshipman at Annapolis, for example, Ollie had used insurance money received after his accident to buy a 427-horsepower Shelby Cobra colored Marine Corps green. When the academy offered its regular familiarization visit for midshipmen to Quantico, Ollie disdained the bus and insisted on organizing his own car convoy. North's Shelby ran out of gas on the highway; he spent much of the trip telephoning around for emergency assistance. In the end, North's Project Democracy turned out very much like his Quantico trip.

Colonel Oliver North did not work in isolation on Project Democracy. His boss was Robert McFarlane, who was directly responsible to the President. Ronald Reagan has said both that he had nothing to do with arms shipments supporting the *contras* and that *he* did support the *contras*—and, as President, he was not constrained by the Boland Amendment. President Reagan certainly has supported the *contras* in numerous weekly radio speeches, in a joint address to the Congress, in receiving *contra* leaders, and in speaking at a *contra* support group fund-raising event. Robert McFarlane's testimony is that he acted at all times with the full authority of the President. Reagan's order, as McFarlane presented it to North and Donald Fortier, was to do anything necessary to ensure success at the next vote on *contra* aid. Part of that mission was keeping the *contra* military force in being and that assignment went to Oliver North.

McFarlane himself performed a critical role as intermediary. In periodic meetings with counterparts from other countries, McFarlane mentioned the *contra* funding problem as a dilemma facing the United States government. The Israelis reportedly rebuffed feelers encouraging them to take an interest. Instead help came from Saudi Arabia, which had never previously shown an interest in Central America, had no diplomatic relations with any country in the region, but had indeed repeatedly invested money in American covert action programs.

In the summer of 1984, Colonel North had Adolfo Calero in his office for one of their more than fifty acknowledged meetings. Ollie gave the *contra* leader the impression that someone was working to raise money and asked for a bank account number where it could be deposited. Calero provided an account in a Cayman Islands bank, hoping for the best. In July there was a deposit of $1 million in UNO's favor, followed by equal sums at monthly intervals through the end of the year. After the third deposit, Calero began to have some confidence in the source of the funds. UNO began making plans.

At the interagency level in the Reagan administration, Central American policy was the province of a Restricted Interagency Group (RIG) of senior officials. Ollie North represented the NSC staff at these meetings, which were chaired by the State Department representative, first Langhorne Motley, then Elliott Abrams. North also belonged to a three-man core group, a sort of restricted RIG. The existence of this core group is disputed by Abrams, the purported chairman, but the RIG has figured in sworn testimony before the Joint Congressional Committee to Investigate the Iran-Contra Diversion. The third member of the core group was Alan Fiers, CIA's chief of Central America Task Force. Abrams's office logs show that this constellation of officials met there seven times during the years 1985–1986, a period in which there were but eighteen meetings of the full RIG.

Whether or not the RIG core group existed, Assistant Secretary of State Elliott Abrams admits the meetings with North and Fiers. In fact, Abrams noticed a certain rivalry between them. That rivalry may have been for the ear of Bill Casey, with whom Oliver North also had a personal relationship. Casey was the first DCI to maintain a hideaway office in the Old Executive Office Building, actually just down the hall from Ollie at Suite 302. On at least two occasions William J. Casey visited North in his office, another time Casey sent a friend who wanted to make a *contra* donation, beer brewer Joseph Coors, and North talked the man into giving $60,000 for a Maule light aircraft. How often North popped down the hall to the DCI's office or they talked on the telephone may never be known. In sworn testimony, Bob McFarlane could not say whether Ollie North had been responding to his orders or to Bill Casey's in North's work on Project Democracy. Always the back alley brawler, Casey's practice was to maintain a wide range of personal contacts for different purposes, some operational. For example, Casey brought back CIA's station chief in Managua from 1982 to 1984, Benjamin B. Wickham, Jr., to be a special assistant, even reportedly working from outside the Agency, on certain aspects of the *contra* affair. North could have been another such link for Casey, a channel outside the purview of CIA's Central America Task Force. Because CIA had been expressly prohibited by the Boland Amendment from assisting the *contras*, in fact a channel such as North's was absolutely necessary if DCI Casey wished to pursue the Nicaraguan secret war.

Adolfo Calero wanted Colonel North's help whether or not North worked for Bill Casey. Calero would take help anywhere he could get it. The Cayman Islands bank account number also went to retired generals John K. Singlaub and Richard V. Secord. Singlaub had been to Honduras in March, was impressed with the FDN camps and the need of the *contra* military for modern antiaircraft weapons. Singlaub volunteered to help raise funds for the rebel umbrella group UNO and later became Calero's best source of arms market weapons. General Secord got the number when his company itself made a donation to UNO.

In addition to the secret means there was an open funding mechanism, through conservative fund-raiser Carl R. Channell, whose National Endowment for the Preservation of Liberty collected over $6 million. "Spitz" Channell courted wealthy donors capable of putting money behind their words and was quite successful at it. With the White House, Channell arranged a series of NSC conference room briefings for big donors. President Reagan himself appeared twice in this series of sessions. At one appearance, in the Roosevelt Room of the White House on January 30, 1986, Reagan's appearance was neatly sandwiched between a talk by Elliott Abrams on the general United States policy and a briefing on Central America from Oliver North.

Channell had developed a one-two-punch tactic he used on likely prospects. First came the gloom and doom NSC briefing, then Channell or an associate would ask the donor for some specific amount that could be used to purchase specific items, like trucks on one occasion, or Maule light aircraft and British Blowpipe surface-to-air missiles on another. Donors were not told that much of their donation money was consumed on overhead, 35 percent or more by some accounts. While most endowment money went to finance TV ads (whose storyboards were critiqued by Elliott Abrams), some $2.2 million went into an account called "Toys" that the donors understood would be for direct support of the *contras*. These funds went through a related corporate entity called International Business Communications to UNO and to Lake Resources, a Richard Secord company. Oliver North appreciated Channell's efforts and sent him a commendation letter on National Security Council stationery. Channell and an associate have since pled guilty to conspiracy to evade taxation charges resulting from their *contra* operations.

Within the White House the Channell effort was complemented by a big campaign from the Office of Public Liaison, dozens of briefings for opinionmakers and interested groups. Colonel North was the preferred speaker, reportedly briefing or giving speeches on Central America over a hundred times from 1984 to 1986. North used a map and slides to put his audiences in the picture. The images he flashed were stark, the claims extravagant. To an audience in Nashville in May 1986, North connected the Sandinistas with immigration to the United States, accused them of suppressing Catholicism, and charged that objections to supporting the *contras* were "the most sophisticated disinformation and active-measures campaign that we have seen in this country since Adolf Hitler." At another briefing for a church group, North flashed a slide of a tomb and asserted the Sandinistas in Nicaragua desecrated the dead. The colonel should have known better. With missions in all Latin America for many tens of decades, the religious have access to information of their own and well knew actual Nicaraguan reverence for the dead. North also told the group that he had been to Angola and thought that too a good cause, and that he was in frequent personal contact with Ronald Reagan. Even opponents like the church group were impressed. "No one," wrote a liaison office staffer, "ever emerges from a North briefing on Central America less than deeply moved."

Ronald Reagan set the accent for the entire *contra*-support network with constant exclamations and exhortations. In February 1985 and again later Reagan called the *contras* "brothers"; in March he termed Calero's crew "the moral equivalent of the founding fathers" and declared to America, "we owe them our help." Later he spoke of a Soviet "beach head" in Nicaragua and called Sandinista leader Daniel Ortega, that July, "a little dictator who went to Moscow in his designer glasses." In case Managua missed the signal, on May 1 Reagan slapped a total trade embargo upon Nicaragua halting all economic relations.

The overriding question was still money to sustain the *contras* pending the next congressional appropriation, so-called bridging money. Here too Reagan played a role, after Bud McFarlane once more took the funding problem to the Saudi Arabians, during preparations for a state visit by Saudi King Fahd. The Saudi king was granted a special privilege, a private tête-à-tête with President Reagan, and the meeting took place as arranged in February 1985. No record exists of what was discussed, but shortly afterward the NSC staff learned the Saudis would extend and even double their previous aid to UNO. Within a month the *contras* received about $24 million in three large deposits, bringing aggregate Saudi aid to the rebels to roughly $32 million, sums on a similar scale to what the CIA had been paying out in the first phase of its involvement. Truly the Saudis permitted the *contras* to keep up their strength at this moment.

Beyond the official connections, a variety of other private sources helped Calero as well. A key operator in this facet of activity was John K. Singlaub, who by now headed organizations called the World Anti-Communist League and the United States Council for World Freedom. Singlaub had been deputy commander of United States forces in Korea during the Carter administration and publicly criticized the President for considering the transfer home of some American troops from that country. The confrontation with Carter led to Singlaub's transfer instead, and later he retired to pursue his political beliefs in private life.

General Singlaub was also a veteran of a long career much given to special warfare. He had been detached to the CIA in its early days, serving in China as chief of base in Mukden. There he began to forge relationships with the nationalist Chinese he later used to solicit funds or material aid, particularly air defense, for the *contras*. In the Korean War, Singlaub had done a tour as CIA's deputy chief of station. For the Army later on, Colonel Singlaub commanded MACV-SOG during the critical years 1966–1968. He still served as a civilian adviser to the secretary of the Army. At least once he presented Bill Casey with a proposal for a round-robin arms deal, involving a communist country, to provide the CIA a supply of Soviet-style weapons.

For the *contra* operation, North's Project Democracy, Singlaub was indispensable. He made direct approaches to Taiwan, followed up by North and McFarlane sending another NSC staff member, Gaston J. Sigur, that brought UNO two donations of $1 million each. Singlaub would have made another appeal at an even higher level save for the intervention of Elliott Abrams. Highly publicized private funding efforts Singlaub made inside the United States proved much less useful, yielding less than $400,000 over two years. Singlaub gave Oliver North a *contra* weapons wish list that was used by the Channell group fund-raising operation. Not least, John Singlaub had the contacts to furnish Adolfo Calero with the cheapest weapons and ammunition the FDN could buy anywhere.

Finally there were a constellation of minor benefactors conjured up by Reagan's appeals whom the President likened to the Abraham Lincoln Brigade in the Spanish civil war. These included Refugee Relief International, which donated a shipment of medical supplies, and Civilian Military Assistance, whose members went to Honduras to help train the FDN troops. There were a host of Cuban Americans eager to enlist in *contra* support, and at least one organization whose officials have been linked to a *contra* arms shipment.

Singlaub was far from the only "private patriotic American," as North liked to call them. As the retired general also noted to Ollie, all the press attention that went to Singlaub and groups like Civilian Military Assistance drew eyes away from Suite 302 of the Old Executive Office Building. Yet though General Singlaub and the others pride themselves on their patriotism, the services they provided were not fundamentally different from those of, for example, Wilson and Terpil in Libya. The secret wars spawned a generation of free-lance cowboys. Project Democracy then brought the ultimate distortion, the office of the President working directly with private citizens on a covert action.

Almost immediately it became apparent that the secret war had assumed a new character. Colonel Bermúdez's FDN columns disappeared from the field; Pastora took ARDE out of the fight. Not only did the single front line fail to materialize, there was nothing in the south at all. The *contras* were obliged to shift to a passive subsistence mode after the CIA pipeline evaporated, while reliance on the private benefactors injected the influence of a range of private agendas. Benefactor aims were not necessarily identical to those of UNO, President Reagan, or the NSC staff.

An early demonstration of this took place even before the Boland Amendment legally took effect. Adolfo Calero was already making his private arrangements to assist Bermúdez's rebels. One was with Civilian Military Assistance, an Alabama-based private group that organized shipments of boots, uniforms, and miscellaneous donated items. By August 1984 nine Americans had been to the FDN camps in small groups, mostly to instruct in hand-to-hand fighting, handling weapons, and marksmanship. Then another group of six traveled to Honduras, including James P. Powell III, of Memphis, and Dana H. Parker, of Huntsville. Powell had been a helicopter pilot in Vietnam, shot down three times, and the FDN had an armed Hughes 500-D at their Aguacate base. Someone asked him to fly it.

Contra military commanders had been considering a bombing attack on a Sandinista military base as a signal that the FDN retained its power. Washington knew of this plan—both the CIA and the NSC. At the end of August, Colonel Oliver North and Duane Clarridge met with Adolfo Calero to convince him to postpone the attack. The Americans argued that the Hughes craft was the only FDN helicopter, and that Bermúdez should conserve his supply of 2.75-inch rockets until supply shipments got organized. Calero appeared convinced and said he would leave orders to cancel the air attack.

On September 1 the air attack happened anyway. *Contra* military commanders selected a base, Santa Clara, they suspected of harboring Cuban advisers. The *contra* air force hit Santa Clara with its three O-2A's, fitted with rocket pods by Summit Aviation, and with the Hughes helicopter, Jim Powell piloting. The *contras* claimed to have killed four Cubans; Managua announced it was a cook at the base and three children. The Hughes helicopter was shot down in the attack; both Americans and an FDN man were killed in the crash. To his superiors Ollie North reported that the Civilian Military Assistance members had pressured local *contra* commanders into going ahead with the mission. To the public UNO spokesmen insisted the helicopter was lost on an emergency rescue attempt.

A month later the Boland Amendment took effect on October 1, the first day of the new fiscal year. The last contingent of seventy-three CIA trainers pulled out of Honduras on the tenth. Langley's orders to its stations were explicit:

> Field stations are to cease and desist with actions that can be construed to be providing any type of support, either direct or indirect, to the various entities with whom we dealt under the program. All future contacts with those entities are, until further notice, to be solely, repeat solely, for the purpose of collecting positive and counterintelligence information of interest to the United States.

Under these restrictions there were narrow limits on what the CIA could do. Langley's national intelligence officer for Latin America, Robert Vickers, and its chief of task force, Allan Fiers, could no longer even know certain things. Soon after Boland went into effect, Fiers rejected a North invitation to attend a meeting with Calero for this reason.

Bill Casey, however, still marched to the beat of his own drummer. Publicly Casey avoided discussions with General John Singlaub, while privately the DCI also refused to talk about the *contras* with him. Casey refused to discuss the *contras* with his friend Joe Coors, but had no hesitation sending Coors down the hall to donate money for a plane to North. Casey joked with North about contributing a million of his own. Casey met with Bud McFarlane, in March 1985, specifically to talk about third country funding options for the *contras*. Several months earlier the DCI was willing to certify to Congress that the CIA had had no involvement in *contra* lobbying activities. The precise role of North for Casey remains a cipher, punctuated most recently by reports that over 1984 and 1985 Bill Casey and Ollie North held a series of meetings with UNO officials at a CIA safe house in Washington. When the time came for Project Democracy to mount its own airlift, Bill Casey also met with General Richard Secord at North's suggestion, and North later took Secord to a meeting with the DCI where Secord was asked to use his contacts in the Middle East to appeal for *contra* aid money.

Meanwhile, Adolfo Calero proceeded to organize his supply network. Procurement of ordinary items was handled by Calero's brother Mario in New Orleans. Arms were shipped directly by the dealers with whom Adolfo contracted. North's legal advisers told him that everything was okay so long as no United States funds were used, nothing went through United States banks, and no American weapons were bought.

Calero made his first arms deal in October 1984. He ordered five thousand G-3 automatic rifles on credit from the RM Equipment Company in Miami. The company got false end-user certificates stating the weapons were intended for Honduras, then purchased the rifles in Portugal.

The biggest weapons deal was between Calero and Energy Resources, one of a web of companies involving General Richard Secord and Iranian-American businessman Albert Hakim. Secord was a partner with Hakim in Stanford Technology Trading Group International in late 1984 when he was asked, presumably by North, to help the *contras* by selling them arms. Secord went to his partner and told Hakim he had been asked to participate to help the President of the United States. Secord simultaneously offered Hakim a chance to participate also, which the latter accepted after assurances that standard profits, with markups of 20 to 30 percent, would be earned. Energy Resources was the result. To Calero, Secord gave the impression that weapons would be sold at cost, and he walked away with an $11.3-million purchases order. The buy included ten thousand automatic rifles of Soviet design (AK-47 and AKMS), rocket-propelled grenades, mortars, and other equipment. Secord's group managed to get Guatemalan end-user certificates and began buying the weapons in Portugal and Eastern Europe in December 1984.

By far the best of Calero's weapons deals was that with General John Singlaub, who worked in conjunction with Barbara Studley of GeoMilTech. Singlaub volunteered to arrange the deal very early, after his March 1984 Honduras visit, then took a long time to put it together. But for his $5.3 million, Calero got another ten thousand AK-47's with fifteen million rounds of ammunition and some SA-7 shoulder-fired antiaircraft missiles, possibly from North Korea. Where Secord's prices had been a little less than those of RM Equipment, Singlaub's were cheaper again by almost half. In retrospect he believes Studley may actually have lost money on the transaction. Here indeed there was no profit.

Buying the weapons was easier than finding them and squeezing them through the pipeline to the rebels in Honduras. Secord's first big shipment the *contras* derisively called the "slow boat from China" because it never seemed to arrive. Calero had to order two air shipments of items needed before the ship came in. Southern Air Transport moved the matériel in February and March, before the vessel *Erria* reached Honduras on May 11, 1985.

For Singlaub the problem was the competition, specifically one Mario Dellamico, a representative in Honduras for RM Equipment. When Singlaub's shipment reached port in July 1985, Dellamico met the ship, claiming to be acting for the Honduran military officer to whom the cargo was consigned. Dellamico got hold of shipping documents that told how little Singlaub had paid for the weapons. Dellamico subsequently tried to get Singlaub to sell *him* weapons at those prices, and when the crusty general refused, threatened to prevent future Singlaub shipments from entering

Honduras. Similarly, Dellamico obtained data on Secord's weapons prices and spread the word that Energy Resources was overcharging—as much as nine dollars for a three-dollar hand grenade. Even Singlaub's original sources for cheap Soviet-style weapons were threatened when Dellamico went to a communist embassy and demanded that he be allowed to purchase weapons at identical prices. The competition among the arms dealers had repercussions that eventually reached directly into the White House.

This occasion was a meeting among North, Secord, Singlaub, and Calero to discuss *contra* antiaircraft weapons. Bermúdez was desperate to get shoulder-fired antiaircraft missiles. Secord offered $180,000 a set for British Blowpipe missiles; Singlaub thought he could get the same missiles for $165,000 but he could not offer trainers to go with them. That deal went to Secord. Singlaub reports North conceded to him that he had the better prices, but after this open confrontation, Singlaub never got another UNO weapons deal.

The NSC staff worked especially hard on operations and intelligence support for Bermúdez and Calero. North used the code name Steelhammer and the alias William P. Goode, among a number of such devices he used in Iran dealings as well. Calero had the code name Sparkplug and the alias Barnaby, after a grandparent. Calero met with North over fifty times, in contrast with Bill Casey, affectionately referred to as "Uncle Bill," whom Calero met with only perhaps six times. There were also four Calero meetings with President Ronald Reagan, at three of which North was present. North and Calero also used an intermediary as go-between. He was Robert Owen, hired by Calero in October 1984 for $2,500 a month plus some expenses. There were over forty meetings between Owen and North, maybe half of them unobtrusively outside the White House. Owen took documents and intelligence information to Calero, passed on important messages, made cash payments at North's direction, cashed traveler's checks given North by Calero, and ran cash for Secord from New York to Washington. Owen used the code name TC, for The Courier, and may have used the alias Armando.

This question of cash funds in the White House remains a perplexing element of the Contragate affair. Calero evidently prevailed upon his Cayman Islands bankers to furnish him with $3 million in unsigned traveler's checks, which UNO used for many kinds of cash payments. After North told him of a need for cash in connection with an operation in progress to find the hostages in Lebanon, Calero provided Steelhammer with $90,000 worth of the checks. Available data suggests that about $50,000 did go to the Lebanese activity, but that Robert Owen distributed roughly $30,000 to various *contra* leaders. North also gave $2,500 to Thomas Dowling, an individual who falsely represented himself as a Roman Catholic priest and gave congressional testimony disputing *contra* human rights abuses. (North also arranged a photo opportunity for Dowling with President Reagan and International Business Communications, part of the Channell group, paid him to write a pamphlet.) To his secretary Fawn Hall, North lent $60 for a beach weekend, while Ollie used $2,440 of the traveler's checks himself. Additional money threads in this plot include a package of cash, possibly $16,000 delivered from Southern Air Transport to North at the White House, a $14,000 security system installed for free at North's home, and "Belly Button," a $200,000 death benefit account Albert Hakim set up for North at the time of the McFarlane mission to Teheran.

Exchange of intelligence, prohibited by the Boland Amendment in effect at that time, was a prominent feature of the *contra* relationship with the NSC staff. A very significant instance occurred in November 1984, when the recent arrival of Soviet gunship helicopters in Nicaragua posed a new threat to the FDN columns. Calero wanted to order an attack on El Bluff, the Atlantic port where the HIND gunships were arriving, being assembled, and initially based. Ollie North asked McFarlane for permission to provide intelligence about El Bluff, and went to the U.S. Southern Command (General Paul F. Gorman) and the CIA's national intelligence officer for Latin America (Robert Vickers) to get the data. North assembled the intelligence into a package that Robert Owen carried to Calero in Honduras in December.

Barnaby seriously toyed with the concept of a strike on El Bluff. He called North on a secure line on November 5, then went to Washington to meet with the NSC aide. In addition to a political strategy for coalition with Alfonso Robelo and Arturo Cruz, Calero talked to North about "borrowing" a T-33 jet from the Honduran air force that could hit El Bluff. A single plane would have had too limited a strike potential, while Honduran cooperation was also a factor. This plan was dropped.

In December a British paramilitary expert, David Walker, formerly commander of the 22nd Special Air Services Regiment, met with North and proposed a commando attack on El Bluff. North and Calero exchanged correspondence on the mission. Calero also consulted General Singlaub regarding the concept of such an attack although not its specific details. A Walker associate is reported to have entered Nicaragua on the ground to test the route, but he found such tight security around El Bluff that a raid seemed impossible. Barnaby abandoned the El Bluff idea altogether. Though Walker received no immediate employment, he did win a place on the crew later, when Project Democracy expanded to include an airlift component.

In February 1985, Ollie North again asked Rob Owen to carry a package of intelligence, including maps, to Calero. Owen met Colonel North just outside the White House Situation Room. The two men discovered that the CIA task force had sent maps pasted down on poster board, not at all suitable to be carried by a secret courier. Owen went back to North's office, where Steelhammer called Allan Fiers with some choice words on CIA competence. Langley apologized, then sent a CIA man to Dulles airport with a reformatted packet that Owen took to Honduras.

Then there was the *Monimbo* affair. Somehow North got wind of a Nicaraguan merchant vessel, the *Monimbo,* that was suspected of carrying arms from North Korea. In a memo to Bud McFarlane on February 6, Steelhammer suggested Calero might finance an attempt to intercept the ship and take its cargo for the *contras.* It would require United States intelligence plus the cooperation of a friendly nation's special-operations unit. Before passing the memo to his boss McFarlane, Admiral Poindexter wrote on it that the United States needed to take action on the *Monimbo,* and the next day he wanted to bring it up at a session of the NSC Crisis Pre-Planning Group. One account is that the project was dropped after failure to get cooperation from the desired third country; McFarlane's testimony is that he never took any action on these proposals.

Arms were of so much interest to North that Owen once called him the *"contra* quartermaster." From his February trip Owen brought back another weapons wish list. In March, Ollie wrote to the Honduran ambassador to the United States requesting a multiple-entry visa for Singlaub as a favor in the mutual interest of the two countries. Singlaub too was supposed to advise Bermúdez on weapons and develop more refined requirements lists. Delivery caused continued headaches as well. In a February 10 letter to North, Rob Owen described security failures on a recent air shipment: The plane had once been impounded by Colombia in a drug arrest, while Summit Aviation had merely put a new coat of paint on it; and part of the crew also had criminal records.

In addition, Steelhammer formulated a military plan that was supposed to bring the *contras* victory. This involved the FDN seizing a portion of Nicaragua and declaring a provisional government, then making a last stand at the place. Puerto Cabezas was apparently mentioned as a likely target, which would have made it the third time around for that long-suffering town. The *contras'* Alamolike stand was supposed to energize support for Reagan's policy and enable a United States naval blockade of Nicaragua, whereupon the Managua government was supposed to fold. This scheme was actually discussed by Elliott Abrams's Restricted Interagency Group but the Pentagon and CIA both rejected it as nonsense. Colonel North nevertheless discussed the plan with William O'Boyle, one of the Channell group's prospective donors.

North busily suggested plans for what the *contras* could do with all the money after the big Saudi donations of early 1985, and he warned Calero that the money was coming. Owen took another packet of intelligence to Calero in April, while Ollie reported to McFarlane that Bermúdez planned a big FDN offensive in June. The *contras* now claimed to have twelve thousand to fourteen thousand men in the field in about forty task forces with eight regional commands. Despite the men, and the delivery of many of the weapons bought by Calero June was most notable for a shooting incident that took place on the Costa Rican border. There was little evidence of any FDN offensive.

The inconclusive performance of Bermúdez and the rebel troops led to a council of war in July. This meeting took place at the Miami airport hotel and involved Calero, Bermúdez, Colonel North, and General Secord. Secord stated his opinion that without an airlift organized soon the *contras* "would be driven from the field and defeated in detail." Secord was then selected to create such an airlift capability. Although friends warned him against such a degree of involvement, Secord accepted the assignment.

Meanwhile, as quiet as North tried to keep his own role, the press got wind of bits and pieces of the story and published accounts that questioned Ollie's activities. Some in Congress noted the reports and began to raise questions of their own. At the National Security Council, McFarlane received inquiries from Congressman Lee Hamilton of the House intelligence committee and Congressman Michael Barnes, chairman of the House foreign affairs committee's Latin America subcommittee.

Congressional inquiries started a flap at the NSC. In answer to Hamilton, Bud McFarlane was content to sign a letter drafted by Colonel North, which asserted a "deep conviction" that no one on the NSC staff was violating Boland. When the Barnes letter came in, McFarlane was with the President at the western White House. He reviewed the file of North's memorandums when he returned to Washington, and found at least half a dozen items that raised legal questions in his mind as to the extent of NSC staff activity. Among them were the *Monimbo* and El Bluff plans, the transfer of intelligence, the matter of the Singlaub visa intervention and others.

Ollie managed to convince Bud that his activities were defensible. Again McFarlane signed a letter drafted by North, this one to Barnes. The letter declared "my actions, and those of my staff, have been in compliance with both the letter and the spirit of the law." Then McFarlane resorted to bluff in the face of Barnes's request for documents bearing on North's involvement. McFarlane refused to surrender any documents or to allow Barnes's staff access to them, but he did invite Barnes to meet him at the White House and said he could review the documents if he wished to. McFarlane then scheduled Barnes for twenty minutes in his office and spent much of the time giving him verbal assurances. The six problem memorandums were immersed in a deep stack of other memos, and Congressman Barnes did not ask to see the documents. North squeaked by this test.

Almost simultaneously the Barnes letter triggered an inquiry by the Intelligence Oversight Board, the private watchdog group in the White House to give the President independent legal advice. IOB counsel Bretton G. Sciarone allowed himself to be satisfied by the assurances McFarlane had given Congress, a five-minute talk with Ollie, plus a single forty-five-minute session with NSC counsel Commander Paul Thompson. The documents Thompson gave Sciarone for review excluded all the problem memorandums; based on the remaining material, the IOB produced a legal opinion backing NSC activity.

Thereafter the problem memorandums were carefully shielded.

North took a list of the file locations of the documents in NSC files. He kept the list taped to the side of his computer. Months later, when it began to appear there would be a real investigation, North checked the papers out of the NSC central registry and altered them, then had Fawn Hall type up revised versions. Whatever else may be said of the IOB legal opinion, Ollie North realized he had a potential legal problem. In the meantime the IOB opinion, exonerating the NSC, said just what North wanted it to. The opinion was retyped onto plain paper without letterhead or date, the evidence suggests, so that North could show it when anyone questioned the legality of his actions.

Bud McFarlane defended Ollie North from a congressional inquiry that could have stopped the NSC *contra* support program. No doubt some participants considered it a crucial moment in the evolution of Project Democracy. It was the first stage in the creation of the airlift force, a unit that gave the private benefactors all the attributes of a standard CIA paramilitary operation.

Lack of supplies continued to hamper *contra* military action at all levels. For Calero the headaches were finding weapons, buying them, and getting them to Honduras. For Bermúdez and Aristedes Sanchez, chief of FDN logistics, supplying the camps in Honduras and getting stuff to columns in the field was the problem. They received general items through Adolfo's brother Mario Calero in New Orleans, and food they mostly bought locally.

Supplies for the task forces in the field went into Nicaragua on the backs of men or mules. Men could not carry very much, while mule trains could not be very big without impeding military action, because the FDN lacked any secure rear area. In the field this translated into patrols that could not stay out very long. Bermúdez could send some columns deep into Nicaragua to exert a presence, but once there, rebel units typically would make one or two ambushes, set a few land mines, and return to base camps in Honduras. The *contra* conflict was a war of alarums and excursions, not a steady exertion of military pressure against an adversary. Congress had it on high authority, from Southern Command chief General Paul Gorman, that the *contras* were incapable of overthrowing the Managua government within the foreseeable future.

Calero and Bermúdez had but one answer for their strategic dilemma. Their solution was spectaculars, missions that did something unusual, got a lot of attention, and suggested the *contras* were still a factor. The Santa Clara bombing was one such spectacular. Another was the foray of the task force under Mike Lima, the *nom de guerre* of an FDN commander taken from radio code, which succeeded in capturing a town in Estelí province for one morning. The El Bluff and *Monimbo* missions would have been spectacular had they been carried out.

Success with spectacular missions, however, was very much a question of the dedication and skill of individuals. Even with a regular organization like the CIA it was difficult to ensure a proper set of skills; with reliance on private benefactors it was tougher still. There was yet another demonstration of this in the summer of 1985 with one more anticommunist adventurer, Sam Hall, who wanted to mount a large-scale Miskito action he called "Rainbow Mission." This was to consist of four or five forces that would enter Nicaragua and then make coordinated attacks on widely separated targets. Hall proposed not only to train the force and coordinate their plans but to go along on the mission. General Singlaub, who initially gave Hall some money, now calls the plan "awesome in its amateurishness and its ambition." Disgruntled in Honduras, Hall met Rob Owen who gave him money for a plane ticket home. "Sam meant well," recalls Owen, "but he just didn't have much judgment."

Far better than depending on spectaculars would be to give the *contras* some real teeth by extending their reach and complicating the Sandinista strategic situation. This meant an airlift to get supplies right to the front, and it also meant doing something about Costa Rica, where the *contra* resistance had fallen apart.

Until 1985 only the Miskito and ARDE operated from Costa Rica and by then both groups were quiescent. The Miskito were divided internally, felt they had been used by the FDN, and were the object of overtures from the Managua government. As for ARDE, it was crippled by the attempted assassination of Pastora plus charges that senior ARDE commanders were running drugs to finance their operations. The CIA and FDN both disliked Pastora. To the degree that either may have been responsible for the La Penca bombing that almost killed Pastora, they may have created their own problems on the southern front. True, Alfonso Robelo joined UNO, but as chief of the ARDE political wing he took few with him and had no troops. Without Pastora the ARDE troops drifted away; any idea that the FDN could immediately step in and gain the allegiance of these rebels was soon laid to rest.

Calero tried from an early date to reactivate the southern front.

He made an arrangement with John Hull, the procontra American farmer, to use his land for $10,000 a month. Then, especially after former Sandinistas Robelo and Arturo Cruz joined UNO, there was a protracted effort to woo the various ARDE factions and their *commandantes*. A man who called himself Armando, whom many believed to be from the CIA, offered weapons to bands that took the field. General Singlaub came to San José and actually negotiated an agreement to supply trainers, weapons, and equipment. The Singlaub agreement, reported over a CIA back channel by Ambassador Lewis A. Tambs, infuriated Elliott Abrams because it purported to commit the United States.

Blandishments had the most success with *commandante* Fernando "El Negro" Chamorro, who agreed to resume operations. Chamorro was known to intimates of this secret war for a 1983 incident in which, facing fire from Sandinista militia, he had crossed back into Costa Rica, phoned Langley, and demanded that the CIA send him mortars. From Calero's traveler's check funds, Chamorro received $230,000 for his organization and $50,000 for himself. (Robelo got $600,000.) But the new southern front was still not very active—the *contras* went up the San Juan River and camped on an island from which they did not budge. The island was a few feet inside the borders of Nicaragua, so technically they could say they were active and engaged.

As usual one of the *commandantes'* main complaints was lack of equipment. An airlift could alleviate that problem. But Secord was the organizer of the airlift, and his opinion was that to get useful loads to the southern front, in the twin-engine aircraft he anticipated using, would require an airfield in Costa Rica to land planes after their missions or for an emergency landing site. The idea of a Costa Rican airfield had come up by August 1985, within a month of the decision for the airlift.

One difficulty with the airfield idea was that it represented a new degree of involvement by the Costa Rican government. San José had been willing to wink at *contra* activities for the most part, making arrests or seizures in only the most egregious cases. Still its official position on the *contra* war was one of neutrality. Allowing land to be used for an airfield, then actual use of the field, was a positive act, an act of commission. The Costa Ricans were only convinced by the intercession of the American ambassador.

Lewis Tambs was new to San José in the summer of 1985. Before his departure from Washington, Tambs had had a series of talks with Ollie North through the spring and early summer. Purporting to speak for the Restricted Interagency Group, North gave Tambs the primary mission task of getting the southern front moving again. Elliott Abrams gave no such order, nor did Secretary Shultz in his written instructions for Tambs, but the ambassador evidently thought Colonel North's order was a real one. Once in San José, Tambs met CIA station chief Joe Fernandez, who told him of the project for an airfield at "Point West." Tambs went to the Costa Ricans and argued that the airfield was in their interest because getting the *contras* into Nicaragua would reduce the *contra* problem in Costa Rica. San José agreed.

Once given the general go-ahead, the Udall Corporation, another Secord-Hakim company, negotiated directly with the Costa Rican government. Their agreement provided that empty aircraft could use the airfield to refuel and that there be no overnight storage there. North sent Rob Owen back to Costa Rica in August, and Joe Fernandez of the CIA provided him with two possible sites for Point West, including information on the landowners. Owen borrowed a camera from Fernandez, surveyed and photographed the sites, and made a map. He took the information to Washington where one of the sites, Santa Elena, was selected.

The landowner at Santa Elena was an American farmer, John Hamilton. When Udall came to him to buy the land, including enough property around the strip proper for a security perimeter, Hamilton went to the United States embassy to check the bona fides of the company. Lewis Tambs consulted with Fernandez and then gave Hamilton a good word on Udall. The farmer sold the land for $1 million immediately, plus a "balloon" payment of $4 million due after three years.

In the meantime, General Secord turned to another former Air Force special-operations veteran, Colonel Richard B. Gadd, to supervise site preparations at Santa Elena, which soon received the code name Plantation. A Gadd company, Eagle Aviation Technology and Services received $100,000 for this work. Plantation was no fancy base, it possessed only minimal facilities: a 6,520-foot cleared dirt strip with irregular edges where vegetation encroached; a barracks building capable of housing maybe thirty men; an open-air shed. But from the beginning there was a security breach at Plantation just waiting to happen—the "secret" airstrip was situated so as to be clearly visible from the air to planes using the standard Pacific-side air corridor to San José's Aeropuerto Juan Santamaria.

Another security breach did occur in the late fall of 1985. The instigator here was Assistant Secretáry of State Elliott Abrams on a visit to San José. Abrams was with Tambs to receive a full CIA briefing on Costa Rica activities from Joe Fernandez and two subordinates. Through the hour-long briefing there was not a word about Plantation. Abrams finally asked, "What about the airfield?" Both Abrams and Tambs saw the CIA station chief turn colors and thought he would have a coronary. Fernandez took Abrams aside, indicated that his men were not cleared to know about the airfield, and pointed out Plantation's location on a map.

While Plantation was being prepared, to be completed in the spring of 1986, only longer-range aircraft, like C-130's, could be used for air missions. Here again Secord turned to Gadd, who once boasted, "Give me an account number and I'll fly anything anywhere." He had in fact done just that, including moving Task Force 160 helicopters to Barbados for the Grenada invasion, and flying Delta team units on exercises and missions. For Richard Secord, Gadd arranged with Southern Air Transport to use civilianized C-130's, called L-100's, for five or six flights to help the *contras.* The Reagan administration had already failed in 1985 with another request for military aid for the *contras,* but came back and won $27 million in "humanitarian" assistance following an incredible series of gaffes by Sandinista leader Daniel Ortega Saavedra. When the State Department was selected, despite its protests, to administer this aid, Colonel North sent their newly formed Nicaraguan Humanitarian Assistance Office (NHAO) to Gadd for airlift services which he arranged through Southern Air Transport.

Gadd and North both played primary roles in setting up the private benefactors' airlift unit. Gadd looked around for aircraft and tried to buy some transports from the Venezuelan air force before he found other planes. Two Canadian versions of the C-7 Caribou were purchased, along with a C-123K from a United States company in March 1986. The C-123 was another of the security breaches so endemic to the private benefactor operation—it was the same plane previously used by the U.S. government in a scheme to implicate the Sandinistas in drug trafficking. To work the planes, Gadd hired nine pilots, three loadmasters, and seven aircraft mechanics. Colonel North found a base for the unit in El Salvador when, in September 1985, he approached Bay of Pigs veteran Felix Rodriguez, then working closely with Salvadoran air force commander General Rafael Bustillo. Rodriguez got the Salvadorans to accord basing privileges at their Ilopango air base, soon codenamed Island. Rodriguez became a local manager for liaison. The pilots and aircrews received $3,000 a month.

If nothing else, the airlift unit had plenty of experience. Chief pilot was William J. Cooper, who had over twenty-five thousand hours in his flight logs and had been Air America's C-123 chief pilot at Udorn, Thailand, flying in support of Vang Pao in Laos. Cooper's deputy, John McRainey, had nineteen thousand flight hours. McRainey and some other members of the unit were also Air America veterans. When asked to participate, McRainey called a friend at CIA who told him Langley knew of the operation although it was not theirs, and advised him to be careful. Two pilots, John Piowaty and Elmo Baker, had flown in Vietnam and Baker had spent five years as a prisoner in North Vietnam. The youngest were Wallace B. "Buz" Sawyer and David Johnson, in their thirties. McRainey joked of the unit as the over-the-hill gang. There was also a British crew made up of David Walker, minimally qualified as a loadmaster, and pilot Iain Crawford, minimally qualified on these American aircraft, and a third man. Of the three American loadmasters, also called "kickers," Eugene Hasenfus had flown with Cooper over Laos. All were nominally employed by a Quarryville, Pennsylvania, company called Corporate Air Services. The men inhabited three houses in fashionable sections of San Salvador.

Felix Rodriguez was less impressed with Mr. Green, a liaison between Secord and Gadd and the crews at Island. "Mr. Green" was actually Rafael Quintero, a fellow Bay of Pigs and Mongoose veteran who was close to Thomas Clines and had worked on some of Edwin Wilson's renegade projects. Later Rodriguez, who used the *nom de guerre* Max Gomez, learned that Clines himself was also involved, working directly with Secord on some of the weapons deals, in which he pocketed about a million dollars. Max Gomez worried about the gloss that could be put on Project Democracy by the pasts of these men, thinking it "the Wilson gang back in business again." But Rodriguez himself brought in another questionable character whom *he* trusted, Luis Posada Carriles, who had been implicated in the 1976 bombing of a Cubana airliner in Caracas that had killed seventy-three persons. Rodriguez also held a commission as lieutenant colonel in the Salvadoran air force although it is illegal for United States citizens to serve in foreign armed forces. The private benefactor operation was not one of pristine purity.

Project Democracy's aircraft were not all they could be. Flying into Ilopango in February 1986 the first C-7 developed engine trouble. It could not make base even after jettisoning its load, including a spare engine and repair manuals, and had to make a forced landing. The incident was reported in the press—yet another security breach at the very outset of the airlift.

On the ground came a close call. On February 5, Gadd called Rodriguez and asked him to pick up a new mechanic who was arriving at Island. Felix sent a man who made the pickup and then came back to tell him the guy was so ancient he seemed ready for an old-age home. That night the new mechanic downed a full case of beer, and he followed up the next day with thirty-six beers. When he began to complain about the accommodations and brag about drug running, kicker Vernon Hughes told Rodriguez of his behavior. The mechanic was sent home before he could learn too much.

General Secord backed up Rodriguez's decision to expel the mechanic. Project Democracy seemed to be one big headache, another part of which was the CIA, reticent on furnishing intelligence support. Secord met with Bill Casey early in February. Both of them were too old, he said, to beat around the bush. "We want every bit of support we can get from you. But instead what we're getting is a lot of questions about the nature of our—of Gadd's organization." Casey made no promises. According to Secord and several associates, CIA cooperation waxed and waned throughout the course of the operation.

The first great moment for the airlift occurred in March 1986. A Sandinista light infantry force pursued FDN troops across the Nicaraguan border and made a strike for some of the *contra* camps. The United States contrived to get the Honduran government to request assistance, whereupon an emergency military aid grant of $20 million plus an airlift were laid on. Southern Command sent fourteen helicopters with fifty American crew to lift one Honduran infantry battalion into the area of the incursions. One CIA pilot was badly injured in the crash of a CIA helicopter trying to survey the combat area.

Within two days of the incursion, Project Democracy aircraft were responding with supply flights into Aguacate, the *contra* airfield in Honduras, a country called Hammerhole in the radio code used by Cooper's crews. Buz Sawyer's flight logs show ten sorties out of Aguacate just between March 24 and 28. In Nicaragua, a Southern Air Transport (SAT) L-100 failed to make radio contact on its initial attempt at a delivery, but succeeded next night in completing the first successful air resupply mission.

There was another SAT flight into Aguacate on the evening of March 24. Aboard was Rob Owen, who had been hired by the Nicaraguan Humanitarian Assistance Office (NHAO) on the strength of a letter he drafted and got signed by Calero, Robelo, and Cruz. Owen was to supervise unloading of NHAO supply shipments because the Honduran government would not allow an on-site American official. The SAT L-100 flew down from Dulles with a load of medical supplies and the trusted courier watched the cargo compartment empty out. As soon as that was accomplished, Owen considered he was on his own time and could do whatever he wanted. In fact he had a second purpose. The L-100 was supposed to reload FDN weapons at Aguacate and fly on to Ilopango from where, the next night, it was to make the first airdrop to the southern front. Because the SAT crew knew none of their contact people at the various points on this mission, Ollie North asked Owen to go along and help them.

This mission was a dump from the start. Owen found no FDN weapons at Aguacate to load onto the L-100. He sought out the two CIA liaison men at Aguacate, who said they knew nothing of weapons, and then *contra* representatives who simply shrugged in ignorance. Owen went back to the chief CIA man who refused to put through a call to the Honduras station chief asking him to use his influence to get the FDN to release the weapons. Finally Owen flew on to Island in an empty L-100. The next day at Ilopango there was a meeting among Owen, Felix Rodriguez, Rafael Quintero, and Colonel James Steele, the United States military advisory group chief in El Salvador. There were phone calls to Gadd, Secord, and North, and Colonel Steele agreed to put through the secure call to the Honduras station chief that had been denied to Owen. Ultimately the Project Democracy managers were forced to scrub the planned airdrop and then had to scramble to inform the affected *contra* units.

The southern front mission was tried again on April 9 with another SAT L-100, after it had delivered a load from New Orleans to Ilopango. The plane took off but could not make contact. Colonel Steele observed the takeoff, then the frustration of the returned crew. The next day, when Secord wanted to try again an hour earlier, Steele tried to insist that the mission not be flown unless radio contact with the *contras* was established first. Secord observed, "This is asinine—no black ops ever use this procedure." The private benefactor was able to get the flight reinstated and the drop was then successfully made.

There was one place in the CIA, an especially important one, where the private benefactors could get all the help they wanted. That was in Costa Rica, where station chief Joe Fernandez had been involved since the initiation of the Santa Elena airstrip project. In March 1985, Rob Owen took Fernandez a sophisticated coding device called a KL-43, produced and provided with daily tapes by the National Security Agency. The KL-43 was from Colonel North, and Fernandez used the machine on April 12 to report the successful L-100 delivery to the southern front.

Fernandez reported to Ambassador Tambs that he had been given the KL-43 device. The diplomat allowed the station chief to go ahead participating in the network North set up. The other nodes on the net were North's NSC office, Secord, Gadd, Calero, Southern Air Transport, Rafael Quintero, and Felix Rodriguez. Fernandez subsequently provided intelligence on Sandinista air defenses and dispositions, weather conditions, and local liaison. That *might* be allowed by a provision of the 1985 Intelligence Authorization Act, which permitted intelligence cooperation with the *contras.* But Fernandez went beyond that to become the contact point to whom the southern front *commandantes* went with their requests for airdrops. The CIA station chief even got into military planning, as demonstrated by his April 12 KL-43 message to North, in which he reported the L-100 drop, another drop by air over the sea for the Miskito, and the sending of eighty new UNO recruits forward with "all remaining cached lethal materiel." As for future plans, Fernandez declared, "My objective is [the] creation of [a] 2,500 man force which can strike northwest and link up with quiche [?] to form [a] solid southern force. Likewise envisage formidable opposition on [the] Atlantic Coast resupplied at or by sea."

This CIA cooperation on the southern front was perhaps the best thing going for Project Democracy at that time. The airlift remained sour, with more accidents and many abortive flights. General Secord thought he could straighten things out, and on April 20 flew to Island, taking North and Colonel Gadd with him. Secord held one meeting with the pilots at the Cooper house in San Salvador's Escalona district. There he told them that the British aircrew would make the flights into Nicaragua so that American nationals could not be captured if anything happened. Secord and North went on to a conference with Colonel Enrique Bermúdez, the *contra* military commander, and Felix Rodriguez. There the subject was getting antiaircraft missiles for the FDN. Secord thought he could get ten launchers and twenty British Blowpipe missiles from a South American country if Felix Rodriguez could get Salvadoran end-user certificates. "Max Gomez" turned to Steelhammer for reassurance; Ollie North made the appropriate gestures. Bermúdez complained of the old, slow aircraft in the lift unit. Here Ollie retorted that if he'd had the money he would have bought an L-100; the planes were donated and the *contras* had to take what they could get. The conversation had fateful consequences, for Felix began to think the Secord aircraft were property of the *contras*. Max Gomez's doubts were one path to the unraveling of Project Democracy.

After these many months the name of the game in Washington was still "bridging" aid. This time the bridge was from the humanitarian aid, which expired in March 1986, and a new $100-million request that could not take effect before the fiscal year changed on October 1. Saudi Arabia had been a generous donor in 1985 but there was little chance for a repeat performance.

"Topfloor," in the radio parlance of Bill Cooper's crews, cast about for alternatives, as did the private benefactors. General John Singlaub prepared a second approach to the Far Eastern country with whom he'd been successful before. He was called off by Abrams shortly before a scheduled meeting at the highest level. That country did donate $1 million more to the UNO.

Ollie North dreamed up the suggestion that brought culpability into the White House. This option was to divert money earned from the Iran arms sales to the *contras*. This too was done, but it ultimately involved only about $3.5 million, not the $12 million or more Steelhammer anticipated, and that amount included the Secord aircraft and the Santa Elena airfield. The discovery of North's memorandum advocating a diversion would later trigger an official investigation, when Justice Department lawyers found it in North's safe on November 21, 1986.

The official United States government approach was to solicit "bridging" aid from third countries, as decided at a National Security Planning Group meeting on May 16. All the principals were present, including Reagan, Bush, Casey, Shultz, Weinberger, political advisers James A. Baker and Don Regan, plus a host of lesser lights. For the NSC staff North was there, along with Central America director Raymond Burghardt. Admiral Poindexter presented the situation as good for the *contras* but liable to change at any moment because their funds were running out. Poindexter presented options for funding such as going to Congress for authority to reprogram other budget funds, or seeking third countries. Secretary George Shultz first argued for the solicitation option. Bill Casey asked whether this had been tried before. Shultz, unaware of the Saudi funding until a bizarre telephone call from McFarlane in June, replied that some approaches had been made but were unsuccessful. Others at the meeting, who were aware of the Saudi donations, also thought solicitation worth exploring, including increased personal involvement from President Reagan. The NSPG decided Secretary Shultz should provide a list of suitable candidate countries.

George Shultz gave this task to Elliott Abrams. Shultz had come a long way since September 1985, when, referring to North, he had actually instructed Abrams to "monitor Ollie." Now Shultz too was ready to seek donors. His instructions to Abrams were merely to avoid countries ruled by dictators and those that are dependent upon United States aid. Abrams felt the donor country had to be an oil magnate to have the requisite cash. He went to the assistant secretary for Middle Eastern affairs, Richard Murphy, to be told none seemed suitable. The only other oil country Abrams could think of was Brunei, a tiny sultanate on the north coast of Borneo in Indonesia. Abrams proposed Brunei and his suggestion was accepted.

The original idea was to have George Shultz make the approach to the Sultan of Brunei during a visit he was about to make to that East Asian country. On the secretary of state's plane crossing the Pacific there were extended discussions among Shultz and top advisers, including Gaston J. Sigur, who was moving from the NSC to State as assistant secretary for East Asian and Pacific affairs. Sigur

and others convinced Shultz to speak with the United States ambassador before talking with the Sultan, and the ambassador, in
turn, convinced the secretary not to make any solicitation during
that visit.

Shultz decided instead that Elliott Abrams should make the solicitation, which was arranged for August 8th. Abrams flew to London, where he used the alias, Mr. Kenilworth, and contacted a high
Brunei government official staying at a hotel. The two diplomats
took a walk in the park. Abrams started with his standard speech on
Central America, a talk he must have given hundreds of times, then
turned to the need for bridging aid. The Sultan's emissary asked
how much money was required. Abrams reckoned NHAO had been
spending at a rate of $3 million a month, so he answered $10 million. The emissary replied that he would have to arrange such a
transaction from home, that he did not have access to these
amounts while traveling. He asked Abrams what was in it for the
Sultan of Brunei. Abrams says he replied nothing, except the grati-
tude of the President and secretary of state. That was the end of the
walk in the park; Abrams handed the emissary a three- by five-inch
file card with a typed bank account number in Geneva.

Assistant Secretary Abrams's file card caused a tremendous diplomatic embarrassment. Abrams had anticipated he would need to
provide an address to send money and got bank account numbers
from both Allan Fiers at CIA and Colonel North at the NSC. The
CIA provided a *contra* bank account in the Bahamas. North gave
Richard Secord's Lake Resources account in Geneva. Abrams decided to use North's number, but Fawn Hall inadvertently tran-
sposed two digits when typing up the file card. The Sultan of
Brunei, however, assumed the account number to be accurate, and
went ahead and deposited $10 million on August 19.

In late August, Brunei asked the United States to confirm deposit
of the money. Elliott Abrams was on vacation at the time, but when
he returned in early September, he called Ollie North to ask about
the money. Steelhammer did not know, but a couple of days later
he called back to say it had not arrived. Abrams thereafter checked
periodically, always to be told there was no money. In one cable he
did not send, Abrams actually raised the specter of embezzlement.
The Sultan's own diplomats reassured the United States that money
transactions sometimes take time.

On December 1, after allegations of impropriety in the *contra* and Iran operations became public in the United States, the State Department cabled that Brunei should stop the deposit if it had not already been made. Delivering this message, the United States ambassador found Brunei officials "visibly shaken" that the United States thought no deposit had been made.

Eventually it turned out that $10 million of the Sultan's money was in the account of a Swiss doctor. The exercise was completely useless except to create a sore point in United States relations with Brunei, and an additional item of controversy in the widening Contragate scandal. But even had the money gone through, it would not have prevented Contragate: Elliott Abrams was mistaken in his assumption that the CIA account was less tainted than Lake Resources.

Richard Secord called the multifarious elements of his far-flung empire "the Enterprise." In collaboration with General Secord, Albert Hakim set up a corporate network with shells on top of shells. There were corporations only to receive money, just to spend money, only to provide services or buy arms, and only to own equipment. Udall Corporation owned Santa Elena and the aircraft at Ilopango. Lake Resources collected the money and was the ultimate umbrella, also running the Iran side of the business. Corporate Air Services provided the flight crews. Flight operations were arranged by Stanford Technology Trading Group International (STTGI) in Washington. Southern Air Transport and Richard Gadd's companies were frequently contracted to provide services, and did many favors as well.

The Enterprise was far-flung operationally as well. For each Iran arms delivery, Secord set up a reporting network in Europe and base in Israel. In early 1986 for a different covert operation, the Enterprise acquired the motor vessel *Erria*, which sailed the Baltic, Mediterranean, Atlantic, and Caribbean at its behest. In the eastern Mediterranean, on Cyprus, there was a parallel effort to free the hostages in Lebanon by the Drug Enforcement Administration. The Enterprise was not responsible for this, but Secord did commit his agent Tom Clines for a time to work with that operation and survey its chances. Then, of course, there was the airlift unit in Central America. It may not be surprising to learn that Richard V. Secord had ambitions of returning to government as director of operations for the CIA.

General Secord had all he could do staying in touch with all of the players and coordinating movements of money, arms, ships, and planes. For detailed management Secord had to rely upon subordinates. Tom Clines did the arms shipments to Central America. Air operations in Central America were the province of Dick Gadd, but he was pretty burned out by the spring of 1986. Secord was doubly pleased at this time, therefore, to hear that his friend Colonel Robert C. Dutton was retiring as deputy chief of staff of the Twenty-third Air Force, which is responsible for USAF special operations and rescue work. Dutton had served with Secord on the Iran hostage missions and trusted his judgment implicitly. Secord immediately offered Dutton a place at STTGI as manager for the Project Democracy airlift.

Dutton came on at the beginning of May at a salary of $5,000 a month. Secord spoke of the legal situation at their very first meeting. Dutton was given a copy of the sanitized IOB legal opinion Bretton Sciarone wrote in 1985, which Secord considered to be sufficient "lawyering" to satisfy him. Secord's instructions were to avoid violating the Neutrality Act by doing nothing on United States soil and by never delivering personnel, only weapons. Dutton immediately left for El Salvador to meet the airlift people and see the equipment. Where Secord could spare one afternoon for his Island visit, Dutton stayed until May 23. He met with the pilots carrying the legal opinion under his arm and reviewed the ground rules with them. Dutton emphasized that William J. Cooper was the boss in San Salvador, that Rafael Quintero was only director of support, and Felix Rodriguez a local facilitator. Dutton initially got a good impression of Felix though later he came to think Rodriguez a meddler. The aircrews did reports of their missions which they sent to Dutton, who passed them to Secord and Colonel Oliver North, whom Dutton considered "co-commanders."

The early intention to limit flights over Nicaragua to third country nationals was abandoned in mid-June. The British crew featured a pilot who had previously only flown helicopters. Moreover, their escapades in San Salvador were drawing unwanted attention to the foreigners, plus a rebuke from military advisory group commander Colonel James Steele on one occasion. Another time British antics led the Salvadorans to bar the whole Cooper unit from Ilopango air base. David Walker's British were phased out of Project Democracy; North and Secord made the decision to send Americans into

Nicaragua. Here came another security breach waiting to happen.

The private communications network was a security breach in progress, with top-secret National Security Agency KL-43 devices and encoding tapes in the hands of persons holding no clearances. Because of his name figuring in the Wilson affair, Secord had failed to attain a CIA clearance in 1983; his Pentagon clearances had later been revoked after failure to file the requisite disclosure papers. Bill Cooper, Quintero, Rodriguez, also lacked clearances. Their use of KL-43 units was convenient operationally but was in all likelihood illegal.

Beyond the use of secret encoding devices there were many ways in which the United States government made the private benefactor activities possible. Colonel Steele provided some intelligence information and weather data, and intervened several times when the Project Democracy people were locked out of Ilopango. Steele also allowed Felix Rodriguez access to the KL-43, provided him a military car and advisory group identification, and at times made him deputy for matters related to the private benefactors. From the United States embassy Rodriguez got a powerful radio to maintain communications with the aircraft on their missions. Felix also got work crews to fix up his house, and the embassy expedited paperwork for Rafael Quintero on loads and personnel movements. From the CIA came the vital cooperation of Joe Fernandez, who sometimes sent his drop zone lists through Quintero and sometimes directly to STTGI.

The degree of CIA involvement was of great interest to Secord and North, who pressed for more of it. On May 16, North sent Admiral Poindexter a memo arguing that the more visible Project Democracy became, with its planes, pilots, and weapons deliveries, the more inquisitive people would become. Steelhammer wrote, "We have to lift more of this onto the CIA," adding facetiously that he needed more than two or three hours of sleep at night. Rather than taking more, Langley suddenly seemed to want less—on May 21, Dutton got a KL-43 message from Quintero that the CIA's people were now saying, after further consultation with their general counsel, that they could not speak with Secord's people at all. That applied to Bill Cooper's crew including Quintero, and specifically enjoined CIA's Joe Fernandez from helping. Secord went to Steelhammer and North followed up with Langley, which remained cool for a time but later in the summer once again warmed up to the private benefactors.

It was at about this time that North took Secord to a meeting with Bill Casey where the discussion, it seemed to Secord, must have been part of an ongoing exchange between Steelhammer and the DCI. Ollie complained that donations were trailing off and mentioned a Middle Eastern country where Secord had contacts he could solicit. Several times North remarked that he himself could not make such solicitations. Secord objected that he was not a United States official and that his contacts would not want to hear from private citizens. This was a far cry from Secord's behavior with Calero in 1985, when he had claimed part of the credit for the Saudi donations. General Secord was also asked how much he needed to keep the airlift going. He estimated a requirement for $10 million. This may have been what led Oliver North to put the Lake Resources account number on the file card he provided Elliott Abrams.

Equipment continued to cause problems for the Enterprise. Drainage was poor at the Santa Elena airfield, which was soggy from the rainy season. When Bill Cooper landed a C-123K there for the first time, it sank into the mud. Poindexter heard of this on June 10 from a computer bulletin board, or "PROF," note that Ollie left for him. A week later a projected airdrop to the southern front failed when North and Joe Fernandez were unable to locate the *commandantes*. In mid-June the Project Democracy managers decided to procure a second C-123K and two new engines after the first plane, ten miles off course due to faulty navigation equipment, hit the trees atop a mountain and sheared off one engine. The plane managed to make Island safely, but the crew were almost killed and pilot John Piowaty joined others in preparing a scathing letter indicting Project Democracy's aircraft maintenance.

The letter went to Felix Rodriguez, whose doubts about the operation were growing rapidly. Felix had met with North in his Suite 302 office at the beginning of May to say he was tired and wanted to bail out, but North was desperate to keep him. A month later, Dutton returned from a June 5–8 visit to Island to report that "Max is the only problem." Rodriguez, according to Dutton, did not understand the concept of the operation. Steelhammer asked Dutton to have Rodriguez come up to "Topfloor," as Washington was called in the radio traffic. "Max Gomez" accordingly presented himself at the old Executive Office Building on June 25.

Rodriguez had a problem just getting in the gate at the White House. That set the tone for the rest of the meeting, where North accused Max of violating communications security by talking about the airlift on an open phone line. Steelhammer claimed he had NSA intercepts to prove it. Rodriguez countered with accusations of faulty maintenance and produced the Piowaty letter. North looked at it and asked, "Is this a joke?" Felix replied that the men who had written the letter had almost been killed. North turned to Dutton, who admitted he knew of the incident but had not thought it worthy of North's attention.

Then Felix Rodriguez asked to speak with Steelhammer alone. When Dutton had left the room, Felix began, "Colonel, I have learned there is stealing going on here." Max Gomez talked of thirty-two-year-old mortar ammunition and the three-dollar hand grenades sold for nine, of which he had learned from Mario Dellamico. Felix brought up the Wilson case and the association with it of Quintero and Thomas Clines. When North then praised Clines as a patriotic American, Felix Rodriguez retorted, "This could be worse than Watergate, it could destroy the President of the United States."

Ollie turned to his television set, which was tuned to the congressional debate on the $100-million aid request. North pointed at the TV. "Those people want me," he said, "but they can't have me because the old man loves my°[ass]."

Max Gomez was isolated in San Salvador with his objections and slowly frozen out of Project Democracy. John Piowaty got promoted by Dutton to chief of maintenance.

The Enterprise tried its best with the airlift. The damaged C-123K went to Southern Air Transport for repairs, while a second aircraft was quickly found. Cooper and a mechanic went up to Tucson, Arizona, to check out the new C-123K and had it at Island before the end of June. Cooper's crews also made their first successful airdrop to the southern front, by Buz Sawyer flying one of the Caribous. The C-7 had such a short range, however, that after the drop it was obliged to land at Aeropuerto Juan Santamaria in Costa Rica to refuel. The Costa Ricans had not given permission for any such thing, but did so after Ambassador Tambs told Joe Fernandez and the military advisory group chief to take care of it.

The airlift went on but remained a shoestring operation. It was tough to find the drop zones and even rarer to find *contras* waiting on them with radio communication and the proper signals. The flights would go to the drop zones, then begin a box search for the *contra* bands, more often than not, returning to Island without completing the mission. In June, Dutton talked with Colonel Steele about a new arrangement of dropping blind into well-defined zones, then having Joe Fernandez simply alert the *commandantes* that supplies awaited them. That was not reliable and was not done. Timing was also a problem. Steele wanted to prohibit daytime flights to minimize the risk of Sandinista air defenses, but night flights were impossible because of poor navigational equipment. Dawn drops found fog up to two hundred feet, while evening missions encountered thunderstorms that built up to fifty thousand feet, far above the ceilings of the aircraft. The poor drainage of the Plantation strip also resulted in three or four incidents in which planes got stuck in the mud. Operation costs were running at $1,800 per flight hour for the C-123's, $1,300 an hour for the C-7's, and $300 per hour for the light Maules.

Relations between Felix Rodriguez and the Enterprise worsened daily. Rodriguez asked what had happened to the Salvadoran end-user certificates he had provided for Blowpipe missiles and was told the deal had been delayed. He finally asked for the documents back but Secord provided nothing. In late July, Rodriguez engaged in some stunts to entertain a visiting South American military friend, whereupon he was accused of stealing an aircraft. There were a few tense days, during which Felix Rodriguez organized Cooper's pilots to fly despite prohibitions from STTGI; then Max Gomez was out of the operation altogether.

In leaving Project Democracy, Felix Rodriguez took two actions that permanently affected the Enterprise. He went to Colonel Bermúdez and told the *contra* commander UNO should consider the planes its property. At Ilopango base, Rodriguez got armed guards assigned to each flight to ensure the planes were not diverted from their missions. In Washington on August 8, Rodriguez met with the national security adviser to Vice-President George Bush, Donald Gregg, a fellow CIA veteran with whom Felix consulted periodically on matters pertaining to El Salvador. Rodriguez went over the same ground he had covered with North at their last meeting. He talked about expensive airplanes, overbilling for pilot hours, the nine-dollar hand grenades, and other items. Felix charged, "Mr. Gadd is engaged in a ripoff," according to notes Gregg made of the meeting. Gregg immediately called North's office and got his deputy in to listen to the "outrageous charges from my friend Felix." Gregg followed up in CIA and Pentagon channels a few days later. These charges created questions about the Enterprise at a high level in the United States government.

A few days later Lieutenant Colonel Ralph Earl, North's deputy, along with Dutton, met with Colonel James Steele of the advisory group. Dutton asked Steele to get the KL-43 unit back from Rodriguez. The colonel merely said he understood the problem.

The big break for Adolfo Calero came in August 1985, when Congress finally passed the $100-million *contra* aid appropriation, to be effective October 1 with the new fiscal year. The NSC staff operators no doubt celebrated among themselves this long-awaited reprieve. But there was less to celebrate than met the eye—Ollie North had been quite correct that more people would become inquisitive as the Project Democracy airlift became more visible. This was a covert operation that began to unravel just as it reached full stride.

For some time the press had been catching bits of revelations regarding the activity. Though the press was still focusing to a considerable degree on John Singlaub, Ollie North's name was coming up in a variety of places in their accounts. So were the names of Robert Owen and Richard V. Secord, now being tied to aircraft sales to the *contras.* North had some success in suppressing stories by two Associated Press reporters investigating the case, but the *Miami Herald* came through with repeated disclosures infuriating Elliott Abrams, among others. There was enough out there now that two American reporters in Costa Rica, Tony Avirgan and Martha Honey, joined with the Christic Institute in a civil lawsuit filed in Miami against about thirty defendants alleged to have been involved in the La Penca bombing of Pastora, in which Avirgan was injured. The defendants included Calero, North, Owen, Singlaub, Secord, and Theodore Shackley, formerly of the CIA. Here again was a time bomb threatening to explode Project Democracy.

Of rather more immediate concern to Ollie North were moves in Congress, as he indicated to Felix Rodriguez at their last meeting. In late June a bill was introduced in the House of Representatives asking the President to provide documentary evidence on North or any other NSC members assisting the *contras.* Ollie's tour of duty at the NSC staff was due to be up in July, and at this juncture Admiral Poindexter himself attempted and failed to get North off the project. Steelhammer rejected suggestions that the time had come to return to the Marine Corps—his work was just too vital to national security. Poindexter then tried to get the *contra* account shifted to the responsible NSC officers for intelligence and regional matters. The admiral swiftly received a series of calls from conservative lawmakers objecting to the shift of North; then the colonel was defended in a piece by columnists Rowland Evans and Robert Novak that accused Poindexter of running the NSC as "a bland paper machine." The admiral backed off. Poindexter lamely explained to North in a PROF note, "I just wanted to lower your visibility so you wouldn't be such a good target for the [liberals]."

Admiral Poindexter nevertheless assigned one of his intelligence aides to accompany North in representing NSC at the meetings of Elliott Abrams's Restricted Interagency Group. The man was Vince Cannistraro, a CIA detailee who was Fiers's predecessor as chief of Central America Task Force and was already collaborating with North on other covert activities. Cannistraro may have been a monitor for Poindexter but he was no check on Ollie's actions.

The House inquiry was compromised away by the White House. The bill disappeared in committee late in July, after which the NSC agreed to allow Colonel North to be interviewed by the House intelligence committee. According to NSC notes of the meeting, North's statements were false: He said he had given no military advice and knew of no military operations; he had had no contact with Singlaub in twenty months and gave *him* no advice; he knew Robert Owen only casually and had never given him guidance. In a PROF note afterward Poindexter gave Ollie the Navy's top accolade, "Well Done."

Below the surface there was other maneuvering going on as well. North and Secord conferred about the disposition of Project Democracy's assets in the context of the CIA coming back into the Nicaraguan secret war come October. Secord discussed this with Dutton, whom he assigned to write a paper summarizing the assets and stating the options. The aircraft and field at Santa Elena plus other holdings of the Enterprise were estimated to value $4.5 million. The options were to sell these assets, to give them to the CIA, or to lease the assets to the CIA for an operating cost of $311,000 a month, more if the planes were used more than fifty flying hours each. North raised the possibility of a CIA purchase with Poindexter in PROF notes during July as well.

At Island the airlift proceeded apace. Judged from Salvadoran telephone company records, whose authenticity Secord disputes, there were numerous calls from the Escalona district houses to STTGI, Secord's home, and Southern Air Transport. There were also calls to North's office, including his unlisted direct number, and to numbers in Costa Rica attributed to Joe Fernandez. The phone bills figured in one of the disputes between Felix Rodriguez and STTGI over setting up a $10,000 contingency fund for the operation in El Salvador. Dutton saw this as Max Gomez reaching for the cash, just as he had insisted on controlling the $50,000 fuel fund for Project Democracy at Ilopango. Dutton didn't want pilots carrying around contingency fund cash and then being tempted to bribe their way out of tight situations. Rodriguez saw late bills piling up, which only raised questions about the Americans, and insists that he took over the fuel fund after a dubious incident in which a large amount of cash was handed to the Salvadoran commander and purported to be for the fund. In any case the phone bills were remarkable in themselves—the three houses in this period ran up bills of $1,119, $1,877, and $1,000, while Rodriguez's office had a bill of $693.

The numerous long-distance telephone calls complemented a very active flight program. The drop zones remained elusive, but in August there was another successful mission to the southern front, requested by Fernandez at mid-month. Again the aircraft landed at San José's Aeropuerto Juan Santamaria where refueling and permissions were handled by the CIA station chief and the military advisory group commander. The southern front *contra* leaders were now beginning to line up outside Joe Fernandez's door with proposals for drops and zones.

Costa Rica had had an election since the start of Santa Elena and the new government took office in May 1986. The president had a new peace plan to replace the stalled Contadora effort and was determined to put new teeth into Costa Rica's official neutrality. On September 3 the government seized the "secret" airstrip at Santa Elena, blocked the runway there, and placed guards at the Plantation site. A few days later North learned the Costa Ricans were going to have a press conference to reveal the Santa Elena base. North spoke to Elliott Abrams, who tracked down Ambassador Lewis Tambs on vacation. The three had a midnight conference call, after which Tambs phoned President Oscar Arias Sanchez and got him to cancel the public revelation.

At the very moment that Steelhammer was scampering to avoid a press conference that would have blown Project Democracy's cover, Dutton was participating in what could also have turned into a major security breach. The STTGI manager went to Island on September 8 and stayed twelve days to get a feel for what the operations were like. As part of this he went along on one of the Nicaragua entry flights, another abortive exercise that failed to make contact with the *contra* recipients. It was rainy, the ceiling was barely fifteen hundred feet, the plane searched for an hour then gave up. By KL-43 on September 9, Dutton asked North for help locating the southern front troops, Ollie replied he would consult Joe Fernandez. Two days later the Salvadorans refused to allow missions by two aircraft together, but then the airlift got lucky. On September 13, Dutton reported on the KL-43 that Project Democracy had delivered 55,000 pounds in two days. Through the rest of the month perhaps seven loads were checked out of the warehouse for the southern front, and 180,000–185,000 pounds were dropped in ten to fifteen missions. North sent his deputy, Lieutenant Colonel Ralph Earl, down to see. At an exultant point Dutton ended one KL-43 message: "Send Fawn—can't continue on milk and cookies."

When Dutton was reporting to North on the negative results of the flight he had been on, Steelhammer realized the STTGI manager had gone into Nicaragua. Ollie asked, "You went on that mission, didn't you?" North felt Dutton knew too much and prohibited him from further flights. As with his complaint to Felix Rodriguez about open phone calls, this was symptomatic of North's great concern for small points of security, but major clues to the operation were scattered about in many places. It was only a matter of time, or of someone going public, until Project Democracy came into the open. Suddenly in September, project personnel were asked to sign secrecy agreements similar to those the CIA uses.

The time came on October 5, 1986. That day one of the C-123K's had been laid on to deliver supplies to an FDN patrol called Sophia at a point where five smoke signals formed an L. The plane was piloted by Bill Cooper and Buz Sawyer, with Eugene Hasenfus as loadmaster. Cooper flew without using any of the standard evasive tactics against antiaircraft missiles and that day his luck ran out. The plane flew over a Sandinista unit, was hit by a missile, and crashed. Hasenfus, who even in Laos had always taken precautions for his personal safety, was the only crewman wearing a parachute, and he jumped and survived. Hasenfus was captured by the Nicaraguans. Unaware of the actual instigators of Project Democracy, Hasenfus told the Sandinistas his plane was employed by the CIA. The fat was in the fire.

The Reagan administration circled its wagons in Washington, where the flap was tremendous. Elliott Abrams's office tried to attribute the plane operation to General Singlaub and claimed the United States had nothing to do with it. The CIA denied any involvement whatsoever. Abrams himself, and CIA Director of Operations Clair George repeated these denials to Congress on October 14. Ollie North intervened with the Justice Department to delay an investigation of Southern Air Transport, where the second Project Democracy C-123 was undergoing repair at the time of the Hasenfus crash. John McRainey flew the plane out for Island late at night when few could be watching.

At every step, however, there were new suggestions of ties to the United States government. Buz Sawyer's personal flight log, recovered from the wreckage of the Cooper plane, showed he had performed flights for the United States military with Southern Air transport (SAT). They also showed SAT personnel, including William Langton, along for some of the *contra* flights. Business cards found in the wreckage suggested a link to the Nicaraguan Humanitarian Assistance Office. The plane itself, tail number N-4410F, was the same one used in the United States entrapment scheme perpetrated on the Sandinistas in 1984. Inquiries in El Salvador quickly revealed the pseudonym Max Gomez and then led to Donald Gregg in the office of the Vice-President. The telephone records tied North explicitly into the action. As if this weren't enough, the Iranian side of the Enterprise's activities was simultaneously coming into the open. Finally the discovery of a North memorandum discussing diversion of Iran arms funds to benefit the *contras* triggered the first of numerous investigations into both sides of the Iran-Contra affair.

Investigations have not yet been completed. The outcome for actors like Richard V. Secord and Oliver North cannot yet be told. But for Ollie it must have begun a nightmare far worse than the trials he had endured, at Annapolis so many years before, when he got himself stuck on the road to Quantico.

Project Democracy never existed in a vacuum. The purpose of the operation was always to "bridge" the *contras* into the bright future when the CIA would come back again. Bill Casey was committed to that, even if he was reticent at times in cooperating with Secord's men. The CIA did nothing to rein in the project, did help when it could, and did everything it could do to get back into the action itself.

Political action remained a feature of Langley's activity throughout this period. Clarridge carefully handed the *contra* account over to North at the very beginning. To help make the *contras* more palatable to Congress, the Agency brokered deals among UNO factions and between Calero's group and the Miskito. It is reported that several million dollars from the CIA supported UNO offices in Europe and Latin America, subsidized *contra* officials, and paid for their trips abroad.

When Congress permitted intelligence and communication cooperation at the end of 1985, the Agency also used this cloak to cover delivery of a reported $13 million in communications gear. This was material aid of a specific and vital sort and certainly allowed Calero to use UNO's own funds for other purposes. Moreover, when the Agency discovered, as early as April 1986, that its Costa Rica station chief was working to support North's operation, it took no steps to bring this to the attention of the appropriate oversight bodies.

In early 1986, when the question was getting Reagan's new *contra* aid requests through Congress, Langley was also quite willing to help. One twelve-page CIA intelligence report in January tried to defend the *contras* against charges of human rights abuses by discrediting studies containing such allegations. Bill Casey personally participated in February, presiding over congressional briefings at which the CIA distributed a classified paper, then collected it at the end of the meetings. The paper characterized lobbying efforts by the consulting firm Agendas International in behalf of Managua as a disinformation and subversion campaign against the United States.

In the summer of 1986, reportedly dissatisfied at the Miskito Indians' refusal to come to terms with Calero, the Agency repossessed equipment previously given to them. That August there was another CIA helicopter crash in which two Americans and two Miskito reportedly perished.

As the time came for the "bridge" to end, the CIA then opened up to the private benefactor operation. Secord alleges an Agency decision at that time to take over the Project Democracy assets.

Ollie North met with CIA officials on October 9, four days *after* the Hasenfus plane crash. The Agency actually did purchase, for $1.2 million, the Hakim-Secord group's last weapons shipment, which was on the high seas en route to Central America when Hasenfus went down.

Of course, Langley had its own plans for its renewed secret war. Under the appropriation $70 million is available for military aid, $27 million for humanitarian assistance, and $3 million to operate a *contra* human rights office. Activity is coordinated by a renewed task force under Army Colonel William C. Comee. Because of the proximity of Aguacate to the Nicaraguan border, and a restriction in the funding authorization against assistance within twenty miles of that border, airlift operations are now carried out from Swan Island, previously the location for the CIA's black radio during the Bay of Pigs operation.

Nicaragua was Bill Casey's last secret war and perhaps his epitaph. Casey was at Langley to see the new program come into effect, but also the widening morass of the Iran-Contra scandal. Casey provided incomplete testimony in three congressional appearances and allowed a false statement to be prepared for him for a November 21, 1986, hearing. The day before he was scheduled to appear under oath before the Senate Select Committee on Intelligence, Casey collapsed in his Langley office. He was admitted to the hospital and diagnosed as suffering from a cerebral tumor. There were other complications as well, and Mr. Casey passed away on May 6, 1987. Casey took the secret of this vest pocket operation with him to the grave.

On the ground the issue remains in doubt. Calero claims a strength of sixteen thousand troops but the war is still a matter of alarums and excursions. A series of successful sabotage strikes in March 1987, by a commando group specially trained by the CIA, only demonstrates the point. In the meantime the *contras* have lost Juan Gomez, their air force chief, and three more aircraft—a C-54, a C-47, and a twin-engine Beechcraft. But Arturo Cruz has resigned from UNO, which still appears the creature of Calero and company. The Sandinistas have mobilized upward of sixty thousand regulars and militia. Despite Elliott Abrams's promise that the *contras* will change the facts on the ground, the Sandinistas have contained the threat. Nicaragua's 1984 elections, denounced as a sham by the United States, still confirmed Sandinista leadership within Nicaragua. Five years of paramilitary action and $300 million have not unseated them, and the administration talks of a $105-million request for 1988.

Bill Casey presided over a revitalization of the CIA's covert action capability. He was proud of that achievement. In the end, however, the many questions raised by the Iran-Contra affair may have the effect of tightening controls over the Agency. In his first appearance before the joint congressional committee investigating the affair, Richard V. Secord, whose ambition was to control CIA operations, was forced into an admission that the old Hughes-Ryan Amendment controls were appropriate. It will be ironic if Casey's legacy is the releashing of the CIA.

The worst aspect of this direct White House involvement in a covert action is the squandering of a President's political capital on a marginal issue. The prestige of the presidency has been openly committed to an effort that by definition lies at the very margins of legality in international relations. Project Democracy muddied the waters even further by skirting the law of the land. There are many wise reasons for eschewing such a policy.

President Reagan's campaign for *contra* aid is a far cry from the days when Dwight Eisenhower refused even to meet with the Dalai Lama for fear of appearing to take sides. Even so, the new wave of paramilitary operations has had similarly indifferent results.

·XX·

PRESIDENTS, POLICIES, AND PARAMILITARY OPTIONS

The controversy over the mining of Nicaraguan ports ended in a compromise between the executive branch and Congress that better defines requirements for the content of Presidential Findings and conditions under which these must be rendered. These definitions are bound to be tested in the years ahead, since the Reagan administration strongly defends its option to resort to covert action as a foreign policy tool; its ideological bent ensures that the administration will perceive plentiful opportunities for the employment of these methods.

There was renewed pressure in early 1986 to resume military aid to the *contras*. There were also vocal demands for similar paramilitary aid to Cambodian rebels and to UNITA in Angola. This time, according to some, we should support anticommunist Cambodians who will fight a Vietnamese puppet government. It is pertinent that *this time* our ally will be the faction headed by Norodom Sihanouk, the ruler overthrown in 1970, who is allied with the communist guerrillas of Pol Pot, formerly our enemy. In Angola over the decade since Operation Feature, Jonas Savimbi has preserved the close UNITA relationship with South African intelligence he forged then. A renewed paramilitary action in Angola would be subject to the same political problems that John Stockwell describes so trenchantly in his account of the 1975 fiasco.

What then of the theorists with even bigger visions? Two of the more prominent exponents of activism in today's era of the unleashed CIA are Dr. Angelo Codevilla, a Senate staff member, and Dr. Roy Godson, a political science professor at Georgetown University. Their vision, expressed in a 1985 paper, was that it is neither superfluous nor beyond our means to supply material assistance to the victims of Communist oppression in Eastern Europe, and to their families. The covert networks to deliver this assistance can be built. Over the long run the "safety net" for those who choose to stand up for their rights, combined with well-timed subversion of the Soviet Union's most obsequious servants, might help to neutralize, and perhaps even to turn Eastern Europe into a liability for the Soviet Union.

While denying that this would amount to nurturing popular anti-Soviet movements, the authors make clear that such covert aid would be part of a policy including political and economic measures and military contingency plans. There are strong echoes of "rollback" here, as well as a return to operations in the "denied areas." Frank Wisner would have approved.

Former intelligence officers almost uniformly support a continued capability for, and reliance on, covert action. This remains true after the recent excesses in Nicaragua, in statements from such figures as William E. Colby and Ray Cline. Retired CIA officers like B. Hugh Tovar and Theodore Shackley have even advanced theories of covert action to supply some intellectual foundation for secret warfare. Shackley considers covert action a "third option" between doing nothing and going to war.

Visions of covert action are based on a wish and a hope. The theories have been preoccupied with tactical considerations, with menus of measures and conditions for success. Neither the visions nor the theories seem to have made much effort to assess the net effect of covert action on American foreign policy. Rather, the argument runs, these techniques have been useful sometimes, and therefore should be maintained in perpetuity, regardless of other considerations.

Writing after the controversy over mining Nicaraguan harbors, McGeorge Bundy noted that "the dismal historical record of covert military and paramilitary operations over the last 25 years is entirely clear." As the NSC adviser to Presidents Kennedy and Johnson, Bundy has some basis on which to make that observation.

The truth is that the record of covert action is not without its successes. Notable among these are the partisan projects during the Korean War and the CIDG and Meo efforts in Indochina. A necessary qualification is that the programs were successful in mobilizing paramilitary forces but were not strategically decisive: neither in

North Korea nor in North Vietnam were adversary forces significantly hampered by the existence or effectiveness of United States paramilitary allies. It is also illuminating that in both cases the operations were wartime programs, which could count on ample resources, including the expertise of military special-warfare forces.

The CIA programs most often cited as successes are Operation Ajax in Iran and Operation Success in Guatemala. Yet these victories had only short-term effects. Action in Iran sowed the seeds for what became virulent anti-Americanism on the part of the successors to the Shah. In Guatemala the overthrow of Arbenz turned the country away from democracy, the supposed aim of the covert action. Neither victory materially affected the balance in the cold war, while, disturbingly, failure *would* have triggered shifts, by forcing those nations into the arms of the Soviet Union.

A paradigm case for this sort of failure has been Cuba. The vendettas conducted by Eisenhower and Kennedy radicalized Fidel Castro, necessitated Cuban reliance on the Soviets, and converted a traditional friend of the United States into an opponent. The covert action also backfired by leading the Cubans and Soviets into nuclear missile deployments, creating a direct military threat to the United States and a crisis that brought us to the edge of nuclear war. In addition, the Cuban-American hostility has become entrenched, with new rounds of proxy or direct sparring in lands as far removed as Angola, Grenada, and Nicaragua.

Operations against the "denied areas" uniformly resulted in failures, and have long since been abandoned. Had these operations been successful, the Soviets would have been confronted with the necessity for a response not confined to a paramilitary level of conflict. This would also be the case today in the event that any scheme like that suggested by Codevilla and Godson were adopted.

The People's Republic of China was one "denied area" where operations rebounded to the detriment of the United States. Adventures with Muslim warlords and Li Mi served to identify the United States with Chiang Kai-shek and the corrupt Kuomintang. The Chinese communists were handed a propaganda tool, a "foreign devil" to use as a symbol in solidifying Mao Tse-tung's control of the nation. The later operation in Tibet was merely incapable of a successful conclusion; it was a spoiling effort by definition.

Indonesia was not a "denied area," but the result there was similar. Sukarno was able to use the apparent American threat as justification for eliminating the last vestiges of opposition to his own rule. This disaster has escaped more intensive examination only because a military coup almost a decade later turned Indonesia back toward the United States' orbit. The effort in Afghanistan, like the earlier one in Tibet, has the characteristics of a cold-war spoiling operation and is really only amenable to a political solution.

Most of the other paramilitary operations surveyed have been unalloyed failures, perhaps excepting the Congo, where the outcome is still disputed among former CIA officers. The ledger of failure includes Albania, Angola, and the Kurds, in addition to efforts in the "denied areas." Track II in Chile failed, but its failure was mitigated by the success of economic pressures and political action that undermined the Allende government. The Chile case also illustrates what *did* work—manipulation of foreign aid and international cash flows. It should be quite clear that a paramilitary capability is not necessary to use that type of technique.

In Nicaragua the issue remains in doubt but the portents still do not favor the United States–sponsored anti-Sandinista forces. "Humanitarian" assistance has given way to military aid once again, but the *contras* have still failed to establish themselves inside Nicaragua. They were unable to triumph in 1983 and early 1984 when conditions most favored them. Since then a united front directorate was forged and has fragmented, while the Miskito and ARDE have gone their own ways. The UNO/FDN retains its pejorative association with Somoza's national guard and has built on its already abysmal human rights record. Force building in the Honduran base camps is literally all that is being accomplished, while the host nation, the sanctuary, has begun to show signs of restiveness at the *contras'* presence. Sandinista military forces have improved their own organization and tactics. There is no evidence that another $100 million for this paramilitary operation, or any amount above that, can transform this basic situation.

In all these CIA operations there is a lesson for prospective guerrillas as well. Being a superpower, the United States acts in its own interests, which are those of the Great Power. There is little true identity of interests between the restive local minority and the Great Power, while there is substantial danger for the local minority in accepting paramilitary aid that may later evaporate at critical moments. Sophisticated guerrillas will avoid playing the United States' game, preventing the CIA from exercising true control, and again vitiating the purpose of paramilitary action.

American national interest suffers each time a paramilitary operation fails. The record shows successes to be few, failures far more numerous, and wartime actions to have been the most useful. It was war that popularized these techniques in the first place. British military historian Michael Howard captures the essence of this development in a lecture he delivered at Oxford University in November 1977:

> The belligerents during the Second World War not only developed weapons of mass destruction: they also developed methods of strategem, subversion and psychological warfare which afterwards remained in their arsenals and became, as it were, institutionalized. In the ideological confrontation that developed after the war and with which we still have to live, honorable men of great ability served their countries by engaging in activities of a kind unjustifiable by any criteria other than the most brutal kind of *raison d'état*, and by the argument that their adversaries were doing the same.

After building a capability expressly to fight the Russians, American secret warriors soon abandoned action in the "denied areas" in favor of interventions in Third World countries. Covert action against the Soviet Union was explicitly referred to in NSC-4/A and NSC-10/2. It took roughly six years, until 1954, for the Central Intelligence Agency to generate its global paramilitary capability; once the forces were built, no further paramilitary operations were attempted against the Soviet Union. This is especially true of the "modern" era, the twenty-five-year period from 1960 to 1985, of which McGeorge Bundy writes.

In terms of its contribution to United States relations with the Third World, paramilitary action has had minimal positive results. The United States committed itself to long-term assistance in Iran, Guatemala, and Chile there that eventually dwarfed the dollar costs of the original CIA projects. The numerous failures contributed nothing. Moreover, it can be argued that the effort as a whole helped fuel the rise of the "nonaligned" movement, neutralism in world affairs, the success of which comes at the expense of cold war strategies. There appears to be much evidence to buttress McGeorge Bundy's assessment of covert action.

Shifting focus to paramilitary action in its own terms, a number of specific weaknesses are visible in the method. These are problems inherent in the use of the technique, including, to some extent, the complementary features of political action and psychological warfare.

Langley has become an avid sponsor of "third force" political movements. Third force movements are noncommunist, preferably anticommunist, but also not fascist. In practice, the third force often turns out to be politically moderate, what would be called Christian democratic in several European countries. In Third World nations, however, third force movements also tend to be associated with established oligarchies in Latin America, or tribes in Africa and Asia. Using such minorities often does little to satisfy general popular aspirations, and often leads only to further upheaval, and additional obligations for United States support of its client groups.

Sometimes there is no third force. The usual political action response is then to create one. These types of artificial groupings tend to have little popular support and are locally perceived as agents for American power. This was the case in Laos with the Committee for the Defense of National Interests; in Albania, with the Committee for a Free Albania; in Angola, with Holden Roberto; and in Zaire, with Joseph Mobutu. While the assumption in using third force tactics is that they will have wide popular appeal, artificial movements have sown few grass roots and are correspondingly fragile.

Where arrays of organized political movements exist, the choice is frequently limited. In Indonesia, Allen Dulles's CIA chose to align itself with separatist military officers and political malcontents. More recently in Nicaragua, the CIA has favored the former National Guardsmen of FDN over the former Sandinistas of ARDE. Too often the United States seems to land on the wrong side of these choices. Langley appears to prefer alleged military expertise over political credibility, and there have been too many cases where the CIA's side with its supposed expertise runs away from the fray.

One special problem of working through local proxies is suffering political liabilities as a result of acts by the local allies. The Indonesian colonels with their smuggling again come to mind, but there is also the drug trafficking by Li Mi's Chinese and Vang Pao's Meo. Allegations of similar activity have been laid at the feet of both sides in the Nicaraguan conflict. In Tibet, Afghanistan, and the Indochinese war a proportion of the CIA's assistance was soaked up by its own allies while still in the pipeline. These kinds of problems not only reduce the effectiveness of covert actions, but they are unavoidable, given the requirement for local allies.

Another kind of special problem arises from the mobilization of local minorities in defense of the nation, as in counterinsurgency in Indochina, which mobilized the *montagnards* in Vietnam and Meo in Laos. In the classical technique, the loyalty of these minority peoples is gained through "nation building," the broad range of measures designed to give a people a stake in the conflict. The problem lies in the contradiction inherent between building nationhood among a minority in the face of the existing sovereignty of the national government, which is itself the object being supported by the CIA covert action. The competition usually can end in only one way, illustrated by South Vietnamese suppression of the *montagnard* autonomy movement and its incorporation of the Mike Forces into the South Vietnamese army. A similar sort of calculation lies behind the decision by the Shah of Iran to betray the Kurdish minority movement. Such actions by governments allied with the United States were not far removed from the Soviet Union's suppression of minorities in the Ukraine, Estonia, Latvia, and Lithuania.

Paramilitary action is also subject to serious operational difficulties. Free-lance raids by the CIA's own allies or others can disrupt carefully planned scenarios, as in the episode where the Kennedy administration became concerned over the uncontrolled activities of anti-Castro Cuban exiles. There is also the problem of the CIA officer who is out of control, the "cowboy" exceeding his instructions. The Central Intelligence Agency is a tightly disciplined organization, but even Langley's reach is limited and there is more than one case of an officer pulling the Agency out on a limb. The record shows that American officers violated orders against direct involvement in the operations against China, Guatemala, Cuba, and Angola, as well as during the campaign in Laos, and these are just the instances we know of. During the Guatemala action a CIA officer took the instructions of a local ally to bomb a neutral freighter. In Laos, a CIA officer assigned to Phoumi Nosavan almost unilaterally changed United States policy. In Nicaragua, a CIA contract officer concocted a guerrilla warfare manual that broke the regulations designed to avoid involvement in assassinations. It is no wonder that Langley paramilitary staffs worry about "cowboys" in the field.

A slightly different problem is the officer who adopts the values and goals of the people CIA is attempting to mobilize. This can lead just as surely to insubordination, since Langley's goals are rarely identical to those of the local minority. The Agency and the military special-warfare forces had difficulties of this sort with the Tibetans, the *montagnards*, and the Meo, as well as the Cubans.

Leaks of information have contributed to several covert action failures, and are unavoidable. Most insidious are leaks that are caused by the adversary's use of classical espionage techniques, because these are unknown to the secret warriors laying their plans. Thus the penetrations of the Soviet and Albanian operations by Kim Philby, as well as the Russians' success at infiltrating the Soviet and Polish operations, contributed measurably to their demise.

Leaks to the press are a better-known problem, but at least a press leak becomes known to Langley, so countermeasures can be taken. In any major paramilitary action, which may involve CIA staff in several countries, military men, various equipment, and hundreds or thousands of local allies, such leaks are basically inevitable. These kinds of leaks occurred during the operations in Indonesia, Tibet, Cuba, Vietnam, Laos, Chile, Angola, and Nicaragua. In some instances covert actions have been canceled because of leaks, but more often the secret warriors merely groan in annoyance and go on to hit the beaches as planned. The paradigm case is the Bay of Pigs, where there were so many leaks and invasion scares in Cuba that Castro's forces were given repeated opportunities to practice mobilizing against the CIA armed exiles.

Finally, even where a covert action is executed completely successfully, with no leaks to the world at large, they are not secrets to the victims. Even a successful paramilitary action can become an embarrassment in retrospect owing to the changing pattern of international relations. Good illustrations here are the operations against China and in Tibet. At the time, the People's Republic of China was considered an enemy, but later the Nixon administration undertook a rapprochement, redefining China as a counterweight to the Soviet Union. The covert actions, successful as they may have been, suddenly became obstacles to the Chinese decision to accept better relations with the United States.

The Central Intelligence Agency exists to serve the President. There would not be paramilitary actions except for presidential desires. Presidents since Harry Truman have been more or less avid users of the technique, and all have used it at least once. We have explored Presidents' control over the CIA in some detail.

Truman was concerned with creating capabilities and undertaking operations with them. Control was mostly left to the subordinates he appointed to the 10/2 and 10/5 panels. It was President Eisenhower, with his extensive experience utilizing staff organizations, who put intelligence control on a more formal basis, by giving explicit coordination and follow-up tasks to the 5412 Group. Through eight years in the White House, however, Ike proved unable to get the Special Group to do everything he wanted it to, and he left the Oval Office frustrated in this regard.

President Kennedy did not appreciate the control arrangements and quickly dismantled them. The Bay of Pigs fiasco just as quickly demonstrated to him the error in this, following which the Special Group was reconstituted. President Johnson continued to use this mechanism with no change except in name.

The Nixon administration left the Special Group mechanism in place, retitled the 40 Committee and with extra presidential watchdogs added. But the group was left to monitor only the less important kinds of covert actions. Decisions on really sensitive operations were increasingly absorbed by the White House and NSC staff dealing directly with agencies involved, as with Track II in Chile. Not only did this reduce the ability of the mechanism to monitor implementation, but it robbed the President of the benefit of the advice of some of the most informed officials.

Conditions improved somewhat during the administrations of Presidents Ford and Carter, but have greatly deteriorated during the years of President Reagan. With the President himself chairing meetings of the National Security Planning Group, the potential for honest denial of United States government approval of covert actions evaporates. The very quality of "covertness" disappears as the administration uses the fact of the paramilitary action as a diplomatic instrument and to score political points. Prevented from using the CIA in one of its operations, the Reagan administration was willing to continue the affair directly through the NSC staff. The President's own public statements leave no doubt which side the United States government takes in the secret war. Executive oversight units like the PFIAB and the Intelligence Oversight Board are encouraging additional covert actions, a technique that President Reagan himself defends. The administration's whole posture is not conducive to close scrutiny of covert action proposals.

Paramilitary actions of doubtful legality are approved and monitored by a special group with its own limitations. The group format makes it difficult to exercise initiative or to give the requisite degree of attention to every proposal. Moreover, the CIA exhibits a proclivity toward holding on to implementation decisions once initial approvals have been secured. Follow-up reviews currently occur only once a year (under the most recent compromise, the congressional committees have only just earned the right to follow-up reviews). These are often cursory amid the rush of events.

The record on presidential control of covert actions is that these have never been under complete *control*, although the White House has total *authority* to order them. The problem with this authority is that *it may not exist*. The legal basis for presidential authority to initiate covert actions rests entirely on the ambiguous "such other functions" clause of the National Security Act of 1947. Yet we have seen several occasions on which the CIA's general counsel concluded that paramilitary action was not within the scope of the 1947 act. If the President instead relies on his authority as Commander in Chief of the armed forces, the problem is that the CIA is not an "armed force." Even if it were, the President would then have to be deemed subject to the War Powers Act of 1973. Moreover, if the CIA is to be considered an unofficial armed force, then the Constitution (Article I, Section 8) expressly reserves to Congress, *not the President*, the right to give letters of marque, which were the eighteenth-century equivalent of grants of unofficial combatant status.

This legal conundrum would not exist if there were a detailed charter that specified permissible missions and methods for the intelligence agencies; but initiatives for charter reform were headed off by the Carter administration in 1978 and 1980. Presidents as politically diverse as Eisenhower and Johnson have consistently opposed intelligence reform. The device of issuing executive orders to regulate intelligence is precisely aimed at avoiding charter revision by law.

One of the most damaging effects of the controversy over William J. Casey's appointment as director of central intelligence is that it diverted congressional attention from broader questions of intelligence reform.

The congressional oversight committees have had a very limited impact. Without an intelligence charter, the committees are forced to play catch-up with Langley, as the administration arbitrarily advances new interpretations of the sketchy existing law. This is the underlying meaning of the continuing struggle between the executive branch and Congress over Presidential Findings and requirements for "full and current" reporting.

To doubtful legality and haphazard control must be added the conclusions that paramilitary operations pose special problems of ensuring effectiveness, and that they have contributed little to American national security. The dilemmas have only been sharpened by the revelations of the Iran-Contra affair, which have added the National Security Council itself to the problem areas associated with paramilitary action. This adds up to a question that requires urgent bipartisan attention, preferably *before* the next paramilitary debacle. Another Bay of Pigs is only a matter of time, while constitutional issues are not resolved overnight.

The general dilemma is further sharpened by the weakness of the War Powers Act. The act excluded the CIA when drafted, on the grounds that it would be covered in omnibus charter legislation, which has yet to appear. Further, the main sanction available to Congress under the act, concurrent resolutions by Congress that can mandate termination of unauthorized hostilities, has recently been ruled unconstitutional by the courts. On both these counts the law requires revision.

One measure that could help clarify the legal status of paramilitary action would be to end the CIA role altogether and put the function squarely within the purview of military special-warfare forces. This would ensure maintenance of the capability for wartime, when it has been demonstrated historically to be most effective, and reduce the propensity to use this technique against the Third World in the service of some cold war strategy. It would also improve the CIA's image and focus it on its classical information function. The secret warriors themselves would then be subject to stricter military discipline and regulations independent of any move toward intelligence charters.

Other areas that today seem to require attention are the activities of private citizens and of the President's own staff. The activities of Secord and company, on the one hand, and Edwin Wilson on the other, vividly illustrate the dangers inherent in a total lack of restraints. Private participation in covert operations should either be proscribed or strictly regulated. Direct participation in covert operations by the staff of the National Security Council is also a thorny problem. This involves the definition of "operations," since the NSC also conducts sensitive private diplomatic missions on occasion, and might have a legitimate role doing so. But the line has to be drawn before covert operations, for the NSC staff has neither resources nor organization for paramilitary implementation. At the same time the NSC staff is so critically placed in the government that it is far too easy for a "cowboy" operator to pull in the bureaucracy behind him. As the case of Oliver North shows, this nation cannot afford very many five-star lieutenant colonels. Though difficult, these problems can nonetheless be resolved.

The real danger inherent in the current framework for covert action is not the CIA as "rogue elephant" but the imperial presidency. America learned about rogue Presidents in the Watergate scandal. In an era in which irresponsible use of covert action techniques can lead to anything, including nuclear confrontation, it is not reasonable to allow a President that much freedom of action. The executive's struggle to limit accountability continues. In the meantime the people of Puerto Cabezas, Nicaragua, have learned the true dangers of paramilitary action: Hosts to the Bay of Pigs invaders, a quarter century later they are attacked by CIA raiders.

ABBREVIATIONS AND ACRONYMS

AIOC	Anglo-Iranian Oil Company
ARC	Air Resupply and Communications
ARDE	Alianza Revolucionaria Democrática (Revolutionary Democratic Alliance in Nicaragua)
BDPS	Bendras Demokratinio Pasipriesinimo Sajudas (United Democratic Resistance Movement in Lithuania)
BOSS	Bureau of State Security (South Africa)
CAT	Civil Air Transport
CCRAK	Covert Clandestine and Related Activities Korea
CDNI	Committee for Defense of National Interests (Laos)
CIA	Central Intelligence Agency
CIC	Counter-Intelligence Corps
CIDG	Civilian Irregular Defense Group (South Vietnam)
CIG	Central Intelligence Group
CORDS	Civil Operations and Revolutionary Development Staff (South Vietnam)
DCI	Director of Central Intelligence
DDCI	Deputy Director of Central Intelligence
DDO	Deputy Director of Operations/Directorate of Operations
DDP	Deputy Director for Plans/Directorate of Plans
DEFCON	Defense Condition
DO	Director of Operations/Directorate of Operations
FAR	Fuerzas Armadas Revolucionarias (Revolutionary Armed Forces of Cuba)
FDN	Fuerza Democrática Nicaraguense (Nicaraguan Democratic Force)
FE	Far East Division (of CIA)

FECOM	Far East Command
FLI	Front for the Liberation of Iran
FNLA	National Front for the Liberation of Angola
FOG	Foreign Operations Group
FRD	Frente Revolucionario Democrático (Democratic Revolutionary Front of Anti-Castro Cubans)
FSLN	Frente Sandinista de Liberación Nacional (Sandinista National Liberation Front in Nicaragua)
FULRO	Front Unifié pour la Libération des Races Opprimées (Unified Front for the Liberation of Oppressed Peoples in South Vietnam)
GAO	General Accounting Office
G-2	U.S. Army Intelligence Branch
HUMINT	Human Intelligence
IOB	Intelligence Oversight Board
ISA	Intelligence Support Activity
IVAG	International Volunteer Air Group
JACK	Joint Advisory Commission Korea
JCS	Joint Chiefs of Staff
JCSM	Joint Chiefs of Staff Memorandum
JM/WAVE	CIA Miami Station (for Cuba operations)
KMT	Kuomintang (Nationalist Chinese)
LCI	Landing Craft Infantry
LLDB	Luc Luong Dac Biet (Airborne Special Forces in South Vietnam)
LS	Lima Site (Laotian airfield)
MACV	Military Assistance Command Vietnam
MIT	Massachusetts Institute of Technology
MPLA	Popular Movement for the Liberation of Angola
NATO	North Atlantic Treaty Organization
NCO	Noncommissioned Officer
NHAO	Nicaraguan Humanitarian Assistance Office
NIA	National Intelligence Authority
NKVD	Soviet Intelligence and Security Service
NLHX	Neo Lao Hak Xat (Lao People's Front in Laos)
NLF	National Liberation Front (South Vietnam)
NSAM	National Security Action Memorandum
NSC	National Security Council
NSDD	National Security Decision Document
NSDM	National Security Decision Memorandum
NSPG	National Security Planning Group
NSSD	National Security Study Directive
NTS	Natsionalno Trudovoi Soyuz (National Labor Alliance in Russia)

NVA	North Vietnamese Army
NVDA	National Volunteer Defense Army (Tibet)
OAS	Organization of American States
OCB	Operations Coordinating Board
OCI	Office of Current Intelligence
OMB	Office of Management and Budget
OPC	Office of Policy Coordination
OPLAN	Operation Plan
OSO	Office of Special Operations
OSS	Office of Strategic Services
OUN	Organization of Ukrainian Nationalists (Russia)
PARU	Police Aerial Resupply Unit (Thailand)
PBCFIA	President's Board of Consultants on Foreign Intelligence Activities
PEMESTA	Piagam Perjuangan Semesta (Charter of Common Struggle in Indonesia)
PEO	Program Evaluation Office (Laos)
PFIAB	President's Foreign Intelligence Advisory Board
PLA	People's Liberation Army (China)
PRU	Provincial Reconnaissance Unit (South Vietnam)
PSB	Psychological Strategy Board
RFE	Radio Free Europe
RIAS	Radio in the American Sector (Berlin)
RIF	Reduction in Force
RIG	Restricted Interagency Group
RLAF	Royal Lao Armed Forces
RLG	Royal Lao Government
SACSA	Special Assistant for Counterinsurgency and Special Activities
SADF	South African Defense Force
SAT	Southern Air Transport
SEALS	Sea-Air-Land Soldiers
SEATO	Southeast Asia Treaty Organization
SGU	Special Guerrilla Unit (Laos)
SIS	Secret Intelligence Service (British)
SOE	Special Operations Executive (British)
SOF	Special Operations Forces
SOG	Special Operations Group (Korea)/Studies and Observation Group (South Vietnam)
SOPAG	Special Operations Policy Advisory Group
SSU	Strategic Services Unit
STTGI	Stanford Technology Trading Group International
UDN	Unión Democrática Nicaraguense (Nicaraguan Democratic Union)

UN   United Nations
UNITA   National Union for the Total Independence of Angola
UNO   Unión Nicaraguense de Oposición (United Nicaraguan
           Opposition)
UNPFK   United Nations Partisan Forces Korea
U.S.   United States
USAF   U.S. Air Force
USAID   U.S. Agency for International Development
USSR   Union of Soviet Socialist Republics
UVO   Ukrayinska Viyskova Orhaniztsiya (Organization of Ukrainian
           Nationalists in Russia)
WH   Western Hemisphere Division (CIA)
WIGMO   Western International Ground Maintenance Organization
           (Congo)

NOTES

The following notes are keyed to the page numbers on which items appear in the narrative. Items are identified by key words from a quotation being cited or short descriptions of the subject concerned, and appear in the narrative on the page indicated. Most of the notes are citations for material in the text. Certain citations, most often those for documentary sources, appear with abbreviations that refer to documentary collections or other sources. Abbreviations are fully identified the first time they appear in these notes, and also repeated in the Bibliography listing sources for the book. Notes that are wholly descriptive or analytical are identified with an asterisk to distinguish them from citations.

Page

I. THE COLD WAR CRUCIBLE

18   "personal snooper": Truman letter to Souers and Leahy. Reprinted in Margaret Truman, *Harry S. Truman* (New York: Pocket Books, 1974), pp. 362–363.

20   National Security Act of 1947: The portion of this law regarding intelligence has been reprinted widely. See, for example, William M. Leary, ed., *The Central Intelligence Agency: History and Documents* (n.p.: University of Alabama Press, 1984), pp. 128–130.

22   "babying the Soviets": letter to James Byrnes. Reprinted in Harry S. Truman, *Memoirs: Year of Decisions* (New York: New American Library, 1965), pp. 604–606.

22   "From Stettin": quoted in Robert J. Donovan, *Conflict and Crisis* (New York: W. W. Norton, 1977), p. 191.

Page
25   "may come with dramatic suddenness": quoted in Walter Millis,
        ed., *The Forrestal Diaries* (New York: Viking Press, 1951),
        p. 387.
27   Houston–Hillenkoetter memo, September 25, 1947.
27   "if the President": Houston letter to the editor, *New York Times*,
        July 26, 1982. In connection with this disclaimer by the former
        CIA general counsel, the reader should be aware that views ex-
        pressed by Mr. Houston following his retirement differ from
        what he told successive directors of central intelligence. Later in
        this narrative we shall encounter legal opinions given by the
        general counsel in 1962 and 1969 that are identical in their es-
        sentials to what he told Admiral Hillenkoetter in 1947.
28   NSC-10/2: "National Security Council Directive on Office of
        Special Projects," June 18, 1948. Reprinted in Leary, op. cit.,
        pp. 131–133.

II. THE SECRET WAR AGAINST RUSSIA

37   "pitilessly destroyed": K. V. Tauras, *Guerrilla Warfare on the
        Amber Coast* (New York: Voyages Press, 1962), p. 93.
40   "secret operations": *The Central Intelligence Agency and Na-
        tional Organization for Intelligence* (Dulles-Jackson-Correa Re-
        port), January 1, 1949 (declassified June 3, 1976), p. 131.
40   "cause the people": Wedemeyer–Bradley memo, August 9,
        1948. Quoted in Alfred H. Paddock, Jr., *U.S. Army Special War-
        fare: Its Origins* (Washington, D.C.: National Defense Univer-
        sity Press, 1982), p. 58.
43   * Zigurd Krumins: The coincidence of Krumins, among all the
        thousands of prisoners in the vast *Gulag* system, being assigned
        as cellmate to Gary Powers, stretches credulity perhaps too far.
        Krumins may have been working for Soviet security in 1960, and
        perhaps was all along. Gary Powers recalls his time at Vladimir
        Prison in considerable detail in his book with Curt Gentry, *Oper-
        ation Overflight* (New York: Holt, Rinehart & Winston, 1970),
        pp. 206–278.
44   "the correct channels": William E. Colby and Peter Forbath,
        Honorable Men: My Life in the CIA (New York: Simon & Schus-
        ter, 1978), p. 91.

Page

III. "WE'LL GET IT RIGHT NEXT TIME"

46   "a clinical experiment": quoted in Anthony Verrier, *Through the Looking Glass* (New York: W. W. Norton, 1983), p. 76.

46   "whenever we want": quoted in Kim Philby, *My Silent War* (London: Granada, 1969), p. 142.

47   "he was like Talleyrand": quoted in Nicolas Bethell, *Betrayed* (New York: Times Books, 1984), p. 59.

48   "prefer not to approach the visa division directly": quoted in *New York Times,* June 20, 1982.

49   "a purely internal uprising": Central Intelligence Agency, Intelligence Memo 218, "Strengths and Weaknesses of the Hoxha Regime in Albania," September 12, 1949 (declassified January 31, 1978). Harry S. Truman Library (hereafter HSTL): Truman Papers: President's Secretary's File (hereafter PSF): Intelligence File, box 249, folder: "Central Intelligence Memos 1949."

49   NSC-58: "United States Policy Toward the Soviet Satellite States in Eastern Europe," September 14, 1949, paragraphs 37, 42. Reprinted in Thomas H. Etzold and John Lewis Gaddis, eds. *Containment* (New York: Columbia University Press, 1978), pp. 211–223.

49   "are there any kings": quoted in *New York Times,* June 20, 1982. op. cit.

49   "settlement of differences": Central Intelligence Agency, ORE 71–49, "Current Situation in Albania," December 15, 1949 (declassified July 5, 1980), p. 6. HSTL: Truman Papers, PSF: Intelligence File, box 256, "ORE Reports 1949 (60–74)."

51   * Poland: The Polish case has not been given detailed study here because it appears to have been initiated by agents operating under Soviet control, rather than by the CIA or the British. Operating under a "false flag," the Polish agents claimed to represent underground nationalists using the acronym WIN. By contrast, in Albania the actions were initiated by the West.

51   "we'll get it right": quoted in Verrier, p. 77.

51   "small part of a big game": quoted in Bethell, p. 160.

51   "in the end": *New York Times,* op. cit.

51   "it's all over": quoted in Howard Hunt, *Undercover* (New York: Berkley Books, 1974), p. 95.

53   * Bandera: This account follows that of John Loftus in *The Belarus Secret* (New York: Knopf, 1982), which also details some

other cases of collaboration with former Nazis. This subject is aired in considerably greater detail in the forthcoming book *Blowback* by Christopher Simpson (New York: Summit, forthcoming).

54   "the Ukrainian people": reprinted in *Pravda*, January 25, 1948.

54   "sometimes amounted to war": Nikita Khrushchev, *Khrushchev Remembers: The Last Testament* (New York: Bantam Books, 1976), p. 198.

55   "fighting for its freedom": telegram, Lachowitch–Truman, August 31, 1947. HSTL: Truman Papers: White House Central Files (hereafter WHCF): Official File, box NA, folder: "1029—Ukraine."

57   "wholesale lying:" Philby, p. 145; cf. pp. 144–146, 140.

57   * On the failure to contact the partisans: A State Department intelligence report as late as March 1952 quoted Soviet press articles as evidence for continuing existence of partisans despite the fact that no contact could be established. Contact was made much more difficult by the OUN field commander's orders to revert to an underground, but some believed the OUN was *avoiding* contact. Bandera, for one, suspected the OUN leadership had been penetrated by the Soviet secret service. He tried to create an even smaller, more secret network in the mid- and late-1950s, which activity made him a target for Soviet assassination efforts.

59   "At least we're getting": quoted in Harry Rositzke, *The CIA's Secret Operations* (New York: Readers's Digest Press, 1977), p. 37.

60   "What did we offer": John C. Campbell interview. HSTL: Oral History number 284, p. 206.

IV. ADVENTURES IN ASIA

65   * American agents: Though little is known of American espionage efforts in this region, considering the embryonic capabilities of the CIA there is every reason to suspect the figure of twenty thousand. On the other hand, there certainly *were* American agents from services other than the CIA. A self-confirmed case is that of Allyn Rickett, a former Marine officer engaged as an observer while attending the prestigious Yenching University. Although Chinese authorities were aware of his involvement, Rickett was not arrested until July 1951, a full year

Page

after the beginning of the Korean War and nine months after the Chinese intervention there. See Allyn and Adele Rickett, *Prisoners of Liberation* (New York: Doubleday, 1973).

70   "unlikely to overthrow": Joint Staff, JSPC 958/15, "Military Support to Anti-Communist Groups in China," February 16, 1951 (declassified April 19, 1976), section L, paragraph 1.

75   "this adventure": Department of State, *Foreign Relations of the United States 1951*, Vol. 6 (Washington, D.C.: Government Printing Office, 1977), p. 288.

76   "Mr. Ambassador": quoted in David Wise and Thomas B. Ross, *The Invisible Government* (New York: Vintage, 1964), p. 131.

77   "What could be more ridiculous": quoted in Chester Bowles, *Ambassador's Report* (New York: Harper & Row), 1954, p. 233.

77   "nothing but difficulty": Goodpaster, "Synopsis of State and Intelligence Material Reported to the President," May 29, 1959 (declassified October 31, 1985). DDEL: DDEP: OSS: Subject Series, Alphabetical Subseries, box 14, folder: "Intelligence Briefing Notes v. I (7)."

V. THE COVERT LEGIONS

81   "lead the CIA": Ray Cline, *Secrets, Spies, and Scholars* (Washington, D.C.: Acropolis Books, 1976), p. 97.

82   "The operators": Victor Marchetti and John D. Marks, *The CIA and the Cult of Intelligence* (New York: Dell Books, 1980), p. 62.

85   "psychological offensive": quoted in Department of State, Assistant Secretary for Public Affairs, "Emergency Plan for Psychological Offensive (USSR)," April 11, 1951 (declassified October 20, 1976), pp. 1, 2, 3, 4, 7. HSTL: Truman Papers: PSF: Subject File, box 188, folder: "Russia, State Department Plan."

86   "the President is serious": Gordon Gray interview, HSTL: Oral History number 167, pp. 51-2.

87   "you just forget about policy": quoted in ibid., p. 55.

88   "we are actually participating": quoted in Alfred H. Paddock, Jr., *U.S. Army Special Warfare* (Washington, D.C.: National Defense University Press, 1982), pp. 60-61.

90   "Now we'll finish off": quoted in Joseph Burkholder Smith, *Portrait of a Cold Warrior* (New York: G. P. Putnam's Sons, 1976), p. 102.

Page

VI. BITTER FRUITS

95   "it would be unfair": Dwight D. Eisenhower, *Mandate for Change: White House Years 1953–1956* (New York: New American Library, 1965), p. 209.

95   "appropriately enthusiastic": quoted in Kermit Roosevelt, *Countercoup* (New York: McGraw-Hill, 1979), p. 10.

98   "If we": quoted in ibid., p. 210.

99   * NSC Special Group: Stephen Schlesinger and Stephen Kinzer in *Bitter Fruit* (New York: Doubleday, 1982). This detailed account of the Guatemala crisis (p. 108), traces the decision for Success to a 5412 Group meeting. In his equally detailed account *The CIA in Guatemala* (Austin: University of Texas Press, 1982) Richard H. Immerman finds no evidence of any such meeting. In fact, the 5412 Group was only formed in 1954, named after an NSC policy paper adopted at that time. The term *Special Group* has had a life of its own as the euphemism for the committee of principals who have dealt with intelligence matters at the NSC level. It is the euphemism more often than the official name, such as 5412 Group, that appears in documents. *Special Group* is used interchangeably with the formal names at each stage of this history.

100   "without United Fruit, you're crazy": quoted in Schlesinger and Kinzer, p. 110.

101   "so they would allow this revolutionary activity to continue": quoted in ibid., p.140.

102   "public opinion": quoted in *Time,* January 11, 1954, p. 27.

102   "agents of international Communism": Eisenhower, p. 507.

103   "the Communist dictatorship": *Public Papers of the President: Dwight D. Eisenhower 1954* (Washington, D.C.: Government Printing Office, 1960), p. 493.

104   "a bad mistake": Robert H. Ferrell, ed. *The Diary of James C. Hagerty* (Bloomington: Indiana University Press, 1983), p. 68. Hagerty was referring to the principle of innocent passage in the international law of the sea, without foreign search or seizure.

105   "suppose we supply the aircraft": quoted in Eisenhower, p. 510.

106   "If you use my airfields": quoted in Schlesinger and Kinzer, p. 193.

106   "went beyond the established limits": quoted in *New York Times,* April 28, 1966. In a September 1979 interview with Schlesinger and Kinzer, however, Bissell qualified this admission

Page

somewhat: "You can't take an operation of this scope, draw narrow boundaries of policy around them, and be absolutely sure those boundaries will never be overstepped" (quoted in *Bitter Fruits*, p. 194).

107   "in Iran": Allen W. Dulles, *The Craft of Intelligence* (New York: New American Library, 1965), pp. 207–208.

VII. "CREATE AND EXPLOIT TROUBLESOME PROBLEMS"

109   * The Solarium study was an interagency report commissioned by Eisenhower in 1953, in which teams competed to present the best analyses of several policy choices. The Killian Report was a study of an outside panel of scientists and technical experts given to the President in early 1955. In that case, Eisenhower responded effectively to a projection of potential scientific developments. The Gaither Report was a similar outside study, which warned of the danger of surprise attack. Its presentation happened to coincide with the Soviet *Sputnik* achievements in 1957, triggering intense pressure for increased military spending. In the Gaither episode, Eisenhower managed to act on the most vital recommendations of the Gaither committee without giving in to the public hysteria for a crash program.

109   "equate the costs": Eisenhower letter to Doolittle, July 26, 1954 (declassified November 11, 1977). Dwight D. Eisenhower Library (DDEL hereafter): Eisenhower Papers (EP): Ann Whitman File (AWF): Administration Series, box 14, folder:"Dulles, Allen (4)."

110   "as long as": "Report of the Special Study Group on the Covert Activities of the Central Intelligence Agency" (Doolittle Report), September 30, 1954 (declassified April 1, 1976), pp. 1, 2. Declassified Documents Reference Service, Fiche 78–139(c).

111   Eisenhower-Doolittle meeting, October 19, 1954: Ann Whitman notes, October 19, 1954. DDEL: EP: AWF: Administration Series, box 14, folder: "Dulles, Allen (4)."

111   "not going to be able": quoted in Leary, ed., *The Central Intelligence Agency*, p. 74. Leary reprints the excellent study of the intelligence community by Church committee staff historian Anne Karalekas, from which this is drawn.

112   "the normal channel": National Security Council, NSC 5412/1, "National Security Council Directive on Covert Operations," March 12, 1955 (declassified March 6, 1977), p. 3. DDEL: EP:

Page

White House Office (hereafter WHO): Office of the Special Assistant for National Security Affairs (OSANSA): Special Assistant series, Presidential Subseries, box 2, folder: "President's Papers 1955 (7)."

112   "the NSC has determined": NSC 5412/2, December 28, 1955, paragraph 3. Reprinted in Leary, pp. 146–47.

116   "such a unit will always be useful": Assistant to the Secretary of Defense (Special Operations). "Outline Plan for the Activation of an International Volunteer Air Group," April 26, 1954 (declassified February 18, 1986). DDEL: DDEP: OSANSA: Special Assistant Series, Name Subseries, box 3, folder: "I—General."

118   "we are already making": Department of State, *Foreign Relations of the United States 1952–1954,* Vol. 13 (Washington, D.C.: Government Printing Office, 1982), p. 1,048.

118   "keep our participation in the background": quoted in Eisenhower, *Mandate for Change,* p. 439.

120   "Fellows, tell me this": quoted in a talk by OCB/NSC staffer Karl G. Harr that is reprinted in Kenneth W. Thompson, ed. *The Eisenhower Presidency* (Lanham, Md.: University Press of America, 1984), p. 108.

120   "increase efforts to disturb" and following: quoted in Department of State, *Foreign Relations of the United States 1952–1954: II: National Security Affairs, Part 1.* (hereafter cited as FRUS). Washington: Government Printing Office, 1984, pp. 416, 419, 418.

121   "a departure from our traditional concepts": quoted in *Washington Post,* December 7, 1984.

121   "who gets it and who gets hurt": quoted in Summary of Discussion, 157th Meeting of the National Security Council, July 30, 1953. FRUS 1952–1954, Vol. II, Part 1, p. 439.

122   "major coups of my tour": Allen Dulles, *The Craft of Intelligence,* p. 80.

122   "Wisner says": Ray Cline, quoted in *Secrets, Spies and Scholars,* p. 164.

123   "pending a decision": Dulles letter to Anderson, May 31, 1956 (declassified September 10, 1984). DDEL: EP: WHO: OSANSA: Special Assistant Series, Subject Series, box 10, folder: "USSR (1)." In *The Craft of Intelligence,* Allen Dulles says no more than that the speech was printed by the State Department. In his memoirs, Eisenhower is completely silent on the subject.

124   "inaccessible as Tibet": Dwight D. Eisenhower, *Waging Peace* (New York: Doubleday, 1965), p. 95.

Page
124 "exactly the end": Colby and Forbath, *Honorable Men,* pp. 134–135.
125 "it was clear": Rositzke, *CIA's Secret Operations,* p. 158.
125 "I am satisfied:" Cord Meyer, *Facing Reality* (New York: Harper & Row, 1980), p. 125.
125 Hungarian students: Richard Nixon, *RN,* Vol. 1 (New York: Warner Books, 1979), p. 224–225.
125 "A few of the scripts": Dulles letter to Goodpaster with memorandum, "Radio Free Europe," November 20, 1956 (declassified March 15, 1982), paragraph 4, pp. 3–4. DDEL: EP: WHO: Office of the Staff Secretary (hereafter OSS): Subject Series, Alphabetical Subseries (hereafter Alpha sub), box 7, folder: "CIA v. I (4)." In fact, British journalist Noel Barber, who covered the uprising and was wounded in Hungary, considers RFE to have been very damaging to the cause of Imre Nagy. Barber cites a constant stream of criticisms of Nagy's efforts to forestall a Soviet intervention, quotes an RFE military expert who considered the ceasefire accommodation a "Trojan horse," as well as other broadcasts advocating rejection of Nagy's reorganized cabinet in favor of a "national provisional government," rejecting the leadership of the defense and interior ministries (loyal not to the Russians but to Nagy), and instructing listeners on how to make Molotov cocktails at a time when Nagy was attempting to calm Hungarian citizens. Noel Barber, *Seven Days of Freedom: The Hungarian Uprising 1956* (New York: Stein & Day, 1974), pp. 62, 128–130. Of the ninety RFE personnel directly involved in the Hungarian broadcasts, only the individual responsible for the Molotov cocktail episode is known to have been dismissed.
126 "whatever doubt": Colby, p. 135.

VIII. ARCHIPELAGO

129 "plans to undertake a coup": Wilbur Crane Eveland, *Ropes of Sand* (New York: W. W. Norton, 1980), p. 180.
131 * Downey-Fecteau release: Chinese release of these captured CIA officers was viewed with such concern at CIA that it is reported the subject dominated the cable traffic of the DDP office involved.
132 "Sukarno's feet to the fire": quoted in Burkholder Smith, *Portrait of a Cold Warrior,* p. 205.
132 "if some plan": ibid.

Page
133   "its fair to say": Richard E. Bissell interview. DDEL: Oral History number 382, p. 16.

135   "drive Lebanon off the front page": quoted in Burkholder Smith, *Portrait of a Cold Warrior,* p. 240.

135   "then you got": Allen–Foster Dulles telephone notes, September 16, 1957, 4:11 P.M. DDEL: John Foster Dulles Papers (hereafter JFDP): Telephone Series (hereafter TS), box 7, folder: September–October 1957 (3)."

135   "continue the present": National Security Council, NSC Agenda note, September 21, 1957 (declassified August 6, 1982), paragraph 6(c). DDEL: EP: WHO; OSANSA: Special Assistant Series, Chronological Subseries, box 5, folder: "September 1957 (2)."

136   "extremely significant": Foster–Allen Dulles telephone notes, November 29, 1957, 10:58 A.M. DDEL: JFDP: TS, box 7, folder: "November–December 1957 (2)."

136   * Though Ambassador Allison strove to contain Washington activism, he relented in the cable that so excited Foster Dulles. Allison apparently refers to this cable in the following passage from his memoirs: "We told the State Department it would be necessary to give these people active encouragement if their efforts were to bear fruit. We did not believe, as Washington seemed to, that it would be sufficient to indicate that if a satisfactory new regime was formed, the United States would promptly open negotiations on aid programs ... I said we believed it was essential to determine in advance what we were prepared to do for such a government and that if this was known, it would give those working for a change added leverage to bring it about." John M. Allison, *Ambassador from the Prairie* (Boston: Houghton Mifflin, 1973), p. 336.

136   "probably the failure": Foster–Allen Dulles telephone notes, December 1, 1957, 12:51 P.M. DDEL: JFDP: TS, box 7, folder: "November–December 1957 (2)."

136   "If this thing goes": Allen–Foster Dulles telephone notes, December 8, 1957, 10:10 A.M. Ibid.

136   "what he would like": Dulles–Herter telephone notes, December 8, 1957, 10:16 A.M. Ibid.

136   "get the British with us": Dulles–Cumming telephone notes, December 12, 1957, 10:46 A.M. Ibid.

137   "going all right": Foster–Allen Dulles telephone notes, January 16, 1958, 5:26 P.M. DDEL: JFDP: TS, box 8, folder: "Memoranda of Telephone Conversations—General February 1, 1958–March 31, 1958 (4)."

137   "Padang group": Central Intelligence Agency, TS 141712-d,

Page

"Probable Developments in Indonesia," January 31, 1958 (declassified October 1985), pp. 1, 3, 4, 10. DDEL: EP: WHO: OSANSA: NSC Series, Briefing Notes Subseries, box 11, folder: "U.S. Policy Toward Indonesia."

137   "my own feeling": quoted in Leonard Mosley, *Dulles* (New York: Dial Press, 1978), p. 471. Mosley incorrectly identifies Cumming as the United States ambassador—the latter remained in Washington as director of intelligence and research throughout the period. The ambassador who replaced Allison was Herbert P. Jones.

138   "You should know": quoted in Allison, *Ambassador from the Prairie,* p. 346.

138   "during the stalling period": Foster–Allen Dulles telephone notes, February 4, 1958, 9:58 A.M. DDEL: JFDP: TS, box 8, folder: "January–March 1958 (3)."

138   "the subject of Archipelago": Allen–Foster Dulles telephone notes, February 5, 1958. Ibid.

139   "The Secretary said": Foster–Allen Dulles telephone notes, February 27, 1958, 4:20 P.M. DDEL: JFDP: TS, box 8, folder: "January–March 1958 (2)." The author has substituted the full name "Allen" and title "Secretary " for "A" and "Sec." as they appear in this quotation.

140   "without intrusion": quoted in *New York Times,* February 21, 1958.

142   "far greater efficiency": Foster–Allen Dulles telephone notes, April 17, 1958, 12:31 P.M. DDEL: JFDP: TS, box 8, folder: "April–May 1958 (3)."

142   "no fight in them": Foster–Allen Dulles telephone notes, April 23, 1958, 12:49 P.M. Ibid.

142   "the East is boiling": Foster–Allen Dulles telephone notes, April 28, 1958, 5:15 P.M. DDEL: JFDP: TS, box 8, folder: "April–May 1958 (2)."

143   "on the other hand": *New York Times,* May 1, 1958.

143   "a lot of confidence in the man": Foster Dulles–Charles Cabell telephone notes, May 19, 1958, 3:02 P.M DDEL: JFDP: TS, box 8, folder: "April–May 1958 (1)."

144   "we must disengage": quoted in Burkholder Smith, *Portrait of a Cold Warrior,* p. 247.

144   "a gift to Sukarno": Brian May, *The Indonesian Tragedy* (London: Routledge & Keegan Paul, 1978), p. 80.

145   "brutal": Lyman Kirkpatrick, *The Real C.I.A.* (New York, Macmillan, 1968), pp. 147–148.

145   "extremely informal": Killian letter to Eisenhower, Decem-

Page

ber 20, 1956 (declassified July 19, 1977), pp. 5, 7. DDEL: EP: WHO: Administration File, box 14, folder: "Allen Dulles (3)."

145   "a group of this type": Memorandum of Conference with the President, December 22, 1958 (declassified December 23, 1981), p. 2. DDEL: EP: AWF: Eisenhower Diaries, box 23, folder: "Staff Notes December 1958."

147   "obviate any tendency": Goodpaster memo to Harlow, January 2, 1959. DDEL: EP: WHO: OSS: Subject Series, Alpha sub, box 7, folder: "CIA v. II (1)."

147   "the criteria": Gray memo to Eisenhower, January 19, 1959 (declassified June 8, 1979). DDEL: EP: WHO: OSS: Subject Series, Alpha sub, box 15, folder: "Intelligence Matters (8)."

147   "the President then referred": Gray, Memorandum of Meeting with the President, June 26, 1959 (declassified October 28, 1981). DDEL: EP: WHO: OSANSA: Special Assistant Series, box 4, folder: "Meetings with the President 1959 (1)."

IX. THE WAR FOR THE ROOF OF THE WORLD

149   Meeting with American: George N. Patterson, *Tibet in Revolt* (London: Faber & Faber, 1960), pp. 120–122.

149   "a nest of spies": Neville Maxwell, *India's China War* (New York: Doubleday, 1972), p. 100.

153   Two accounts of inception: Patterson, *Tibet;* and John F. Avedon, *In Exile from the Land of Snows* (New York: Knopf, 1984), p. 47.

153   "buried in the lore": L. Fletcher Prouty, *The Secret Team* (Englewood Cliffs, N.J.: Prentice-Hall, 1973), p. 351.

154   * Scarce cotton: It is worth noting that one of the first industries the Chinese established in Tibet was a huge textile plant with machinery brought from Shanghai. The mill at Lhasa employed twelve thousand workers plus a thousand administrators.

154   First airdrop: Michel Peissel, *The Secret War in Tibet* (Boston: Little Brown, 1972), p. 87.

157   "I saw the weapons": quoted in Han Suyin, *Lhasa, The Open City* (London: Triad Panther Books, 1979), p. 70.

160   "between two volcanoes": quoted in Avedon, *In Exile from the Land of Snows,* p. 52.

160   "one of the strangest": Michel Peissel, *The Secret War in Tibet* (Boston: Little Brown, 1972), p. 116.

Page

161 "the new social experiment": Gray memo to Lay, November 1, 1958, DDEL: EP: WHO: OSANSA: Special Assistant Series, Subject subseries, box 11, folder: "Basic National Security Policy."

161 "if the Tibetans are able": Department of State, "Uprisings in Communist China," undated (declassified July 31, 1985), p. 4. DDEL: WHO: OSANSA: NSC Series, Briefing Notes subseries, box 5, folder "Communist China."

161 "the Tibetan uprisings": Synopsis of Intelligence, March 23, 1959 (declassified June 8, 1982). DDEL: EP: WHO: OSS: Subject series, Alpha sub, box 14, folder: "Intelligence Briefing Notes v. I (5)."

162 "What Is the Home Ministry Doing": reprinted in Chanakya Sen, *Tibet Disappears* (New York: Asia Publishing House, 1960), p. 176.

163 "We have informed": Synopsis of Intelligence, April 1, 1959 (declassified December 9, 1983), pp. 2–3. DDEL: EP: WHO: OSS: Subject series, Alpha sub, box 14, folder: "Intelligence Briefing Notes v. I (6)."

163 "You must help us": message received April 2, 1959 (declassified July 9, 1981). DDEL: EP: WHO: OSANSA: Special Assistant Series, Alpha sub, box 15, folder: "Intelligence Matters (9)."

164 "recognizing independence or sovereignty": Christian Herter-Henry Cabot Lodge Telephone Notes, October 6, 1959, 1:05 P.M. (declassified January 23, 1986). DDEL: Christian Herter Papers, box 12, folder: "CAH Phone Calls 5/4/59–12/31/59 (2)."

165 "We Tibetans": Gompo Tashi letter to Eisenhower, December 9, 1959. DDEL; EP: WHO: OSS: International Series, box 13, folder: "Tibet (2)."

165 "Channels considered by the embassy": Thomas McElhiney-Goodpaster Memo, December 15, 1959. DDEL: EP: WHO: OSS: International Series, box 13, folder "Tibet (2)." McElhiney acted for the executive secretariat of the Department of State in treating the Tibetan gifts as a miscellaneous protocol matter left over from Ike's visit to India. The White House raised no objection.

166 "reorient his thinking": Gray, Memorandum of Meeting with the President, September 15, 1960 (declassified December 11, 1981). DDEL: EP: OSANSA: Special Assistant series, Presidential Subseries, box 5, folder "1960 Meetings with the President v. II (6)."

167 "consultations he had had": Gray, Memorandum of Meeting

Page
       with the President, November 28, 1960. Ibid., folder: "1960 Meetings with the President v. II (3)."
167   "deeply unhygienic tribesmen": John Kenneth Galbraith, *A Life in Our Times* (Boston: Houghton Mifflin, 1981), p. 395.
168   "particularly insane enterprise": ibid.
168   * Captured documents: Avedon (p. 124) places this incident in 1966, but the release of the Chinese political journals was reported in the press at the time. The documents were even given extensive analysis in a scholarly paper by J. Chester Cheng, "Problems of Chinese Communist Leadership As Seen in the Secret Military Papers," *Asian Survey* (June 1964), pp. 861–872.
169   "resulted in a bonanza": Ray Cline, *Secrets, Spies and Scholars,* p. 181.

X. CUBA I: "ANOTHER BLACK HOLE OF CALCUTTA"

172   "I am Che": quoted in Marvin D. Resnick, *The Black Beret* (New York: Ballantine Books, 1969), pp. 141–142.
173   "far from stable": Central Intelligence Agency, Memo to DCI, February 4, 1959 (declassified July 15, 1981), pp. 1, 3. DDEL: EP: AWF: Dulles-Herter Series, box 8, folder: "Dulles, February 1959."
174   "incredibly naive": Richard Nixon, *RN.* Vol. 1, p. 250.
174   "Castro cautiously indicated": Herter memo to Eisenhower with attachment "Unofficial Visit of Prime Minister Castro," April 23, 1959 (declassified December 22, 1976). DDEL: EP: Dulles-Herter Series, box 9, folder: "Herter, April 1959 (2)."
175   "anti-Communists have an interest": quoted in James Martin Keagle, *Toward an Understanding of US Latin American Policy* (Princeton University: Ph.D. dissertation, 1982), p. 90.
175   "In view of the special sensitivity": Herter memo to Eisenhower, November 5, 1959 (declassified February 3, 1981). DDEL: EP: WHO: OSS: International Series, box 4, folder: "Cuba (1) [1959]."
176   "thorough consideration": quoted in U.S. Congress. Senate (94/2) Select Committee to Study Governmental Operations with Respect to Intelligence Activities (hereafter Church Committee), *Interim Report: Alleged Assassination Plots Involving Foreign Leaders* (hereafter *Alleged Assassination Plots*) (Washington: Government Printing Office, 1975), p. 92.
176   "over the long run": quoted in Church Committee, *Alleged Assassination Plots,* p. 93.

Page

177   March 10, 1960 NSC: Church Committee, *Alleged Assassination Plots*, pp. 93, 114–116. When asked about his comments during the committee's mid-1970s investigation, Admiral Burke insisted he was referring to the general plans that led to the Bay of Pigs and not to any specific notions of attempting assassinations.

177   * "Black Hole of Calcutta": A small storeroom in the palace of this city, used in 1756 by the Indian ruler of Bengal to imprison British and other foreigners who had not escaped the revolt he was attempting. Several dozen persons perished of wounds, heat, or suffocation in the "Black Hole."

177   "Allen, this is fine": Gordon Gray interview. Quoted in DDEL: Oral History number 352, pp. 27–28.

178   "to bring about the replacement": Central Intelligence Agency, "A Program of Covert Action Against the Castro Regime," March 16, 1960 (declassified April 9, 1982). DDEL: DDEP: WHO: OSS: International Series, box 4, folder: "CIA Policy Paper re Cuba."

179   Pluto memo: *Operation Zapata: The "Ultrasensitive" Report and Testimony of the Board of Inquiry on the Bay of Pigs.* Frederick, Md.: University Publications of America, 1981), p. 4.

179   Stans quotes Dulles and Eisenhower: quoted in Thompson, ed., *The Eisenhower Presidency*, p. 219.

182   "timetable of various events": Gray, Memorandum of Meeting with the President, July 6, 1960 (declassified October 25, 1977). DDEL: EP: WHO: OSANSA: Special Assistant Series. Presidential subseries, box 4, folder: "1960 Meetings with the President v. I (1)."

190   "turning over the government": Gray, Memorandum of Meeting with the President, December 5, 1960 (declassified May 23, 1983), p. 3. Ibid., box 5, folder: "1960 Meetings with the President v. II (2)."

192   declassified memoranda: Memorandum of December 5, 1960, op. cit. Also Gray, Memorandum of Meeting with the President, January 9, 1961 (declassified May 23, 1983), ibid.

193   "now boys:" Gordon Gray interview. Quoted in DDEL: Oral History number 352, p. 37.

XI. CUBA II: FROM PLUTO TO MONGOOSE

198   "a bail-out operation": Robert L. Dennison interview. U.S. Navy Oral History. Reprinted in *U.S. Naval Institute Proceedings* (October 1979), p. 111.

Page
199   "I stood right here": quoted in Theodore Sorensen, *Kennedy*
        (New York: Bantam Books, 1965), p. 332.
201   "My observations": Mañuel Artime et. al., "We Who Tried,"
        Life (May 10, 1963), p. 34.
203   * Diversions: Another aspect of diversionary operations involved
        a U.S. Navy submarine that surfaced at the other end of Cuba,
        firing star shells, and otherwise tried to mimic landing activities.
        Finally came the business CIA was supposed to be about in all
        this—fomenting an uprising within Cuba. Some thirty-five
        Cubans were landed to activate resistance on the island, but
        their role was conceived as impeding Castro's response to the
        invasion rather than mounting the effort that would overthrow
        him. The Cubans were uniformly unsuccessful and were then
        caught up in Castro's massive security sweep that preceded the
        landings. Twenty-five of the Cuban agents were captured and
        fifteen of them executed. Ten managed to flee to the Venezuelan
        embassy in Havana where they sought political asylum and left
        Cuba under a safe conduct some months later. Among the escap-
        ees was Felix Rodriguez, who achieved revenge of sorts in 1967,
        when he was among the Americans who assisted Bolivian efforts
        to capture Che Guevara. Rodriguez conversed with Guevara for
        several hours after his capture, one of the last persons to see Che
        alive. Later still, Rodriguez went to Vietnam for the CIA and
        would play a prominent role in the National Security Council
        covert operation in Nicaragua.
207   "We're already in it": quoted in Peter Wyden, *Bay of Pigs: The
        Untold Story* (New York: Simon & Schuster, 1979), p. 271.
207   "I certainly would": quoted in Richard Nixon, *RN*, Vol. 1, pp.
        287–288, 289.
207   "chief apparent causes": Eisenhower diary, April 22, 1961. Rob-
        ert H. Ferrell, ed., *The Eisenhower Diaries* (New York: W. W.
        Norton, 1981), p. 386.
207   "proper legal cover": Richard Nixon, *RN* Vol;. 1, p. 289.
208   "prevention of communist entry": Eisenhower diary April 22,
        1961. Ferrell, ed., op. cit.
208   "this story could be called": Eisenhower diary, June 7, 1961.
        Ferrell, ed., p. 390.
208   Taylor Report, June 7, 1961: *Operation Zapata*, pp. 41, 42.
210   "a legendary figure": quoted in Arthur Schlesinger, *A Thousand
        Days* (Greenwich, Conn.: Fawcett Books, 1965), p. 258.
210   Dulles's rebuttal: See Lucien S. Vandenbroucke, "The Confess-
        ions of Allen Dulles: New Evidence on the Bay of Pigs," *Diplo-
        matic History* (Fall 1984), pp. 365–375.

Page

210   "splinter . . . into a thousand pieces": quoted in Taylor Branch and George Crile, "The Kennedy Vendetta," *Harper's* (August 1975), p. 50.

213   "more dynamic action": Central Intelligence Agency, "Memorandum of Mongoose Meeting Held on Thursday October 4, 1962" (declassified May 7, 1976).

215   "Can you imagine": quoted in Brock Brower, "Why People Like You Joined the CIA," *Washington Monthly* (November 1976), p. 59.

215   "the basic decision": Burris memo to Johnson, "Cuba (NSC Meeting, January 25th)," January 25, 1963 (declassified April 28, 1978). Lyndon Baines Johnson Library (hereafter LBJL): Johnson Papers (hereafter JP): Vice-Presidential Security File, box 6, folder: "Memos from Burris, July 1962–April 1963."

216   "I am concerned": Rusk, draft letter, March 28, 1963 (declassified June 17, 1977). LBJL: JP: Vice-Presidential Security File, box 4, folder: "NSC (I)."

XII. COLD WAR AND COUNTERINSURGENCY

219   "I think the answers": Joint Chiefs of Staff, "CIA Study on Peripheral Wars," September 21, 1955. National Archives: Modern Military Branch: Records Group 218: Radford 1953–1957, box 48, folder: "381 Net Evaluation 1955."

219   "operational" questions: Allen–Foster Dulles telephone notes, March 21, 1958. DDEL: JFDP: TS, box 8, folder: "January–March 1958 (1)."

220   "Our nuclear power": John F. Kennedy, *The Strategy of Peace*, ed. Allan Nevins (New York: Harper & Brothers, 1960), p. 184.

221   Taylor recollections: Maxwell Taylor, *Swords into Plowshares* (New York: W. W. Norton, 1972), pp. 178–179, 184–185.

222   "an analogous advisory function": ibid., p. 197.

223   * Special Forces teams: Designations for the various types of teams carried an "F" prefix during the 1950s—"FA" Teams, "FB," "FC." The nomenclature presented in the text applied in the 1960s and after. Since Special Forces operations appear in this narrative only in the later period, I have used the later type designations throughout.

224   Rostow speech: Department of the Army, Office of the Chief of Information, Special Warfare U.S. Army (Washington, D.C.: Department of the Army, n.d. [1962], pp. 25, 23.

Page
225   "symbol of excellence": Kennedy letter to United States Army,
           April 11, 1962. Reprinted in ibid., p. 3.
225   OPLAN 10-1: Duncan Campbell, *The Unsinkable Aircraft Car-*
           rier (London: Michael Joseph, 1984), pp. 137–139, fn. 18 pp.
           68–69.
226   "For the first time": Tom Compere, ed., *The Army Blue Book*
           (New York: Military Publishing Institute, 1960), p. 80.
229   "no statutory authorization": Houston memo to McCone, OGC
           62-0083, "Legal Basis for Cold War Activities," January 15,
           1962 (declassification date not available). This and other legal
           memorandums of the CIA general counsel quoted in the narra-
           tive are included in the documentary appendix to Jay Peterzell,
           "Legal and Constitutional Authority for Covert Operations,"
           paper presented at the twenty-fifth annual meeting of the Inter-
           national Studies Association, Washington, D.C., March 1985.
234   "classic Communist effort": quoted in Madeleine G. Kalb, *The*
           Congo Cables (New York: Macmillan, 1982), p. 53.
235   "harrowing . . . bought": quoted in Richard D. Mahoney, *JFK:*
           Ordeal in Africa (New York: Oxford University Press, 1983),
           p. 38.

XIII. VIETNAM

239   Lansdale's case: His own account is *In the Midst of Wars* (New
           York: Harper & Row, 1972).
240   "combat area of the cold war": quoted in Lansdale Report, Jan-
           uary 17, 1961. Department of Defense, *United States–Vietnam*
           Relations 1947–1967 (hereafter *US-GVN Rel*), Vol. 2, Book
           IV.A.5 (Washington, D.C.: Government Printing Office, n.d.
           [1971], pp. 66–77.
241   "This is the worst one": quoted in Walt W. Rostow, *The Diffu-*
           sion of Power (New York: Macmillan, 1972), p. 265.
241   "Somehow I found him": quoted in U.S. Congress, Senate (98/2),
           Foreign Relations Committee, *Report: The U.S. Government*
           and the Vietnam War: Executive and Legislative Roles and Rela-
           tionships (hereafter *USG & VN War*), (Washington, D.C.: Gov-
           ernment Printing Office, 1984), Part II, p. 13.
242   "none of us": quoted in ibid., p. 36.
242   "expand present operations": Gilpatric Report, May 6, 1961.
           US-GVN Rel, Vol. 11, p. 84.
243   "increased covert offensive": Taylor-Rostow Report, November
           3, 1961. *The Pentagon Papers: The Senator Gravell Edition: The*

Page

Defense Department History of United States Decisionmaking on Vietnam, Vol. 2 (Boston: Little Brown, n.d. [1972]), p. 653.

244   * Lansdale in Indochina: Then an Air Force lieutenant colonel, Lansdale maintains he was kept in Vietnam longer than he wished. Accorded a meeting with the brothers Allen and John Foster Dulles, Lansdale startled the secretary of state with the statement that he had no wish to stay through the referendum on reunification scheduled for 1956 by the Geneva agreement of 1954. Lansdale recalls himself as being less interested in Vietnam than in what he read of another contemporary event—the April 1956 disappearance of British underwater warfare expert Commander Crabbe, who vanished while swimming beneath the Soviet heavy cruiser *Ordzhonikidze,* which had conveyed Nikita Khrushchev to a state visit in England. Crabbe was widely believed to have been acting for the Secret Intelligence Service.

247   "should never have done it": quoted in *USG & VN War,* Part II, p. 203.

250   "The policy arbiters": quoted in Church Committee, *Final Report,* Vol. I, *Foreign and Military Intelligence* (hereafter *Foreign and Military Intelligence*) (Washington, D.C.: Government Printing Office, 1976), p. 56.

251   "a beginner's credulity": McGeorge Bundy in *New York Times,* June 10, 1985.

255   "only the crash allocation": Major General Robert R. Ploger, *U.S. Army Engineers 1965–1970* (Washington, D.C.: Department of the Army, 1974), pp. 192–193.

257   "cumbersome governmental mechanisms": Helms memo to McCone, "CIA Proposals for Limited Civilian Political Action in Vietnam," March 31, 1965 (declassified September 1985). LBJL: JP: National Security File (hereafter NSF): Country File—Vietnam (hereafter CF-VN), box 194, folder: "McCone's 12 Points."

258   "you really think that": quoted in Stewart Alsop, *The Center* (New York: Harper & Row, 1968), p. 145.

XIV. THE HIGH PLATEAU

264   *Border incident: On September 16, Phoumi claimed that six battalions of Vietnamese troops had invaded Laos and killed fifty people. An international commission sent to investigate the

Page

incident found no evidence of North Vietnamese troops and a toll of no more than five dead.

267 * Alert: United States military forces operate using a graduated scale of five states of readiness, ranging from peacetime disposi- ton (DEFCON 5) to combat engagement (DEFCON 1).

267 "must not allow": Goodpaster, Memorandum of Conference with the President, December 31, 1960 (declassified May 23, 1983). DDEL: EP: WHO: OSS: International Series, box 9, folder: "Laos (2)."

268 "understood nothing": quoted in Roger Hilsman, *To Move a Na- tion* (New York: Doubleday, 1967), p. 125.

273 falsification: Ralph W. McGehee, *Deadly Deceits* (New York: Sheridan Square Publications, 1983), pp. 82–84.

275 "a most reluctant militarist": William H. Sullivan. *Obbligato 1939–1979* (New York: W. W. Norton, 1984), pp. 210, 213.

275 "were quick to recognize": Theodore Shackley, *The Third Op- tion* (New York: Reader's Digest Press, 1981), p. 72.

275 "agency . . . was flat out": Richard Helms interview. LBJL Oral History, II, p. 18–19.

275 "when I found": Sullivan, *Obbligato*, p. 211.

277 "Air America did a magnificent job": William Colby interview, LBJL Oral History, I, p. 54.

278 "greatest single asset": quoted in Burkholder Smith, *Portrait of a Cold Warrior*, p. 205.

279 "all our Yankee Team": Cable, Sullivan-Rusk, Vientiane 2054, June 21, 1965 (declassified February 14, 1984). LBJL: JP: NSF: Aides' Files: Bundy; box 3, folder: "Bundy Memos v. 11 (June 1965)."

281 "the biggest job": quoted in Charles A. Stevenson, *The End of Nowhere* (Boston: Beacon Press, 1972), p. 217. Also see William C. Westmoreland, *A Soldier Reports* (New York: Dell Books, 1980), pp. 355–357, 514–516.

282 Intelligence Estimates on Laos: U.S. Military Assistance Com- mand, Vietnam, Office of the Assistant Chief of Staff J-2, "Cur- rent Summary of Enemy Order of Battle in Laos," editions of (a) 15 December 1967 (declassified February 17, 1982) and (b) 15 August 1968 (declassified February 12, 1982). (a): LBJL:JP: NSF: CF-VN, box 176–177, folder "Vietnam Order of Battle Reports Vol. III." (b): ibid., box 178, folder "Vietnam Order of Battle Reports Vol. IX."

283 "wasn't a bag of rice": quoted in Stevenson, *The End of No- where*, p. 217.

284 Symington hearings: *New York Times*, October 29, 1969; Jan-

Page

uary 23, 1970; quoted in Stevenson, *The End of Nowhere*, p. 209. Houston-Helms memo, October 30, 1969, is appended to Peterzell, "Legal and Constitutional Authority for Covert Operations," ms. 1985.

285   "Symington got up": Helms Oral History, II, p. 6.

286   Helms-Stennis talk: quoted in Helms Oral History, II, p. 21.

286   * *The Politics of Heroin in Southeast Asia* (New York: Harper & Row, 1972) was written by Yale Ph.D. candidate Alfred W. McCoy with Cathleen B. Read and Leonard P. Adams II. Langley reportedly got hold of a copy of the manuscript and threatened legal action to deter its publication. This tactic failed. Release of the book rekindled public concern regarding drug trafficking in the war. The CIA inspector general's report is detailed by the Church committee in *Foreign and Military Intelligence* (pp. 227–230).

290   "We were caught": Henry A. Kissinger, *White House Years 1969–1973* (Boston: Little Brown, 1979), p. 451.

291   "the American mission has lost any interest": quoted in *New York Times*, February 25, 1970.

293   * The extent of CIA complicity in the Sukarno coup in Indonesia in 1965, as well as Hugh Tovar's knowledge of the general's plans, remains a matter of historical controversy. See the *Harper's* symposium, "Should the U.S. Fight Secret Wars?" (September 1984), pp. 33–47.

294   "As we discussed": quoted in Arnold R. Isaacs, *Without Honor* (Baltimore: Johns Hopkins University Press, 1983), pp. 178–179.

295   Douglas S. Blaufarb, *The Counterinsurgency Era* (New York: The Free Press, 1977), pp. 166–168.

XV. GLOBAL REACH

299   * Dap Chhuon plot: William Colby (*Honorable Men*, pp. 149–150) confirms that CIA recruited and supplied the radio operators, but he attributes the "plot" to South Vietnamese and Thai intelligence agencies the CIA was unable to dissuade.

301   "Green Beret affair": John Steven Barry, *Those Gallant Men* (Novato, Calif.: Presidio Press, 1984).

302   "What we knew at the time": Lieutenant General Sak Sutsakhan, *The Khmer Republic at War and the Final Collapse* (Washington, D.C.: U.S. Army Center for Military History, Indochina Monograph, n.d. [1980], p. 55.

Page

302   "we neither encouraged": Kissinger, *White House Years*, p. 463.

303   "Lon Nol may well have been encouraged": quoted in William Shawcross, *Sideshow* (New York: Simon & Schuster, 1979), p. 122. It may be worth noting that the first volume of Kissinger's memoirs, in galleys at the time the Shawcross account appeared, was reworked by the former secretary of state to defend himself from its charges.

303   "What the hell do those clowns do": quoted in Richard Nixon, *RN*, Vol. 1, p. 553.

303   "Let's get a plan": quoted in Kissinger, *White House Years*, p. 465.

303   "I want Helms": ibid.

306   "That crazy Blackburn": quoted in Benjamin F. Schemmer, *The Raid* (New York: Harper & Row, 1976), p. 146.

308   Helms on Komer: quoted in Colby and Forbath, *Honorable Men*, p. 245. Komer's own account has him putting nothing over on anyone. LBJ called him into the office one day, recalls Komer, and suddenly said, "Bob, I'm going to put you in charge of the other war in Vietnam." Puzzled, Komer asked, "What's the other war in Vietnam? I thought we had only one." LBJ retorted, "That's part of the problem. I want to have a war that will build as well as destroy." The President proceeded to insist Komer take the pacification job and the NSC aide gracefully acquiesced. Quoted in Bob Brewin and Sydney Shaw, *Vietnam on Trial* (New York: Atheneum, 1986), p. 234.

310   "one situation we obviously missed": ibid., p. 275.

312   "I look upon this organization": *Public Papers of the Presidents: Richard Nixon, 1969* (Washington, D.C.: Government Printing Office, 1971), p. 203.

312   "the American people need to understand:" ibid.

313   "The mountain tribes": Central Intelligence Agency, ORE 71-48, "The Kurdish Minority Problem," December 8, 1948 (declassified July 5, 1978), p. 1 HSTL: Truman Papers: PSF: Intelligence File, box 258, folder: "ORE Reports 1948 (67–78)."

314   Kurdish messages; CIA station chief; official's retort: quoted in William Safire, *Safire's Washington* (New York: Times Books, 1980), pp. 83–84, 85–86. These documents were uncovered by the Pike committee investigation (see next chapter) and reprinted in *The Village Voice*, February 16, 1976, but in this source Safire supplies the names of principals that were sanitized.

317   "Had I believed": Kissinger, *White House Years*, p. 669.

Page

317   "I don't see": quoted in Seymour Hersh, *The Pursuit of Power* (New York: Summit Books, 1983), p. 265.

317   "I am not interested in": quoted in Armando Uribe, *The Black Book of American Intervention n Chile* (Boston: Beacon Press, 1974), p. 33.

317   "make the economy scream" and "the President came down hard": quoted in Church Committee, *Alleged Assassination Plots*, p. 227–228. In a sworn deposition he gave the committee, Richard Nixon declared: "I do not recall discussing during the September 15, 1970 meeting specific means to be used by the CIA to attempt to prevent Mr. Allende from assuming the Presidency of Chile. I recall the meeting as one that focused upon the policy considerations which should influence my decision to act and upon the general means available. As I have previously stated, I recall discussing the direct expenditure of funds to assist Mr. Allende's opponents, the termination of United States financial aid and assistance programs as a means of adversely affecting the Chilean economy and the effort to enlist support of various factions, including the military, behind a candidate who could defeat Mr. Allende in the Congressional confirmation procedure.

   "I do not recall specifically issuing instructions that the activity being conducted by the CIA in Chile not be disclosed to the Department of State or the Department of Defense." Reprinted in *New York Times*, March 12, 1976.

318   "As far as I was concerned": quoted in Church Committee, *Alleged Assassination Plots*, p. 254.

321   ° American citizens: Charles Horman was a writer from New York, Frank Teruggi a journalist from Chicago. Both were apprehended by Chilean security about a week after the coup— Horman on September 17, Teruggi on the 20th. Both died, although the Chilean government denies responsibility, while in the custody of the Chilean military, as far as can be determined. At least seventeen other Americans, mostly doctoral candidates and other students but including at least one priest and a professor of physics, were also arrested. The others were freed after State Department intervention, which seems to have been less earnest in the cases of Horman and Teruggi. Horman's disappearance has been dramatized in the movie *Missing*, based on the book by Thomas Hauser, *The Execution of Charles Horman* (New York: Harcourt, Brace, Jovanovich, 1978).

321   ° Helms: Much later, when memories had dimmed (in 1983), President Ronald Reagan quietly awarded Helms the nation's

highest intelligence decoration, the National Security Medal.

322   "I have determined": National Security Council, NSDM-40, "Responsibility for the Conduct, Supervision and Coordination of Covert Action Operations," February 17, 1970 (declassified June 8, 1976).

323   "It is true": U. Alexis Johnson with Jef Olivarius, *The Right Hand of Power* (Englewood Cliffs, N.J.: Prentice-Hall, 1984), p. 347.

323   * Italian elections: The 1972 Italian election operation supported political parties, organizations, and twenty-one individual candidates. Included were $3.4 million to one party, $3.4 million to an organization created and supported by the CIA, and $1.3 million to other organizations and parties. This brought total CIA spending for political action in Italy to $65 million since 1948. According to the Pike committee, the 1972 operation was a quick fix launched after a CIA-commissioned survey in 1970 concluded that the Italian communist party had a chance for electoral victory. American officials feared that the example of Allende's Chile would encourage other countries, like Italy, to take a similar path.

XVI. "ROGUE ELEPHANT" TO RESURRECTION

327   HUGE CIA OPERATION: *New York Times,* December 22, 1974.

327   "press and political firestorm": Colby and Forbath, *Honorable Men,* pp. 388, 391.

328   "fudge the truth": Thomas Braden, "What's Wrong with the CIA?" *Saturday Review* (April 5, 1975), p. 24.

328   "a few war stories": quoted in Marchetti and Marks, *The CIA and the Cult of Intelligence,* p. 305.

329   "not a question of reluctance": quoted in Harry Howe Ransom, *The Intelligence Establishment* (Cambridge: Harvard University Press, 1970), p. 169.

329   "we plan to use": Bundy memo to Johnson, October 13, 1965. LBJL: JP: NSF: Aides' Files: Bundy, box 5, folder: "Bundy Memos v. 15 (Sept. 23–Oct 15, 1965)."

330   "Because they leak!": marginal note in Rostow memo to Johnson, June 1, 1966 (declassified September 25, 1979). LBJL: JP: NSF: Agency File, box 5, 8, 9, 10, folder: "CIA v. II." President Johnson was specifically referring to revelations about the United States intervention in the Dominican Republic, which

were widely attributed to sources within Senate Foreign Relations Committee.

330   * Harry C. McPherson: This was not the first time McPherson had acted as White House intermediary in a delicate intelligence matter. He had also been the action officer in the prolonged Heine-Raus libel suit, in which a prominent Estonian émigré sued after another émigré began denouncing him as an agent of the Soviet services. Defendent Jiri Raus, national commander of the League Estonian Liberation, petitioned the White House. Though Raus's lawyer was carefully informed there could be no such assistance from Langley, DDP Richard Helms eventually contributed several affidavits to the court, declaring that Raus had been acting at the CIA's behest, and then that the Agency had ordered the defendant not to testify at his trial, on national security grounds. The suit brought by Eerik Heine was eventually thrown out of court.

331   "Don't waffle": quoted in Thomas Powers, *The Man Who Kept the Secrets* (New York: Pocket Books, 1981), p. 221.

333   "Well, Bill": quoted in Colby and Forbath, *Honorable Men,* p. 395.

334   Ford's reminiscences: Gerald R. Ford, *A Time to Heal* (New York: Berkley Books, 1980), pp. xxiv, 258; cf. pp. 223–224. Italics in the original.

335   "stick it to Kissinger": ibid., p. 344.

335   "an election year": quoted in Daniel Schorr, *Clearing the Air* (New York: Berkley Books, 1978), p. 196.

335   Pike Report: "The CIA Report the President Doesn't Want You to Read," *The Village Voice* (February 16, 1976), pp. 69–94. The committee also produced five volumes of hearings and two of proceedings, including very interesting examinations of intelligence analysis.

336   * Assassination plots: The Church committee investigation in this area greatly concerned former Eisenhower administration officials including Gordon Gray and John S. D. Eisenhower. Both encouraged colleagues from the President's staff to give evidence that Ike had never approved any sort of assassination project. The Church committee eventually accepted this view, but confronted with evidence of plots carried out during that period against Lumumba, Castro, and Trujillo, ended by concluding that the assassinations had been sanctioned by Allen Dulles (the DCI) and not the President.

337   Church committee findings: *Foreign and Military Intelligence,*

Page

pp. 424–431. Though the atmosphere surrounding release of the Church committee report was better than that of the Pike committee, the CIA did attempt to get substantial deletions in the documents, some of which were made. Suggested deletions included references to the Bay of Pigs as a paramilitary operation, to Laos, and to testimony given in public before television cameras. Langley succeeded also in suppressing all of the committee's case studies on covert operations save for that pertaining to the destabilization of Chile.

337   "rogue elephant": quoted in Ford, *A Time to Heal*, p. xxiv.

337   "a regiment of cloak-and-dagger men": *Foreign and Military Intelligence*, p. 564.

339   "probable disclosure": from May 1, 1975 memo quoted in Nathaniel Davis, "The Angola Decision of 1975: A Personal Memoir," *Foreign Affairs* (Fall 1978), p. 111.

340   "at the direction": Pike committee report, *Village Voice* (February 16, 1976), p. 85.

340   "the CIA recommended": U.S. Congress (94/2) Government Operations Committee. *Hearings: Oversight of U.S. Governmnt Intelligence Functions* (Washington, D.C.: Government Printing Office, 1976), p. 440. In February 5, 1976, testimony Kissinger conceded, however, that "it is quite possible that the CIA will say in a certain case, not applying it now to the specifics . . . the CIA will say, we are in favor of this, but we do not believe it can be kept secret.

"In that case it might be technically registered that they are opposed to the covert operation because they do not believe it can be kept covert, even though they support the substance" (ibid.).

341   ° Davis resignation: Davis left without any public statement of his views. He became ambassador to Switzerland. His replacement on the interagency committee was William G. Hyland, at that time director of State's Bureau of Intelligence and Research. Hyland has recently provided his own account of Angola that raises additional questions. Here Hyland argues that the initial funding for Roberto "scarcely caused a ripple in Angola," no doubt reasoning from the small amount of money ($300,000) involved. It was the fact of the CIA support rather than the amount, however, that energized Roberto, who could have some confidence that more would be forthcoming and indeed proved correct in that belief. Roberto ordered FNLA troops into the field and started the fighting based on it. This was not the first time that a paramilitary action was begun with only a small in-

vestment, and the amount involved should not be deemed to excuse the activity. Hyland also argues that Kissinger's involvement "was late and hesitant." This squares with Kissinger's overriding focus on East-West issues and comes from an observer in close contact with the secretary, who was in a position to see Kissinger's daily concerns. On the other hand, the claim throws open the question of where the Angola secret war came from. Hyland agrees that both CIA and State were reticent. If someone (i.e., Kissinger) were not pushing there would have been no Angola intervention. Kissinger *was* already involved in Portuguese matters and therein may lie the key—the intervention began with Portugal and was later fought for Angola. Hyland's account does have the virtue of providing high-level confirmation for the chronology of intervention—he confirms that Cuban intervention followed that by the United States and did not precede it. William G. Hyland, *Mortal Rivals* (New York: Random House, 1987), pp. 130–147; quotations from p. 137.

341   "we've been given a job": quoted in John Stockwell, *In Search of Enemies* (New York: W. W. Norton, 1978), p. 95.

344   "He read it": quoted in Stockwell, *In Search of Enemies*, p. 22.

345   Ford comments: Gerald Ford, *A Time to Heal*, p. xxv.

347   * Daniel Gearhart: The executed American hardly fit the "macho man" image of a mercenary. Daniel Gearhart had never been in Special Forces. He was a skydiving enthusiast and parachute rigger at the Southern Cross Para Center in Downsville, Maryland. He was the type who, on a dive, would pull his ripcord early while others went down in free fall. Beset by domestic problems, Gearhart startled his friends when he showed up one day to make the simple statement that he was leaving for Angola to be a mercenary.

348   * Presidential Findings: Instituted by the Hughes-Ryan amendment, Presidential Findings are a form of certification to Congress that a proposed project has top-level approval. Findings are declarations. An example might be: "I have determined that x is a problem, so I have authorized y operation." Findings as restraints on covert action have been of dubious value since the beginning, because the certifications need meet no tests other than a President's willingness to make the statement. As shall be seen, the intelligence community was also able to exploit the imprecision of the law in specifying the occasions upon which findings were required and the scope of the authority conveyed by any given finding. The sense of the legislation was that Congress should be "fully and currently informed" on all covert ac-

Page

     tions. Defining that phrase has subsequently been a matter of continuing controversy.

350   "Being confident": Stansfield Turner, *Secrecy and Democracy* (Boston: Houghton Mifflin, 1985), p. 194.

355   "Eureka" briefing: Hearings of the Joint Congressional Committee to Investigate the Iran-Contra Diversion [hereafter cited as Contragate Hearings], Richard V. Secord testimony, May 6, 1987. As the Contragate investigation continues at this writing, the printed hearings and committee reports are not yet available for citation. Quotations presented in this narrative are from the author's notes and are cited by witness and date of testimony.

355   "The talent necessary": Turner, op. cit., p. 177.

XVII. NEW WAVE COVERT ACTIONS

357   "yearned for peace": Jimmy Carter, *Keeping Faith* (New York: Bantam Books, 1982), p. 471.

357   "going to war": quoted in *Washington Post*, October 7, 1982.

359   "The invasion of Afghanistan": Carter, *Keeping Faith*, p. 471.

359   Sadat confirmed: *New York Times* and *Washington Post*, September 23, 1981.

360   "some price for their invasion": Zbigniew Brzezinski, *Power and Principle* (New York: Farrar, Straus & Giroux, 1983), p. 434.

363   "a box score mentality": Jack Anderson, *Washington Post*, April 27, 1987.

364   antiaircraft guns: *Washington Post*, January 13, 1985.

366   Andrew Eiva: *New York Times*, May 25, 1983; *Washington Post*, September 8, 1984; Jack Anderson, June 14, 1984.

367   Cuban exiles in Letelier assassination: Taylor Branch and Eugene M. Propper, *Labrinth* (New York: Penguin Books, 1983).

368   Iran Rescue: Businessmen William Gaylord and Paul Chiapparone were freed from a Teheran prison in May 1979 in a scheme financed by their employer, H. Ross Perot. The tale is told in Ken Follett, *On Wings of Eagles* (New York: William Morrow, 1983).

369   "a disgrace to the United States": quoted in Bernard Diederich, *Somoza and the Legacy of U.S. Involvement in Central America* (New York: E. P. Dutton, 1981), p. 187.

369   Green Berets in Libya: *New York Times:* August 26, 1981; December 9, 1981. Phillip Taubman, "The Secret World of a Green Beret," *New York Times Magazine*, July 4, 1982.

Page

370   Wilson and CIA personnel: Seymour Hersh, "Exposing the Libyan Link," *New York Times Magazine*, June 21, 1981; also his "The Quaddafi Connection," ibid., June 14, 1981.

370   Walters on retired intelligence officers: *New York Times*, September 23, 1981.

372   "no basis for concluding": quoted in *New York Times*, July 30, 1981. After a further extension of this investigation the assessment was reiterated in a Senate intelligence committee release on December 1, 1981.

375   Opposition to covert-action proposals: *New York Times*, July 5, 1982, December 19, 1982, August 5, 1983: *Washington Post*, December 16, 1984, March 31, 1986. Also see Bob Woodward, *Veil: The Secret Wars of the CIA*. New York: Simon & Schuster, 1987, *passim*.

376   Executive Order 12333: reprinted in *New York Times*, December 5, 1981.

377   Casey-Reagan on Iran: Mansur Rafizadeh, *Witness: From the Shah to the Secret Arms Deal, An Insider's Account of U.S. Involvement in Iran* (New York: Morrow, 1987), p. 347.

378   "groping through a maze": quoted in *Washington Post*, December 19, 1986.

380   "a riskier policy": quoted in Report of the President's Special Review Board [hereafter cited as Tower Commission report], February 26, 1987, p. B-6.
       "improvement of ties": ibid., p. B-7.

383   "no course of action": quoted in *Washington Post*, November 3, 1985.

384   "redraw the map of North Africa": quoted in *Washington Post*, February 20, 1987.

384   "our timetable": ibid.

385   "collision course": *Wall Street Journal*, August 25, 1986.

394   * Pentagon study: The group Singlaub chaired concurred with his own views on "low-intensity conflict," the latest jargon for brushfire wars. This reflected the composition of the study panel, which included such prominent secret warriors as General Edward Lansdale and General Harry Aderholt, the man who had designed the Lima Site airfield system for Laos. Aderholt, as president of the private Air Commando Association, has also worked with Singlaub in raising funds for the *contras* and in arranging shipments of supplies.

XVIII. BILL CASEY'S WAR

397   Presidential Finding: *Washington Post,* April 3, 1983.

397   United States program: *Washington Post,* March 10, 1982.

399   Argentine involvement: *New York Times,* May 31, 1982, December 3, 1982; *Washington Post,* May 16, 1982, December 3, 1982.

399   Money from Argentines: Shirley Christian, *Nicaragua: Revolution in the Family* (New York: Random House, 1985), p. 197.

399   Negotiations: Roy Gutman, "America's Diplomatic Charade," *Foreign Policy* #56, Fall 1984.

400   "We were all hugging": quoted in *New York Times,* March 18, 1985.

402   Héctor Francés: *Miami Herald,* December 1, 1982; *Washington Post,* December 2, 1982; *New York Times,* December 19, 1982. A transcript of the videotaped statement by Francés was published in the Managua FSLN newspaper *Barricada* on December 2, 1982. An English translation appears in *The Black Scholar* (v. 14 #2) March/April 1983, pp. 2–16. *Washington Post* correspondent Christopher Dickey believes that Francés may not have been a true defector, that his statement may have been extracted by the Sandinista sources who, Dickey laims, originally provided the videotape to the press. Christopher Dickey, *With the Contras* (New York: Simon and Schuster, 1985), p. 154.

403   "we want to give democracy a chance": quoted in *New York Times,* December 9, 1982.

405   "Lau was still": quoted in Edgar Chamorro, "Confessions of a Contra," *The New Republic* (August 5, 1985), p. 22.

406   CIA officers and manual: *Washington Post,* October 24, 1984; *Newsweek,* November 26, 1984, p. 42.

408   Possible air proprietaries: *New York Times,* April 3, 1983, November 8, 1983; *Washington Post,* September 1, 15, 18, and 19, 1984.

408   "may well be": quoted in *New York Times,* November 8, 1983.

409   Civil Military Assistance: September 5, 6, 1984, December 13, 1984.

409   Casey trips: *Washington Post,* March 10, 1981; *New York Times,* December 3, 1984.

411   "not one of the happiest episodes": Contragate Hearings, McFarlane testimony, May 13, 1987.

411   Navy tests mines: *New York Times,* June 1, 1984.

413   Revised Presidential Finding: United States Congress (98/2),

Page

Senate Select Committee on Intelligence, *Report*, January 1, 1983 to December 31, 1984. Washington, D.C.: Government Printing Office, 1985, pp. 5–6.

414　Chamorro is approached during debate over the Boland amendment: Edgar Chamorro, "Confessions of a Contra," pp. 20–21.

415　Senate Intelligence Committee demands explanations: Committee Report, op. cit., pp. 7–10.

416　"unilaterally controlled latino assets": quoted in *Washington Post*, April 18, 1984.

416　"no way to run a railroad": Committee Report, op. cit., p. 8.

XIX. PROJECT DEMOCRACY

419　"crisis caused by the Congress": quoted in *New York Times*, June 1, 1984.

423　"occasional peacock": Mona Charen, "What White House Women Think About White House Men," *The Washingtonian* magazine, September 1986, p. 188.

423　"do an Admiral Yamamoto": quoted in *Washington Post*, November 30, 1986.

427　"active-measures campaign": reprinted in *Washington Post*, December 21, 1986.

427　"deeply moved": Mona Charen, op. cit.

427　Quotations from Reagan speech: *New York Times*, March 2, 1985; April 1, 1985; June 6, 1985.

430　"cease and desist": quoted in National Security Archive, *The Chronology: The Documented Day-by-Day Account of the Secret Military Assistance to Iran and the Contras* (New York: Warner Books, 1987), p. 66.

432　"slow boat from China": Contragate Hearings, Calero testimony, May 20, 1987.

435　"*contra* quartermaster": Contragate Hearings, Owen testimony, May 19, 1987.

436　"defeated in detail": Contragate Hearings, Secord testimony, May 5, 1987.

439　"awesome in its amateurishness": Contragate Hearings, Singlaub testimony, May 21, 1987.

439　"Sam meant well": Contragate Hearings, Owen testimony May 19, 1987.

442　"What about the airfield": Contragate Hearings, Elliott Abrams testimony, June 2, 1987.

Page

442   "Give me an account number": Contragate Hearings, Owen testimony, May 19, 1987.

443   McRainey joke: *Newsweek,* February 9, 1987, p. 26.

443   "Wilson gang back in business": Contragate Hearings, Rodriguez testimony, May 27, 1987.

444   "We want every bit of support": Contragate Hearings, Secord testimony, May 5, 1987.

446   "This is asinine": Secord KL-43 message, quoted in *Washington Post,* June 14, 1987.

446   "My objective": quoted in Tower Commission report, p. C-8.

448   "monitor Ollie": Contragate Hearings, Elliott Abrams testimony, June 2, 9, 1987.

454   North-Rodriguez meeting: Contragate Hearings: Robert C. Dutton testimony, May 27, 1987; Felix Rodriguez testimony, May 27, 1987. Quotations are from Rodriguez testimony.

455   "engaged in a ripoff": ibid., Rodriguez testimony.

457   "bland paper machine": Evans and Novak, *Washington Post,* July 21, 1986.
        "I wanted to lower your visibility": *The Chronology,* op. cit., reprinted p. 423. Poindexter had also asked North to lower his visibility in May, as well as to speak to no one except Poindexter (including Casey) about his operational roles. Tower Commission report, p. C-10.
        "Well Done": Tower Commission report, p. C-10.

459   "Send Fawn": quoted in *New York Times,* June 2, 1987.
        "You went on that mission": Contragate Hearings, Robert C. Dutton testimony, May 27, 1987.

XX. PRESIDENTS, POLICIES, AND PARAMILITARY OPTIONS

465   "supply material assistance": Angelo Codevilla and Roy Godson, "Intelligence (Covert Action and Counterintelligence) As an Instrument of Policy," paper presented at the twenty-fifth annual meeting of the International Studies Association (Washington, D.C., March 1985), p. 11.

465   "dismal historical record": Bundy, *New York Times,* June 10, 1985.

468   "The belligerents": Michael Howard, *The Causes of Wars* (Cambridge: Harvard University Press, 1983), p. 30.

BIBLIOGRAPHY

DOCUMENTS

a. Harry S. Truman Library (National Archives and Records Administration) collections:
   President's Secretary's File (PSF): Intelligence File
   PSF: Korean War File
   PSF: NSC Meetings File
   PSF: Subject File
   White House Central File (WHCF): Confidential File
   WHCF: Official File
   Records of the Psychological Strategy Board
   Dean Acheson Papers
   Clark Clifford Papers
   Oral Histories
b. Dwight D. Eisenhower Library (NARA) collections:
   Eisenhower Papers (EP):
   Ann Whitman File (AWF): Administration Series
   AWF: DDE Diaries
   AWF: Dulles-Herter Series
   White House Office (WHO): Office of the Special Assistant for National Security Affairs (OSANSA): Special Assistant Series: Alphabetical Subseries
   WHO: OSANSA: Special Assistant Series: NSC Subseries
   WHO: OSANSA: Special Assistant Series: Presidential Subseries
   WHO: OSANSA: Special Assistant Series: Subject Subseries
   WHO: Office of the Staff Secretary (OSS): International Series
   WHO: OSS: Subject Series
   WHCF: Administration File

John Foster Dulles Papers: Telephone Series
Oral Histories
c. Lyndon B. Johnson Library (NARA) collections:
   Johnson Papers (JP):
   Declassified and Sanitized Documents Unboxed Folders
   National Security File (NSF): Agency File
   NSF: Aides' Files
   NSF: Country File: Laos
   NSF: Country File: Vietnam
   NSF: Files of Special Committee of NSC
   NSF: Subject File
   Official File: Harry McPherson File
   Vice-Presidential Security File
   Oral Histories
d. Declassified Documents Reference Service (DDRS): This is a microfiche documents collection first issued in 1975. It is organized into a Retrospective series plus subsequent annual sets. In citations the year of the set is given, followed by a card number and then an alphabetic document position identifier (example: (78)—234—g).
e. Freedom of Information Act: These are documents cited with only the name of an agency and a declassification date, which were released under official declassification regulations.
f. Unclassified Executive Documents: This refers to a variety of White House, State Department, and Department of Defense memorandums, reports, and releases that are not secret but form portions of the public record.
g. Congressional Documents: (All such documents are cited by the Congress and session numbers (e.g., 96/1), the originating committee, and the title.

Senate

Foreign Relations (98/2). *Report: The U.S. Government and the Vietnam War: Executive and Legislative Relationships* (2 parts). Washington, D.C. Government Printing Office (GPO), 1984.
Government Operations (93/2). *Hearings: Legislative Proposals to Strengthen Congressional Oversight of the Nation's Intelligence Agencies.* Washington, D.C. GPO, 1974.
Government Operations (94/2) *Hearings: Oversight of U.S. Government Intelligence Functions.* Washington, D.C.: GPO, 1976.
Rules and Administration (94/2). *Hearings: Proposed Standing Committee on Intelligence Activities.* Washington, D.C.: GPO, 1976.
Select Committee to Study Governmental Operations with Respect to In-

telligence (Church Committee) 94/1. *Interim Report: Alleged Assassination Plots Involving Foreign Leaders.* Washington, D.C.: GPO, 1975.

(94/1) *Staff Study: Covert Operations in Chile, 1963–1973.* Washington, D.C.: GPO, 1975.

(94/2) *Final Report* (in 6 parts with accompanying volumes of hearings), especially books I, IV, VI. Washington, D.C.: GPO, 1976.

Select Committee on Intelligence (94/2) *Hearing: Nomination of E. Henry Knoche.* Washington, D.C.: GPO, 1976.

(95/1) *Annual Report,* May 1977. Washington, D.C.: GPO, 1977.

(95/2) *Hearings: National Intelligence Reorganization and Reform Act of 1978.* Washington, D.C.: GPO, 1978.

(98/2) *Report,* January 1, 1983 to December 31, 1984. Washington, D.C.: GPO, 1985.

House

Foreign Affairs Committee (Historical Volume, 94/1) *Hearings: The United States and Chile During the Allende Years 1970–1973.* Washington, D.C.: GPO, 1975.

Permanent Select Committee on Intelligence (95/2). *Hearings: Disclosure of Funds for Intelligence Activities.* Washington, D.C.: GPO, 1977.

Select Committee on Intelligence (Pike Committee) 94/1. *Hearings* (in 5 parts). Washington, D.C.: GPO, 1975.

h. Leaked Documents: A number of authentic government documents have entered the public record by means of unauthorized disclosure. These range from Reagan administration decisional documents on Central America (*New York Times,* April 7, 1983) to large portions of the Pike Report (*Village Voice,* February 16, 1976). Among the most significant of leaked documents—really a full-scale collection in its own right—is the secret decision-making study assembled for the Department of Defense to explain United States involvement in the Vietnam War. This latter has been published in several complementary editions. See Neil Sheehan et. al., eds., *The Pentagon Papers* (New York: Bantam Books, 1971). Department of Defense, *United States-Vietnam Relations, 1945–1967* (12 parts) (Washington, D.C.: GPO, 1971), also, *The Pentagon Papers: The Senator Gravell Edition: The Defense Department History of United States Decisionmaking on Vietnam,* 4 vols. (Boston: Little Brown, n.d. [1972]) four volumes.

II. BOOKS

Official Histories

DEPARTMENT OF THE AIR FORCE—*The United States Air Force in Southeast Asia*

Ballard, Jack S. *Development and Employment of Fixed-Wing Gunships, 1962–1972*. Washington, D.C.: Office of Air Force History, 1982.

Bowers, Ray L. *Tactical Airlift*. Washington, D.C.: Office of Air Force History, 1983.

Futrell, Robert F., with Martin Blumenson. *The Advisory Years to 1965*. Washintgon, D.C.: Office of Air Force History, 1981.

DEPARTMENT OF THE ARMY

Ethnographic Study Series

Schrock, Joann et. al. DA 550–105. *Minority Groups in the Republic of Vietnam*. Washington, D.C.: Department of the Army, 1966.

Indochina Monographs

Hoang, Colonel Ngoc Lung. *Intelligence*. Washington, D.C.: Center for Military History, 1981.

Sananikone, Major General Oudone. *The Royal Lao Army and U.S. Army Advice and Support*. Washington, D.C.: Center for Military History, 1978.

Sutsakhan, Lieutenant General Sak. *The Khmer Republic at War and the Final Collapse*. Washington, D.C.: Center for Military History, n.d. (1978).

Vietnam Studies

Hay, Lieutenant General John H., Jr. *Tactical and Materiel Innovations*. Washington, D.C.: Department of the Army, 1974.

Heiser, Lieutenant General Joseph M., Jr. *Logistic Support*. Washington, D.C.: Department of the Army, 1974.

Kelly, Colonel Francis J. *U.S. Army Special Forces, 1961–1971*. Washington, D.C.: Department of the Army, 1973.

Ploger, Major General Robert R. *U.S. Army Engineers, 1965–1970*. Washington, D.C.: Department of the Army, 1974.

DEPARTMENT OF THE NAVY

Field, James A., Jr. *History of United States Naval Operations—Korea*. Washington, D.C.: GPO, 1962.

Other Books

Acheson, Dean. *Present at the, Creation: My Years in the State Department.* New York: New American Library, 1970.

Adams, Nina S., and Alfred McCoy Smith, eds. *Laos: War and Revolution.* New York: Harper & Row, 1970.

Allison, John M. *Ambassador from the Prairie or Allison Wonderland.* Boston: Houghton Mifflin, 1973.

Alsop, Stewart. *The Center: People and Power in Political Washington.* New York: Harper & Row, 1968.

Ambrose, Stephen E. *Eisenhower: The President.* New York: Simon & Schuster, 1984.

———, with Richard H. Immerman. *Ike's Spies: Eisenhower and the Espionage Establishment.* Garden City, N.Y.: Doubleday, 1981.

Amter, Joseph A. *Vietnam Verdict: A Citizen's History.* New York: Continuum, 1982.

Anderson, Jack, with George Clifford. *The Anderson Papers.* New York: Ballantine Books, 1974.

Andreski, Stanislav. *Parasitism and Revolution: The Case of Latin America.* New York: Shocken, 1969.

Austin, Anthony. *The President's War.* New York: Lippincott, 1971.

Avedon, John F. *In Exile from the Land of the Snows.* New York: Knopf, 1984.

Ayers, Bradley. *The War That Never Was.* New York: Bobbs-Merrill, 1976.

Ball, George W. *The Past Has Another Pattern: Memoirs.* New York: W. W. Norton, 1982.

Ballantine, Joseph W. *Formosa: A Problem for United States Foreign Policy.* Washington: Brookings Institution, 1952.

Barnett, Frank R., B. Hugh Tovar, and Richard H. Shultz, eds. *Special Operations in U.S. Strategy.* Washington, D.C.: National Defense University Press with National Strategy Information Center, 1984.

Barron, John. *KGB: The Secret Work of Soviet Secret Agents.* New York: Bantam Books, 1974.

———. *KGB Today: The Hidden Hand.* New York: Berkley Books, 1985.

Barry, John Steven. *Those Gallant Men: On Trial in Vietnam.* Novato, (Calif.): Presidio Press, 1984.

Beam, Jacob D. *Multiple Exposure: An American Ambassador's Unique Perspective on East-West Relations.* New York: W. W. Norton, 1978.

Beck, Melvin. *Secret Contenders: The Myth of Cold War Counterintelligence.* New York: Sheridan Square Publications, 1984.

Beckwith, Colonel Charlie A., with Donald Knox. *Delta Force.* New York: Harcourt Brace Jovanovich, 1983.

Beitzell, Robert. *The Uneasy Alliance: America, Britain and Russia, 1941–1943.* New York: Knopf, 1972.

Bethell, Nicolas, *Betrayed.* New York: Times Books, 1984.

Bernert, Philippe. *SDECE Service 7: L'extraordinaire histoire du Colonel LeRoy-Finville et de ses clandestins.* Paris: Presses de la Cité, 1980.

Betts, Richard K. *Soldiers, Statesmen and Cold War Crises.* Cambridge: Harvard University Press, 1977.

Bilmanis, Dr. Alfred. *Baltic Essays.* Washington: Latvian Delegation, 1945.

———. *Dictionary of Events in Latvia.* Washington, D.C.: Latvian Delegation, 1946.

———. *Latvia as an Independent State.* Washington, D.C.: Latvian Delegation, 1947.

———. *Latvia Between the Anvil and the Hammer.* Washington, D.C.: Latvian Delegation, 1945.

Blaufarb, Douglas S. *The Counterinsurgency Era: U.S. Doctrine and Performance, 1950 to the Present.* New York: Free Press, 1977.

Bloch, Jonathan, and Patrick Fitzgerald. *British Intelligence and Covert Action.* London: Junction Books, 1983.

Blum, Howard. *Wanted: The Search for Nazis in America.* Greenwich, (Conn.): Fawcett, 1977.

Blum, Robert M. *Holding the Line: The Origins of the American Containment Policy in East Asia.* New York: W. W. Norton, 1982.

Bohlen, Chester E. *Witness to History 1929–1969.* New York: W. W. Norton, 1973.

Boorstein, Edward. *Allende's Chile: An Inside View.* New York: International Publishers, 1977.

Bower, Tom. *The Pledge Betrayed: America and Britain and the Denazification of Post-War Germany.* Garden City, N.Y.: Doubleday, 1982.

Bowles, Chester. *Ambassador's Report.* New York: Harper & Brothers, 1954.

———. *Promises to Keep: My Years in Public Life, 1941–1969.* New York: Harper & Row, 1971.

Boyle, Andrew. *The Fourth Man.* New York: Dial Press, 1979.

Bradsher, Henry S. *Afghanistan and the Soviet Union.* Durham: University of North Carolina Press, 1983.

Brogan, Patrick, and Albert Zarca. *Deadly Business: Sam Cummings, Interarms and the Arms Trade.* New York: W. W. Norton, 1983.

Brown, Anthony Cave. *Wild Bill Donovan: The Last Hero.* New York: Times Books, 1982.

Brzezinski, Zbigniew. *Power and Principle: Memoirs of the National Security Advisor, 1977–1981.* New York: Farrar, Straus & Giroux, 1983.

Buchsbajew, Alexander. "Toward a Theory of Guerrilla Warfare: A Case Study of the Ukrainian Nationalist Underground in the Soviet Union and Communist Poland." Ph.D. Dissertation, City University of New York, 1984.

Byrnes, James F. *All in One Lifetime.* New York: Harper & Brothers, 1958.

Caldwell, Malcolm, and Lek Tan. *Cambodia in the Southeast Asian War.* New York: Monthly Review Press, 1973.

Campbell, Duncan. *The Unsinkable Aircraft Carrier: American Military Power in Britain.* London: Michael Joseph, 1984.

Carter, Jimmy. *Keeping Faith: Memoirs of a President.* New York: Bantam Books, 1982.

Chernyavsky, V., ed. *The CIA in the Dock: Soviet Journalists on International Terrorism.* Moscow: Progress Publishers, 1983.

Chorley, Katharine. *Armies and the Art of Revolution.* Boston: Beacon Press, 1973.

Christian, Shirley. *Nicaragua: Revolution in the Family.* New York: Random House, 1985.

Cline, Ray S. *Secrets, Spies and Scholars: Blueprint of the Essential CIA.* Washington, D.C.,: Acropolis Books, 1976.

Colby, William E., and Peter Forbath. *Honorable Men: My Life in the CIA.* New York: Simon & Schuster, 1978.

Compere, Tom, ed. *The Army Blue Book.* New York: Military Publishing Institute, 1960.

Cook, Blanche W. *The Declassified Eisenhower: A Divided Legacy of Peace and Political Warfare.* New York: Penguin Books, 1984.

Cookridge, E. H. *Gehlen: Spy of the Century.* New York: Pyramid Books, 1971.

————. *The Many Sides of George Blake, Esq.* Princeton: Vertex, 1970.

———— *The Net That Covers the World.* New York: Henry Holt & Company, 1955.

Cooper, Chester L. *The Lion's Last Roar: Suez 1956.* New York: Harper & Row, 1978.

————*The Lost Crusade: America in Vietnam.* New York: Dodd, Mead, 1970.

Corr, Gerard H. *The Chinese Red Army.* New York: Shocken, 1974.

Corson, William R. *The Armies of Ignorance: The Rise of the American Intelligence Empire.* New York: Dial Press, 1977.

Crozier, Brian, with Eric Chou. *The Man Who Lost China: The First Full Biography of Chiang Kai-shek.* New York: Scribner's, 1976.

Dabringhaus, Erhard. *Klaus Barbie.* Washington: Acropolis, 1984.

Davis, Nathaniel. *The Last Two Years of Salvador Allende.* Ithaca: Cornell University Press, 1985.

Deane, General John R. *The Strange Alliance: The Story of Our Efforts at Wartime Cooperation with Russia.* New York: Viking, 1947.

Dempster, Chris, and Dave Tompkins. *Firepower.* New York: St. Martin's Press, 1980.

De Silva, Peer. *Sub Rosa: The CIA and the Uses of Intelligence.* New York: Times Books, 1978.

Dickey, Christopher. *With the Contras: A Reporter in the Wilds of Nicaragua.* New York: Simon & Schuster, 1985.

Diederich, Bernard. *Somoza and the Legacy of U.S. Involvement in Central America.* New York: E. P. Dutton, 1981.

Dinerstein, Herbert S. *The Making of a Missile Crisis: October 1962.* Baltimore: Johns Hopkins University Press, 1976.

Dinges, John, and Saul Landau. *Assassination on Embassy Row.* New York: Pantheon Books, 1980.

Dobriansky, Lev E. *The Vulnerable Russians.* New York: Pageant Press, 1967.

Donovan, Robert J. *Eisenhower: The Inside Story.* New York: Harper & Brothers, 1956.

———. *Conflict and Crisis: The Presidency of Harry S. Truman, 1945–1948.* New York: W. W. Norton, 1977.

———. *Tumultuous Years: The Presidency of Harry S. Truman, 1949–1953.* New York: W. W. Norton, 1982.

Dorschner, John, and Roberto Fabricio. *The Winds of December: The Cuban Revolution, 1958.* London: Macmillan, 1980.

Dulles, Allen. *The Craft of Intelligence.* New York: New American Library, 1965.

Dulles, Eleanor Lansing. *American Foreign Policy in the Making.* New York: Harper & Row, 1968.

———. *John Foster Dulles: The Last Year.* New York: Harcourt, Brace & World, 1963.

Eagleton, Senator Thomas F. *War and Presidential Power: A Chronicle of Congressional Surrender.* New York: Liveright, 1974.

Eisenhower, Dwight D. *Mandate for Change: White House Years 1953–1956.* New York: New American Library, 1965.

———. *Waging Peace: White House Years, 1956–1961.* Garden City, N.Y.: Doubleday, 1965.

Epstein, Edward Jay. *Legend: The Secret World of Lee Harvey Oswald.* New York: Ballantine Books, 1978.

Estonia: My Beautiful Land. Gottingen: Estonian Committee, 1946.

Etzold, Thomas H., and John Lewis Gaddis, *Containment: Documents on American Policy and Strategy, 1945–1950.* New York: Columbia University Press, 1978.

Evans, Les, ed. *Disaster in Chile: Allende's Strategy and Why It Failed.* New York: Pathfinder Books, 1974.

Eveland, Wilbur Crane. *Ropes of Sand: America's Failure in the Middle East.* New York: W. W. Norton, 1980.

Fabian, Bela. *Cardinal Mindszenty: The Story of a Modern Martyr.* New York: Scribner's, 1949.

Fain, Tyrus G., Katharine Plant, and Ross Molloy, eds. *The Intelligence Community: History, Organization, and Issues.* New York: R. R. Bowker, 1977.

Farago, Ladislas. *Burn After Reading.* New York: McFadden, 1966.

———*War of Wits: The Anatomy of Espionage.* New York: Paperback Library, 1954.

Ferrell, Robert H., ed. *The Diary of James C. Hagerty: Eisenhower in Mid-Course, 1954–1955.* Bloomington: Indiana University Press, 1983.

———, ed. *The Eisenhower Diaries.* New York: W. W. Norton, 1981.

Fitzgibbon, Constantine. *Denazification.* London: Michael Joseph, 1969.

Ford, Corey. *Donovan of OSS.* Boston: Little Brown, 1970.

Ford, Gerald R. *A Time to Heal: The Autobiography of Gerald R. Ford.* New York: Berkley Books, 1980.

Franck, Thomas M., and Edward Weisband, eds. *Secrecy and Foreign Policy.* London: Oxford University Press, 1974.

Gabriel, Richard A. *Military Incompetence: Why the American Military Doesn't Win.* New York: Hill and Wang, 1985.

Gaddis, John L. *Strategies of Containment: A Critical Reappraisal of Postwar American National Security Policy.* New York: Oxford University Press, 1982.

Galbraith, John Kenneth. *A Life in Our Times.* Boston: Houghton Mifflin, 1981.

Garwood, Darrell. *Under Cover: Thirty-five Years of CIA Deception.* New York: Grove Press, 1985.

Gehlen, Reinhard. *The Service: The Memoirs of Reinhard Gehlen.* New York: Popular Library, 1972.

George, Alexander, and Richard Smoke. *Deterrence in American Foreign Policy: Theory and Practice.* New York: Columbia University Press, 1974.

Gerassi, John. *The Great Fear in Latin America.* London: Collier Books, 1965.

Godson, Roy, ed. *Intelligence Requirements for the 1980s.* Vol. 1, *Elements of Intelligence,* rev. ed. Vol. 4, *Covert Action.* Vol. 5, *Clandestine Collection.* Washington, D.C.: National Strategy Information Center, 1983.

Goldwater, Barry M. *With No Apologies: The Personal and Political Memoirs of a United States Senator.* New York: Morrow, 1979.

Gonzalez, Luis J., and Gustavo A. Sanchez-Salazar. *The Great Rebel: Che Guevara in Bolivia.* New York: Grove Press, 1969.

Gott, Richard. *Guerrilla Movements in Latin America*. Garden City, N.Y.: Doubleday/Anchor, 1970.

Goulden, Joseph C. *Korea: The Untold Story of the War*. New York: Times Books, 1982.

————. *Truth Is the First Casualty*. Chicago: Rand McNally, 1969.

Goulding, Phil G. *Confirm or Deny: Informing the People on National Security*. New York: Harper & Row, 1970.

Gramont, Sanche de. *The Secret War*. New York: Dell Books, 1962.

Gray, Robert Keith. *Eighteen Acres Under Glass*. Garden City, N.Y.: Doubleday, 1982.

Green, Steven. *Taking Sides: America's Secret Relations with a Militant Israel*. New York: Morrow, 1984.

Gromyko, Anatoli A. *Through Russian Eyes: President Kennedy's 1036 Days*. Washington: International Publishers, 1973.

Hagen, Louis. *The Secret War for Europe: A Dossier of Espionage*. New York: Stein & Day, 1969.

Halberstam, David. *The Best and the Brightest*. New York: Random House, 1972.

Haldeman, H. R., with Joseph DiMona. *The Ends of Power*. New York: Dell Books, 1978.

Halpern, Manfred. *The Morality and Politics of Intervention*. New York: Council on Religion in International Affairs, 1963.

Hammond, Thomas T. *Red Flag over Afghanistan: The Communist Coup, the Soviet Invasion, and the Consequences*. Boulder, Colo.: Westview Press, 1984.

Hauser, Thomas. *The Execution of Charles Horman: An American Sacrifice*. New York: Harcourt Brace Jovanovich, 1978.

Heinz, G., and H. Donnay. *Lumumba: The Last Fifty Days*. New York: Grove Press, 1969.

Herring, George C., Jr. *Aid to Russia, 1941–1946: Strategy, Diplomacy: The Origins of the Cold War*. New York: Columbia University Press, 1973.

Hersh, Seymour M. *The Price of Power: Kissinger in the Nixon White House*. New York: Summit Books, 1983.

Hilsman, Roger. *To Move a Nation: The Politics of Foreign Policy in the Administration of John F. Kennedy*. Garden City, N.Y.: Doubleday, 1967.

Hilton, Ralph, ed. *Tales of the Foreign Service*. Columbia: University of South Carolina Press, 1978.

Hinckle, Warren, and William W. Turner. *The Fish Is Red: The Story of the Secret War Against Castro*. New York: Harper & Row, 1981.

Hoare, Colonel Mike. *Mercenary*. New York: Bantam Books, 1979.

Holt, Robert T. *Radio Free Europe*. Minneapolis: University of Minnesota Press, 1958.

Hoopes, Townsend. *The Devil and John Foster Dulles.* Boston: Little Brown, 1973.

Hughes, Emmet John. *The Ordeal of Power.* New York: Dell Books, 1962.

Hunt, E. Howard. *Give Us This Day.* New Rochelle, N.Y.: Arlington House, 1973.

————. *Undercover: Memoirs of an American Secret Agent.* New York: Berkley Books, 1974.

Hymoff, Edward. *The OSS in World War II.* New York: Ballantine Books, 1972.

Immerman, Richard H. *The CIA in Guatemala: The Foreign Policy of Intervention.* Austin: University of Texas Press, 1982.

Isaacs, Arnold R. *Without Honor: Defeat in Vietnam and Cambodia.* Baltimore: Johns Hopkins University Press, 1983.

Johnson, Haynes. *The Bay of Pigs: The Leaders' Story of Brigade 2506.* New York: W. W. Norton, 1964.

Johnson, Lyndon Baines. *The Vantage Point: Perspectives of the Presidency, 1963–1969.* New York: Harper & Row, 1972.

Johnson, U. Alexis with Jef Olivarius McAllister. *The Right Hand of Power.* Englewood Cliffs, N.J.: Prentice-Hall, 1984.

Joesten, Joachim. *They Call It Intelligence.* London: Adlard-Schuman, 1963.

Jurgela, Constantine R. *History of the Lithuanian Nation.* New York: Lithuanian Cultural Institute, 1948.

Kalb, Madeleine G. *The Congo Cables: The Cold War in Africa from Eisenhower to Kennedy.* New York: Macmillan, 1982.

Karnow, Stanley. *Vietnam: A History.* New York: Viking Press, 1983.

Kaufmann, William W. *The McNamara Strategy.* New York: Harper & Row, 1964.

Keagle, James Martin. "Toward an Understanding of U.S. Latin American Policy." Ph. D. Dissertation, Princeton University, 1982.

Keesings' Research Report No. 8: *Germany and Eastern Europe Since 1945.* New York: Scribner's, 1973.

Kennedy, John F. *The Strategy of Peace,* ed. Allan Nevins. New York: Harper & Brothers, 1960.

Kennedy, Robert F. *Thirteen Days: A Memoir of the Missile Crisis.* New York: New American Library, 1969.

Khrushchev, Nikita. *Khrushchev Remembers,* trans. Strobe Talbott. New York: Bantam Books, 1971.

————. *Khrushchev Remembers: The Last Testament.* New York: Bantam Books, 1976.

Kirk, Donald. *Wider War: The Struggle for Cambodia, Thailand, and Laos.* New York: Praeger, 1971.

Kirkpatrick, Lyman. *The Real C.I.A.* New York: Macmillan, 1968.

————. *The U.S. Intelligence Community.* New York: Hill & Wang, 1973.

Kissinger, Henry A. *White House Years, 1969–1973.* Boston: Little Brown, 1979.

————. *Years of Upheaval.* Boston: Little Brown, 1982.

Klare, Michael T. *War Without End: American Planning for the Next Vietnams.* New York: Knopf, 1972.

Kovrig, Bennett. *The Myth of Liberation: East Central Europe in U.S. Diplomacy and Politics Since 1941.* Baltimore: Johns Hopkins University Press, 1973.

Krock, Arthur. *Memoirs: Sixty Years on the Firing Line.* New York: Funk & Wagnalls, 1968.

Kwitney, Jonathan. *Endless Enemies: The Making of an Unfriendly World.* New York: Congdon & Weed, 1984.

Langer, Paul F., and Joseph J. Zasloff. *North Vietnam and the Pathet Lao.* Cambridge: Harvard University Press, 1970.

Lansdale, Edward Geary. *In the Midst of Wars: An American in Southeast Asia.* New York: Harper & Row, 1972.

Lasky, Melvin J., ed. *The Hungarian Revolution: A White Book.* New York: Congress for Cultural Freedom, 1957.

Laskey, Victor. *JFK: The Man and the Myth.* New York: Macmillian, 1963.

Lazo, Mario. *Dagger in the Heart: American Policy Failures in Cuba.* New York: Funk & Wagnalls, 1968.

Leary, William M., ed. *The Central Intelligence Agency: History and Documents.* N.p.: University of Alabama Press, 1984.

————. *Perilous Missions: Civil Air Transport and CIA Covert Operations in Asia.* N.p.: University of Alabama Press, 1984.

Lebar, Frank M., and Adrienne Suddard, eds. *Laos: Its People, Its Society, Its Culture.* New Haven: Human Relations Area Files Press, 1960.

Ledeen, Michael, and William Lewis. *Debacle: The American Failure in Iran.* New York: Vintage Books, 1982.

Lernoux, Penny. *Cry of the People: The Struggle for Human Rights in Latin America—The Catholic Church in Conflict with U.S. Policy.* New York: Penguin Books, 1982.

Lettis, Richard, and William E. Morris. *The Hungarian Revolt: October 23–November 4, 1956.* New York: Scribner's, 1961.

Lewis, Flora. *A Case History of Hope: The Story of Poland's Peaceful Revolutions.* Garden City, N.Y.: Doubleday, 1958.

Llerena, Mario. *The Unsuspected Revolution: The Birth and Rise of Castroism.* Ithaca: Cornell University Press, 1978.

Lobe, Thomas, *United States National Security Policy and Aid to the Thailand Police.* Denver: University of Denver Monograph in International Affairs, 1977.

Loftus, John. *The Belarus Secret,* ed. Nathan Miller. New York: Knopf, 1982.

Logoreci, Anton. *The Albanians: Europe's Forgotton Survivors.* Boulder, Colo.: Westview Press, 1977.

Ludovici, L. J. *Tomorrow Sometimes Comes.* London: Longacre Oldhams, 1957.

Lukas, Richard C. *Eagles East: The Army Air Forces and the Soviet Union, 1941–1945.* Tallahassee: Florida State University Press, 1970.

Lundestad, Geir. *America, Scandanavia and the Cold War, 1945–1949.* New York: Columbia University Press, 1980.

McCauley, Martin, ed. *Communist Power in Europe, 1944–1949.* London: Macmillan, 1988.

McClellan, David S. *Dean Acheson: The State Department Years.* New York: Dodd, Mead, 1976.

McCoy, Alfred W., with Cathleen B. Read and Leonard P. Adams II. *The Politics of Heroin in Southeast Asia.* New York: Harper & Row, 1972.

McGarvey, Patrick J. *CIA: The Myth and the Madness.* New York: Saturday Review Press, 1972.

McGehee, Ralph W. *Deadly Deceits: My Twenty-five Years in the CIA.* New York: Sheridan Square Publications, 1983.

Mader, Julius. *Who's Who in CIA.* Berlin: Julius Mader, 1968.

Mahoney, Richard D. *JFK: Ordeal in Africa.* New York: Oxford University Press, 1983.

Marchetti, Victor, and John D. Marks. *The CIA and the Cult of Intolligence.* New York: Dell Books, 1980.

Marcum, John. *The Angolan Revolution,* 2 vols. Cambridge: MIT Press, 1969, 1978.

Martin, David C. *A Wilderness of Mirrors.* New York: Harper & Row, 1980.

Martin, John Bartlow. *Adlai Stevenson and the World.* Garden City, N.Y.: Doubleday, 1978.

Masterman, J. C. *The Double-cross System.* New York: Avon Books, 1972.

Mastny, Vojtech. *Russia's Road to the Cold War: Diplomacy, Warfare and the Politics of Communism.* New York: Columbia University Press, 1979.

Matthews, Kenneth. *Memories of a Mountain War: Greece, 1944–1949.* London: Longman, 1972.

Maxwell, Neville. *India's China War.* Garden City, N.Y.: Doubleday/Anchor, 1972.

May, Brian. *The Indonesian Tragedy.* London: Routledge & Keegan Paul, 1978.

Medhurst, Kenneth, ed. *Allende's Chile.* New York: St. Martin's Press, 1972.

Meeker, Odeen. *The Little World of Laos.* New York: Scribner's, 1959.

Meyer, Cord. *Facing Reality: From World Federalism to the CIA.* New York: Harper & Row, 1980.

Michener, James. *The Bridge at Andau.* New York: Bantam Books, 1963.

Mickelson, Sig. *America's Other Voice: The Story of Radio Free Europe and Radio Liberty.* New York: Praeger, 1983.

Miller, Richard I. *Dag Hammarskjold and Crisis Diplomacy.* New York: Pyramid Books, 1961.

Millis, Walter, ed. *The Forrestal Diaries.* New York: Viking Press, 1951.

Misiunas, Romuald J., and Rein Taagepera. *The Baltic States: Years of Dependence, 1940–1980.* Berkeley: University of California Press, 1983.

Monahan, James, ed. *Before I Sleep: The Last Days of Dr. Tom Dooley.* New York: Farrar, Straus & Cudahy, 1961.

Moore, Robin. *The Green Berets.* New York: Avon Books, 1965.

Moraes, Frank. *The Revolt in Tibet.* New York: Macmillan, 1960.

Morris, David J. *We Must Make Haste Slowly: The Process of Revolution in Chile.* New York: Vintage Books, 1973.

Morris, Roger. *Uncertain Greatness: Henry Kissinger and American Foreign Policy.* New York: Harper & Row, 1977.

Morrow, Robert D. *Betrayal.* Chicago: Henry Regnery, 1976.

Moser, Charles, ed. *Combat on Communist Territory.* Washington, D.C., Free Congress Research and Education Foundation, 1985.

Mosley, Leonard. *Dulles: A Biography of Eleanor, Allen and John Foster and Their Family Network.* New York: Dial Press, 1978.

Murphy, Robert. *Diplomat Among Warriors.* Garden City, N.Y.: Doubleday, 1964.

Nagy, Imre. *On Communism: In Defense of the New Course.* New York: Praeger, 1957.

Nessen, Ron. *It Sure Looks Different from the Inside.* New York: Playboy Press, 1978.

Nevin, David. *The American Touch in Micronesia.* New York: W. W. Norton, 1977.

Nixon, Richard Milhous. *RN: The Memoirs of Richard Nixon* 2 vols. New York: Warner Books, 1979.

O'Ballance, Edgar. *The Kurdish Revolt, 1961–1970.* London: Archon Books, 1973.

Operation Zapata: The Ultrasensitive Report and Testimony of the Board of Inquiry on the Bay of Pigs. Frederick, Md.: University Publications of America, 1981.

Osborne, John. *The Last Nixon Watch.* Washington, D.C.: New Republic Press, 1975.

———. *The White House Watch: The Ford Years.* Washington, D.C.: New Republic Press, 1978.

Oseth, John M. *Regulating U.S. Intelligence Operations: A Study in Definition of the National Interest.* N.p.: University Press of Kentucky, 1985.

Paddock, Alfred H., Jr. *U.S. Army Special Warfare: Its Origins.* Washington, D.C.: National Defense University Press, 1982.

Paine, Lauran. *The CIA at Work.* London: Robert Hale, 1977.

Palacios, Jorge. *Chile: An Attempt at "Historic Compromise.": The Real Story of the Allende Years.* Chicago: Banner Press, 1979.

Parmet, Herbert S. *Eisenhower and the American Crusades.* New York: Macmillan, 1972.

————. *JFK: The Presidency of John F. Kennedy.* New York: Dial Press, 1983.

Patterson, George N. *Tibet in Revolt.* London: Faber & Faber, 1960.

Peissel, Michel. *The Secret War in Tibet.* Boston: Little Brown, 1972.

Penkovskiy, Colonel Oleg. *The Penkovskiy Papers,* trans. Peter Deriabin. New York: Avon Books, 1965.

Persico, Joseph E. *Piercing the Reich: The Penetration of Nazi Germany by American Secret Agents During World War II.* New York: Viking Press, 1979.

Peterzell, Jay. *Reagan's Secret Wars.* Washington, D.C.: Center for National Security Studies, 1984.

Petrusenko, Vitali. *A Dangerous Game: CIA and Mass Media.* Prague: Interpress, n.d. [1976].

Philby, Kim. *My Silent War.* London: Granada Books, 1969.

Phillips, David Atlee. *The Night Watch: Twenty-five Years of Peculiar Service.* New York: Atheneum, 1977.

Pincher, Chapman. *Their Trade Is Treachery.* New York: Bantam Books, 1982.

————. *Too Secret Too Long.* New York: St. Martin's Press, 1985.

Powers, Francis Gary, with Curt Gentry. *Operation Overflight.* New York: Holt, Rinehart & Winston, 1970.

Powers, Thomas. *The Man Who Kept the Secrets: Richard Helms and the CIA.* New York: Knopf, 1979.

Prouty, L. Fletcher, *The Secret Team.* Englewood Cliffs, N.J.: Prentice-Hall, 1973.

Ransom, Harry Howe. *Central Intelligence and National Security.* Cambridge: Harvard University Press, 1958.

————. *The Intelligence Establishment.* Cambridge: Harvard University Press, 1970.

Resnick, Marvin D. *The Black Beret.* New York: Ballantine Books, 1969.

Richelson, Jeffrey T. *The U.S. Intelligence Community.* Cambridge: Ballinger, 1985.

Rickett, Allyn, and Adele Rickett. *Prisoners of Liberation: Four Years in a*

Chinese Communist Prison. Garden City, N.Y.: Doubleday/Anchor, 1973.

Robbins, Christopher. *Air America: The Story of the CIA's Secret Airlines.* New York: G. P. Putnam's Sons, 1979.

Roberts, Chalmers. *First Rough Draft: A Journalist's Journal of Our Times.* New York: Praeger, 1973.

Roosevelt, Kermit. *Countercoup: The Struggle for the Control of Iran.* New York: McGraw-Hill, 1979.

Rositzke, Harry. *The CIA's Secret Operations.* New York: Reader's Digest Press, 1977.

————. *The KGB: The Eyes of Russia.* Garden City, N.Y.: Doubleday, 1981.

Rostow, Walt W. *The Diffusion of Power, 1957–1972: An Essay in Recent History.* New York: Macmillan, 1972.

Royal Laotian Government, Ministry of Foreign Affairs. *White Book on the Violations of the 1962 Geneva Accords by the Government of North Vietnam.* Vientiane, 1969.

Rubin, Barry. *Paved with Good Intentions: The American Experience with Iran.* New York: Oxford University Press, 1980.

Safire, William. *Safire's Washington.* New York: Times Books, 1980.

Sartre, Jean-Paul. *Sartre on Cuba.* New York: Ballantine Books, 1961.

Schemmer, Benjamin F. *The Raid.* New York: Harper & Row, 1976.

Schlesinger, Arthur F., Jr. *Robert Kennedy and His Times.* Boston: Houghton Mifflin, 1978.

————. *A Thousand Days: John F. Kennedy in the White House.* Greenwich, Conn.: Fawcett Books, 1965.

Schlesinger, Stephen, and Stephen Kinzer. *Bitter Fruit: The Untold Story of the American Coup in Guatemala.* Garden City, N.Y.: Doubleday, 1982.

Schorr, Daniel. *Clearing the Air.* New York: Berkley Books, 1978.

Sen, Chanakya, ed. *Tibet Disappears: A Documentary History of Tibet's International Status, the Great Rebellion, and Its Aftermath.* New York: Asia Publishing House, 1960.

Sergeyev, F. *Chile: CIA Big Business,* trans. Lev Bobrov. Moscow: Progress Publishers, 1981.

Shackley, Theodore. *The Third Option: An American View of Counterinsurgency Operations.* New York: Reader's Digest Press, 1981.

Shawcross, William. *Sideshow: Kissinger, Nixon and the Destruction of Cambodia.* New York: Simon & Schuster, 1979.

Sihanouk, Norodom (as related to Wilfred Burchett). *My War with the CIA: The Memoirs of Prince Norodom Sihanouk.* Baltimore: Penguin Books, 1974.

Simpson, Colonel Charles M. III. *Inside the Green Berets: the First Thirty*

Years: A History of the U.S. Army Special Forces. San Francisco: Presidio Press, 1983.

Sivachev, Nikolai V., and Nikolai N. Yakovlev. *Russia and the United States: U.S.-Soviet Relations from the Soviet Point of View.* Chicago: University of Chicago Press, 1979.

Smith, Joseph Burkholder. *Portrait of a Cold Warrior.* New York: G. P. Putnam's Sons, 1976.

Smith, Walter Bedell. *Moscow Mission, 1946–1949.* London: Heinemann, 1950.

Snepp, Frank. *Decent Interval.* New York: Random House, 1977.

Sorenson, Theodore. *Kennedy.* New York: Bantam Books, 1965.

Steenberg, Sven. *Vlasov.* New York: Knopf, 1970.

Sterling, Claire. *The Time of the Assassins.* New York: Holt, Rinehart & Winston, 1983.

Steven, Stewart. *Operation Splinter Factor.* Philadelphia: J. B. Lippincott, 1974.

Stevens, Vice-Admiral Leslie C. *Russian Assignment.* Boston: Little Brown, 1953.

Stevenson, Charles A. *The End of Nowhere: American Policy Toward Laos Since 1954.* Boston: Beacon Press, 1972.

Stockwell, John. *In Search of Enemies: A CIA Story.* New York: W. W. Norton, 1978.

Stoessinger, John G. *Henry Kissinger: The Anguish of Power.* New York: W. W. Norton, 1976.

Strong, General Sir Kenneth. *Intelligence at the Top.* Garden City, N.Y. Doubleday, 1967.

———. *Men of Intelligence.* New York: St. Martin's Press, 1971.

Stueck, William W., Jr. *The Road to Confrontation: American Policy Toward China and Korea, 1947–1950.* Chapel Hill: University of North Carolina Press, 1981.

Sullivan, William H. *Obbligato, 1939–1979: Notes on a Foreign Service Career.* New York: W. W. Norton, 1984.

Sulzberger, Cyrus L. *A Long Row of Candles: Memoirs and Diaries, 1934–1954.* New York: Macmillan, 1969.

———. *An Age of Mediocrity: Memoirs and Diaries, 1963–1972.* New York: Macmillan, 1973.

———. *The Last of the Giants.* New York: Macmillan, 1970.

Suyin, Han. *Lhasa, the Open City: A Journey to Tibet.* London: Triad Panther Books, 1979.

Szulc, Tad. *The Illusion of Peace: Foreign Policy in the Nixon Years.* New York: Viking Press, 1978.

Szulc, Tad, and Karl E. Meyer. *The Cuban Invasion: The Chronicle of a Disaster.* New York: Ballantine Books, 1962.

Taber, Robert. *M-26: The Biography of a Revolution.* New York: Lyle Stuart, 1961.

Tanham, George K. *Trial in Thailand.* New York: Crane Russak, 1974.

Tauras, K. V. *Guerrilla Warfare on the Amber Coast.* New York: Lithuanian Research Institute, 1962.

Taylor, General Maxwell D. *Swords into Plowshares.* New York: W. W. Norton, 1972.

————. *The Uncertain Trumpet.* New York: Harper & Brothers, 1959.

Thayer, Charles W. *Guerrilla.* New York: New American Library, 1963.

Thayer, George. *The War Business: The International Trade in Armaments.* New York: Simon & Schuster, 1965.

Thies, Wallace J. *When Governments Collide: Coercion and Diplomacy in the Vietnam Conflict, 1964–1968.* Berkeley: University of California Press, 1980.

Thomas, Lowell J., and Edward Jablonski. *Doolittle: A Biography.* Garden City, N.Y.: Doubleday, 1976.

Thomas, Lowell, Jr. *The Silent War in Tibet.* Garden City, N.Y.: Doubleday, 1959.

Trewhitt, Henry L. *McNamara.* New York: Harper & Row, 1971.

Troy, Thomas F. *Donovan and the CIA.* Frederick, Md.: University Press of America, 1981.

Truman, Harry S. *Memoirs.* Vol. I, *Year of Decisions.* Vol. II, *Years of Trial and Hope.* New York: New American Library, 1965.

Truman, Margaret. *Harry S. Truman.* New York: Pocket Books, 1974.

Tully, Andrew. *CIA: The Inside Story.* Greenwich, Conn.: Fawcett Books, 1962.

Turner, Admiral Stansfield. *Secrecy and Democracy: The CIA in Transition.* Boston: Houghton Mifflin, 1985.

Twining, General Nathan F. *Neither Liberty nor Safety.* New York: Holt, Rinehart & Winston, 1966.

Ulam, Adam B. *Expansion and Coexistence: Soviet Foreign Policy 1917–1973,* 2nd ed. New York: Praeger, 1974.

Uribe, Armando. *The Black Book of American Intervention in Chile.* Boston: Beacon Press, 1975.

Valeriani, Richard. *Travels with Henry.* Boston: Houghton Mifflin, 1979.

Verrier, Anthony. *Through the Looking Glass: British Foreign Policy in an Age of Illusions.* New York: W. W. Norton, 1983.

Volkman, Ernest, *Warriors of the Night: Spies, Soldiers and American Intelligence.* New York: Morrow, 1985.

Wagoner, Fred E. *Dragon Rouge: The Rescue of Hostages in the Congo.* Washington, D.C.: National Defense University Research Directorate, 1980.

Walters, Lieutenant General Vernon A. *Silent Missions.* Garden City, N.Y.: Doubleday, 1978.

Walton, Richard J. *Cold War and Counter-Revolution: The Foreign Policy of John F. Kennedy.* Baltimore: Penguin Press, 1972.

Weintal, Edward, and Charles Bartlett. *Facing the Brink: An Intimate Study of Crisis Diplomacy.* New York: Scribner's, 1967.

Weisberger, Bernard A. *Cold War, Cold Peace: The United States and Russia Since 1945.* New York: American Heritage Press, 1985.

Weissman, Stephen R. *American Foreign Policy in the Congo, 1960–1964.* Ithaca: Cornell University Press, 1974.

West, Nigel. *The Circus: MI 5 Operations, 1945–1972.* New York: Stein & Day, 1983.

Westmoreland, General William C. *A Soldier Reports.* New York: Dell Books, 1980.

Weyl, Nathaniel. *Red Star over Cuba.* New York: Hilman-McFadden, 1961.

White, Theodore H. *The Making of the President, 1960.* New York: Pocket Books, 1961.

Whitson, Colonel William, with Chen-hsia Huang. *The Chinese High Command: A History of Communist Military Politics, 1927–1971.* New York: Praeger, 1973.

Wicker, Tom. *On Press.* New York: Berkley Books, 1979.

Wilensky, Harold L. *Organizational Intelligence.* New York: Basic Books, 1967.

Williams, Phil. *Crisis Management: Confrontation and Diplomacy in the Nuclear Age.* New York: John Wiley & Sons, 1976.

Williams, William Appleman. *The United States and Castro.* New York: Monthly Review Press, 1962.

Windchy, Eugene E. *Tonkin Gulf.* Garden City, N.Y.: Doubleday, 1970.

Wise, David. *The Politics of Lying: Government Deception, Secrecy and Power.* New York: Vintage Books, 1973.

———, and Thomas B. Ross. *The Espionage Establishment.* New York: Random House, 1967.

———. *The Invisible Government.* New York: Vintage Books, 1964.

———. *The U-2 Affair.* New York: Random House, 1962.

Wittner, Lawrence S. *American Intervention in Greece, 1943–1949.* New York: Columbia University Press, 1982.

Wohlstetter, Roberta. *Pearl Harbor: Warning and Decision.* Stanford: Stanford University Press, 1962.

Wyden, Peter. *Bay of Pigs: The Untold Story.* New York: Simon & Schuster, 1979.

Yakolev, Nikolai. *CIA Target: USSR.* Moscow: Progress Publishers, 1982.

Yergin, Daniel. *Shattered Peace: The Origins of the Cold War and the National Security State.* Boston: Houghton Mifflin, 1978.
Zumwalt, Admiral Elmo R., Jr. *On Watch: A Memoir.* New York: Quadrangle, 1976.

ARTICLES

Adler, Emmanuel. "Executive Command and Control in Foreign Policy: The CIA's Covert Activities." *Orbis*, Vol. 23, No. 3, Fall 1979.
Allende, Hortensia Bussi de. "Chile and CIA Intervention, 1964–1973." Presentation at Yale University conference, The CIA and World Power, April 5, 1975.
Artime, Mañuel, José Perez San Roman, Erneido Oliva, and Enrique Ruiz-Williams (with Haynes Johnson). "We Who Tried." *Life*, May 10, 1963.
Astor, Gerard. "Henry Kissinger: Strategist in the White House Basement." *Look*, August 12, 1969.
Baldwin, Hanson W. "The Future of Intelligence." *Strategic Review*, Vol. 4, No. 3, Summer 1976.
Barnds, William J. "Intelligence and Foreign Policy: Dilemmas of a Democracy." *Foreign Affairs*, Vol. 47, No. 2, January 1969.
Beck, Kent M. "Necessary Lies, Hidden Truths: Cuba in the 1960 Campaign." *Diplomatic History*, Vol. 8. No. 1. Winter 1984.
Blackstock, Paul W. "The Intelligence Community Under the Nixon Administration." *Armed Forces and Society*, Vol. 1, No. 2, February 1975.
Braden, Thomas. "What's Wrong with the CIA?" *Saturday Review*, April 5, 1975.
Branch, Taylor, and George Crile. "The Kennedy Vendetta." *Harper's* August 1975.
Brower, Brock. "Why People Like You Joined the CIA." *Washington Monthly*, Vol. 8, No. 9, November 1976.
Brown, John H. "The Disappearing Russian Embassy Archives, 1922–1949." *Prologue*, Vol. 14, No. 1, Spring 1982.
Chamorro, Edgar. "Confessions of a Contra." *The New Republic*, August 5, 1985.
Cline, Ray. "Policy Without Intelligence." *Foreign Policy*, No. 17, Winter 1975–1976.
Codevilla, Angelo, and Roy Godson, "Intelligence (Covert Action and Counterintelligence) as an Instrument of Policy." Paper presented at the International Studies Association conference, Washington, D.C., March 8, 1985.

Cooper, Chester L. "The CIA and Decisionmaking." *Foreign Affairs,* Vol. 70. No. 1, January 1972.

Dalia Lama. "A Vast Sea of Chinese Threatens Tibet." *New York Times,* August 9, 1985.

————. "China and the Future of Tibet." *Worldview,* October 1977.

De Graffenreid, Kenneth. "Intelligence and the Oval Office." Paper presented at the International Studies Association conference, Washington, D.C., March 8, 1985.

Drenkowski, Dana. "MERC Work: Does the Geneva Convention Apply?" *Soldier of Fortune,* December 1984.

Drew, Elizabeth. "A Reporter at Large: Brzezinski." *New Yorker,* May 1, 1978.

Elliff, John T. "The Legal Framework for Intelligence Activities." Paper presented at the American Political Science Association conference, Washington, D.C., September 1, 1984.

Ellsworth, Robert F., and Kenneth Adelman. "Foolish Intelligence." *Foreign Policy,* No. 36, Fall 1979.

Fallows, James. "Crazies by the Tail: Bay of Pigs, Diem and Liddy." *Washington Monthly,* Vol. 6, No. 7, September 1974.

Gutman, Roy. "America's Diplomatic Charade." *Foreign Policy,* No. 56. Fall 1984.

Gwertzman, Bernard. "Cyrus Vance Plays It Cool." *New York Times Magazine,* March 18, 1979.

Halperin, Morton H. "Clever Briefers, Crazy Leaders and Myopic Analysts." *Washington Monthly,* Vol. 6. No. 7, September 1974.

Harkness, Richard, and Gladys Harkness. "The Mysterious Doings of CIA." *Saturday Evening Post,* October 30, November 6 and 13, 1954.

Hersh, Seymour. "Exposing the Libyan Link." *New York Times Magazine,* June 21, 1981.

————. "The Qaddafi Connection." *New York Times Magazine.* June 14, 1981.

Johnson, Loch. "Congress and the CIA: Monitoring the Dark Side of Government." Paper presented at the American Political Science Association conference, Washington, D.C., September 1, 1979.

Kalb, Madeleine G. "The CIA and Lumumba." *New York Times Magazine,* August 2, 1981.

Kaplan, Fred H. "Our Cold War Policy—Circa 1950." *New York Times Magazine,* May 18, 1980.

Keegan, John. "The Ordeal of Afghanistan." *The Atlantic,* November 1985.

Kerby, Robert L. "American Military Airlift During the Laotian Civil War, 1958–1963." *Aerospace Historian,* Vol. 24, No. 1, Spring 1977.

Leacacos, John P. "Kissinger's Apparat." *Foreign Policy*, No. 5, Winter 1971–1972.

William M. Leary, and William Stueck, "The Chennault Plan to Save China: U.S. Containment in Asia and the Origins of the CIA's Aerial Empire, 1949–1950." *Diplomatic History*, Vol. 8, No. 4, Fall 1984.

Lelyveld, Joseph. "The Director: Running the CIA." *New York Times Magazine*, January 20, 1985.

McCone, John. "Why We Need the CIA." *T.V. Guide*, January 10, 1976.

Martin, David C. "The American James Bond: A True Story." *Playboy* Magazine, April 1980.

Morris, Roger. "Kissinger and the Brothers Kalb." *Washington Monthly*, Vol. 6. Nos. 5–6, July–August 1974.

Nocera, Joseph. "The Art of the Leak." *Washington Monthly*, Vol. 11, Nos. 5–6, July–August 1979.

Paterson, Thomas G. "If Europe, Why Not China? The Containment Doctrine, 1947–1949," *Prologue*, Vol. 13, No. 1, Spring 1981.

Peterzell, Jay. "Legal and Constitutional Authority for Covert Operations." Paper presented at the International Studies Association conference, Washington, D.C., March 8, 1985.

Phillips, John. "The Days of the Dulleses." *New York Review of Books*, May 4, 1978.

Ransom, Harry Howe. "CIA Accountability: Congress as Temperamental Watchdog." Paper presented at the American Political Science Association, Washington, D.C., September 1, 1984.

Roberts, Adam. "The CIA: Reform Is Not Enough." *Millenium: Journal of International Studies* Vol. 6, No. 1, Spring 1977.

Rositzke, Harry. "America's Secret Operations: A Perspective." *Foreign Affairs*, Vol. 53, No. 2, January 1975.

Schmitt, Gary. "Oversight: What For and How Effective?" Paper presented at the International Studies Association conference, Washington, D.C., March 8, 1985.

"Should the U.S. Fight Secret Wars?" (Symposium). *Harper's*, September 1984.

Shrivastava, B. K. "The United States and Recent Developments in Afghanistan." *International Studies*, Vol. 19, No. 4, October–December 1980.

Smith, Joseph Burkholder. "The CIA in Vietnam: Nation Builders, Old Pros, Paramilitary Boys, and Misplaced Persons." *Washington Monthly* Vol. 9, No. 12, February 1978.

Szulc, Tad. "How Kissinger Runs Our 'Other Government.'" *New York*, November 30, 1974.

———. "Putting the Bite Back in the CIA." *New York Times Magazine*, April 6, 1980.

————. "Shaking Up the CIA." *New York Times Magazine,* July 29, 1979.

Taubman, Phillip. "Casey and His CIA on the Rebound." *New York Times Magazine* January 16, 1983.

————. "The Secret World of a Green Beret." *New York Times Magazine,* July 4, 1982.

Treverton, Gregory F. "Reforming the CIA." *Millenium: Journal of International Studies,* Vol. 5, No. 3, Winter 1976–1977.

Vandenbroucke, Lucien S. "Anatomy of a Failure: The Decision to Land at the Bay of Pigs." *Political Science Quarterly,* Vol. 99, No. 3, Fall 1984.

————. "The Confessions of Allen Dulles: New Evidence on the Bay of Pigs." *Diplomatic History,* Vol. 8, No. 4, Fall 1984.

Weissman, Steven R. "CIA Covert Action in Zaire and Angola: Patterns and Consequences." *Political Science Quarterly,* Vol. 94, No. 2, Summer 1979.

Welles, Benjamin. "H——L——S of the CIA," *New York Times Magazine,* April 18, 1971.

INDEX